A Dictionary
of
Continental Philosophy

A Dictionary
of
Continental Philosophy

Edited by John Protevi

Yale University Press
New Haven and London

First published in the United States in 2006 by Yale University Press.

First published in the United Kingdom in 2005 by Edinburgh University Press.

Typeset in 11 on 13 Ehrhardt by Iolaire Typesetting.
Printed and bound in Great Britain by Antony Rowe Ltd, Chippenham, Wilts.

Library of Congress Control Number: 2005931727

ISBN-13: 978-0-300-11605-2 (cloth : alk. paper)
ISBN-10: 0-300-11605-5 (cloth : alk. paper)

A catalogue record for this book is available from the British Library.

The paper in this book meets the guidelines for permanence and durability of the Committee on Production Guidelines for Book Longevity of the Council on Library Resources.

10 9 8 7 6 5 4 3 2 1

Contents

Preface

Rationale for the present work

The *Edinburgh Encyclopedia of Continental Philosophy* (*EECP*) has found a home among the leading reference works of various formats ('Readers', 'Companions', 'Histories') now available for readers interested in continental philosophy. These works, consisting of large essays (5–10,000 words) on major figures, movements and topics in the field, serve certain purposes very well, but cannot serve all the needs of readers interested in help with continental philosophy, in particular those new to the field. Limited by the very size of the entries to a restricted number of subject headings, these works are not as nimble or user-friendly as they could be for quick orientation and as guides for further study. For instance, a reader wanting a quick orientation on a particular term used in continental circles (for example, 'difference') must be able to associate that term with a particular author and then wade through a long essay hoping for a discussion of it. And while that discussion may provide cross-references to uses of the term in other philosophers, it may again not do so. With *A Dictionary of Continental Philosophy* (*DCP*) we aim then to complement the *EECP* by providing brief entries on a much wider range of subject headings. Along with explicit cross-references, these mini-orientations will enable readers to quickly and accurately target their subsequent research in the *EECP* and other resources.

Working definition of 'continental philosophy'

'Continental philosophy' has always been an exceedingly difficult term to define. In fact, it may even be impossible to define. After all, Nietzsche tells us in *On the Genealogy of Morals* that 'only that which is without history can be defined', and not only does continental philosophy have a history, but most – although perhaps not all – of its practitioners would agree with Nietzsche that a historical treatment (or what he would call a 'genealogy') of philosophical texts is vitally important. Thus, in lieu of a definition, this Preface offers a (synchronic) operational treatment and a (diachronic) genealogy of continental philosophy.

By an operational treatment, we mean that we shall treat as continental those thinkers who are now or who have been at some time in the past so labelled by a reasonable portion of the philosophical or general intellectual community, whether or not that labelling constitutes a set whose essence can be defined by a set of necessary and sufficient conditions that demarcates it from other types of philosophy. Indeed we will not even bind ourselves to what Wittgenstein would call a family resemblance, since the fact that philosophers as diverse in aim, method and style as Hegel and Nietzsche, Deleuze and Levinas, Heidegger and Habermas, Irigaray and Gadamer, have all been called continental philosophers would seem to strain even that generous way of treating groups.

By a genealogy of continental philosophy we mean to trace not only the history of the term, but also the various movements whose convergence and divergence have made up the shifting field of continental philosophy over the years. First, what is the genealogy of the term 'continental philosophy'? As Simon Glendinning points out in his article on Analytic Philosophy in the *DCP*, it was first used as a term of opprobrium by the Oxbridge philosophers of the 1950s for those 'not like us', those over there on 'the Continent'. Over the years 'continental philosophy' has come to lose its geographical sense, however, due to the strong interest in such a philosophy in the Anglophone world – it makes little sense to call someone working with Derridean concepts in North America, Australia (or indeed the United Kingdom or Ireland), a 'continental philosopher' if that term is intended geographically! It has also lost some but not all of its polemical sting when used in analytic circles, and in fact it has come to be adopted as a positive self-designation by many, as evidenced by the shift of the title of the influential journal *Man and World* to its current *Continental Philosophy Review*.

Second, the genealogy of the various convergent and divergent movements of continental philosophy is often begun by citing a certain appropriation of Kant and has come to include the philosophical and intellectual movements of German Idealism, Marxism, phenomenology, hermeneutics, existentialism, Frankfurt School Critical Theory, that branch of feminism sometimes called 'French feminism', structuralism and poststructuralism, the French 'philosophy of difference' of the 1960s, philosophies based on or influenced by Freudian and Lacanian psychoanalysis, and the multitude of subfields produced by the intersections and mutual influences these movements have exerted on each other.

Indeed the best reason for offering an operational and genealogical treatment of continental philosophy rather than a definition of it lies in precisely the sort of combinatorial explosion that results when these movements are put into relation with one another. The resulting field provides an ever-shifting profusion of positions, theses, methodologies and so forth, no one of which can be said to unify the field. (The logic of Derrida's 'quasi-transcendentality' could be cited here: any term that aspires to rise from an empirical field to a transcendental ordering or conditioning position will leave behind it a mark of its absence from the field.) Among the factors in the field of continental philosophy are: (1) a reaction to the transcendental turn of Kant; (2) a materialist 'overturning' of Hegel; (3) the 'overcoming of Platonism'; (4) a focus on corporeality or embodiment, often combined with a focus on gender; (5) a type of 'linguistic turn' via Saussure; (6) the disbelief in 'grand narratives'; (7) the structuralist or poststructuralist 'death of the subject'; (8) the philosophical implications of the 'new sciences' variously called catastrophe theory, chaos theory, or complexity theory; and many other themes, almost all of which can be combined with each other. For example, one could imagine a cross of the readings of Deleuze and Guattari by Brian Massumi and Elizabeth Grosz as a poststructuralist feminist appropriation of complexity theory to consider gendered embodiment in globalised capitalism. Only a genealogy considering multiple factors can offer ways to consider such a field; a definition seeking to isolate an essence could only be arbitrary and produce artificial distinctions. To twist Deleuze's famous citation of Spinoza: 'we don't know what the body [of continental philosophy] can do'. An essential definition pretends to tell you what a body can do; a genealogy only tells you what a body has done (although it may show what it might do in the (near) future).

Using our operational and genealogical method, then, we will attempt to cover in the *DCP* the major figures, topics and technical terms of the movements and themes sketched above. We begin our treatment of philosophers with Kant and include contemporary figures of note. The inclusion of figures presents difficult problems of judgement, however, which we will illustrate with financial metaphors. With regard to historical figures, we must balance the contemporary interest in their work (their current 'value') with their historical importance, as measured both by the highest point of interest in them at any one time

(their 'peak price') and by their 'staying power', the length of time they
sustained such interest. With contemporary figures we must balance
the current interest in their work against our best guesses as to the
future 'worth' of their philosophical 'stock'. We have tried for a
reasonable depth in covering figures, but in certain cases we decided
not to commission an article on a figure in order to save room for
technical terms.

Format of entries and principle of selection

The *DCP* consists of some 450 entries of limited size (a few reach 2,500
words for major figures, topics and movements, but most are between
250 and 1,000 words). We took advantage of the specialised knowledge
of the commissioned authors in generating the list of technical terms,
on the principle that the distributed cognition of experts would be far
superior to the ability of any one generalist to generate such a list of
specialised terms.

In addition to figures clearly associated with continental philosophy,
we also treat (1) figures such as Freud and Saussure, who, while not
philosophers, have influenced many continental philosophers; (2)
Anglo-American philosophers or philosophical movements such as
Davidson, James and Rorty, or Pragmatism and Speech Act Theory,
where there is appreciable resonance with the work of continental
thinkers; (3) fields and movements such as Complexity Theory and
Semiotics, which, while not strictly speaking philosophical, are closely
linked to continental thinking; and (4) fields and movements such as
Cinema, Critical Legal Studies, Ecocriticism, Geography, Queer
Theory and Postcolonial Theory which have been influenced by
continental philosophy.

Target readership, aims and purpose of the work

We address the *DCP* not only to professional philosophers who would
identify themselves as 'continental', but also to beginning students in
philosophy and other humanities disciplines, to professional philosophers in the analytic tradition and to the educated lay public. We aim
for the *DCP* to be a standard reference tool for the above readership. It
provides authoritative, accurate and objective (yet sympathetic) treatments of thinkers, topics and technical terms in clear, jargon-free
language. As one of the foremost difficulties of continental philosophy
is the specialised terminology and complex writing style of many of
its figures, the articles in the *DCP* will provide an encouraging

introduction to the field for those at first intimidated by its difficulties. But in providing this help, the articles will at the same time attempt to explain what philosophical reasons led those thinkers to adopt those terms and styles in the first place. Accuracy without jargon or paraphrase and simplicity without superficiality or naiveté have been the foremost editorial criteria.

Cross-referencing

We provide '*See also*' references at the end of articles on figures to point to articles devoted to technical terms associated with their work or to point to where they are discussed in articles on movements or fields. We do not do so in the reverse direction, that is from technical term articles to major figures. In general, we do not provide references to figures mentioned in an article on a movement or field.

Bibliography

Due to the size of the volume, there is no cumulative bibliography. Bibliographical references are kept to a minimum in the articles, with only the title (of the translation when available) and date of original publication, as in: *Being and Time* (1927). We do not provide the date of books in entries on technical terms, expect in certain cases, such as when a comparison to other dates is made or when the book in question is not mentioned in the article on the figure associated with that term. The availability of bibliographic information via the Internet has, we believe, obviated the need for including much of it in a work of this kind.

Acknowledgements

The *DCP* is truly a collaborative work. I'd like to thank the contributors for their professionalism and expertise; the members of the Editorial Advisory Board: Giovanna Borradori, Simon Glendinning, Richard Kearney, Leonard Lawlor and Paul Patton for their helpful advice at many stages of the project; Jackie Jones (who came up with the idea for the *DCP* in the first place), James Dale, Anna Somerville, Carol Macdonald and all the people at Edinburgh University Press for their good judgement and cheerful support; my student workers Michael Roetzel, Souleymane Fofana, Janet Terry and Sarah Lundmark and the clerical staff at the Department of French Studies at Louisiana State University, Connie Simpson and Louise

Lanier, for their hard work and patience with my endless requests for paper, more paper; my colleagues in the Department of French Studies for abiding my absent-mindedness while finishing this volume; and my students, friends and teachers, who have all helped me grapple with philosophy over the years. As I write these lines, I'm struck by the impossibility of trying to thank my wife, without whose love and good humour I would never have been up to this task. Finally, I'd like to dedicate my work on this volume to Joseph J. Kockelmans, who first introduced me to the study of continental philosophy at Penn State, and whose generosity and wisdom has continued to inspire me in my teaching and writing.

John Protevi
Baton Rouge, January 2005

The Dictionary

A

ABJECTION A notion developed by Kristeva in *Powers of Horror* (1980), where she couples psychoanalysis with anthropological research, in particular Mary Douglas's analysis of defilement in *Purity and Danger* (1969). Douglas maintains that defilement is defined and ritualised in order to protect the borders of the body and society. As Kristeva describes it, the abject is what is excluded in order to set up the clean and proper boundaries of the body, the subject, the society or nation. Above all, it is ambiguity that must be excluded or prohibited so that identity can be stabilised. Bringing together Freud's analysis of the prohibition of incest with that of Lévi-Strauss, Kristeva suggests that ultimately the threatening ambiguity of the abject always comes back to the maternal body, which must be excluded in order to constitute and shore up both individual and social identity. Like all repression, however, the abject maternal is bound to return, and its return can be transformative or even revolutionary.

K. Oliver

ABSOLUTE One of the most crucial and yet very often misunderstood terms in Hegel's philosophy. In the Introduction to the *Phenomenology of Spirit*, Hegel defines 'the absolute' simply as 'whatever in truth is'. This contrasts with mere appearances, semblances or half-truths. Hegel's 'absolute' is thus an expression of realism, of the view that something exists and is whatever it is, regardless of whatever we say, think or believe about it. This realism is consistent with Hegel's 'idealism', because Hegel's idealism is a moderate form of ontological holism: the identity conditions of things are given by their causal characteristics and by constitutive contrasts among their manifest characteristics. Hence the identity conditions of things are mutually interdependent. The only ontologically self-sufficient being is the world-whole, which exists only in and through its various aspects or constituents, namely particular objects, events or other specific phenomena. Hegel contends that the world as a whole has a certain discernable structure and historical *telos*, consisting in the gradual development and achievement of human reason, knowledge and freedom. Through our collective, historically and socially based knowledge of the world-whole to which we belong, the world-whole comes to know itself. The world-whole is thus both substance – it is literally all that does exist, has existed or will exist – and subject: through humanity, the world-whole achieves self-knowledge and not only facilitates but ultimately achieves rational freedom, embodied in human communities.

In the *Phenomenology of Spirit*, the *Philosophy of Right* and in his lectures on absolute spirit, Hegel contends that the modern world is humanly intelligible and inhabitable, that it sufficiently facilitates our individual and collective freedom, and that it thus deserves our affirmation – and our cooperation in ongoing political and social reform. Conversely, Hegel also tried to show that various forms of alienation result mainly from failing to understand the modern world and one's place within it.

K. Westphal

ABSTRACT MACHINE A term used by Deleuze and Guattari in *A Thousand Plateaus* to describe the most abstract level at which systems assemble themselves. Both 'abstract' and 'machine' are terms of art. 'Abstract' has no connotation of conceptual generality, but should rather be understood as being in proximity to the free creative processes of production at the heart of the real. 'Machinic' also has a specialised sense, designating processes that cannot be referred to intentional control, and that therefore have only an oblique relation to actual (technical) machines.

An abstract machine lies between the pure immanence of the flow of matter and processes directly involved in the construction of a particular system, so-called machinic assemblages. Consequently, in an abstract machine, matter is only partly formed or 'intense', prior to the construction of any stable formed substances. In this intense state, matter is neither passively waiting for forms to be impressed upon it, nor is it simply a blindly surging chaos. Rather it is imbued with many of the characteristics of fully constituted stable systems, but as 'traits' or embryonically. These traits actively probe for new creative potentials or 'becomings' in ways that fully realised systems cannot (just as embryos can fold and twist in ways organisms cannot).

Not all abstract machines generate novelty, however; there are also abstract machines of stratification, which create hierarchies and stereotyped behaviour patterns.

A. Welchman

ABSURDITY (1) The quality of being deeply irrational. Modern philosophical interest in the absurd can be traced back to Kierkegaard's interpretation of Abraham's sacrifice in *Fear and Trembling*. That Abraham was ready to sacrifice Isaac to God was not absurd, Kierkegaard argued. What was absurd was Abraham's faith in the continuing validity of God's promise that through Isaac he would have many descendants or, as Kierkegaard put it, that he would get Isaac back. Abraham thus epitomises the 'knight of faith' who continually makes a 'double-movement' of renunciation and hope. How far Kierkegaard himself is committed to such an absurdist view of faith is debatable, although influential commentators such as the Russian existentialist Lev Shestov (1866–1938) made it central to their portrayal of Kierkegaardian existentialism. For many in the twentieth-century, however, the question of the absurd was no longer limited to exceptional religious situations (such as Abraham's), but belongs to life as such and, for the modern consciousness at least, is unavoidable.

G. Pattison

ABSURDITY (2) The twentieth-century philosopher with whom the notion of 'the absurd' is perhaps most closely associated is Albert Camus. In *The Myth of Sisyphus* (1942), Camus identifies himself as an 'absurdist' by contrast with 'existentialists' such as Sartre – a contrast that is usually not noticed or respected by many historians of philosophy, who tend to classify Camus as himself an existentialist. For Camus, 'the absurd' consists in the lack of fit, or congruence, between the rational categories through which we think and the vast universe which eludes all attempts at comprehensive explanation and justification. Our existence, then, is ultimately absurd – an insight that Sartre had already attributed to his protagonist, Roquentin, at the moment of self-revelation which is the climax of Sartre's early novel *Nausea* (1938). In contrast to Sartre's rather dismal portrayal of Roquentin, Camus ends his essay with the famous line: 'We must imagine Sisyphus happy'; such happiness comes from the way Sisyphus accepts absurdity and rejects any hope for a final fit of reason and world.

W. McBride

ACTIVE FORGETTING The process of corporeal re-attunement Nietzsche recommends as a corrective to the asceticism that circumscribes the agency of modern subjects. In Essay II of *On the Genealogy of Morals*, Nietzsche reverses the received wisdom of his day by presenting memory as an unreliable, recently emergent faculty which has been acquired at immeasurable cost to human beings. He describes the forcible investiture of memory as involving a long, painful process, which occupied much of human pre-history, culminating in the establishment of the 'morality of mores'. The aim of this process, he speculates, was to make human beings more regular and calculable, so that they might receive the benefits and bear the responsibilities of life in civil society.

Nietzsche concludes from this account of the acquisition of memory that forgetting is actually more natural to human beings, even if remembering has become our second nature. Rather than treat forgetting as an inertial force or defect (whether moral or physiological), he identifies it as 'an active and in the strictest sense positive faculty of repression', which enables individuals to bypass consciousness as much as possible in their absorption of adventitious experiences. He thus identifies forgetting as essential to the creation of the 'monological' works of art that he most admires. Having 'forgotten the world', as he puts it in Section 367 of *The Gay Science*, an artist may create without regard for those 'witnesses' who may view and evaluate this creation.

Nietzsche occasionally suggests that a regimen of 'active forgetting' may enable (some) human beings to alter or suspend their participation in the ascetic disciplines that define the agency of modern subjects. As envisioned by Nietzsche, a regimen of 'active forgetting' thus involves a deliberate undoing (or unlearning) of the ascetic routines that have become second nature to us. Inasmuch as these routines have enforced the self-division and self-estrangement that fault the agency of modern subjects, a regimen of 'active forgetting' may succeed in recovering for its practitioners a partial measure of self-possession and self-identity. While a complete 'return to nature' (or recovery of a 'second innocence') is simply out of the question, some human beings may be able to 'forget' some aspects of their ascetic training, thereby granting themselves novel opportunities for spontaneous displays of self-assertion. Although a regimen of 'active forgetting' cannot absolve one of the burden of one's history, it may allow one to suffer this burden without also suffering from it.

Our best example of the practice of 'active forgetting' may be Nietzsche's own *Ecce Homo*, in which he purports to explain 'how one becomes what one is'. In *Ecce Homo*, Nietzsche purports to demonstrate how (and that) he has come to 'forget' so much of the ascetic heritage that had stifled him earlier in his life, such that he may now present himself as a world-historical 'destiny'.

D. Conway

ACTOR-NETWORK THEORY (ANT) A research programme associated with some Science and Technology Studies theorists during the 1980s to the mid-1990s; its theoretical death was announced in *Actor*

Network Theory and After (1999). The most notable ANT figures are Madeleine Akrich, Michael Callon, Bruno Latour, John Law and Antoine Hennion. They developed a critical vocabulary – 'inscriptions', 'regimes of delegation', 'the centrality of mediation', 'the sociology of translation' and 'the enrolment of allies' – that enabled theorists to examine the production of technoscientific knowledge in its varied, relational contexts.

Latour highlights two ideas as central to ANT. The first, a semiotics of materiality, allows analysts to treat all entities – not just linguistic ones – as being relationally constituted, as assuming temporary identities based upon associations with other 'actants'. The second is a methodological bracketing of all a priori classificatory categories; this allows analysts, unencumbered by modern classifications of the natural and the cultural, or the human and the non-human, to observe and describe networks of heterogeneous association.

From a critical perspective, because ANT highlights the vast infrastructure that enables technoscientific facts to be accepted as authoritative, it can be understood as a methodological corrective to traditional histories and theories of discovery that revolve around an isolatable, heroic figure of genius. Despite the importance of this narrative shift, a number of feminists and social theorists have criticised ANT for its putative overemphasis on the Machiavellian aspects of networking, that is for depicting scientists as using any available means to establish centres of control.

E. Selinger

ACTUAL/VIRTUAL DISTINCTION A modal distinction proposed by Deleuze as a replacement for the real–possible distinction, and as a way of reformulating the relationship between the empirical and the transcendental (the latter being the 'ground' or 'condition' of the former). The concept of the possible is problematic in two ways. We tend to think of the possible as pre-existing the real, and the real as a possibility that has been instantiated in existence. But this process of realisation is subject to two rules. On the one hand, since not every possibility is realised, realisation involves a limitation by which some possibles are supposed to be repulsed or thwarted, while others are allowed pass into the real. On the other hand, the real is supposed to resemble the possible it realises: the concept of the thing is already given as possible, and simply has existence added to it when it is realised, in a kind of brute leap. But this is where an illusion manifests itself: if the real is supposed to resemble the possible, is it not because we have retrospectively or retroactively 'projected' a fictitious image of the real back into the possible? In other words, it is not the real that resembles the possible, but the possible that resembles the real. The possible thus fails as a transcendental or grounding concept because it is simply traced off the empirical. The error, writes Deleuze in *Logic of Sense*, 'is to conceive of the transcendental in the image and resemblance of what it is supposed to found'.

Replacing the real–possible couplet with the actual–virtual couplet, Deleuze argues in *Difference and Repetition*, is the only way to provide a true concept of the transcendental field. For Deleuze, the virtual and the actual correspond, but they do not resemble each other. A principle of difference reigns throughout, with Deleuze marking the distinction between virtual differentiation and actualisation as differenciation. Virtual differentiation occurs via the composition of 'multiplicities' or 'Ideas', that is, sets of differential elements, differential relations and singular points. The virtual differs from the actual, and the process of actualisation does not proceed by limitation but by differenciation; the virtual differs from itself in being actualised. The transcendental thus no longer outlines the conditions of possible experience, but accounts for the genesis of *real* experience: it forms an intrinsic genesis, not an extrinsic conditioning. But to be a condition of real experience, the condition can be no broader than what it conditions; the virtual must therefore be determined along with the actual that it conditions, and it must change as the conditioned changes (conditions are not universal but singular). The search for new and actual concepts can be infinite, since there is always an excess of the virtual that animates them (there can therefore be no a priori categories, in the Kantian sense).

D. Smith

See also: transcendental empiricism

ADESTINATION A term used by Derrida to indicate the deconstruction of communication. When pronounced with its definite article, the French word (*l'adestination*) is indistinguishable from its opposite (*la destination*). It can therefore be understood as another version of *différance*, but whereas the latter term intevenes most explicitly in the concept of the sign, adestination effects the deconstruction of communication. It is the necessary and irreducible structural possibility that a letter can not arrive, built into the letter by means of its address or posting, for once it is consigned to the postal system and to uncontrollable mechanisms of delay, nothing can guarantee that it will arrive. Only once it has arrived can it be said with certainty to arrive.

Derrida develops the term in his debate with Lacan, who concludes his analysis of Poe's *Purloined Letter* with the assertion that a letter always arrives at its destination ('Le Facteur de la vérité' in *The Post Card*). That assertion is for Derrida a sign of psychoanalysis's recourse to the truth of a transcendental signifier. In 'Envois' (*The Post Card*) he performs adestination by writing postcards which are addressed to a loved one but which are, as it were, purloined by the reader, and which, by a complicated set of narrative effects, expose their precious contents to the chance and destiny of the postal system.

D. Wills

ADORNO, THEODOR (1903–69) German philosopher and member of the Frankfurt School, which attempted to connect Marxist theory with investigations of present material conditions. Adorno trained as a classical pianist and composer and his earliest writings were in music criticism, a field always central to his concerns, though he wrote on a range of issues in cultural studies, sociology, literary criticism and philosophy. Shortly after Adorno joined the Institute for Social Research at the University of Frankfurt, Hitler rose to power and the Institute was shut down. Adorno then moved to Oxford before settling in America for the duration of The Second World War. After the war, he returned to Frankfurt, helping to reconstitute the Institute and serving as its director during the last years of his life.

These periods of exile and return were Adorno's most productive: during the former he wrote *Dialectic of Enlightenment* (with Horkheimer) (1944), a genealogical critique of subjectivity and instrumental rationality, and *Minima Moralia* (1951), a melancholy assessment of the damaged character of modern 'private life', which is asked to serve as refuge from the societal structures that, in turn, distort it. During the latter, Adorno composed *Negative Dialectics* (1966) and *Aesthetic Theory* (1970), critical assessments of the cognitive character of, respectively, philosophical reason and aesthetic judgement, as well as the divide that has occurred between them.

Throughout all his works, Adorno traces, and subjects to critique, the rise of 'identity thinking', the reduction of objects to instances of general concepts. In this endeavour Adorno does not only produce a history of thinking but, coinciding with Weber's thesis of the 'rationalisation' and 'disenchantment' of the modern world, he also traces the rise of a form of social organisation that renders individuals little more than occasions for the application of abstracted, universal rules. Rationality and society mirror and inform one another: reason is social and society is, more or less, a product of reason. The tendency towards societal rationalisation is exemplified by the ever-expanding centrality of exchange value in capitalist society and culture, the subsumption of the determinate qualities and uses of each thing and person to a singular quantity (abstract labour time) that renders it indifferently equivalent with every other. The ascendance of exchange value in capitalism is, however, only an instance of a tendency endemic to the development of rationality as such, which is driven by the imperative of self-preservation to reduce the world to a system of general principles that allow for control. In being directed towards overcoming fear, liberating us from the fate of natural forces and ending suffering, such identity thinking recoils upon human beings by reducing our material singularity to the status of a 'specimen', an object of administration and control. For Adorno, this reductive tendency unmasks such reason as irrational and places it in an immanent relation to genocide, understood as 'absolute integration'.

Such rationality is not simply false – if it were, it would be useless for the control of nature. Rather, it is the systematic drive to render nature entirely determinable through a deductive order of concepts that distorts reason (and the rational subject) and renders it incapable of accounting for, and responding to, its own material ground in the object and in experience. Indeed, the triumph of such reason, and of the socio-historical world it expresses and informs, distorts experience, both because rational structures come to shape individual engagement with the world and because rationalised society shapes objects and individuals. Embedded in, and constituted by, this history, no individual is free to simply live or think differently. Thus Adorno continually insists that attempts to think outside the subject/object opposition are misguided: the opposition is a socio-historical development, one that is false but also real.

Rather than attempting an impossible escape, Adorno produces an immanent critique of the products of modernity, revealing their internal antagonisms and contradictions – the scars by which identity thinking attests to its always incomplete effort to free itself from the non-identical – as well as the suppressed hopes within such products for another mode of life. Still, he does endeavour to articulate strategies for a thinking that would not be identity-based, an effort that informs his often difficult 'paratactic' manner of writing, in which the modes of deductive argumentation are dispensed with in order to render a text in which every claim is at an equal distance from its object. The negative critique of concepts is also an effort to arrange concepts into 'constellations', a series of relations which is neither deductive nor subsumptive, but which, clustered around a thing, might grasp its historical singularity, 'the side which to a classifying procedure is either a matter of indifference or a burden'.

What haunts this effort is the difficult dialectic of revolution: the suspicion that no new manner of thinking could develop entirely without a transformation of society, matched with the fear that any revolution pursued under the present regime of thought will reproduce terror. The position of art intimates this dilemma: as a form of cognition grounded in the sensible and not guided by determinative judgement, art inscribes the possibility of an alternative, reflective form of knowledge and praxis. Yet the status of art in the modern world – a sphere disconnected from and unable to influence the economic, political and moral spheres wherein rationalisation holds sway – renders art incapable of the social transformation toward which it gestures. Art's autonomy is the key to its persistence as a different mode of knowledge *and* the source of its inability to be translated into societal change. For Adorno, the position of dialectical philosophy, or critical theory, is analogous to that of art: it holds open a small space of freedom and hope precisely through its relentless practice of critique.

M. Bray

See also: Cinema; Critical Theory; dialectic of enlightenment; Enlightenment; negative dialectics

AESTHETIC JUDGEMENT That form of judgement, examined by Kant in his *Critique of Judgement*, which concerns beauty. In the 'Transcendental Aesthetic' of the *Critique of Pure Reason* Kant distinguished between aesthetic as a doctrine of 'a priori sensibility' and the 'critique of taste'. The aesthetic judgement belongs largely to the latter, and is analysed in the first part of the *Critique of Judgement*. This form of judgement has for Kant two fundamental peculiarities: it involves the ascription of a quality (beauty) inseparable from a feeling (pleasure), and is reflective, meaning that it does not apply a concept to an object in the manner of the 'determinate' judgements analysed in the first *Critique* but seeks out its concept by reflecting upon its acts of judgement.

In the Analytic of the aesthetic judgement of taste Kant explores the characteristics of such judgements in terms of the basic headings of the table of the categories established in the first *Critique*, namely quality, quantity, relation and modality. The quality of such judgements consists in the absence of 'interest' – they are as indifferent to the materiality as they are to the rational ideas informing their objects. The quantity of such judgements consists in their 'universal validity', but this universality is founded neither upon the subjective summing of individual judgements nor on the universality of the concept. The relation informing an aesthetic judgement consists in 'purposiveness without end' that is neither the material structure of its object nor its intelligible perfection. Finally, the modality proper to aesthetic judgement is necessity, but not one based on 'objective principles'.

Kant's procedure with respect to the aesthetic judgement in the third *Critique* is self-consciously aporetic – he devotes more attention to describing what it is not rather than defining its positive qualities. The searching and inconclusive character of the investigation extends to the discussion of the deduction of such judgements and to their proximity with the experience of the sublime. It has also contributed to the intense discussion provoked by the aesthetic judgement which saw a remarkable renaissance late in the twentieth century in the writings of Arendt, de Man, Derrida and Lyotard.

H. Caygill

AESTHETICS That philosophical discipline which reflects on questions provoked by art works and artistic production, often – but not always – in conjunction with the notion of 'aesthetics' as the realm of the senses. One of the major works in continental aesthetics is Heidegger's 'The Origin of the Work of Art' (1936), which argues that to understand art we must turn to actual works whose work-being has been covered over by a language governed by the concepts of 'form' and 'matter', and by practices focused on the utility of objects detached from their origins. Heidegger wants to show that the nature of art is to be the truth of being setting itself to work in the work of art, the unconcealedness of being, since whenever art happens, something is brought out of nothing in a founding leap, opening a world and setting it up on earth. Derrida counters in 'Restitutions' (in *The Truth in Painting*, 1978) that the work of art is silent, meaningless, unless its involvement in the world is disclosed in our pre-comprehension of the world. A return to origins, to the pure presence of the object, would require the erasure of all signs, memory and imagination. The most we can accomplish is to capture the presence of a work as a representation, with the result that the more we know of the world, the farther we are from an understanding of the work of art as a pure origin. What is at issue is the hold language has over what it describes in the work of art. Wendy Steiner (*The Colors of Rhetoric*, 1982) describes this conflict as one in which prose works engage the established linguistic signifying system while visual arts emphasise the thingly nature of the work of art, yet the language system defines both.

Lyotard points out in *The Postmodern Condition* (1979) that thought strives for determinations by setting up a system, theory, programme or project in anticipation of the work of art, yet there is pain at the thought that nothing might happen and sublime pleasure that works of art appear where there might have been nothing. In this account, contemporary art is not discourse, but the dissolution of discourse, the collapse of the logical, discursive sequence. As Kant made clear in the *Critique of Judgement* (1791), visual pleasure reduced to zero in the encounter with the sublime engenders an orientation for thought to the super-sensible which is no longer limited by the demands of discursive reason. Yet, as Hegel observes in the *Lectures on Aesthetics* (1820–9), Kant fell back into the division into subjective thought and objective things and to the perverse idea that subverts art to moral ends outside the sphere of art. Still, according to Heidegger, Hegel inaugurates the 'age of the world picture', bringing what is present-at-hand before oneself as something standing over against oneself, forcing it into this relationship as the norm where 'man' takes precedence over every other possible centre. Such subjectivism stands in defiance of the idea expressed by Merleau-Ponty in *Phenomenology of Perception* (1945), that in thought, history and life, the only surpassings we know are concrete, partial, encumbered with survivals, saddled with deficits.

Following these lines of thought, we can say that the disruption of representation in modern art does not confine itself to the aesthetic dimension. The creation of new spatial and temporal relations, new forms and visual norms has its counterpart in the decentring of 'man' in the cosmos. Thus the work of art is not the communication, expression or conveyance of meanings, nor is it the privileged expression of a being at the world. In any case, expression requires far more than anonymous embodiment, it calls for denotation, designation, the force of speaking and being spoken. Words are not just sounds, expressions are not just perceptions; one must distinguish the 'sense' of perceptions from their physical and psychological aspects.

Where does the trajectory taken by continental aesthetics leave us? We may find ourselves with Barthes (*The Pleasure of the Text*, 1975), with an anti-hero, the reader-spectator at the moment she takes pleasure in the text-spectacle which abolishes logical contradiction, mixes every language or semiotic system and accepts every charge of illogicality, a sanctioned Babel: subtle subversion rather than *oppositional* confrontation. Or, perhaps, as Deleuze and Guattari assert in *What is Philosophy?* (1990), we can come to understand the work of art in terms of a block of sensations, percepts without a perceiver, sensations and affects that exceed any lived being, inhabiting, instead, the work of art.

Contemporary aesthetics influenced by continental philosophy, we may conclude, posits a work of art detached from fixed social, aesthetic and metaphysical objectives yet recognises that the work of art is influenced by the space and time we occupy, the space and time of media, of economic, political and military power. But beyond this we find as well, the space and time that constructs our perspectives, that space and time of social relations and environmental impacts, that space and time of our world and our cosmos. In this way, the complexity of the work of art can no longer be evaded, and we encounter its multiple layers of sense as they emerge from its myriad influences – including its relations to other works of art – such that the work of art now functions within a network of influences, an effect of their illuminations, a perspective emerging from the stars. As such it evokes not only the question, why is it that I am alive here and now to see, to sense this light radiating from the work of art? but also the question, what is this world, this universe, that intertwines its events, that spatio-temporalises itself, radiant and diffusive in myriad directions making it possible, once again, for beauty to emerge?

D. Olkowski

AFFIRMATION A notion developed prominently by Derrida as 'another thinking of the eternal return' ('Pas' in *Parages*, 1986) and articulated through two words, 'come [*viens*]' and 'yes [*oui*]', and through reference, in particular, to Maurice Blanchot and James Joyce. It is a major preoccupation and, as Derrida says of the *oui*, something that has 'for a very long time . . . mobilised or traversed everything I have been trying to think, write, teach, or read' ('Ulysses Gramophone'). By means of *oui* and *viens* he attempts to develop an affirmative 'force' of language, a type of tonality or even musicality that functions as it were before or outside of language, an affirmativity that renders possible every performative speech act (in Austin's terms) such as a promise or a consent, and which thereby allows for meaning in excess of any programmable information.

Emptied as it were of semantic content, *oui* and *viens* operate on the one hand as the very e-vent of a language as invitation, consent or call to the other. On the other hand, to the extent that they are within language – and since there are no singular utterances – they necessarily function as repetitions or citations of themselves. This opens the threat of mechanical parody, and even of eschatological closure, as well as the chance of a response come from the other, but never the simple symmetry of another 'yes' or even a 'no', and indeed not even from a simple identifiable other; rather 'the light dancing *yes* of affirmation, the open affirmation of the gift' ('Ulysses Gramophone').

D. Wills

AFRICAN PHILOSOPHY We focus here on African philosophy in its relation to recent continental philosophy. We thus only mention, but do not discuss, multi-disciplinary (linguistic, ethnographic, historical) studies of pre-colonial African thought, as well as the lively debates surrounding Africa's role, including that of Egypt, in the network of ancient Mediterranean cultures from which Greek culture emerged. Nor do we discuss the vast impact of Islamic cultures, including those of North Africa, on contemporary philosophy in Europe and other parts of Africa. Finally, we must neglect the thought of Du Bois and others on the complex relations of African, African-American and European thought.

Instead, we begin with Father Placide Tempels's *Bantu Philosophy* (1945), which, according to a standard account, was 'the first [text] to attribute a developed philosophical system to an African people'. Tempels' work flew in the face of dominant anthropological conceptions of the alleged primitive mentality of Africans, instead recognising African rationality by calling its thought a 'philosophy'. *Bantu Philosophy* must be taken into account here as it helped set the context for future debates on the field designated by the term 'African philosophy'.

Tempels's affirmation of African rationality in *Bantu Philosophy* was enthusiastically received among African intellectuals even while being condemned by many white Europeans; the heightened tensions at the beginning of the era of intensified anti-colonial struggle cannot be underestimated in assessing this reception. Yet Tempels' work cannot be simply hailed as positive in all regards. His 'progressive' argument for a developed African philosophical system came at the expense of homogenising an intellectual African heritage that is in fact historically, geographically and culturally diverse; furthermore, *Bantu Philosophy* preserves a hierarchy privileging Europe over Africa, regarding African thought as a junior partner to the full flowering of European thought.

Despite (or, rather, because of) these shortcomings, almost all subsequent discussions of African philosophy have felt obliged to come to grips with the reception of *Bantu Philosophy* in so far as that reception reveals a complex set of problems that continue to challenge notions of 'Africa' and 'philosophy'. In particular, one must be wary of the way an affirmation of African reason as 'African philosophy' potentially leads to collectivist and homogenising understandings that are founded upon racist rather than empirical groupings. On the one hand, there might only be some notion of race or 'blackness' that functions as the unifying category under which are gathered all the profound historical and cultural differences of human life on the continent of Africa. On the other hand, simply rejecting the notion of 'African philosophy' might reinstate the racist notion of a 'primitive mentality'. Therefore, consideration of *Bantu Philosophy*, the text and its reception, provides the following challenge: that one be wary of rejecting the honorific of 'philosophy' even as one interrogates the supposed unity of 'Africa'. Thus the major questions fuelling the recent growth in interest in the field of 'African philosophy' are: What is African about African philosophy? What kinds of questions characterise the practice of African philosophy? And lastly, what is specifically philosophical about these questions?

A prominent participant in the discursive field formed by texts interrogating the pairing of 'African' and 'philosophy' is Paulin Hountondji. In his 1976 book *African Philosophy: Myth and Reality*, Hountondji cautions against the false collectivisation of African thought that might accompany the term 'African philosophy'. Hountondji defines 'African philosophy' as 'a set of texts written by Africans and described as philosophical by their authors themselves'. That is, the utility of the term is determined or grounded by the geographical origin of authorship and self-conception of practice. Through this definition, Hountondji intends to designate a philosophical field wherein the word 'African' is a geographic and not a metaphysical descriptor. In Hountondji's words, positioning 'African Philosophy' as metaphysically particular constitutes 'a metamorphisation of the "primitive mentality" into a "primitive philosophy"'. By situating 'African' as a solely geographic descriptor, Hountondji seeks to preclude the simplistic way a thought still hostage to colonialist prejudice, even in a politically postcolonial age, might unify conceptions of the African intellect. Hountondji's definition is consistent with the practice evident in the terms 'German philosophy', 'French philosophy', and so on. However, this geographic treatment proves wholly inadequate in capturing both important strains within the field as well as the historical exigencies that condition the pairing of 'African' and 'philosophy.'

In his 1992 book *In My Father's House*, Kwame Anthony Appiah writes that Hountondji's geographic definition 'knowingly sidesteps what has been one of the cruces of philosophical debate in postcolonial black Africa', that is 'what sorts of intellectual activity should be called "philosophy"'. Appiah's criticism of Hountondji illustrates not only an inadequacy of the geographic definition but also a powerful

contribution that 'African philosophy' promises to continental philosophy – a careful reflective stance toward the very practice of
philosophising. Appiah accurately points out that, given the divergent
schools of analytic and continental thought, 'Western academic
philosophy may have a hard time agreeing on its own definition'
and that contemporary African philosophers 'have inherited the two
warring traditions'. Appiah illustrates the inadequacies of the two
dominant means of defining the practice of 'philosophy'. First of all,
('analytic') attempts to define philosophy through its employment of
'rational argumentation' fail to set it apart from other theoretical
disciplines. And secondly, ('continental') attempts to define philosophy
as the study of a specifiable canon are frustrated by the question,
'Whose canon?' Appiah continues on to define philosophy as a *family
of questions* that has historically been the subject of philosophical
contemplation. Appiah's definition is persuasive in many ways. However, the most striking dimension of his essay remains his ability to
illustrate how the problematics of the term 'African philosophy' can
prompt a reflection in which any practitioner of philosophy, analytic or
continental, European or African, has a vested interest. Namely, the
question 'What is philosophy?'

Within this same work Appiah also identifies a fruitful conceptual
contribution to 'Africa's real problems' as the foremost purpose of the
field of 'African philosophy'. This notion of 'Africa's real problems'
touches upon another important topic of debate in the field of African
Philosophy, that is the role of the critique of Eurocentrism and the
work provoked by the onset of the postcolonial age. The historical
reality of imperial colonial projects throughout the African continent
left indelible marks upon both Western and African intellectual life.
The project of critiquing Eurocentrism and addressing the colonial
experience characterises the Negritude movement of the 1940s and
1950s, as led by Aimé Césaire and Léopold Senghor. More recent
philosophers, such as Tsenay Serequeberhan and Lucius Outlaw, have
also foregrounded this critical project within the field of African
philosophy's concern.

In *On Race and Philosophy* (1996) Outlaw stands with Appiah
against Hountondji's geographical orientation. Outlaw aims to situate,
via the lens of deconstruction, the critical project of African philosophy
as thinking of philosophy 'not [as] structured by universal and necessary norms, but by norms conditioned by social, historical contingencies'. Benefiting from deconstruction's attention to strategy and
construction rather than an allegiance to self-evident or transcendental
axioms, Outlaw wants to instigate the critique and displacement of first

principles like 'Western philosophy' (53). By questioning and displacing the dominance of 'Western philosophy', Outlaw seeks to direct the discipline toward 'a fabric of historicity' that draws the practice of philosophising, in Africa and the West, together. Outlaw's deconstructive stance is one of many efforts to bridge the seeming divide between 'African philosophy' and 'Western philosophy' via an interrogation of the pairing 'African' and 'philosophy'. The work of Hountondji, Appiah, Serequeberhan and Outlaw thus illustrates how fostering a critical relationship between African and continental philosophy can contribute to a necessary and constructive interrogation of both the practice of raciological thinking and the practice (and discipline) of philosophy.

S. Hansen

See also: African Socialism; Césaire; Fanon; negritude; Postcolonial Theory

AFRICAN SOCIALISM A humanist socio-political and socio-economic ideology that sought to adapt socialism to the African settings of the postcolonial era. It had a number of variants, some of the most notable ones being Julius Nyerere's *Ujamaa* ['familyhood'], Léopold Senghor's integration of negritude with socialism, Kwame Nkrumah's formulation of socialism based on the philosophy of 'Consciencism', and Kenneth Kaunda's formulation of socialism based on 'Humanism'.

In *Socialism and Rural Development* (1967), Nyerere rejects Marx's assertion that the history of every society has been a history of class struggle, by asserting that the traditional African society was based on extended families which unconsciously lived according to three basic principles of *Ujamaa*: 'mutual respect, sharing of joint production and work for all'. Two basic factors that prevented this traditional society from full flowering, Nyerere insists, were the acceptance of one form of human inequality, that of women's marginalisation, and the failure to break away from poverty due to ignorance and a small scale of operations. Nyerere's vision of Modern Tanzanian Socialism, then, was to combine the traditional three principles of *Ujamaa* with the modern knowledge and techniques learnt from technologically developed countries so as to defeat poverty and build a relatively well-off egalitarian society. Tanzania institutionalised the vision of *The Arusha Declaration and TANU's Policy on Socialism and Self-Reliance* (1967).

Nyerere's *Ujamaa: Essays on Socialism* (1968) attempts to provide an accessible text that highlights the link between the *Ujamaa* philosophy and *Ujamaa* policies. Here he reasserts the claims he made in *Ujamaa: The Basis of African Socialism* (1962) that Africans do not need to be converted to socialism since it is rooted in the African past and reaffirms that 'socialism is an attitude of mind'. His conceptualisation of socialism as a moral and humane outlook, in contrast to the exploitative capitalist mindset, ideologically legitimised the nationalisation of some private firms, the establishment of cooperative *Ujamaa* villages, the introduction of policies set out in his *Education for Self-Reliance* (1967) and the enforcement of the ruling party's anti-capitalist Leadership Code, which were all meant to foster socialist values and thus create an egalitarian society.

Senghor's *On African Socialism* (1964) starts from Marx and Engels but seeks to retain only those methods and ideas that would help solve the problems of Francophone Africa in the postcolonial era, which, we should remember, was also the time of the Cold War. His socialism rejects both capitalist individualism and Communist materialism in its allegedly 'scientific' guise in favour of a middle course of 'democratic' or 'open' socialism 'which goes so far as to integrate spiritual values, a socialism which ties in with the old ethical current of the French socialists'. While it recognises the need for state intervention and control of key economic activities, it never neglected what it saw as the need for integrating traditional African communal values as encapsulated in Senghor's philosophy of negritude into modern economic society.

In *Consciencism* (1964), Nkrumah proposes 'philosophical consciencism', which aims to harmoniously synthesise the 'original humanist principles underlying African society' with Islamic and Euro-Christian influences. Like Nyerere, he also asserts that there were no classes of a Marxian kind in traditional African society. In its quest to adapt modern technology inherited from colonialism without embracing the dehumanisation inherent in capitalism and neo-colonialism, Nkrumah's version of African socialism embraced two tenets of scientific socialism, namely dialectics and materialism.

Kaunda's (1974) *Humanism in Zambia and a Guide to Its Implementation Part II* 'was a statement of philosophical theory on the meaning of human existence'. Drawing from the Christian belief that humanity was created by a master designer for a purpose, it asserted that to use a 'concretely existing' human being as a means to any end abrogates his or her humanity since it dehumanises both the user/exploiter and the used/exploited. Based on its assumption that the traditional African society was communal and centred on the human, Kaunda argued that 'Man's "truth" lies in Man as man-in-community' while his 'untruth' lies in the 'isolated self' characteristic of capitalist manipulation. Since it viewed socialism as 'a stage of human development attained just before that final which is humanism', it therefore sought to 'to devise a social, political and economic order which is based on Man's truth rather than Man's untruth'. The Zambian State was to be structured for the service of humanity, which, he felt, could only be realised in a socialist state which upholds 'the noble principle of egalitarianism'.

C. Chachage

See also: African Philosophy; negritude

AGAMBEN, GIORGIO (1942–) Italian philosopher who works on aesthetics, the philosophy of language, metaphysics and political philosophy. Agamben draws on Heidegger, Benjamin, Derrida, Foucault, Arendt, Schmitt and others to address the question of human finitude, action and community in the political context of late modernity.

In works such as *The Coming Community* (1990), Agamben explores a conception of community based on a treatment of human finitude distinct from that found in the work of writers such as Derrida and Nancy, who continue to acknowledge the Heideggerian concern with mortality. By contrast, Agamben approaches human finitude in terms of life, and thus also the power of life and the powers to which life is subjected. The influences on Agamben at this point are several, including Heidegger's understanding of art as a founding event that precedes the sphere of judgement. Heidegger himself recognises the act of political foundation as implicated in this structure, and Agamben can be read as undertaking a more developed exploration of this perspective. Constituent power, as expressed in such a founding moment, is quite different from the constituted power articulated in terms of law. However, pre-juridical power takes the form of a revolutionary violence that is presupposed by the constitution of law, leading to a conception of sovereignty with paradox at its very core.

While many past thinkers have recognised a similar paradox in sovereignty, Agamben's strength lies in the originality with which he formulates this paradox and then proceeds to think through it from within, from the very position in which we find ourselves today. The paradoxical presupposition by law of the power that founds the state of law is perceived by Agamben as making the inside and the outside indistinguishable. In *Homo Sacer* (1995), he thereby develops the idea of sovereignty in terms of the exception to law, and describes the contemporary situation as one in which the violence of the pre-juridical permeates a political order presented as an extended state of emergency in which the normal condition of law is suspended. This radicalised and prolonged condition of law as exception no longer bears on a classical conception of human life as *bios*, life as a form of living characteristic of an individual and of the community to which he or she belongs, but on *zoē*, the bare fact of life itself. In his analysis of the contemporary political order, Agamben sees power work to reduce the human to bare life, a reference back to the Roman conception of *homo sacer*, a human being who could be killed without incurring legal penalty. Human life is thereby included in the juridical order as exception, as that which is exposed to the immediate exercise of power, to the point of death. As this order becomes a global reality, so new forms of political thought and action are required and are in fact emerging. Agamben has sought to identify these in ideas such as that of a politics of gesture and in the way the classical figure of the citizen is being displaced by that of the refugee.

D. Webb

See also: biopower; Death; state of exception

ALETHEIA The Greek word for 'truth', which comes to play an important role in Heidegger's philosophy. Heidegger understands this notion quite literally, and translates it as 'disclosedness' (*Erschlossenheit*), or 'unconcealment' (*Unverborgenheit*). He hopes thereby to show that our modern concept of truth – inherited from late Antiquity and the Middle Ages, strengthened in the philosophies of Descartes, Kant and many others, and operating also in the sciences as something that is taken for granted – testifies to a relation to nature, and so to Being itself, that is radically different from the Greek one. What we call 'truth', namely the agreement or correspondence between fact and theory, or between a thing and the concept of that thing, has little in common with what the Greeks understood, and most of all experienced, with that word. Truth for them, and for Heidegger who tries to revive what the Greeks intimated, meant the coming into presence of beings, out of hiddenness or concealment. This coming into presence out of concealment was a source of constant questioning and wonder. Philosophy was intimately bound up with this need to question truth understood as unconcealment. In *Being and Time*, and in the texts leading up to it, Heidegger understands existence, or Dasein, as the site of the *aletheuein*, or the disclosing, from out of which beings become manifest. Later on, it is being itself that is understood as truth or unconcealment. Hence the formulation: 'the truth of being'. But the essence of truth (as concealment, or *lethe*), remains concealed in unconcealment. Only what Heidegger calls 'thought' (*Denken*) is able to do justice to this hidden essence of truth.

M. de Beistegui

See also: Truth

ALIENATION (1) A term widely used in contemporary social thought to refer to a situation in which a human product or attribute appears as independent and hostile. The concept originates in Hegel's philosophy and was taken up by Feuerbach, who criticises Christian religion as an alienated expression of human attributes (*The Essence of Christianity*). The term 'alienation' is used to translate two closely related German words: *Entfremdung* (estrangement) and *Entäusserung* (externalisation). Its main modern currency is due to the influence of Marx's account of 'alienated' or 'estranged' labour (*entfremdete Arbeit*) in *Economic and Philosophical Manuscripts*, the unpublished notes of the young Marx written in 1844. They appeared for the first time only in 1932 and were not translated into English until 1959. Their impact since then has been enormous.

According to Marx, productive activity is our 'species activity' (*Gattungswesen*), our 'essential activity'; it is potentially fulfilling and an end-in-itself. However, alienated labour is experienced as a mere means to satisfy material needs and as a forced activity. Likewise, the products of labour are experienced as hostile and independent powers working against the worker. Marx also holds that our relationship to God, the state and economic and social structures can take an alienated form, in which they too are experienced as independent and hostile. Some argue that Marx's use of the term is characteristic of an early, philosophical and humanist, period of his thought and that he abandoned the concept in his later work (Althusser, *For Marx*, 1965), while others dispute this interpretation (Mészáros, *Marx's Theory of Alienation*, 1970). Alienation has now become a major term of social theory and social criticism; it is one of the few terms of Marxist philosophy which has passed into the common language. In the process, however, it has lost its specifically Hegelian philosophical basis and is used in a variety of ways to refer to conditions of meaninglessness, powerlessness, isolation, self-estrangement and so on.

S. Sayers

ALIENATION (2) While Marx's conception of alienation emphasised the workers' objective condition, many later writers placed greater emphasis on alienation as a psychological phenomenon, as in the idea of 'alienated youth'. In mid-twentieth-century existentialism, particularly in Sartre's thought, the notion underwent a philosophical revival as a way of characterising an inevitable aspect of human existence. If we are indeed 'thrown' into a world not of our making, as both Sartre and Heidegger insist, then alienation, otherness, is part of being human. The related notions of 'otherness' and 'the other' are also crucial themes for numerous other continental philosophers such as Levinas and Ricoeur.

W. McBride

ALIENATION (3) Beauvoir uses the term 'alienation' in two distinct but related senses. One refers to the process of identity formation; the other describes our relationship to freedom. In both cases, Beauvoir taps into its Hegelian, Marxist, Lacanian and existential-phenomenological meanings. Understood in terms of the dynamic of self-recognition, alienation refers to the process by which the child maps itself onto its body image and explores this image for keys to its identity. Beauvoir argues that within patriarchy, boys alienate themselves in a body part, the penis, and identify with its powers; in this way, they see themselves as embodied agents. No such body part is made available to the girl, who is directed to dolls; alienating herself in these passive doubles of her body, the girl experiences herself as lacking agency. These sexed alienations of identity formation create sexed experiences of alienated freedom. Each sex alienates itself from the ambiguities of freedom differently, and neither embraces their embodied freedom. Men identify themselves as absolute subjects, while women experience themselves as objectified bodies. With men alienation is self-initiated, and they are therefore responsible for their bad faith. With women (and other marginalised groups), alienation is the effect of oppression, not of a choice to evade the responsibilities of freedom. For men, the antidote to alienated freedom is ethical conversion. Women, however, must retrieve their bodies from its alienations and reclaim their alienated subjectivity.

D. Bergoffen

ALTHUSSER, LOUIS (1918–90) French philosopher and communist who contributed to Marxist theory, psychoanalysis, literary criticism and philosophy of science. As advisor to students at the École Normale Supérieure, he influenced a generation of French thinkers. Most well known for his works from the early 1960s advocating a structuralist rereading of Marx, Althusser engaged the deepest problems of political theory and practice until the early 1980s when mental illness greatly reduced his philosophical acumen.

Combating the idealistic tendencies of post-Stalinist Marxisms, Althusser proposed in his first collection of essays *For Marx* (1965) to distinguish the young Marx who wrote of 'species being' and 'alienation' from the mature Marx of *Capital* who had abandoned philosophical anthropology for a genuinely materialist philosophy of history and dialectic. Since such a break was never made explicit by Marx and in order to expose it in Marx's texts, Althusser developed a close reading strategy that combined Lacanian psychoanalysis, Levi-Straussian anthropology and Bachelardian philosophy of science.

The result was a Marxism purged of metaphysical speculations on the *telos* and essence of man, and concerned solely with an analysis of the materialist logic of economic and social structures in history.

In *Reading Capital* (1965), Althusser and his collaborators sought to render explicit these economic and social structures, to define the different levels of production (economic, political, ideological and scientific) and to show the way in which these four practices constitute the socio-economic totality. Here Althusser's work is recognisably structuralist and his conclusion that structures, not man, make history leads him to advocate an anti-humanist position. In Althusser's structural Marxism, there is no spirit of man striving to realise itself in history nor is there a necessary economic contradiction that will lead to a proletarian revolution. Instead, there are only specific and analysable productive practices that constitute the social totality and which overdetermine the subjects (states, persons, classes) that exist within that totality.

Departing from this original, rather Spinozistic thesis that the different levels of production have no relation one to the other, Althusser from 1966 until his death strove to work out the interrelations among economics, politics, philosophy, science and ideology and to specify the content of each practice. Out of these revisions, Althusser is best known for his suggestion from *Sur la reproduction* (1995) that ideological state apparatuses interpellate the subject and thus are responsible for subjectification. In such works as *Lenin and Philosophy* (1969) and *Response to John Lewis* (1972), he also advanced the thesis that science produces non-ideological knowledge and that philosophy is that practice which separates ideological from non-ideological knowledge, thereby making a political intervention. It is this type of intervention that may best describe the intent and function of Althusser's philosophy taken as a whole.

W. Lewis

See also: epistemological break; Ideological State Apparatuses; interpellation; Marxism; overdetermination; problematic; Structuralism; uneven development

ANALYTIC PHILOSOPHY For the purposes of this account, that movement of modern philosophy which has distinguished itself through a contrast to an 'other' that it names 'continental philosophy'.

Although analytic philosophy has a disputed history, on all accounts it is intertwined with that of 'continental philosophy'. For many British philosophers of the 1950s the developments which marked its birth arose from what Gilbert Ryle called 'the Cambridge transformation of the theory of concepts'. The heroes here are Russell, Moore and Wittgenstein. According to Ryle in *The Concept of Mind* (1949), the basic feature of this Cambridge transformation was the realisation, 'forced by logical considerations', that concepts are not a species of 'Platonic universal or essence'. Ryle outlined the new 'Anglo-Saxon' theory and practice with characteristic clarity:

> Concepts are not things that are there crystallised in a splendid isolation; they are discriminable features, but not detachable atoms, of what is integrally said or integrally thought. They are not detachable parts of, but distinguishable contributions to, the unitary senses of sentences. To examine them is to examine the live force of things that we actually say. It is to examine them not in retirement, but doing their co-operative work.

Analytic philosophy, on this view, is essentially conceptual analysis. Not that Ryle regarded this feature of it as itself especially innovative: it stands squarely in the tradition of philosophy 'familiar to us *ambulando* since Socrates'. On the other hand, however, Ryle takes 'the Cambridge transformation' to bring about a fundamental cleavage within the contemporary Western tradition, for it establishes a crucial contrast with the ongoing practice of what he calls 'Continental philosophers', those philosophers who, he supposes, regard philosophy as some kind of quasi-perceptual intuition of essences. (Husserl's phenomenology, Ryle's only example, is at least a prima facie fair target here.)

Ryle's insistence that the analytic movement has its origins in distinctively 'Anglo-Saxon' developments has been strongly contested from within by Michael Dummett. According to Dummett in *The Origins of Analytic Philosophy* (1994), Russell and Moore are bit-parts only and alone on centre stage is Frege – who was German and thus geographically speaking 'continental'. With Frege, Dummett argues, two basic 'beliefs' that define analytic philosophy are arrived at for the first time: 'first, that a philosophical account of thought can be attained through a philosophical account of language, and secondly, that a comprehensive account can only be so attained'.

More recent research by Ray Monk in 'Bertrand Russell's Brain-child' (*Radical Philosophy*, 78, 1996) has suggested that both of these historical pictures are, in reality, 'myths'. If this is so it is perhaps not altogether surprising. For its own history as a movement is not typically regarded as a *philosophically* significant issue for analytic philosophy anyway. However, Monk's dissatisfaction with complacent and overly simplified historical accounts is not isolated, and in the last few years there has been a substantial amount of soul-searching among analytic and analytically trained philosophers concerning the details and philosophical significance of their historical roots.

In part this historical turn reflects that 'what is integrally said' by the statements of philosophers who belong to the analytic movement has remained stubbornly resistant to a purely conceptual or theoretical analysis of a distinctive analytic method. Indeed, there are many philosophers today who standardly count as analytic philosophers who totally reject the 'conceptual analysis' conception which sharply distinguishes philosophical from scientific or empirical studies of phenomena. Yet despite all sorts of methodological and stylistic differences there remains a powerful underlying unity to the analytic movement. How is this unity to be understood?

One way of attempting to grapple with this question is by attending to what analytic philosophy has, throughout its history, grasped as what it is *not*, namely 'continental philosophy'. This is where matters (and especially myths) of history become crucially important. For while analytic philosophers are prepared to differ profoundly about the origins and methods of the movement, they tend to agree that, wherever it began and however it is pursued, its development is inseparable from the perception of a fundamental division within the contemporary philosophical culture. It belongs to the self-understanding of analytic philosophy that there is a 'gulf' between the way philosophy is studied in the analytic tradition and the way the same subject is studied in what it calls the continental tradition – where that term is not to be taken geographically but is intended to refer to a profoundly alien strain of philosophy that first developed on the European mainland.

So, analytic philosophy is essentially not-continental-philosophy. This approach to the identity and unity of the movement raises significant problems of its own since it is not at all clear that there is a distinctive way or set of ways of doing philosophy which can be identified as the contrasting continental tradition. Nevertheless, even if the very idea of continental philosophy is something of an invention of the analytic movement, the (constructed) idea does, as Ryle put it, 'show up by contrast' its predominant features. There are various ways in which one might want to represent this contrast, but the following list gives a fair indication of the sorts of things that are usually (and usually indefensibly) in view:

Analytic	Continental
Argument	Rhetoric
Science	Literature and Art
Analysis	Speculation
Clear	Obscure
Precise	Vague
Logic	Metaphysics
Reason	Passion

Of these contrasts the second – a contrast regarding what one might call 'methodological affiliation' – is perhaps the most normatively significant. The idea here is that the primary way of achieving and displaying the kind of knowledge (conceptual or not) that philosophy should aim at is, as A. W. Moore has put it, 'through the affirmation of truths'. Like science, analytic philosophy, in this way, involves 'a *commitment* to the truth' that, supposedly, is not in view, or at least not so securely in view, in what it calls continental philosophy.

This commitment – which is not, it should be stressed, itself a purely theoretical matter – has given the contrast between analytic and so-called continental philosophy a profoundly evaluative accent. While himself sceptical that one can seriously speak of the differences 'between so-called continental and Anglo-Saxon philosophies' solely in terms of intraphilosophical 'questions of style, method or even problematic field', Derrida in *Who's Afraid of Philosophy* (1978) gives an accurate summary of the reality of the 'gulf-seeking' rhetoric of the analytic movement as one which guarantees that 'the minimal conditions for communication and co-operation are lacking . . . the same interference or opacity can prevent philosophical communication and even make one doubt the unity of *the* philosophical, of the concept or project behind the word *philosophy*, which then constantly risks being but a homonymic lure'.

We are very close with this worry to R. M. Hare's view, expressed some twenty years earlier and with strident confidence, that philosophy as it stands in our time is not (or is no longer) one: there are, he stated in 1960, 'two different ways' in which philosophy is now studied, ways concerning which 'one might be forgiven for thinking . . . are really two quite different subjects'. As Dummett has put it more recently 'we have reached a point at which it is as if we're working in different subjects'.

But the exquisite complications formatted by the 'one might be forgiven' and 'as if' in these formulations call for further reflection. On the one hand, such moments of scrupulousness leave open a space for projects and approaches that would – and indeed today do – weaken the sense of such radical separation. (The 'embodied mind' school, the project of 'naturalising phenomenology', the work of Hubert Dreyfus and Manuel DeLanda's work on Deleuze and the philosophy of science are good examples of this growing trend.) On the other hand, however, since such gestures are essentially withdrawals from the suggestion that there really are two different subjects here, they also remind us that recourse to the distinction belongs to a movement of self-differentiation within a quite heterogeneous (and profoundly contested) subject. Indeed, it is arguable that the construction of the category of continental philosophy has been the *sine qua non* of the formation of the analytic movement: calling a work by that name has enabled self-styled analytic philosophers to render inaccessible to themselves whatever they have been interested in underestimating.

S. Glendinning

ANTIPHILOSOPHY A term used by Lacan in several senses.

(1) It indicates one of the disciplines – along with linguistics, topology and modern logic – necessary to the psychoanalyst's schooling. Lacan intimates that psychoanalysis, an ethics of singularity, should not take itself for a philosophy, when the latter is defined as a vision of the world that absorbs singularity in a totalising structure. Thus, for Lacan, psychoanalysis will never replace philosophy and instead constitutes itself as an antiphilosophy. (Conversely, calling psychoanalysis an 'antiphilosophy' encourages philosophy to liberate itself from psychoanalysis, as Deleuze and Guattari do in *Anti-Oedipus* (1972).)

(2) The categorisation of psychoanalysis as 'antiphilosophy' is also the consequence of philosophy's categorisation, by Lacan, as an avatar of the Master's discourse in the theory of discourses proposed in *Seminar XVII, L'envers de la psychanalyse* (1969–70); here, Lacan also follows Freud, when the latter assimilates a philosophical system to a paranoid psychosis, that is a vision of the world that is coherent only because it eliminates the Real. Philosophy, for Lacan, is a discourse of mastery, and as such, it is positioned in exact opposition to the analyst's discourse, which is non-mastery because it takes into account the unconscious.

(3) Finally, antiphilosophy heralds a psychoanalytical rereading and criticism of the entire tradition of Western philosophy, which can be summarised as follow: philosophy is regularly accused by Lacan of not noticing that thinking depends on speaking, that we are thinking beings only because we are speaking beings, as evidenced by Hegel's not noticing that, in the master–slave dialectic, a third linguistic structure positions the master and the slave and masters them.

A. Leupin

ANTI-THEODICY A notion which denotes a response to catastrophic suffering, unique perhaps to the Jewish tradition, which comes from within religion, but does not justify the relationship between God and radical evil. In often sharp contrast to the canon of theodicy, anti-theodicy recognises the existence of evil, while negating its value as just desserts or as a divine pedagogy, the mysterious means to some greater good, most typically reward in the hereafter and human freedom. No attempt is made to ascribe theological meaning to genuine evil or to square the way in which it disrupts the equilibrium between divine power and divine benevolence. Instead of justifying God, expressions of protest and incomprehension provide a premium to acts of solidarity with suffering people and to the covenant that binds God to them. It thereby performs an end-run around a logical problem that has historically stumped metaphysical theology and the philosophy of religion, not by avoiding or otherwise assuaging the severity of the problem but by confirming, even amplifying the tension that is inherent to it. While it sometimes appears in the Hebrew Bible as well as in rabbinic Midrash and Talmud, its presence there remains rare. It dominates, however, the post-Holocaust Jewish philosophy and theology that begins to emerge in the late 1960s in works by Levinas ('Useless Suffering'), Richard Rubenstein (*After Auschwitz*), Eliezer Berkovits (*Faith after the Holocaust*), and Emil Fackenheim (*God's Presence in History*; *To Mend the World*).

Z. Braiterman

ANXIETY (German *Angst*, French *angoisse*, English angst, anguish or dread) (1) A concept which denotes an object-less fear or disquiet, and which makes its definitive entry into modern philosophy with Kierkegaard's *The Concept of Anxiety*. Aspects of this are anticipated in Schelling's speculative reflections on *The Ages of the World*, but where Schelling adopts a cosmological perspective, Kierkegaard focuses on the particular individual. Although *The Concept of Anxiety* is preoccupied with the question of the Fall, anxiety itself is not sin. Instead, it is the state between the immediacy of nature and the advent of self-conscious freedom. It is spirit 'dreaming' in man, a 'nothing' that disturbs nature yet which nature cannot identify. There is no necessity for the freedom anticipated in anxiety to realise itself as fallen (there is no sense of original or inherited sin), yet spirit is repeatedly overwhelmed with vertigo at the prospect of its own infinite freedom and 'grasps at finitude', becoming guilty of its failure to realise itself. But by making us dissatisfied with a merely worldly life anxiety can also encourage us to seek the way to genuine freedom.

G. Pattison

ANXIETY (2) In Heidegger's *Being and Time* and 'What is Metaphysics?', anxiety (*Angst*) is a distinct mood or 'attunement' in which there
is no specific object that can be identified as the source of anxiety. One
is afraid of spiders or of the dark, but, Heidegger claims, one is not
anxious about anything, that is about anything specific. Does this mean
that there is no such thing as anxiety? Not at all. It does mean, however,
that in anxiety we are confronted with 'nothing', and that this confrontation is the very source of the feeling. But the nothing that is in
question here is not simply to be dismissed as insignificant. There is a
reality of 'the nothing', a distinct experience of the absence of any
specific thing that is the cause of an extraordinary unease. Normally,
our way of being in the world is the busy, 'concerned' and absorbed
way of being, in which we are surrounded with familiar things (and
other fellow human beings): things to do, things that are in the way,
people to meet and so on. But in anxiety, all such beings seem to have
vanished, all such familiarity seems to have dissolved, leaving us face to
face with ourselves, with the uncanny experience of brute existence.
This is precisely what interests Heidegger as an existential phenomenon, namely the fact that, every once in a while, we are confronted
with ourselves as being-in-the-world, or with our own essence as
existence. Anxiety testifies to the possibility for Dasein of being
revealed to itself as the being that it is. Anxiety is not a state in which
Dasein wants to remain, however, and so we often find ourselves
immediately thrown back into the world of concernful absorption. It
is only with the phenomenon of 'resolute disclosedness' that such a
possibility will be secured.

M. de Beistegui

   See also: 'the nothing'

ANXIETY (3) Sartre, borrowing from both Heidegger and Kierkegaard,
retained the idea that anxiety (*angoisse*) is a special, 'privileged' mood
that opens us to fruitful reflections on the human condition, while
discarding Kierkegaard's religiosity. Sartre accepted Kierkegaard's
distinction between fear, of which there is always a specific, identifiable
object', and anxiety, which is open-ended and global in scope, based as
it is, according to Sartre, on an awareness of our freedom and of the
absolute existential and ethical responsibility which is its correlate.

   Heidegger always maintained that *Angst* neither was nor should be a
normal, everyday mood. In an interview shortly before he died, Sartre
flippantly remarked that he had not personally experienced *angoisse*,
but had emphasised it because it had been so much in vogue during the
early years of existentialism's prominence (in the 1940s and 1950s). Be

this as it may, 'angoisse' became closely associated with existentialism in the popular consciousness, and this no doubt contributed to the widespread but basically superficial, inaccurate view of it as a movement of gloom and doom.

W. McBride

APEL, KARL-OTTO (1922–) German philosopher chiefly known for his attempt to provide a transcendental foundation for ethics in the universal and necessary conditions for communication – a concept he shares with his more famous friend and collaborator, Jürgen Habermas. His importance for contemporary German philosophy extends much farther than this, however: Apel was the first German philosopher to engage Anglo-American philosophy of language in the postwar period and he was the first to introduce American pragmatism to a new generation of German philosophers (including Habermas). These interventions occurred during a time when German philosophy was awash in hermeneutical ontology and philosophical anthropology, neither current providing much in the way of rigorous epistemological and ethical analysis and argumentation. Apel subsequently blazed the path toward a more responsible form of normative philosophising in over twenty books, including *Towards a Transformation of Philosophy* (1980), *Charles Peirce: From Pragmatism to Pragmaticism* (1981), *Understanding and Explanation: A Transcendental-Pragmatic Perspective* (1984), *Selected Essays: Towards a Transcendental Semiotics* (1994) and *The Response of Discourse Ethics* (1994).

Apel's philosophical career was auspicious from the outset. Soon after completing his dissertation exploring a Kant-inspired epistemological interpretation of Heidegger in 1950 under Erich Rothacker (also the director of Habermas's first dissertation), Apel set out to examine the history of hermeneutics and linguistics along a trajectory that would eventually lead him first to Wittgensteinian speech-act theory and Anglo-American philosophy of language and later to Peircian semiotics and pragmatism. The culmination of this line of research – a programme he variously dubbed 'transcendental semiotics' or 'transcendental pragmatics' in distinction from Habermas's programme of universal pragmatics – was a two-volume masterpiece, *Transformation der Philosophie* (1973). Consisting of essays written over fifteen years, this collection laid out Apel's attempt to undertake a transcendental grounding of the humanities and sciences in terms of a theory of knowledge-constitutive interests – a project whose impact on Habermas's own *Knowledge and Human Interests* (1968) can hardly be overestimated.

In the 1980s, Apel began devoting himself increasingly to elaborating a discourse ethic which contrasted with Habermas's in significant respects. While both philosophers agreed that moral reflection had to take the form of a rational dialogue embodying pragmatic norms ideally specifying the equality, freedom and universal inclusion of all those affected, they disagreed on how this ethical principle itself was to be justified. According to Habermas, philosophy, understood as pure rational reflection, was not sufficient to this task, requiring supplementation from empirical and hermeneutical social science. So construed, the rational reconstruction of universal pragmatic norms of rational speech would forever remain fallible, thereby undercutting their transcendental (purely reflective) necessity. Apel, by contrast, insisted that such a transcendental justification was both possible and necessary. Without it, he claimed, critical reason itself is left with no other foundation than conventional tradition – a condition that contradicts its own normative claim to universal validity.

Unlike Habermas, Apel has not situated himself squarely within the critical theory tradition of social science. However, what he lacks in interdisciplinary breadth is more than compensated for by his encyclopaedic knowledge of philosophy. More recently, his criticism of Eurocentric philosophy, partly initiated by his decade-long engagement with the Argentinian-Mexican philosopher Enrique Dussel, has also led him to adopt a highly critical stance with respect to global poverty.

D. Ingram

See also: discourse ethics; universal pragmatics

ARCHAEOLOGY Foucault's name for the method of analysis he uses in his first three major books: *Madness and Civilisation*, *The Birth of the Clinic* and *The Order of Things*; Foucault offers a detailed account of this method in *The Archaeology of Knowledge*. By use of this term foreign to the discipline of history, Foucault distinguishes his work from the historiography typical of the history of ideas, which tends to be preoccupied with demonstrating the continuous development of intellectual phenomena such as scientific theories, philosophies or world-views. Foucault is not attempting to trace a causal series or demonstrate logical continuity through change, nor is he interested in locating the origins of ideas and identifying the subjects who produced them. Instead, he endeavours to examine the system of rules that allow for the formation of a given set of discursive structures or the regularity of a given set of discursive practices at a specific time. He describes his analytic approach as vertical, or as spatial rather than temporal – hence the term archaeology – and eschews what he calls interpretation, meaning that he does not attempt to reconstruct a theme, structure or historical unconscious underlying historical events. Rather, he attempts to describe rules of formation that are immanent in the practices of speakers and authors of texts, not the repressed unconscious of history, as he puts it, but the positive unconscious, the rules discourses follow but do not explicitly formulate.

L. McWhorter

ARCHE-WRITING A term introduced by Derrida in his early work to refer to a differential structure common to both speech and writing. It thereby functions as it were at the origin ('arche'), before speech, yet in such a way as to negate the classical sense of an origin as primordial source. Synonymous with 'trace', called the 'movement of differance' (*Of Grammatology*), it is the new sense that Derrida wants to give to the term writing – as it were between quotation marks – following the third moment (displacement) of the deconstruction of the opposition between it and speech: 'the alleged derivativeness of writing . . . was possible only on one condition: that the "original," "natural," etc. language had never existed, never been intact and untouched by writing, that it had itself always been a writing' (*Of Grammatology*). In other words, although speech is presumed to be the origin of language, it can function the way it does – representing thinking and serving to communicate – only because it is a differential system of marks or traces rather than some natural expression of a self-present consciousness. In this way it in fact possesses the characteristics ascribed to writing. Arche-writing would in this sense be what renders language possible, the movement outside of itself of the supposed origin (speech) that is understood to be always already in effect. It is also an example of Derrida's practice of 'paleonymy' whereby he continues to employ an insufficient or 'discredited' term, in the first place because it retains something of the sense of that previous word, and in the second place in order to rework and displace that sense as part of his project of reworking and displacing traditional thinking.

D. Wills

ARCHITECTONIC Pertaining to architecture or construction, but with a further meaning implying control, as an architect might direct a construction crew. From this comes the philosophical sense of an overall plan for the construction of knowledge. The term became prominent when used by Kant to describe the plan guiding the articulation of his system. His architectonic consisted of basic divisions of philosophy into theoretical and practical parts, with a sequence of procedures of analysis, justification and discussions of antinomies within each part, guided by the set of basic organising categories and ideas of totality that he developed from an analysis of logic and applied again in his discussions of knowledge, morality, art and natural forces. After Kant, the term names the overall structure of thought that provides systematic guidance for which philosophical questions should be asked and in what order, and what shape their answers should follow. Philosophers now investigate the differing architectonics behind other systems, for instance those of Hegel or Aristotle. A systematic architectonic can lead thought to questions and insights that otherwise might be overlooked, but as a form of rationality and control, architectonic is opposed by those who see thought as more anarchic and fragmentary and think an architectonic constrains insight and creativity. Nietzsche and Deleuze thus provide concepts and insights which cannot be gathered into a system, and Kant and Nietzsche would give very different answers to the question whether thought and life should or could be architectonically organised, and whether this would be a fulfilment or a betrayal.

D. Kolb

ARCHITECTURE The art of building edifices for human use; an architect is a master builder who directs construction. Often architecture implies more than constructing shelter; it also symbolises and centres a community's values and ways of life. As an art form, architecture mixes the aesthetic with the practical in ways that confound many theories of pure or fine art. Architecture builds shelters for human dwelling. Its fundamental action can be taken as erecting structures, putting up posts and columns to support a roof, or as hollowing out a space, digging a hole or enlarging a cave. The gendered connotations are hardly accidental.

Modern architecture proclaimed itself the expression of pure function, with a sleek new aesthetic of the efficient machine, away from over-decorated nineteenth-century eclecticism. It would express basic social functions, not random cultural meanings. But apart from an occasional masterpiece, the new aesthetic joined the drive for efficient building to produce a new level of monotony and inhuman geometry. Postmodern architecture was then proclaimed to liberate the imagination and local cultures from the dead hand of efficient geometry. It too failed its promises, turning into a weak decorative *mélange*, and leading to further reactions including a more expressive neo-modernism.

Philosophy contributed to the modernist architectural revolution by critiques of historicism, and then to the postmodern architectural revolution by critiques of modernity's attempt to control and rationalise, and then to the further reactions by means of Heidegger's deconstructive attacks on the finality and firmness of any structure. Heidegger argues that the task of architecture is to enable true human dwelling, which is not just roofs and walls but a shared world of meaning and projects. He sees little hope for such dwelling when architecture has become the tool of efficiency and technological control of the environment.

The influence of philosophy on architecture comes and goes, but the influence of architecture on philosophy remains constant and deep. In many ways, the image of architecture defines what it means to think. The Roman architect Vitruvius defined three qualities that a building should have, usually translated as 'commodity, firmness and delight'. A building must be useful and fulfil its function; it must be strong and enduring; it must bring aesthetic pleasure. These apply to systems of thought as well. They must be useful for their purposes, firmly knit together and bring intellectual pleasure in their inhabitation. Terms from architecture are everywhere in discussions of thinking: we speak of structures of thought which are built on foundations that stand on their own with solid bases. Or they lack foundations and collapse. Justification or truth is passed up and down along the parts of these structures just as are weight and stress along the parts of a building. A structure of thought provides areas to wander among and connections between them, and it defines an interior and an exterior. One structure provides a place where we can dwell, that we take for granted as we do our house, while another structure may be strange, foreign or authoritative and grand, or perhaps an imposing ruin.

These images are not quite metaphors. The way a column supports a roof and the way a premise supports a conclusion seem equally original. But the emphasis on structure in thought and philosophy needs to be questioned. Why do we think of thinking in terms of argument and items supporting other items, rather than, say, as paths leading to discoveries? The question of architecture is thus the question of system and structure. Architecture in both matter and in thought can be seen as making shelter and a home, but also as restricting and disciplining. Much recent philosophy has been preoccupied with developing flexible and powerful notions of structure, in logical calculi and in analyses of language and categories of thought. The Kantian and Hegelian wings of continental philosophy have celebrated thought's architecture, seeking to extend the firmness and reach of structure and the systematics of thinking. Others in continental philosophy have been concerned to question the reach and nature of structure and to celebrate the fragmentary, the ruin, the incomplete and unstructured, the momentary and intense instead of the synoptic and complete.

Critics of architecture ask what the demand for architectural structure in self and thought tries to shelter us from. The raging physical elements of air and water and fire have their analogues for thought. Do structure and system counter a chaos of unordered experiences? But Kant has argued that there is no unordered experience, since for there to be experience at all there must be architecture and order of thought and selfhood. Is structure then a bulwark against raging passions and feelings that do not fit into accepted categories? From the unconscious and the carnival, the barbaric and impulsive and fearful? Bataille argues that we must experience beyond the accepted limits, beyond structure, if we are to live fully. Deleuze tries to show how regulating structures always have spaces that allow unintended lines of flight moving into possibilities not controlled by established laws. Derrida argues that no architecture, in thought or in concrete, is as firm as it appears to be. Indeed its firmness is an effect brought about by a deeper and more basic mobility and slippage, and to say 'deeper and more basic' is again an architectural image. There is no avoiding structure and architecture, but this needs to be thought, built and lived in the context of its process of becoming and its slippage and self-transgression, which it tries to deny.

These philosophical critiques of the notion of structure and architecture have been influential in the arts, but attempts to apply them to actual buildings have not been very successful. While architects claim to have been inspired by these philosophical ideas, the requirements of gravity and shelter continue to dominate, though new materials and new technologies may allow these demands to be less obvious in construction, as in thought.

D. Kolb

ARENDT, HANNAH (1906–75) German-born political philosopher who is chiefly famous for her Cold War study of totalitarianism linking Nazism and Stalinism. A student of Heidegger and Jaspers, under whom she completed her doctoral thesis on Augustine (1928), Arendt immigrated first to France (1934) and later to the United States (1941) to escape persecution by the Nazis. During and after the war she held the directorships of several Jewish refugee and cultural organisations and later served as chief editor of Schocken Books before assuming academic positions at the University of Chicago (1963) and the New School for Social Research in New York (1967). The impressive range of her erudition spanned such diverse topics as Zionism and the Jewish Question, the plight of stateless refugees, Eichmann and the nature of evil, the French and American Revolutions, Kant and the nature of judgement, the crisis of culture in mass society, the decline of the public sphere in the modern world, and above all the nature of freedom and its relationship to political action. Her most important books include *The Origins of Totalitarianism* (1951), *The Human Condition* (1958), *Eichmann in Jerusalem: A Report on the Banality of Evil* (1965), *On Revolution* (1963), *On Violence* (1970), *The Life of the Mind*, 2 vols. (1978) and *Lectures on Kant's Political Philosophy* (1982). During her lifetime she received many honours, including the prestigious Sonning Prize for Contributions to European Civilisation (1975). Among her most famous acolytes is Habermas, who, like most others currently writing on deliberative democracy, shares her view that true power can come only from individuals speaking and acting in concert.

Although Arendt's fascination with political action resonates more closely with Jaspers' existential philosophy of communication than with Heidegger's existential ontology of being, it was Heidegger who perhaps exerted a more profound influence on her thought. Heidegger himself had been a student of Husserl, whose phenomenological method of philosophising he would later appropriate and modify. Husserl had argued that our natural attitude towards the world, in which we unquestioningly accept the 'givenness' of objects, conceals the subjective flow of experience out of which the sense of such a world is originally constituted. More importantly, he and Heidegger argued that the objectifying modes of understanding the world definitive of modern science and technology go even further in concealing the primal sources of meaning and value, thereby contributing to a crisis of nihilism.

Arendt shares Heidegger's concern that the modern age's twin obsessions with science and technology, on the one hand, and economic production and consumption, on the other, have concealed and endangered our most authentic ways of understanding and being. Both of them therefore return to pre-modernity – more precisely, the ancient Greek *polis* – for clues in disclosing the world in its originality. However, whereas Heidegger located the primal source of meaning and value in the monumental work of art, Arendt located it in democratic action. This difference would later take them in opposite political directions. Heidegger's supreme estimation of the revelatory power of the lone thinker/poet/artist to found a new world and new community of being – coupled with his contempt for public opinion and political debate – harmonised comfortably with the Nazi's *Führerprinzip* and their ideology of a unitary *Volk*.

Arendt's entire philosophy, by contrast, is premised on the derivative nature of artistic creativity as a form of world disclosure and constitution. In her opinion, artistic creation no less than economic production is an instrumental activity that can be undertaken in isolation and can therefore be assimilated to the objectifying will to dominate so characteristic of science and technology. Only in political action, where a plurality of persons display their unique individuality in spontaneous and unpredictable response to one another, does a public space of meaning and value, and therewith a common world of appearance, first emerge in all its glory. So-called artistic creativity can serve to 'memorialise' these deeds in permanent narratives and monuments, but it cannot substitute for them.

Arendt's tripartite distinction between cultural fabrication, economic production (labour) and political action underpins her theory of freedom, understood as a kind of singular eruption (or birth) interrupting the continuity of life. Whereas economic activity is necessitated by biological need and cultural fabrication reinterprets what has already happened, political action itself is characterised by initiating something totally new, unique and distinctive – the stuff out of which histories are told. It is here where we detect Arendt's own deep ambivalence with respect to modernity. The undermining of tradition and authority generates a crisis of nihilism, but it also underscores our responsibility to act, or give ourselves new meaning and value, without relying upon the past or any other external or transcendent authority. This is doubtless why the French and American Revolutions intrigued her so much: here, for the first time, we witness people trying to reconstitute their political identities – indeed, their very freedom – without any foundation save their own voluntary consent. Some of this radical spontaneity, she believed, still existed in New England town hall meetings and Soviet worker councils.

Despite her effusive praise of the American Revolution and its founding fathers, Arendt generally adopted a rather pessimistic and negative assessment of modern mass democracy. In contrast to the French Revolution, the American Revolution did not have to concern itself with the problem of widespread poverty. This enabled it to focus almost exclusively on establishing strong constitutional guarantees of individual freedom. However, this original neglect of the 'social question' did not save the new republic from having to deal with slavery and the race question; nor did it save the republic from its own obsession with commerce and economic progress – an obsession that would later lead to the growth of the social welfare state. For Arendt, the imperative to maintain economic growth invariably comes at the expense of political freedom; indeed, greater citizen participation imposes unpredictable and contradictory demands on government leaders that are viewed by them as severely limiting their capacity to scientifically manage social problems efficiently. Hence, government officials have a powerful incentive to either limit citizen participation to passive voting or manipulate it through propaganda. Either way, active and public deliberation is in some sense violated. But there is further danger in depoliticising the citizenry. Once citizens are reduced to a passive mass of isolated atoms, nothing remains to resist the totalitarian tendency of the state to dominate all aspects of their lives.

D. Ingram

See also: natality

ASIAN PHILOSOPHY In our context, not Asian thought per se, but Asian thought in its connection with European philosophy. It is hard to say exactly where the confluence of Asian thought with European philosophy begins: M. L. West, in *Early Greek Philosophy and the Orient* (1971), argues that ancient Greek philosophy was influenced by Persian philosophy. If this originary blending is indeed the case, any strict distinction between 'Asian' and 'European' philosophy is revealed as a construction.

If we nonetheless assume there is some utility in making the distinction, a clear case of contact between already established traditions is found in Schopenhauer, especially *The World as Will and Representation*. While Schopenhauer was certainly influenced by Plato and Kant, he was also influenced by some of the first Buddhist texts to be translated into modern European languages. These translations were partial and erroneous by comparison with what is available today; they, and Schopenhauer's absorption of them, are largely responsible for the widespread, but false, notion among contemporary Europeans and Euro-Americans that Buddhism is a negative and nihilistic system of thought.

Human ideas, according to Schopenhauer, are a reflection of human will. Human will, like the cosmic will it reflects, is not a product of human consciousness or motive, but something which precedes and subtends it, a blind force without direction. The world as we know it is an ongoing expression of this cosmic will. Human ideas are expressions of human will, as worldly manifestations express the will of the cosmos. Humans may temporarily escape the vagaries of will by contemplation of pure ideas – philosophy – or through aesthetic contemplation – the arts. Permanent liberation from blind will can only be achieved by a reasoned rejection, through compassion for other beings, of the individual self and the will to prolong individual life. Schopenhauer's theses reflect a rather crude apprehension of some tenets of ascetic Buddhism and had an influence on Nietzsche, Bergson and literary figures such as Dostoevsky and Proust.

Much of the interest in the confluence of traditional Asian and contemporary European thought has centred on Heidegger and Derrida. One of Heidegger's most eminent students, Gadamer, is said to have encouraged scholars to compare his teacher's work to Asian thought; this is not merely, as Graham Parkes suggests in *Heidegger and Asian Thought* (1990), because both Heidegger and Asian thinkers reject the strict adherence to a discourse of logical ratiocination. Rather, Heidegger's familiarity with Zen thought through the work of D. T. Suzuki and conversations with Keiji Nishitani and others is well documented, though his affinities with Buddhist thought seem to predate those direct contacts and arise from his own interpretation of the European tradition, culminating in his displacement of a subject who represents objects to itself by a field or an opening within which both subject and object arise. In Japan, this affinity was quickly recognised: a Japanese translation of *Being and Time* was published in 1939, only twelve years after the work appeared in German, and was followed by numerous revised transla-tions. This affinity came to define the so-called Kyoto School of philosophy, sometimes characterised as 'Buddhist phenomenology' and presided over by Nishitani, whose major work is translated as *Religion and Nothingness* (1983).

The affinity between Asian thought and Derrida's thought seems to rest on a common rejection of philosophy as dependent on a restricted sense of identity-based logic or 'logocentrism' which seeks to establish relations between already-unified entities, rather than delve into the differential fields from which those identities arise. Indeed there has been a good deal of interest in Derrida's thought in Japan, echoing the earlier interest in Heidegger. Among Western writers, Robert Magliola's *Derrida on the Mend* (1984) is notable for its attempt to reconcile Derrida and Buddhism with Catholicism, while Bernard Faure has applied the methods of Foucault and Derrida to Zen discourses and histories in *Chan Insights and Oversights* (1996).

We should not neglect attempts to use Asian philosophy to answer long-standing questions in Western philosophy. François Jullien, for example, has explored in *Detour and Access* (2000) many useful ways in which Chinese thought may inform – and explode – modalities of Western philosophy, particularly the representational model of language: instead of being merely representational and functional, language and the arts might be something which humans produce, as a rose bush produces flowers; this would be a natural phenomenon instead of one characterised by artifice.

The most promising ongoing collaboration between Asian and Western philosophy, however, might very well be the attempt to bring Buddhist insights to bear on questions of cognitive science and 'naturalised phenomenology'. Given a first philosophical formulation by Francisco Varela and his collaborators in *The Embodied Mind* (1991), Varela and his research team have subsequently brought people highly trained in Buddhist meditation into the laboratory for experiments in the field of 'neurophenomenology'. These and other instances of Asian/Western collaboration are recorded in a series of works done by the 'Mind and Life' group, of which *Destructive Emotions* (2003) is the latest; these works involve a team of Western philosophers and scientists in dialogue with the Dalai Lama and a group of his followers and provide a fascinating example of inter-cultural encounter and collaboration with great promise for mutual enlightenment.

J. Humphries

ASSEMBLAGE (*agencement*) A term used by Deleuze and Guattari in *A Thousand Plateaus* to describe, at its most general, the set of inter-articulated processes that actualises a particular abstract system, making it real. In an assemblage, however, no one does the assembling, even if people are part of it. Assemblages show that the composition of complex systems is not dependent on forms, structures, intentions or anything cognate with them: the abstract system that an assemblage implements is itself also constructed by the activity of the assemblage. In this respect, assemblages are an important generalisation of self-organising systems. Self-organising systems are generally conservative since they aim at self-maintenance. But assemblages are defined by the changes they can induce, both in other assemblages and also in themselves, ultimately becoming something else entirely. This creativity belongs to matter itself, to which assemblages are immanent. Assem-blages therefore not only implement real systems, which are always to some extent hierarchical in nature; they also present an alternative flat mode of organisation and reorganisation, forming a series with other terms used by Deleuze and Guattari like 'rhizome'.

Assemblages have a special affinity with ethological constructs, especially those of territorial animals. The ability to demarcate a territory requires a minimum proto-semiotic capability, which shows that matter is not just body or content, but also and at the same time 'expression'. Matter is in and of itself expressive, but territoriality marks an important threshold in the development of the autonomy of expression.

A. Welchman

ATTUNEMENT (*Befindlichkeit*) For Heidegger in *Being and Time*, the way in which existence always finds itself in a mood; this essential structure indicates a crucial aspect of existence, which he calls 'facticity'. In the early 1920s, and under the influence of Dilthey, Heidegger referred to existence as 'factical life', thus emphasising the phenomenon of life as the fundamental *fact* that must be the starting point of philosophy. Life is what is known and understood from within, that behind which philosophy cannot go so as to explain it. *Being and Time* clarifies the facticity of life by showing how we always find ourselves disposed to the world, that is open to it, not as a result of some choice, or some decision, but passively as it were. When we ask: 'How are you today?' we ask about the factical, thrown aspect of existence. It is a question of disposition, of attunement, of moods. Heidegger places a huge importance on moods, as they disclose one specific way in which the world unfolds for us. They provide essential clues as to how we understand the world, how the world is there for us, before any theoretical interpretation of it. Fear, anxiety, boredom, awe, love: these are all dispositions, ways in which the world resonates for us. They all testify to the fact that we exist in the world as thrown (*geworfen*), and not simply as projection (*Entwurf*), as contingency, and not only as possibility and freedom. Our historicity itself is made up of irreducible, factical situations, as well as of decisive choices, and defining possibilities.

M. de Beistegui

AUFHEBUNG A German language term used by Hegel and Marx, with three distinct connotations: to cancel or nullify, to preserve, and to lift or raise up. The obsolete English term 'sublate' is now used exclusively to mean whatever Hegel means by *Aufhebung*. Interpreting the use of 'Aufhebung' in any particular sentence requires discerning which of its connotations are relevant, and what is the relative stress on each should two or more of its connotations be relevant, which is fairly common since Hegel delighted in words with multiple and apparently contradictory connotations. Typically, he used all three connotations of 'Aufhebung', though their relative stress may vary with context. In particular, Hegel used 'Aufhebung', both in the *Phenomenology of Spirit* and in the *Science of Logic*, to designate the outcome of a constructive internal critique of a plausible, though inadequate view, where its insights and oversights are accounted for in a superior successor view. In Marx's writings, 'Aufhebung' may be fairly translated negatively as 'abolish' when Marx speaks of the destruction of old economic or political orders. However, disregarding the positive connotations of 'Aufhebung' obscures Marx's view that new economic or political orders only develop through the exhaustive development of their predecessors, taking over many materials and practices from them, investing them with new significance in the new order.

K. Westphal

AURA A term used by Benjamin to describe the singularity of a work of art. An age of mass reproduction extinguishes the aura. As a result, authenticity and tradition lose their aesthetic relevance, just as cult value and ritual lose their position as the basis of art. The historical changes that result in the loss of aura are not confined to the world of art. Benjamin describes a general 'liquidation of the traditional value of the cultural heritage' and he also describes a transformation of human sense perception itself; both coincide with the disappearance of the aura of artworks. The lyrical but alienated reveries of Baudelaire, Benjamin observes, 'indicated the price for which the sensation of the modern age may be had: the disintegration of the aura in the experience of shock'.

Photography and film announce the loss of the aura. They bring new conditions of alienation to the artist and the artwork, but they also bring new prospects for advancing revolutionary politics through art. Benjamin uses the screen actor to illustrate the first consequence. The final form of the actor's performance is a reel of photographic images, a displaced presence, which can be edited and remounted indefinitely. As a result, Benjamin writes, 'for the first time – and this is the effect of the film – man has to operate with his whole living person, yet forgoing its aura'. Yet because the auratic value of art has been replaced by exhibition value, art becomes more closely integrated with the politics of the masses.

P. Lewis

AUTHENTICITY (*Eigentlichkeit*) For Heidegger in *Being and Time*, an existential modification of inauthenticity, a mode of being characteristic of Dasein in its average, everyday comportment. This is the comportment according to which Dasein, while understanding its own being implicitly, does not understand it on the basis of its own, singular self, as 'being-towards-death'. In other words, Dasein understands itself as an improper (*uneigentlich*), impersonal, anonymous self that is no different from any other self. This is what Heidegger calls 'das Man', or 'the One'. Authenticity, on the other hand, signals the possibility for Dasein of grasping itself, in its essence, and this means as the being that exists, or is in the world, on the basis of this ownmost, uttermost and unsurpassable possibility that is death. The phenomenon of anxiety (*Angst*) already provided a phenomenological clue regarding the possibility for Dasein of grasping itself on the basis of itself, or as being-in-the-world. It is with the phenomenon of 'resolute disclosedness', however, that the possibility of authenticity, or ownness, will be established definitively.

M. de Beistegui

AUTO-IMMUNITY A term used by Derrida in his later work, meaning the self-attack of an entity in the name of its own self-preservation, often in relation to questions of religion but more specifically where religion intersects with politics and technology. It may be understood to some extent in the context of his earlier ideas of parasitism and the virus. The term 'auto-immune indemnification' is also used, emphasising both exemption or self-protection ('immunity' referred originally to exemption from public service or taxation such as that bestowed on religious entities) and a sense of the holy or sacro-sanct (*indemnis* is Latin for 'unscathed' or, literally, 'un-damned'). The term's most explicit reference is to the biological process: if the immune system produces antibodies to fight off foreign antigens, auto-immunity is the means by which the organism attacks its own immune defences in order to protect itself (from its own self-protection). It is thus the double-bind of self-protection that amounts to a confusion between what threatens from inside or from outside, but which becomes necessary to avoid the body's rejection of a transplanted organ.

   In 'Faith and Knowledge' (1996) auto-immunity is used to describe the nationalist or fundamentalist rejection of technoscience – without which religion can no longer, and in fact could not ever function – as a phenomenon of reaction against the machine, which reaction being 'as automatic (and thus machinal) as life itself'. By extension, life itself opens itself to the auto-immune supplementarity of what is beyond it, both to the automaton and to religion. In *Voyous* (2003) Derrida returned to the idea in the context of the '*auto-co-immunity*' of the community, and more particularly democracy's attempts at self-protection against the threat of terrorism, attempts which often involve the supposedly temporary and expedient sacrifice of democracy itself.

D. Wills

AUTOPOIESIS The process whereby a system or machine, conceived as a unified network of processes and relations of production, perpetually regenerates its components and maintains its topological unity. Used to single out those systems that 'produce themselves', it is juxtaposed to allopoiesis, which refers to systems or machines having something other than themselves as their product.

Coined by the Chilean biologist Humberto Maturana in 1972 and developed in collaboration with Francisco Varela, namely in *Autopoiesis and Cognition* (1980), the theory of autopoiesis proposes a systematic, non-vitalist model of living systems couched in terms of their structural organisation and operational autonomy. Philosophically, it could be understood as a manner of employing the theoretical instruments of contemporary life science and systems theory to dispel the problematic or merely regulative character of self-organisation postulated in Kant's *Critique of Judgement*. The theory of autopoietic machines thus aims to sever the Kantian equation of autonomy with teleology, function and intentionality, such that the individuality of living beings (whether natural or artificial) can be understood simply in terms of relations of production between components and the rules that govern these interactions. The theory of autopoiesis has been the object of criticism for its relative indifference to the Darwinian revolution and its difficulty in accounting for the generation of the living.

While Maturana and Varela indicate that autopoiesis is always defined according to its instantiation in a given 'machine', the concept has been adopted, in an expanded sense, by thinkers such as Luhmann and Guattari for the consideration of social phenomena.

A. Toscano

BACHELARD, GASTON (1884–1962) French philosopher, most widely known in the English-speaking world, and especially in English departments, for his nine works on poetic imagination which have inspired generations of literary critics. In France, however, his philosophical reputation was built by work in the philosophy of science, on which he published twelve books. He is the originator of the notion of 'epistemological break', which was later picked up and exploited for his own purposes by Althusser. Bachelard succeeded to the chair of history and philosophy of science at the Sorbonne in 1940 and continued in that position until retirement in 1955. As a consequence, his approach to the philosophy of science became a standard part of the education of French philosophers. The impact of his thought can be seen not only on figures such as Canguilhem and Foucault, but more broadly in the approaches taken by many if not most French scholars to the history and philosophy of the sciences. His work has had little direct impact on philosophers of science working in English, however, since of his twelve works in this area, only two have been translated: *La Philosophie du non* (1940) appeared in 1969 as *The Philosophy of No* and *Essai d'une philosophie du nouvel esprit scientifique* (1934) appeared in 1984 as *A Philosophy of the New Scientific Mind*.

Bachelard is frequently classified as a neo-Kantian. This is fair to the extent that there are broad similarities between him and, say, Cassirer and the pragmatists James and Dewey. Knowledge always involves a knowing subject and an object of knowledge; epistemology is the study of the dynamics of the interplay between these two poles. The history of science is also the history of the 'scientific mind', which is reconfigured in response to changes in our conception of the reality studied by science. Science so conceived is very much a human project, and this residual humanism has been criticised by those (such as Lecourt and Latour) who have advocated removing the knowing subject from discussion of knowledge as part of their rejection of Cartesian epistemology. However, Bachelard also firmly rejects the Cartesian framework. If he is a humanist, his humanism is, as Mary McCallester Jones tells us in *Gaston Bachelard, Subversive Humanist* (1991), of a distinctly subversive kind. He goes much further than James or Dewey in stressing the significance for science of its material basis in laboratory instrumentation and technique, emphasising the respect in which the phenomena studied by modern science are laboratory constructs (products of what he calls phenomeno-technique), where knowledge of the techniques of manufacture contribute crucially to knowledge of the phenomenon. Bachelard's emphasis throughout is on the activities of scientists, whether theoretical or experimental, and on the way in which these activities bring about changes in our understanding. It is in the transition from one theory or set of practices to another that learning occurs, not in the accumulation of 'facts'.

M. Tiles

See also: epistemological break; Epistemology; problematic; Space

BAD CONSCIENCE (*schlechtes Gewissen*) Nietzsche's term for the baseline level of suffering that afflicts all human beings, simply by dint of their non-negotiable participation in civilisation. As Nietzsche explains in *On the Genealogy of Morals*, the founding condition of civilisation is that its participants learn to police their natural impulses and introject the animal vitality that would otherwise express itself in outward displays of cruelty and appropriation. Rather than direct their native energies toward others (as Nietzsche suggests is both natural and creative and healthy), civilised human beings direct their cruelty and aggression against themselves.

The 'bad conscience' is Nietzsche's term for the ensuing experience of self-inflicted suffering, which he regards as nothing more than the opportunity cost of sharing in the burdens and blessings of civilisation; he believes that the strongest amongst us will see it for that and demand no further explanation or justification. For most human beings, however, the gratuitous suffering of the bad conscience is unendurable on its own terms and actually calls into question the value of life itself. According to Nietzsche, human beings seek to avoid only those experiences of suffering, like the bad conscience, that are perceived as unjustified. Human beings will endure, and even crave, any form of suffering that is perceived or presented as meaningful, no matter how outlandish the pretext of justification. This is why guilt (*Schuld*) has been such an enduringly appealing interpretation of the pain of the bad conscience. According to the priests who champion this interpretation, human beings suffer from the pain of the bad conscience because they *deserve* to suffer, because their very being is faulted in some mysterious way. The suffering of the bad conscience is thus explained, and guilty parties need no longer be troubled by the prospect of meaningless suffering. That the priests' explanation of the feeling of guilt is patently false does not detract from its explanatory power.

D. *Conway*

BAD FAITH (*mauvaise foi*) (1) A concept developed by Sartre in *Being and Nothingness*, with a view to demonstrating that negation or negativity is at the heart of human existence. He defines bad faith as a lie that one tells oneself while knowing that it is a lie. Sartre's most famous examples of bad faith are of a café waiter who engages in certain rituals of service – gestures, phrases – as if he were entirely and without remainder a café waiter, and of a woman on a date who offers her partner her hand while feigning ignorance of his sexual desires. Sartre's point is that much human behaviour consists of such complex role-playing as we seek to give ourselves some fixed identity or essence whereas we are in fact protean, indefinitely flexible.

Protestations of sincerity may themselves manifest bad faith. Indeed faith itself is what Sartre calls a 'metastable' phenomenon: zealous believers seek to convince themselves of their absolute certainty, but doubt always threatens. The question arises whether it is possible to avoid being in bad faith. In a footnote in *Being and Nothingness*, Sartre suggests that it is, to wit, by living in 'authenticity' (a notion dear to Heidegger as well), but does not explore the issue further there.

W. McBride

BAD FAITH (2) While Beauvoir and Sartre share the concept of bad faith, which refers to the self-deceptions by which we refuse the ambiguities and evade the responsibilities of freedom, there are important differences between their analyses. Sartre, grounding bad faith in the ontology of freedom and anxiety, identifies all refusals of freedom's dialectic of transcendence and immanence, and all acquiescence to authorities or ideas that deny freedom, with bad faith. Beauvoir does not. She distinguishes between those who can challenge authorities or ideas that deny freedom and those who cannot, between those who deny their freedom and those who are robbed of it. Only the former are in bad faith. The latter are victims of oppression. Thus, out of her attentiveness to our embodiment and facticity, Beauvoir links the possibilities of lived freedom to the materialities of our lives. She argues that extreme material deprivation and/or pervasive and powerful ideologies create situations where we experience ourselves as either unfit for freedom or objectively (by natural or divine laws) precluded from it. To call submission to these conditions of unfreedom 'bad faith' would be to absolve the oppressor of their bad faith, their refusal to recognise the other as free.

In another departure from Sartre, Beauvoir ties the faith of bad faith to the nostalgia for childhood, a contingency of our existence, as well as to an ontology of freedom as ambiguous. She argues that as children we lived a privileged metaphysical existence where we experienced the joys of freedom but not its responsibilities. Bad faith is thus a refusal to grow up, a search for parent substitutes in political, religious or other authorities. It is the desire for the child's objectively ordered and stable world and a denial of the ambiguities of the adult condition. Unlike the child whose distance from the responsibilities and tensions of freedom is innocent, adults who refuse their freedom are dangerous. Seeking to live and be justified by the authority of another (human, natural or divine), they are the arm of the tyrant's power and the face that peoples the mob.

For Beauvoir, advocating ontological solutions to bad faith is utopian. We must combat it materially and psychologically. The nostalgia for childhood must be critiqued and demystified. The defence 'I was just following orders' must be rejected.

D. Bergoffen

BADIOU, ALAIN (1937–) French philosopher, novelist and play-wright, the immense depth, breadth and rigour of whose writings designate him as the most significant heir of French poststructuralism. He has produced a fully-fledged system, in which particular fields of inquiry are grounded in ontology. Its basic axiom is that being is pure multiplicity, which leads to the conclusion that accurate ontological formalisation is only to be found in a philosophical interpretation of modern set theory.

Badiou's ontology is dualistic, as the title of his 1988 *magnum opus* indicates: *L'Etre et l'événement* ('Being and Event'). Being is pure multiplicity, but cannot appear as such. It is always already deployed in structures in which particular laws render multiplicity into discernible elements. At this structural level, multiplicity is named, arranged and classified into sets and subsets, to the extent that nothing remains that would not be counted and accounted for. This is the level of ontological normality, including the categorical underpinning of nature and nat-ural sciences, but also including state institutions intervening in social reality. Within this level, knowledge is purely nominalistic and truth mere 'veridicality'. Consequently, for truth and freedom to become real, normality must be ruptured. The 'event' takes ontology to this 'abnormal' plane, in which a subject can also be conceptualised.

Underneath structures, multiplicity pre-exists in disordered fashion. In that guise, it escapes structural ordering, it is ontologically illegal and indiscernible, it is tantamount to nothing: Badiou's name for Being is the 'void' (*vide*). The event is the manifestation of this void. It signals that, immanent to the structure, a potentiality for free creation exists which structural knowledge cannot explicate or tolerate. Truth is then defined as the fidelity to the promises of the past event. It consists in an infinite process of verification of the event's effects within the struc-tural situation, leading to the transfiguration of the latter and the creation of faithful subjectivities. The subject is the instance that supports the truth-procedures through thought and action. Badiou lists four such generic procedures: love, art, science and politics. In love, the subject is the couple; in art, the work; in science, a new theory; in politics, the collective.

Philosophy for Badiou is thus ontologically revolutionary, or con-versely, only revolutionary politics are philosophically valid. He rejects any politics based on state reform, mainstream interpretations of justice and democracy, or identity, as they operate within structural and meta-structural logic. Ultimately, they only serve the interests of state power and capital. They cannot articulate the two criteria of political truth: universality and equality. Similarly the contemporary ethical turn is the subjective manifestation of the resignation to structural forces. Badiou's ethic of truths is based on the principle of faithfulness to revolutionary events that can alone transform human creatures into free subjects. Finally, philosophy is not itself a generic procedure. It does not produce truths, but simply articulates those created elsewhere. Political philosophy can only be conducted as 'metapolitics', and aesthetics as 'inaesthetic'. Through the many texts he has devoted to the arts and great artists, Badiou has shown in theory and with his own works the specific potential for truth and emancipation that artistic creativity unfolds.

J-P Deranty
See also: event; fidelity; metapolitics; multiplicity; singularity; void

BAKHTIN, MIKHAIL (1895–1975) Russian philosopher who, along with his intellectual circle, produced important works on language and culture during the formative years of the Soviet Union. Stalin's purges led to the disappearances of some of the circle's members and to Bakhtin's arrest and exile to the provinces. Liberalisation in the Soviet Union of the 1960s permitted Bakhtin's return to Moscow as well as his rediscovery by the Soviet and international academic community. His writings strongly influenced Kristeva, Todorov and other recent French thinkers, and have also been greeted enthusiastically by many Anglophone scholars working in literature, cultural studies, linguistics, psychology and philosophy.

Bakhtin's work can be divided into three areas of emphasis. The first and earliest of these is ethically and phenomenologically oriented, and reflects the influence of Kant and neo-Kantianism on Russian intellectuals in the early part of the twentieth century (*Toward a Philosophy of the Act*, 1919–21; *Art and Answerability*, 1919–24). In this phase of his work, Bakhtin concentrates on the creativity of active subjects the open-endedness of the effort to unify their surroundings, their relation to other subjects, and the ethical 'answerability' of those who would disown any of these aspects of their involvement with the world.

But the two theoretical emphases that have excited most contemporary thinkers emerge later in Bakhtin's career: dialogism and his theory of carnival and the grotesque body. Bakhtin's dialogism presumably begins with books that many scholars believe were published under the name of other members of Bakhtin's circle, V. N. Voloshinov and P. N. Medvedev, in order to evade Stalin's prohibitions against exiled intellectuals and other possible dissidents (*Freudianism: A Critical Sketch*, 1927; *Marxism and the Philosophy of Language*, 1930; *The Formal Method in Literary Scholarship*, 1928). In these books, both formalistic and romantic subject-centred views are criticised in the name of a dialogic conception of language coupled with historical materialism. Bakhtin's later works on language and culture (*The Dialogic Imagination*, 1975; *Problems of Dostoevsky's Poetics*, 1929 and 1972; and *Speech Genres and Other Late Essays*, 1979) drop explicit reference to Marxism but continue to develop his dialogism and his notions of 'hybridisation' and 'heteroglossia/monoglossia'. According to this work, the voices or 'social languages' of the community are shot through with one another (hybridised), and the words and objects to which they refer are inseparable from and reflect these multiple sociolinguistic world-views. Heteroglossia and the tendency of the community to produce new social languages oppose subordinating this diversity to a monoglossic or master language.

Bakhtin's treatment of carnival and the grotesque body (*Rabelais and His World*, 1965) assists in the struggle of heteroglossia against monoglossia. The role-reversals and parodies that make up carnival help to undermine the master language and ruling groups of society. The grotesque bodies discussed by Bakhtin and portrayed most spectacularly in Rabelais' novels – bodies that are primarily orifices and protuberances and are plugged into one another and their surroundings – debunk classical sculpture and other traditional portrayals of bodies as smooth, well-formed and self-contained. Bakhtin's emphasis upon language, difference and the production of novelty has thus led many to view him as an early postmodernist.

F. Evans

See also: dialogism; heteroglossia/monoglossia

BARTHES, ROLAND (1915–80) French literary scholar, cultural theorist and semiotician, who in 1976 became the first person to hold the chair of 'literary semiology' at the Collège de France. Barthes's approach to cultural criticism evolved from a structuralism influenced by Saussure and the Danish linguist Louis Hjelmslev into a more poststructuralist inflection, in which he went beyond Saussure's focus on purely verbal signs, applying it to a wide range of social phenomena. The Saussurean legacy of the arbitrariness of signs led Barthes to stress that even signs which appear 'transparent' – such as in photography and film – are in fact dependent on social and cultural conventions (or codes) which have to be learned before such signs can be 'read'.

Barthes's best-known work is *Mythologies* (1957), a collection of essays examining taken-for-granted assumptions embedded in popular culture. His early work was largely responsible for establishing structuralist semiotics as a major approach to reading cultural practices. He formally outlined the method in *Elements of Semiology* (1964) and applied it in *The Fashion System* (1967). These two works focused on formal structural analysis, but in much of his work the reading of textual and social codes was a tool for a loosely neo-Marxist ideological analysis – serving to unmask what he saw as the dominant social values of the bourgeoisie.

Barthes adopted from Hjelmslev the notion that there are different orders of signification (levels of meaning) in semiotic systems. The first is that of denotation, where there is a sign consisting of a signifier and a signified. Connotation is a second order which uses the denotative sign as its signifier and attaches to it an additional signified. Barthes argues that these orders combine to produce ideology in the form of myth, which serves the ideological function of naturalisation—in other words, making dominant cultural and historical values, attitudes and beliefs seem entirely 'natural', normal, self-evident, timeless, obvious common sense – and thus objective and true reflections of 'the way things are'. Despite an oft-quoted assertion in 'Le message photographique' (in *Image–Music–Text*, 1977) that 'the photographic image . . . is a *message without a code*', Barthes went on to argue that the apparent identity of the signifier and the signified in this medium is a powerful illusion. No sign is purely denotative – lacking connotation. Thus his final formulation is 'every sign supposes a code'.

Although Saussure argued for the arbitrariness of the relationship between the signifier and the signified, poststructuralists assert their total disconnection. While the advent of poststructuralism is often associated with the publication of Barthes's *S/Z* in 1970, Barthes already refers to an 'empty signifier' in 1957 ('Myth Today' in *Mythologies*). In later work he shows a poststructuralist concern both for what became known as 'intertextuality' (the text as 'a tissue of quotations') and for the reader as 'a producer of the text' – heralding 'the death of the author'.

D. Chandler

See also: codes; Literary Theory; Poststructuralism; semiotics; signifier and signified; Structuralism

BATAILLE, GEORGES (1897–1962) French philosopher and novelist whose wide-ranging interests led to important contributions in philosophy, art history, religion, economics and literary criticism. Although he often distanced himself from philosophy as a discipline – 'I am not a philosopher, but a saint, perhaps a madman', he wrote in 1943 – he studied philosophy first with the Russian émigré and mystic Lev Shestov, then in the seminars of Alexandre Kojève and Alexandre

Koyré at the École des Hautes Études. His writings bear witness to the influence of Hegel, of mystics such as Boehme and Eckhardt, and especially that of Nietzsche, to whom he devoted a book (*On Nietzsche*, 1945).

Bataille frequently addresses themes that traditional philosophy neglects or marginalises. In 'The Psychological Structure of Fascism' (1933), Bataille describes the processes of homogenisation by which human societies exclude 'every non-useful element'. The homogenous or 'productive' society, based on the principle of classical utility, operates according to the capitalist values of productive expenditure (acquisition, conservation, expansion), values reproduced discursively in the orderly rationalism of philosophy. The heterogeneous world, on the other hand, comprises various forms of 'non-productive expenditure', objects and states having no exchange value and that tend to provoke a strong and often ambiguous affective reaction (simultaneous attraction and repulsion). As the waste-matter of the homogeneous world, heterogeneous reality arrives 'with a force or a shock' and has a disturbing, even revolutionary potential; examples include human excrement and bodily secretions, vermin, garbage, body parts, words carrying an erotic suggestion, unconscious processes such as dreams and neuroses, criminals, madmen, poets. In 'The Notion of Expenditure' (1933), Bataille insists again on the insufficiency of the principle of classical utility; evoking the bloody sacrifices of the Aztecs and the practice of potlatch among the Tlingit Indians of the American Northwest (as analysed by Marcel Mauss), he asserts the value to society of 'the principle of loss', of a non-rational economics of excess and 'unconditional expenditure', and of sacrifice ('the production of sacred things').

Many of Bataille's texts from the 1940s deal with experiences (laughter, erotic experience and trauma) that resist 'intellectual translation' and that consequently find no place in the discursive systems of philosophers. In *Inner Experience* (1943), which is at once an intimate journal, a philosophical treatise and a poetics, Bataille sets out to describe an especially intense experience he knew at first through the practice of yoga, then later in a more spontaneous fashion. 'Born of non-knowledge', this ecstatic experience represents 'the extreme limit of the possible'; fundamentally unknowable, it serves as the point of departure for an extensive critique of philosophy from Descartes to Hegel and Heidegger. Philosophy, Bataille maintains, has remained ignorant of or has deftly spirited away any experience that cannot be reduced to the faculty of the understanding; in so doing, it has neglected an essential part of human experience (the 'accursed' part, as Bataille calls it elsewhere). Although Bataille tried to distinguish the inner experience from the experience of mystics such as Saint Theresa of Avila and Saint John of the Cross, from whose writings he quotes liberally, he was criticised by Jean-Paul Sartre in a scathing review ('A New Mystic') that dismissed Bataille's enterprise as 'an adventure that is beyond philosophy'. Bataille was well aware that his interests situated him on the margins of the various philosophical and literary groups of his time. Dismissed by Sartre, he was excommunicated from the Surrealist movement by André Breton, who called him 'pathological' in his *Second Manifesto of Surrealism* (1930).

Many of the themes Bataille introduces in *Inner Experience* are elaborated in subsequent works: laughter and non-knowledge in *Guilty* (1944); the impossible in *The Hatred of Poetry* (1947, re-titled *The Impossible*, 1962); sovereignty and expenditure in *The Accursed Share* (1949); and eroticism in *Erotism* (1957). His later works examine various expressions of violence, especially in its intimate relation to eroticism, which Bataille considered crucial to our understanding of human nature (see *The Trial of Gilles de Rais*, 1959, a long essay on the fifteen-century aristocrat and child-murderer, and *The Tears of Eros*, 1961, a study of erotic violence in art).

Bataille published (often pseudonymously) a number of novels, such as *Story of the Eye* (1928) and *The Blue of Noon* (1936), as well as short narratives such as *Madame Edwarda* (1937) and *My Mother* (1966) which dramatise the primacy of experience over language. His often pornographic fiction, deeply influenced by Sade, explores the themes of human sexuality, eroticism and violence. Some of his literary criticism is collected in *Literature and Evil* (1957), the thesis of which is that certain writers, in whom we find 'a complicity in the knowledge of Evil' – for example, William Blake, Charles Baudelaire, Emily Bronte, Franz Kafka, Jean Genet – point the way to a 'hypermorality' that eschews the prescriptive moralism of religions and philosophies.

In the late 1920s and 1930s Bataille founded a number of mostly left-wing groups and reviews, notably *Documents* (co-founded with Georges-Henri Rivière), 'Contre-Attaque' (a union of 'revolutionary intellectuals' including André Breton, Yves Tanguy and Pierre Klossowski), the College of Sociology (with Michel Leiris and Roger Caillois), and *Acéphale*. In 1946 Bataille founded the journal *Critique*, a general review of publications in all domains of the human sciences both in France and abroad. He directed this review, which remains one of the most respected journals in Europe, until his death. 'If it were necessary to give me a place in the history of thought', Bataille wrote, 'it would be I think for having discerned the effects, in our human life, of the "fading of the discursive real" ' (Postscriptum to *Inner Experience*, 1953). Bataille set in motion a deconstruction of the complicity between discourse and the real that has been carried on by others. His influence on French philosophy has been immense: Foucault, Deleuze, Derrida, Kristeva, Baudrillard and others have acknowledged a debt to his work.

P. *Connor*

See also: Death; expenditure

BAUDRILLARD, JEAN (1929–) French cultural theorist widely and misleadingly presented as the chief proponent of postmodernism. Conflations of Baudrillard's descriptions of advanced capitalism as a consumer society of simulation with his own position abound, despite the criticisms he levels at just such a society.

Baudrillard's major contributions are threefold: (1) a theory and analysis of consumer society; (2) a theory of simulation, in which codes regulate the reproducibility of 'copies' freed from any putative 'original', coupled with notorious theses about hyperreality (that which is realer than the real) which remain relevant for analyses of contemporary practices of surveillance and digital culture; (3) a poetical and anthropological conception of a radical principle, symbolic exchange, which as an anti-semiology is opposed to simulation. Baudrillard's theoretical project is an effort to understand the complex and shifting relationship between simulation and the symbolic, which he first thought transgressed simulation, and then thought was immanent to it, before finally being conceived as singular with regard to it.

The System of Objects (1968) attempts a psychosocial reorientation of structuralism which accommodated what would be otherwise considered external to a system. Baudrillard thus refigures consumption as an active process, providing social rank through the code of status provided by advertising. Objects dematerialised into signs are consumed and manipulated in their systematic differences with other signs, entailing the abolition of a lived, non-arbitrary, visceral human relationship with objects.

The analysis of how purpose becomes counter-purpose, developed in *The System of Objects*, deepens in *Consumer Society* (1970). The calculus of objects that is the manipulation of signs or 'semiurgy' (sign work), traps us while giving us an excuse for not participating in the world and with one another in unmediated ways. Mediatic mass communication thus replaces metabolic communion. This is an early lament for the diminishment of symbolic communion in consumer culture. In *Consumer Society* the influence of anthropology is beginning to be felt. Baudrillard's turn to so-called primitive societies of the gift, which were truly affluent, whose temporality was the rhythm of collective activity before time became money and whose unity was not rent asunder in cold, clinical communication, provided the groundwork for his theory of symbolic exchange. The industrial production of differences that allegedly allow individuals to be themselves, to have their own style and personality, simultaneously erase singular differences between persons for the sake of replacing them with signs of difference, more and more subtly and minutely defined, in conformity with abstract, artificial models.

For A Critique of the Political Economy of the Sign (1972) exposes the ideological dimension of use value as a repository of Marxist idealism, as an abstraction hidden under the cloak of immediacy and particularity but already infused with equivalence. Baudrillard learned a great deal about the pitfalls of theorising symbolic exchange from this analysis of Marxist myth-making, in which he demonstrated the homology between sign and commodity forms (exchange value is to signifier as use value is to signified) and the non-convertibility between logics of value (use value, exchange value, sign value and symbolic exchange). Whereas use value, exchange value and sign value converge in two-sided object forms integrated into a functional syntax and controlled by a code determining their circulation, symbolic exchange emerged as the heterogeneous other of homogeneous political economy and semiology, subversive of all theories of value. At this stage of Baudrillard's thought, symbolic exchange transgresses the field of value, into which it is not convertible.

In *The Mirror of Production* (1973), the fatal malady of capitalism is its inability to reproduce itself symbolically, the relations of which it instead simulates; likewise, the failure of historical materialism was that it could not escape the categories of political economy, insufficiently analysing production and labour. In other words, Marxism is haunted by these mirrors of social activity and remains trapped in the logic of representing what it sought to radically critique. As an alternative, Baudrillard proffers symbolic exchange: an incessant, agonistic cycle of non-economic exchange perfused with value-eroding ambivalence and extra-material spiritual significance.

The symbolic as transgressive, as Baudrillard specifies in *Symbolic Exchange and Death* (1976), can also be thought as immanent to operational codes from which all value (figured as work, the social, consumption, economy, even the distinction between life and death) emanates. His strategy forces a rediscovery of the symbolic obligation through the challenge of a destabilising counter-gift, forcing a worthy repayment in kind. The stake of this symbolic exchange is death understood as a social relation between living and dead ancestors, arrived at through initiation rites like those described by the anthropologist Robert Jaulin. Baudrillard reclaims this kind of social over biological death against its statistical entombment and monopolisation by functionaries of modern church and state.

The third moment of Baudrillard's thought, in which the symbolic is singular with regard to simulation, is clearly seen in *The Vital Illusion* (2000), where it is an eccentric, antagonistic, self-destructing, anomalous figure in a world of cloning. As vernacular language resists universal digitisation, singularity valorises imperfection and the beautiful frailty of never being fully present to ourselves. These antidotes to nihilism are perhaps best expressed in the idea that the murder of the real, the perfect crime – simulation of the world – is never perfect. Respite is found in a passionate appreciation of the world's illusoriness.

This trend is consolidated in *Impossible Exchange* (2001). Here the circle of symbolic exchange is threatened by collapse, since exchange is now impossible – the general equivalent displaced, otherness become incomparable – and the condition of thought is stuck in a paradoxical inability to confirm, justify or measure itself against any principle outside itself. Yet in this reigning speculative disorder Baudrillard valorises singularity as an absolute particular lacking self-being and hence that which has no equivalent. Dialoguing with Jean Nouvel in *The Singular Objects of Architecture* (2002), Baudrillard deploys singularity – unrepresentable, untranslatable, exhausted in itself – as an antidote to simulation that bears a virulent power against hyperreality.

Like the symbolic, singularity is immanent to globalised exchanges and is an 'integral monstrosity' that may be regained or perhaps glimpsed in the anti-globalisation movement's 'antagonistic and irreducible' demonstrations, as he wrote in *Screened Out* (2002).

G. Genosko

See also: simulation; symbolic exchange

BEAUVOIR, SIMONE DE (1908–86)

BEAUVOIR, SIMONE DE (1908–86) French philosopher and writer who achieved world-wide fame with the publication in 1949 of *The Second Sex*. Beauvoir is recognised among philosophers for developing the ethical implications of our ambiguously lived freedom, for her unique analysis of intentionality, and for her insistence that human existence, lived in the horizon of the failure to be, be embraced generously, lucidly and joyfully.

Calling herself a writer, an existentialist, a humanist and, belatedly, a feminist, Beauvoir articulated her philosophical commitments in novels, short stories, memoirs, intimate accounts of her experience of her mother's and Sartre's dying and death, and philosophical essays. She tells us that writing in these diverse genres is no accident. It reflects her objection to abstract philosophical systems, her commitment to the existential phenomenological method and her insistence that philosophy be grounded in the material concrete. While philosophy provides us with the intelligibilities of experience, the novel and the memoir disclose the thickness of its complexities. For Beauvoir, the novel, the memoir and the philosophical essay need each other. While literature reminds us that the lived world exceeds all reflective categories, philosophy alerts us to the meaning and value of subjectivity.

Writing fiction and memoirs where the world is disclosed, and philosophy where it is given formal structure, Beauvoir instantiates her concept of ambiguity and enacts her description of intentionality. This description, found early in *The Ethics of Ambiguity* and influential throughout her writings, takes Husserl's formula, 'consciousness is always consciousness of . . .' into the lived world of desiring consciousness. There are, Beauvoir tells us, two modes of consciousness as 'consciousness of . . .': an original mode that expresses our attachment to being, which she calls the desire to disclose being, and a subsequent mode which expresses our capacity to sustain certain meanings of the world, which she calls our desire to be. The first moment of intentionality reveals the truth of our spontaneous freedom; the second expresses the truth of the project. This doubled way of being 'consciousness of . . .' is inescapable. It is the ambiguity that lies at the heart of our existence and that spills over into the ambiguities of existing between life and death, in solitude and bond to the other, and as subject of/to the world and an object in it.

This ambiguity of intentionality is complicated by the ambiguity coiled within the desire to be. This desire lures us to bad faith and the project of tyranny. It also, however, grounds projects of liberation and justice. As the intentionality of the desire to be, I choose one of the disclosed meanings of the world and give it being. I alone am the ground of this choice. In choosing I raise the ethical question: 'If I am the free source of all value, are all of my choices justified?' Beauvoir says no. Our ambiguous freedom carries within it the criteria by which we can distinguish the moral from the immoral project.

Making this distinction requires attention to the ontology of freedom: its grounding in a finite subject (none of my projects may be established as absolute); its necessary entanglement with others' freedom (our projects intersect, affect and need the other); and its embodiment (it is vulnerable to objectification). Immoral projects violate my bond with others by degrading their freedom. This degradation may target the body or consciousness; for consciousness may be disabled through the body, and the body may lose its instrumentalities through consciousness. Targeting the body, immoral projects enslave others in regimes of mechanised and/or futile labour; they humiliate, torture and render them abject. Targeting consciousness, immoral projects conjure up mystifications and ideologies that constitute others as necessarily subject(ed) to the authority of the other (Nature, God, the state, the superior race).

Rebellion, Beauvoir says, is the only adequate response to these evils. History seems to bear her out – except in the case of women. Thus the question of *The Second Sex*, 'Why don't women rebel?' It is said that they are not oppressed, that their subordination to men is natural, divinely ordained, but this is said of all exploited peoples. Examining biological, psychological, dialectical, literary, religious and mythical justifications of women's subordination and providing phenomenological descriptions of how one is not born a woman but becomes one, Beauvoir determines that women, like other exploited groups, are mystified (by ideologies of femininity); are reduced to their bodies (woman as womb/sex); are restricted to repetitive labour (sustaining the existence of men and children); and are sometimes complicit in their oppression (glad to be absolved of the responsibilities of freedom). Unlike other oppressed groups, however, women are isolated from each other. They do not say 'we'. They form unique, intimate bonds with their oppressors. Through this bond they are displaced from the position of the other, the one who will rebel, and situated as the inessential other, the one barred from the master–slave dialectic.

Unlike Beauvoir's earlier works, *The Second Sex* does not advocate rebellion. It provides another route to justice. This route evades the violence (though not the conflict) that Beauvoir often identifies as the evil that unavoidably contaminates our pursuit of justice. This may reflect the unique situation of men and women, or it may reflect a new direction in Beauvoir's thinking. The liberated, independent woman will be man's other in equality. She will have equal access to the economic, political and social materialities of freedom. More focused on embodiment than before, Beauvoir now posits that as men's equal, women will live the difference of their bodies on their, not patriarchal, terms. Further, she identifies the erotic intimacies of the couple as a material realisation of our ambiguous intentionalities and looks to a post-patriarchal world where men and women recognise each other as both subject and object, autonomous and in need of each other.

The problem of the inessential other is not confined to women within patriarchy. Beauvoir's *Coming of Age* describes the ways in which inessential otherness awaits us all. Addressing the problem of aging again requires attention to embodiment and ambiguity. Again, Beauvoir argues that justice requires that the material conditions of freedom be met in such a way as to engage the joys of its generous spontaneities.

D. Bergoffen

See also: alienation (3); bad faith (2); Death; essentialism; Existentialism; Feminism; inessential other; Nature, Philosophy of; project

BECOMING That which traditional philosophy distinguished from being. *Becoming* is that which is changing, what is contingent, in constant process and flux, whereas *being* is that which is unchanging, necessary and eternal. Heraclitus' statement 'One cannot step into the same river twice' is often seen as a formula summarising the philosophy of becoming. In the nineteenth century, Nietzsche and Bergson developed philosophies that elevated change over permanence, becoming over being. In the twentieth century, Deleuze explored the paradoxes of becoming in *Logic of Sense* ('it is at the same moment that one becomes larger than one was and smaller than one will become') and proposed a new definition of the concept: becoming refers to an objective zone of indistinction or indiscernibility that always exists between multiplicities, a zone that immediately precedes their respective natural differentiation. To take a literary example: in Emily Bronte's *Wuthering Heights*, Catherine and Heathcliff are caught up in a double becoming ('I *am* Heathcliff', says Catherine) that is deeper than love and higher than any 'lived experience', a profound passion that traces a zone of indiscernibility between the two characters, and creates a block of becoming that passes through an entire series of complex affects. Such a conception of becoming has received its scientific expression in the contemporary sciences of chaos and complexity, which have explored zones of objective indetermination and disequilibrium in physical and mathematical systems. Ilya Prigogine (*From Being to Becoming*, 1980) is perhaps the best known exponent of the primacy of becoming in the sciences.

D. Smith

See also: eternal recurrence

BEING-TOWARDS-DEATH (*Sein-zum-Tode*) A concept which enables Heidegger to bring closure to the existential analytic of *Being and Time*. Throughout the existential analytic, Dasein is threatened with dispersion: inasmuch as existence is ecstatic, that is thrown into the world, and projecting itself into a world of possibilities, this thrown projection seems limitless and paves the way for alienation. So Heidegger asks: can Dasein be conceived as a whole, or as a totality (indeed not made of parts, but of existentials), or must it be seen as irreducibly fragmented? Is there something that holds it together, and makes every Dasein *a* Dasein? The answer is: death. Death is the ultimate horizon, the horizon as such, from out of which Dasein projects itself and opens up its world. Dasein is the being that is *towards* death. Death is this possibility that is still outstanding: when every other possibility has been exhausted, death remains, and so testifies to the fact that there is always something about Dasein that is not quite complete: so long as Dasein is, there remains something outstanding. But death is a possibility unlike others, in so far as it cannot be realised, or actualised, without negating Dasein itself. As a result, death is the ultimate, as well as the primordial, possibility. It is against the backdrop of death, as this horizon or this limit towards which we always find ourselves thrown that all other possibilities, and indeed existence itself, unfold.

M. de Beistegui

BENJAMIN, WALTER (1892–1940) German philosopher, cultural critic and literary theorist. Born into affluence, Benjamin found a subject of lifelong philosophical importance in the 'endless flâneries' (strolls) of his youth. Berlin *circa* 1900 was a place of explosive growth, and a major motif of Benjamin's mature works reflects his ardent fascination with the connection between the industrial economic conditions of modern urban life and the forms of individual and collective consciousness. Benjamin wrote on a wide range of literary and philosophical subjects, and he invested this eclecticism with the idea that a complete 'historical schematism' could be revealed in minutiae, in the dust and debris of modernity. Inspiration and support for this idea came from an exposure to the thought of Simmel, whose lectures Benjamin had attended, from Goethe's notion of the *Urphäno-men*, and from studies of Freud's work.

The unfinished *Arcades Project* was in many respects a culmination of these important strands in Benjamin's research, to which one must also add the methodological influence of French surrealism and, above all, of Marxism. In place of interpretation, *The Arcades Project* relies for its compositional force upon the 'principle of montage', by which Benjamin tried to achieve a 'profane illumination' of structural corre-spondences between material and cultural forms of the nineteenth century. Not merely a novel way of reflecting on the past, 'the new dialectical method of doing history presents itself as the art of experiencing the present as waking world, a world to which that dream we name the past refers in truth'. Benjamin's application of psycho-analysis to culture, as the collective dream of an epoch, combined with his appropriation of historical materialism, led him to conceive of the 'dialectical image', a point at which the present might dispel the dream consciousness it has inherited from the past.

Owing to the oddity of its conception and to the untimely end of the work with Benjamin's death, the bibliographic status of *The Arcades Project* is unclear. It can be approached as an incomplete manuscript, as a research notebook, as a finished text awaiting its assignment to an as yet non-existent genre or as none of these things. Benjamin himself referred to the work as 'the theatre of all my struggles and all my ideas'.

Benjamin's 'The Work of Art in the Age of Mechanical Production' (1936) gives the nature and prospects of a modern aesthetic theory that is 'useful for the formulation of revolutionary demands in the politics of art'. Benjamin's exposition includes the famous thesis: 'That which withers in the age of mechanical reproduction is the aura of the work of art'. The 'aura' is whatever might have secured for the work of art its unique presence, originality and place in a tradition. Mechanical reproduction floods the cognitive world with simulations, extinguish-ing the aura, but it also 'emancipates the work of art from its parasitical dependence on ritual', thereby conferring upon art a new political power in relation to the masses.

P. Lewis

See also: aura; Baudrillard; Cinema; Critical Theory; dialectical image; simulation

BERGSON, HENRI (1859–1941) French philosopher, who, after an initial period of widespread acclaim, fell out of fashion, but today occupies an important position in continental philosophy. So important was Bergson in his first appearance that he was elected a member of the *Académie française* in 1914, was awarded the Nobel Prize for Literature in 1928 and had his work described by no less than William James as marking a Copernican turn in philosophy akin to that of Kant. For years his work was studied by all schoolchildren in France. However, from the 1930s onwards, in part because of this very institutional success, and in part because of a perceived spiritualist tendency in his work, Bergson fell dramatically out of favour, until in the late 1950s and early 1960s Deleuze almost single-handedly precipitated a return to Bergsonism. Today, Bergson once again occupies a central position in continental philosophy. However, in keeping with the Deleuzean method, this rejuvenated Bergson is significantly different from the one who made such an impact in *fin-de-siècle* France.

Bergson initially trained to be a mathematician, winning first prize for the Concours Général with his 'plane solution of Pascal'. While teaching philosophy in the early 1880s, as he recounts in a subsequent letter to James, Bergson began to formulate his own distinctive philosophical position as a consequence of two insights that were to have a crucial impact on his later work: the rejection of mechanism, particularly as it is found in Spencer; and the recognition that 'scientific time has no *duration* [*durée*]'. The former insight would inform *Creative Evolution*, while the latter would determine all of Bergson's philosophical work, beginning most strikingly with *Time and Free Will*, published in 1888 as one of two doctoral theses submitted to the University of Paris. The other was *What Is Aristotle's Sense of Place?*, a topic which, intriguingly, was also to play a pivotal role in Heidegger's reflections on the themes of motion, time and continuity in Aristotle during lecture courses from the 1920s.

In *Time and Free Will*, Bergson shows that space and time constitute two different multiplicities. Time, or duration, is continuous, qualitative and differential, whereas space is discrete, quantitative and divisible. Therefore only the latter is measurable, and all attempts to render time quantitatively measurable, such as those of the natural sciences, will effect an implicit spatialisation of time, thereby reducing time's essential nature. Moreover, since the method of the intellect is analytical, it is condemned always to miss time, so Bergson proposes a new philosophical method of 'intuition'. This method does not begin and end with duration, however, for Bergson further argues that many traditional philosophical problems result from the inappropriate application of the analytic tendency of the intellect, such that recasting these problems in their true temporal guise would render them soluble. Bergson fulfils this project in the final chapter of *Time and Free Will*, showing how the 'problem' of free will results from applying spatial reasoning to the flow of the mind.

Similarly, *Matter and Memory* (1896) resolves the traditional problem of the interaction of mind and matter by means of a new theory of memory, which rejects the assumption of memory as a store or repository on the basis of the spatiality of these metaphors, offering in its place new temporally determined explanations of perception, habitual memory, recollective memory and recognition.

We can clearly see from this approach that Bergson is a self-avowed dualist. Uniquely, however, he does not begin from the assumption of the separation of the dualities, as do Plato and Descartes. Rather, he seeks to show how, for instance, space emerges from time. This method reaches its apotheosis in *Creative Evolution* (1907), in which he criticises the mechanistic assumptions of neo-Darwinism, primarily because they are unable to account for the movement of evolution. Although ridiculed throughout much of twentieth-century biology and philosophy, largely because of his poorly understood notion of *élan vital*, Bergson's critique of reductionist mechanism is finding a new audience today in the emerging sciences of complexity. However, the philosophical heart of *Creative Evolution* resides in its dualist ontology, in which Bergson characterises matter and life as two tendencies, showing the ontological process by which these tendencies emerge as such. The core of this demonstration returns to the 'theory of difference' underpinning Bergson's original theory of multiplicities, and it is this 'differential' Bergson which struck a resonant chord with Deleuze, accounting in part for Bergson's renaissance in contemporary continental philosophy.

A further contributory factor is Bergson's conception of metaphysics as a necessary complement to scientific investigation. Affirming the reality of, as well as the difference in kind between, matter and spirit (or memory or life), Bergson argues for the necessity of two methods, namely scientific intellect and philosophical intuition, to investigate these distinct realities. Already evident in *Matter and Memory* and *Creative Evolution*, this approach is most strikingly applied in *Duration and Simultaneity* (1922). Again poorly received, and hastening Bergson's philosophical decline, this work sought to engage Einstein's theory of special relativity. Although marred by mathematical errors in his discussion of the 'twins paradox', the value of this poorly understood work lies in its demonstration that Einstein is offering a theory of measurement rather than a theory of time, and thus special relativity requires a supplementary philosophical theory of duration. Again, Bergson's position, if not the detail of his critique, has found a new scientific audience who share the perspective that there is no time in relativity theory.

Bergson also published an essay on *Laughter* (1900) and two collections of papers, *Mind-Energy* (1919) and *Creative Mind* (1933). His last substantive work was *The Two Sources of Morality and Religion* (1932), which applied the findings of his earlier investigations, and particularly his dualist perspective, to ethics, drawing a key distinction between what he termed open and closed societies.

R. Durie

See also: becoming; Cinema; creative evolution; duration; intuition; *Lebensphilosophie*; Memory; multiplicity; Time

BIOLOGY, PHILOSOPHY OF While there is no unified, specialised domain within the continental tradition to match the epistemological or analytical designation of a philosophy of biology, it is undeniable that a persistent and variegated investigation of the biological sciences has been a crucial component in the genealogy of continental philosophy. More precisely, the very development of the biological sciences, starting with the simultaneous coining of the term 'biology' in 1802 by Lamarck and Treviranus, has always contained a marked philosophical component, whether in an Aristotelian, Kantian, materialist or other guise.

As Cassirer argues in *The Problem of Knowledge* (1906–20) and as Canguilhem corroborates in his numerous writings on the history of biology and epistemology, the debate pitting vitalist against mechanist accounts of biological phenomena was given one of its most systematic and lasting formulations in the second half of Kant's *Critique of Judgement* (1790), 'The Critique of Teleological Judgement'. Ever since that text, and passing through the vicissitudes of evolutionary theory, embryology, genetics, systems theory, autopoiesis and so on, the biological problems of production, individuation, autonomy, purpose and organisation have frequently been at the forefront of philosophical speculation. However, precisely because of the very sensitive role of the problem of the organism in Kant – where, via the question of regulative judgement, it thematises the very consistency of the critical philosophy – post-Kantian speculation regarding biology has never simply been an epistemological reflection on the categories used by biologists, but has always implicated philosophy's self-image. Conversely, philosophical speculation regarding the status of living beings has played an active, if perhaps ideological, role in the development of the biological sciences themselves – notice the way the vitalism/mechanism debate, for instance, is explicitly thematised in Lorentz's studies on ethology and Monod's writings on genetics.

Following Kant, Schelling's *Naturphilosophie*, initially more preoccupied with chemical and electromagnetic phenomena, latched onto the problematic idea of organisms as self-organising beings to present that point of indifference between the objective and subjective domain so central to Schelling's early philosophy, as well as to provide a template for philosophy and art. It also took inspiration from biology to formulate the distinctly non-Kantian possibility of a thinking from the point of view of production. In Hegel, the organism is both a distinct phase in the unfolding of the philosophy of nature and a symbol for the realisation of the concept, for the manner in which an ideal plan concretely and temporally comes to be in the world. The emphasis here, contra Schelling, is on the organism as concrete negation, as dialectical articulation of identity and difference. Both Schelling and Hegel's writings testify to a philosophical ideal, of Aristotelian provenance, which regards living beings as the concrete and singular instantiation of the ideality and universality of the concept, as well as the symbolic exhibition of the dynamic totality aspired to by philosophy itself. In this current of thought – for which biology is primarily understood via anatomy, physiology and embryology – philosophy reconfigures its own structure and telos through a focus on certain guiding traits of living organisms, such as self-affection, creativity and unity.

This current of thought was arguably interrupted and transformed by the Darwinian revolution and the postulation of random variation and natural selection as the 'mindless' mechanisms behind the generation of biological design. Nietzsche's acute critical response to the challenge of Darwinism is thus a key moment in the development of the continental tradition, as recently argued by Keith Ansell Pearson in *Viroid Life* (1997). At the crossroads of Schopenhauer's identification of life with will and F. A. Lange's Darwinian scepticism vis-à-vis Kantian teleology, Nietzsche integrated much of the biological speculation of his time into his model of interpretation and his thought of the will to power, even picking up on some of the most advanced critiques of Darwinism (witness his attack on the understanding of function in *The Genealogy of Morality*). Despite Heidegger's defence of Nietzsche against charges of 'biologism', it seems evident that in the latter's work it is virtually impossible to separate speculation on biological themes from philosophical argument.

By virtue of Schelling's influence on Victor Cousin and Félix Ravaisson, certain aspects of the post-Kantian and non-Darwinian tradition of philosophy of biology entered into the current of French spiritualism and played a considerable role in the formation of Bergson's thinking of creative evolution. In Bergson, the tendency to model thought on life becomes even more intense, arguably leading to the creation of a full-blown biophilosophy. Here the focus shifts onto the image of life as self-differentiating production and duration, and the post-Kantian concern with the organism as a symbol of thought is considerably attenuated, rendering possible Deleuze's later espousal of a vitalism centred on the notion of 'non-organic life'. This attempt to think life *against* the notion of the organism makes of Deleuze's thought perhaps the boldest attempt to rethink the role of biology in continental thought. In this respect, his original usage of embryological and genetic models of difference in *Difference and Repetition* (1968), his work with

Guattari on the Cuvier-St Hilaire debate in *A Thousand Plateaus* (1980) and his foregrounding of such seminal biophilosophers as Gabriel Tarde, Gilbert Simondon and Raymond Ruyer makes Deleuze's work into a unique synthesis of the biological elements in the continental tradition.

This philosophy *from* rather than *of* biology, this biophilosophy, is interestingly offset by a more political reading of the speculative significance of the life sciences. One should here at least cite the Althusserian works of Dominique Lécourt, namely on the Lyssenko affair; Foucault's writings, much indebted to Canguilhem, about the relationship between the discourse on life and the discourse on man; and Agamben's researches, beginning with *Homo Sacer* (1995), on the articulation between the metaphysics of life and the biopolitics of sovereignty, exclusion and extermination. The recent interest in biological themes within the phenomenological tradition, on the other hand, is perhaps closer to the inaugural Kantian formulation of the problem. Here we note interest in Heidegger's lectures on von Üexkull's ethology in *Fundamental Concepts of Metaphysics* (1930) as well as in Merleau-Ponty's account of the vitalism-mechanism debate in *The Structure of Behaviour* (1939) and his lectures on the concept of nature. Here it is once again the organism and not 'life' or 'production' which takes centre stage, as is clear in the accounts of embodied cognition that motivate the project of a 'naturalised phenomenology'.

A. Toscano

See also: complexity theory; German Idealism; *Lebensphilosophie*; Materialism; naturalising phenomenology; Nature, Philosophy of; organism; vitalism

BIOPOWER A term Foucault introduced in 1976 which names configurations of power relations that concern themselves not with exercising the old sovereign's right to put subjects to death or demand the sacrifice of their lives in war but, rather, with exercising the power to make human beings live. Networks of biopower are institutionalised relations and practices that function to oversee, regulate, and direct populations so as to increase or decrease fertility and longevity, manage public health and mortality, control epidemics and maintain living environments. Biopolitical strategies may include governmental programmes for public hygiene, state- or corporate-sponsored campaigns to improve workers' morals and physical fitness, mandatory vaccinations, tax or wage incentives for marriage and family planning, state regulation of fertility, public surveillance and crime management, insurance, and a host of related social and economic programmes.

Biopower emerges out of normalised disciplinary power in the nineteenth century; it differs from disciplinary power in that it does not
focus on individuals (as disciplinary power does) except as members of
populations, but the two types of power are complementary in the
development of contemporary forms of state and corporate management of human lives. Foucault discusses biopower in Part V of *The
History of Sexuality, Volume One* (1980) and chapter 11 of '*Society
Must Be Defended*' (2003). In both texts, he links the rise of biopower
with the rise of state racism in the twentieth century, suggesting that
the imperative to manage populations typically involves or leads to a
desire to 'purify' them.

L. McWhorter

See also: Agamben; state of exception

BLANCHOT, MAURICE (1907–2003) French thinker whose theoretical and literary work centred on the possibilities of redefining
traditional notions of language and its relationship to the speaking
subject. In approximately thirty works published between 1941 and
1994 he developed a style of writing beyond the traditional distinction
between essays and fictional works, so that works such as *Thomas the
Obscure, Death Sentence* and *The Madness of the Day* were often called
by Blanchot *récits*.

Already in one of his early and very influential essays ('Literature
and the Right to Death', 1949) Blanchot determined literary language
as one of the privileged objects of his thinking. In contrast to ordinary
language which 'limits equivocation', in literary language 'ambiguity is
in some sense abandoned to its excesses'. Thus literature gives us to see
what is at stake in any language, namely, not only that language is
ambiguous (that it can say more than one thing at once) but that 'the
general meaning of language is unclear: we do not know if it is
expressing or representing'.

Reacting to the Hegelian thesis that writers do not take action in the
world but through writing only mime such an action without actually
initiating it, not negating anything and therefore not risking their life
(the ultimate risk and thus the horizon of any action), Blanchot
maintains that, far from only employing limitless imagination (which
for Hegel would be an affirmation withdrawn from the negative of
reality), writing necessarily stumbles upon the limit that differentiates
being from non-being, life from death. What is more, literary language
is indeed a negation for it can begin to speak only as the fundamental
lack that is expressed through it: 'No fullness, no certainty can ever
speak; something essential is lacking in anyone who expresses himself.

Negation is tied to language'. Literary language is a void that forces me to 'say nothing', which is why in every speaking void, nothingness or death 'speaks in me'. As 'death speaking', literary language is a 'deferred assassination' that first negates the speaking subject itself. Literary language is thus the exposure of the subject (writer, author) to its own possibility of dying.

In one of his major works, *The Infinite Conversation* (1969), the answer to the question of whether language is expressing or representing is answered through a radical 'formula': 'speaking is not seeing'. This formula, which condenses the fundamental stakes of Blanchot's theoretical and literary efforts, divorces speaking from representation. We do not speak about what we see, we do not think 'according to the measure of the eye'. However, to say that 'speaking frees thought from the optical imperative' is at the same time to disturb the traditional ideas of truth, testimony, lie, error and so on, all of which, in one way or another, insist on the adequate representation of what we see in what we say. What is more, by speaking of what is not visible or present, speaking takes the speaking subject (absorbed in the visual, in the process of representing what is or what was present) unawares, comes from behind his back and disrupts him. Disruption means turning the self away from itself, which is the real force of what are called 'tropes' (turns). In this turning away, in this disruption (and not merely interruption) of the subject that abandons itself to self-oblivion lies the truly negative force of speaking. Speaking speaks the absence, the void or self-oblivion. What speaks when no one is speaking is the very being of language (something Blanchot will also call the 'neuter'), which in speaking or affirming itself affirms only its 'void' (nothing visible, nothing to say other than nothing), affirms its own absence and thus negates the force of presence (of the I, of the visible).

In *The Space of Literature* (1955) this disruption is called 'the other night'. By this term Blanchot referred to the breakdown of the regime of the optical and thus of the representational force of language. Described as the moment in which ' "everything [that] has disappeared" appears', the other night does not refer simply to a nocturnal space of obscure representations but to the disappearance of all representations (including representation of the self) and the appearance of 'nothing representable'. To use one of Blanchot's famous examples, when Orpheus turns back to see Eurydice, thus committing the very act he was forbidden to commit, not only does he not manage to see her but in turning back he himself vanishes, turning away from himself toward the 'nothing to be seen'. He is lost in the 'other night', and 'lost absolutely'.

In *The Writing of the Disaster* (1980), absolute loss is referred to as disaster in which all referents are destroyed. The paradox of the 'absolute loss' that arrives with disaster is that not everything is lost with it. What remains after the disaster is a 'language without referent' or, as Blanchot also puts it, 'the excessiveness of uncodifiable law'. Since the disaster always arrives as an event, as an incalculable breakdown of law and reference (as catastrophe of the world) Blanchot calls its force the 'outside'. Outside is not a simple exteriority vis-à-vis an interiority of the subject, but the destruction of both interiority and exteriority. Outside is 'where being lacks without giving place to non-being', a negation of the difference between being and non-being. Paradoxically, the outside is in the manner of (being of) what *is* not. In it any firmness of existence is annihilated. What therefore remains after the disaster is the outside: no interiority, no self, no intended meanings but the being of language that speaks. This speaking of what is left to be is the letting be of language itself. This speaking of the disaster is what Blanchot then calls writing, which is not to be confused with the written. Such a writing does not 'give speech to be seen', it does not represent speaking. Rather, it is both the violent movement of a 'crisis' or of the disaster and the (impersonal) telling of what is left after its arrival.

B. Arsić

See also: Death; *désœuvrement*; narrative voice

BLOCH, ERNST (1885–1977) German philosopher, theologian and social critic. In Berlin, at Simmel's seminars on the philosophy of culture and the aesthetics of modernity, he met Benjamin and Buber, and developed a view of the Russian Revolution as a cathartic event that Germany should join in order to redeem itself from the base bellicose impulses expressed in the First World War. His monograph on a fifteenth-century heretic monk, *Thomas Münzer als Theologe der Revolution* (1921), is a passionate study in the genealogy of this 'other' Germany, distinctly anti-Bismarckian and non-hegemonic. In Heidelberg, Bloch became part of the intellectual circle of Max Weber, whose focus was the critique of capitalism in terms of the 'Protestant ethic' and secularisation. His life-long friendship with Lukács dates back to those years. As Hitler came to power, Bloch went into exile in Europe and the US. But at the zenith of Stalin's totalitarian rule, he left America for East Germany. There, in tandem with Lukács in Hungary, Bloch contributed to the formation of a new generation of Marxist intellectuals, such as Agnes Heller, who played a crucial role in the European uprisings of 1956 and 1968. In the end, however, his critical angle on the Soviet regime made him lose his post at the University of Leipzig. In 1961, just after the construction of the Berlin Wall, Bloch crossed the Iron Curtain back to West Germany, where he taught at the University of Tübingen until his death in 1977.

Bloch's roots lay deep in the culture that anticipated the Weimer Republic, enlivened by a new focus on Kierkegaard and Kant and the avant-garde dismantling of tradition. His first major work, *The Spirit of Utopia* (1918), written in an experimental philosophical style inspired by expressionism, provides a synthesis of these elements. 'Spirit' is for him the essence of utopia, assumed as both the pivotal metaphysical principle and the driving force behind all moral, social and creative progress. Utopia, however, is not an intellectual construct but rather a concrete aspect of ordinary everyday existence, which is the job of philosophy to capture and interpret. The fragmentary and occasional style of *Spuren* (1930) and *Heritage of Our Times* (1935) seeks to give voice to such concrete utopian fragments.

In the second edition of *The Spirit of Utopia* (1923), Bloch presents for the first time his highly original combination of Marxism, messianism and utopianism. In it, his commitment to Kant as philosopher of the individual normative call recedes in favour of a more Hegelian picture, in which history is endowed with a rational design. Yet, in contrast with Hegel, such rationality can never be fully determined or even expressed. In this sense, the human urges for redemption, the absolute and happiness are not subjective states of mind but necessitated and validated by the very structure of reality.

The Principle of Hope (1955–9) offers a phenomenology of the utopian states of consciousness. These include individual desires, works of art as well as the collective expressions of utopian aspirations embedded in mass cultural products. The careful analysis of these states reveals what Bloch has called the 'ontology of the not-yet', namely, the structure of a reality still to come, which may serve not only as a guide for action but also, and perhaps even more deeply, as a source of metaphysical hope.

G. Borradori

BODY WITHOUT ORGANS | BwO (*corps sans organes* | *CsO*) a phrase coined by Artaud and adapted by Deleuze and Guattari in *Anti-Oedipus* and *A Thousand Plateaus* as a name for the single substance of their materialist monism.

Everything is a complication of the BwO; and, consequently, the BwO is also the point at which anything can become anything else. In *A Thousand Plateaus* Deleuze and Guattari use the phrase 'plane of consistency' to suggest the place where everything is consistent with, that is can be transformed into, anything else. 'BwO' then takes on a more specific use: a BwO describes the way in which the components of some particular system or assemblage can be rendered consistent. The dominant social register of *Anti-Oedipus* leads such secondary bodies to be understood as describing particular blocs of social consolidation akin to modes of production in Marx.

The BwO is, however, not given but produced: the actions of a system generate new connections, becomings and transitions, which render it consistent with other systems. The scope of these becomings is not calculable in advance. As the doctrine of a single substance suggests, the BwO owes much to Spinoza. But the term 'body' also resonates with Spinoza's suggestion that we don't know yet what a body can do. Although the BwO is matter in its most informal state and leaves traces on systems mostly through operations of destructuring, it is nevertheless creative, since these operations are the motor of change and complexity.

A. Welchman

BOURDIEU, PIERRE (1930–2002) French sociologist, anthropologist, political essayist, philosopher and theorist of social action, with powerful and influential writings on education, art, power, language, culture and sundry social phenomena. Of perhaps greatest interest for philosophy is his practice theory of action, which was arguably the leading theory of social action in the final third of the twentieth century. This theory is presented largely in two treatises, *Outline of a Theory of Practice* (1972) and *The Logic of Practice* (1980), and a collection of lectures and interviews, *In Other Words* (1990). Two major conceptual innovations mark this theory: habitus and field.

Bourdieu opposed theories that attribute human action either to free will or to objective structures that force particular actions. He argued that what generates action are, instead, batteries of dispositions he called habitus. Habitus can be likened to a collection of skills or practical senses: business sense, moral sense, a sense of reality, a 'sense for the game'. Unlike free will, these skills or dispositions are not under people's conscious control. Unlike objective structures, habitus does not force any particular actions. Habitus, instead, generates actions – possibly innovative actions – that are appropriate to and sensible in the particular situations in which people act. People acquire a habitus as they learn to participate in the practices about them, and the actions habitus subsequently generates perpetuate the practices in which it was acquired. Indeed, absent external influence and with allowance for drift, habitus almost guarantees the endless perpetuation of the practices it incorporates.

Human practices are carried out, and habitus acquired, in domains of practice called fields. Examples are politics, cooking, agriculture, art and education. The actions that habitus generates sustain not just the practices in which it was acquired, but also the fields in which these practices transpire. Fields are characterised by stakes, what is at issue in them: the practices that transpire in a field resemble games played there for particular stakes. In pursuing these stakes, moreover, actors utilise a variety of capitals – not just economic capital (for example, money or land) but symbolic and cultural capital as well (for example, reputation or charisma). One of Bourdieu's great innovations was widening the notion of capital to embrace non-economic factors that people can draw on in pursuing what is at stake in their practices. Correlatively, he expanded the theory of economic rationality, according to which people maximise economic utility and capital, into a theory holding that people maximise all types of capital: the sensible and appropriate actions that habitus generates maximise capital. The distribution of capitals is also a key element in the objective structure of fields (and groups), which is charted by the methods of empirical social science. Along with practices, this structure is perpetuated in the actions that habitus generates.

According to Bourdieu, a society can be thought of as a whole of homologous fields. In empirical work he applied these theories to different societies, including Kabylia society in Algeria and contemporary French society.

T. Schatzki

See also: habitus

BRENTANO, FRANZ (1838–1917) German philosopher chiefly remembered today for his re-introduction of the term 'intentionality', and for his effect on Husserl, who called him 'my one and only teacher in philosophy'. After training in philosophy and theology at the University of Würtzburg, Brentano became Professor of Philosophy at the University of Vienna in 1874, then, after marrying six years later, *Privatdozent* for a further fifteen years. During this period he encountered such students as Meinong and Husserl. He retired in 1895, working for the rest of his life as a private scholar in Switzerland and Italy.

As a Catholic scholar, Brentano's philosophical training began with Aquinas and, in particular, Aristotle. Despite his antipathy towards Aristotle, Brentano nevertheless respected the integrity of his philosophy sufficiently to devote considerable scholarship to his work, resulting in his doctoral thesis 'On the Manifold Sense of Being [*Seienden*] in Aristotle', a text which was to be given to the young Heidegger and one which was to exercise a significant influence on his early philosophical development. Brentano was more overtly critical of Thomist philosophy, and reserved his most vehement polemic for the speculative systems of German idealism and the contemporary vogue for scepticism, a critical stance shared by Husserl.

Brentano sought philosophical allies among French Positivists and British Empiricists, aiming to apply the methodology of the natural sciences to philosophy. This approach is evident in Brentano's major work, *Psychology from an Empirical Standpoint* (1874). At the outset of the *Psychology*, Brentano stated that his 'standpoint in psychology is empirical: Experience alone is my teacher'. He also argued that the psychologism or genetic psychology practised by such schools was meaningless if a prior elucidation of their basic concepts were not offered. Such a task was undertaken in what Brentano called his 'descriptive psychology'.

The ground for such a descriptive psychology is found in the distinction Brentano effected between general introspection, which he deemed unreliable, and inner perception, the immediate awareness of our own psychological phenomena, which yielded certain and reliable data. This is the case to the extent that immediate awareness is restricted to the immediate present, or the fringe of 'immediate memory' which accompanies this present, since in both immediate awareness and immediate memory, phenomena are given directly, whereas the phenomena of past and future times are given indirectly. In this methodological claim it is possible to discern a theory of internal time consciousness which was to have significant influence on Husserl.

Of greater influence still, however, was Brentano's determination of the attribute which distinguishes psychological phenomena from physical phenomena. This quality is intentionality, a notion derived from Scholastic philosophy, which designates the 'reference to a content, the directedness toward an object' of all psychic phenomena. Thus psychic phenomena uniquely 'contain objects in themselves by way of intention'. The task for descriptive psychology consists in the classification of the types of such psychical acts, according to the 'quality' with which they refer to objects. It was this discovery of the structure of intentionality, and the task of the classification of acts according to quality, which was to exert the decisive influence on Husserl, the founder of phenomenology.

R. Durie

See also: Intentionality; Phenomenology

BRITISH IDEALISM The name given to the school which dominated British philosophy during the final quarter of the nineteenth and the early years of the twentieth century, introducing the ideas of classical continental idealism to native streams of thought. The key figures were T. H. Green, F. H. Bradley, Bernard Bosanquet, John and Edward Caird, Henry Jones, Andrew Seth Pringle-Pattison, James Seth, D. G. Ritchie, J. S. Mackenzie, William Wallace, J. M. E. McTaggart, R. B. Haldane and J. H. Muirhead. They made contributions across the broad range of philosophical topics, most notably in ethics, metaphysics, logic, theology, social and political philosophy, aesthetics and philosophy of history. There was not, of course, complete homogeneity, but it is possible to pick out the following key features which were typical of their views and which make their common classification historically useful.

Perhaps the most characteristic mark of their philosophy was its strongly metaphysical character. For the British Idealists, questions of ethics, logic, religion and the like, if pursued to any great depth, demonstrated themselves to be at heart metaphysical. The result was a creative flowering of speculative metaphysics, and the period saw the construction of several subtle and complex new systems. This point provides us too with one of the greatest differences between the British Idealists and the analytic school which followed them. No doubt in part as a reaction, their successors sharply rejected any dependence of the other branches of philosophy on metaphysics, and often even rejected metaphysics itself, with the result that most English language philosophy in the twentieth century has been strongly antimetaphysical.

A second common feature of the movement – reflected in their name – is that they were all idealists, where this is to be understood in the manner of Kant and Hegel rather than the native fashion of Berkeley. The ideas of classical continental idealism were known in Britain in the first half of the nineteenth century, but not widely. From the 1860s, however, they suddenly became very fashionable; in a culture traditionally noted for its empirical realism, the notion that reality was not separate from mind was embraced with enthusiasm, and there appeared a flood of translations, commentaries and independent idealist analyses. Notwithstanding its importance, it should be remembered that the following of Kant and Hegel was never slavish; it was indeed more one of general tone than detail.

Another distinctive aspect of British Idealist philosophy was its advocacy of systematic, holistic and even monistic patterns of thought. In logical terms, this stress on unity can be seen in their championing of such Hegelian doctrines as identity-in-difference, the unity of finite and infinite, the notion of the concrete universal, organic development and, perhaps most importantly, the coherence theory of truth, according to which truth is a function not of correspondence to some 'external' world but of the inner coherence and comprehensiveness of any given system of propositions. In metaphysical terms, these drifts of thinking led most of them into a kind of Absolutism, according to which reality consists in one great monistic whole. The most famous such position is that of F. H. Bradley, whose *Appearance and Reality* (1893) argues against the notion of relation and hence against pluralism.

Monism as extreme as Bradley's has implications for the self which many find uncomfortable: a sense of being lost or submerged in something greater. In consequence, there arose an important division within the school. A number of figures, who became known as the personal idealists, put forward accounts which, while still idealistic and systematic, nonetheless respected the irreducible distinctness of persons. In practice this covered quite a range of positions. For some, such as McTaggart, in *The Nature of Existence* (1927), the system was little more than a community of distinct spirits. But others, like Andrew Seth Pringle-Pattison in *The Idea of God* (1917), regarded it as possible to assert a much stronger unity. This problem of how to reconcile the facts of personality with the unity of the world became a dominant subject for the whole movement.

At issue was distinctness of persons, not just from one another but from God, and this introduces a fourth common theme in their thought: the movement was from the first a philosophy of religion. In the second half of the nineteenth century, many felt that the conflict between the claims of religion and the findings of natural science (especially evolutionary theory) – as well as the findings of historical Biblical research – was becoming a veritable cultural crisis. Intellectuals searched for a rational basis for belief, something many thought they found in Hegelianism, which they felt gave them a non-miraculous universe, but one nonetheless shot though with spirit, value and purpose. But although almost all of the British Idealists presented philosophies religious in motivation, they differed about details, for instance about whether or not the whole system should be called 'God'.

There was also in their thought a strong emphasis on political, social and ethical matters, shown in works such as Bradley's *Ethical Studies* (1876), Green's *Prolegomena to Ethics* (1883) and Bosanquet's *The Philosophical Theory of the State* (1899). In such works their holism led to a social conception of the individual and a trenchant opposition to the individualistic modes of thought, such as utilitarianism, which had predominated hitherto.

A final common thread may be found in their readings of history –
be it intellectual, religious or moral – as essentially developmental and
progressive. This is particularly evident in a philosophy such as that of
Caird, in whose *The Evolution of Religion* (1893) development is seen as
the key for uncovering the underlying unity of things.

This progressivism was one factor in the eventual undoing of the
school, for after the First World War such confidence in human
progress found few sympathetic ears. Although the movement continued until the 1920s, it was in decline, and soon it was eclipsed and
forgotten. Indeed, it is only in very recent years that their work has
been rediscovered and that it has been possible to begin to make any
kind of informed judgements about their worth and contribution.

W. Mander

BUBER, MARTIN (1878–1965) German philosopher frequently asso-
ciated with religious existentialism. Buber's work reflects the world of
German modernism and mandarin letters, not professional philosophy.
Buber combined the influence of Nietzsche, Dilthey and Simmel with
the Zionism of Herzl and Nordau, the utopian socialism of Gustav
Landauer and the Hebrew prophetic and hasidic mystical traditions.
His mature work is coterminous with the phenomenology of Max
Scheler and Rudolf Otto. Unlike Husserl, Buber was less interested in
the intentional structure of human consciousness per se, less interested
in subjectivity than in intersubjectivity. While widely pilloried in the
critical literature, already in the 1920s and up until this day, as a
hopeless romantic, Buber came more and more to focus his attention on
the gray realities of everyday life and the political and ethical exigencies
that define the life of dialogue. As well as producing essays on
philosophical anthropology, Kierkegaard, Kafka and the image-work
in art (*Between Man and Man*, *The Knowledge of Man*), Buber was an
early critic of Heidegger and Sartre (*Eclipse of God*, 1952). A critique of
the isolated individual and an emphasis upon the shape of community
in the confluence of life and form lend coherence to the entire corpus of
his writing.

In the early work leading up to the First World War, the current
Nietzsche-vogue and the flowing contours of German-speaking *art
nouveau* meet up with Hasidism, a form of East European pietism based
upon mystical devotion, intentional acts and charismatic authority. *The
Tales of Rabbi Nahman of Bratzlav* (1906) and then *Legends of the Baal
Shem* (1908) earned early literary fame for Buber, while *Ecstatic
Confessions* (1909) and *Daniel* (1912) further increased his reputation
in the world of German letters. Dionysian *Erlebnis* (experience in the

sense of that which one lives through) is fundamental to all the early works. The undistilled essence of pure experience grasped intuitively by the integrated self, such *Erlebnis* extends knowledge beyond the relative limits and finite concepts hemming in human cognition. *Erlebnis* constitutes the root power in the break of myth and mysticism from the rigid form of inert religion and bourgeois convention. The absolute and unconditional touched in Dionysian *Erlebnis* are made real through Apollonian form-creation: creative, organic acts at the physical centre of the chaos of brute sensation. Religiosity and renewal are lent art's lush tonal shape and sensual texture.

In the wake of the First World War, Buber looked past the stylised individual subject to highlight the life of relationship between multiple subjects. His masterpiece remains *I and Thou* (1923), the basic tenets of which he was to modify but never to abandon; it is the key to his mature thought on everything from Zionism and Hasidism, on the Hebrew Bible and its translation, on Arab–Jewish conflict in Palestine, and on continental philosophy. Complicating the unified shape of *Erlebnis*, the text's profoundly dualistic world-view embodies the clashing colour combinations in Expressionistic poetry and painting. Human inter-subjectivity affirms the polymorphous I–YOU encounter. Resting upon the claim that no isolated 'I' exists apart from relationship, revelation transforms each party into ultimate and mysterious centres of value whose presence eludes the concepts of instrumental language. The revelation of YOUR presence calls ME into an open-ended relationship that defies sense, logic and proportion, whereas the I–IT relationship assumes the fixed form of objects that one can measure and manipulate.

Z. Braiterman

See also: antitheodicy; Jewish Philosophy

BUTLER, JUDITH (1956–) American philosopher working in feminist and queer theory, psychoanalysis and continental philosophy, known for her work on gender, sexuality, power and identity.

In *Gender Trouble* (1990) – considered one of the central texts in queer theory – Butler advances the performative model of gender, whereby the categories 'male' and 'female' are understood to be the consequence of the repetition of certain acts instead of natural or necessary categories. Arguing against the essentialist assumption that certain gendered behaviour is natural, Butler claims instead that it is the culturally informed performance of certain gendered roles that gives rise to identity. In this sense, what is taken to be the 'nature' or 'essence' of gender is actually manufactured through a sustained and stylised sequence of acts. Seen in this way, identity is not the expression of some inner, core self; it is rather the dramatic effect of contingent and culturally specific performances. For this reason, Butler is noted for her critique of the sex/gender distinction. Rather than understanding gender as the culturally inscribed overlay of a natural and material sex, Butler argues instead that sex itself is materialised through gendered social and linguistic practice.

Butler's analysis of the relation between discourse and materiality is furthered in *Bodies That Matter* (1993) to consider the ways in which sexual difference is discursively demarcated. Here Butler advances her argument that sex is not a natural given that is superimposed by gender, but rather represents those very norms that govern the materialisation of bodies. Motivating Butler's argument for the conventional and historic nature of gender is her criticism of the cultural assumption of normative heterosexuality, or those cultural rules that dictate conformity with hegemonic – and heterosexual – standards of cultural intelligibility. The exposure of the artificial and conventional dimensions of compulsory heterosexuality has the effect of displacing its necessity, and moreover of liberating those identities that do not conform to the conventional rules that govern normative sexual expectation. Butler's interest in liberating sexual identities that have been rendered abject through the framework of compulsory heterosexuality is furthered in *Antigone's Claim* (2000) where she explores the possibility of radical new forms of kinship.

In *Excitable Speech* (1997) and *The Psychic Life of Power* (1997), Butler continues her analysis of the relationship between language, power and subjectivity, furthering her investigation of the ways in which power and action are determined by the subject's taking up of certain linguistic and cultural norms. A central theme throughout her writing is the claim that the social self is the object of certain discourses of power and legitimacy rather than the autonomous subject of constitutive acts.

A. Murphy

See also: Feminism; Queer Theory; Sex and Sexuality

C

CAMUS, ALBERT (1913–60) French writer, identified with the existentialist movement primarily through his philosophical essay, *The Myth of Sisyphus* (1942), and through his literary essays and novels, most notably *The Plague* (1947) and *The Stranger* (1957). *The*

Myth of Sisyphus, which Camus presents in part as a response to the temptation to commit suicide in light of the 'absurdity' of a universe that eludes ultimate comprehension by human reason, critically examines various philosophical and literary figures, including the religious existentialists Kierkegaard and Shestov, whom he accuses of 'philosophical suicide' by virtue of their 'leaps' of faith. It concludes with the heroic image of Sisyphus, condemned by the Greek gods eternally to roll his stone up a hill, only to see it roll back down whenever he reaches the crest; the clear-eyed Sisyphus, Camus declares, must be considered happy.

The Plague imagines the Algerian city of Oran under siege from a virulent, recrudescent bubonic plague and quarantined from the outside world. It is a moral study of the cowards and the heroes among its central figures – Camus was always, first and foremost, a moralist – as well as an allegory of France under German occupation. *The Stranger* traces events in the life of a 'loner', an otherwise unexceptional member of the community of French colonisers in Algeria into which Camus himself had been born, who more or less accidentally kills an Arab and is eventually condemned to death largely because of his failure to exhibit conventionally expected emotions. (Camus was a strong opponent of capital punishment.)

Camus had left Algeria as a young man and settled in Paris, where during the war years he was heavily involved in the French Resistance and befriended Sartre, Beauvoir and other members of the nascent existentialist movement. He later became alienated from them over a critical review in Sartre's journal, *Les Temps Modernes*, of his second major philosophical essay, *The Rebel* (1951), presented as a study of the problem of (political) murder and a plea for moderation. Sartre accused him of taking an untenable stance, outside of history, with his view that political revolution, as distinguished from personal revolt, is always doomed to failure; Camus accused Sartre of excusing the totalitarian Communist regimes with their claims to being the revolutionary vanguard.

Despite his literary successes, Camus' final years were clouded by the bloody war in Algeria, concerning which he refused to take the anticolonialist stance common among French intellectuals. He had been raised there, he had a deep love of its Mediterranean climate that he frequently expressed, and had also there acquired his love of philosophy from his proto-existentialist *lycée* teacher, Jean Grenier. Moreover, his mother still lived there. What is perhaps his single most famous declaration, to the effect that if he had to choose between his mother and justice he would choose his mother, expressed his personal anguish. He died prematurely, in an automobile accident, while the Algerian War was still at its height in the winter of 1959–60.

W. McBride

See also: absurdity (2); Existentialism

CANGUILHEM, GEORGES (1904–95) French philosopher of science primarily interested in biology and medicine; beyond the notable contributions of his own work, he is also known for having influenced the thought of Foucault. Initially a pacifist, Canguilhem later played an active role in the French Resistance, with his friend Jean Cavaillès. He submitted his thesis in 1943; in 1948 he became the inspector general of philosophy and in 1955 succeeded Gaston Bachelard to the Chair of History and Philosophy of Sciences at the Sorbonne.

The 1943 thesis had two French publications, in 1950 and 1966, before appearing in English in 1978 as *The Normal and the Pathological.* Here Canguilhem mounts a sustained attack on the idea that medicine can be rendered fully scientific by defining health as normality. Medical practice in France had defined disease as departure from a norm, presumed to be fixed. To shape medical practice in this way makes norms normative, makes them ideal states to be attained and sustained. Canguilhem turns this approach on its head by defining health in terms of the individual organism's ability to adapt to changing circumstances. Each individual organism establishes its own norms, from which it follows that there may be considerable diversity within a population of healthy individuals. One of Canguilhem's most important philosophic contributions is to have stressed the distinctiveness of the life sciences (for example in his *La Connaissance de la vie*, 1952). Questions of life and death, or conditions that pose a threat to life, have no place in physics. Life, Canguilhem insists, involves self-preservation by means of self-regulation. Here he rejects the materialist reductionism of many molecular biologists while trying to steer clear of vitalism. The point is that life introduces evaluative descriptions; it needs specific conditions for survival and flourishing; other conditions pose threats to life.

Canguilhem's other major contribution is his distinctive conception of the nature and role of the history of science, something he both discussed explicitly and demonstrated in his own work in the history of the life sciences, in works such as *Etudes d'histoire et de philosophie des sciences* (1968) and *Ideology and Rationality in the History of the Life Sciences* (1977). Where Bachelard stressed the need for epistemology to be historical, Canguilhem argues that history of science – being the history of a form of knowledge – must be written as epistemological history. His histories trace the development of a science through successive revisions of a concept, as in his work on the reflex arc. But this is not necessarily a continuous or logical progression, for the historian also has to face, as Bachelard already pointed out, the issue of what to count as science and how to account for the transition between what was once counted as part of science but now is not.

M. Tiles

See also: Epistemology; problematic; vitalism

CAPUTO, JOHN (1941–) American philosopher noted for his recent work on the intersection of deconstruction and religion in such works as *The Prayers and Tears of Jacques Derrida* (1997) and *On Religion* (2001). Caputo has also written extensively on the relationship between Meister Eckhart and Martin Heidegger in *The Mystical Element in Heidegger's Thought* (1978), and on that between Heideggerian mysticism and scholastic metaphysics in *Heidegger and Aquinas* (1982). In 1987, he published *Radical Hermeneutics*, which sought to underscore the fragility and highly contingent nature of all human beliefs and practices through a blend of Kierkegaardian pathos and Nietzschean drama. This was followed in 1993 by *Against Ethics*, in which Caputo argued for a non-foundational ethics of responsibility in which only appeals for mercy by fellow human beings should count as a genuine source of obligation.

Throughout *Radical Hermeneutics* and *Against Ethics* it was becoming clear that Jacques Derrida was replacing Martin Heidegger as Caputo's foremost intellectual inspiration. The reason for this was starkly revealed with the publication in 1993 of *Demythologising Heidegger*, a critique of the National Socialist ideology Caputo found in Heidegger's work. Most of Caputo's writings from 1993 to the present have attempted to interpret and distil Derrida's work for an English-speaking audience, as in, for example, *Deconstruction in a Nutshell* (1997), a work that functions as a lucid commentary on a roundtable discussion with Derrida. Here, the ethical and prophetic element of deconstruction is emphasised to the detriment of those who would claim that it signals nihilistic disintegration. Caputo highlights Derrida's appeal on behalf of justice as 'the impossible', or as something that serves to keep us from maintaining that the present context (political, religious, philosophical) is anything more than a provisional formation that has the potential to be continually reformed.

In both *The Prayers and Tears of Jacques Derrida* (1997) and *More Radical Hermeneutics* (2000), Caputo pays close scrutiny to how Derridean deconstruction helps foster a religious awareness that rejects the fanatical in favour of a notion of faith which, in the tradition of Kierkegaard's *Fear and Trembling*, emphasises uncertainty and blindness. These books have formed the basis for serious debate on the impact of deconstruction on religious thought. Since 1997, Caputo has provided a context for this discussion in a series of international conferences, first at Villanova University and now at Syracuse University, the proceedings of which have been published as *God, the Gift, and Postmodernism* (1999) and *Questioning God* (2001).

M. Dooley

See also: Religion, Philosophy of

CASEY, EDWARD (1939–) American philosopher, widely published in philosophical psychology, psychoanalytic theory and recent French thought, whose primary work has traced an influential trajectory from the abstract formalism of Husserlian philosophy of mind to concrete embodiment in a philosophy of place.

In *Imagining* (1976) and in the first chapters of *Remembering* (1987), Casey presented exemplary 'phenomenological studies', eidetic analyses of intentional structures and objective correlates (noetic and noematic 'phases') of 'mental acts'. In *Imagining*, for example, Casey isolated three 'acts' (imaging, imagining-that and imagining-how), and several distinct layers of presentation (focal content, imaginal world-frame, horizon). Rejecting hierarchies that would either denigrate or overly elevate imagination, Casey argued for the independence and self-sufficiency of imagination as 'pure possibility', fully disengaged from the life world; at once controlled and spontaneous, marked by indeterminacy both in background 'aura' and focal object, imagination was seen as self-contained and apodictically self-evident.

Beginning with a *Review of Metaphysics* article 'Keeping the Past in Mind' (1983), Casey came to reject the confined 'mentalism' of the received intentionalist paradigm, with its formalistic representational assumptions and 'detachment from the surrounding world'. By his own account, Casey turned from the ethereal 'thin autonomy' of imagination to 'thick' matters of memory and place, through a broadened phenomenology of embodied experience. For Casey, memory is not 'contained' in the mind, but 'out there', in bodies, in language and activities shared with others such as commemoration, and in landscapes.

Thus, in Part Two of *Remembering*, Casey offered an account of 'mnemonic modes' he termed 'intermediary', since they draw mind into the environing world: reminding, recognising, reminiscing (continuous with indicative signs, perception and language, respectively).

Part Three pursued memory still further 'beyond mind'; here, Casey developed an initial Jamesian account of the embodied horizon or 'fringes' of primary memory, via Whitehead's 'causal efficacy' and Merleau-Ponty's 'operative intentionality', into a strong thesis concerning the centrality of the 'emplaced' body to all memory: it is only in the echoes and retentions of the body 'feeling itself feel' that the experience of the past as past first becomes possible. Through detailed analysis of body memory, place memory and commemoration, Casey's goal was not just to 're-place memory' but to 're-member the body in place', and in the company of others.

Moving from an emphasis on the body as centre, Casey's recent work – *Getting Back Into Place* (1993), *The Fate of Place: A Philosophical History* (1999) and *Representing Place: Landscape Paintings and Maps* (2002) – explores the priority of place as common ground, and the connection between its modern occlusion and the emergence of today's alienated and desolate subjectivity. Drawing on Heidegger and Bachelard, Casey's 'topo-analysis' is distinctive in emphasising embodiment (dimensionality, direction, 'primal depth', spatial levels), horizonal, articulatory and intentional 'arcs', and an a priori body-place; along with rich historical and phenomenological analyses of ideas of place and representations of places, both built and wild, Casey outlines important contributions to environmental ethics. Overall, Casey's work constitutes an impassioned journey back into the dense 'flesh of the world', the telluric rootedness of emplacement.

R. Switzer

See also: Geography

CASSIRER, ERNST (1874–1945) German philosopher and historian of ideas, who contributed to (1) epistemology and philosophy of science; (2) the history of modern philosophy and science, including an edition of Kant's works; and (3) the philosophy of myth, language, culture and art.

Cassirer belonged to a prominent Breslau Jewish family and worked with Hermann Cohen of the Neo-Kantian Marburg School. Because of the German university system's anti-Semitism, his *Habilitation* required the intervention of Dilthey to pass and he was only Privatdozent in Berlin (1906–19), despite his productive and influential scholarly activity. His early publications included groundbreaking studies in the history of epistemology and science as well as original works in the philosophy of science that transformed Marburg neo-Kantianism in relation to the revolutions in logic, mathematics and physics.

In *Substance and Function* (1910), Cassirer replaced the traditional philosophy of substance with the logic of function by establishing the relational rather than species character of concepts. Whereas the theory of the concept expresses the totality of pure relational structures, reality is the determinate and complete limit toward which concepts converge through their successive relational application. In this work, and in *Kant's Life and Thought* (1918) and *Einstein's Theory of Relativity* (1921), Cassirer deepened the functional, non-substance, character of the concept. He reinterpreted Kant's productive synthesis in light of symbolic forms progressively generating the scientific object. Space and time are not forms of intuition but fundamental modes of symbolically constituting the object. Rejecting Kant's duality between sensibility and understanding, knowledge is a coordination of signs instead of a picturing of things. Einstein's theory of relativity did not disconfirm the priority of Euclidean geometry in ordinary intuition, but confirmed that these involve symbolic understanding.

In the early Weimar Republic, Cassirer became a full professor at the newly founded University of Hamburg. He used the resources of the Warburg Library for the three-volume *Philosophy of Symbolic Forms* (1923–9). This magnum opus examined all human experience and thought as symbolically mediated. For Cassirer, humans are primarily symbolical animals acting and understanding through the symbolic forms which are constitutive for human thought and practices. Language is the condition of the possibility of all thought as discursive, and it has its counterpart in myth. Whereas language is discursive, myth is poetic and disclosive, revealing a pre-cognitive but structured world-understanding. Cultures are understood through their respective mythical-linguistic systems. The human enactment of language constitutes different worlds requiring a philosophy of symbolic forms to recognise and evaluate them. Since all humans employ symbols and consequently reason, this implies the commensurability of everything human instead of cultural relativism or ethnocentric particularism. The symbolic character of human life establishes a connection running through all the various symbolic systems through which humans understand themselves and others.

Cassirer was vilified by German right-wingers as a Jewish liberal, especially when he became the first Jewish rector of a German university (1929–30). He argued for universalism, rationality, humanism and democracy on the basis of an 'other' liberal German tradition found in Kant, Goethe and Schiller. He debated Heidegger in the famous Davos disputation (1929), attended by Levinas and Carnap. Whereas Cassirer represented neo-Kantian rationalism and liberal humanism, Heidegger challenged established structures and ideas.

National Socialism forced Cassirer into exile. In *An Essay on Man* (1944) he revised and expanded his philosophy of culture by exploring its anthropological context. In *The Myth of State* (1946) he articulated the totalitarian, symbolic and particularistic roots of National Socialism and demonstrated the destructive potential of manipulated symbolic forms.

E. Nelson

CASTORIADIS, CORNELIUS (1922–97) Greek-born French philosopher, revolutionary theorist and psychoanalyst. Born in Constantinople (Istanbul), he and his family were deported after the Greek–Turkish War of 1922. As an adolescent he became involved with the Communist Left, but under the influence of the powerful ideological and paternal figure of Alexandros Stinas, he abandoned the Stalinist policies of the official Communist party. He became an active Trotskyite and member of the Fourth International during the Second World War and the German Occupation of Greece. After the liberation, Castoriadis was targeted for assassination by both the Communists and the Conservatives, who were entangled in a disastrous civil war. In 1945, Castoriadis left for France where he was to establish himself as a professional economist at the Organisation for Economic Cooperation and Development. At the same time, in collaboration with Claude Lefort, he established the influential political group and journal *Socialisme ou Barbarie* (1949–67). He wrote under pseudonyms until the late 1960s when he was granted French citizenship.

During this period of intense political involvement, Castoriadis gradually formed his theoretical orientation; and indeed what distinguishes him is the originality of his central ideas, which are in many ways unclassifiable within the dominant categories of postwar thought as expressed by Heidegger, existentialism or structuralism. During this period Castoriadis also dissociated himself from the dominant forms of socialist organisation and theory, privileging the autonomous and spontaneous action of the working class as opposed to the imposition of an official partyline from above. The repression in East Germany and Hungary in the 1950s convinced him that Soviet Communism was in its essence a totalitarian 'state capitalism' which, through its control over institutional structures, conditioned citizens to heteronomy and subordination.

Castoriadis's project of autonomy found its most complete expression in *The Imaginary Institution of Society* (1975), which proposes a liberation theory that combined post-Marxist insights, critical theory and psychoanalysis. In this seminal book, Castoriadis struggled to establish an ontology of change, innovation and creativity as self-conscious and autonomous praxis in history. He criticised 'the logic of identity' that dominated Western thinking after Plato by stressing that 'society is intrinsically history – namely self-alteration'. The main thrust in his ideas is how self-reflective theory and communal praxis can create autonomous, thoughtful and contemporaneous citizens who confront the dominant imaginary institutions of their society and uncover their self-alienating logic, even when they discover it within their own psyche.

Psychoanalysis helped Castoriadis to further establish his theory of the autonomous subject as 'psychical monad' in search of its own completeness. All psychical life is constituted on something missing; as he himself put it, 'the psyche is its own lost object'. In this search for unification, the psyche incessantly produces new imaginary meanings and representations which constitute the very essence, the active self-reflection, of the self-conscious subject. The motivating energy beyond and behind creativity was called by Castoriadis 'magma' – a notion some have criticised as indicating a 'metaphysical cosmology'. Magma should, however, not be interpreted metaphysically, but as a heuristic device in order to establish a conceptual grounding of both creative 'drive' and creative potential. Magma indicates the undifferentiated realm of potentialities before their mental crystallisation through cultural formations. Castoriadis's analysis of the subject offers a coherent and rational interpretation of how autonomous subjectivity may emerge within the internalised constraints of any societal structure.

In later years, he continued to elaborate on his ideas, distancing himself from postmodernism in a number of highly polemical essays such as 'The State of the Subject Today'; in this he tried to elucidate the question of the subject as 'the question of the human being in its innumerable singularities and universalities' and explain human interaction as 'the overcoming of mutual exteriority'. In the last decades of his life, he returned to classical Greek philosophy; his lectures on Plato's *Statesman* are crucial for appreciating his social vision. Overall, his philosophy can be seen as a neo-humanism aimed at the theoretical empowerment of the individual to realise its effective freedom within the historical framework of existing political institutions.

V. Karalis

See also: *Socialisme ou Barbarie*

CATEGORICAL IMPERATIVE A central concept in Kant's critical account of moral action, as developed in the *Groundwork of a Metaphysics of Morals* and the *Critique of Practical Reason*. It is a member of a set of possible imperatives, understood generically as any proposition that realises a particular aim or 'end'. The necessity investing such propositions – what makes them 'imperatives' – is distinguished from the necessity of theoretical propositions such as those analysed in the *Critique of Pure Reason* which concern judgements of what is; imperatives are concerned only with what ought to be. The necessity involved in such an 'ought' is located by Kant in the relationship between an objective rational law and a subjective will. According to him, this relation can be either 'hypothetical' or 'categorical', the propositions of the former involving reference to a condition or an 'if'. The family of hypothetical imperatives is made up of hypothetical assertoric imperatives – technical imperatives or 'rules of skill' – and hypothetical possible imperatives or 'counsels of prudence'.

Kant regarded most previous moral philosophy as involving the use of hypothetical imperatives that view action in terms of the end to which it is dedicated. The categorical imperative, however, has no reference to realising an aim, but involves only the form of the action. It is given a number of formulations, but the most definite is that in the second *Critique* which states 'act as if the maxim of your action were to become through your will a universal law of nature'. The categorical imperative is to be used as a 'canon' or rule for estimating the moral worth of maxims and actions – assessing the maxim informing an action and not its appropriateness to attaining an end. Kant justified the categorical imperative by means of a law that commands without incentive to achieve any particular aim, namely duty. The absolute character of duty is the source of categorical necessity or 'obligation' and being beyond particular aims and interests is a source of freedom.

The categorical imperative has been the subject of much attention since its first formulation, with much of the suspicion falling on its 'formal' character. Critics such as Hegel, Schopenhauer and Nietzsche saw in its very formality the presence of veiled interests and contents. Although this strain of criticism continues to be developed, it has more recently been qualified by defences of the formality of the categorical imperative as a canon or test of the consistency of the maxims informing action.

H. Caygill

CAVAILLÈS, JEAN (1903–44) French philosopher of science and mathematics. Cavaillès was active in the French Resistance and died at the hands of the Gestapo after his arrest in August 1943. In 1940 he was taken prisoner of war but escaped during his transfer to Germany, and resumed teaching at the University of Strasbourg while also playing a leading role in the Resistance. In August 1942 he was captured while attempting to embark for England. It was while he was in prison in 1942 that he wrote his last book, *Sur la logique et la théorie de la science*, completing it and escaping with his book in his pocket toward the end of 1942. In March 1943 he succeeded in leaving for England, returning to France in May only to be rearrested in August. A copy of his book had been left with his sister. It was edited by Canguilhem and Ehresmann and published in 1946. A second edition appeared in 1960 with a preface by Gaston Bachelard.

Other published works by Cavaillès are *Remarques sur la formation de la théorie abstraite des ensembles* (1938), *Correspondance Cantor-Dedekind* (with Emmy Noether, 1937) and 'Transfini et continu' (1941, published posthumously in 1947). These were collected and published in one volume, with a preface by Raymond Aron and introduction by Roger Martin, in 1962 under the title *Philosophie Mathématique*.

One can understand why Canguilhem and Bachelard should have attached their names to Cavaillès's last work. He concludes it by saying it is not a philosophy of consciousness but a philosophy of the concept which can yield a theory of science. The generative necessity is not that of an activity, but of a dialectic. Writing of the history of science he says, that which comes after is more than what was before, not because it contains it, nor because it extends it, but because it necessarily comes from it and bears in its content the singular mark of its superiority. These were already themes announced by Bachelard and later put into practice by Canguilhem with his focus on concepts when writing the history of science. But Cavaillès tackles issues which neither Bachelard nor Canguilhem confront, issues concerning the place of logic in science and mathematics. In so doing, Cavaillès follows up on debates between Frege and Husserl as well as considering the work of Russell, Hilbert and Gödel. Cavaillès offers a history of the theory of sets which is at the same time a critique of claims that it can provide a foundation for the rest of mathematics. This thesis, together with his critique of developments in formal logic and of the positions of logicism, formalism and phenomenology, leads him to a philosophy which cannot be readily identified with any of the usual trio of philosophies of mathematics touted in the first half of the twentieth century (logicism, formalism and intuitionism). His work remains of interest in that it can help us think beyond the confines of those more familiar positions, but it must be noted that it is also difficult to approach, since it jumps straight into issues, presupposing a considerable background on the part of the reader. Unfortunately Cavaillès was not allowed to live long enough to write the introductions that he knew were required.

M. Tiles

CERTEAU, MICHEL DE (1925–86) French polymath whose major intellectual contributions were to the fields of religion, the theory and practice of history, contemporary ethnography and cultural policy. Underlying these contributions was a methodological orientation that he would describe, in *The Practice of Everyday Life* (1980), as 'a science of singularity'. Such a science is, of course, problematic in that it attempts to find general patterns in material practices that are irreducibly specific. For example, if you walk to work on a wet Tuesday morning, preoccupied by the events of the previous evening, this walk is unrepeatable in its specificity. But what can be said about it at a general level? Certeau's solution to this problem is to move from the level of interpretation to the level of operations. Rather than asking what does this walk mean, a question of interpretation which remains tied to the specific, he asks what 'ways of operating' are *shared* by such specific acts of walking? His goal, then, is to discover a 'logic' or a grammar for these singular practices: the rules of combination, condensation and displacement, by which a singular performance actualises a repertoire of operations. So, this walk, while always particular, instantiates an amalgam of habit, memory, desire, physical propensities and abilities, practices of negotiation and so on, which are common to walking in general.

Certeau's approach is dedicated to culture as practice, but it sees practice not in terms of pragmatism but as activity orchestrated by repression and resistance. Certeau's work can usefully be described as a form of cultural psychoanalysis; a psychoanalytic approach that recognises its subject as collective, as social. In the essays collected in *The Writing of History* (1975) and *Heterologies: Discourse on the Other* (1986), Certeau analyses the work of historians, ethnologists, psychoanalysts and novelists. For Certeau, ethnological writing (the description of other worlds: the past, madness, the foreign, 'folk' culture and so on), legitimated by institutions that remain outside the object of study, necessarily institutes a fundamental repression. Ethnological writing writes over the culture it seeks to describe, repressing the heterogeneity of this culture, and substituting descriptions of its own desire. Reading accounts, for example, of indigenous cultures in the Americas at the time of colonial conquest is to read about the anxieties, ambitions and desires of the colonisers. However, as in psychoanalysis, repressed material is never simply obliterated; it remains in distorted forms, as a resistance, always threatening to reappear.

There is an implicit ethical challenge in Certeau's work. The task of describing the workings and manifestations of power is never enough. We also have an ethical responsibility to repressed and resistant culture. This might mean a speculative practice of reading that is peculiarly attentive to what is suppressed in the text, or it might require a description of walking attentive to the touch of the foot on the road, the effects of weather, choices of itinerary, and the play of memory and desire.

B. Highmore

CÉSAIRE, AIMÉ (1913–) Franco-Martiniquean poet, dramatist, social critic and politician who was a cofounder of the *négritude* movement. His critique of colonialism and capitalism has become one of the key resources in postcolonial thought and struggle.

Césaire's *Discourse on Colonialism* (1950), which was written before he became disillusioned with Communism's emphasis on class struggle at the expense of racial struggle, offers a powerful Marxist critique of European/Western civilisation's inability to solve the problems it has created for itself; in classic dialectical fashion, the 'civilising' process enacted in the colonies in fact 'decivilises' the colonisers, as their violence directed at the colonised ends up brutalising them. Although he admits that 'it is a good thing to place different civilisations in contact with each others', he questions the way colonial expeditions employed the 'dishonest equations *Christianity = civilisation, paganism = savagery*' to establish a kind of contact that was decivilising and dehumanising to both the coloniser and the colonised. Césaire quotes a number of European racist and pro-colonial texts from authors such as Ernest Renan, Carl Sigers and Jules Romains and Comte de Gobineau, in support of his claim that Nazism is far from an aberration, but was instead the essence of colonialism; it only became a horror to Europeans when it was employed in Europe rather than far away. In a famous and powerful indictment that deserves to be quoted at length, Césaire writes:

> People are surprised, they become indignant. They say: 'How strange! But never mind – it's Nazism, it will pass!' And they wait, and they hope; and they hide the truth from themselves, that it is barbarism, the supreme barbarism, the crowning barbarism that sums up all the daily barbarisms; that it is Nazism, yes, but that before they were its victims, they were its accomplices; that they tolerated Nazism before it was inflicted on them, that they absolved it, shut their eyes to it, legitimised it, because, until then, it had been applied only to non-European peoples; that they have cultivated Nazism, that they are responsible for it, and that before engulfing the whole edifice of Western, Christian civilisation in its reddened waters, it oozes, seeps, and trickles from every crack.

In thus locating Nazism at the heart of European civilisation, Césaire called for the dialectical destruction of the bourgeois class that benefited from the 'barbarism' of colonialism long before it had to confront it at home.

In the mid-1950s Césaire became convinced that racism and colonialism could not be subordinated by a narrow Old Left view of the centrality of class struggle based on the urbanised industrial working class. In doing so, he rejects the false 'universality' predicated of the European proletariat by official Marxist dogma. Far from expressing essential human nature, the European proletariat is European at base, not simply 'human'. The only universal to be countenanced for Césaire is a universal rife with the particularities of racial, geographical and cultural difference. Here we see themes that will resonate with many of the themes of the New Left, poststructuralist and postcolonial movements.

Césaire's later work includes a historical study of Toussaint L'Ouverture and the Haitian Revolution, as well as dramatic works criticising the rise of postcolonial dictatorships. An adaptation of Shakespeare's *The Tempest* written in 1969 is a powerful exploration of the psychodynamics of colonialism using Césaire's magnificent poetic gifts.

C. Chachage

See also: *négritude*; Postcolonial Theory

CHIASM A notion introduced by Merleau-Ponty in *The Visible and the Invisible*. It may be represented by the Greek letter χ (*chi*), in which there is an intersection of two unequal lines. Merleau-Ponty was struck by the reversibility inherent in Husserl's account of bodily experience, in which one and the same phenomenon can be experienced either actively (touching) or passively (touched). When I see an object, Merleau-Ponty argues, following Bergson, I believe my perception is the object itself; but I know that others have perceptions of the same object which differ from mine, and which I therefore determine to be images. However, I also know that this relation is reversible, and that these others believe that their perceptions are of the object itself while, for them, my perceptions are images. The intersection of the unequal lines in the chiasm denotes the intersection of perception as thing and perception as image. Nothing in itself, since it refers to perceptions which can never be given simultaneously to one person (just as in touching, the phenomenon can be active or passive, but never both at once), the chiasm is nevertheless something, namely the object as visible. Merleau-Ponty thus begins to move from a phenomenology to an ontology of perception. The intersection of the chiasm designates that which is neither perceived not perceivable, and as such is literally invisible, while yet being the condition of visibility of any thing. In this way, the chiasm is the intertwining of the visible and the invisible.

R. Durie

CINEMA An art form with a particularly rich relation to continental philosophy. We will treat three aspects of that relation: (1) philosophical writings referring to cinema; (2) writings on cinema referring to philosophy; and (3) films engaged in a philosophical project.

Philosophical treatments of cinema. Early in film history, philosophers often rejected cinema. Their concerns might be roughly divided into two types: a critique of the cinema as illusion, and a concern that cinema might have a degenerative effect on individual and social life.

In *Creative Evolution* (1907), Bergson uses cinematic movement as an example against which to define true movement. For him, both cinema and perception produce the illusion of movement from a series of still images instead of attending to the 'becoming of things'. Bergson argues that duration and movement are both defined by their continuity and that a part of a movement is qualitatively different from the full movement, so that a reconstituted movement can only be a false one. In *Creative Evolution*, Bergson uses the cinema as an image of what he defines as flaws in ordinary perception.

In 1944, Adorno and Horkheimer produced perhaps the most sustained philosophical critique of cinema's social function in an essay on 'The Culture Industry'. They find that cinema's aesthetic development was limited by economic conditions of capitalism and that in the context of capitalist society, the cinema plays a regressive role in human development. 'The Culture Industry' needs to be read in conjunction with a much more optimistic piece written by Adorno's close correspondent, Walter Benjamin, in 1937, 'The Work of Art in the Age of Mechanical Reproduction'. In that essay Benjamin argues that film, photography and other forms of mass reproduction cause works of art to lose their aura and cult value. That is to say, the new technologies change the relations of ownership governing aesthetic production and circulation. Benjamin saw progressive potential in film and photography, but to release that potential, a reorganisation of the film industry would be required.

In 1949, Heidegger starts his essay on 'The Thing' by associating cinema with television and radio, communications technologies he accuses of destroying distance by causing the remote to appear present.

What should be distant in space and time can be conjured by such technologies, which destroy distance and therefore nearness as well. The essay contrasts the images produced by modern communication technologies with a jug considered as a thing and then meditates on the word 'thing' or *Ding*. Heidegger points out that 'thing' meant 'gathering' in Old High German. Playing off the word's etymology, Heidegger turns it into a verb and asserts that the thing gathers together earth, sky, divinities and mortals in what he calls 'the fourfold'. Nearness, which cinema helps destroy, is the work of the jug in its 'thinging'.

By all accounts, Deleuze produced the most important writing about cinema by a philosopher after the Second World War in his two-volume study *Cinema*. Deleuze rereads Bergson's philosophy of duration and movement as a theory of cinema, leading Deleuze to the conclusion that the universe is inherently cinematic. Deleuze argues that Bergson understood the cinema as false movement because he wrote in a period of film history when the camera itself did not move. According to Deleuze, once movement *of* the image, or reframing within the shot, was added to movement *in* the image, cinema could be understood as presenting true motion. In Deleuze's account, cinema can be divided into two periods, replicating the Kantian revolution in philosophy. In the first period, from the invention of cinema to the end of the First World War, films figure time as the measure of movement, while in the second period, which extends to the present day, certain films start to present time in and of itself.

Late in his career, Derrida began to appear in films and to develop a theory of the medium as a technology of phantoms. As well as a variety of interviews, Derrida co-authored a book on the process of film-making, *Tourner les mots: Au bord d'un film*, with Safaa Fathy, the director of *D'Ailleurs, Derrida*. Derrida both explores the possibility of thinking within the conditions imposed by filmmaking and meditates on the ontological status of the cinema as a sort of haunting, or non-Aristotlean, being.

Stanley Cavell reads popular films philosophically, arguing that films both provide a vision of the world and take up philosophical themes in their narratives. His work on cinema grounds itself in criticism, or 'readings', of individual films. By looking at films as serious investigations of the ways in which conceptual problems affect social life and analysing his own 'natural relation to the movies', Cavell developed a sort of cinematic *Lebensphilosophie*.

Philosophically informed film theory and criticism. Parallel to these philosophical developments, film theory has sought to develop philosophical concepts starting from the premises of cinema. From its very beginnings, cinema has been accompanied by a discourse reflecting on it. In part, that discourse had to establish cinema's legitimacy as an art and as an object of academic study. In order to do so, early theorists applied the concepts of classical aesthetics to the cinema. These theorists often sought to identify the properties unique to the cinema, relying on ideas taken from Kant linking aesthetic pleasure to the work's formal organisation and from Lessing about works of art expressing their material base.

In 1915, Hugo Münsterberg developed a neo-Kantian film theory in which the images on screen become mental images producing the real movie in the mind of its spectator which converts the series of still images into moving ones and grants it attention, memory and emotion. By transforming reality into an object of the imagination, certain films become aesthetic in so far as they attain purposiveness without a purpose and replace the relations between appearances in the world with mental relations.

In the 1920s, Russian filmmakers developed elaborate theories of montage, according to which the meanings of individual images are determined by the relations between images in a film. The writings of Dziga Vertov, Sergei Eisenstein, Vsevolod Pudovkin and Alexander Dovzhenko all develop the ideas of film teacher Lem Kuleshov. Kuleshov argues that an image of a man looking followed by an image of a plate of food makes the man's face look hungry, whereas the same image of the man followed by the image of a knife makes the man look murderous. The four principal montage theorists each developed their ideas according to a different dialectical model.

Rudolf Arnheim's 1932 *Film As Art* develops concepts similar to those of Münsterberg, but deploys them in an argument about the specificity of film as medium. He attempts to prove that cinema was not a syncretic art such as opera. Defining cinema as the unique art of the moving image afforded the medium a place alongside the other fine arts; it also set up a criteria according to which the cinema could be judged: the more purely a film expressed the essence of the medium, the more aesthetically perfect it was. Films that used the medium to create thrilling sensations were judged have no artistic value. By the same token, he argued against changes in cinematic technology such as sound and colour, because they diluted the rigour of the medium by changing its material conditions. Unfortunately for Arnheim, changes in cinematic technology have always outstripped theories of cinematic specificity by adding new capacities to cinema, going beyond the very qualities that had been said to be specific to the medium.

In the 1960s Christian Metz developed a semiotic theory of the cinema based on Saussure, positing the images, sounds and editing structures of a film as signifiers referring to signifieds. Metz compared film to language and concluded that film is a language without a language system, in other words that the rules of cinematic language are potentially redefined with every film. Metz's next project linked his semiotic work to Lacan, focusing on the pleasure audiences take in the cinema. Metz's psychoanalytic theory centres on the identification between the audience and both the gaze of the camera, which becomes the spectator's own gaze during a screening, and the characters in the film. Metz argued that cinematic identification unifies the split subject posited by Lacan. The Metzian notion of unification was taken up by psychoanalytic and Marxist film theorists, who were led to think the question of the subject in order to account for the economics of cinema, whose patrons pay for a specific form of pleasure.

A major advance in film theory was made by Laura Mulvey and other feminist film theorists who posited the camera gaze as a gendered, male gaze; accounting for the pleasure experienced by female audience members thus became a serious issue. These theorists critiqued the universalist claims of previous writers by revealing that such claims were made from a specific point of view, that of the male spectator, and that this male spectator was also the cinema's ideal addressee. As feminist film theory developed, it initiated an auto-critique that pointed out the ways in which earlier feminists made assumptions about the race, sexuality and class of female spectators.

Recently, cognitivist film scholars have attempted to use philosophy to correct what they posit as the fallacies of previous film theorists. The 1990s saw a strong reassertion of Aristotelian and Kantian reasoning in film studies. Scholars associated with cognitivism and neoformalism, such as David Bordwell, Kristen Thompson and Noel Carol, sought to inaugurate a 'post-theory' era in which empirically driven 'mid-level' research would be regulated by classical reasoning to produce knowledge about film cultures. These scholars invoke philosophy to correct what they take to be the errors of what they label 'grand theory' by pitting a classical regime of thought against the premises of their interlocutors.

Philosophical films. Films have taken up philosophy in three principal forms: (1) movies about philosophers; (2) movies that organise their narratives around philosophical problems; and (3) movies that are themselves philosophical investigations. The films named here are only examples from among the many films of each kind.

1. *Wittgenstein* (Jarman) presents scenes from the eponymous philosopher's life in way that illuminates his work and sexuality. The

film takes up the difficult project of relating the philosopher's work to his life. In so doing, *Wittgenstein* uses all of cinema's resources to depict a culture of thought.

2. Popular high-budget films, such as *Blade Runner* (Scott, 1982), *AI: Artifical Intelligence* (Spielberg, 2001) and *Terminator 2* (Cameron, 1991) attempt to think the relationship between humans and machines. In such films the non-human tends also to function as an allegory of the cinema itself. The cinema provides an ideal forum for such questions since it is itself a mechanical device seemingly capable of perception. Other popular films such as *The Matrix* (1999) have taken up philosophical themes such as the nature of reality, the effects of simulacra and the function of ideology. *The Matrix* in particular was popularly received as a philosophical film and produced a spate of academic publications tracings its various references.

3. Experimental films often attempt to address philosophical problems through the medium. Many schools of avant-garde cinema have used films to ask the question 'What is cinema?' and thereby broach a series of philosophical problems such as the relation between word and image and the limits and definition of an aesthetic object. Avant-garde and experimental film has also taken up the question of cinema's essential characteristics. For example, an early film by Man Ray entitled *Emak Bakia* (1926) introduces images produced without using a camera but rather through the process of contact printing, thus opening up the question of whether a camera is a necessary component of filmmaking. Flicker films such as Peter Kubelka's *Arnulf Rainer* alternate black and white screens in an attempt to reduce cinema to its most basic components.

L.-G. Schwartz

CIORAN, E. M. (1911–95) Romanian-born existential philosopher who moved to Paris in 1937, where he spent the rest of his life, writing in French. Renowned as a formidable prose stylist, Cioran is a philosopher of man's tragic destiny.

In *On the Heights of Despair* (1934), Cioran displays a remarkable discernment of affective states such as boredom, anxiety, enthusiasm, melancholy, joy, despair and ecstasy. Whereas in most phenomenological descriptions affect moves between the limits of anxiety and boredom, in Cioran, life begins at these limits, they are the source of everything else. Organic, affective participation in being is often the measure of truth and those whose thoughts are alive are always correct; there are no arguments against them. In his work, Cioran discovers a subjectivity which wells out of life like a spring. But, yet, life produces exuberance as well as void, both positive and negative affective states. The problem is that of expression, how to capture the inner lyricism brought on by the suffering and loving man without sacrificing the inner fluidity to outer objectification. Matter, far from inert, is rather the living content, which is moreover infinite. Form is what limits, finishes, makes finite and removes the perspective of the universal and the infinite.

In *Tears and Saints* (1937), Nietzsche influences Cioran's aesthetic spirituality where contradictions are consonant with a rich spiritual life and he who does not love chaos is not a creator. There is a tension between a Nietzschean critique of religion and Cioran's own practice of suffering and related valorisation of illness. Cioran says that we are equally divided between becoming and eternity and that this largely accounts for the tragedy of our condition. A nexus between these divisions may be tears. Tears are both the gateway to eternity, where we live in God, and the material trace or form of infinity or becoming that music is best able to capture.

A Short History of Decay, published in French in 1949, marks a crucial step in the thought of Cioran: the exile from his language and from his country completes his metaphysical exile. It is indeed into a negative, final and radical metaphysics that his *élan vers le pire* (impulse toward the worst) takes us, as Cioran applies himself to rethinking thought in its absurdity and in its torn subjectivity, in its essence and in its affects, to its extremities and to its root, to digging up what it tries not to reveal, to come to terms with the weight of philosophical shadow. Because one is unable to abolish death (*The Trouble With Being Born*, 1973), one has to 'start knowledge again', even if it means one has to 'think against oneself', even if one has to definitely leave history (*The Fall into Time*, 1964). The powerful originality of Cioran's pessimism, as black as it is stimulating, lies in the paroxysm of lucidity reached by Cioran in his desperate existence, full of humour, as expressed in his *Notebooks*, written between 1957 and 1972.

C. Kinkead

CIXOUS, HÉLÈNE (1937–) Algerian-born French philosopher. An extraordinarily fecund writer who refers to her work as 'poetical', she is also an eminent professor, who was entrusted in 1968 with the creation of the experimental Université de Paris VIII at Vincennes, before founding in 1974 the only extant Centre de recherches en Etudes féminines in France. She has remarkably collaborated with Ariane Mnouchkine, director of the Théâtre du Soleil, for whom she started writing plays, and with Antoinette Fouque, founder of the Mouvement de Libération des Femmes, who published her work for years in the publishing house Editions des femmes.

Cixous's writing has been called a 'writing of thought', but the thought in question resists being reduced in concepts. Even the phrase *écriture féminine* (feminine writing), which has been associated with her name, does not stand for any systematic theory. Instead, Cixous calls for, signs or interprets writings which address differently the question of sexual difference. For Cixous, one of the impasses of the thinking about sexual difference is that it is structured by hierarchical binary oppositions such as male/female and active/passive. On the contrary, poets are invested by Cixous with the ability to write the unthinkable, that which exceeds phallocentrism, or as she says after Jacques Derrida, phallogocentrism. In that sense, not only does the poetical unfold a new thought, it also achieves historical-political effects disrupting the phallocentric order, which is never therefore hermetically closed off. Clarice Lispector, Kafka, Kleist, Joyce, Shakespeare and Stendhal are among the poetical writers admired and interpreted by Cixous.

Her first novel, *Dedans* (1969), was awarded the *Prix Médicis*. Transgressing the generic borders between fiction, autobiography, and essay, Cixous develops motifs haunting her oeuvre ever since, such as the way her father's premature death served as a point of departure for her writing; her childhood in Oran and Algiers as a Jew deprived of French citizenship under the Vichy regime and growing up in a colonial context, which taught her the 'lucky chance' of exteriority; and the exceptional linguistic condition in which she became a French speaker (her father's language), whose mother tongue was, however, German, in a larger multilingual background including Arabic and Hebrew. She ascribes to these factors her uniquely complex relation to Frenchness, identity and to the French language itself, which, in her writing, becomes marked by alterity, already in a process of translation. This complication doubtless contributes to the fact that a great part of her oeuvre remains to be translated in other languages. Underlining what resists or prevents translation also allows Cixous to probe the ethical question of what or who has been silenced and disregarded. While it is crucial for Cixous to write what has been repressed, it is as important not to subsume alterity and to let it resonate without re-appropriation. One of her latest publications, *Rêve je te dis* (2003), is a selection of her dreams, the introduction of which testifies to Cixous's admirative, yet critical, familiarity with Freud's investigation of the unconscious.

B. Weltman-Aron

See also: Death; *écriture féminine*; Feminism; Poststructuralism

CODES A key concept in structuralist-inspired semiotics. Saussure stressed that signs are not meaningful in isolation, but only in relation to each other. Later, Roman Jakobson emphasised that the production and interpretation of texts depends upon the existence of codes or conventions for communication which are at least partly shared. Codes thus represent a social dimension of semiotics. They can be broadly divided into social codes (such as 'body language'), textual or representational codes (such as aesthetic realism) and interpretative codes or ways of reading (such as feminism). Within a code there may also be stylistic and personal subcodes (or 'idiolects'). Not all signs are as 'arbitrary' as the linguistic ones on which Saussure focused, but many semioticians argue that even photographs and films involve codes which have to be 'read'. It is the familiarity of such codes which leads texts which employ them to seem like recordings or direct reproductions of reality. The signified comes to seem identical with the signifier, giving the illusion of what Barthes called a 'message without a code'. He and others sought to 'denaturalise' codes in order to make more explicit the underlying rules for encoding and decoding texts, and often also with the intention of revealing the operation of ideological forces. Some codes are fairly explicit; others are much looser (and their status as codes disputed). Some theorists (such as Eco) have even argued that our perception of the everyday world involves codes.

D. Chandler

COGNITIVE SCIENCE An interdisciplinary field with increasingly important connections to phenomenology and other fields in continental philosophy. Its contributors come from philosophy, psychology, neuroscience, linguistics, computer science and artificial intelligence; their methods are also increasingly used by anthropologists, economists and other social scientists. The leading idea of the traditional school of cognitive science, computationalism, is that cognition involves representations and computational processes as the means by which many natural and artificial systems adapt to their surroundings, achieve equilibrium or otherwise fulfil a goal. Since the mid-1970s, cognitive science has replaced behaviourism as the dominant paradigm in psychology.

As a characterisation of cognition, cognitive science has moved from abstract rules and representations ('classical computation') to massive parallel processing ('connectionism') and most recently to an emphasis upon the body's, and through it, the mind's, embeddedness in the world ('dynamical cognition'). The Turing Machine is the model for classical computation: it represents inputs in terms of discrete symbols, specifically strings of '0's and '1's, and then obeys sets of 'if-then' production rules in order to convert the inputs into a particular output, for example these visible marks into a meaningful sentence. Although classical computation may capture some of our more sophisticated deliberations, many researchers complain that it is too fragile and over-intellectualised a system to adequately capture all our cognitive processes. Connectionism, in contrast, mimics the brain more closely and involves swarms of simple neuron-like nodes that are activated simultaneously – in 'parallel' – by their surroundings. The resulting activation pattern is distributed over all the nodes and is determined in part by the various 'weighted' positive and negative 'connections' that hold among the many simple nodes. This activation pattern or representation of the input is distributed rather than being a discrete symbol, and the computation rules involved are extremely general rather than consisting of the specific production procedures favoured by classical computation. But this still leaves us stuck within our skulls. Thus various forms of 'dynamical cognition' attempt to treat the brain, body and environment as variables within a common system. Some of these forms still involve representations and computations (Andy Clark, *Being There*, 1997), but others attempt to portray the system in terms of positions, distances, regions, and paths in a space of possible states, that is geometrically (Tim van Gelder, 'The dynamical hypothesis in cognitive science', *Behavioral and Brain Sciences*, 1998, 21: 5).

For many continental philosophers, this movement toward 'putting brain, body and world together again' is heading in the correct direction but cannot obtain its goal. Among others, Maurice Merleau-Ponty, Hubert Dreyfus, Francisco J. Varela, Evan Thompson, and Eleanor Rosch (*The Embodied Mind*, 1991) and Fred Evans (*Psychology and Nihilism*, 1993) argue on phenomenological grounds that computational forms of cognition cannot take place successfully unless subjects and their situations are already internally related and involve the transformation of a relatively indeterminate situation into one that is temporarily more definite – a continually re-enacted 'movement of transcendence'. In a Nietzschean vein, Evans also argues that the computational model of mind remains dominant despite its shortcomings because it reinforces and mimics the technocratic aspects of contemporary society and is ultimately a form of 'passive nihilism', that is, acquiescence to algorithmic or technocratic routines of contemporary society. The thematisation by Manuel DeLanda and Brian Massumi of the relevance of non-linear dynamics or 'complexity theory' for Deleuze's philosophy promises to open another connection between continental philosophy and cognitive science, and is closely related to work begun by Varela on 'neurophenomenology'.

F. Evans

See also: Biology, Philosophy of; naturalising phenomenology

COMPLEXITY THEORY A broad label covering a host of contemporary approaches in scientific theory, including chaos theory, biophysical investigations into the origin of life, theories of dissipative structures, cellular automata, theories of autocatalysis and self-organisation, non-linear dynamics and artificial life.

Though many of the theories collected under this term present rival explanations or models of the same phenomena, they share a concern with the laws or parameters governing the emergence of structure or form from the interactions of lower-level components, or with the passage from chaotic flows to ordered systems. Following on from the foregrounding of the concept of 'information' in postwar cybernetics and systems theory, complexity theory is distinguished by its preference for substrate-independent models which diagram the possible paths and individuations of systems, rather than for the statement of physical laws aimed at the deduction and prediction of natural phenomena. Ranging from mathematics to physics, from biology to chemistry, and often applied to the vicissitudes of social systems, complexity theory is characterised by a generally anti-reductionist stance, wary of the ontological and epistemological commitments of classical scientific theory to a supposedly deterministic variant of materialism. Its contention is that new practices of modelling, reliant on advances in computer science and simulation, can provide far more adequate accounts of the unpredictable or creative behaviour of systems (whether physical, chemical, biological, artificial or social) than those founded on the classical idea of the laws of nature.

Though some thinkers, such as Gilbert Simondon and Raymond Ruyer, seem to have anticipated the philosophical challenge of complexity theory, the groundbreaking work in this respect is Ilya Prigogine and Isabelle Stengers's *La Nouvelle Alliance* (1979), republished in a considerably revised version in English as *Order Out of Chaos* (1984). Building on Prigogine's work on dissipative structures and engaging in a wide-ranging critique of the philosophical premises of the reductionist approach, Prigogine and Stengers were the first to make an explicit connection between these developments in scientific theory and contemporary continental philosophy, namely Deleuze's ontology of difference and singularity as expounded in *Difference and Repetition*. Ever since, numerous authors, especially in the Anglophone world, have turned to Deleuze to provide the speculative armature (or even the ontology and epistemology) of complexity theory – chief among these are Manuel DeLanda and Brian Massumi.

This current of thought regards Deleuze's (and Deleuze and Guattari's) work as the source of a 'new materialism' which, via concepts such as intensity, singularity, event, stratification – all of which tellingly were initially drawn from the sciences – can provide the intellectual tools to think the emergence of novel structures and behaviours out of the dynamic processes of production and interaction characterising material systems. Though imputing such an aim to Deleuze remains contentious, such an approach follows programmatic indications in *A Thousand Plateaus* toward a general theory of material becoming, whose models would range over traditionally distinct fields – from evolutionary theory to history, from political organisation to technological evolution. As demonstrated by its focus on self-organisation, this uptake of complexity theory in continental philosophy is principally motivated by an attempt to produce a non-representational, non-intentional and non-teleological, that is a fundamentally non-Kantian, thinking of matter.

A. Toscano

See also: Biology, Philosophy of; Materialism

COMTE, AUGUSTE (1798–1857) French philosopher and founder of sociology, positivism, the history of science and the 'Religion of Humanity'. Born during the French Revolution, Comte remained loyal to its republican and secular ideals but was repelled by its chaos. Influenced by Enlightenment thinkers, by the socialist Saint-Simon and by his engineering training at the École Polytechnique, Comte concluded in the early 1820s that a new intellectual synthesis would lead to a moral restructuring that would produce social and political harmony. In his organic community, all classes, parties and sexes would unite in working for the good of the whole.

The *Cours de philosophie positive* (1830–42) outlined his intellectual synthesis, called 'positivism', which insisted that knowledge be based on the 'positive' or scientific method. The positivist system included not only the major sciences but the last area that had been until recently in the hands of priests and metaphysical philosophers: the study of society. Comte called this new scientific discipline 'sociology' in 1839. Consisting of two parts, social statics, which focused on order, and social dynamics, which investigated progress, sociology represented the keystone of positivism because it united all the sciences around the study of society, that is humanity.

Sociology had two principles. The first, the law of three stages, explained that as the mind advanced from one mode of thinking to another, it generated a different theoretical system, which shaped society and politics. In the theological stage of history, which was further subdivided into the fetishist, polytheist and monotheist stages, the human mind attempted to grasp the first causes of phenomena and used supernatural ideas to connect isolated observations; politics and society were characterised by divine-right monarchy, militarism and slavery. The metaphysical stage linked observed facts by means of personified non-supernatural, but non-scientific abstractions such as Nature; politics was embodied in the doctrines of popular sovereignty and natural rights, and society witnessed the birth of industry. In the positive stage, the human mind would abandon the search for first causes and would relate facts by descriptive laws confirmed by observation. Social relations would be based on industry. In politics, positive philosophers would become the new spiritual or moral power. Aided by workers and women, they would check the new temporal power, that of the industrialists. The second principle of sociology, the classification of the sciences, stated that the sciences went through the three stages according to the increasing complexity of their subject matter and their closeness to humans. The sciences reached the positive stage in the following order: mathematics, astronomy, physics, chemistry, biology and sociology. Each science relied on the ones preceding it in the hierarchy.

Both the law of three stages and the classification of the sciences expressed the inevitable triumph of scientific thought. Once the study of society and by extension politics became a science based on the observation of concrete facts instead of dogmas, social theory would attain the certainty and unquestionable authority of the natural sciences and offer cures for social ills. Because all ideas would be scientific and everyone would agree on fundamental principles, there would be intellectual harmony, the first major step toward the creation of a stable society and the positive stage of history. The second major step involved infusing society with 'altruism', a word that Comte coined. To him, people were highly developed when they displayed intelligence and love for others, both of which he considered intertwined and in need of cultivation, especially to ensure fruitful action. Thus after having synthesised ideas, Comte systematised feelings. The *Système de politique positive* (1851–54) introduced the new secular 'Religion of Humanity', his new science of morality, and the global political and social system of the positive age. His Religion included a calendar based on secular saints, new positivist sacraments, a cult of

Woman and rituals to revive the emotional spontaneity of fetishism.

Emile Littré, John Stuart Mill, George Henry Lewes and Harriet Martineau popularised Comte's doctrine. It permeated sociology, philosophy, history and history of science, literature and political movements in France, Latin America and the United States. Brazil's flag, in fact, features Comte's motto 'Order and Progress'.

M. Pickering

See also: positivism

CONSTITUENT/CONSTITUTED POWER Linked concepts defining popular sovereignty and its formal institutionalisation in a constitution, respectively, central to the Anglo-European tradition of radical republicanism that culminates in the American and French Revolutions. Recently, Negri has derived concepts parallel to these from Spinoza's political writings and traced them through modern political philosophy from Machiavelli and the English Civil War to the present as a non-dialectical alternative to the dominant dialectical theories of contractual or state sovereignty associated with Rousseau and Hegel. In *The Savage Anomaly* (1981), Negri argues that Spinoza distinguishes between the Latin terms *potestas* and *potentia*: *potestas* (Italian *potere*, French *pouvoir*, German *Macht*) refers to power in stabilised, institutionalised, delegated or representational forms, while *potentia* (Italian *potenza*, French *puissance*, German *Vermögen*) refers to power in fluid, dynamic, unmediated or non-representational forms prior to and in excess of its alienation into institutions. In *Insurgencies* (1992), Negri redefines *potestas* as constituted power and *potentia* as constituent power, which correspond in his work to Deleuze and Guattari's linked concepts of reterritorialisation and deterritorialisation. Despite its ontological priority over constituted power, constituent power manifests itself most clearly in the periodic revolutionary crises that overthrow existing institutions and states, only to be mediated, codified and stifled once again in the new constitutional arrangements that end each revolution. These arrangements of constituted power can never be definitively or permanently stabilised, however, and the multitude's ongoing struggle for radically non-representational forms of democracy regularly reopens the constituent process.

T. Murphy

CONSTITUTION An epistemological term for the process of establishing objects of thought (*Gegenstanden*). There are two main ways of understanding such constitution: (1) to constitute an object is to create it; or (2) to constitute X is to constitute it *as* an object of consciousness, to bring it to conscious awareness. Both uses concern fundamental concepts or structures of practice involved in our 'constitution' of objects; either use can concern how we recognise, organise or interpret sensory information. The former use plainly has idealist implications; we literally construct the object in question. The latter does not, at least not by itself. The term comes from twentieth-century phenomenology, and has been used retrospectively to explicate the idealist and realist aspects of Kant's and Hegel's views. While Kant claimed to identify twelve basic concepts or categories fundamental to human thought as such, post-Kantian philosophers often stress forms of historical change or cultural variety among our basic concepts. Both the static Kantian and historical Hegelian views can be interpreted as raising the same issues regarding idealism and realism mentioned above.

K. Westphal

CONTRADICTION (*Widerspruch*) (1) Literally, 'speaking against', it is the violation of the logical law whereby an unambiguous statement cannot be both true and false at the same time. Traditionally, something cannot both have and lack a property in the same regard at the same time. Provocatively, one thesis of Hegel's dissertation (1801) is: 'identity is the rule of falsehood; contradiction is the rule of truth'. Hegel understood and used formal logic well. His characteristic use of 'contradiction' instead concerns an ontological dispute between atomism and holism. Hegel's 'idealism' is a form of moderate ontological holism, whereby the identity conditions of things are mutually inter-defined. 'Individuals' thus depend on the whole to which they belong, while the whole likewise depends on its individual constituents. Hegel argued that moderate holism is true, and that atomism fails to capture this important truth. 'Identity' became associated with 'atomism' by the common (though mistaken) belief that the logical law of identity entails metaphysical atomism.

While formal-logical contradiction entails the impossibility of some (alleged) thing, for Hegel, 'dialectical contradictions' are necessary for the existence of something. For example, any one perceptible thing only exists through its multitude of properties, and vice versa. The concept 'physical object' thus integrates two counterposed quantitative determinations, unity and plurality. Many of Hegel's 'dialectical contradictions' can be expressed logically with biconditional ('if and only if') statements. For example, something is a single perceptible object if and only if it integrates a plurality of properties, at least some of which are perceptible. The logical law of non-contradiction governs synchronic relations; it holds either timelessly or at any given time, but entails virtually nothing about temporal (diachronic) processes. Hegel claims to find 'dialectical contradictions' in processes, such as the tension between what something is (actuality) and what it tends to become (potentiality).

K. Westphal

CONTRADICTION (2) In Marxist dialectical philosophy, contradiction is the 'unity of opposites'. All concrete things are contradictory because they combine opposed and conflicting aspects and forces within themselves, and because of this they develop and change. This philosophy has been controversial since it was first developed from Hegel and made into a standard part of orthodox Marxist philosophy, dialectical materialism, by Engels (*Anti-Dühring*, 1878).

The notion of contradiction plays a central role in Marx's theory of history, in which it denotes the fundamental conflicts which drive forward social development and change. According to Marx, contradictions of this sort are inherent in all hitherto existing social formations. In developing his account of Marxist philosophy, Engels uses the term in a more metaphysical fashion. According to Engels, the law of the unity of opposites is one of the basic principles of dialectical thought. Contradictions are at work in all things: in nature, society and thought. For Engels, the idea of a 'dialectic of nature' is a crucial and distinctive tenet of dialectical and materialist philosophy; this is one of the most frequently criticised and disputed tenets of Engels's interpretation of dialectical materialism. Many philosophers, among them Russell and Sartre, have argued that the concept of contradiction can be applied only to human rational processes, not to mere things. Natural entities, they argue, are related only externally and causally to each other, but never logically. Common as they are, these views are rejected not only by Engels, but equally by other dialectical philosophers, including Hegel and Lenin. Where Marx stands on the question of whether dialectic operates in nature is much disputed.

S. Sayers

CORPOREAL FEMINISM That subset of feminist theory emphasising the importance of lived, sexed, embodiment, taking as its starting point the claim that the sexed body is central in the figuring of experience. Drawing in particular on insights from the phenomenological tradition, corporeal feminists such as Judith Butler, Moira Gatens and Elizabeth Grosz argue that sexual difference cannot be theorised apart from the particular experience of sexed embodiment. In so far as corporeal feminism is oriented around the claim that the body is central in the figuring of subjectivity, it may be read as a critique of the philosophical tradition's privileging of reason and the mind over and above embodied experience. For this reason, corporeal feminism might be read as a critique of Cartesian dualism, attacking the assumption that the ready dissociation of mind and body, reason and emotion, is even possible. While corporeal feminism draws attention to the sexually specific dimension of embodiment, this return to the body need not provoke the accusation of essentialism. This is because corporeal feminism advocates an understanding of the body as culturally and historically specific and is in this sense far removed from the idea of a natural or essential body that prefigures culture. Corporeal feminists argue for the inadequacy of theoretical frameworks that fail to take the historical and political significance of the sexed body seriously in the elaboration of subjectivity.

A. Murphy

See also: Embodiment; Feminism; Gender

COSMOPOLITANISM The notion that one's identity is not determined solely nor primarily by any racial, national or ethnic background. Diogenes and the ancient Cynics began the cosmopolitan tradition by forming the notion that an individual could have a primary identity apart from the one he or she inherited from the polis. In de-emphasising the value of class, status, national origin and gender, the Cynics simultaneously placed great emphasis on the value of reason and moral purpose. Here is the revolutionary idea that the Cynics achieved which is a given in the Western concept of personality and its concomitant dependence on dignity: regardless of how much one is deprived of the concrete goods that are constitutive of social identity, one possesses a larger universal identity grounded in reason, moral purpose and, above all, human dignity. Today, when contemporary cosmopolitans speak in terms of a universal human identity that they share with others, they are invoking concepts bequeathed to them by the ancient Cynics.

The concept of world–citizenship in the sense of belonging to all of humankind gained ascendancy in the Hellenistic era. It is among the core features of Stoic thought, which, along with its great rival Epicureanism, were reactions to the gradual disappearance of the small city-state in an age of empire. (One of the reasons for the current upsurge in interest in cosmopolitanism, it goes without saying, is our own relation to empire.) As Philip of Macedonia and then his son Alexander imposed an overarching monarchy on the Greeks and conquered new territories, not only did the *poleis* cease to be the sole seat of political authority for citizens, they were no longer insular safe havens in which local identities could be formed.

The cosmopolis, that vastly growing space beyond the insular polis, the place that heretofore had been the home of barbarians, was conceived of as a place where social and cultural distinctions were irrelevant compared to an essential sameness to all human beings, who are bound together, regardless of their backgrounds, by their subjection to natural law. Human beings may live in a multiplicity of ways, but there is a law that holds the variations in their actions and behaviours to a recognisably human model. The people in one village may live in an area populated with plants, some of which are poisonous and some of which are not; those of another may live off the meat of animals. In the first scenario someone has to learn how to detoxify plants and classify them and establish it as an art or science. In the second scenario, one has to establish procedures for effective hunting and so on. In both cases, each individual must live by the evidence of his or her senses. That is what is to be expected, as human beings are conceptual animals, and this shared nature provides the basis for a universal humanity. So goes the reasoning of the Stoics. Today, a contemporary cosmopolitan would point out that, for example, in no culture would you find mothers arbitrarily offering up their young to strangers, that individuals in all cultures have capacities for responding to shame and loss of dignity, and that such examples are just a few among several that are the shared core features that all humans have and that override local particularity.

Cosmopolitanism stands in sharp contrast to two very important political categories in our contemporary world: pluralism and multiculturalism. Pluralists defend the view that individual identity is to be configured within the parameters of a conceptually neat ethnic, national or racial paradigmatic prism. Pluralists are not separatists, but they do insist that the boundaries that make separate identities distinct (Italian, German, Native-American, for example) are protected and kept in place. Group solidarity and group identity, then, are the important values upheld by those in the pluralist camp. Multiculturalists are more likely than pluralists to acknowledge an overarching national or international community, but want to insist on the abstract nature of all such communities as well as critiquing the way one particular culture tends to pass itself off as pure, transparent or universal for the community in question. Multiculturalists also insist on recognising the contributions of seemingly 'marginal' cultures to such allegedly pure cultures.

Cosmopolitans, on the other hand, in keeping with the pro-individual stance first evinced by Diogenes, are of the view that human socialisation takes place in the world where human intercourse takes place: in the multiple spaces that we inhabit and among the myriad of human beings with whom we interact and exchange stories, experiences, values and norms. Strong cosmopolitanism repudiates the tendencies of cultural nationalism and racial ideologists to impute moral value to morally neutral features – accidents of birth such as skin pigmentation, national origin and ethnic background. Strong cosmopolitanism argues that there is no one fundamental culture to which any one individual is biologically constituted and leaves the question of identity entirely to the individual. That is, individuals ought to be able to cull their own identities based on the extent to which their experiences and their life roles have allowed them to experience themselves as the persons they take themselves to be, rather than the passive wearers of tribal labels assigned to them by their culture or by the society at large.

In the field of political philosophy, one must distinguish between cosmopolitan law and international law. Cosmopolitan law protects the rights of citizens of the world by making their relations to the state a concern of the world community, while international law pertains to the relations among sovereign and self-legislating states.

Kristeva and Derrida are among the continental philosophers whose writings have contributed to cosmopolitanism. Kristeva's cosmopolitanism can be found in two texts, *Nations without Nationalism* and *Strangers to Ourselves*. The latter is a psychoanalytically inspired scholarly work that traces the genealogy of foreignness. In it she develops notions of strangeness and Otherness that reside in each individual. If we accept the foreigner within us, then we are less likely to be disturbed by the political foreigner in our nations. For Kristeva, being a cosmopolitan means that she has, against origins and starting from them, chosen a transnational or international position situated at the crossing of boundaries. Derrida's *On Cosmopolitanism and Forgiveness* is a treatment of the cosmopolitan ethos by means of an examination of the tensions between refugee and asylum rights. Derrida develops an ethic of hospitality and forgiveness as a viable cosmopolitan response.

Moral cosmopolitanism draws the following conclusion from the above arguments: geographic demarcations among groups of peoples, and national, ethnic and racial differences among human beings, are irrelevant factors when determining moral obligations persons have towards each other. Moral cosmopolitanism further holds that tribalism hijacks our moral lives because it works according to a specious logic of false separatism. That is, tribalism takes the morally neutral markers of human beings such as their nationality, ethnicity and morphological markers – the latter codified into various racial categories – and imbues them with moral relevance, punishing and persecuting persons solely on the basis of characteristics which are accidents of birth and which tell us nothing about them as moral human beings.

J. Hill

CREATIVE EVOLUTION Bergson's first two books, *Time and Free Will* and *Matter and Memory*, explored the dualisms of time and space and mind and matter respectively. However, Bergson remained unsatisfied with his account of the interaction between the dualities in each of these works. In *Creative Evolution*, he explores the dualism of life and matter from an ontological perspective, and in many ways this represents the culminating achievement of Bergson's philosophy. Because the essential characteristic of life is *duration*, the movement of evolution is fundamentally unpredictable, that is to say, creative, a fact designated by Bergson's concept of *élan vital*. But the creativity of life and evolution mean that they are not susceptible to the analyses of mechanistic science. However, matter does seem perfectly adapted to scientific analysis. What then is the source of the dualism of matter and life? Bergson's claim is that life and matter are both 'tendencies', the one towards greater complexity of interpenetration of 'parts', the other towards greater separability of parts. From the outset, these two tendencies exist in a state of 'reciprocal implication'. As a tendency towards separability, matter works to divide out lines of evolution. Life, the *élan vital*, on the other hand, works towards the indivisibility of the whole, allowing for the preservation of hereditary characteristics in an organism's adaptation to environmental change. Because the two tendencies are in opposition, neither achieves its ultimate end, and so the creativity of life and evolution always expresses itself as a response to the constraints of matter.

R. Durie

CRITICAL EPISTEMOLOGY A project developed by Michèle Le Doeuff from notions in the work of Alexendre Koyré and Gaston Bachelard; it also draws upon an extended critique of the epistemology of Francis Bacon. Le Doeuff holds that in seeking knowledge we strive for universality. Therefore, we offer what we think to whoever may receive it, and are answerable to whoever may criticise it. This rules out an absolute foundation for knowledge, which would be a system of ideas beyond reciprocal correction. For instance, one might understand philosophy in terms of psychoanalysis, but that is not therefore a foundation for it. Philosophy equally has an understanding of the psychoanalytic enterprise.

In seeking knowledge we use and listen to argument, which implicitly involves imagery and other tropes. We cannot dispense with all tropes, since in eliminating one figure of speech we import others. At the same time, these images and metaphors are subject to critical reason. We aim at universality in our various forms of reasoning, but cannot install argument as the primary foundation for the use of imagery and metaphor, nor imagery and metaphor as the primary foundation for argument. Philosophy would be a measuring stick for all rationality only if (impossibly) it could justify itself. Its general weakness is not an excessive allegiance to reason, but a tendency to overreach itself. Failing to practise pure reason, philosophers tend to allocate 'unreason' to some special source that undoes its efforts. Though not intrinsically sexist, philosophy may raise up 'woman' as an icon of unreason's threat to it. Philosophy might thus mystify 'woman', but the process has been as likely to seize upon 'the child' or 'backward races'.

M. Deutscher

See also: Feminist Epistemology

CRITICAL LEGAL STUDIES (CLS) A term referring both to formal associations of legal academics organised in the United States and Great Britain, and to a form or style of legal theorising that takes 'critical' – in the sense of left-progressive and philosophical – perspectives on law. The name was coined in the late 1970s in the United States with the formation of the Conference on Critical Legal Studies, an association of legal academics who shared a commitment to left-theoretical approaches to the study of law. The Critical Legal Conference (CLC) was formed subsequently in Britain by legal academics with similar commitments. The American Conference became largely moribund by the early 1990s. The CLC, on the other hand, remains active, holding annual conferences and sponsoring an academic journal (*Law and Critique*), and has increasingly expanded its reach to include scholars from outside Great Britain.

From its inception, both as institution and as intellectual style, Critical Legal Studies included a broad and far from consistent range of theoretical approaches under its umbrella. In the American context, CLS as an intellectual movement was a congeries of notions adopted from a variety of sources: (1) Legal Realism (an earlier approach that attempted to look past the formalism of legal reasoning to the actual social and psychological determinants of legal decision-making); (2) the Law and Society movement (a sociological approach that studied the social functioning of the law); (3) a left-political orientation rooted broadly in Marxist critiques which viewed law as an ideological obfuscation of underlying political power relations; and (4) an interest in applying new ('postmodern') philosophical approaches, many but not all of them continental, to the critique and analysis of law. Most prominent among these philosophical influences were Derrida and, to a lesser extent, Habermas and Foucault, along with the neo-pragmatists Richard Rorty and Stanley Fish.

It ought to be said that much (although not all) of the American CLS work that relied on continental sources was relatively unsophisticated, in part because CLS writers usually approached these sources narrowly from the limited perspective of the immediate concerns of the left legal academy. What American CLS writers found particularly relevant in contemporary continental philosophy was its rejection of metaphysics, its critique of rationality and its focus on language as a, if not the, primary subject of philosophical investigation, all of which resonated with the antiformalist impulse shared by CLS's various schools. One irony of this limited incorporation of continental philosophical insights was that it resulted in a tendency to fall back into a more abstract form of the very formalism and political liberalism that were the ostensible primary targets of CLS critique. To cite the most prominent example, the strand of CLS thinking known as its 'indeterminacy wing' frequently relied on the work of Derrida in arguing that all legal language was fundamentally indeterminate, and thus that the law's pretension to consistent and rational application could not be sustained. In particular, these writers detected within the law (and language and reason more generally) the repetition of binary oppositions that structured legal arguments even while preventing any determinate conclusion from being drawn. What issued from this analysis, then, was a view of law as formal in the extreme. Law was seen as structured by binary oppositions that were significant solely with regard to their internal structural opposition, without regard to their substance. As a result, legal decisions were thought to be determined solely on the basis of the individual political preferences of the legal decision maker, a 'subjectivisation' of the law that amounts to a radicalisation of the liberal reduction of the collective social good to the individual preferences of the collective's constituents. In fact, what is elided in CLS's immediate reduction of law to politics – a reduction that was a central tenet of its doctrine – is the mediating element that forms a central concern of much contemporary continental philosophy (including Derrida's), and that distinguishes it from liberalism: the ethical relationship to the Other. CLS, in other words, tended to ascribe the indeterminacy and open-endedness of legal language and rational argumentation to the primacy of the subject, whereas for Derrida and others in the continental traditions this openness to the future is instead the 'trace' of the indelible, ethical relationship to otherness inscribed in the language and rationality of the law.

Consistent with the equation of law and politics, the strong (although, again, not unanimous) tendency of American CLS was to reject the legitimacy of law in any form, including the legitimacy of the legal protection of individual rights. This total rejection, which throws out even seemingly progressive elements of law, like the protections against discrimination on the basis of race and gender – protections that were in fact the hard-won goals of previous political struggles – was a primary reason that the CLS movement splintered in the late 1980s and 1990s into a number of separate movements that took a more nuanced view of the political validity of law, including Critical Race Theory, Feminist Legal Theory and Latina/Latino Critical Legal Theory, among others. (It should be noted that despite their identity-group origins, many of these schools of thought have taken a critique of identity politics as one of their central goals.)

In Britain and elsewhere outside the United States, the CLS movement shares many of the American movement's characteristics, including a diversity of sometimes conflicting theoretical perspectives, a commitment to progressive critique of the law and philosophical approaches that are deeply indebted to continental theory. In contrast to the American version, however, the movement remains vital, even while giving rise to its own versions of Critical Race Theory and similar offshoots. This may be attributable in part to its greater philosophical sophistication. Legal academics outside the United States have employed continental theory with far greater rigour and diversity of sources than the American critical scholars. There is now a budding literature analysing law from the perspectives of Lacanian psychoanalytic theory, the critical theory of the Frankfurt School and the writings of continental theorists generally, including – along with Derrida and Foucault – Levinas, Agamben and Deleuze, among many others.

A. Thurschwell

CRITICAL THEORY A term coined in the 1930s to describe the unique blend of Marxist social theory and German Idealism (later supplemented by Freudian psychology) developed by members of the

Frankfurt Institute for Social Research. Notable members of the 'Frankfurt School' included Horkheimer, Adorno, Marcuse, Benjamin, Erich Fromm, Leo Lowenthal, Otto Kirchheimer, Franz Neumann, Frederick Pollock and (more recently) Habermas. Together, they pioneered pathbreaking studies on the authoritarian personality and the breakdown of the nuclear family; the mass psychology of fascism and anti-Semitism; the effects of mass production and mass consumption and the emergence of a mass culture industry; the decline of the labour movement and the rise of managerial elites; the transition from liberal capitalism to corporate welfare capitalism; and, most famously, the emergence of modern nihilism and totalitarianism in an age of scientific reason (the 'dialectic of enlightenment').

Throughout its history, the School retained a certain consistency in its critical orientation, despite the widely divergent and at times radically shifting viewpoints of its affiliates. The Institute's first period (1923–31) witnessed the early collaboration of Georg Lukács and Karl Korsch, neo-Hegelians who explicitly criticised the crude positivism and economic determinism of Marxist orthodoxy. In their opinion, the dialectical conception of reason underlying Marx's account of history as a process propelled by class struggle could not be reduced to natural science – the province of what Hegel called analytical reason – but had to be conceived as revolutionary praxis.

This rejection of scientific reductionism also informed the Institute's second period (1931–41), in which the explicit synthesis of analytic-empirical social science and dialectical moral philosophy became even more pronounced, albeit not necessarily in ways that augured well for revolutionary praxis. To begin with, the new generation of critical theorists – spearheaded by Horkheimer, Adorno, Pollock, Neumann, Kirchheimer and Marcuse – was much less optimistic than their predecessors about the success of the Bolshevik Revolution in Russia, and were also less optimistic about the capacity of the proletariat to achieve revolutionary class consciousness. They pointed to structural features of the emergent corporate-welfare state – economic regulation coupled with guaranteed welfare benefits and high employment fuelled by military spending – that serve to mitigate economic crises and thwart international proletarian solidarity. In accordance with this revision, they affirmed the importance of democratic political struggle and the role of culture (ideology) in advancing or hindering the emergence of critical aptitudes generally.

Here, for the first time, we begin to detect a fateful turning away from the original thematic underlying Marxism: the role of theory in guiding revolutionary practice. With the end of labour militancy and the rise of reactionary social movements, critical theorists increasingly turned their attention toward more academic philosophical problems concerning epistemology and metaphysics. Even by these standards, however, the School's third period stands out as something of a radical reversal in its former direction. Writing in exile during the darkest moments of the war, Adorno and Horkheimer collaborated on *Dialectic of Enlightenment* (1947), which argues that rationality as such – be it analytical or dialectical – degenerates into a mere tool for self-preservation. Instead of fulfilling its promise of emancipation, enlightenment emerges as a system of scientific-technological domination in which all embers of critical reflection are extinguished.

Horkheimer and Adorno drew starkly pessimistic conclusions from this diagnosis. Dubious of any form of revolutionary praxis, they later sought to recover repressed intimations of utopian reconciliation and liberation in theology and aesthetics, respectively. Marcuse, who by the 1960s had emerged as the other leading exponent of critical theory, was less pessimistic in this regard. In his opinion, what Adorno and Horkheimer diagnosed as the dialectic of enlightenment was in truth a contingent distortion of scientific-technological rationality caused by the growth imperatives of capitalism. Drawing upon classical metaphysics and aesthetics, he maintained that scientific-technological rationality could be transformed under socialism in ways that would redeem its original emancipatory potential.

Marcuse's break with Adorno and Horkheimer over the dialectic of enlightenment anticipates the fourth and final period of the School's history, inaugurated by Habermas in the early 1960s. Like Marcuse, Habermas was closely involved with the New Left student movement. Unlike him, however, his solution to the dialectic of enlightenment did not take the form of a speculative reconceptualisation of science and technology. Instead, he argued that moral-practical reason and critical emancipatory reflection are already present in everyday communicative interaction. As he later put it, the idea of reaching an uncoerced agreement (mutual understanding) that we associate with rational persuasion implies notions of dialogical reciprocity (equality), receptivity and openness (freedom), and inclusiveness (solidarity) that can be appealed to as critical standards in questioning the moral legitimacy and justice of institutions that purport to be democratic. In effect, the change in philosophical paradigm inaugurated by Habermas – from a philosophy of subjective consciousness to a philosophy of intersubjective communication – signals a departure from Marxism, with its emphasis on labour as the chief vehicle of dialectical praxis. Yet the ties to Marxism remain in Habermas's criticism of the inherent contradiction between capitalism and democracy, for him the principal institutional embodiment of dialectical reason.

The legacy of the Frankfurt School lives on not only in the writings of Habermas and his followers, but in the thought of many other contemporary continental philosophers who take their bearings from Nietzsche and Heidegger. Foucault noted the remarkable similarity between his poststructuralist analysis of power and the theory of domination elaborated by first-generation critical theorists. Lyotard and Derrida likewise noted a similar convergence of their postmodern views of language, reason and knowledge and the critique of identity-thinking and progress elaborated in different ways by Adorno and Benjamin. Whether this new poststructuralist and postmodernist reception of critical theory – with its profound rejection of any revolutionary pretension of achieving total historical knowledge for the sake of total emancipation and reconciliation – marks its end or continuation has yet to be determined. But this too, after all, seems fitting for a school of thought that seemed all too self-conscious of its own historical contingency and indeterminacy.

D. Ingram

CRITIQUE the examination of judgements and claims with an eye to establishing their legitimacy, especially as practised in the philosophy of Kant. In the preface to the first edition of the *Critique of Pure Reason* (1781) Kant notes that 'Our age is, in especial degree, the age of criticism and to criticism everything must submit'. His own three critiques, of pure reason, practical reason and judgement, thus contribute to and further develop the practice of criticism. Yet Kant conceived criticism not only as a destruction of the claims based on 'habit' by philosophy, 'sanctity' by religion and 'majesty' by legislation, but also the constructive assurance of 'lawful claims' – claims that in the case of reason would be defended by a revolutionary tribunal that 'is no other than the *critique of pure reason*'. Without this tribunal, Kant claimed towards the end of the first critique, reason will find itself in a state of nature and thus at war with itself. Critique thus on the one hand submits all judgements and claims to 'the test of free and open examination' while on the other providing a decision on what is a legitimate judgement by means of the decrees of the critical tribunal.

As introduced in the first *Critique*, the practice of criticism not only involves the powerful institutions of religion and politics, but also reason itself. While conducted in the name of reason, critique does not exempt reason from its investigation. Much of the difficulty of the first *Critique* may be indeed be traced to the tension between pursuing critique by means of reason, and submitting reason to the same critique. Kant believed that over time the critique of reason would reach a point in which the 'eternal and unalterable laws' of reason would become visible, and thus justify a halt to the destructive work of critique. Yet the sense of an internal limit to critique assumed by this conviction is by no means itself justified in the pages of the critical philosophy, that is it is not secured critically. The dangers are evident in the essay 'An Answer to the Question: What is Enlightenment?' where the public sphere of 'free and open examination' central to Kant's description of the 'age of criticism' returns as the age of enlightenment, or in other words 'the century of Frederick' – the same Prussian monarch whose official culture of 'indifferentism' or 'argue as much as you like and about whatever you like, but obey' was the object of barely veiled criticism in the Preface to the first *Critique* written five years before.

The association of freedom and criticism that informs Kant's writings of the critical period ensured that the limits of freedom determined the limits of critique. The freedom to reason beyond the limits of space and time is critically limited in the Transcendental Dialectic of the *Critique of Pure Reason* although it is restored in the *Critique of Practical Philosophy*. Yet for subsequent philosophers, Kant provided both a positive and negative example. Marx and Nietzsche lauded the project of total critique and its corollary of unlimited freedom – even or especially the critique of the institutional conditions that made critique itself possible – but were wary of attempts to establish internal limits to freedom and critique. The two aspects of Kant's concept of critique returned to prominence in the postmodernism debate where philosophers such as Lyotard, Foucault and Derrida who extended the freedom of critique into the core of rationality itself were criticised by Habermas for abandoning critique in the name of 'irrationalism'. Thus the concept and the limits of critique continue to provoke philosophical debate even two centuries after Kant's formulation of the 'Age of Criticism'.

H. Caygill

CROCE, BENEDETTO (1866–1952) Italian philosopher known for his work on aesthetics and literary criticism, and for his philosophy of history, known as absolute historicism. His 'philosophy of the spirit', an attempt at systematic philosophy, consisted of an Aesthetics, Logic, Practical Philosophy (Economics and Ethics) and Theory and History of Historiography. Croce, however, only apparently follows in the wake of Giambattista Vico, his acknowledged predecessor, and Hegel. Croce is a complex and radical thinker who has to be read, rather, against the Vichian and Hegelian language that inform his writings.

Croce's writings on aesthetics and literary criticism span his career, from *Aesthetics as Science of Expression and General Linguistics* (1902) to *Literature and Poetry* (1936), by way of a series of works on aesthetics, as well as literary criticism both on Italian and European authors. First impressions aside, Croce's conception of the aesthetic is very much modern, resting on a linguistic model of the sign, implying a conception of art as allegory that Croce develops and expands in *Literature and Poetry*. This aesthetic conception makes Croce a perceptive reader of literature. His analyses of Dante and Ariosto are, in fact, an elaboration of the allegory and irony, respectively, which characterise the work of these authors. Even his controversial reading of Pirandello can be shown to be not only an adequate assessment of this author's works but also an instance of his lifelong preoccupation with literature and its relation to philosophy.

Croce's most important contribution, however, is in the field of history, which for him occupies a precarious place between art and philosophy. For Croce history is not only subsumed under the concept of art but is also one and the same with philosophy. Thus, if history belongs to art rather than to science, and, history is, at the same time, at one with philosophy, then art and philosophy share history as a common ground. This history is conceived as being, first of all, contemporary, since it is only because of our present interests that we are moved to investigate the past. In the second place, this history is not a history of good and evil; such a simplistic morality tale cannot be a mature history, but is only a history which has not yet been thought through, remaining prey to feelings and imagination. Thirdly, history has no longer to do with men but with humanity, a standpoint he called 'cosmic humanism'. Finally, history is not resolved into a simple unity, which for Croce is either theological or mythological, but into a complex unity which is that of life itself and is therefore always uncertain and always riven by difference. At the ethical level, then, the spontaneity of life becomes the expression of freedom and of the good which characterises history. His *History of Europe* (1932) and *History of the Kingdom of Naples* (1925) are illustrations of how this ethical universal is fully revealed in history.

M. Verdicchio

CYBERNETICS A term coined in 1947 by Norbert Wiener from the Greek word meaning to govern or steer, it designates a research project devoted to modelling machine operation on human behaviour. In its first formulation, cybernetics focused on the science of communication and control in animals and machines; it thus encompassed the 'study of messages, and in particular of the effective messages of control', as Wiener remarks in *The Human Use of Human Beings* (1950). Drawing upon electrical engineering, mathematics, neurophysiology and information technology, cybernetics studied actions, feedback and response in systems of all kinds. The early contributions of cybernetics include feedback control devices, automation of production processes and computers.

Cybernetics quickly evolved beyond its narrow technoscientific context thanks in no small part to a series of postwar conferences convened by Warren McCulloch under the auspices of the Josiah Macy Foundation. The so-called Macy conferences brought together an impressive array of researchers from a host of disciplines – including prominent figures from the social sciences like Gregory Bateson, Heinrich Klüver, Lawrence Kubie, Lawrence Frank and Margaret Mead – whose work helped spread cybernetic discourse to anthropology, psychology and other social sciences, and ultimately to the humanities and the arts. Because it focuses not on things but on ways of behaving, cybernetics forms a metadisciplinary language useful for describing a wide array of systems in living, social and technological worlds.

Largely on account of this metadisciplinary status and the collaboration of a multidisciplinary host of researchers, cybernetics developed in a direction that must be clearly distinguished from Artificial Intelligence and, more broadly, from computer science as it has developed in the wake of the digital computer. Whereas AI pursues the goal of machine intelligence and values implementation, cybernetics is and has always been concerned with epistemology, how we come to know and the limits associated with how we know what we know. This epistemological focus initially became apparent in the claim by cybernetics that organisation (rather than materiality) of systems yields their identity, and it has only intensified with the development of 'second-order cybernetics'.

In second-order cybernetics researchers thematise self-reference in processes of observation and knowledge production; it is the fruit of the realisation that, as Heinz von Foerster puts it, 'the science of observed systems' cannot be divorced from 'the science of observing systems' since it is we who observe. This self-mapping of observing and observed systems has the effect of foregrounding our own subjectivity, or more generally, the perspective of the knowing system, as a contingent yet unavoidable limit to what can be known. In addition to von Foerster, prominent researchers associated with second-order cybernetics include Maturana and Varela (co-originators of the theory of 'autopoiesis' of living systems) and Luhmann (proponent of functionalist systems theory in sociology).

Several recent studies have been devoted to the history of cybernetics. Steven Heims's *The Cybernetics Group* (1991) meticulously describes the Macy conference interactions; Jean-Pierre Dupuy's *The Mechanisation of the Mind* (2000) traces the genealogy of cognitive science from cybernetics; and N. Katherine Hayles's *How We Became Posthuman* (1999) presents a thick cultural history of cybernetics.

M. Hansen

See also: Cognitive Science

DASEIN A term that means 'existence' in ordinary German, literally 'being-there', it is employed by Heidegger to designate the human being in its relation to being. In *Being and Time*, Heidegger argues that the question of being must be enacted by means of a reflection on the essence of the human, but that this must be understood in a radically non-anthropological and non-subjective way. Through the use of 'Dasein', Heidegger attempted to break with the notion of the human as the 'rational animal', as well as with the modern Cartesian tradition of the subject, instead defining the human strictly in its relation to being. Dasein thus designates the essence of the human, understood as openness to being. This is why the term Dasein, as Heidegger clarified in his 1949 introduction to *What is Metaphysics?*, designates in the same stroke our relation (opening) to being and being's relation to us (openness). In Heidegger's later thought, the term is often hyphenated (*Da-sein*) in order to stress the sheer relatedness to being, a relatedness which is not posited by us but comes from being (*Sein*) itself. Heidegger thus emphasised further the non-anthropological scope of his thinking of Dasein, which now names the co-belonging of being and the human (*Ereignis*), a belonging into which humans are thrown and called to inhabit and in which they stand as humans.

F. Raffoul

DAVIDSON, DONALD (1917–2003) American analytic philosopher whose arguments against epistemological foundationalism and the reification of mind are frequently compared to those of exemplary figures in the continental tradition. Central to his highly systematic philosophy is an interpretation-based account of linguistic understanding which employs the work of formal semanticists such as Tarski to clarify the concepts and knowledge required for the interpretation of linguistic utterances. 'Truth and Meaning' (1967) argues that knowledge of the truth conditions of utterances suffices for understanding them; hence semantics can eschew metaphysical distinctions between the meaning of a declarative sentence and circumstances under which it would be true. Subsequent essays develop a metatheory of 'radical interpretation', specifying how interpreters could test whether a theory of truth conditions is interpretative for an alien language. Davidson argues that the criterion of hermeneutic success is that the truth theory correctly predicts circumstances of utterance for arbitrary sentences of a language. This implies that the 'meaning' of a term reflects its place in the totality of a speaker's linguistic activity – a 'holistic' view reminiscent of Saussure's claim that meaning resides in the differences between linguistic elements.

Davidson argues that public activity can only count as evidence for an interpretation if, applying the so-called 'principle of charity', interpreters assume that speakers have largely true beliefs. This claim implies that the possibility of massive error presupposed by foundationalists since Descartes is unintelligible. For, as he argues in the 'The Myth of the Subjective' (1987), the content of mental states, like sentences, is only fixed under charitable interpretations of an agent's activity within a common world. Davidson thus undermines subjectivist appeals to intrinsically contentful 'Ideas' as a basis for philosophical reflection.

Davidson holds, however, that interpretations are underdetermined by considerations of charity. There are, in consequence, no 'deeper' mental or semantic facts that could allow an interpreter to decide between similarly adequate interpretative theories. In 'On the Very Idea of a Conceptual Scheme' (1974), notions of charity and semantic indeterminacy are put to work against empiricist and transcendentalist pictures of mind 'forming' the world from unconceptualised 'content', a stance which Davidson takes to underlie relativism and strong incommensurability claims. Strong Kantian parallels can be found, though, in 'Thought and Talk' (1975) and 'Rational Animals' (1982), where it is argued that only creatures possessing a concept of belief can have beliefs and that an understanding of objectivity emerges in the intersubjective context of linguistic interpretation.

Despite the Saussurean parallels noted above, Davidson's interpretation-based approach to meaning is at odds with a synchronic view of language as a structure pre-existing singular acts of utterance or inscription. There are strong resonances here with the critique of structural linguistics and conventionalism to be found in Derrida's early work. Like him, Davidson often uses literary examples to question formalist presumptions. Thus 'A Nice Derangement of Epitaphs' (1986) employs instances of unconventional but intelligible speech produced by, among others, Sheridan's Mrs Malaprop to argue that the notion of a shared system of rules has little explanatory role in semantics – a line of reasoning comparable to Derrida's use of the notion of iterability to deconstruct philosophical appeals to convention or shared practice.

D. Roden

DEATH A major concern for continental philosophy, in which several interrelated themes can be discerned: the death of the self and of others; death as negation (in thought, language and the world); and the experience of mourning, dying, sacrifice and killing. In many works by continental figures, death is a key to understanding subjectivity, ethics and politics. While each theorist represents the work of death differently, for each it is finitude and negativity that is at the heart of human existing.

Death understood as negativity, as the negation or annihilation of an aspect of conceptual or material existence, structures Hegel's reflections on human experience in the *Phenomenology of Spirit* (1807). Hegel's dialectics may be understood as a negation and sublation that makes death into a productive transformation in so far as the original term or object is incorporated into a higher concept or stage. At the same time, death as the end of a particular human life is also evident in Hegel's reflection: the different ways the master and the slave approach the fight to the death become a trope for the attainment of recognition and full human consciousness. Hegel's observation that death 'is of all things the most dreadful, and to hold fast what is dead requires the greatest strength' indicates that facing death, as life's end and as non-actuality more generally, is imperative for human existing. It is this 'tarrying with the negative', embracing the negative rather than denying it by describing it as nothing or as false, that enables subjectivity and coming into being more generally.

For Bataille, Hegel's account construes death as a productive tool for the attainment of consciousness so that death becomes an instrument in a servile search for wisdom ('Hegel, Death, and Sacrifice', 1955). Instead, Bataille proposes that death facilitates the experience of pleasure and laughter; it is not a sober process of seeking higher truth and self-consciousness but a revelation of the joy of life. Bataille proposes that it is only an uncontaminated experience of death, such as the experience of sacrifice, that makes humanity manifest. Sacrifice is not subordinated to fulfilling a human need but creates heightened sensibilities revealing the passionate nature of human existing.

Heidegger focuses on the subject's relation to death and on how this structures human existence or Dasein (*Being and Time*, 1927). Rejecting earlier philosophical definitions of the human as rational thinking being, Heidegger proposes that Dasein is the being for whom its being is a question. Further, he suggests that it is awareness of mortality that distinguishes human existence from animals and gods. But this awareness is more than an abstract understanding that each of us and everybody will die. Rather, it is the awareness of my particular lifespan. This realisation of a limited time is not conceived as a time line from birth to death, from past through present to my future nothingness, but involves a differing experience of time such that the past that constitutes me now and the future as my current potentiality are of the now and within the present. Death, for Heidegger, is the possibility of impossibility such that the illusion of endlessness is shattered and possibilities come into existence. Death thus ends possibilities but also, by limiting endlessness, creates possibilities.

Heidegger further defines this authentic experience of being-to-ward-death. It is non-relational, not to be outstripped, certain and also indefinite. It involves recognising that death is ownmost, as no other can replace me in facing my death. This ownmost character of being-towards-death indicates that each must die: there is no possibility of avoiding death by having another die in my place, for I will myself nonetheless die. While this appears uncontentious, Levinas rejects elements of Heidegger's analysis, especially the implication that authentic Dasein is constituted through this isolated and individualistic process of being-towards-death and that the deaths of others are irrelevant to Dasein's being and death.

In contrast to Heidegger, Levinas sees ethics and the relation to the other, rather than the existential-ontology of the individual Dasein, as primary. Levinas reads beneath Heidegger's insistence that death is ownmost and non-substitutable a lack of concern for the other who dies. In contrast, for Levinas, I am responsible for the other, including for the other's death, whatever the circumstances: 'It is for the death of the other that I am responsible to the point of including myself in his death' (*God, Death, and Time*, 1993). More generally for Levinas, the ethical face-to-face relation indicates that the other has priority over the self and this necessitates being hostage to the other, even sacrificing oneself for the other. Levinasian ethics prioritises the other and the death of the other in instituting the responsibility of the self, over-coming the individualism that haunts Heidegger's thought on death.

While Heidegger and Levinas focus on the end of human life, Blanchot reintroduces the broader concept of death as negativity. While Hegel, in addition to the specific death of the individual subject, speaks of death as negation and change in general, Blanchot articulates the relation between the dying of the self and others and the death that is inherent to literature and language more generally. For Blanchot, unlike the earlier accounts, death cannot be made into a positive attribute through a mastery that transforms it into the basis for the achievement of subjectivity and authentic existence. Instead, Blanchot reveals the dissipation and meaninglessness of the experience of dying which renders us powerless. However, Blanchot acknowledges both sides of death: it does provide us with possibilities, yet it imposes a passivity that turns these possibilities to ash. Blanchot thus reformu-lates Heidegger's summation of death as the possibility of impossibility by recognising death's other side as the impossibility of possibility (*The Space of Literature*, 1955). The experience of passivity in the experience of dying enables a responsiveness and receptivity that opens the self to the other. Through this openness that emerges in dying the singular human being engages with, and creates, community. Unlike Heidegger who individualises death, Blanchot conceives death as the basis for sociality.

Derrida, affirming the importance of the other's death, analyses the effects of mortality on friendship and on ethics and politics more broadly. For Derrida, friendship is founded on the knowledge that the other is mortal and will die. This raises the issue of how to respond to the other's death, both at the moment of death and in anticipation of that death. The psychoanalytic accounts of mourning and melancholia are rethought to suggest that both a possible mourning and an impossible mourning fail to respect the mortal and deceased other. Both involve internalising others – preserving them by making them a part of the self – but the former assimilates others, destroying their difference, while the latter incorporates others whole, maintaining their alterity but excluding them from attachment and engagement with the self (*Memoires for Paul de Man*, 1988). Derrida argues that the self is constituted through these interiorisations of others and that this immediately raises the ethical question of how to internalise in a way that maintains the other's alterity while enabling engagement with others.

At a broader ethical and political level, Derrida conceives of death as a gift (*The Gift of Death*, 1992). Engaging with Levinas's critique of Heidegger, Derrida proposes that death is ownmost and constitutes my singularity, but also that it is only through this singularity that I can assume my primary responsibility for the other and for her death. For Derrida, 'responsibility demands irreplaceable singularity. Yet only death or rather the apprehension of death can give this irreplaceability . . .' It is only from this position of singularity that I can sacrifice myself for the other, can die for the other. Derrida also acknowledges the paradox of this situation for in giving the gift of death, for example by sacrificing myself for another, I thereby deny this ethical gift to another other and so act unethically. For Derrida, ethical action toward a singular other always also involves unethical action toward yet other others.

Jean-Luc Nancy also reflects on the relation between death, ethics and politics (*The Experience of Freedom*, 1988). He formulates this in relation to his critique of the everyday understanding of community as founded on a commonality of heritage, history, geography, biology, culture and so on. Instead, he proposes that community 'is revealed in the death of others'. It is the finitude of others that demands our exposure of self to, and our sharing with, others. Finitude enables the creation of being-with-others across difference such that community may include rather than exclude the stranger, the foreigner, the other. Giorgio Agamben considers the relation between death and the political from yet another perspective (*Homo Sacer: Sovereign Power and Bare Life*, 1995). He proposes that the polity is constituted through a legitimation of killing the excluded other. The state not only regulates society through Foucauldian technologies of surveillance and police, but also enacts zones of exclusion in which those deemed non-citizens could be killed without a legal ascription of murder.

Women philosophers too have reflected on the experience and the ethics and politics of death. While these reflections are often overlooked in the debates about finitude, they form a significant undercurrent, sometimes diverging from and sometimes conforming to the more recognised positions developed by men philosophers. Simone de Beauvoir considers how immortality would undermine the experience of being human in her novel *All Men Are Mortal* (1946); in *The Blood of Others* (1945) she investigates, in the context of the resistance to fascism, the ethics of killing and sacrifice, and of asking others to risk death for a political cause.

Irigaray's work as a whole could be construed as an investigation of the philosophical, and social, negation or killing of the feminine. This becomes explicit in *Speculum of the Other Woman* (1974), where Irigaray critiques Hegel's representation of Antigone's death. For Hegel, Antigone represents women's law and Creon man's law, both of which are sublated within the later stage of ethical community. For Irigaray, this account occludes the transition, in Sophocles' *Antigone*, from a matriarchal to a patriarchal system. For Irigaray, Antigone's death is emblematic of the repression of femininity enacted by a transition of political power from a female line to a male line represented by Creon.

Cixous also investigates the relation between death and femininity in her early essay 'Castration or Decapitation?' (1976). Drawing on psychoanalytic accounts of ego formation, Cixous suggests that if masculinity is organised around the castration complex, then femininity, lacking this threat, is regulated by a threat of decapitation. She suggests that it is man who teaches woman this awareness of death and of the Law of the Father.

Sarah Kofman follows another trajectory in her late work *Smothered Words* (1987). This work engages with Blanchot's reflections on the holocaust, Robert Antelme's account of his internment, as well as reporting on Kofman's father's death in Auschwitz. By bringing together disparate texts – philosophical, literary, historical, (auto)biographical – and by allowing a certain disjunction between the demands of historical reportage and subjective experience, Kofman reaches toward what Blanchot calls the passivity of the work. Rather than formulating a coherent synthesis through a mastery that conveys meanings and intentions, Kofman explores the unworking of writing, the negativity and finitude of writing. She thus resists the active ethic of production that underlies much Western thought and that finds abhorrent expression in the production of death in the concentration camps.

L. Secomb

DEBORD, GUY (1931–94) French writer, filmmaker and social critic, best known as the author of *The Society of the Spectacle*, a slim volume published in 1967 which stands as one of the most original and enduring critiques of late twentieth century capitalism. Drawing on the work of Hegel, Marx and Lukács, Debord develops the idea that the alienation inherent in capitalist modes of production extends into every area of everyday experience, transforming the entire social world into a commodified version of itself. This is the spectacle, a system of manufactured needs and processed desires, which perpetuates the logic of survival long after its imperatives have disappeared, and is capable of capturing – or recuperating – even the most radical attempts to expose and disrupt its dominion.

In the early 1950s, Debord became involved with the Lettrists, whose ideas and activities had much in common with the earlier movements of Dada and Surrealism. The Situationist International emerged from the 1957 issue of the Lettrist journal *Potlatch*. While the function of art remained one of its abiding concerns, the Situationist International developed into a movement committed to the wholesale revolution of every aspect of everyday life, from architecture and urban planning to the most intimate human relationships. This was a highly intellectual but by no means academic exercise: the Situationists promoted the active *détournement* (subversion) of the highly mediated relations of the spectacle, in part through the creation of spontaneous, participatory situations from which a radical, desiring subjectivity can emerge as a revolutionary force. These themes were developed in the Situationists' journal, *Internationale Situationniste*, and several other publications, including Raoul Vaneigem's *The Revolution of Everyday Life* (1967). Debord was nonetheless both the main protagonist and central theorist of the movement, and *The Society of the Spectacle* was its most influential and substantial text.

Debord published many articles as well as writing film scripts and producing a series of experimental films. His autocratic, sometimes enigmatic style contributed to the mythologising of a movement marked by splits and exclusions, and controversy surrounded him long after the collapse of the movement in the early 1970s. In 1989 Debord published *Comments on the Society of the Spectacle*, in which he argued that the spectacle had extended into an integrated global system, confirming his earlier analyses of capitalism, and making its contestation more necessary and more difficult as well.

The Society of the Spectacle had an enormous influence at the time of its publication – just a year before the revolutionary events of May 1968 – and on a wide variety of subsequent analyses and activities. His dialectical critiques and totalising revolutionary position were dismissed by later theorists of postmodernity, but his influence can be read in the works of writers such as Baudrillard and Lyotard. His films were rarely seen, but they too had an impact on radical filmmakers such as Chris Marker, and his ideas have informed guerrilla artists, punk rockers and anarchist activists. They have also, as he knew they would, been taken up and recuperated by advertisers, management theorists and other managers of spectacular society.

S. Plant

DECONSTRUCTION The term now most commonly used to refer to the work of Derrida. He used the word, which already existed in French, to translate and reinforce the affirmative value of what

Heidegger called *Destruktion* or *Abbau*, distinguishing it from 'destruction' or 'demolition' and referring instead to a 'de-sedimentation' or to a critique of systems that would take place with respect not just to their structures but also to their foundations. Deconstruction was never proposed as a method, in spite of attempts to apply it as a form of literary analysis, and Derrida has insisted that it is not a critique that one performs without also being something that takes place in a given set of circumstances. Deconstruction is thus as much an echo or affirmation of struggle against hierarchy; it is the 'maximum intensification of a transformation already in progress'. To the extent that analyses such as those in the work from 1967–72 have become classic examples in the Derridean œuvre, deconstruction can be understood to involve diagnosing oppositions as hierarchies, demonstrating that the denigrated side of the opposition is essential to the prioritised side, and displacing the opposition itself in a 'third term' that indicates the 'general economy' from which the opposition was drawn.

Derrida has expressed surprise at the extent to which the word entered academic, and now common, parlance and for a time he used it sparingly, insisting that it be understood as 'a word in a chain with many other words – such as trace or *différance* – as well as with a whole elaboration which is not limited only to a lexicon' (*The Ear of the Other*). Perhaps the most extensive 'definition' of deconstruction can be found in the letter Derrida writes to a Japanese translator ('Letter to a Japanese Friend'), where the suggestion is finally that deconstruction should reinvent itself by being translated. This is in line with another more elliptical formulation – what Derrida calls the only definition be ever attempted – namely, '(no) more than one language [*plus d'une langue*]' (*Memoires for Paul de Man*).

D. Wills

DEDUCTION An integral part of Kant's critical philosophy, in which the basic categories or principles of each work are justified. In the *Critique of Pure Reason* these are the categories or pure concepts of the understanding, in the *Critique of Practical Reason* the principles of pure practical reason and in the *Critique of Judgement* the principles of the aesthetic judgement of taste. The method of deduction is introduced in the first *Critique* in terms of the legal technique of distinguishing between rights and claims in terms of the question of fact and the question of right. The first determines factual possession, the latter legal or legitimate possession. In the case of the categories, the deduction is dedicated to proving the legitimate possession of the pure concepts of experience that make possible experience. Kant considered the deduction one of his most original contributions, distinguishing his 'transcendental' from an 'empirical' deduction. The latter sought the legitimation for the possession of concepts in experience (and is attributed by Kant to Locke and Hume) while the former, Kant's self-perceived contribution to metaphysics, was to show that the concepts are justified as the conditions of experience. The transcendental deduction consisted in the proof that experience is not possible without the pure concepts of the understanding.

Kant offered two versions of the deduction of the categories in the two editions of the *Critique of Pure Reason* (1781/1787) which contain fascinating and debatable differences. Nevertheless, the basic objective remains largely the same in both versions. Just as appearances are governed by the forms of intuition of space and time – an object cannot appear but in space and time – so too are they regulated by the 'unity of apperception', which is perceived either subjectively in the activities of consciousness or objectively in the fact of consciousness. Whether the emphasis in the deduction is laid upon the synthetic or combinatoric activities of consciousness, the basic aim of showing that the unity of consciousness distributed across the categories is the condition, not the outcome, of experience remains the same.

H. Caygill

DELANDA, MANUEL (1952–) Mexican philosopher and leading figure in the 'new materialism' developing in the wake of Deleuze and Guattari. DeLanda's work combines research into history, biology, technology and economics to investigate a wide variety of topics at the intersection of philosophy and the scientific researches known as non-linear dynamics or complexity theory. DeLanda's basic concern is 'morphogenesis', the production of stable structures out of material flows; such production is not the result of a form being imposed on a chaotic matter ('hylomorphism'), but occurs when a physical, biological or social system reaches a threshold that triggers immanent processes of material self-organisation.

DeLanda's *War in the Age of Intelligent Machines* (1991) is nominally an examination of the role of information technology in military history, but is really an examination of social-military morphogenesis, as with, for example, Napoleon's mobilisation of the citizenry created by the French Revolution. DeLanda is careful to note, however, that his application of non-linear dynamics findings in physics and biology to social systems remains analogical and not yet scientific, as mathematical models of sufficient complexity to analyse social systems have yet to be developed.

In *A Thousand Years of Nonlinear History* (1997), DeLanda widens his field of vision to examine economics, biology and linguistics. DeLanda appeals to non-linear dynamics researches and Deleuzoguattarian terminology to move from the geological to the social, investigating the interplay of 'the flows of lava, biomass, genes, memes, norms, money' out of which come the stable and semi-stable structures of the natural and social world. Relying on the historians Ferdnand Braudel and William McNeill, the biologists Stuart Kauffman and Brian Goodwin, and the linguists William Labov and Zelig Harris, DeLanda distinguishes 'hierarchies' and 'meshworks' (interactive networks, or what Deleuze and Guattari call 'rhizomes') as two basic structural forms found in many natural and social registers (although never purely, but always in mixed form).

In *Intensive Science and Virtual Philosophy* (2002), DeLanda continues with the topic of morphogenesis, but this time in the guise of a 'reconstruction' of Deleuze's *Difference and Repetition* that explains the mathematical background of Deleuze's ontology and epistemology. DeLanda explains Deleuze's ontology as anti-essentialist, that is as insisting on tracing the genesis of actual forms from intensive material processes (those that change their nature when pushed beyond critical thresholds); the virtual realm is made up of the repeatable structures of such processes. The Deleuzean 'ontological difference' is produced by the purification of mathematical concepts, which eliminates any reference to identity to produce a pure differential virtual field. For DeLanda, Deleuzean epistemology asks us to treat physics problematically rather than axiomatically. In this approach, the achievements of theoretical physics are seen not as linguistically interpreted general laws, but as correctly posed problems, that is as the posing of the distribution of what is singular and ordinary (that is, what is important and not). DeLanda's reconstruction thus stresses that Deleuzean ontology discloses not a closed world capturable by sentences, but an open world to be explored.

J. Protevi

See also: Complexity Theory; Materialism

DELEUZE, GILLES (1925–1995) French philosopher, associated with the poststructuralist movement, and most famous for the two-volume work *Capitalism and Schizophrenia* (1972, 1980), written in collaboration with the radical psychoanalyst and political activist Félix Guattari. Rather than radicalising structuralism and phenomenology as did Jacques Derrida, Deleuze's work changed the direction of French philosophy in inaugurating a new materialism fused out of Marx and

Freud; *Capitalism and Schizophrenia* remains the emblematic philosophical work for the generation of 1968 and the only one to match the speed and turbulence of bottom-up social change during that time.

Deleuze's philosophical work can be untidily but functionally divided into three periods: first, an early phase of scholarly works that examine individual philosophers (Hume, Bergson, Kant, Nietzsche and Spinoza); second, a short middle period of two books, *The Logic of Sense* and *Difference and Repetition*, published in the late 1960s in which Deleuze achieved a genuine independence of thought and no longer expressed himself vicariously though commentary; and third, a late period, characterised by a collaborative writing technique, whose most important product is the two-volume *Capitalism and Schizophrenia*. The taxonomy is untidy because it doesn't begin to do justice to the range of Deleuze's non-philosophical work. He wrote widely on literature (books on Proust and Kafka), art (a book on Francis Bacon) and film (the two volumes of *Cinema*). But the periodisation retains a heuristic validity for a philosophical introduction to Deleuze's work.

Deleuze's most basic philosophical instinct is against anthropomorphism: we should not assume that the universe can be grasped with the concepts of our everyday common sense, which presupposes a stable world of persons and objects capable of being hierarchically ordered and subject to natural laws. The task of philosophy is to invent new concepts that answer to exteriority, not to rely on the ones we already have, those of interiority. Moreover, the relations between interior and exterior are not symmetrical: from the inside, the exterior appears as the fugitive limit of a primarily epistemological problematic; but from the outside, an interior can be carved out by processes of folding or torsion. Starting from the concepts of interiority therefore it is impossible to think the outside, but not vice versa.

Interiority is construed quite widely in Deleuze's critique. It clearly includes phenomenology and any kind of idealism in which the world is subordinated to consciousness. But Deleuze argues that the same image of thought is operating in non-idealist philosophy that nevertheless takes for granted the fact that the world of empirical objects is individuated in accordance with the conceptual categories of consciousness. In fact Deleuze argues that the image of interiority extends further than this, to any thinking that is a function of the higher political interiority of the state. This is particularly legible in Deleuze's careful construction of a kind of counter-canon of philosophers who have operated only at the margins of state and academic acceptability.

Kant is a paradigm philosopher of consciousness, representation, interiority and the state, so Deleuze is understandably ambivalent about him. But they in fact have a more intimate intellectual connection than the slim book Deleuze devoted to Kant might suggest. Kant argued that the stable and ordered empirical world of neatly delineated subjects and objects is not actually given but could be the target of a critique showing how it is produced. Kant's name for this intellectual process was transcendental philosophy, and Deleuze is heir to it, but Deleuze maintains that Kant botched the project by tracing the structure of the transcendental field from the empirical, so that the Kantian categories preserve the structures of empirical consciousness at a higher level. For Deleuze, the transcendental cannot 'resemble' the empirical because it would then be in a representational and not a productive relation to the empirical. Deleuze's transcendental field is an ensemble of production processes that are therefore 'pre-individual, non-personal and a-conceptual'.

Such a negative characterisation of the transcendental could easily lead back to a liminal thematic, as elaborated extensively by Heidegger and his followers. This is not at all what Deleuze has in mind. The stable and ordinary objects of the empirical world do indeed occlude their production processes, but, while stability is normal, not everything is ordinary. Deleuze, in contrast to a philosophical tradition whose examples are all banal (Descartes' wax, Kant's ship and building), is interested in extraordinary cases: complex systems like cell differentiation, in which intensive production processes rise to the surface.

In the late 1960s Deleuze published two books in short succession – *Difference and Repetition* (1968) and *The Logic of Sense* (1969) – which established him as a philosopher in his own right. While making frequent use of his earlier monographs, especially those on Hume and Bergson, these two texts are notable for a deliberate deviation from the philosophical canon in the use of concepts from other disciplines.

For example, Deleuze outlines the key concept of difference through thermodynamics, which distinguishes between extensive and intensive properties (a distinction that Deleuze also takes over). Extensive properties, like volume, are decomposable, so that if you break something in half, each half has exactly half the volume of the original. Intensive properties, like temperature, are not decomposable. If you break something in half, each half has exactly the *same* temperature as the original. *Intensive* differences, like thermal gradients, are therefore quite unlike extensive differences between two already constituted entities. They do not presuppose identity; rather they set up dynamic processes that *result* in stable, extensive, objects whose intensive differences have been cancelled and are at equilibrium. Such extensive objects – like the banal examples of the tradition – cover up the intensive conditions of their own production, creating the illusion that these processes do not take place. But this illusion is objective because, in a stable situation, differences really *have* been cancelled. In rare situations, far from equilibrium, however, transcendental processes are directly visible: in the intensive and morphogenetic chemical gradients traversing a developing embryo for instance.

A second important source of philosophical novelty for Deleuze is geometry, and specifically the notion of a multiplicity derived from the nineteenth-century mathematician Riemann. Riemann showed that the curvature of a two-dimensional surface could be attached to the surface itself, rather than requiring the plane to be inserted into a space with a supplementary third dimension. This supplementary dimension or enclosing space is the crucial presupposition of interiority, permitting connection only on the basis of commonality or identity. The fact that multiplicities do not need this supplement enables them to connect heterogeneous elements or differences without unifying them, pre-serving their mutual exteriority. Deleuze describes multiplicities as virtual but real; they are progressively actualised into stable extensive systems. Deleuze rejects the notion of possibility as, like the Kantian transcendental (= condition of possibility), another tracing from the empirical. Possibilities are simply non-extant combinations of extensive properties. A virtual multiplicity, on the other hand, which Deleuze often describes as a surface or plane, enables novel connections to be made between heterogeneous production processes, and hence allows new forms to arise.

Deleuze never abandons this array of new concepts, even though *Anti-Oedipus* (1972), the first volume of the collaborative *Capitalism and Schizophrenia,* rejects the decorous philosophical tone of Deleuze's earlier books for a high-octane multidisciplinary ride journeying into the socio-psychic realm. The manifest content of *Anti-Oedipus* is its fusion and simultaneous critique of Marx and Freud. By making social production basic, Marx can only appeal to ideology as an explanation when people whose objective conditions are revolutionary nevertheless persist in collaborating in their own oppression. But ideology gives ideas an autonomous force, vitiating Marx's materialism (turning Hegel right side up again). Conversely, Freud makes desire basic, but at the cost of separating it from all socio-political reality: there is always, according to the generalised reductionism of psychoanalysis, a daddy lurking underneath the boss.

Deleuze and Guattari's solution in *Anti-Oedipus* is to identify transcendental production with a desiring-production that is immediately both productive and libidinal, so that desire is political and social production suffused with libido. There is no reductionism here in either direction: desire isn't just interest, and politics isn't just mummy and daddy. This enables them to show how desiring-production can be turned back against itself in a psychic repression that allows capitalist subjects to collaborate in their own political oppression. The primary figure of this repression-oppression is the Oedipus complex of classical psychoanalysis, seen through a rather French intellectual lens as a structural condition of culture.

At first glance these concerns are rather remote from those of Deleuze's work from the 1960s. But the ability of desire to turn against itself is a psycho-political spin on the twin ideas that stable extensive systems presuppose but occlude their intensive production processes and that interiority is produced by folding exteriority. Stable subjects of capitalist consumption are produced as zones of interiority in strict correlation with extensive commodity objects. Deleuze and Guattari effectively generalise Marx's observation that markets separate producer from product so that finished products (commodities) obscure their real processes of production (human labour).

Marx's point has a second component: capital not only disguises production, it actually appears as the ground of production, taking the place of labour. This point also gets generalised: each mode of production (there are three in the baroque architecture of *Anti-Oedipus*) has a 'body' akin to the body of capital which arrogates production to itself and disguises the role of desiring production. In societies without a state, things seem to emanate from the earth itself; in non-capitalist state societies, the state itself (paradigmatically embodied in a despot) appears as the origin of all production.

These bodies inherit and extend the sense of the virtual in Deleuze's earlier work, and give political content to the objective illusion by means of which the extensive envelops its intensive conditions.

Underlying all social production is desiring-production as such, intensive processes that are not enveloped by their extensive products. Even at this level, described by Deleuze and Guattari in psychoanalytic terms as primary production, a body is produced, the body without organs. Primary production therefore also contains a constitutive illusion that makes possible all the structures of secondary or actual production. But the body without organs stresses the positive role played by the virtual, or more strictly by the heterogeneous ensemble of all virtual bodies. While it is not actually the agent of production (earlier Deleuze had described this role as 'quasi-causal'), it is still crucial for the generation of novelty because it allows intensive processes to reconfigure extensive systems. It does so by enabling heterogeneous elements to connect. This process is sometimes called deterritorialisation in accordance with the way the body of the earth is displaced as the seeming source of production in the transition from primitive (territorial) societies to state societies.

A Thousand Plateaus (1980) takes Deleuze's problematic of transcendental production beyond the political turn of *Anti-Oedipus* back into the scientific domains of his earlier work, but with a vastly expanded range of reference, happily, in fact joyously, integrating musicology into ethology at the same time as giving a metallurgical account of nomadism. The tone of the book is quite different again from *Anti-Oedipus*, albeit no less racy. The last familiar intellectual coordinates (Marx and Freud) have been abandoned in favour of free invention. Even its organisation is novel, divided as it is into plateaus, without a continuous argument or order, and each connected to all the others by subterranean passages (rhizomes, in the vocabulary they develop in the book itself). Several terms from Deleuze's other works find their way into *A Thousand Plateaus*, but less on the basis of continuity than because they were also sources of material.

Easily the densest plateau, 'The Geology of Morals' addresses the formation of what they now call strata, again modifying the sense of what an extensive system is. What Deleuze and Guattari really object to is the doctrine of form and matter, which essentially takes form as given, making the production of form an impossible topic. They propose to replace such a hylomorphism with a matrix of four terms: content / expression and form / substance, none of which correspond to form and matter.

This terminology can seem arbitrary, but such complexity is quite normal outside philosophy. Organisms, for instance, are composed of proteins (form of content) that are themselves composed of chains of amino acids (substance of content); but both of these are (re)produced by a completely different set of molecules, nucleic acids like DNA (forms of expression), which are themselves made from components, nucleotides (substances of expression), which are different in nature from the amino acid substances of content. Expression (nucleotides and nucleic acid sequences) does not *form* or *resemble* content (proteins and amino acids) because they share nothing in common. Instead they enter into 'a state of unstable equilibrium . . . reciprocal presupposition' or feedback: at the molecular level, expression codes for content; but natural selection causes content at the level of molar population aggregates to re-code expression.

The concept of form presupposes and therefore reduplicates the organisation of the empirical. By eliminating it, Deleuze and Guattari hope to develop a materialism whose explanatory terms can be redeployed at all levels of production from the geological to the social. Deleuze shows, for instance, that Foucault's account of panopticism distinguishes between the form of content of the prison system, a distribution of light in which a viewer can see but not be seen, and a form of (linguistic) expression that is not about prisons at all, but rather about a new content of expression, the idea of delinquency. Expression does not represent content, but the two presuppose each other.

Such processes – which Deleuze and Guattari call stratification because they all involve the same processes as the construction of geological strata – are responsible for fabricating organised, hierarchical and stable systems, zones of interiority and extensive objects. And just as before, the intensive processes responsible for producing stable systems come to prominence in other kinds of system. These intensive systems are called rhizomes. Unlike the hierarchy of the strata (like the Panopticon), rhizomes exhibit lateral connectivity, linking irreducibly heterogeneous components. Using a biological register, Deleuze and Guattari often contrast rhizomes with tree-like or arborescent systems. The latter formalise the notion of hierarchy, by organising nodes into layers such that each node makes contact with its neighbour in one layer only, via a node located higher up the tree. In the Panopticon, prisoners make contact only via the warder; according to your organisational chart, the boss mediates your relation with your colleagues, and so on. In a graphic illustration of a rhizome, Deleuze and Guattari point to the actions of viruses that splice genetic material from living species, that is to say, neighbouring leaves on the tree of life, who thereby become directly allied rather than mediated through their filiation, that is their joint relation to a common ancestor higher up the tree. Network replaces hierarchy.

This kind of thing is always happening; rhizomes are always sprouting out of trees and strata, creating unexpected connections. And for a good reason: strata are consolidations of a material flow that is itself not stratified, so that strata themselves are always provisional, liable to decompose and perhaps to recompose, to destratify.

Although *A Thousand Plateaus* is the only book of Deleuze's to do this explicitly, in fact each of his works, despite very different styles, tones and areas of interest, connects the others into an œuvre that is itself multiple, a rhizome.

A. Welchman

See also: abstract machine; actual/virtual distinction assemblage; becoming; body without organs; Cinema; Death; desiring-production;

deterritorialisation; Difference; differentiation; Geography; haecceity; hylomorphism; Idea; immanence; intensive difference; line of flight; Memory; Metaphysics; minor literature; multiplicity; Nature, Philosophy of; nomadology; order word; organism; Poststructuralism; plateau; repetition; schizoanalysis; simulacrum; singularity; Space; speech acts; stratification; Time; Thought; transcendental empiricism; vitalism; war machine

DEMOCRACY-TO-COME (*à venir*) A term developed by Derrida in a series of texts, beginning with 'Force of Law' (1989) and *The Other Heading* (1991) and extending to *Voyous* (2003), in which an idea of democracy, and the political future in general, is argued for in terms not simply of perfectibility but of the promise or arrival of what cannot be foreseen or predicted. The term plays on the French word for the future (*l'avenir*) as that which is yet to come (*à venir*), but also carries the sense of what is unknown or even impossible about that future. Derrida notes that the term is a syntagm that does not constitute a sentence and that might not, in the final analysis, be reducible to a sense. However, it remains the performative promise – sometimes referred to as a 'structural messianism' without content or without religion – upon which any sense of politics or justice must be based, and without which no political or ethical e-vent can come to pass.

Democracy-to-come would not therefore refer to a stabilised system of government, and certainly not to a form of politics that has arrived, even within those countries that seem to enjoy it, but rather to the destabilising challenge to any politics. Enunciated in the context of the fall of the Berlin Wall, democracy-to-come becomes an increasingly explicit critique of the American and European model of a triumphant neo-liberal capitalism which has done nothing to alter the scandalous fact that, as he writes in *Specters of Marx*, 'never have violence, inequality, exclusion, famine, and thus economic oppression affected as many human beings in the history of the earth and of humanity'.

D. Wills

DERRIDA, JACQUES (1930–2004) Algerian-born French philosopher whose work has often been subsumed under the aegis of 'deconstruction', a word he first used to translate what Heidegger called *Destruktion* or *Abbau*. Derrida radicalised both phenomenology and structuralism in addressing classic epistemological and ontological issues in the philosophical tradition (knowledge, substance, being, time) as well as questions of language, literature, aesthetics, psychoanalysis, religion, politics and ethics. He produced a remarkable body of writings that refer not only to philosophers from Socrates to Levinas, but also to writers and artists, including among others Shakespeare, Joyce, Mallarmé and Cezanne.

Perhaps more than any other figure in continental philosophy, Derrida has provoked both admiration and scorn. In 1984 the Halleck Professor of Philosophy at Yale University accused him of 'terrorist obscurantism'; in 1992, along with eighteen of her colleagues from three different continents, in an attempt to block his being awarded an honorary doctorate from Cambridge – an attempt that ultimately failed – she contended that 'Derrida's work does not meet accepted standards of clarity and rigour . . . [it] defies comprehension'. Such vehement opposition no doubt derived from the radical challenge to thinking implied in his theses, and from his refusal to treat the intractable questions of Western thought in anything other than the complicated terms in which they are posed, a refusal to presume that changes in that tradition can be achieved through any simple strategy. Indeed, his work may be said to have functioned, on both sides of the Channel, or the Atlantic, or the Pacific, as a consistent *heterotopia* within continental philosophy, as an *ec-centric* or *exorbitant* experience of philosophy itself.

Derrida began his career as a Husserl specialist, and many of the hallmarks of deconstruction can be seen in the analyses of Husserl's work on historicity and ideality, time-consciousness and intuition. His first major publication was a long Introduction to his 1962 translation of 'The Origin of Geometry' (from *The Crisis of the European Sciences*, 1938), followed by *Speech and Phenomena* (1967) where the emphasis on voice and its relation to 'trace' and 'differance' was introduced. For Derrida, Western thinking has consistently modelled itself on the *logos* or voice as unmediated expression of thought and intention, and guarantor of truth and integrity, in contrast to which writing was represented as a fall outside of such a self-present origin into absence and error. Yet – as Derrida showed by analysing treatments of language in thinkers as diverse as Plato and Saussure, Rousseau and Condillac, as well as Husserl – writing does not in fact differ structurally from speech: speech as well as writing functions by introducing 'spacing' between itself and, say, the thought that produces it; it similarly introduces difference, and therefore the necessary and irreducible possibility of miscommunication between what issues from a speaker's mouth and what enters a listener's ear, even when that speaker and listener are the same, and even when the voice speaks silently in self-communion. Spacing and absence are therefore constituents of any utterance whatsoever; indeed, they are the structures that make language and communication possible even as they make it subject to chance, or as Derrida put it, 'undecidable'.

The now 'classic' deconstructions of the period 1967–72 follow something of a pattern in analysing the philosophical impulse that privileges presence, what Derrida at the time, following Heidegger, called 'metaphysics': the diagnosis of opposition as hierarchy (speech over writing); the demonstration that the supposed derivative term is essential to the prioritised one (speech is also constituted by the absence thought to be specific to writing); the displacement of the opposition, and a general reconfiguration of the differences involved, by means of another term ('arche-writing' or 'trace' as the structure of 'spacing' common to both speech and writing).

Derrida also inherited explicitly from Heidegger, and by extension from Nietzsche, although he differed in important respects from each. His analyses of the classic texts of philosophy, for example of Plato in 'Plato's Pharmacy' (in *Dissemination*, 1972) or of Aristotle in 'White Mythology' (in *Margins*, 1972), often underscored the rhetorical means by which philosophy seeks to distinguish itself from literature (à la Nietzsche), yet also offered rereadings of the specific etymological sedimentations of the terms employed (à la Heidegger). But he resisted occupying the symmetrical other side of what he critiqued, as Nietzsche was often reduced to doing, considering that to be an ineffectual response which in many respects preserves the status quo. And, while remaining vigilant concerning Heidegger's conservative recourse to poetry, or to the earth, he thought the latter moved too fast in proclaiming the end of metaphysics (Nietzsche being for Heidegger its last gasp), and in suggesting that we can henceforth (re)think outside of the tradition. In this respect Derrida also marked his distance from Deleuze concerning philosophy's 'creation' of concepts, but, as he wrote in his eulogy for his friend, he put their differences down to 'the "gesture," the "strategy," the "manner" of writing, of speaking, of reading', Deleuze being 'the one among all those of my "generation" to whom I have always considered myself closest'. Finally, any mention of influences upon Derrida's thinking cannot fail to underline his unqualified respect for Blanchot, a thinker or writer who was perhaps situated in an even more equivocal relation than was Derrida to the institution of philosophy.

'Exorbitant' is a word used in *Of Grammatology* (1967) to refer to the methodological quandary posed by the relation between an author's life and work, a relation Derrida wanted to be understood as 'textual' beyond any purely linguistic sense, referring to any network of traces and calling into question the limits of that network, introducing a problematics of the margin or border when considering any constituted identity, hence his now famous formulation 'il n'y a pas de hors-texte', which translated literally means 'there is no outside-the-text'. If the statement can also be read to mean there is nothing that is not text, it is again by no means in the sense that the textual is only or primarily linguistic, that there are only words; rather, that there are permanent and irreducible questions concerning what delimits any constituted identity – a text, a life, a history, a being – and that there is a permanent and irreducible labour of reading and interpretation involved in any analysis of such questions.

Derrida's writings consist almost exclusively of analytical readings and interpretations which, in the process, perform a problematics of reading and interpretation. Thus the essay 'Signature event context' (in *Margins of Philosophy*, 1972), which led speech act theorist John Searle to argue that Derrida had so seriously misread and misunderstood Austin, ends (and so ends the entire volume) with a series of versions of Derrida's proper name – printed initials, printed name and a hand-written signature – which pluralise and displace the author as source and controlling centre of what s/he writes, and which progressively edge the author's name into the margins of the textual space, radically disorienting the hierarchical arrangements (title, headings, author, words, blank spaces) by means of which readers presume to gain a purchase on the meaning of a text. How indeed can we rigorously analyse the effects of a so-called creator of a piece of writing who is held to be, in turn or simultaneously, outside of and absent from the text (often to the extent of being dead), printed on its edges as a name on a title page, and located as it were invisibly throughout its main body as intended meaning? For Derrida, no analysis is possible that does not take account of such uncanny dislocations and any reading that thinks it can avoid them will necessarily fall into the spaces or abysses that open up between or among them.

One obvious reason why writing is considered to break away from the speech that supposedly engenders it derives from its never having been simply a phonetic medium. It is also graphic in the sense of being visual. This is something that poetry has exploited, most radically in Mallarmé's *Un coup de dés* (*A Dice-throw*, 1897), and Derrida attempted to have his own writings function both according to principles of chance and in visual terms. His multiple signatures at the end of 'Signature Event Context' were already an example of that, but it was more explicit and much more developed in *Glas* (1974), where two columns of text, one on Hegel and one on Genet, play as it were silently off each other across the putative empty space between them. In other cases he disjoined in a dramatic way the main body of a text from its notes ('Living On: Border Lines', 1979), introduced seemingly arbitrary ellipses ('Envois' in *The Post Card*, 1980) or embedded a collaborative and competing text within another ('Circumfession', in *Jacques Derrida*, 1991). At the same time, from 1978, he wrote a series of pieces on the visual arts proper, addressing in particular the function of the frame as the very matter that a theory of aesthetics such as Kant's *Critique of Judgement* ignores, but which, as the means of 'entry' into the work proper, cannot not concern any theory of that work. *The Truth in Painting* (1978), which groups together four essays on the visual arts, concentrated on how discourses on the plastic arts presume to be able to cross over the frame and enter unproblematically into the work in order to locate its centre and truth. In contrast, Derrida proposed that one pay attention to the work of the signature, undecidably a part and not a part of the work, repeating therefore the structure of the frame within the work, dividing and subverting its integrity, disseminating its truth.

Undecidability derives from the 'iterability' which, for Derrida, structures every mark. It is only because every mark (and every sign, every word and so on) is iterable or able to be 'cited', that it can function within a system of communication or sense. No single event of the mark or sign would be capable of doing that, for then every utterance would create a new private language. Yet because the mark is iterable, it is dislocatable, able to be untethered from any saturable context. What enables it to function within a system of communication and sense also disables it or disseminates it. That sort of aporetic 'structure' had been found by Derrida to function within the economic systems – systems that attempt to control the limits of their functioning – that govern various ethico-political presumptions of everyday life: the gift, responsibility, justice, hospitality, decision itself. Beginning with *Glas*, but more extensively in the period from the mid 1980s to his death, Derrida's work concentrated on analysing those aporetic operations. For there to be a gift that operates outside of the economy of exchange (the expectation of something given in return) one would have not to know that one was giving (*Given Time*, 1991); any truly rigorous responsibility involves forms of *irresponsibilisation* (being responsible to one at the expense of all the others) (*The Gift of Death*, 1992); justice, unlike the law, requires the law to be rewritten in every judgement and therefore disables the law ('Force of Law', 1992); unconditional hospitality requires leaving the door open without any heed to even the identity or form of whoever might arrive, anything less is a calculation (*Of Hospitality*, 1997); a decision worthy of the name, far from being the moment whereby the conscious human agent imposes itself, requires an irreducible undecidability, an absolute unpredictability of the decision, an 'unconscious' decision, one made by the other (*Politics of Friendship*, 1994). Derrida argued that an ethics of any consequence and especially one that can rise to the complexities of the contemporary situation, rather than ending because of such aporias, can only begin by taking them into account, by reasoning with and as it were through them. That will inevitably require a displacement of traditional thinking, a radical rethinking of the very foundations, such as philosophy has always taken to be its most pertinent task.

The Derridean aporia should also be understood as a recasting of dialectical thinking and of the logic of the paradox. The aporia is neither resolved nor transcended; instead, as was just suggested, it calls for a type of sidestep that amounts to a complex renegotiation of the terms of thinking, one that takes place via a signifying network of modifiable concepts – beginning with 'writing', 'trace' or 'mark' – that are sometimes called 'quasi-transcendentals'. Such terms refer more to strategic manoeuvres than to concepts in the classical sense, and to the extent that they can be systematically recognised it is by virtue of their being double, both constative and performative, seeking to 'put into practice [both] a *reversal* of the classical opposition [e.g. between speech and writing] *and* a general *displacement* of the system' ('Signature Event Context', in *Margins of Philosophy*, 1972). The two sides of this double gesture work in some sort of competition one with the other, operating what Derrida, playing on the French, refered to as a relation of *band* to *contraband*, one side erecting a thesis in a more traditional sense and the other side subverting that thesis in a way that appears logically or philosophically illicit, as it were smuggling the concept away from itself.

A consistent *contraband* in Derrida's work is performed by means of the proper name, for what renders us unique or most 'properly' ourselves is also a signifier of death; it is what is used to refer to us in our absence and will continue to refer to us once we are permanently gone. This has led to his philosophy's being a complicated practice of autobiography, or what might better be called 'signatory writing', and it brings him back to Nietzsche as well as to Freud who, Derrida suggests in a section of *The Post Card* devoted to a detailed analysis of *Beyond the Pleasure Principle*, 'produc[es] the institution of his desire' and 'graft[s] his own genealogy onto it' as if 'an autobiographical writing, in the abyss of an unterminated self-analysis g[a]ve to a worldwide institution *its* birth'. When it comes to his own autobiography, he has maintained that he can't produce a constative rendition of his life – 'like "I-was-born-in-El-Biar-on-the-outskirts-of-Algiers-in-a-petit-bourgeois-family-of-assimilated-Jews-but . . ."' – yet a series of texts deal in diverse ways with the material facts of his existence. *Glas* encrypts his father's name; *Monolingualism of the Other*, while again disclaiming 'some autobiographical or . . . intellectual bildungsroman', develops a theory of language in the context of his childhood in Algeria; 'Envois' recounts, among other things, a long and complicated love-story; 'Circumfession' is written as a vigil of his mother's final days, 'A Silkworm of One's Own' begins with the words 'Before the verdict, my verdict . . .', and 'Correspondence', which consists of postcards written from various foreign destinations, describes his relation to travel.

In 'Correspondence', Derrida spoke of writing as being, for him, more capable than travel of producing the unexpected or unforeseeable event 'whose arrival will stop the form of writing, *from the outside*, be its decisive caesura'. One can understand Derrida's entire project as an insistent attempt to produce that event, knowing nevertheless that, if it is to truly be an event, if it is to be unpredictable, it precisely cannot be produced. It can only happen: as promise, as chance and indeed as catastrophe. But it is such an insistence on the event that gives his work its urgency as well as its timeliness, taking his reasoning into the thick of the world's most pressing questions and problems, such as post-Soviet Marxism (*Specters of Marx*, 1993), religion and nationalisms ('Faith and Knowledge', 1996), media and technology (*Echographies*, 1996), and the so-called war on terrorism (*Voyous*, 2003). And such an insistence also means that the work itself functions as a type of supplication, even a *sufferance* to the extent that that word still refers to a type of patience or waiting, for it is less the sheer volume or the sometimes maddening difficulty of Derrida's writings than the very performance of each and every one of them that has them waiting, waiting to be read, holding out the chance that that reading will come to be their event.

D. Wills

See also: adestination; affirmation; arche-writing; auto-immunity; Cinema; Critical Legal Studies; Cosmpolitanism; Death; deconstruction; democracy-to-come (*à venir*); différance; Difference; Epistemology; Ethics; framing; gift; hospitality; iterability; Language; logocentrism; Memory; Metaphysics; onto-theo-logy; parasite; pharmakon; Poststructuralism; Repetition; responsibility; signature; simulacrum; Space; spectrality; speech acts; Subject; supplement; Thought; Time; undecideability

DESIRING-PRODUCTION A term that fuses Marx and Freud, used by Deleuze and Guattari in *Anti-Oedipus* to describe a universal production process.

Deleuze and Guattari do not merely combine Marx and Freud but offer symmetrical critiques of both. Marx views desire as something superficial, determined (even if perhaps just in the last instance) by a base consisting only of economic production and social relations of production. Freud on the other hand views desire as basic, projecting social relations back onto the determining structure of an incestuous family romance. Desiring-production refuses both of these attempts at reductionism because desiring-production is simultaneously libidinally and socially productive. In fact, desiring-production goes deeper still, to a point of universal production where the distinction between nature and culture is no longer operative. Desiring-production synthesises psycho-social reality under determinate historical conditions. These conditions, however, transcend the flow of desiring-production itself, canalising it into unified subjects and objects (e.g. capitalist subjects and commodities). Generalising Marx's account of commodity fetishism, social life as a whole occludes the conditions of its own production. In the detailed architectonic of *Anti-Oedipus*, one of the three syntheses of desiring-production is illegitimately deployed in the formation of each historical mode of desiring production.

Because desiring-production itself drives history, each social revolution, culminating in capitalism, involves a general freeing up of the resources of desiring-production, a 'deterritorialisation'. This is then followed by the use of new instruments of repression to control the now liberated flows. Capitalism for instance liberates productive potential, which is, however, forced into the straitjacket of commodities.

A. Welchman

DESOEUVREMENT ('worklessness') A term that refers to Blanchot's thesis that the work (of art) is the effect of the non-work or the un-power of being, in other words that artistic creativity requires the relinquishment of subjective control. Power, for Blanchot, even in the broadest sense of capacity or ability, always refers to domination, whereas the work (of art) arrives only from the utmost un-power of passivity, of 'acting' without intention. Far from being the effect of the intention of an I or ego (of the author), the work is possible only when the I suffers its own total abjection. 'Not-writing' or worklessness is not the same as 'I don't want to write' or 'I cannot write', as the latter cases still relate to power by referring to its loss, to the lost capacity of a still existing I. In order for not-working to 'work' a transition from I to 'it' (the 'neuter' form of the third person singular subjective pronoun, *il*) has to take place. For that transition Blanchot coined the word *subissement*, from the infinitive *subir*, to 'undergo' or to suffer, and the adverb *subitement*, which means 'suddenly'. *Subissement* would thus mean the sudden suffering of letting oneself go from oneself. 'This is abnegation understood as the abandonment of the self', Blanchot explains. Only out of this utmost impersonal passivity of the absence of work will the work start shaping itself. In *The Writing of the Disaster* Melville's Bartleby will function as a figure of such a non-working, as a figure of a non-author whose 'I would prefer not to' is the giving up of the *author*-ity to speak.

B. Arsić

DESPAIR A concept originally denoting the loss of hope, but in modern philosophy seen as a kind of split consciousness or divided self, reflecting the German *Verzweifelung*. In the Preface to his *Phenomenology of Spirit*, Hegel claims that despair in this sense deepens Cartesian doubt (*Zweifel*) in such a way as to lead to a new basis for philosophy. Pursuing the splitting of a concept or form of life to its end will set the stage for a reintegration at a higher level. Rejecting the implication of a necessary movement from despair to reconciliation, Kierkegaard portrayed despair as the basic state of anyone who has not decisively chosen their life through faith. This may either take the form of not daring to be a self at all (despair of weakness) or of affirming an arbitrary and wilful self (despair of defiance). But what can the person who is in despair do about it? He can despair! How does this help? Because in despairing he accepts his truth and thus finds a point of unification of all that is divided within him. Yet this kind of saving despair must be chosen and willed. For Sartre, however, despair is no longer the way to faith but, once more, the abandonment of any hope based on eternal values or truths that might save us from having to choose our values for ourselves. As such, Sartre says, despair is the condition of modem philosophy.

G. Pattison

DETERRITORIALISATION A term used by Deleuze and Guattari in *Anti-Oedipus* and *A Thousand Plateaus* to describe processes of creative destructuring.

Strictly speaking, deterritorialisation is the process of leaving or dismantling a territory, but Deleuze and Guattari's use of the term becomes increasingly general. In *Anti-Oedipus* it refers paradigmatically to the transition from non-state to state societies. For the former, social production always appears, in myth for instance, to emerge from the earth itself. In state societies, notably the ancient empires, however, social production is referred not to the earth but to the body of the despotic emperor, who is the magical source of all value. The transition involves deterritorialisation because of the displacement of territory or the earth from its central organisational role.

In *A Thousand Plateaus* Deleuze and Guattari extend their account beyond a social register into a biological one (territorial animals) and simultaneously broaden their understanding of deterritorialisation to include any process of rupture in the consolidation of matter operating at the level of substance (they call the symmetrical process at the level of form 'decoding'). Such processes are creative because they unblock the underlying absolutely deterritorialised matter flow and make new configurations of matter possible. Deterritorialisation is ambiguous because it is often attended with compensatory processes that forge new territories or impose other rigid types of order. Empires are deterritorialising, for instance, because they replace direct territoriality with an abstract principle of citizenship; but they also invent a bureaucratic apparatus to code the material flows, controlling them in a different way.

A. Welchman

DIALECTIC A term closely associated with Hegel's philosophy, which uses it in several senses. The 'dialectical' method of the *Phenomenology of Spirit* examines philosophical concepts or principles in connection with their purported domains of objects or events as embodied in 'forms of consciousness'. Each form of consciousness is examined on its own terms, internally, to determine the extent to which its key concepts or principles are in fact adequate for their intended domains, and whether their intended domains are also the proper and relevant domains for the concepts, principles and issues under consideration. Hegel's method is modelled in part on Greek tragedy and addresses Sextus Empiricus' 'Dilemma of the Criterion' – the problem of how to justify basic criteria of truth, without dogmatism, vicious circularity or infinite regress. The 'dialectical' method of the *Science of Logic* analyses concepts and other functions of judgement in abstraction from their concrete use, though (in a different way) with regard to their internal coherence and adequacy for their intended domains. 'Dialectical' relations are relations among two or more distinct concepts, objects or events, where these relations are fundamental to the character and behaviour of each relatum. These relations may be synchronic or diachronic, and may be constitutive or conflictual. 'Dialectical' explanations explain phenomena by highlighting their dialectical relations and behaviour.

K. Westphal

DIALECTIC OF ENLIGHTENMENT A phrase taken from the title of a work co-authored by Adorno and Horkheimer, it proposes that some forms of reason produce irrational results. *The Dialectic of Enlightenment* (1947) was the first direct response to the monumental challenge facing German intellectuals after the Second World War: taking responsibility for a culture with an 'unmasterable past'. In addition to its great historical significance, the book inaugurated three main strands of late twentieth-century debate: (1) the meaning of modernity and postmodernity; (2) the philosophical significance of the Holocaust; and (3) the definition of totalitarianism.

In *Dialectic*, Adorno and Horkheimer launch these questions by tracing a genealogy of the Enlightenment's sovereign respect for rationality and its political import. Their argument evolves as a critique of rationality and, more generally, Western reason, which they see inextricably connected to domination. The liberating function of reason with respect to myth and superstition becomes itself a myth, the myth of the Enlightenment, which prevents reason from examining itself critically. What remains concealed and unbridled is the instrumental essence of reason that infects modernity with a strain of self-destructiveness. This is why, with the rise of capitalism and bourgeois society, reason seems to have turned against itself and mutated into totalitarianism and authoritarian conformism.

The history of twentieth-century continental philosophy unfolds as a set of answers to this bleak picture. On the one hand, Habermas, the leading thinker of the second generation of Frankfurt School theorists, claims that while the legacy of the Enlightenment remains healthy, the project of modernity has not run its full course. Therefore, to combat the threat of totalitarianism and genocide, we need more, rather than less, Enlightenment and modernisation. On the other hand, Heidegger, Derrida and Foucault all claim, each in their own way, that what Derrida was to call the 'auto-immunity' of enlightened reason may be contained and controlled but not completely overcome. To achieve this goal, albeit in different ways, all three of them recommend a minute and patient interpretive work aimed at unmasking reason's largely illusory promises.

G. Borradori

DIALECTICAL IMAGE A key concept in the thought of Benjamin, who used it as the methodological cornerstone of *The Arcades Project*. Benjamin never rigorously defined the term, but it is in fact a highly idiosyncratic extension of Marxian dialectics. Marx had theorised an acceleration of the process by which capital realises a profit through the sale of commodities in the marketplace. Benjamin saw that this acceleration had reached a condition of simultaneity: the economic physiognomy and the cultural physiognomy of modern life converged absolutely.

The dialectical image captures this convergence, which becomes a moment of revelatory importance in the study of history. This 'dialectics at a standstill' had both a synchronic and a diachronic significance in Benjamin's esoteric version of historical materialism. Synchronically, it expanded on Marx's concept of commodity fetishism. An ambiguity of paired social and economic relations characterises the dialectical image, an ambiguity that is not epistemological but rooted in the concrete conditions of history itself. In 'Paris, Capital of the Nineteenth Century', written as a synopsis of his *Arcades Project*, Benjamin explained that 'such an image is afforded by the commodity per se: as fetish. Such an image is presented by the arcades, which are house no less than street. Such an image is the prostitute-seller and sold in one'. Diachronically, the dialectical image enters Benjamin's historiography as the saving possibility in which the present perceives not merely particular events of the past but also how it has come to invest these events with present significance.

P. Lewis

DIALECTICAL MATERIALISM The name given to the official philosophy of Marxism-Leninism by its proponents in the Communist Parties of China, Cuba, the erstwhile Soviet Union and its followers in the International Communist Movement. Usually contrasted with 'historical materialism', which designates the theory of history and social philosophy of Marxism, the term was probably first coined by G. Plekhanov in 1891; it was not used by either Marx or Engels. However, in situating his own philosophy, Marx describes himself as a follower of Hegel who turns Hegel's idealism the 'right way up' and sets it 'on its feet'. According to Engels, Marx rejects Hegel's idealism in favour of materialism, and yet he retains Hegel's dialectical method and thus avoids the mechanical form of materialism which had been common among earlier Enlightenment philosophers.

These contrasts are spelled out by Engels in *Anti-Dühring* (1878), *Ludwig Feuerbach and the End of Classical German Philosophy* (1886) and *Dialectics of Nature* (1927). These works constitute the fullest accounts of their philosophy by Marx and Engels. This position is further developed by Lenin, *Materialism and Empirio-Criticism* (1908), and by subsequent Marxist-Leninist philosophers. In *Dialectics of Nature* Engels sets out what he claims to be three fundamental laws of dialectic (unity of opposites, transition of quantity into quality, negation of the negation). These have remained controversial even among avowed Marxists. Indeed, the very idea of a materialist dialectic is disputed by many philosophers otherwise sympathetic to the Hegelian aspects of Marx's thought, such as Lukács and Sartre. Cohen (*Karl Marx's Theory of History*, 1978) and other 'analytical' Marxists have even tried to interpret Marxism without any reference to Hegelian dialectical ideas at all, but this results in fundamental distortions of Marx's thought.

S. Sayers

DIALOGISM A term that can mean simply that our relation to others, God and nature is structured like a dialogue, but its stronger and more exact meaning is that subjects, words and the objects of perception or thought are inseparable from the linguistic or gestural exchanges between interlocutors. For example, Gadamer in *Truth and Method* views history or tradition as the unending and multifaceted transformation of itself into its truth. This transformation takes place through the dialogic exchange – the 'fusion of horizons' – of its participants. History includes these participants in its self-transformative movement by providing them with the subject-matter for their dialogic and creative exchanges, and the participants provide history with the agents it needs for its self-transformation. Because being is inseparable from language and these exchanges, it is also ultimately dialogical.

Bakhtin grants a central role to dialogue also, but without Gadamer's subordination of it to history or tradition. For Bakhtin, dialogue is ultimately creative 'hybridisation'. Even when we speak face to face and in the same 'social language', our words and the objects denoted by them carry the meanings of the other voices that make up our dialogic community. This intersection or interplay of voices constitutes our setting and our destiny; ultimately these exchanges are part of a larger contest between a tendency to produce more social languages (heteroglossia) and a counter tendency (one less favoured by Bakhtin) toward a univocal master language (monoglossia). Dialogue, then, is much more than a mere exchange of words between individuals; it re-enacts the tensions implicit in any social framework.

F. Evans

DIFFÉRANCE A neologism invented by Derrida to mean variously what gives rise to the possibility of difference; or what amounts to a difference without recognising itself as such; or what both defers or delays, and differs at the same time (the verb *différer* in French has both those senses). The word distinguishes itself from 'difference' only in its written form, its difference from difference being a silent one, thereby robbing the spoken word of the 'priority' it assumes over the written, but without introducing itself as a new priority. It is introduced in Derrida's early work on Husserl to account for the differential structure, or 'spacing', that opens up historicity and time-consciousness to its supposedly excluded 'other'.

Derrida insists that *différance* is neither a word nor a concept, nor something that can be understood according to the concept of the sign. By its reference to time-delay it introduces absence into a system of signification that presumes, impossibly, to represent what is present and what supposedly remains present-to-itself throughout the movement (and hence its absence-from-itself) into representation. But the delay or absence inherent in *différance* also has to be understood as something other than a simple postponement, for if it gives rise to difference it is in the sense of precipitating it, 'binding itself necessarily to the form of the instant, in imminence and in urgency', as Derrida puts it in *Specters of Marx*.

D. Wills

DIFFERENCE Against a dominant trend in Western philosophy, which, beginning with Aristotle, thinks difference as logically and ontologically subordinated to identity, a number of twentieth-century continental philosophers (Deleuze and Derrida especially) attempt to free difference from the grip of identity, and show how it is in fact the movement of difference itself that produces the apparent stability of the world of fixed identities (of substances and essences).

For Aristotle, and a whole tradition after him, something (or someone) is different from something (or someone) else only to the extent that they can be subsumed under the identity of a common genus, or kind. Two things can differ only in some particular respect, only on the basis of something they have in common. An apple is different from a banana only to the extent that they are both pieces of fruit. An apple, on the other hand, cannot be said to be different from a hammer, precisely to the extent that the genera 'fruit' and 'tool' cannot be subsumed under a higher, ultimate term that would be common to both. As such, they are simply 'other'. Difference and alterity are thus two different concepts. The former presupposes the unity of a kind, and so is only ever specific (it *specifies* a genus), whereas the latter indicates pure heterogeneity, of which, strictly speaking, there is nothing to say. Whether explicitly or implicitly, identity is primary, and defines a thing in its essence, whereas difference is only ever *secondary* and *derivative*. As such, differences are not essential to the definition (or concept) of a thing. There is a concept of difference, but difference itself is never sufficient to provide the concept of a thing. It does not define the essence (the quiddity) of a thing. It merely indicates some quality of that thing. It does not address that thing in its 'form', but only in its material contingency. Throughout, difference is subordinated to what is known as the principle of identity.

In short, differences as traditionally concerned are qualitative, material, contingent, secondary and derivative.

Against this dominant, Aristotelian conception of difference, a number of twentieth-century thinkers, among whom Deleuze and Derrida figure most prominently, have attempted to show how, in fact, it is differences themselves, and the material, contingent qualities they exhibit, which generate the apparent stability, permanence and self-identity of the concepts that classical metaphysics took as its point of departure. Drawing on advances made in the natural sciences (evolutionary biology, thermodynamics), on recent developments in the social sciences (psychoanalysis, structuralist anthropology, linguistics and semiotics), as well as on proto-differential discourses in philosophy, such as those of Nietzsche, Bergson and Heidegger, these thinkers insist that differences are not accidents occuring to pre-given, self-identical and already constituted substances, but the very background and process against which these seemingly stable and permanent entities are generated. While agreeing that differences address things with relation to the question *qualis* (or 'how?'), and so indicate something like qualities, they refuse to envisage them as material contingencies happening to a substance defined primarily as form and given in advance. Rather, they claim we should understand them as *events* generating pseudo-identities on the basis of a purely differential logic. This means that, far from pointing to stable essences, and to the permanence and self-presence of something like a substance, concepts only ever point to the way in which self-identical and self-present entities are always and already inscribed in an endless chain of displacement and deferal, thus revealing them as metaphysical illusions.

The 'real' world, if we may speak in this way, is thus no longer that of fixed identies and abstract forms, but that of differential processes and structures that result in the illusion of identity and permanence.

At the heart of the philosophies of difference is the ambition to dislodge (and at the same time account for) these metaphysical illusions, and to place philosophy on the path of the discovery of the spatial and temporal dynamisms that are secretly at work behind metaphysics' commitment to self-presence and self-identity. There is a differential space and a differential time that precedes logically that of identity (of classical metaphysics), and to which thought is now to be returned. In the process, and through this reversal, difference can no longer be thought as subsumed under identity, and so as specific difference. It cannot even be thought dialectically, that is as non-identity and as contradiction. For even in speculative dialectic difference turns out to be a moment in the constitution of identity. It is now identity that is a 'moment'of an originary difference, or the 'effect' of a differential logic that can never point to an absolute point of departure or an absolute point at which this logic would terminate. Difference is without beginning or end: it is the pure movement of a term that is never there, a 'term' that is always lacking in its own place, both already no longer here and not yet here, at once late and early, present and absent; and yet, in this double movement, in this spatiality in excess of presence, and this temporality in excess of permanence, everything takes place and sense is produced. The philosophies of difference reveal how, in the phenomenal realm, the seemingly most stable systems, and, in the philosophical realm, the drive to presence and identity, are in fact sustained and under-mined by a purely differential economy.

Twentieth-century continental philosophy thus proposed substitut-ing a principle of difference for that of identity. This is the 'principle' that declares that, for any given superficial identity, whether that of a substance, an essence or a physical system, there is always a deeper, hidden manifold of differences, the 'law' which philosophy articulates. This is the principle that stipulates that, contrary to what Aristotle and the ensuing tradition argued, not only is heterogeneity thinkable, it is also the condition of possibility of thought – even of metaphysical thought – itself.

M. de Beistegui

DIFFEREND A concept developed by Lyotard in *The Differend* (1983) to designate an irresolvable conflict. Two sides of a differend cannot agree to a resolution of an opposition in a common language. This is because any such language or set of rules and goals must favour one side over the other, to the point where one side loses something all-important in the resolution. Lyotard was concerned that terrible events, such as the Holocaust, were betrayed if they were accounted for strictly in terms of acts and descriptions of events. The wrong is so great that it is a betrayal to treat it only in terms of numbers or sums, for example in terms of reparations or comparisons with other genocides. In a differend, something lies beyond accounts and financial values, beyond descriptions and identifications. The question then becomes 'How to do justice to a differend?' Lyotard's answer is firstly that we must testify to the differend, that is show that there is something that cannot simply be resolved or represented. But how can we present the unpresentable? Secondly, therefore, we must appeal to feelings in addition to understanding and knowledge. Only feelings can testify to the differend. In particular, the feeling of the sublime combines pleasure and pain to put us in a state where we sense a presence (pleasure) but equally sense the impossibility of its representation (pain). The differend, then, is a way into an ethics and politics of the sublime, where philosophy adds a testimony for that which is forgotten or excluded, to the resolution of conflicts and the instigation of common measures and rules.

J. Williams

DIFFERENTIATION A term with different uses in biology, mathematics and philosophy. In biology, it refers to the various processes (folding, migrating, dividing and so on) whereby a cell attains its adult form and function. In mathematics, it refers to the process whereby one attains the derivative of an equation (the opposite of integration). In philosophy, it refers to the movement of specification of concepts whereby a genus is divided into its species ('rational' is the *differentia* that divides the genus 'animal' into the species 'human' and 'non-human'). In *Difference and Repetition*, Deleuze attempted to bring all three meanings together in a single philosophical concept: 'We tried to constitute a philosophical concept from the mathematical function of differen*t*iation and the biological function of differen*c*iation.' The calculus – or more precisely, the theory of differential equations – provides Deleuze with his model of purely immanent Ideas (ideal multiplicities defined by their elements, relations and singularities). These Ideas are actualised spatio-temporally through the intervention of intensive quantities (intensity is prior to extensive space), but every actualisation entails a differen*c*iation of an already differen*t*ial Idea. One thus finds in Deleuze a purely differential philosophy of immanent processes that replaces the traditional philosophical move of employing self-identical essences as a principle of individuation.

D. Smith

DILTHEY, WILHELM (1833–1911) German philosopher who contributed to hermeneutics, life-philosophy (*Lebensphilosophie*), interpretive psychology and the philosophy of the human sciences. His work can be divided into three periods: (1) an early period involving empiricist, historicist and romantic tendencies; (2) a middle pragmatic period emphasising psychological inquiry; and (3) a late hermeneutical period.

The early Dilthey developed the epistemological project of 'the empirical without empiricism' in order to unfold a 'critique of historical reason' that would validate the human sciences. In his critique of empiricism, Dilthey argued for the irreducible richness and variety of experience understood from out of itself. Experience is bound to meaning-relating activities and structures that are only understandable in their life-context (*Lebenszusammenhang*). He also used this description of lived-experience to reject traditional metaphysics. Metaphysics conceives the world through a unified point outside the world, assumed to be inherently intelligible, in order to represent the world as a systematic totality. Metaphysics thus separates knowledge from its historical context and the 'totality of human nature'.

In his *Life of Schleiermacher* (1870) and *Introduction to the Human Sciences* (1883), Dilthey interpreted the processes of life immanently and in relation to a dynamic context that is never fully visible. This 'inner' perspective of life implies the original givenness of meaningful structures and processes. 'Inner' thus refers to the life-context, which is inherently worldly and social, while 'outer' refers to the abstraction of objects from their life-nexus. The primary intention of the human sciences is the explication of individuality in its life-context. Individuality presents itself as both the goal and limit of understanding since it cannot be fully articulated. The 'hermeneutical circle' is the unending and irreducible intersection of and movement between individual and context, singular and whole. This dynamic is productive of understanding.

During his middle period Dilthey developed his arguments for the 'acquired psychic nexus', the tension and differentiation of self and world in the experience of resistance, and the categories of life. The acquired psychic nexus indicates the complexity of overlapping functions of the individual as it develops in a historical situation. Dilthey's 'proof' of the external world through the experience of resistance indicates the cogivenness of self/world. Epistemological categories have their basis in the historical and social character of life. Categories such as substance and cause are derived from the prereflective categories of life through which the world is experienced.

In his final period, Dilthey focused on the hermeneutical and social character of sense and meaning in the context of Hegel's objective spirit, which signifies the constitutive role of intersubjectivity for human practices and products. Dilthey analysed historical life in *The Formation of the Historical World in the Human Sciences* (1910) through the relation of lived-experience (*Erlebnis*), expression (*Ausdruck*) and understanding (*Verstehen*). He also developed a 'philosophy of world-views' in order to account for the genesis and conflict of systems of interpretation of meaning. World-views express the tendency to unify experience. Yet the conflict inherent in life (*Widerstreit*) prevents the closure of life in conceptual systems, since they inevitably face their limits in the antinomies and aporias generated by life itself.

E. Nelson

See also: *Lebensphilosophie*

DISAGREEMENT (*mésentente*) The fundamental concept in Jacques Rancière's political philosophy, it undermines the sociological grounding and the institutional focus of classical and contemporary theories of justice. Rancière intends it to be an alternative to Habermas's politics of consensus and to Lyotard's 'differend'. Rancière agrees with these thinkers that politics can be conceptualised as a form of argumentation testing the validity of truth-claims. He remarks, however, that the speech situation in which political discussion takes place should not be taken as a given. On the contrary, the genuine political question concerns the very existence of a shared situation of speech. The hierarchical logic structuring social orders recognises only some beings, some interests and some issues as valid partners and valid objects in the search for consensus or compromise. By asserting the radical equality of all speaking beings, politics are polemical in essence, a challenge to the inegalitarian logic of the social, and more particularly to the expert discourses prevalent in 'post-democratic' societies. The understanding (*entente*) aimed for in standard political discussion, which typically finds its expression in laws and the formal recognition of rights, relies on the existence of a more fundamental misunderstanding (the other sense of *mésentente*) and disagreement over who can understand and be understood and what there is to understand. Rancière's vision of *mésentente* as the real basis of politics thus differs essentially from Lyotard's differend since its radical egalitarian principle leads to the vindication of a common language beyond the heterology of language games.

J.-P. Deranty

DISCLOSEDNESS/RESOLUTE DISCLOSEDNESS (*Erschlossenheit/Entschlossenheit*) Terms used by Heidegger in *Being and Time* to designate the general character of Dasein as the site of truth, and the authentic moment of Dasein's self-revelation. *Erschlossenheit* designates the truth-character of Dasein: Dasein is the being who, in simply being the being that it is, or in existing, opens up or discloses a world. This disclosedness, however, and somewhat paradoxically, is made possible by the ultimate possibility and horizon of Dasein, namely death. Death is the possibility of the end or the total closure of existence. At the same time, however, it is also the possibility that opens up all other possibilities, the possibility that makes disclosedness as such possible. *Entschlossenheit* characterises one distinct possibility, one distinct way in which Dasein can be disclosed to the world and to itself, and that is as this finite, essentially temporal being that it is. In 'resolute disclosedness', Dasein relates to its own being as 'being-towards-death'. It is a moment of total individuation. As such, it is the highest possibility, for in it Dasein comes face to face with itself as the 'ek-sistent' being or as truth. In *Entschlossenheit*, it is the essence of existence as *Erschlossenheit* that is taken up again or repeated, yet the way in which it is taken up makes all the difference for existence. Specifically, it amounts to the difference between authenticity and inauthenticity, between the loss or dissolution of individuality and total individuation. Ultimately, this repetition amounts to a doubling and hence an intensification of existence. It is existence brought to the second power, existence existed to the full and made fully transparent to itself.

M. de Beistegui

DISCOURSE ETHICS An approach to ethics mainly developed by Apel and Habermas (with important historical antecedents in the Socratic method of dialogue and in the social and political writings of Mill, Kant and George Herbert Mead) that appeals to models of free, equal, undistorted and inclusive communication as a touchstone for moral deliberation. Its major claim is that moral deliberation is a collective process of reasoning that is best exemplified in democratic forums. In this respect it is quite antithetical to modes of moral deliberation that take as their point of departure the lone individual who relies for guidance solely on subjective moral feelings and judgements, such as the 'inner voice' of moral conscience, reason, natural sentiment or divine revelation. Such feelings and judgements no doubt guide our actions, but discourse ethics recommends that they be shaped and transformed in ongoing discussions with others who feel and think differently, for only this process provides a critical check on our irrational and otherwise contentious opinions. Even in the moment of decision, when discussion has ceased and one must act, persons should always try to imagine how others – those actually affected by one's decisions as well as the 'ideal' community of humanity – would regard their choice. This raises two important qualifications in the application of discourse ethics. First, discourse ethics works best in political arenas, in which persons are deliberating together about shared norms of social cooperation. For discourse ethics, only norms that have the general and uncoerced consent of all are truly binding for each taken individually. Second, discourse ethics sharply distinguishes 'sub-rational' discussions whose resolutions are 'constrained' and less binding from those that approximate the conditions of ideal speech.

D. Ingram

DREYFUS, HUBERT (1929–) American philosopher who has made remarkable contributions to the two ways of doing 'continental philosophy' in North America. On the one hand, he has written scholarly books about specific contemporary European philosophers. For example, he has published books on Heidegger (*Being-in-the-World*, 1991) and Foucault (with Paul Rabinow, *Michel Foucault: Beyond Structuralism and Hermeneutics*, 1983; *Heidegger and Foucault on the Ordering of Things*, forthcoming); an anthology on Husserl (*Husserl, Intentionality and Cognitive Science*, 1982) and another on Heidegger (*Heidegger: A Critical Reader*, 1992); and an edited translation of some of Merleau-Ponty's essays (with Patricia Allen Dreyfus, *Sense and Nonsense*, 1964) as well as numerous articles on Merleau-Ponty. On the other hand, Dreyfus has 'applied' phenomenology and other methods originating in contemporary European thought to problems in psychology, technology and other areas that have been dominated by quantitative methods and analytic philosophy in North America. In this regard, he has published critical books on cognitive science and artificial intelligence (*What Computers Can't Do: A Critique of Artificial Reason*, 1972, 1979, 1992); expert systems and skill acquisition (with Stuart E. Dreyfus, *Mind over Machine: The Power of Human Intuitive Expertise in the Era of the Computer*, 1986); capitalism and democracy (with Charles Spinosa and Fernando Flores, *Disclosing New Worlds: Entrepreneurship, Democratic Action, and the Cultivation of Solidarity*, 1997); and the Internet (*On the Internet*, 2001). These publications, as well as the many honours Dreyfus has received and the number of editorial boards to which he has been appointed, attest to his central role in the growth of North American continental philosophy.

Dreyfus's criticism of cognitive science and other attempts to reduce human cognition to computational rules or algorithms is almost always three-pronged. First, he shows that the discipline in question over-states the case for its expected success. Second, he demonstrates that the optimism of these researchers is due to unwarranted assumptions they make about the nature of cognition and its surroundings. Third, he provides an alternative, non-computational account of cognition that solves the problems blocking the computational paradigm. In *What Computers Can't Do*, for example, Dreyfus shows that in each new phase of research in cognitive science – cognitive simulation, semantic information processing, micro-world manipulation and knowledge representation – researchers claimed that their early suc-cesses in specific contexts would soon allow them to create programs that could duplicate general human intelligence. But this optimism was and is still not fulfilled. In order to explain this immediate but unwarranted optimism, Dreyfus shows that cognitive scientists assume that we initially encounter a world of discrete, fully determinate features or objects, and that computational rules are all that is required for processing the 'information' that these sorts of entities provide. In response to these assumptions, Dreyfus argues along with Merleau-Ponty and Heidegger that we first grasp the world as a whole: our minds are embodied and our bodies are always already engaged with our surroundings. Only on this basis are we then able to recognise, manipulate or otherwise make sense of the specific aspects of our world. Moreover, phenomenology or some other qualitative method is re-quired for understanding our body's non-computational grasp of the world and the more specific forms of cognition based on that grasp.

F. Evans

See also: Cognitive Science; naturalising phenomenology; Psy-chology

DROMOLOGY A term coined by Paul Virilio in *Speed and Politics* for the study of the way speed is inherently connected to wealth creation, a link that can be seen in the political economy of speed. For Virilio, the political economy of speed can be observed in the historically increas-ing velocity of state apparatuses, as they affect geographical space and the human body. Dromology studies the inexorable acceleration of human societies wherein the fastest speeds are the exclusive preserve of the social elite and the slowest speeds are the all-embracing realm of the socially disadvantaged.

In *A Thousand Plateaus* Deleuze and Guattari cite Virilio's dromo-logical texts while elucidating their 'nomadological' treatise of the war machine. In this treatise, Deleuze and Guattari propose that 'nomad existence has for "affects" the weapons of a war machine'. A nomadic way of life is therefore premised on they way weapons and tools have different speeds, since weapons, unlike tools, have a 'projective character'. Moreover, Deleuze and Guattari refer to Virilio's conception of dromology when examining contemporary processes of militarisation. Indeed, the war machine triggers a vector of speed so identifiable with it that Deleuze and Guattari in homage to Virilio have named it 'dromocracy'.

J. Armitage

DURATION (*durée*) In *Time and Free Will*, Bergson argues that both philosophy and science tend to conceive of time as an empty, homogenous medium, within which temporal events can be compared with one another and thus quantitatively measured. However, this way of thinking is appropriate to space rather than time, and whenever time is conceived in this way, it is thereby 'spatialised'. When experienced directly, we find that temporal events *endure*. Time, or duration (*durée*), is characterised by the 'succession without distinction' or the 'mutual interpenetration' of its parts. Time is thus continuous, whereas space is discrete. As a consequence, the parts of time or of temporal events cannot be set alongside one another, and thus quantitatively compared and measured, as can spatial entities, because they melt into one another. The difference between the parts of time or temporal events is qualitative rather than quantitative. Bergson thus defines 'pure duration' as 'a succession of qualitative changes, which melt into and permeate one another, without precise outlines, without any tendency to externalize themselves in relation to one another, without any affiliation with number: it would be pure heterogeneity'. While the process of intuition leading to this definition is quasi-phenomenological, Bergson's account of the relation between time and memory (in *Matter and Memory*) differs fundamentally from Husserl's. Moreover, in *Creative Evolution*, he proceeds to explore the metaphysical and ontological dimensions of his initial theory, exploring the implications of the argument that evolution and life are fundamentally durational.

R. Durie

DUTY (*Pflicht*) A central concept in Kant's critical moral philosophy, the point of departure of which is the notion of a 'possible pure will' considered in abstraction from human volition. The latter is indeed considered to be a mixture of pure will and 'sensuous motives' which points to a tension within human volition. From the standpoint of the pure will, human volition is subject to restraint through duty. Duty ensures through the categorical imperative that action is consistent with the law of the pure will but is also the occasion for a feeling of respect (*Achtung*) for the law. Moral action is that which is fully in accord with duty. The *Critique of Practical Reason* situates this account of duty in a broader theological context, anticipating the link between divine commands and duty developed in *Religion within the Limits of Reason Alone*. The main application of the concept of duty to practical philosophy is, however, to be found in the *Metaphysics of Morals*. There Kant developed a complex series of distinctions between juridical and ethical, positive and negative and perfect and imperfect duties. Juridical duties are those conducted according to duty, but not necessarily *from* duty, the latter comprising ethical duties. Positive duties command while negative duties forbid possible courses of action; imperfect duties are broadly, while perfect duties are narrowly, formulated. These distinctions are mobilised in a complex system of moral and legal casuistry that nevertheless never loses sight of the theological context from which the concept of duty emerged.

H. Caygill

EARTH AND WORLD A term that appears in Heidegger's work in the 1930s. The concept of world was omnipresent in the early work, where 'worldhood' designated the very being of Dasein. The concept of earth appears in the later work only, however, and almost always alongside that of world. This pair of notions must be thought on the basis of the essence of truth as involving a double and internally strife-ridden movement of clearing and concealing, as in the problematic of '*aletheia*'. In 'The Origin of the Work of Art' (1935), Heidegger claims that the work of art (and no longer simply existence) is a happening, or an instance, of truth; the way in which the work of art puts truth to work is by setting up the 'strife' of world and earth. The world signifies that which first lets things be, lets them come to presence. It is the open expanse in which things and human beings find their place and are related to one another. (This is a de-subjectivising of Husserlian intentionality or Kantian transcendental subjectivity.) The earth, on the other hand, signifies the force that harbours, secures and so conceals things from world. Earth resists the drive to openness and disclosure of world; it withdraws from all efforts to disclose and penetrate it; it is essentially undisclosable and self-secluding. (This seclusion testifies to the de-subjectivising of traditional philosophy that Heidegger undertakes: the opening up of a world is not a subjective act, so we can say that the origin of the open or the world is not open to us or under our control; rather, it pulls away and hides, as earth.) Earth and world are bound together by an eternal strife, each pulling in a different direction as it were. In the age of technology and consumed metaphysics, the withdrawing and self-secluding power of earth has all but withdrawn. Art and 'meditative thought', as in a practice of *Gelassenheit* alone, can still intimate its power.

M. de Beistegui

ECO, UMBERTO (1932–) Italian semiotician and novelist, who achieved international fame with the publication in 1980 of *The Name of the Rose* – a murder mystery which reflects both his semiotic and medieval interests. This celebrity semiotician (an oxymoron that can only be employed for Eco) believes that mainstream contemporary philosophy should not sideline semiotics. In *A Theory of Semiotics* (1976) he declared that 'semiotics is concerned with everything that can be *taken* as a sign'. In this work he sought to combine aspects of European structuralism and the semiotics of Peirce.

One of Eco's central concerns is reflected in the title *The Role of the Reader* (1979). As Peirce had noted, a sign is not a sign until it is interpreted – a notion pursued further in Eco's *Semiotics and the Philosophy of Language* (1984). While Saussure had established that signs always relate to other signs, within his model the relationship between signifier and signified was stable and predictable. Drawing upon Peirce's notion of the 'interpretant', Eco coined the term 'un-limited semiosis' to refer to the way in which the signified can function in its turn as a signifier for a further signified. 'Open' texts can have multiple interpretations, although unlike many postmodernists Eco regards such interpretations as subject to constraints; for Eco, such constraints demand a detective reader seeking an interpretation jus-tified by the evidence. Like the structuralist semioticians Eco also locates signs within codes – to which one must refer in interpreting signs. These include both denotative and connotative codes. Eco's codes are more open, dynamic and related to social context than conventional structuralist models; meaning is dependent on users' variable competence in using codes and subcodes. 'Aberrant decoding' occurs thus when a text is decoded by means of a different code from that used to encode it.

A Theory of Semiotics should be read in conjunction with *Kant and the Platypus* (1999) – an exploration of the relationship between language, cognition and reality. Eco has declared that his abiding concern is with the ways in which we give meaning to the world. In a stance which critics interpret as idealism but which does not, as Saussure had done, 'bracket' reference to a world beyond the sign system, Eco insists that language does not merely mediate reality but is involved in its construction. Hence his provocative declaration that 'semiotics is in principle the discipline studying everything which can be used in order to lie'.

D. Chandler

ECOCRITICISM A loose collection of interpretive stances which emerged as a discernable 'school' of literary criticism and theory in the mid-1990s (centred in the journal *ISLE: Interdisciplinary Studies in Literature and the Environment*). Ecocriticism includes a variety of projects concerned with the relation of literature and the environment: the study of 'nature writing' from any critical perspective whatsoever (in an attempt to move such writing from the margins to the centre of the literary canon); conversely, the study of any text whatsoever from an ecological perspective (in an attempt to show the universal relevance of such a perspective); perhaps most significantly – following upon the recognition that 'nature' is in part defined by cultural forms such as language, art and literature – the attempt to alter for the better the human comportment toward the non-human world by promoting literary and artistic works that will help foster new and beneficial understandings of 'nature'.

It is in pursuing this latter project that ecocriticism draws upon continental philosophy, most notably upon the 'deep ecology' formulated by the Norwegian philosopher Arne Naess. From the perspective of 'deep ecology', much contemporary environmentalism is 'shallow' in that it does not question fundamental norms and, in its anthropocentric understanding of nature's value, fails to challenge the capitalist exploitation of nature. In his effort to overcome the dualistic division between human self-interest and the interests of non-human nature, Naess draws especially upon his reading of Spinoza's *Ethics*, which for Naess urges us to develop the most expansive possible sense of self, ultimately to identify ourselves with others, including the other which we call 'nature'. Naess, by identifying the interests of humankind with the interests of nature, offers an alternative to previous environmental ethics, which have attributed to nature a value that is either 'intrinsic' (entirely unrelated to humankind) or 'instrumental' (entirely dependent on human use). Ecocriticism has also been drawn to Heidegger's later writings (the early Heidegger's insistence on an absolute distinction between human existence and animal life does not appeal to ecocritics), especially for their critique of the world-view of modern technology (which sees all things as raw materials or resources for human domination) and for the notion of 'letting things be' (*Gelassenheit*), which in Heideggerian terms means holding open the clearing in which the being of entities may be allowed to emerge, rather than claiming to hold definitive knowledge concerning 'what things are'.

G. Stone

ÉCRITURE FÉMININE ('feminine writing') A phrase used by Hélène Cixous in the mid-1970s to address what she perceived then as the impasses of discourses on sexual difference which construe difference as a binary opposition and thereby generate unceasing controversies over essentialism. In three essays, 'The Laugh of the Medusa' (1975), 'Sorties' in *The Newly-Born Woman*, written with Catherine Clément (1975), and 'Coming to Writing' (1977), Cixous insists that difference should not be construed 'on the basis of socially distributed "sexes" ' ('Sorties'). The feminine, which is not necessarily the female, is hospitable to alterity, opening to it without appropriating calculations, giving itself away without return. If Cixous privileges 'writing woman', it is because historically woman has not been allowed to write her own 'instinctual economy', her body, her *jouissance*, which might effectively undo prevailing notions of sexual difference, and invent another history. Examples of rethinking difference include recasting bisexuality as the co-location of both sexes and not the fantasy of one complete being ('Sorties'), as well as questioning the metaphysical opposition between the human and the animal ('Coming to Writing'). Cixous insists that the practice of feminine writing cannot be theorised and coded; it responds to no existing programme.

B. Weltman-Aron

EIDETIC REDUCTION The act by which the Husserlian phenomenologist gains access to the essences (or 'eide') that he or she studies. What is meant by 'essence' and its terminological equivalent, 'eidos', is an invariant structure of pure intentional experience that is inseparable from the transcendent sense of such experience's subjective and objective dimensions. The key moment of the eidetic reduction is the cognitive regard's withdrawal of attention from the contingent and empirical aspects of experience, such that the *eide* they adumbrate are highlighted and made capable of being thematically apprehended. This focus on the essential is accomplished by a process of 'variation' in which elements of the target experience are systematically changed, until such change renders the target experience unrecognisable as that from which it began. That which cannot be so changed in the process of variation is the essence or *eidos*. The resultant thematic apprehension of the *eidos* is characterised by Husserl as 'essential' or 'eidetic' seeing.

B. Hopkins

EK-SISTENZ ('ek-sistence') A term used by Heidegger in his 'Letter on Humanism' (1946) to describe the essence of the human: the human is the being that is open to being, that is, open to the Open itself. It is the being who is disclosed and exposed to the facticity of the 'there is', open not only to this or that being, but to the fact that beings are, and to the fact that 'being' is itself in excess of 'beings', that is, open to the 'ontological difference'. The human is the being who has always and already been drawn into the clearing of being, who always moves itself within a pre-understanding of it. In his later work (from the 1930s onward), Heidegger interprets this openness to the Open as such in historical and destinal terms: the destiny (or the fate) of the human is to be drawn into the truth of being, and its history is played out in the manner in which it responds to this call, or to the way in which it hears this address of being. Ek-sistence signals the destiny of the human being, as the being whose being is freed for truth. It is because the human being is made to respond to the call of being that it is responsible for it. The distinct responsibility of the human lies in its responsiveness to the truth of being.

M. de Beistegui

ÉLAN VITAL ('vital impulse') One of the most notorious, and mis-understood, of all philosophical concepts, *élan vital* is invariably cited by both scientists and philosophers who wish to dismiss Bergson as a mere metaphysician or as an outmoded vitalist. But Bergson himself is explicitly critical of naive vitalism, is adamant that metaphysics can be of value to science and argues that *élan vital* is a notion derived from actual experience. In *Creative Evolution*, Bergson demonstrates that reductive, mechanistic, science is unable to account for the movement of evolution. The notion of *élan vital* designates those aspects of life and the movement of evolution which are irreducible to mechanistic explanation. Among these are the tendency of evolution towards greater complexity and the indivisibility of the whole organism, expressed in the co-ordination of its parts, which contributes to the ability of an organism to adapt to environmental changes. But the most significant stems from Bergson's account of duration. If evolution could be explained by mechanism, then, Bergson argues, the forms adopted by life in the future could be deduced according to the principle of mechanistic determinism. However, to the extent that duration is the 'essential attribute of life', such forms are unpredictable in the strict sense, just as, in time, the future cannot be predicted on the basis of the past or present. In the final analysis, therefore, *élan vital* is the mark of the irreducible temporality of life, and hence of evolution, and thus designates the fundamental creativity of both life and evolution.

R. Durie

EMBODIMENT A term with two philosophical senses: (1) the concrete expression of human being in a body; (2) the concrete expression of ideas, concepts and meanings in things, linguistic signifiers or social institutions. Both these senses can have negative or positive implications.

Implied in both senses of embodiment is the idea of the incarnation or expression in material form of a non-material attribute which is assumed to precede its embodiment. So, for example, within the context of Descartes' philosophy where human existence is said to centre on a thinking, non-material substance, the embodiment of that consciousness (in a biomechanical, causally determined body) is viewed as incidental and subsequent to the essence of human being. Similarly, if concepts are assumed to be immaterial entities, then their embodiment in and expression through material signifiers is said to be secondary to the origin and essence of meaning. In both cases embodiment tends to be viewed as a problem: a potential hindrance to achieving rational subjectivity in the case of human embodiment, and the source of the corruption of meaning in the case of the embodiment of ideas and concepts. However, these two general senses of embodiment already assume a dualism (between mind and body, reason and passion, meaning and expression, culture and nature) that continental philosophers find highly questionable. Where that dualism is in question, the meaning of embodiment takes on a more specific and positive significance: the expression of human being in a body, and of ideas and meanings in material signifiers, becomes a primordial rather than an incidental and secondary feature of human existence and the expression of meaning.

With respect to human existence, this positive doctrine of embodiment consists in various accounts of this embodied state that revise accepted understandings of corporeality and the corporeal dimension of human agency, perception, thinking, sociality and so on. In so far as human existence is thereby characterised in a way that falls between materialism and idealism, the human body is characterised as irreducible to a biophysical, causally determined mechanism of Cartesian philosophy and of some forms of contemporary materialism. And insofar as these models of embodiment deal with the incorporation of social norms and ideas in instances of human existence, there is a convergence between accounts of human embodiment and embodiment with respect to the expression of meaning.

Contemporary continental philosophers interested in embodiment tend to follow one of three approaches: (1) a Spinozist, monist account that requires radical revision of the very notion of the embodiment of a mind; (2) a materialist investigation of the role of the body in the formation of subjectivity through 'subjectivising' practices; (3) a phenomenological description of the role of the body in the workings of subjectivity.

The first approach relies on Spinoza's critique of Descartes' substance dualism. In Spinoza's monism the mind is an 'idea of' the body; mind and body are the same substance conceived under two different 'attributes' (what the 'intellect perceives of a substance as constituting its essence'). Therefore the human body does not contain a mind nor do bodies incorporate pre-existing ideas; rather, every 'mode' of extension is identical with the 'idea of' that mode. In this way the very idea of 'embodiment' is brought radically into question.

Two aspects of Nietzsche's accounts of embodiment have been influential for materialist accounts of subjectivising practices. First, his account in the Second Essay of *On the Genealogy of Morals* (1887) of the social constitution of the responsible subject through the 'mnemotechnics of pain' proposes that moral norms are incorporated through punishment; in this way, the conscious expression of moral ideas presupposes a prior 'interpretation' by bodies subjected to such practices. Second, Nietzsche's doctrine of 'will-to-power' includes the idea that bodies, including human bodies, are 'works of art'; bodies are forces, sets of effects or 'quanta of power' in relation to other quanta of power that, through resistance, measurement, evaluation and interpretation, form complexes of power and meaning. Both these ideas of embodiment foreshadow Foucault's influential thesis that the human body is the locus of subjection (social control and subject formation). In *Discipline and Punish* (1975) Foucault argues that the human body is the site of the operation of 'micro-techniques of power', such as disciplinary power, which, in concert with prevailing social norms and knowledges of the human sciences, form self-regulating bodies that enact ideas that do not need to pass through consciousness. In *A Thousand Plateaus* (1980) Deleuze and Guattari develop the idea of a 'body without organs' more reminiscent of Nietzsche's quanta of power: the body without organs describes the corporeal intensities, powers and flows that exceed and defy organisation and regulation into a meaningful, proper body.

The third, phenomenological, approach, which focuses on embodied subjectivity, is best exemplified by Merleau-Ponty, who claims that we live our body and perceive another body, not as a body-in-itself ('objective body') in objective space but a body in meaningful situation ('body subject'). The central thesis of his *Phenomenology of Perception* (1945) is the primacy of perception of the body as I live it: against the privileging of 'objective thought' within philosophy Merleau-Ponty argues that perception, and hence knowledge, is pre-reflective and grounded in a body acting through the world in which it is embedded (where the 'world' is at once social and material). One feature of embodied perception, so understood, is that meaning is necessarily ambiguous and open to transformation; another related feature is that embodiment is intercorporeal such that meaning comes as much from the world and the other as from oneself. As these ideas of ambiguity and intercorporeality are developed through Merleau-Ponty's later work, he tends to drop the emphasis on perception by a 'body subject' favouring instead the primacy of sensibility through 'flesh' (the 'intertwining' of bodies and of ideas and the corporeal). Throughout his work, Merleau-Ponty brings together human embodiment with the embodiment of meaning, understanding both in terms exemplified by the following formula: the body expresses existence, not as a symbol of an external or inner idea; the body expresses existence (and therefore meaning) as it realises it through sensibility in the 'undividedness of the sensing and the sensed' ('Eye and Mind').

Since the 1980s corporeal feminists have adopted these perspectives in their efforts to develop and refine the notion of embodiment, thus revising understandings of sociality, ethics, aesthetics, politics and biomedical practice.

R. Diprose

See also: Corporeal Feminism; Feminism

EMPIRE Antonio Negri's term, developed in collaboration with Michael Hardt in their 2000 book of that name, for the socio-political constitution of contemporary capitalist globalisation. Unlike traditional models of imperialism, which functioned through the polarity between a metropolitan European national centre and a colonised non-European periphery, Empire is not centred in any nation-state that controls the system, and consequently it has no periphery; centres of capitalist accumulation exist even in the most impoverished nations, and even the US, the 'sole superpower', is subject to Empire's overall command. This functional universality of capitalist relations characterises the real subsumption of global society within capital. Empire operates through anti-democratic non-governmental organisations like the International Monetary Fund (IMF) and World Trade Organisation (WTO), as well as multinational corporations, all of which subordinate nation-states as more or less interchangeable instruments for the management of labouring populations. These populations, whose flexibility and mobility mirror the features of the capital that commands them and the commodities they produce, are subject to constant processes of surveillance, measurement and reorganisation that Hardt and Negri, following Foucault, call biopower or biopolitics. The rule of Empire claims to suspend history in a perpetual present which is constituted as a continuous state of exception or emergency; since it has no external enemy upon whom to wage war, it justifies its deployment of violence as police action, legitimated by international consensus, against terrorism and subversion. The only possible opposition to Empire must arise from the denationalised labouring populations that comprise the multitude, the heretofore unorganised collective political subject of globalisation.

T. Murphy

ENACTION The process whereby a world is brought forth by the interaction or structural coupling between an embodied agent and its medium or environment; also the study of the manner in which a subject of perception creatively matches its actions to the requirements of its situation. The term was coined by Francisco Varela, Evan Thompson and Eleanor Rosch in *The Embodied Mind* (1991), and applies a number of Varela's own theses about biological autonomy to cognitive science. The enactive approach tries to present itself as a middle path between the cognitivist vision of an essentially representational mind and connectionist models of the emergence of mind from networks of neuron-like units. While sympathetic to the aim of cognitive science, the concept of enaction belongs to the project of a 'naturalised phenomenology'. It relates to the notion of 'being-in-the-world', and borrows from Merleau-Ponty's early work on the structure of behaviour, as well as from aspects of Piaget's evolutionary epistemology.

Varela and his colleagues depict action (or sensori-motor behaviour) as perceptually guided just as perception is dependent on action. On this ground, enaction is used to repudiate both radical subjectivism (or idealism) and radical objectivism (or realism), both of which are viewed as wedded to an untenable representational stance. Like Merleau-Ponty, Varela and his colleagues are concerned with the 'bringing forth' (enactment) of meaning out of a history of embodied perceptual activity, reliant on sedimented cultural and phylogenetic factors and not grounded in any transcendental subjectivity or material structure (whence the role of Buddhist anti-foundationalism in this approach).

A. Toscano

ENGELS, FRIEDRICH (1820–95) German communist social theorist, philosopher and revolutionary, and close associate of Marx. The son of a textile manufacturer, Engels became attracted to radical and Left Hegelian ideas while in school. After military service and before taking up a career in the family business he became involved with Young Hegelian circles in Berlin. After a visit to England he wrote *The Condition of the Working Class in England* (1845), a pioneering work of social analysis and criticism of industrial conditions in Manchester. He met Marx soon after writing this book and the two jointly wrote a series of works in which the fundamental principles of Marxism were first worked out: *The Holy Family* (1844), *The German Ideology* (written 1845, first fully published 1932) and *The Communist Manifesto* (1848). He fled Germany after the defeat of the 1848 revolutions and settled in Manchester in 1850, where he worked for the family firm and helped Marx financially and intellectually.

Over the years, Engels became increasingly interested in philosophy and the natural sciences; this interest resulted in *Anti-Dühring* (1878) and *Ludwig Feuerbach and the End of Classical German Philosophy* (1886). His notes on the natural sciences were published posthumously as *Dialectics of Nature* (1927). Together these works provide the fullest accounts of Marxist philosophy. Engels's pamphlet *Socialism: Utopian and Scientific* (1880, an abridged portion of *Anti-Dühring*) is one of the clearest accounts of Marxism as a social and political theory, and one of the most widely read works of Marxism. He also wrote a substantial work based on notes of Marx, *Origin of the Family, Private Property and the State* (1884), which has had a major influence in the field of anthropology. After Marx's death in 1883, Engels devoted much of his considerable energy to editing and publishing the second and third volumes of *Capital* (1885, 1894). As the leading figure of the communist movement after Marx's death, he also conducted an enormous correspondence as well as playing a leading role in founding the Second International.

His contribution to the philosophy of science has been very

controversial. In *Dialectics of Nature*, he attempts to codify the basic principles of Marxist philosophy, which came to be called 'dialectical materialism', into three fundamental 'laws of dialectic': (1) the law of the unity of opposites; (2) the law of transition of quantity into quality; (3) the law of the negation of the negation. These 'laws' became part of the orthodox philosophy of official communist parties throughout the international communist movement for much of the twentieth century. They are rejected and dismissed by many other philosophers, including many sympathetic to Marxism and even to dialectic. Engels's insistence that there is a 'dialectic of nature' is similarly controversial. Nevertheless, Engels has a clear and straightforward literary style, which avoids the Hegelian formulations of which Marx is so fond. His works have been the main popular expositions of Marxism and have probably been read at least as widely as those of Marx himself. He was engaged in preparing the fourth volume of *Capital* (subsequently published as *Theories of Surplus Value*, 3 volumes, 1905–10) when he died in London in 1895.

S. Sayers

See also: contradiction (2); dialectical materialism; historical materialism; ideology; Marxism

ENLIGHTENMENT (*Aufklärung*) A process of critical self-questioning that arises as a double-sided aspect of modernity, at least as conceived of in Kant's essay, 'What is Enlightenment?' (1784). On the one hand, it expressed the 'age of criticism', identified as the defining mark of Kant's time in the *Critique of Pure Reason*: the process of enlightenment is the release from tutelage, enacted through the public, rational critique of religious and metaphysical sureties that hold sway, not because of their immanent rationality, but through the weight of external authorities. On the other hand, enlightenment pushes beyond criticism through reason's capacity to provide a positive foundation for the moral ordering of individual and social life. The self-enacted release from tutelage was not a launch into the chaos of individual assertion, but into the harmony of universal law. And, if a people were not yet enlightened, they could be provided for, in the meantime, by a monarch who allows the public use of reason, and makes laws that the people could approve, if they were motivated solely by respect for the rational law. Thus, if the critical aspect of enlightenment, in Kant's account, precedes the onset of its positive instantiation, it does so only through the decisiveness of political power. So political power itself is inured against the practical thrust of critique: 'You are free to question, only *obey*!' becomes the motto for a people whose path towards self-administration tends to become progress towards an ever-delayed goal. Critique, severed from political action, lives in the hope that a rational culture will produce enlightened administrators who alone retain an agency capable of enacting the enlightenment's positive aspirations.

Recent efforts at assessing enlightenment as a process have generally been less optimistic about the potential of an ostensibly universal reason to negotiate the divide between critique and the administration of powers. If one follows Marx and Nietzsche in seeing rational structures as products of and intercessions in historical fields of power, then the transcendental universality that underwrote reason's promotion of harmony as the end of history comes under suspicion. In his late work on 'political rationality', Foucault offered such a critique: ideas of law as the progressive actualisation of universal norms masks the extent to which all laws are embedded in determinate practices of power, including the modern state forms of disciplinary, pastoral and bio-political power, which structure the very lives of individuals and populations.

This does not mean that Foucault dispenses with enlightenment altogether. Rather, he finds in Kant's essay the model for a critical attitude in which the present moment interrogates its meaning and practices by articulating its relationship to the past. And, as for Kant, such an articulation is a liberatory practice, in so far as it involves a coming-to-awareness regarding forces that delimit our possibilities and pleasures. Only, for Foucault, this critical element of enlightenment is decisively separated from the universalist aspirations of Kant's historical and political writings. What the critical attitude embodies, rather, is an effort to dispense with grand narratives, to recognise the present's relationship to the past as a complex web of emergence and descent. 'Enlightenment' is modelled by genealogical critique; its practices of freedom lie not in the grounding of transcendental norms of reason but in its unmasking of such norms as the product of contingent events, singular constellations in determinate fields of power. The present shakes off the weight of the past by recognising the past in its determinacy, as constituted by a web of powers and discourses.

If Foucault, thus, reconceives and recuperates the critical aspect of enlightenment, his conception of its 'positive' aspect is more ambiguous, at least when compared to Kant's progressive, rational history. Foucault, no doubt, would have insisted that the ambiguity and provisional status of positive political formulations is precisely what one must embrace in a history of singular events. But others, including Habermas, have insisted that Foucault provides no positive ground according to which political improvements can be pursued and assessed, a failure that would vacate the hopes embedded in enlightenment discourse. For Habermas, Foucault's genealogy is grounded in an 'ontology of power', which provides no space for the conception of freedom, precisely because all positions are equally determined by structures of power that eclipse the agency of any subject.

Habermas does not entirely reject Marxist and Nietzschean notions of reason's implication in structures of power, but he does attempt to limit the extent of that implication. The positive hopes of enlightenment rationality can be rescued, he insists, by the recognition and affirmation of a divide within the modalities of reason itself. Modern thought has generally understood reason as solely instrumental, as a tool for mastery, in light of which all efforts to know are efforts to control and determine. But neither this link between knowledge and power, nor its critical exposition, exhaust the potentials of reason in Habermas's mind. Rather, the communicative function of reason – the structures through which discussion, exchange and consensus are achieved – can be understood to provide a basis for the articulation of a positive practice and goal. The tacit structures and commitments of communicative speech, that is, reveal a 'quasi-transcendental' set of norms that function as guidelines for the production and organisation of speech communities, which, in their processes of decision-making, would be free from the dominating aspects of power. The positive aspect of enlightenment can be saved precisely through the articulation and enactment of such a set of norms, which needs neither to remain unaware of, nor resign itself to, the intersections of reason and social power.

That critics of Habermas have been sceptical of the manner in which such 'quasi-transcendental' norms can find articulation outside of, and enactment within, the social fields of power suggests the extent to which – in its broad terms – the debate over enlightenment remains in the shadow of its Kantian dilemma: to what extent can reason's reflective ability to map the powers that shape its understanding provide an index and guide for actual practices of liberation?

M. Bray

ENVIRONMENTAL PHILOSOPHY The term for a relatively recent movement incorporating a variety of philosophical issues concerning the human relation to the natural environment. Originally formulated in the 1970s as a branch of applied ethics – so that it was at the time largely associated with analytic philosophy – environmental philosophy has become a vital component of continental philosophy as well. In doing so, its scope has expanded to include not just 'environmental ethics', but also issues of an aesthetic and theological character; the possibility of a new philosophy, and perhaps even a new metaphysics, of nature; environmental dimensions of policy and technology; and the issues of bioregionalism and geopolitical praxis.

Early 'environmental ethics' explored the extent to which existing ethical theories could be expanded to include the natural environment; it also proposed new ethical formulations that to varying degrees challenged the boundaries of then current moral philosophy. Figures associated with such early work include Baird Callicott, Eugene Hargrove, Don Marietta and Holmes Ralston. All of them have remained active the field, but none have been very strongly influenced by continental philosophy. Founded in 1979, the journal *Environmental Ethics* published much of this early work and continues to be the leading journal in the area; for some time now it also publishes articles that go well beyond the limits of the ethical.

Many figures in continental philosophy can be seen as precursors to environmental philosophy. In the nineteenth century, Schelling's *Naturphilosophie*, Feuerbach's emphasis on the embodied and species character of human existence, Kropotkin's ecological view of human society and Nietzsche's call to 'be true to the earth' should all be seen as anticipations of environmental sensibilities. In the twentieth century, we find Heidegger's emphasis on poetic dwelling, on saving the earth and his technology critique; Merleau Ponty's phenomenology of the 'lived body'; and Bachelard's poetics of the elements. Max Scheler, in *The Nature of Sympathy* (1912), devoted an important section to the human sense of unity with the cosmos (*kosmiche Einsfühlung*).

Philosophers of the Frankfurt School of neo-Marxism, especially Horkheimer and Marcuse, often dealt with themes related to environmental issues. Also leading into issues of environmental philosophy was the work of Hans Jonas and Carl Mitcham. Jonas, a student of Heidegger's, eventually concluded that Heidegger's understanding of human existence was inattentive to its biological medium, and in *The Phenomenon of Life* (1966) and *The Imperative of Responsibility* (1979), he articulated a view of nature, humanity and the contemporary world that sought to redress the putative omission. Mitcham drew upon a variety of sources in continental philosophy to develop a sustained body of work, beginning with *Philosophy and Technology* which he co-edited in 1973, exploring the concrete implications of science and technology for society. All of these develop environmentally charged issues, articulating insights into nature and the human relation to it that we have just begun to assimilate.

Work in environmental philosophy proper by continental philosophers began in earnest in the 1980s, and from the beginning had a much wider range than its more analytic counterpart, although by the same token less focused as to what constitutes its proper domain. Many authors of this period shared a background in phenomenology which encouraged them to see both the phenomenological emphasis upon the *Lebenswelt* ('lifeworld'), and its critique of the 'natural attitude', as providing important correctives to the scientific understanding both of the natural environment and of the character of environmental crisis. From this period comes perhaps the earliest, and still undoubtedly one of the best, works devoted to environmental philosophy by a continental philosopher, *The Embers and the Stars*, published in 1984 by the Husserl scholar Erazim Kohák, a Czech philosopher who lived and taught for many years in New England; readers often remark that he seems to breathe the very air of Emerson and Thoreau. In addition to a basically phenomenological approach, Kohák's book also exhibits two other features that have often characterised continental environmental philosophy: a willingness to engage the philosophical issues at an existential and even personal level, and correspondingly an unabashed use of lyrical or poetic kinds of discourse that are not often employed in analytic circles.

Heidegger's philosophy had some measure of influence on what has come to be called 'deep ecology', a term first employed by Norwegian philosopher Arne Naess, and work exploring the implications of Heidegger's thought for environmental philosophy was published by Bruce Foltz and Michael Zimmerman beginning in the mid-1980s, while Albert Borgmann elaborated a technology critique drawing heavily upon Heidegger. At the same time, a closely related movement in architectural theory and city planning was exploring ties with continental philosophy (especially Heidegger's understanding of 'dwelling'); examples of thinkers in this field are Robert Mugerauer, David Seamon and Ingrid Stefanovic.

Continental work in environmental philosophy blossomed in the 1990s. Edward Casey's work on the philosophy of place (beginning with *Getting Back into Place* in 1993) had important implications for environmental philosophy, as did John Llewelyn's *Middle Voice of Ecological Conscience* (1991), and John Sallis's *Stone* (1994), along with much of the work published by Alphonso Lingis, Stephen David Ross and Bruce Wilshire. David Abrams's *Spell of the Sensuous* (1996) brought to a wide range of readers the environmental implications of the work of Husserl and Merleau-Ponty. Environmental philosophy developing, from a continental background, themes related to ecofeminism included work by Trish

Glazebrook, who has also published a work on Heidegger's philosophy of science, and Elaine Miller, who explores the 'vegetative' understanding of the soul in nineteenth-century German philosophy. Robert Kirkman explores issues of scepticism in the philosophy of science in *Skeptical Environmentalism* (2002), while Robert Frodeman's *Geo-Logic* (2003) and Mark Bonta and John Protevi's *Deleuze and Geophilosophy* (2004) show the powerful implications of continental thought for understanding the earth sciences.

The widespread interest in this intersection of continental philosophy and environmental philosophy was also expressed in the founding of the International Association for Environmental Philosophy in 1997 and the journal *Call to Earth* in 1999 which began publication in a new format in 2004 as *Environmental Philosophy*. Three collections of articles, presenting work written either entirely or largely by continental philosophers, suggested that environmental philosophy had become a major area of scholarship and research in continental philosophy: *Earth Matters: The Earth Sciences, Philosophy, and the Claims of Community*, edited by Robert Frodeman (1999); *Eco-Phenomenology: Back to the Earth Itself* edited by Charles S. Brown and Ted Toadvine (2003); and *Rethinking Nature: Essays in Environmental Philosophy* (2004), edited by Bruce Foltz and Robert Frodeman.

                                                                    B. Foltz

EPISTEME Foucault's name for the objects of his archaeological method of analysis. An episteme is a set of relations or rules of formation that, at a given place and time, unite the set of discursive practices that make up an apparatus of knowledge-production. Although descriptions of epistemes in *The Order of Things* (1966) were often taken to be descriptions of historical 'world-views' or 'conceptual schemes', Foucault insists – particularly in *The Archeology of Knowledge* (1969) – that an episteme is not a collection of propositions or concepts or a type of rationality that permeates and governs a group of disciplines or sciences; instead, it is a set of dynamic relations that exist only in their concrete occurrences in discursive regularities across fields of knowledge in a particular historical epoch. These relations are not hidden beneath the surface of the discursive practices they organise but are, rather, what Foucault calls the 'positive unconscious' of discourses, the operative rules of formation of discourses that are manifest in those discourses but not reflected upon them. After about 1970, Foucault discarded the term, perhaps because he found it difficult to dissociate it from the concept of alternative conceptual schemes that was circulating in the 1960s. In his later works, which he called genealogies rather than archaeologies, he does not take epistemes as his objects of analysis. Instead, he seeks to analyse apparatuses (*dispositifs*) of what he calls 'power/knowledge' and *askeses*, or techniques of self.

L. McWhorter

EPISTEMOLOGICAL BREAK/RUPTURE (*brisure épistemologique*) A term coined by Bachelard to mark two kinds of discontinuity. The first is that of a break between scientific and non-scientific thought. Non-scientific thinking accepts intuition as reliable; it holds many things as self-evident truths, as beyond question, whether on the basis of experience or tradition. Modern science begins with challenges to intuition (Galileo challenges the self-evident truth that the earth is stationary, for example); it demands reasons, evidence and explanations. But this break does not occur just once and for all. At any time a science operates with framing principles that it puts beyond question (for example, conservation of mass in Newtonian mechanics), but which may need to be challenged. The second kind of break is then the shift in status (in the epistemological value) of a principle, from necessary truth to something open to empirical challenge; this second sort of break is a reconfiguration of the conceptual framework of scientific inquiry. Bachelard's claim was that such a 'correction of concepts' was one of the mechanisms of scientific progress, thus implying that the sciences do not develop gradually by the steady accumulation of knowledge. Rather they have a history punctuated by discontinuities (analogous to the scientific revolutions postulated by Kuhn).

Althusser made the term widely known by giving it a specific application in the context of his interpretation of the development of Marx's thought. He claimed there was an epistemological rupture between Marx's early humanist or 'ideological' thought and his later more firmly materialist and scientific thought. Althusser did not subscribe to other aspects of Bachelard's epistemology, which he and other French Marxists regarded as insufficiently scientific and materialist.

M. Tiles

EPISTEMOLOGY That branch of philosophical inquiry which concerns itself with the scope, limits and conditions of human knowledge in general. Philosophy of science raises similar issues with regard to the methods and procedures of the sciences. 'Continental' thinkers tend to treat philosophy of science as a sub-branch of epistemology, while 'analytic' philosophers tend to treat the methods of the physical sciences as their chief source of guidance in epistemological matters.

The Kantian background. Both traditions may be said to have their starting-point in Kant, who claimed to have reconciled the twin doctrines of 'transcendental idealism' and 'empirical realism' (*Critique of Pure Reason*, 1781). Thus he strove to steer between the arguments of continental rationalists (such as Descartes and Leibniz) who took it that knowledge could be justified only on the basis of certain innate or a priori ideas and the arguments of British empiricists (such as Locke and Hume) who held that all knowledge was the product of sensory or phenomenal cognition. Kant's alternative maintained that the conditions of possibility for knowledge included a priori factors: the intuitions of time and space and the categories, unified in the 'transcendental unity of apperception'. Thus, according to Kant, 'concepts without intuitions are empty' while 'intuitions without concepts are blind'. Hence his proclaimed 'Copernican revolution' in philosophy: only by taking both conditions into account (that is, the necessity that knowledge be acquired on the basis of certain a priori factors yet also under certain empirical constraints) could thinking escape the chronic oscillation between a 'common sense' Humean empiricism devoid of rational guidance and a pure-bred rationalist philosophy devoid of empirical content.

The Kantian project ran aground – so it is often maintained – on the sheer impossibility of explaining how two such disparate realms as those of sensuous intuition and concepts of understanding could ever achieve the kind of synthesis which Kant's argument required. Nor is there much help to be had from those notoriously murky passages where Kant alludes to the joint exercise of 'judgement' and 'imagination', this latter conceived as 'a blind but indispensable function of the soul, without which we should have no knowledge whatsoever, but of which we are scarcely ever conscious'. For in the absence of any more rigorous or adequate definition it would seem that Kantian epistemology is condemned to just the kind of stalemate or seesaw movement between 'blind' sense-data and 'empty' concepts which it strenuously sought to overcome.

One could write the history of later developments in the two traditions as a series of sharply differing responses to this problem bequeathed by Kant's First *Critique*. On the analytic side, proponents of logical positivism and logical empiricism proposed simply to cut out those obscure appeals to a priori knowledge and to focus rather on different kinds of statement and their justificatory grounds. In which case – so they argued – only two kinds should count as genuinely meaningful: empirical statements (like those of the physical sciences) whose truth or falsity could be checked against the observational evidence and analytic statements whose truth was self-evident just in virtue of their logical form.

Another tradition of thought – Husserlian phenomenology – remained faithful to Kant's project by continuing to raise questions about the various modalities of human experience, knowledge and judgement, while subjecting that project to a rigorous critique with regard to its grounding presuppositions. For Husserl, philosophy could only live up to its true vocation and avoid the twin perils of a naive or unselfcritical positivism and a reactive scepticism or irrationalism by taking absolutely nothing for granted in the way of empirical or logical self-evidence. Rather it should operate by suspending or 'bracketing' all such assumptions and questing back – through a radicalisation of Cartesian sceptical doubt – to a stage of inquiry where thought encounters the a priori necessary forms and structures of perceptual and cognitive judgement. That is to say, Husserlian 'transcendental phenomenology' is transcendental in so far as it claims to argue from the very conditions of possibility for knowledge and experience, and phenomenological in so far as it concerns those particular modes of judgement which explain the genesis and structure of our knowledge in fields such as logic, mathematics and the physical sciences.

However – as Derrida has argued – there is a tension between those terms, 'genesis' and 'structure', which cannot be resolved and whose presence in Husserl's texts calls for a deconstructive reading. On the one hand Husserl's project involves the genetic idea that knowledge (for example, geometrical knowledge) is first acquired and thereafter 'reactivated' in the minds of certain individuals. On the other, it requires that such truths be conceived as existing objectively and for all time quite apart from any relation to particular, historically situated human knowers. Thus Husserl's arguments are again caught in an oscillating movement between the twin poles of a genetic account which brings truth within reach of human knowledge and a structural account that locates truth in the realm of 'absolute ideal objectivity'.

Indeed, continental epistemology has often tended to veer between a phenomenological perspective that retains a prominent role for the knowing, thinking or judging subject and a structuralist perspective that on principle rejects any ultimate appeal to the subject as locus of knowledge or truth. Derrida brings out the strictly unavoidable tensions that characterise Husserl's exemplary and rigorous attempt to think through the antinomy of 'genesis' and 'structure'. For there is plentiful evidence in Husserl's own texts that knowledge could not possibly have advanced beyond the founding intuition of the 'original geometer' – nor could that founding intuition have served as a basis for later discoveries – except for the fact of their material inscription. Thus Derrida raises significant questions with regard to the realist (or Platonist) claim that truth can somehow objectively transcend the deliverance of present-best knowledge or epistemic warrant. Yet he also sees clearly enough – unlike anti-realists such as Dummett – that this *must* be the case if one is to explain how geometry and the other formal and physical sciences have indeed made progress by rejecting certain erstwhile 'self-evident' items of knowledge. Thus the question has been raised on both sides as to how far – if at all – truth can be a matter of apodictic warrant or of a priori reasoning from the conditions of possibility for knowledge and experience in general. Where these approaches differ is mainly with respect to their treating that question either from a logico-semantic or from an epistemological standpoint. That is to say, analytic philosophy is characterised for the most part by its emphasis on logic as (in Dummett's words) the 'basis of metaphysics' and its refusal to follow thinkers like Kant and Husserl in their quest for some ultimate grounding in the forms, structures or modalities of human knowledge.

The Subject in Question. Continental philosophy has nevertheless taken a turn against the subject-centred epistemological paradigm that prevailed in the French rationalist tradition after Descartes and in the German transcendental-idealist line of descent from Kant. Hence those various 'decentrings' of the subject (the Cartesian 'subject-presumed-to-know') periodically announced over the past half-century by existentialists, structuralists, poststructuralists, Lacanian psychoanalytic theorists and – albeit with qualification – by Derrida in his readings of Husserl. It is also evident in the work of Habermas, who seeks to redeem the 'unfinished project' of modernity by adopting a linguistically oriented approach (or 'theory of communicative action') based on the appeal to certain normative values implicit in our various, everyday or specialised modes of discourse. Thus Habermas shares the French theorists' desire to move beyond that old (presumptively discredited) foundationalist paradigm even though he criticises what he sees as their reactive tendency to break faith with every last principle of enlightened, progressive or emancipatory thought. In short, this turn toward language and away from epistemological concepts and categories has been a prominent feature of much recent thinking in both traditions. However – as I have said – there is a difference of emphasis between them and one that unites such otherwise sharply opposed representatives of 'continental' philosophy as Derrida and

Habermas. This is the belief that such issues cannot be confined to the purely logico-semantic domain but must involve some account – some jointly historical and philosophical working-through – of the various antinomies (such as that between 'genesis' and 'structure') which continue to solicit just that kind of epistemo-critical reflection. Thus neither Habermas nor Derrida would go so far with the linguistic turn as to reject such thinking as merely a delusive remnant of old-style Cartesian, Kantian or Husserlian epistemological concerns.

Other thinkers on the 'continental' side have pushed much further in that direction. Most influential among them has been Foucault, who started out by proposing an 'archaeology' of knowledge which treated truth-claims of whatever kind as a product of various historically shifting discursive formations (*The Order of Things*, 1966). Later on – from the mid-1970s – he adopted a Nietzschean 'genealogical' approach whereby they became just so many products of an epistemic 'will-to-power' which passed itself off as a pure, disinterested quest for knowledge and truth. Foucault argued very strongly against any version of the Kantian or phenomenological claim that knowledge might be grounded – or discover its ultimate 'conditions of possibility' – in an appeal to the subject as locus or guarantor of truth. Thus, in a famous passage from *The Order of Things*, he describes Kant's conception of the subject as just a kind of linguistic mirage, a 'strange empirical-transcendental doublet' which marks nothing more than a transient phase in the short-lived history of humanist thought. All the same there is a striking tension between this idea of the knowing subject as a fictive construct engendered by various (no doubt multiple or heterogeneous) discourses and Foucault's later stress on the power of strong-willed individuals to shape their own lives in accordance with certain ethical or aesthetically inspired values and commitments. For, as Derrida pointed out at some length in an early essay on Foucault's *Madness and Civilisation* (1961), it is strictly impossible for thinking to renounce the 'security' of rational discourse without either lapsing into sheer, unintelligible nonsense or forwarding its case – like Foucault – in a form that inescapably subscribes to the protocols of rational argumentation. Thus Foucault rather blatantly invites the charge of performative self-contradiction when he claims to be speaking 'in the voice' of madness.

There is also a certain ambiguity about just how far Foucault's sceptical or discourse-relativist arguments should be taken to extend. In his early works they are mainly applied to the social and human sciences, along with those disciplines (such as clinical psychology) at what might be called the 'softer' end of the natural science scale. On the other hand he also has much to say about biology and the life sciences, which are likewise treated as having undergone a series of 'epistemological breaks' (or discursive mutations) from one period to the next. Indeed some philosophers of biology have adduced his work in support of their claim that we should give up thinking about 'natural kinds', such as animal or plant species, as if they could be specified in terms of certain unique identifying features (Dupré, *The Disorder of Things*, 1993). And from here it is but a short distance to the notion – espoused by thinkers like Richard Rorty – that 'reality' is entirely a product of those various language-games, discourses, 'preferential vocabularies' and so forth, by which scientists conventionally choose to describe this or that range of putative realia (Rorty, *Objectivity, Relativism, and Truth*, 1991).

Bachelard and Canguilhem. Among the most relevant contexts here is that distinctively French tradition in history and philosophy of science whose chief representatives were Gaston Bachelard and Georges Canguilhem. Like Foucault, these thinkers focus on the various successive revolutions in scientific thought that were marked by large-scale 'epistemological breaks'. However they are not relativists, nor do they detach their account of these changes from any idea of progress or advancement in scientific knowledge. On the contrary: for Bachelard and Canguilhem it is crucial to distinguish *histoire sanctionée* (the history of valid, productive or knowledge-conducive hypotheses) from *histoire perimée* (those which have since been discredited or proved incapable of further development). They also have much to say about the role of metaphor in scientific theory-formation, a role most pronounced during periods of pre-revolutionary ferment when scientists are forced back upon such modes of oblique, metaphoric or analogical description for want of any other (more direct or literal) descriptive resources. Hence Bachelard's well-known example of the cellular structure of organic tissue, one that started out with strongly-marked 'affective' connotations (for example, that of the beehive as an emblem of cooperative labour), but was then subject to an ongoing process of 'rectification and critique' whereby those connotations were progressively shed and the metaphor transformed into a fully operative scientific concept. In other cases no such process occurred since the metaphor in question resisted any effort to subtract its affective or anthropomorphic residues, at which point it became (in Bachelard's phrase) an 'obstacle to thought'.

This kind of argument has a long prehistory, going back as it does to Aristotle's claims for the heuristic role of 'good' (creative and knowledge-promoting) metaphors in the discourse of the physical sciences.

Where it differs most markedly from Foucault's approach – as likewise from Kuhn's account of scientific paradigm-change – is in offering certain specific criteria of progress or conceptual advancement, and also in treating such progress as a matter of creative insights, perceptions or discoveries on the part of scientists working under given historical conditions of knowledge. This is why Bachelard described his approach as a kind of 'applied rationalism' (*rationalisme appliqué*), one that owed at least a partial allegiance to the line of thought descending from Descartes and the seventeenth-century rationalists. Its emphasis on 'rectification and critique' can be seen as upholding the Cartesian doctrine of 'clear and distinct ideas' to the extent that it involves a progressive purging of common-sense (anthropomorphic) beliefs which must otherwise block the attainment of conceptual clarity. On the other hand Bachelard rejects any notion that scientific knowledge could somehow transcend the historical context of its own emergence, or – in disciplinary terms – that philosophy of science could do without the insights provided by history of science. What is required, rather, is a jointly rationalist and 'applied' (that is, historically informed) approach that gives due weight to both sides of this constantly evolving dialectic between scientific reason and the various factors that have promoted or hindered its development to date. Thus Bachelard's philosophy of science has much in common with Derrida's deconstructive reading of Husserlian phenomenology, that is to say, his exposure of the various deep-laid antinomies that resulted from Husserl's strenuous attempt to reconcile the conflicting claims of 'genesis' and 'structure'.

Misperceptions of 'continental' thought. So there is something askew about the widespread perception – at least among analytically trained philosophers of science – that continental thinkers over the past century have taken a disastrously wrong turn which began with the 'psychologistic' aberration of transcendental phenomenology and ended up with the extreme 'textualist' stance of deconstructive mavericks like Derrida. Indeed one could argue to opposite effect: that analytic philosophy in the wake of logical empiricism lay open to attack from a Quinean or Kuhnian paradigm-relativist quarter just because it ignored those epistemological problems that were addressed by thinkers in the post-Kantian 'continental' line of descent. Among them was the single greatest problem for anyone defending Kant's claim with regard to synthetic a priori truths, that is his reliance on Euclidean geometry as a paradigm instance of truths that were both self-evident to reason and a source of empirically verifiable knowledge. That claim was soon afterwards called into question by the discovery that there existed non-Euclidean geometries that were logically consistent or capable of axiomatisation even though they possessed no kind of intuitive self-evidence. And then it turned out – with the advent of Einstein's relativity theory – that the best current hypothesis concerning the structure of physical reality was one that required a decisive break not only with Euclidean geometry but also with Kant's other great example of a priori knowledge: Newtonian physics.

Thinkers in the mainland European line of descent – unlike their analytic counterparts – never lost sight of the requirement that philosophy respect both the objectivity of truth and also its progressive coming-to-light through various historically dated though scientifically valid theories, conjectures or hypotheses. That is to say, there is more insight to be had through Derrida's deconstructive yet scrupulously faithful reading of Husserl than through a treatment of the issue – like that to be found in recent analytical debate – which decrees that we can either have objective (recognition-transcendent) mathematical truths or humanly attainable mathematical knowledge, but surely not both unless at the cost of downright self-contradiction.

The harder one looks at the kinds of work carried on by thinkers in the 'two traditions', the less it appears that they have really pulled apart in the way described by so many standard doxographic accounts. On the one hand there is a large body of mainland European thought – some of which I have summarised above – that engages issues in epistemology and philosophy of science with a high degree of analytic rigour, albeit from a standpoint informed by distinctive interests and priorities. On the other, it is clear that certain 'continental' trends which are often held up as examples of how they do things differently over there in fact find a close analogue in developments nearer home. Among them are the various post-empiricist 'turns' – linguistic, sociological, cultural, hermeneutic, paradigm-relativist and so forth – that have lately emerged within the Anglophone sphere. These sometimes take a lead from continental sources, as with recent moves to revitalise the currency of mainstream (analytic) epistemology by an infusion of Heideggerian 'depth-hermeneutic' concerns. So likewise with work in philosophy of science that has drawn on Foucauldian and poststructuralist ideas with a view to challenging received conceptions of scientific method and truth

Sociology of knowledge. Thus there is something distinctly skewed about the way that 'continental' philosophy has so often been thought of (by 'analytic' types) as the source of everything most squarely opposed to the virtues of rational and truth-seeking logical inquiry. One major focus of these debates has been the 'strong' programme in sociology of knowledge, a movement that rejects any notion of scientific truth as transcending the conditions of its historical, cultural or ideological production. That is to say, we should treat all scientific theories or truth-claims as strictly on a par for the purposes of sociological investigation, whether those that still count among the best (most scientifically acceptable) candidates for truth or those that have since been discredited or subject to radical revision. Such is the strong 'principle of parity' according to which any judgement regarding the truth or falsehood of a given hypothesis must itself be a product of certain prevalent ideological values, and hence apt for treatment in sociological terms (Bloor, *Knowledge and Social Imagery*, 1976). Along with this goes the reflexive principle whereby the claims put forward by the strong sociologists should likewise be regarded as culture-relative and in no way exempt from such treatment. All the same – as critics of the doctrine are wont to remark – this show of even-handedness still leaves sociology very much in command of the field since it has managed to dictate the rules of the game and to determine its outcome in advance. Thus any counter-argument from the scientific-realist quarter will routinely be met with the response that it reflects nothing more than a cultural investment in the preferred self-image of science as a disciplined, progressive and ideologically neutral quest for knowledge and truth. In which case, quite simply, nothing could count – least of all any version of the realist case for convergence on truth at the end of inquiry – as an adequate answer to the strong sociologists.

One might gather from recent exchanges in the so-called 'science wars' that this was a disease of exclusively continental origin, a virus spread about by cultural theorists like Bruno Latour whose anthropologically oriented studies of 'laboratory life' reduce the quest for scientific truth to a matter of pragmatic 'negotiation' between rival claimants motivated solely by ideological interests. Yet the strongest proponents of this way of thinking are those in the 'Edinburgh School' – David Bloor chief among them – who arrived at it on grounds having less to do with their espousal of 'continental' sources than with their claim to have travelled through and beyond the constraints of old-style logical empiricism. And if one looks without prejudice at Latour's work then one will find it (contrary to widespread report) very far from adopting an outlook of wholesale social constructivism or paradigm relativism. Rather it is the kind of work that results from the conjunction of sociological interests – the study of how science actually 'gets done' in various localised contexts or settings – with an approach to epistemological issues which has clearly learned a good deal from the examples of Bachelard and Canguilhem. (See especially Latour,

The Pasteurisation of France, 1988.) If Latour's version of *rationalisme appliqué* simply tends to privilege the 'applied' over the 'rationalist' component then he is still fully justified – it seems to me – in rebutting any charge of cultural relativism or sociological imperialism.

C. Norris

EPOCHÉ, or 'bracketing' The fundamental methodological principle of Edmund Husserl's phenomenology, which establishes the pure field of appearance of objects. The epoché, which can also be known as the 'phenomenological' or 'transcendental' reduction, is concerned with the problem of the relationship between subjective acts of thinking and the objectivity of (1) the formal aspects of cognition (that which pertains to the thinking of any object whatsoever) and (2) the material dimensions of being (that which pertains to things in so far as they are thought to exist in the world). In other words, the epoché tries to account for the way the concepts of material and formal reality carry the sense of being non-contingent and independent of empirical, psychological subjectivity ('transcendent' to such subjectivity), even though these concepts appear in experiences and thought processes that are in some sense subjective. The epoché addresses this problem by redirecting cognitive awareness, from its naive belief in the independent reality of the objects of its knowledge and experience ('the natural attitude'), to the thematic apprehension of what shows up in this belief – *precisely as it shows up*. This is not a doubting of the reality of those objects in a Cartesian sense – the phenomenologist does not believe the objects are false or simply illusory – but a 'bracketing' or putting to one side of the sense of the object as independent of psychological subjectivity. The consequence of this is the reduction of the transcendent being of the concepts and objects of knowledge and experience to their phenomenological being; hence the name 'phenomenological reduction'. When the objects thus attended to are psychological acts, their empirical being is reduced to their transcendental being; hence the name 'transcendental reduction'.

B. Hopkins

EREIGNIS A key term in the later Heidegger's lexicon. Like the Greek *logos*, or the Chinese *Tao*, Heidegger claims in *Identity and Difference* (1957) that *Ereignis* is untranslatable. Unlike its ordinary usage in German, where it means 'event', *Ereignis* in Heidegger's work does not express something that is taking place or happening, some specific, actual event. Rather, it designates the unique, founding event, which is continually taking place, namely the event of presence itself. It is in presencing that things are given their 'proper' place, in presencing that they appear. As such, it is another name for Heidegger's constant concern, 'being'. Just as 'Dasein' or 'being-there' is Heidegger's de subjectivising of Husserl's 'consciousness', *Ereignis*, the presencing of things, is a desubjectivising of Husserl's 'intentionality'. Rather than being the act of a subject, *Ereignis* or presencing is an event that occurs in and to humans. As part of this desubjectivising, Heidegger stresses that presencing is not grounded in any self-present subject. This means that presence unfolds from out of an originary concealing. But this structure of truth as revealing is hidden by our fascination with the beings so revealed, so we can say the event of presence is simultaneously the event of the concealing of concealment itself. Heidegger expresses this by saying that *Er-eignis* is *Ent-eignis*, that is, ap-propriation is ex-propriation.

But why is *Ereignis* 'appropriation' in the first place? The event of presencing always implicates the human in a certain way. As such, *Ereignis* also designates the historical and destinal constellation that links the human and being; this is Heidegger's reworking of Hegel's thematising of historical difference in categorial structures, though without the latter's sense of 'spiritual' development. It designates the co-belonging of the human and being, or their community of destiny. It is the event of their reciprocal ap-propriation. The ownness or the properness of the human consists in being drawn into the clearing, in being delivered over to its open expanse. In other words, the humanity of the human being consists in its being transpropriated to being (*dem Sein vereignet ist*). Similarly, the ownness or properness of being consists in the fact that is turned (*zugeeignet*) towards the human, in the fact that truth destines itself to the human. The event of this double and reciprocal 'ap-propriation', of this dependency (*Vereignung*) and this address (*Zueignung*), is what Heidegger calls *Ereignis*. It is the unceasing event through which the human and being are transpropriated into one another. The verb *ereignen*, Heidegger reminds us, comes from the old German *er-aügen*, which meant: to grasp with one's gaze, to gaze upon, to draw into one's gaze, in short, to ap-propriate. Thus what is appropriate to the human is to grasp our own being ex-appropriated, that we are not in control, that being is an event, not the act of a subject. Hence the call to a 'letting-be' or *Gelassenheit*.

M. de Beistegui

ESSENTIALISM The belief in a single metaphysical nature that causally determines the identity and characteristics of a specific group of entities. The term essentialism marks a stage in the history of feminism and is now commonly used as a condemning adjective to describe certain forms of feminism as outdated and retrograde. Though social constructivism is the dominant theory of identity today, some argue essentialist claims can and should be strategically used in feminist politics.

The essentialist phase was dominated by white, middle-class, heterosexual women who sought to isolate women's experiential specificity in order to overcome the problems of liberal feminism, in which male and female subjects were posited as the same. Though these feminists rejected the surface claims of essentialism, their work often served surreptitiously to reinstate them. Women of colour and lesbian feminists were the strongest force in bringing this specific brand of essentialism into question and insisting on the differences among women.

Feminists have rejected essentialism not just because cultural identity is irreducible to anatomy, but also because of the way the identity of any one woman is constituted through the interplay of various factors, including race, class, sexuality and nationality. Several notable postmodern and continental feminists have been accused of essentialism, though this charge neglects the imaginary, psychic, symbolic and social dimensions of their use of the term 'sexual difference'. What primarily distinguishes the postmodern feminism of figures such as Irigaray, Kristeva and Cixous from the 'essentialist' brand of feminism is their rethinking of subjectivity as fragmented and incompatible with any form of essentialism.

S. Keltner

ETERNAL RECURRENCE (*ewige Wiederkehr*) The centrepiece of an imaginative exercise, presented by Nietzsche, which is meant to measure one's capacity for affirming life as it is, stripped bare of all metaphysical fictions and comforts. In the most influential formulation of the idea of eternal recurrence, as found in Section 341 of *The Gay Science* (1882), we are asked (though not directly by Nietzsche) how we would respond if we were to learn that the cosmos as we know it has recurred in every detail and will continue indefinitely to do so. Two general responses are anticipated: we will either gnash our teeth in despair (and thereby fail the test of affirmation), or we will rejoice and *will* the eternal recurrence (thereby passing the test of affirmation.)

The idea of eternal recurrence is apparently modelled in some way on an epiphany Nietzsche experienced in 1881 while walking in the mountains near Sils-Maria. 'Six thousand feet beyond man and time' is how he described his experience at the time, suggesting that he had been transported mysteriously to a consummatory, trans-historical insight. Translating this personal epiphany into a communicable teaching proved extremely challenging, however, and Nietzsche's readers remain divided on the question of how successful he was in doing so. Even today, scholars vigorously dispute what, if anything, this teaching is meant to convey to Nietzsche's readers. Although some of his notebook entries present the eternal recurrence as a hypothesis pertaining to physics and/or cosmology, most readers agree that its intended meaning is broadly diagnostic, perhaps even suggestive of a revolutionary new ideal of human flourishing. Indeed, there is widespread scholarly agreement that the idea of eternal recurrence is one of Nietzsche's most original and influential teachings.

Nietzsche describes the idea of eternal recurrence as the 'fundamental conception' of his greatest work, *Thus Spoke Zarathustra* (1883–5). The central character's struggles to embrace this idea, as a condition of promulgating it to others, furnish the book with its central dramatic narrative. Throughout his various journeys and speeches, Zarathustra strives to grow into the role supposedly reserved for him as the teacher of the eternal recurrence. While his personal growth is in many respects remarkable, and even quasi-heroic, the open-ended conclusion of the book casts some doubt on the success of his endeavour to embrace (and so impart) the teaching of eternal recurrence. In the final scene of the book, he sets out to meet his ideal companions (whom he calls his 'children') and, presumably, to commence the post-moral, post-theistic epoch of human history. The dramatic trajectory of the book suggests that a successful meeting between Zarathustra and his 'children' could take place only in the event that he has in fact succeeded in becoming the teacher of the eternal recurrence. But the book closes on a famously inconclusive note; the narrator neither confirms nor denies the eventuality of this fateful meeting between Zarathustra and his 'children'. We therefore cannot know if Zarathustra has in fact grown into the role reserved for him, or if he has simply failed once again to connect with his chosen audience. Similar doubts may be said to cloud Nietzsche's own attempts to promulgate the teaching of eternal recurrence.

D. Conway

ETHICS The development of ethical theories in the twentieth century in the continental tradition has taken place against the background of Nietzsche's celebrated critique of morality, and also as a response to the horrors of that century. While there have been many noteworthy developments in the areas of feminist ethics, the 'discourse ethics' of Habermas and the work of the later Foucault, we will focus on Nietzsche, Heidegger, Levinas and Derrida.

Nietzsche's attacks on morality have often been described as a nihilistic enterprise of destruction of values leading to the impossibility of ethics. Consequently, continental philosophies of ethics, which are in their very basis post-Nietzschean thoughts, have also been accused of moral relativism and nihilism. However, one notes that Nietzsche's critiques are not the simple dismissal of ethics as such, but rather an attack on a certain way of understanding ethics: Nietzsche targets what he terms 'life-denying' ethical philosophies, which he sees in Christianity and of course Platonism, which both posit another world beyond this world in the positing of ideals. What is thus at issue is the positing of the ethical values of 'good' and 'evil' as transcendent values lying beyond this world, a movement indicating an implicit rejection and hatred for this life in this world (as betrayed by the presence of guilt and shame as cornerstones of such ethics). This is the sense of Nietzsche's genealogy of morals: to return to its actual soil in life itself, and to reveal the material, historical, 'human, all-too human' origins of ethics and values, as opposed to some ideal provenance. Nietzsche actually calls for a life-affirming ethics, known as his philosophy of the overman and of joyful wisdom.

The proper site of ethics, which is Nietzsche's question, is at the centre of the phenomenological enterprise, in which ethics is grounded on a phenomenal basis (as opposed to being left groundless in abstract theorising on so-called applied and theoretical ethics). Hence, in Heidegger's work, the question of ethics arises out of the very event of being and its givenness. Ethics needs to be understood in terms of being, and of what Heidegger calls 'Dasein', the human being conceived in its relation to being itself. Traditional accounts of ethics are indeed phenomenologically destroyed or deconstructed in Heidegger's work, but in order to retrieve a non-metaphysical, non-theological, more original sense of the ethical. For instance, when Heidegger takes issue with the theme of empathy in *Being and Time*, it is not in order to condemn an ethical motif as such, but to show how the problematics of empathy are still too dependent on Cartesianism and ego-based philosophies. Instead, Heidegger retrieves what he calls the dimension of 'being-with', which is the originary being-with-others of Dasein, rendering moot the question of accessing through empathy another mind. Similarly, when Heidegger takes issue with ethics as a metaphysical discipline in 'Letter on Humanism', it is with the intent of uncovering a more originary sense of ethics as 'authentic dwelling' and 'standing-in' the truth of being. Ultimately for Heidegger, as he himself states in the 'Letter on Humanism', the thinking of being is an 'originary ethics' because being is not some substantial ground, but an event which calls for a responsible engagement and praxis.

With Levinas, ethics is situated in the relationship to the other person, and is presented by Levinas as an alternative to violence and dehumanisation, as witnessed in the Nazi regime and the Holocaust. It is also situated in opposition to traditional ontology and the privilege of knowledge in Western philosophy, which always reduce the other to a principle of identity, or the Same. Levinas aims at reversing the traditional hierarchy in which ethics is reduced to being a branch of ontology, and seeks to raise ethics to the level of first philosophy. As opposed to the negation of the other and its humanity, the ethical experience – however rare it may be – enacts a respect for and a concern for the other. Levinas describes this experience as the face to face with the other, in which I am faced with the destitute and vulnerable nature of the other. Faced with such vulnerability (ultimately the mortality or irremediable exposure to death of the other), I am called to care for the other and to attend to the other as other. Ethics understood in this way represents what is truly human in human beings, a new humanism (which Levinas calls 'humanism of the other human') which breaks with ego-centred philosophies and opens onto the infinite character of the alterity of the other to whom I am responsible. Ethics for Levinas thus means: responsibility for the other.

Derrida problematises further the question of the site and possibility of ethics in terms of what he calls 'aporetic ethics'. Derrida sees the locus of the ethical in an experience of the aporia of ethics, the possibility of ethics in a certain experience of the impossible. When speaking of ethics, Derrida does not mean a system of rules, of moral norms, and to that extent he readily concedes that he does not propose an ethics. What interests him in ethics is instead 'the aporias of ethics, its limits', what he calls the an-ethical origins of ethics: not to point to the simple impossibility of ethics, but on the contrary to reveal aporia as the possibility of ethics. For instance, ethical decision is based on a 'not-knowing': a responsible decision can never be part of a calculable horizon; it cannot consist in the application of a rule. A leap into the incalculable is necessary for any decision to take place. 'It is when "I do not know the right rule" that the ethical question arises', he writes. Derrida thus locates the an-ethical origin of ethics: 'What I do is thus both an-ethical and ethical. I question the impossible as possibility of ethics'. This also reveals the alterity from which the ethical arises. In his words, 'This is what I meant earlier by heteronomy, by a law come from the other, by a responsibility and decision of the other – of the other in me, an other greater and older than I am'. Responsible decision (a kind of 'passive decision' or 'of the other') is openness to the incalculable, to the absolute other. If the decision takes place in a leap into the unknown, then an alterity is its condition: 'for a decision to be a decision, it must be made by the other in myself'. Responsibility is then understood as responsiveness to the opening of the incalculable, an incalculable which remains inappropriable for the subject.

F. Raffoul

EVENT (*événement*) A concept of fundamental interest to Heidegger, Derrida, Foucault and Deleuze, it also forms the fundamental truth-criterion in Badiou's logic, epistemology, ethics and aesthetics. Among the different types of ontological situations, some are recognisable in the general situation, while their elements are not. For example, during the French Revolution, all the elements constituting that situation could theoretically be described ad infinitum, but the factors triggering the revolution remain inaccessible to historical inquiries, qua revolutionary. Badiou names such situations 'event-sites' (other possible examples are: a couple falling in love and periods in scientific or aesthetic history at the cusp of major revolutions). The event's definition is: the site itself, with all its immanently present yet structurally unpresentable elements, plus the signifier making the site one ('I love you', 'Cantor', 'Haydn', 'Russian Revolution' and so on). The event comes from the 'void' of the situation, and, by naming it, makes it visible. Since the void is the invisible foundation of the situation and its laws, the event naming this void is itself illegal: unfathomable, institutionally and structurally. It also represents an inescapable challenge forcing the situation to change, in particular, the nominalistic language and knowledge operating within the normality of the situation (through the identification of elements and their classifications). The event founds the possibility of truth. It is also the criterion of ethics. The good is defined as a consistent acting maintaining 'fidelity' to an event. Evil is acting on the basis of a pseudo-event (a rupture of the situation not founded in its void), the betrayal of an event once recognised, or the attempt to force the whole of reality from the premises of a real event.

J.-P. Deranty

EXISTENTIAL ANALYTIC The term Heidegger uses for Part One, Division One of *Being and Time*, emphasising its preliminary and preparatory role. It is to provide a genuine access to the fundamental question Heidegger wishes to raise in *Being and Time*, namely the question regarding the sense of the being of not only Dasein, but all beings. The justification for choosing Dasein as the access to the question, and as the point of departure for the elaboration of a 'fundamental ontology', is justified in the Introduction to *Being and Time*: in so far as being is always the being of a particular being, it is necessary to interrogate a specific being with respect to its being. And since our own being is at issue in reawakening the question of being, since we cannot bracket or suspend entirely this being that is at issue in raising the question, we should start by clarifying our own being. This leads to the first Division of the book, and ultimately to the identification of the being of Dasein as 'care' (*Sorge*), or as the three basic and integrated structures (also known as 'existentials') of existentiality, facticity and being-fallen. The movement of the analytic is as follows: having identified the basic trait of existence as being-in-the-world, Heidegger decomposes this basic phenomenon in three phases: the first clarifies how we need to understand the 'in' of being-in-the-world; the second develops the meaning of world and 'worldhood'; the third reveals that this being-*in* is also a being-*with* (and specifically with other Daseins).

M. de Beistegui

EXISTENTIALISM The name given to the thought of a wide range of continental philosophers and literary figures holding in common some form of focus on concrete human being or 'existence'. To some, particularly from the nineteenth century, it has been applied retrospectively, since 'existentialism' did not yet then name a movement. To others, such as Gabriel Marcel, whose *Metaphysical Journal* (1927) was among the earliest works to suggest this name, it has sometimes been applied against their will – in Marcel's case, because it had later become identified with Jean-Paul Sartre, whose thought Marcel detested. It is therefore difficult to draw clear borders separating 'existentialists' from others in a way that invites broad agreement.

Nevertheless, there is some consensus about which philosophers to identify in the first instance as 'existentialists': Sartre and Simone de Beauvoir, who accepted this label, and Søren Kierkegaard from the first half of the nineteenth century, whom Sartre invoked as an intellectual ancestor. This historical connection is paradoxical, because Sartre and Beauvoir were atheists whereas Kierkegaard was a person of deep religious faith. In fact, one common way in which historians classify existentialist philosophers is to distinguish between theistic existentialists, of whom Marcel is perhaps the most prominent after Kierkegaard (Nikolai Berdyaev and Lev Shestov are others), and the non-theists.

The idea of commonalities between theistic and non-theistic existentialists was emphasised by Karl Jaspers in a discussion of Kierkegaard and Friedrich Nietzsche in *Reason and Existence* (1935). Jaspers stressed, among other things, their common rejection of Hegel's ultra-systematic thought, their common critique of mainstream notions of 'rationality' and ethics, and their insistence, against abstract, universalistic thinking, on the individual human being as unique and always concretely 'situated' in place and time. There is now considerable disagreement as to whether to classify Nietzsche as an 'existentialist' – many current writers, for example, prefer to see him as anticipating post-existentialist 'poststructuralism' – but there is no doubt that he, along with Fyodor Dostoevsky on the literary side, was among the great sources of inspiration from the late nineteenth century for later existentialists, Jaspers included.

Jaspers' reputation tends to be overshadowed, however, in the catalogue of putative twentieth-century German existentialists, by that of Martin Heidegger. Heidegger's *Being and Time* (1927), by any measure a twentieth-century classic, strongly influenced Sartre, as well as many others. Heidegger's explicit invocation of Kierkegaard concerning the concept of anxiety that was so central to the thought of both of them (as well as subsequently to Sartre); his rejection, indebted to Nietzsche, of what he characterised as mainstream Western metaphysics' approach to 'being' through abstract categories; his stress on ethical responsibility and 'authenticity'; and numerous other features make it tempting to trace a history of the existentialist tradition through Heidegger's work, as most historians still do. Nevertheless, there are reasons for questioning this classification, notably certain implications of Heidegger's later 'turn' (*Kehre*) of thought and above all his repudiation, in his 'Letter on Humanism' (1947), of the anthropocentric or 'humanistic' existentialism espoused by Sartre. This letter was a reaction to the publication, which Sartre himself later regretted because of its oversimplifications, of a Sartrean lecture entitled *Existentialism Is a Humanism* (1946).

Although Sartre's long, technical, systematic treatise *Being and Nothingness* (1943), published during the Second World War and the German occupation of France, was a critical success and hence crucial to giving existentialism its postwar identity, the term had already begun to be widely used in Italian, French and English, as well as German. For example, Nicola Abbagnano in Italy (*Introduzione all' esistenzialismo*, 1942), Jean Wahl in France and Dorothy Emmet in Great Britain had already employed the label in published works. In her article, 'Kierkegaard and the "Existential" Philosophy' (1941),

Emmet argued for existentialism's contemporaneity by evoking a Kierkegaardian sense of dread occasioned by the outbreak of the War. (She also showed an awareness, achieved by some only fifty years later, of Heidegger's involvement with National Socialism.) In a similar vein, it would be mistaken to dismiss the importance of the symbolism (Paris café life, jazz, sexuality) accompanying the postwar image of Sartrean-Beauvoirian existentialism. With its strong emphasis on the reality and value of human freedom, it captured the spirit of liberation from conservative conventions combined with deep anxiety over the future which characterised that time of the nascent Cold War and concern over the atomic bomb. In other words, this philosophy, which emphasised the actual 'situation' of the human individual, was itself very much 'situated' in time.

One way of epitomising this and related existentialist insights is the slogan, 'existence precedes essence'. Sartre discussed this assertion in his aforementioned lecture, and it may help illuminate Kierkegaard's outrage at the alleged reduction of both God and human beings from existents to abstract essences by Hegel, as well as Sartre's denial that there is any fixed 'human nature' or essence and Beauvoir's famous pronouncement in *The Second Sex* (1949) that one is not born a woman but rather becomes one. On the other hand, there are elements in the thought of Sartre's and Beauvoir's one-time associate Albert Camus, who is often denominated an existentialist, that resist this slogan, reflecting a sense of fate and Greek moderation which has a more 'essentialist' ring. (Another long-time collaborator of theirs, Maurice Merleau-Ponty, while sharing their interest in the phenomenological method and sociopolitical issues and often included under the 'existentialist' label, also resists such labelling in numerous ways.) Camus' early teacher, Jean Grenier, was responsible for first publishing most of the writings of an obscure French contemporary of Kierkegaard's, Jules Lequier, a Catholic, who had challenged the determinism of both science and mainstream Christian philosophy in the name of a hypothesis of radical human freedom and, apparently by way of testing this hypothesis, eventually committed suicide. Were Lequier and Kierkegaard together, as some claim, the first European proto-existentialists? Or should that honour be accorded to the seventeenth-century figure Blaise Pascal, who in a way anticipatory of Kierkegaard challenged 'orthodox' philosophies in the name of 'existential' faith? To pursue such questioning is to affirm the pervasiveness of the spirit of existentialism in continental philosophy and beyond.

W. McBride

EXPENDITURE (*dépense*) A cardinal notion in the economic writings of Bataille, extrapolated from Marcel Mauss's analysis of gift-giving ceremonies among North American Indians in *Essay on the Gift* (1925). In 'The Notion of Expenditure' (1933), Bataille introduces the theme of 'non-productive expenditure' (*la dépense improductive*) to designate activities in which individuals or societies expend energy in a gratuitous way, without expectation of returns or profits. By insisting on the importance to society of non-productive expenditure and of a 'principle of loss', Bataille seeks to put an end to the stifling conformity that bourgeois economics and the logic of capitalism breeds. The goal of a society based on the principle of classical or material utility is the production, acquisition and conservation of goods; while pleasure is not alien to such a society, it is present only in an impoverished, 'tempered' form. All types of 'violent pleasure', being irreducible to the principle of utility, are considered 'pathological'. Examples of non-productive expenditure include the gift-giving ceremony of *potlatch*; the construction of sumptuary monuments; ostentatious luxury; wars; laughter, gambling and the arts; and the orgy and other forms of 'perverse sexuality'. These activities, at least in their 'primitive' forms, stand opposed to the activities that serve to continue the productive life of a society. For Bataille, 'the greatest form of social expenditure' is 'the unleashing of class struggle'. Bataille develops the idea of expenditure in *The Accursed Share* (1947), where he considers Aztec sacrifice and the Marshall Plan as examples.

P. Connor

EXPERIENCE Getting hold of something in consciousness (*Erfahrung*), or living through the events and actions of one's existence (*Erlebnis*). The role of 'experience' in modern philosophy from Descartes to the present is pivotal, but determining what experience is has proved controversial. Many twentieth-century philosophers strive to get beyond the stereotypical opposition of a rationalism that posits intellectual experience as the primary source of knowledge and an empiricism that posits sense-experience as the primary source of knowledge, but none more persistently than Husserl and Merleau-Ponty.

Some thinkers try to supplant any focus on experience by disclosing sub- or trans-experiential processes and structures that would determine human value, action and identity. Examples of such purportedly originative factors are the formal structure of language or linguistically determinable prototypes (structuralism), subconscious dialectics modelled on linguistic operation (Lacanian psychoanalysis); or social processes and practices (Foucault, Bourdieu). Yet all this seems only to presuppose a certain functioning of experience that, though taken for granted and depended upon, is nonetheless displaced as naive and unimportant to the interpretive and critique programmes in question.

Be that as it may, we shall focus on three major points of still active phenomenological accounts of experience. (1) Experience is not an input-output or information-processing system. To conceive it this way is to presuppose the validity of a whole pre-given structuring of being that in fact is supposed to be established from the processes in question – all of which amounts to simply begging the question. (2) Experience is fundamentally sensuous in its character, but it will not be adequately grasped on a matter-form schema in which brute sensation or sheer sensuous vagueness is contrasted to clearly formed conceptual cognition. Experience is instead an integrating and integrated fullness of engagement; it is not a consciousness preoccupied immanently with its own contents, but with an all-embracing milieu. There is differentiation, but not between raw sensation and fully formed concepts, but in sensation itself in its aesthetic, kinaesthetic and affective modalities. Sensation is itself immediately qualified in vision, touch and hearing; in being oriented up-down, near-far and so on; and in being pleasing, displeasing or otherwise affectively laden. The grasp of categorial arrangements is also already in play in sensation: for example, whole and part, likeness or dissimilarity, and so on. In other words, experience as perceptual is already a rich differentiation that does not divide neatly into sensuous formlessness and conceptual form, sense against intellect. (3) Experience is not just the reception of, or resistance to, input (roughly, experience as *Erfahrung*); far more than that, it is a living through what goes on (experience as *Erlebnis*). And analogous to what biological study through the twentieth century makes so clear, living being, life, is constitutively a process of interplay and exchange with a whole milieu; and in the case of human being, the plenum both of this living being and of its life-milieu is all-encompassing in its richness and its integrative fullness.

The above features allow us to begin to specify the condition of 'sense' in the phenomenological account of experience. Yet one further consideration is needed to complete the delineation of the 'sense' in experience. Sense as such is not just sensuous quality internally represented; sense as sensuous quality is the *manifestness* of that which appears in the conscious experience. Here is what phenomenology means by the 'intentionality' of consciousness: experience is consciousness opened out to qualitatively concrete, manifestly appearing being; furthermore, we live this engagement in a fullness of sensuous interplay

in the milieu of that manifestness. The world, then, is the all-embracing milieu of living engagement and manifest appearing. The sense of
the sensing in experience in the world is the integrative consolidation of
many sense-modalities (vision, hearing, touch, feeling, movement) in
the very manifestness of a particular object in terms of perceptual
quality, and standing out thus in its milieu.

Here is a conception of experience and of sense that cannot be
reduced to some level of sheer physical structure. Here is where sense
and experience have to be seen as *sui generis* with respect to the
categories of physical science; for the primary feature of sense is that
it is the qualitative manifestness of being, not in terms of sense-data
isolates but in terms of the integrative synthesis of manifestness in
qualitative multi-modality. It is in this way that experience functions
not simply as an underlying fundament upon which a superstructure of
more sophisticated conceptual elaborations is otherwise constructed,
but as the engagement with being that sustains conceptual thought by
permeating it with the sense that is refashioned in and as the conceptual
order.

Much more needs to be worked out to clarify the phenomenological
notion of experience, but we have here at least a general understanding
of the nature of experience that emerges from the investigations of
Husserl and Merleau-Ponty.

R. Bruzina

FACE (*visage*) A term in Levinas's philosophy that represents the other
as an absolutely concrete, singular human being. Far from representing
the assemblage of features by which an individual is known, the face
represents the impossibility of an adequate representation of the other.
For Levinas, there is a fundamental difference between the way things
are given to consciousness (the order of ontology) and the way human
beings are encountered (the order of ethics): things are given in sensible
experience through the mediation of forms or concepts, whereas a face
is present in experience only through its refusal to be contained in a
form. The face is defined as 'the way in which the other presents
himself, exceeding *the idea of the other in me*'. There can be no
phenomenology of the face because, strictly speaking, the face does
not appear; it manifests itself in an 'expression' whose content does not
state anything other than the expression itself. Levinas often describes

the relationship to the Other in terms of the welcome of the face, where this welcome is neither a voluntary, active receiving of the other, nor an involuntary, passive (and therefore violent) imposition. To welcome a face – to have a 'face-to-face relation' (*rapport face-à-face*) with another – is to enter into a relationship with an exteriority in which neither term absorbs or dominates the other, and in which the possibility of an ethical commitment first arises.

D. Perpich

FANON, FRANTZ (1925–61) Franco-Martiniquean doctor, psychiatrist, social philosopher and revolutionary who developed a powerful critique of colonialism and racism which has become one of the key resources in postcolonial thought and struggle.

Fanon was born in the then-French colony of Martinique, volunteered to fight with the Free French forces, and finished his studies in France after the war. His later work as a psychiatrist in colonial Algeria was important in developing his theoretical reflections, but they first took shape before his move with *Black Skins White Mask* (1952). Based on his experiences in Martinique and France, Fanon's main concern in this text is 'the liberation of the man of colour from himself'. He employs Sartrean existentialism and Freudian psychoanalysis to analyse 'a massive psycho-existential complex' that has been created by the way colonialism and its heritage has forced a juxtaposition of the white and black races in politically charged situations. This complex is psychologically characterised by the black man's inferiority complex and the white man's superiority complex. Existentially, it implies that the 'black man is not a man' while it ensures that the 'white man slaves [that is, labours intensively] to reach a human level'. Fanon moves beyond Freud's ontogenic perspective, which emphasised individual factors, by appropriating Marx as he, Fanon, asserts that the black man's alienation or inferiority is not an individual question but rather is primarily economic and hence structural. In order to create what he referred to as a new humanism, which is characterised by a disalienation that makes it possible for one to discover, love and understand man regardless of race or locality, Fanon argues for the need to move beyond the historical constructions that seal the black man and the white man in their antagonistic past.

After his psychiatric work in colonial Algeria and his move to Tunisia to work for the Algerian independence movement, Fanon wrote several important works. In *A Dying Colonialism* (1959), he optimistically highlights the positive aspects and prospects of the then ongoing Algerian revolution in transforming the colonised and creating a new humane society, while his *Toward the African Revolution* (1961) is mainly concerned with the interdependent link between anti-colonial struggles, African unity and pan-humanism. *The Wretched of the Earth* (1961) is his last analysis of the process of decolonisation and the pending pitfalls it entailed for newly independent nation-states. In a revolutionary humanistic tone that calls for a destruction of the Manichean world of black and white, the colonised and coloniser, Fanon rejects Gandhi's *sagayatra* philosophy, which Fanon construes as 'turning the other cheek' and therefore a political compromise that betrays the will of the masses, which for him had become the peasantry rather than the urban workers. Fanon here develops a profound dialectical theory of violence, calling for a total and cleansing violence. Since violence is the essence of colonialism, it follows that 'decolonisation is always a violent phenomenon' which at the level of the individual 'frees the native from his inferiority complex'. A staunch revolutionary, Fanon felt decolonisation will have been for naught if it simply replaces the colonial white bourgeoisie with a native black one. In this demand to think race and class together, Fanon prefigures what will become one of the major themes of the New Left.

C. Chachage

FEMINISM The term 'le feminisme' first appeared in the 1890s in France and was appropriated shortly thereafter throughout Europe and America. The term initially signalled the various political campaigns and philosophical reflections supporting the emancipation of women throughout the late eighteenth and nineteenth centuries, including the right to vote and the demand for equal educational and political opportunities. If the term seemed to cover a well-defined landscape at the end of the nineteenth century, its status following that period has been subject to ceaseless difficulty. No single definition exhausts the term 'feminism' and no single movement, camp or strategy adequately represents its history, although most would agree that feminism seeks to criticise and to change practices of masculine domination. Concretely, however, no such general claim can be meaningful, as there are perhaps as many 'feminisms' as there are feminist sensibilities. Any definition of feminism, then, must necessarily be accompanied by qualification in order to avoid repeating just the sort of exclusionary or hierarchical practices that feminism has sought to remedy.

One of the most influential trends for approaching the diversity of feminist thinking has been to account for its history according to the metaphor of two waves, along with a question concerning a possible third. The first wave of feminism is associated with the liberal feminism of the nineteenth and early twentieth centuries, which consisted of egalitarian claims enabling some of the most important feminist gains of the twentieth century. The second wave of feminism was inaugurated with a critique of the conceptual basis of the first. The second wave insists that though important achievements were made during the first wave – gains we are still realising today – its philosophical premises are fundamentally flawed, and liberal feminism ultimately cannot achieve its goal as a liberatory movement as long as it relies on arguments claiming the essential sameness of women and men. For the first wave, there are no essential differences dividing the sexes that legitimate women's subordination to men, while the second wave insists that there are indeed differences that matter – though certainly not those that legitimate women's subordination. Thus, if the first wave is characterised by 'sameness,' the second wave is characterised by 'difference'. Moreover, though the first wave is generally speaking immersed in the tradition of liberalism, the second wave is characterised by a variety of philosophical and political alliances. Finally, a 'third wave' is currently being postulated by younger feminists, who take notice of 'riot grrl', 'girl power' and new activist stances which continue to grow within the variety of intellectual and cultural practices that make up contemporary youth culture.

Despite its popularity, there are many difficulties with the metaphor of waves. First, the metaphor suggests a movement of fall and retreat beneath a successor. This misses the long-standing dominance of liberal feminism, for instance, in American culture. Second, the metaphor suggests that later developments in feminism are essentially tied to earlier ones. Third, the characterisation of the waves tends to privilege countries like America, England and France as the forerunners of all 'subsequent' feminisms, thus neglecting other traditions. This neglect is nowhere more apparent than in translation trends. Anglo-American feminism, from its beginning, has been widely translated into other languages, and French feminism is now translated just as widely, but Italian, Spanish, German, Eastern European and Latin American feminisms, as well as Asian, African and Third World feminisms, have only just begun to be translated. Considering these other traditions of feminist theory corrects the bias that pervades what has become accepted, through translation choices, as the waves of feminist theory. Though in broad strokes the 'waves' image reveals a large, historical sweep that illuminates and organises an initial entrance into feminism, it ignores, for example, the fact that German-speaking feminists never had a liberal moment, but saw from the beginning a problem in liberalism's politic and law; German, Austrian and Swiss feminisms critically engage German philosophy in thereby creating a unique position, deserving of more attention, that offers alternative perspectives on the essential themes of feminism.

As a corrective to the metaphor of waves, a geography of feminism(s) can be laid out according to philosophical and disciplinary allegiance or national and international affiliation. Feminism has become an essential component in every academic discipline of the humanities and the sciences, giving rise to feminist philosophy of science and technology, feminist evolutionary biology, feminist legal theory, feminist religious studies and so on; there are liberal, libertarian, Marxist, socialist, existentialist, psychoanalytic, postmodern, global and ecological feminists; various positions arise through attention to the intersections of gender with race, class and sexuality; and national and international historical delineations like Anglo-American, French, Italian and Latin American or 'first' and 'third-world' also outline various feminist perspectives. However, even this seemingly exhaustive list misses the ambiguity of its various feminist positions. A feminist stance is not necessarily reducible to a single category or history, and many delineations repeat the hegemony they are meant to overcome, such as the suspect categories of the first and third worlds. Nevertheless, all of these interpretive difficulties have a positive value in so far as they indicate the vibrant health of academic feminism as a discourse tied to ongoing feminist struggles.

If 'feminism' in general is difficult to trace, 'continental feminism' is no less so. 'Continental' feminism, like 'continental' philosophy, is an English-speaking category that extends to any feminist working within the framework of European philosophy and feminism, but not to any specific philosophical allegiance or geographical location. Nonetheless, we can identify two of the most important tendencies of continental feminism as those inspired by (German) critical theory and by (French) poststructuralism. Feminisms inspired by the critical theory of Horkheimer, Adorno, Marcuse and Habermas blend feminist concerns and issues with Marxism and psychoanalysis. Seyla Benhabib, Nancy Fraser and Iris Marion Young, for example, examine the role of gender in the distinction between theory and practice; in the concepts of reason, power, history and critique; in philosophies of modernity; in the social and political notions of justice, difference and group identity; and in critiques of dominating and fascist practice. Critical theory feminism has been widely influential in democratic theory by generating a critique of the concepts of democracy and objectivity as they have been articulated within a capitalist framework. Further, some critical theory feminists have also worked with the thought of

poststructuralist figures such as Lacan, Derrida, Foucault and Deleuze, though we shouldn't interpret this as an uncritical appropriation
and application; it is more like an interrogation within a general
philosophical culture. Critical theory-based feminism, has, however,
taken something of a back seat in continental philosophy as practised in
the Anglophone world to the feminism developed in France within the
general milieu of poststructuralist theory.

Despite the anachronism involved, discussion of French poststructuralist feminism must begin with the existential phenomenology of
Beauvoir, who is often considered the 'mother' of the second wave. *The
Second Sex* is arguably the most important feminist treatise of the
twentieth century and is the touchstone for many feminist theories that
arise in its aftermath. In the English-speaking world, *The Second Sex*
was received with enthusiasm as providing an ironclad argument
against biological essentialism; it also initiated what can be called
'difference feminism'. Beauvoir was received in English-speaking
countries as initiating a distinction between sex and gender when
she claimed that there is no important anatomical difference that
determines socio-cultural differences. This means that sexual difference must be interrogated at the level of history, culture and society in
order to outline the existential situation from which feminist thought
emerges. The difference feminism of the Anglo-American world
argued against essentialism in Beauvoirian fashion, but fell under
the critical scrutiny of women of colour and lesbian feminists who
sought to open the category of gender itself to further differentiation
and argued that the specificity outlined by this difference feminism was
restricted to white, middle-class, heterosexual, Western women. Subsequently, this specific brand of difference feminism has come to be
associated with essentialism itself. The critique of essentialism, both
following the existentialist critique provided by Beauvoir and that
provided by later feminists, has opened various other feminist camps,
including Judith Butler's influential theory of gender performativity.
Butler integrates her early reading of Beauvoir with later poststructuralist theory, particularly the work of Foucault and Derrida; her work
has been devoted to the deconstruction of subjectivity and the theorisation of gender as a performance within a socio-cultural matrix of
power, making it crucial to those working within continental feminism,
especially those at its intersection with queer and critical race theory.

Difference feminism in France also takes up Beauvoir's claim
concerning the arbitrariness of gender localisation and the need for
a critical examination of history and culture contributing to hierarchised gender differences. However, generally speaking, the difference

feminisms of France – which we might hereafter refer to as 'sexual difference feminism' – claim that Beauvoir's existential framework led her to the same egalitarian presuppositions of sameness, thereby situating her closer to liberal feminism than she might have thought. For Beauvoir, human subjectivity is marked by a dialectical ambiguity between transcendence and facticity. Traditionally, Beauvoir argues, men have been associated with transcendence and women with facticity. The solution, for her, seems to lie in women's achievement of transcendence, thereby bringing women and men to the same status. Further, the social constructivism of her thought tends to neglect the importance of an account of dynamic materiality and the body; the consequent neglect of the body as any real force within patriarchal culture makes of nature a mute, passive entity. Following Beauvoir, French feminists in general, along with feminists inspired by French feminism and philosophy, have sought a more complex account of the body and a more nuanced account of the sex/gender border.

'French feminism' in America, until recently, has been narrowly defined as the work of Luce Irigaray, Julia Kristeva and Hèléne Cixous, though feminism is much more diverse in France itself, where Sarah Kofman, Monique Wittig, Michèle Le Doeuff, Catherine Clément and Christine Delphy all offer insightful perspectives. Delphy was in fact one of the first to offer a critique of the category of 'French feminism' when she claimed that it is an English-speaking construction that results in the neutralisation of genuine feminist concerns. Nevertheless, because Irigaray, Kristeva and Cixous have exercised considerable influence outside of France as representative of 'French feminism', they have become necessary, if controversial, figures in any discussion of 'continental feminism'.

Irigaray, Kristeva and Cixous were initially received by Anglo-American feminists as essentialists. All three rely on a notion of 'sexual difference' and a commitment to recasting the importance of corporeality within knowledge and language. However, the charge of essentialism, as has been pointed out by American feminists working within the continental tradition, neglects the symbolic and the social imaginary in which these theorists work. Further, the way 'sexual difference' has been employed by these thinkers cannot be understood in terms of the sex/gender distinction used in Anglo-American feminism; this conceptual incongruence has caused many problems in the Anglo-American reception of French feminism. For the French, sexual difference is often cast as a *genre*, and while the term *genre* can be roughly translated as 'type' or 'kind', such a translation misses the socio-historical dimension of the term. (Historically speaking, *genre* is a term used in French courts to denote a specific group that is demanding rights before the law.) Equally troubling is its translation as 'gender', for sexual difference as a difference of *genre* connotes a certain malleability lacking in the English sense of the phrase 'sexual difference'. Further, neither 'sex' nor 'gender' can adequately account for the ambiguity of embodied existence in the work of these thinkers. This is not to say that the French never speak of a distinction between 'sex' and 'gender'. However, their accounts of sexual difference belie any easy interpretation within an English-speaking feminist framework. Sexual difference in the French tradition examines the ambiguous border of materiality and its imaginary and symbolic codification. This has resulted in a strong turn to language and psychoanalysis in thinking sexual difference.

French feminism's concern for language is connected to Derrida's reading of the history of philosophy as logocentric. For Derrida, the philosophical systems of the West are governed by a privileging of presence and unity, which denigrates any form of difference or otherness. French feminism insists that the logocentrism characterising the history of philosophy is also sustained through a privileging of the phallus. 'Phallogocentrism' is thus defined as a patriarchal logic of reason that orders itself according to the subordination of the feminine; this ordering forms the heart of our very language and modes of thinking. To combat the phallogocentrism of Western modes of thinking, French feminism has sought to create a discursive space of *écriture féminine* in which the female body and feminine sexuality disrupt traditional forms of discourse. What this 'feminine writing' means for the French feminists, however, varies. Irigaray and Cixous draw on metaphors of fluidity and multiplicity to characterise feminine being and sexuality in order to disrupt the stability of (male) discourse. Julia Kristeva, though she has denounced the possibility of any distinctly feminine writing, has delineated the maternal body as a site that calls phallogocentric discourse into question. Monique Wittig's theoretical and literary work on the potentiality of another site of meaning isolates the lesbian body as the (disruptive) other of philosophical discourse. All seek to open an imaginary space for rethinking difference that disrupts traditional, discursive productions of hierarchised identity. The body, for these thinkers, is a site of *jouissance* that contests traditional articulations of subjectivity, truth and sexual difference.

The concern for language is connected to their work in psychoanalysis, as it highlights the importance of language in subjects formed by practices instantiating sexual difference. Psychoanalysis, understood as an articulation of the formation of the 'I' of enunciation, outlines the preconditions for the appearance of a subject upon entering into sign-systems. Psychoanalysis does not presume the givenness of the subject but seeks to uncover the processes that make possible a speaking subject through relation to the imaginary and symbolic codification of the socio-historical world. Most importantly, Irigaray, Kristeva and Cixous utilise the insights of psychoanalysis without attributing a universal, ahistorical status to the discourse itself. Rather, the insights of psychoanalysis are applicable to psychoanalysis itself, resulting in the characterisation of psychoanalysis as a Western, modern discourse subject to the same limitations of the discourses it shows up as marked by sexual difference. Psychoanalysis gives us, therefore, an account of the modern subject(s) within a patriarchal cultural formation. For instance, Kristeva claims that psychoanalysis arises within the weakening of a socio-symbolic system of meaning in order to mark the failure of patriarchal authority. For Irigaray, psychoanalysis provides insight into the sexuate nature of discourse and is thereby essential in the raising of the question of sexual difference itself.

Despite the undoubted depth, breadth and rigour of their work, the riches of which are still being absorbed, the ongoing attention to feminists other than the trio of Irigaray, Kristeva and Cixous promises a future with more diversity and growth for continental feminism.

S. Keltner

FEMINIST EPISTEMOLOGY That branch of philosophical reflection concerned with the intersection of feminist critiques of male domination and questions about knowledge production. Feminist epistemologists in the Anglophone world have drawn from both continental philosophy and from Anglo-American empiricism and pragmatism, and while the latter two influences have been strongest, there is an appreciable confluence between the interests of many continental philosophers and those of many feminist epistemologists, whatever their training or vocabulary. For instance, most feminist epistemologists have rejected the view that epistemic agents must be 'objective' – as that is understood by 'the ontological tyranny' (see below) – and have set in its place the view that epistemic agents are 'situated.' They also reject epistemological individualism – the idea that autonomous individuals produce knowledge – in favour of conceiving knowledge production as a social process.

Feminist epistemologies and philosophies of science tend to be naturalised in the sense set out by Lynn Hankinson Nelson: subject to the same criteria as knowledge production in the sciences; grounded in sciences relevant to theories of theorising, such as empirical psychology, social psychology, cognitive science, evolutionary biology and sociology; and following the symmetry principle, that is having consistent methodological principles for explaining consensus and dissent, and progressive and less than progressive episodes in knowledge production, and for explaining both in the same terms.

Naturalised epistemologies and philosophies of science aim to be empirically adequate, accounting for a rich body of facts about knowledge production and/or having broad scope, that is applying to a range of cases in the history of knowledge production (such as the history of science). Feminist naturalised epistemologies are, like mainstream ones, naturalised to a greater or lesser extent. Some eschew norms other than those found in the sciences, while others retain a stronger normative role for epistemology and philosophy of science. Naturalised epistemologies and philosophies of science are useful to feminists because they enable understanding of how knowledge is actually produced and so make it possible to suggest changes that help to end the systematic subordination of women to men.

Thus primary concerns include the relationship between knowledge and values; the nature of epistemic agents; the balance between naturalising and normative considerations; the nature of objectivity and how to achieve it; and pluralism, underdetermination and epistemological relativism.

Standpoint and community. Sandra Harding's 'standpoint' theory exemplifies work in feminist epistemology arising from European thought. Rejecting the views that gender relations are natural or the result of individual choices made by autonomous individuals, she and other early standpoint theorists argued that the relations between men and women are institutionalised. Dominant accounts of gender as well as race and class relations are thus seen as 'ideologies' legitimating gender, economic and other socio-political hierarchies as natural and inevitable.

Harding and others (notably Nancy Hartsock) make an analogy between the Marxist notion of the proletariat as the economically subordinated group under capitalism and women as the subordinated group under patriarchy. They also take up the Hegelian/Marxian insight that the material conditions of people's lives shape their understandings of the social and natural world. Feminist standpoint epistemologists thus generalise from class as an epistemically relevant variable to the view that all agents of knowledge are 'situated'; in other words, that as epistemic agents, their social locations are relevant to the content of their knowledge and to the methods and standards used in producing it. This constitutes a rejection of the rational man as presented in modernist epistemologies as objective, as having no point of view, as well as a rejection of the Marxist notion of the proletarian as the unitary, universal knower whose social location – and any social differences between him and other proletarians – is irrelevant to the knowledge he produces and maintains.

A standpoint is not to be confused with a social location. A social location is found at the intersection of categories used to stratify societies such as gender, class, race, ethnicity, sexuality, religion, age, abilities and so on. Thus working-class, lesbian, Muslim, Pacific Islander living in the Philippines constitutes a social location. A standpoint is an achievement, the result of analysis by a group of people (who might share a social location). For Harding, in her 1993 essay 'Rethinking Standpoint Epistemology', standpoints arise in the first instance when people occupying a subordinate social location analyse the conditions of their lives and engage in political struggle to change them. Although the proletariat achieves a supposedly universal standpoint by escaping ideological mystification, the agents of knowledge as feminist standpoint theory understands them do not escape their situations, for their lives are embedded in socially constructed discursive and practical formations. Even feminist standpoints do not escape the influence of social forces – though they are less partial and less false than masculinist ones. This is so because they ask critical questions about received belief and about the beliefs constituting their own standpoint.

The anti-individualism of much feminist epistemology is manifest when Harding argues that knowledge is produced by groups of people in 'epistemic communities'. These are local and heterogeneous; thus different epistemic communities – of which scientific communities are a good example – can differ in many ways from one another, and although different epistemic communities might produce similar, compatible accounts of the same domain of the natural or social world, they can produce conflicting accounts. Second, all epistemic communities are, like scientific communities, internally heterogeneous inasmuch as they are made up of people who are epistemically significantly different from one another.

Objectivity. If standpoints do not escape the influence of social forces, there is no guarantee that they see the world 'as it is'. Moreover, if epistemic communities are heterogeneous, and if different communities of scientists investigate the same domain but produce conflicting theories about it, how can they objectively decide among the theories? In response to these difficulties, many feminist epistemologists adopt

Elisabeth Lloyd's analysis of objectivity as based upon 'the ontological tyranny'. Contemporary analytic philosophers recognise that the meaning of 'objectivity' and of 'objective' is not 'transparent, simple, stable and clear' and have offered various accounts of it. In an important 1995 article in *Synthese*, 'Objectivity and the Double Standard for Feminist Epistemologies', Lloyd identifies four distinct meanings of 'objective' appearing in these accounts: (1) detached, disinterested, unbiased, impersonal, invested in no particular point of view (or not having a point of view) and predicated of knowers who are detached, disinterested and so on; (2) public, publicly available, observable, or accessible (at least in principle); (3) existing independently or separately from us. (Note that meanings (2) and (3) denote a relationship between reality and knowers in which reality is observable, publicly available and exists independently of knowers.) Finally, (4) 'objective' means really existing, Really Real, the way things really are; in this sense 'objective' denotes a status of independent existence regardless of any relationship it has to knowers.

All four definitions are at work in the philosophical picture lying behind 'the ontological tyranny': 'objective' characterises a relationship between knowers and reality-as-independently existing, and methodologically, the knower must be detached, because investment in a particular belief or attachment to a point of view ('bias') 'could impede the free acquisition of knowledge and correct representation of (independent) reality'. The ontological tyranny begins with the claim that 'objective' reality 'equals all of the Really Real' and is 'converged upon through the *application of objective methods*'. The Really Real can be known since it is publicly accessible to those who use these objective methods and who are properly detached or distinterested. This view assumes (1) that the Really Real is completely independent of us; thus (2) objective knowledge of this Reality requires an 'objective method' characterised by detachment, because (3) any attachment or point of view might interfere with our independence from the reality we wish to know, and (4) this reality is publicly accessible, if it is accessible at all. The ontological tyranny appears in philosophically popular forms; Lloyd dubs one of these, 'Type/Law Convergent Realism'. In this view, objectivity will result in a convergence on One True Description of reality. Thus real knowledge 'carves Nature at its joints'. This epistemological criterion for knowledge presupposes the metaphysical view that, as Lloyd puts it: 'Nature *has* joints, i.e., "natural" objects and/or events, and kinds, and laws, which could serve (ideally) to guide inquirers' to discover them.

There is no consensus on the best alternative understanding of objectivity. Yet some philosophers hold a 'double-standard' inasmuch as they problematise objectivity while demanding that feminist philosophers not problematise it and accept a view of it based upon the ontological tyranny. Lloyd also argues that once philosophers abandon Type/Law Convergent Realism, they must recognise that in addition to 'resistances by reality', socio-cultural factors are 'necessarily involved in the development of knowledge and concept-formation'. Anthropologists are virtually unanimous in holding that 'sex and gender roles lay the *foundations* of every human society's other social practices', therefore, any epistemology and philosophy of science that includes social interests and values as integral to the acquisition of knowledge should include values and interests related to sex and gender.

Scientific methods developed to ensure objectivity by preventing an individual scientist's interests and personal values from biasing the results of her research are useful, but provide only 'weak objectivity', Harding points out. Feminist and other science studies reveal these methods as too weak to identify widely shared, unnoticed beliefs, interests and values about gender. Harding suggests 'strong objectivity' as a partial solution of this problem. To make it more likely that widely held beliefs and values be examined, Harding, with most feminist epistemologists, calls for greater diversity within knowledge communities, for their self-reflection and for more democratic knowledge procedures. When women within marginalised and dominant groups achieve their own standpoints, these standpoints can contribute to the strong objectivity of scientific and other knowledge accounts. If the standpoints are used to critique dominant accounts of nature and of the social world, they can reveal hidden androcentric, Eurocentric or class-based assumptions.

Holism. Lynn Hankinson Nelson's epistemology and philosophy of science takes up a pragmatist holism recognising no bright line between scientific, philosophical and common-sense theories. It is also naturalised, distinguishing good and bad knowledge production by a balance among the norms of empirical success, predictive success and explanatory power. Epistemology in general describes and explains how knowledge is acquired and epistemology of science how scientific knowledge is acquired. Neither justifies knowledge; instead, the aim is to give an empirically adequate description of the production of knowledge and to suggest changes for improvement in the social processes currently characterising knowledge production.

Rejecting a sharp distinction between theory and observation, Nelson argues that the evidence for a hypothesis includes the observational consequences of the hypothesis and a large set of theories, including common-sense theories, within which it is embedded. Thus she offers a methodological principle for a naturalised feminist account of evidence: evidence is constituted by observations and theories, themselves supported by evidence and by other theories. Moreover, observations themselves depend on theories, and science studies show us that evidence is holistic, that socio-political assumptions function as part of the evidence for a hypothesis or theory. Countering the received view that socio-political values are 'non-cognitive' – not subject to correction the way statements of fact are, and hence cannot enter the context of justification in good epistemic work – Nelson argues that feminist case studies of good scientific work reveal that their influence upon epistemic justification does not necessarily lead to bad science. It is the lack of empirical success that makes poor science. A number of feminist epistemologists reject the received view, most notably Elizabeth Anderson, whose Co-operative Model of Theory Confirmation makes clear the role of such values in science and the influence of science upon such values. On the basis of case studies, Nelson also argues that knowledge is produced and maintained by communities. While individuals put forward candidates for knowledge, they do not know anything autonomously. Even an individual's beliefs depend upon language and theories learned from communities and must meet community standards of reasonableness.

Relativism. We find a strong consensus in feminist epistemology and philosophy of science that work in the history and sociology of science reveals change in standards and methods in the sciences over time with new discoveries, new theories and models, shifting interests and many other reasons. Standards and methods differ from domain to domain and, within the same domain, can vary locally, from laboratory to laboratory. The work of Helen Longino will exemplify feminist responses to the charge that this historical relativism entails pernicious epistemic relativism.

In Longino's account, scientific knowledge, a paradigm for all knowledge, is produced through practices carried out primarily by communities of scientists. Attempts by logical empiricists and post-positivists to find a logical relation between propositions expressing hypotheses or theories and those expressing observational data have failed; therefore, Longino argues, scientific hypotheses are under-determined by sensory perceptions in the sense that perceptions alone tell us nothing about hypotheses, models and theories. Scientists determine which perceptions function as data relevant to a hypothesis and so as evidence for it on the basis of background assumptions they hold. These include both 'cognitive values', which Longino dubs 'constitutive values' – for example, accuracy, simplicity, predictability and so on – arising from the goals of science, and 'contextual values', that is beliefs, socio-political values and interests, including assumptions about gender.

Synchronically and diachronically, different scientific communities arrive at different, sometimes conflicting, theories and models of the same (or apparently the same) phenomena. Hence, epistemologists and philosophers of science search for general norms to determine the superiority of one theory or set of theories and so to avert the radical epistemological relativism suggested by this state of affairs. In her 2001 book, *The Fate of Knowledge*, Longino offers four norms distinguishing knowledge from opinion. Added to traditional empiricist norms such as valid reasoning and empirical adequacy, these norms constitute requirements for the effective criticism without which science and other epistemic practices do not meet our shared understanding of knowledge. They include: (1) venues or 'publicly recognised forums for the criticism of evidence, of methods, and of assumptions and reasoning' – where criticism is given nearly the same weight and presented in the same venues as original research; (2) uptake of criticism, not just toleration of it so that, over time, beliefs and theories change in response to the critical discourse; (3) public standards for evaluating theories, hypotheses and observational practices which are subordinated to the overall cognitive aims of the community and can themselves be criticised and changed in reference to other standards, goals or values held temporarily constant by the community; and (4) tempered equality or equality of intellectual authority within cognitive communities to expose hypotheses to the broadest range of criticism. This equality must be tempered to ensure the diversity of perspectives necessary for effective critical discourse. Thus the exclusion of women and minority men from scientific education and professions is a cognitive failure. In so far as feminist science scholars as well as historians and sociologists of racist practices have documented the role of sex, gender and racial assumptions in the sciences, to ensure that the requirement of tempered equality is met, a community must 'take active steps to ensure that alternative points of view are developed enough to be a source of criticism and new perspectives'. This would ensure that feminist perspectives are among those developed and considered.

Clearly these requirements do not ensure that only one hypothesis or theory prevails. Longino rejects the ontological tyranny and its monism, the view that the aim of science is to find the One True Description of reality using only one general approach. As a contextualist, Longino holds that statements cannot be detached either from their truth conditions or from the context in which their truth conditions are determinable. Thus, they cannot be compared without a third context which gives us the terms in which to compare them. She has a number of arguments for the pluralism she adopts according to which different accounts, including those that conflict, should be understood by analogy with maps having different systems of projection, such as the Mercator or the Peterson projections. And conflicts between theories should be resolved, if possible, by limiting the domain of application of at least one of the conflicting theories. Since this is not always possible, research in some domains might go on until humans die out. Whether monism or pluralism is correct is an empirical question; it may turn out that the natural world is too complex to be captured through a single theoretical approach and pictured in one unified account or that humans are incapable of finding the One True Account. These questions should not be decided a priori by an epistemology or philosophy of science.

Longino proposes three new definitions of knowledge, including the content of knowledge, knowledge-producing practices and the knower. Having a good justification has been understood to distinguish knowledge from opinion. In her new definitions, Longino replaces justification with epistemic acceptability. Her technical definition of 'epistemic acceptability' demarcates content which is the content of knowledge and turns on her new success category, conformation – of which truth is only one mode – to replace both correspondence and coherence theories of truth as the one mark of epistemically acceptable beliefs or knowledge.

E. Potter

See also: critical epistemology; Feminism; Feminist re-readings of the tradition; Haraway; Keller; Le Doeuff

FEMINIST RE-READINGS OF THE TRADITION

That branch of work in the history of philosophy dedicated to re-reading the canon of philosophy by evoking gender. This project bifurcates along the axes of (1) attention to women and (2) investigation of the symbolic imaginary regarding the feminine/masculine. Feminist attention to gender in the history of philosophy has not only resulted in the recovery of 'lost' or 'silenced' women philosophers, it also calls into question models of philosophy and philosophical concepts emerging from a privileging of the masculine.

Attention to women. Canon formation is a topic fraught with controversy. While none would dispute the inclusion of Plato or Kant, there is often contestation concerning which aspects of their corpus are most central, with epistemological texts, for example, often overprivileged in analytic histories of philosophy. Some also question the 'great man' model, in which an appropriate history of modern philosophy would include Descartes, Hobbes, Hume, Leibniz, Locke and Spinoza, but need not mention Pascal, Pufendorf or Vico.

Feminist philosophers of history have contributed to this investigation of canon formation by decrying the forgetting of women philosophers. They have worked to recover the voices and import of philosophers like Jane Addams, Mary Astell, Sor Juana Inés de la Cruz, Jacqueline Pascal, Anna Maria van Schurman and Mary Wollstonecraft. This work has demonstrated that the lack of women philosophers in contemporary histories of philosophy is due neither to the absence of women philosophers nor to the significance and value of their work, but is the result of complex values that inform the narratives of philosophy and determine what questions and styles count as philosophical and whose voices are sufficiently influential to be chronicled. It is sometimes even the result of where we look for philosophy, attending only to the academy and the seminary, and excluding those locations where women are most likely to be found in certain historical periods, such as the convent and the salon.

This attention to women has also included a chronicling of philosophers' perceptions of woman. Through this lens feminists have uncovered a systematic perception of woman as inferior and man as the true form. This has led philosophers of sexual difference such as Luce Irigaray to argue that woman has been defined not in terms of true difference, but in terms of lack according to an A (male) / − A (female) logic well illustrated by Hegel's claim that although women are educable, they are not capable of activities like science or philosophy that demand a universal faculty. Through such a logic, women and indeed the feminine receive no positive definition, no true difference, but are merely an inversion of the masculine. Such investigations have led to the realisation that the very concepts of philosophy have been inscribed by this conception of man and thereby the masculine as the true form.

Symbolic imaginary. This attention to gender has revealed that many of the central categories of philosophy are formed through the exclusion of the feminine. Genevieve Lloyd's early study of the 'maleness' of reason in *The Man of Reason* (1984) demonstrated the ways in which conceptions of rationality have privileged traits historically associated with masculinity and control or transcendence of those historically associated with the female such as the body, the emotions and the passions. Michèle Le Doeuff (*The Philosophical Imaginary*, 1989) has argued that this philosophical imagery of gender is inscribed in dominant philosophical conceptions of reason and thus is not an instance of sexism that can be ignored or excised, for it is at the core of the values from which this central category emerges.

Feminists rereading the canon often find in the work of forgotten women philosophers resources for refiguring the central categories of philosophy. Linda Shapiro ('Princess Elizabeth and Descartes', 1999), for example, turns to the work of Princess Elizabeth in the context of her dialogues with Descartes to locate a resource for rethinking the mind–body dualism. Shapiro finds in her writing a way of respecting the autonomy of thought without denying that reason is dependent on embodiment, including, but not limited to, one's gendered being. And she argues that in reading the work of Elizabeth in conjunction with Descartes' *Passions of the Soul*, a text written at her request, one can both trace the influence of Elizabeth's philosophy upon Descartes' and recover an enriched conception of the interaction of the functions of the soul and the body that is neither a reductionist materialism nor a substance dualism.

Feminist efforts to reveal the denigration of the feminine in the history of philosophy is thus only the first step of a much larger inquiry. Feminists engaged in rereading the tradition are developing reading strategies motivated by our feminist commitments and by a historiography attentive to gender that contribute to a deeper engagement with the texts of philosophy. These strategies emerge out of the feminist critiques of the gendering of the central concepts of philosophy and employ it and more recent attempts to reclaim the feminine as a basis for developing an enriched historiography that foregrounds forgotten elements of texts, as well as ignored authors to advance new ways of thinking about reason, morality and other philosophical concepts. By identifying the denigration of feminine traits and the reasons for the forgetting of gender, we could begin to participate in new ways of reading historical texts that permitted or enacted unifications of emotion, intellect and imagination.

This realisation has led to various efforts to identify and refigure the role of the feminine in the texts of canonised philosophers (Irigaray) and to examine the specifically feminine sites of philosophy (Conley). In this fashion feminist historians of philosophy have begun to identify resources for engendering the central concepts of philosophy in ways not predicated on the forgetting of gender. These reading strategies are diverse and reflect the different positions and training of feminists themselves. Some like Michèle Le Doeuff, Penelope Deutscher, Sarah

Kofman and Luce Irigaray bring deconstructive methods to bear on canonical texts. Others like Annette Baier, Barbara Herman and Martha Nussbaum read through the lens of contemporary feminist revaluing of the emotions. Yet others like John Conley and Susan James work to recover forgotten voices and ignored themes.

In such attention to neglected aspects of historical texts we are motivated by our own feminist wonder at the relation between reason and emotion in the play of the canon, a feminist inspired desire to find a place in-between mind and body, a third way. In this sense, our desires are enacted in our reading strategies.

N. Tuana

FEUERBACH, LUDWIG (1804–72) German philosopher associated with the 'Young Hegelians'. Having enrolled in 1824 at the University of Berlin to study theology, Feuerbach soon thereafter turned to philosophy. His doctoral thesis of 1828, entitled *De Ratione, una, universali, infinita* ('On Reason, One, Universal, and Infinite'), was rooted firmly in Hegel's metaphysics, but also challenged important elements of Christian doctrine and indicated the future direction of Feuerbach's critical research. In *Thoughts About Death and Immortality* (1830), Feuerbach expanded upon ideas he had presented in his dissertation, arguing openly against the concept of personal immortality. At the same time, he affirmed the immortality of reason and spirit in the absolute sense, just as Hegel had done. For the impiety of his views, Feuerbach lost his teaching post at the University of Erlangen and never returned to academic life. Through the decade following Hegel's death in 1831, he worked as an independent scholar, making important contributions to the growing body of work associated with the Young Hegelians but also maintaining some distance between himself and the organisational centres of the movement in Berlin and Halle.

By 1839, Feuerbach had grown more strident in his criticism of the idealist and speculative tendencies in Hegel's thought. His *Essence of Christianity* (1841) was among the most influential tracts produced by the Young Hegelians, acting in some respects as a catalyst for the movement as a whole. In this work, Feuerbach initiated what has come to be known as the anthropological turn in modern German philosophy, which had until then been guided, if not defined, by its spirit of idealism, by largely epistemological concerns and by its contempt for the sensuous foundations of human experience. The basis of Feuerbach's anthropological materialism is his claim that the real composition of human subjectivity resides as much in the objects of contemplation and in sensuous experience as it does in the mind or spirit.

Much of Feuerbach's lasting renown is due to the special significance attached to his work by Marx and Engels. In his brief critical notes on Feuerbach, eventually published in 1886 as the *Theses on Feuerbach*, Marx penned his celebrated maxim: 'The philosophers have merely *interpreted* the world in various ways; the point is to *change* it'. In abbreviated form, this was the statement of Marx's break with Feuerbach, whose materialism was seen as too contemplative and therefore unhistorical. For his part, Engels had seen fit to write a lengthy work, entitled *Ludwig Feuerbach and the End of Classical German Philosophy* (1886), which in some sense gave Feuerbach the valedictory place in the history of ideas that Hegel had once occupied. Engels's praise was not unqualified, however, and he saw Feuerbach as the last exhausted gasp of speculative approaches to the human condition.

Feuerbach married into wealth and was able to spend his most productive years free from financial concerns. Following the ill-fated revolution of 1848, to which he had attached some hopes, and following the collapse of his wife's family fortune, he retired to a life of provincial introspection and malaise.

P. Lewis

FICHTE, JOHANN GOTTLIEB (1762–1814) German philosopher associated with the German Idealist movement. While taking his point of orientation from Kant's Critical philosophy, Fichte was concerned to rectify philosophical difficulties he saw arising from Kant's system. Specifically, he wanted to eliminate Kant's notion of a thing-in-itself and ground philosophy in a single principle: subjectivity. By deducing his system from this first principle, Fichte thought he could overcome the dichotomy between freedom and necessity, and between practical and theoretical philosophy.

Working at the University of Jena, Fichte articulated the foundation and details of his system, which he called the *Wissenschaftslehre* or 'Doctrine of Science'. *Wissenschaftslehre* is not the name of a single text, but of a system whose conception Fichte articulated in many lectures and writings. The central concept is that of the self-positing I, a principle of subjective self-constitution that is the highest condition for the possibility of all experience, objects of experience and moral action. Fichte stresses the fact that the I is not a fact (*Tatsache*), but an act (*Tathandlung*, his own coinage), and he often calls it an act of intellectual intuition. The I must be distinguished from an empirical consciousness; it is infinite and not accessible to experience, since it acts to ground experience. Fichte stresses that the I cannot ultimately be rationally justified as a first principle – it can only be recommended to people with a lively sense of their own inner essence as free beings. The other candidate for a first principle, Fichte argues, material objectivity, leads to a morally unacceptable determinism and cannot account for consciousness.

Starting from the I, Fichte proceeds to ask about the conditions for the I's act of self-positing. He discovers a number of successor principles, such as the existence of a not-I. That is, the I posits its own limit in the process of self-determination. This is the source of our experience of objects, or impressions 'accompanied by a feeling of necessity'. Fichte also deduces conditions such as spatiality, temporality and causation out of the I's self-positing act.

In 1798, Fichte began articulating a philosophy of religion 'in accordance with the principles of the *Wissenschaftslehre*'. He was accused of atheism and an enormous public controversy ensued, which ended in his expulsion from Jena and exile to Berlin, where he helped found the university. In addition to continuing work on the *Wissenschaftslehre*, Fichte continued his life-long devotion to public education, pointing out the consequences of some of his ideas for political and moral practice. Although he had been a staunch and outspoken liberal early in his career, his later writings took a more conservative turn and today he is widely known for his *Addresses to the German Nation* (1808). Although this is viewed as a founding document in the history of German nationalism, it should be recalled that these talks were held under French military occupation, which Fichte reviled; they are mainly concerned with questions of German sovereignty, education and the relation between national and linguistic identity.

J. Norman

See also: German Idealism; intellectual intuition; transcendental ego

FIDELITY (*fidélité*) The notion in Badiou's philosophy connecting truth and the event. Any situation (personal, historical, scientific or aesthetic) is structured around its own void, and the event makes the void visible by naming it. Within the situation, however, it remains totally undecidable whether or not the event belongs to it since the situation recognises only that which can be structurally defined, and the event, as originating in the void, by definition escapes structural laws. It is always doubtful that an event ever took place (see the treatment of the French Revolution in contemporary historiography).

Only an interpreting intervention can produce this decision by retro-actively apprehending the situation from the perspective of the event. This intervention introduces an immanent rupture in the situation: it discerns all the elements and posterior events whose existence and meaning depend on the circulation of the event's name. This practice that makes out the features of the event's phantasmatic presence within a situation is fidelity. Against the veridicity achieved by structural languages, fidelity produces a truth (*vérité*), defined as the set of all the terms connected to an event. Fidelity also induces subjects, and is thus the criterion of ethics. In natural terms, a human being is only a member of a species (human) belonging to the animal genre. A subject is never given. Only when a human animal responds actively to the appeal of an event by engaging in a fidelity-procedure, does it transcend its animality and become a subject of that truth.

J.-P. Deranty

FINK, EUGEN (1905–75) German philosopher and Husserl's last research assistant, who worked closely with him in the entire period of Husserl's retirement (1928–38) which culminated in *The Crisis of European Sciences and Transcendental Phenomenology* (1936). This was the work that captured so much interest in the postwar philosophic renaissance in Europe and in the same period figured in the increasing interest in continental ways of thinking on the part of North American philosophers. Having studied with both Husserl beginning in 1925 and Heidegger after the latter's return to Freiburg in 1928, Fink was able to see the validity of the mutual critique that the thinking of each could exercise on the other. This together with his own broad grasp of philosophers such as Hegel and Nietzsche allowed him also to see richer options than Husserl had at hand for recasting the conceptions that both guided the detailed analyses in Husserl's extraordinarily wide-ranging investigations and were to be corrected by the results of those analyses.

Carrying out thus a crucial aspect of Husserl's own phenomenolo-gical programme, Fink showed an exceptional ability to grasp Husserl's work integratively rather than in terms of the individual themes of particular manuscript studies. This integrative capacity is manifest in Fink's *Sixth Cartesian Meditation* (1988), which, written for Husserl in 1932, undertakes a radical analysis of the character and limits of transcendental method. For example, his defining the issue of trans-cendental phenomenology as the constitution of the world ('The Phenomenological Philosophy of Edmund Husserl and Contemporary Critique', 1933) enabled him to distinguish the core of Husserl's work from NeoKantianism, while allowing him to point to the fundamental ambiguity of Heidegger's conception of *Dasein*, a critique he unfortunately never brought to published form and that remains in his as yet unpublished *Nachlass* notes. Since the temporality and spatiality of the world as the arena of being as appearing framed not only experiential life but also intellectual and reflective cognition, especially to the extent that this was intuitionally grounded and linguistically articulated, phenomenological work itself could not be conceived as taking a perspective on the constitution of the world from a position beyond the world.

It was also only in terms of this same limitation, however, that any question of being could be raised, whether by Husserl in transcendental phenomenology or in the transformed phenomenological practice of Heidegger's fundamental ontology – which Fink saw as predicated upon the ambiguity of *Dasein* as both within the world as constituted and the very dynamic that structured the world as world. Fink's resolution of the problem lay in his clear delineation of two fundamental dimensions to the programme of phenomenological investigation. One was that of detailed investigation; the other was that of the elaboration of concepts to guide and then to articulate the results of the analysis, the 'speculative' dimension ('Die intentionale Analyse und das Problem des spekulativen Denkens', 1951).

It was this 'speculative' dimension, then, on which Fink concentrated in his own work after Husserl's death and especially in the years after the Second World War.

R. Bruzina

FLESH (of the World) (*la chair du monde*) A phrase made popular by Merleau-Ponty's *The Visible and the Invisible*. With it, Merleau-Ponty was developing an ontology based on embodiment: the whole world (being) is made of flesh; the world itself is a union of the soul and the body, the word made flesh, incarnation. Thus Merleau-Ponty's ontology was distinctly anti-Cartesian, and by that token was able to influence much feminist thinking since now we have a non-reductionist view of bodies: bodies are not just what a science of mechanisms tells us; they are not simply machines.

The term (*chair*) comes into French philosophy as a translation of Husserl's use, in *Ideas II*, of the term 'Leib', which, unlike 'chair' and 'flesh', is etymologically connected to life (*Leben*). It is not always translated into French by 'chair'; sometimes it is 'le corps propre', 'one's own body'. Through this translation of 'Leib' we can see the problem it raises; there is no alterity, only that which belongs to oneself. Thus the generation of French philosophers after Merleau-Ponty criticised 'flesh'. Derrida showed there can be no 'one's own' as such; there is always the contamination in my own body of the other. For their part, Deleuze and Guattari developed an idea of a 'body without organs', which is 'machinic' but not mechanistic. And Foucault's still unpublished fourth volume of *The History of Sexuality*, on the Middle Ages, was to be called *Les aveux de la chair* (*Confessions of the Flesh*), implying thereby that 'the flesh' is not a universal term, but one that is pre-Cartesian, indeed medieval.

L. Lawlor

FLORENSKY, PAVEL (1882–1937) Arguably Russia's most important philosopher – and one of Europe's greatest polymaths, who is often compared to Leonardo, Pascal and Leibniz – his work is now being read by an increasingly large and appreciative audience in the West, especially in Germany where his *Collected Works*, in ten volumes, are currently being translated. Of Russian and Armenian ancestry, Florensky grew up in the Caucasus Mountains where he developed a mystical affinity for nature that never left him and which may be taken as a key to his writings, as he suggests in the posthumously published work, *To My Children: Recollections of a Youth in the Caucasus* (1992). A brilliant mathematician, physicist and engineer (inventor of a famous industrial lubricant and editor of the Soviet *Technological Encyclopedia*), while at the same time a distinguished linguist (who knew more than a dozen languages), art historian, theologian and philosopher, Florensky was ordained an Orthodox priest in 1911, and insisted on wearing his priestly cassock, cross and cap while conducting his university lectures and scientific research even during the era of Stalinist purges. For this, he was sent to the labour camps in Siberia in 1933; he was eventually executed by the KGB at the infamous Solovki Monastery gulag and buried in a mass grave, a loss lamented in Solzhenitsyn's *Gulag Archipelago*.

Florensky's major work, *The Pillar and Ground of Truth* (1914), in many ways invites comparison with Heidegger's *Being and Time*, especially in linking traditional ontology themes with studies of individual existence as it is lived. At the same time, the work draws heavily on the tradition of Byzantine philosophy and theology, unifying dichotomies in ways that may seem strikingly paradoxical to Western conceptuality: he employs a philosophical approach akin to phenomenology, even as he deals both with metaphysical and logical issues that would seem immune to such an approach; he affirms both the Parmenidean dialectic of unity and the Heracleitean dialectic of difference; he maintains Plato's noetic (and metaphysical) emphasis on the invisible while affirming Aristotle's discursive (and epistemological) focus on the visible; and he affirms German Idealism's insight into the triune structure of being while insisting on Kierkegaard's demand that such understanding must proceed from existential experience. And it is indeed one of the primary claims of *The Pillar and Ground of Truth* that truth must necessarily appear antinomial to discursive thought, that it is something to be encountered only in 'discontinuities'. In a series of twelve letters, which each like a haiku poem combines seasonal and affective ambience with metaphysical insight, he proceeds from the principle of identity (A = A) to an affirmation of radical otherness (A + [− A]), maintaining that 'the act of knowing is not just gnoseological but also an ontological act', that 'knowing is a real going of the knower out of himself', and hence that genuine knowledge entails a union of love with the known. The work is perhaps best known for its brilliant elaboration of the Divine Sophia, or Holy Wisdom, a numinous depth of nature and cosmic ordering that Florensky understands aesthetically, and that has powerful implications both for feminist and for environmental philosophy.

The major collection of his later essays was published posthumously in Russian as *From the Watersheds of Thinking* (1990). In aesthetics, Florensky was associated with the Russian Symbolists, and some of his more important essays on the theory and history of art have been translated into English in the volumes *Iconostasis* (1996) and *Beyond Vision: Essays on the Perception of Art* (2002).

B. Foltz

FOUCAULT, MICHEL (1926–84) French philosopher usually classified as a poststructuralist, with a profound impact across the breadth of the humanities and social sciences. Foucault was not interested in finding the universal structures of history or society or language (as structuralists often were); in fact, he refused to assume that there were any unchanging structures at all in history, society or language, insisting that we approach phenomena with the expectation that investigation will reveal them to be historically emergent and thoroughly contingent. He did, however, adopt the structuralist idea that human subjectivity could not be the foundation for knowledge, a view that sets him apart from philosophers such as Kant and Hegel, for example, who hold that the characteristic features or activities of subjectivity generate and guarantee our knowledge.

Subjectivity and subjectivising practices. Foucault critiques the notion of subjectivity operative in European philosophy from

Descartes through Husserl and puts forth alternative 'knowledges', which he calls 'genealogies'. He insists:

> One has to dispense with the constituent subject, to get rid of the subject itself to arrive at an analysis which can account for the constitution of the subject within a historical framework. And this is what I would call genealogy, that is, a form of history which can account for the constitution of knowledges, discourses, domains of objects, etc., without having to make reference to a subject which is either transcendental in relation to the field of events or runs in its empty sameness throughout the course of history. ('Truth and Power', 1980)

In short, Foucault wants to think through Western history and current networks of knowledge and power without resorting to any sort of universals at all, including a universal form of subjectivity.

This raises two big questions for anyone trained in the history of Western philosophy. First, how will Foucault justify his own knowledge claims if he refuses to ground them in the foundation that philosophers have used for the last four hundred years, namely universal subjectivity? Second, how will Foucault account for subjectivity as a phenomenon if he denies it any sort of transcendental status? While most of Foucault's critics have been especially interested in the first question, often asserting that he fails to ground his claims at all, most of Foucault's adherents and sympathisers have been far more interested in the second question, as was Foucault himself. Both questions will be addressed here, beginning with Foucault's own.

'My objective', Foucault asserts, looking back over the previous two decades of his research, 'has been to create a history of the different modes by which, in our culture, human beings are made subjects' ('The Subject and Power', 1983). If subjectivity is not a universal given, if subjects emerge in history and change through history, some account must be given of how these events occur. Of course, the means by which humans are made into subjects vary historically, just as the types of subjects that they become vary. Therefore no single theory of what Foucault called 'subjectivisation' is possible. Instead, it is necessary to study the many historically specific ways that different sorts of subjects have been created, and this is exactly what Foucault does.

Retrospectively, Foucault identifies three modes of subjectivisation under study in his work from about 1961 until 1983. The first involves forms of inquiry or sciences. For example, Foucault studies the genealogies of the twentieth-century sciences of linguistics, economics and biology in *The Order of Things* (1966). In this work he demonstrates that how Westerners have understood themselves in relation to language, labour and physical life has changed considerably over the last four centuries. (Hence, to take any one of these characteristics of 'the subject' as definitive of or foundational for knowledge, as many thinkers have, is to build a house on shifting sand.) These changes are closely tied to institutional, political, economic, technological and other cultural changes; they are not due to a refinement in scientific knowledge or an advance in rationality (nor are they completely reducible to changes in the means of production, as a Marxist analysis might have it). Furthermore, how people think, talk and theorise about themselves as language users, productive labourers and material entities helps shape the capacities and limits of their subjectivities.

A second mode by which humans are transformed into subjects Foucault labels 'dividing practices'. At a given time, dominant theories and institutional structures group people into categories. For example, some people are held to be sane, while others are insane; some are sick, while others are healthy; some are criminals, while others are normal, non-violent and law-abiding. Being placed into such groups not only determines the parameters of an individual's life – especially if the members of the group one is placed in are typically incarcerated; it also shapes a person's self-image and experience of him or herself in far-reaching ways, in effect instilling in that person a kind of subjectivity. Foucault studies these practices of subjectivisation in several books, including *Madness and Civilisation* (1961), *The Birth of the Clinic* (1963), *Discipline and Punish: The Birth of the Prison* (1975) and *The History of Sexuality, Volume One* (1976). His most influential study in this regard is *Discipline and Punish*, wherein he shows how modern power functions as 'normalisation', identifying and rendering all individuals measurable according to statistical norms.

The third mode of subjectivisation Foucault identifies and studies encompasses methods, routines, practices and disciplines that a person undertakes more or less consciously in an attempt to alter his or her own subjectivity. Very generally these self-shaping activities or techniques of the self might be called ethical practices, because they are engaged in as a way of establishing oneself in an *ethos*, a more or less chosen, self-aware way of life. Foucault's last works are devoted to the study of such practices. These include the second and third volumes in the *History of Sexuality* series, *The Use of Pleasure* and *The Care of the Self* (1984). Here Foucault examines the self-forming activities of the classical Greeks and Romans – such as dream interpretation, self-examination at bedtime, keeping a journal of helpful adages and memories, fasting and so on – and shows how these activities gave a sense of rightness, proportion, meaning or purpose to life in the ancient world. These practices were meant to strengthen a person, make him (or occasionally, in the Roman world, her) resistant to the opinions of the crowd or to the fears and cravings of the body when independent or dangerous action was necessary, and overall to create a beautiful life. Foucault is interested in the Greeks and Romans in great part because their ethical practices were so different from, yet often also so similar to, the techniques of self that developed in medieval Christianity. Many of the actual activities were the same – self-examination and fasting – but the type of self to be shaped was quite different. Whereas the Greeks wanted to become firm masters of themselves, the Christians wanted to become totally submissive to God and to the representatives of God on earth. Christians adapted pagan exercises to their own purposes, changing them in important ways even while perpetuating them.

This inquiry into ancient practices or 'technologies of the self' raises the question of what practices of the self are current in modern, post-Enlightenment society. Foucault was very interested in that question, although he did not write a book on the topic. In a number of interviews he notes that in Western societies in the twentieth century there is no single, agreed-upon idea about what counts as a good or beautiful life, and belief in any sort of universal standards for, or purpose of, human life or selfhood is in decline. Whether that loss makes us happy or terrifies us, Foucault thinks, we are all faced with it. 'From the idea that the self is not given to us', he says, 'I think there is only one practical consequence: we have to create ourselves as a work of art' ('On the Genealogy of Ethics', 1983). In Foucault's view, this task of self-creation is the real business of philosophy.

This activity of self-stylisation is not mere whimsy, as some of Foucault's detractors have suggested. No real work of art, no matter how joyously playful it may be when it assumes its final form, can come into being without laborious cultivation of skill, knowledge and insight. Just as with great painting, music and poetry, so with great philosophy, artful and beautiful self-stylisation. One could read all of Foucault's philosophical writing as the product of his own philosophically artistic, self-transformative labour. He writes books, he says in the introduction to *The Use of Pleasure*, in order to think differently from the way that his society, his culture, his time and his personal history have led him to think, which means in order to live, to be, differently from the way that, at any given time, he is.

Here, as in many other places, Foucault's work shows the influence of Nietzsche, who spoke often of self-overcoming, the self-transformations that occur as one resists and works one's way out from under the values and beliefs that one has inherited and taken for granted. Foucault engages in genealogical study in part to loosen the grip that his culture's values, sciences, and philosophical categories have on him. For him, philosophical writing can be said to be an *askesis*, a technology of the self.

Genealogy and power. Geneaological work is especially suited for this kind of self-overcoming project. A genealogy presupposes a time prior to something's or someone's coming into existence. It is a tracing of the ancestors of a given person or concept or phenomenon, of the contingencies and clashes that resulted in the familiar forms, objects and subjectivities that populate our world. History, shaped by the metaphysical commitments of modern philosophy, too often takes the form, Foucault writes, of 'an attempt to capture the exact essence of things, their purest possibilities, and their carefully protected identities'. But if we really pay attention to history, we will discover that there is nothing permanent behind the succession of appearances of events and things, no 'timeless and essential secret, but the secret that they have no essence or that their essence was fabricated in a piecemeal fashion from alien forms' ('Nietzsche, Genealogy, History', 1977). As we learn this about our own basic concepts – such as sexuality, sanity or health – we may be shaken; we may find ourselves changing in response to the destabilisation of the ideas that form our own subjectivities.

Foucault's investigations into the genealogies of sciences, subjectivities, and categories leads him to consider the concept of power. Often historical change occurs because of conflicts, multiple factions in struggle. One group or individual seeks to influence the behaviour of others or to control some aspect of a situation; others resist that effort, and something new is born of that strife. Power, then, seems to be central to genealogical accounts of historical change.

But Foucault found traditional accounts of power inadequate to illuminate the kinds of forces and struggles he was investigating. He began to rethink power through the early 1970s. The result, by 1975, is what he calls his 'analytics of power', which is set forth in *Discipline and Punish* and more explicitly in *The History of Sexuality, Volume One*. Power is not to be understood as an all or nothing situation, where one faction possesses power and another lacks it. Power is not a possession at all; it is a relation of struggle. This means that resistance is internal to power. Whenever we resist someone's attempt to force us to behave a certain way, we are engaging in a power relation. Power relations occur at every level of society, including personal relationships. Networks of power form when the same clashes with similar outcomes occur repeatedly over a period of time across a whole field of relations.

Thus a struggle between a husband and a wife over who will do household chores is a power relation at what Foucault calls the micro-level. But thousands of similar clashes with similar outcomes across an entire social field could constitute a network of force relations that might be analysed as 'sexism' or as 'the battle of the sexes'. Networks of power cannot exist without the repetition of power relations at the micro-level. But struggle at the micro-level is affected by the existence or non-existence or collapse of networks. Power relations are mutually reinforcing, then. And the networks they form are not usually intentional creations of any person or group; instead they are the relatively stable institutionalisation of repeated micro-events. If a certain network becomes so reinforced, so stabilised, that there is little or no chance that micro-relations can do anything but repeat previous events without alteration, then power relations have hardened into a situation of domination where genuine struggle (and hence significant *relation*) is no longer possible. Such occurrences are relatively rare, fortunately, at least over long periods of time. Most power formations are not in fact very stable and can be altered by changes at the micro-level. Genealogical study must keep both micro-level struggles and macro-level social institutions and cultural forms in view so as to take account of how concepts, subjectivities, knowledges and other phenomena form, give rise to differences and disintegrate. Studies that pay attention only to the macro-level – only to the top of the existing hierarchy, such as the sovereign or the ruling class – often overlook the most important events in the history of configurations of power.

But if everything is shaped in history and relations of power, what of Foucault's own claims about contingency, history and power networks? Some critics have claimed that Foucault's work undercuts itself, because by insisting that nothing is permanent he leaves himself with no solid ground (like universal truths of subjectivity or laws of logic) from which to make judgements. Why should anyone believe what Foucault has to say?

In fact Foucault does not make sweeping claims about the contingency of all of history and every conceivable concept. Rather, he simply refuses to assume anything is not contingent. He shifts the burden of proof to those who would claim universal truth or metaphysical absolutes. In the meantime, he shows that many things we have heretofore taken to be universal or necessary or absolute in fact are not, and he shows this by giving historical accounts that follow the rules of good historical practice in the present day. All Foucault must do in order to engage in effective genealogical practice is to produce plausible genealogies that challenge the status of cherished ideas. And he does that very well. That is why his genealogies can function as social critique and why they are so likely to transform their readers. Thus, Foucault's genealogies can be a self-overcoming experience, an element in the creation of a new *ethos* not only for Foucault, but for Foucault's readers as well.

L. McWhorter

See also: archaeology; biopower; Embodiment; Enlightenment; episteme; Epistemology; French Maoism; Gender; Genealogy; Geography; governmentality; heterotopia; normalisation; panopticon; Poststructuralism; Queer Theory; Sex and sexuality; Simulacrum; Structuralism; techniques of the self; Thought

FOUR-FOLD (*Geviert*) A word that appears in the early 1950s in Heidegger's idiom and marks a new development in his thought, as is evident from the ssays in *Poetry, Language, Thought*. Like the word *Gestell*, though in a sense that is altogether different, it suggests a power of gathering ('*Ge-*'), or the gathering together of different – in fact, four (*vier*) – horizons, which together make up the fabric of the real, or the unfolding of the truth of Being: earth, sky, mortals and divinities. Following in the footsteps of certain works of art, and of poetry in particular (Hölderlin, Rilke), 'meditative' or 'genuine' thought, as a form of 'Gelassenheit', is the thought that, unlike metaphysical, calculative thought, is able to see everyday 'things' (such as houses and bridges) as the concrescence of earth, sky, mortals and divinities. In meditative thought, and in poetic thinking, human beings are envisaged as being *on* and *of* the earth, as dwelling on the earth and belonging to it. Our being rests in our capacity to safeguard the earth, to protect it from thoughtless exploitation and to defend it from the attacks of technology. The earth is the place of growth (*phuein* in Greek, from which *phusis*, or nature, is derived), from which things grow skyward. Sky suggests divinities that visit and depart and in departing gesture towards mortals who dwell on earth. 'Being' originally names the unified presencing of the fourfold of earth, sky, divinities and mortals – in the things. To open thinking to this onefold presencing in things is indeed to preserve the unconcealment and secure the concealment at play in being.

M. de Beistegui

FRAMING (*cadre*) A Derridean term for the undecidable border between inside and outside and thus as the neglected but necessary emphasis for any theory or practice of aesthetic analysis. He points to how, in Kant's *Critique of Judgement*, the frame is strangely grouped with columns supporting buildings and clothing on statues as an example of something accessory to the work of art. Derrida shows how the work (*ergon*) constantly calls upon a whole series of framing supports (*parerga*) – not just the frame itself, or the wall or space that the work divides, but also the concepts of authorship and authenticity, as well as the museum – in order to define itself and determine its institutional status.

The French word for frame (*cadre*) is derived from the Latin for '(four) square' (*quadrus, carré*) and is related to *carte* (map, chart, card). Derrida plays on these senses especially in 'Envois' (*The Post Card*) where, among other things, it is a matter of the relation between private (inside) and public (outside) correspondence, and between image and writing. For the undecidability of the frame's status means that framing effects come to invade and 'corrupt' the surface of the work itself, creating a graphic heterogeneity that is both pictorial and discursive. In the same book Derrida draws attention to the importance of framing for literary analysis, finding that Lacan, in a move typical of approaches to the aesthetic object in general, presumed to bypass such effects in his haste to arrive at what he supposed to be the central truth of Poe's *Purloined Letter*.

D. Wills

FRENCH MAOISM A Marxist-Leninist political and philosophical movement that enjoyed a wide influence on French thought and had a limited influence on French society. Contemporaneous with other Chinese-inspired radical movements, French Maoism differed from Italian Maoism and the American Black Panther Party inasmuch as the revolutionary violence it advocated was largely rhetorical and in the wide support it attracted from French intellectuals.

The Maoist 'revolution' in France did not start in the county and move to the city. Quite the contrary, French Maoism began in Paris around 1963 as a dissident intellectual movement within the French Communist Party (*Parti Communiste Français* or PCF). Frustrated by the PCF's inability to 'de-stalinise' and inspired by the Sino-Soviet split, small radical groups began to look to Mao's philosophy and to the Cultural Revolution for new models of revolutionary theory and practice. Althusser's *For Marx* (1965), a leftist critique of Stalinism (and of its alternative Marxist Humanism) that owed much to Mao's text *On Contradiction* (1937), is the most significant theoretical output of this period of the movement. Inspired by scholastic debates, some of Althusser's students at the École Normale Supérieure formed an avowedly Maoist revolutionary cell. When student revolts began in

May of 1968, these 'Chinese' stood on the sidelines, judging the whole spectacle to be bourgeois and counter-revolutionary. After the demonstrations widened to include workers, the Maoist students attempted to direct the revolution 'from within' by venturing into factories and trying to board trains for the country. Frustrated at summer's end by the State's successful reconstitution, this original cell splintered, producing yet more cells. Increasingly popular and activist, these groups grew to have a far greater impact on French intellectual and political life in the early 1970s than did any of the 'theoretical' Maoists of the 1960s.

Marked by admiration for the Chinese model of bringing the revolution to the masses, by 'third world' sympathies, by anti-sovietism (as well as anti-capitalism) and by calls for 'armed struggle', political French Maoism is perhaps best distinguished by its spirit of populism and spontaneity. Always with 'the people', Maoists were eager to fight for any radical cause so long as it appeared liberatory. Though there is no archetypical Maoist philosophy, its spirit influenced much French thought during the early 1970s. Sartre applauded Maoist actions and saw their 'adaptability' as the requisite model for continued class struggle. In literary theory, the journal *Tel Quel* and its editors Kristeva and Sollers explicitly aligned themselves with Maoism, arguing that not only a political revolution but also a 'revolution in language' was necessary to break down 'phallogocentric' orders. Foucault's *Discipline and Punish* (1975) was inspired by his conversations with imprisoned Maoist activists. These discussions and his researches resulted in an action group, the *Groupe d'information sur les prisons* (GIP), which successfully agitated for prison reform. Aligned with the members of GIP and other intellectuals, Maoist groups also enjoyed some success in transforming French public attitudes towards women and homosexuals. Though many of these changes have endured, Mao's death in 1978 and revelations about his dictatorial practices effectively ended French Maoism as a theoretical and political movement.

W. Lewis

FREUD, SIGMUND (1856–1939) Viennese neurologist and founder of psychoanalysis. Freud's initial formation in neuropsychiatry has nothing to do with the field he created later. It will give his work a scientistic bent that at times confuses his theory, whose real object is the signifier's symbolic effects on man. However, he will never abandon his claim for a scientific status for psychoanalysis, lest it be confused with magic, religion or a traditional, hermeneutic 'art of interpretation'. The discovery of the unconscious comes from two sources: first, his practice as a psychiatrist forces him to identify mental illnesses that have no identifiable physical causes – hysterical female patients play a determining role here; second, a dream in 1897 on the anniversary of his father's death, which will lead him later to the laying out of the Oedipus complex and to the redaction of *The Interpretation of Dreams*, begun the same year.

The Freudian discovery can be summarised in two words: 'It (or *Id*) thinks'; there is in man an agency that thinks beyond the grasp of conscious thinking. Freud will devote his life to mapping out his breakthrough and its consequences. His first description of the human psyche (known as the first topography) distinguishes three agencies: unconscious, consciousness, preconscious; there relationships are envisioned in the terms of nineteenth century thermodynamics and neurobiology: for example, the preconscious is like a dam containing the huge energy reservoir of the unconscious, and consciousness is an apparatus responding to external stimuli. The second topography, built around 1918 and ushered in by the publication of *Beyond the Pleasure Principle* and *The Ego and the Id*, will get rid of this neurological background by renaming the three agencies the id, the ego and the superego; Freud shifts to an anthropomorphisation, with the id as a locus for drives and desires, the ego representing the individual, the superego standing for parental authority and cultural and societal rules and constraints. In parallel, the first, monist conception centred on the libido is substituted by a dualist view, which sees the psyche as the locus for a struggle between two primordial forces Eros (the libido) and Thanatos (the death drive). Following his central reference to the Oedipus complex, which is present in his work from the very beginning to the end, Freud boldly extends his foray into the terminology borrowed from mythology. He thus shifts the emphasis of psychoanalysis from neurology to the effects of symbolism: 'The theory of drives is, so to speak, our mythology. Drives are mythical beings, great by their indetermination' (*Standard Edition*, XXIII, p. 148); however, the references to natural sciences remain ensconced in the work (for example, the death drive as a return to the non-organic). The real object of psychoanalysis remains ambiguous in its founder's own mind.

The fundamental hypothesis of psychoanalysis is the shift from natural (animal) instinct for reproduction of the species (in German, *Instinkt*) to the notion of drive (in German, *Trieb*), that is a desire that does now obeys symbolic and linguistic determinations instead of the Darwinian law of reproduction of the species. As such nothing in the human domain should escape the purview of psychoanalysis, as Freud's work itself, with its numerous branchings out into religion, literature, mythology and art, testifies. As far as philosophy is concerned, the relationship of psychoanalysis with it is an uneasy one.

Freud's influence on philosophy has been immense, especially in France, often under the influence of Lacan's reading of his work. For confirmation, one may mention Derrida, Deleuze and Guattari, among others. However, Freud's relationship with and impact on philosophy is, for the most part, negative and critical: he sees philosophy as mythical, inasmuch as most philosophers do not take the scientific revolution of the seventeenth century into account. Hence, in *Totem and Taboo* (Chapter II, section 4) psychosis is described as 'a caricature of a philosophical system', and Kant's a priori mental categories are viewed as 'projections of the psyche' (*Gesammelte Werke*, XXII, p. 132). In, brief, philosophy, for Freud, is another belief system. These objections to Western philosophy are addressed to its main trend from Socrates up to Hegel's '*absolute* knowledge', a trend that believes that man can gain a self-explanatory, wholly conscious of itself, view of being. This goes against the essence of Freud's discovery, which supposes that consciousness is not the whole of thinking, that there is another stage, the unconscious, where thinking occurs beyond the grasp of consciousness. Since psychoanalysis denies the possibility of a wholly self-revelatory consciousness, it cannot be assimilated to philosophy and, unlike philosophy, it has no world-view (*Weltanschauung*) to propose, no all encompassing interpretation of human thought (an old temptation of philosophers). Reason is the master of only a small part of the human house, its light doesn't reach into the basement and consciousness is not the essence of the psyche. This leads Freud to link psychoanalysis, not to Western philosophy, but to the decentring of humanity produced by Copernicus' heliocentrism. Hence Freud deliberately puts psychoanalysis and his entire life work under the aegis of the scientific revolution ushered in by Galileo in the seventeenth century: 'In my opinion, psychoanalysis is not able of building for itself a special vision of the universe. Psychoanalysis does not need to do so: being a part of science, it can throw its lot with science' (*New Introductory Lectures on Psychoanalysis, Seventh Lecture*, 1932). This claim for scientific status for psychoanalysis is not without causing ambiguities in Freud's and his followers' work, in so far as Freud will cling up to his death to metaphors borrowed from the natural sciences, whereas the objects of psychoanalysis are effects of language on mankind. So, psychoanalysis has to borrow its methodology from a science of language, not hard sciences. But that is another story that will be written by Lacan.

A. Leupin

FRIEND–FOE RELATION According to Carl Schmitt, an ultimate political distinction to which all political actions and motives can be traced back. The political itself can ultimately be understood through this distinction between friend and foe.

In *The Concept of the Political* (1927), Schmitt shows to what extent friend and foe are political categories. The index of the relationship is the foe. The foe is not a public rival or a personal opponent, but rather, a real possibility for a totality of combatants who stand opposed to another such totality. The point of intersection of the friend–foe distinction is accordingly battle or war, which illuminates why all political concepts bear a polemical character. This polemical character of political discourse is nevertheless only the echo of a principal battle of the parties which must be construed as civil war in matters of internal politics and as war between states in international affairs. Thus the concepts of friend and foe achieve their significance through battle, that is through the real possibility of a mutual killing. War, however, is only the most extreme realisation of this real possibility; enmity thus does not immediately entail a military implementation.

If religious, moral, economic and ethnic oppositions are not political differences as such, they nevertheless receive a political significance when they are grasped as friend–foe relations. Political unities are friend and foe not only in that they bring the possibility of war into play, but also when they are in the position to not regard their political opponents as foes, that is to prevent a war.

P. Trawny

FUNDAMENTAL ONTOLOGY A term which designates Heidegger's project as a whole in the years preceding and leading up to the publication of *Being and Time* in 1927. 'Fundamental' is to be understood in two interrelated senses. First, ontology is fundamental since the question it raises, namely that concerning the sense of being, is the most basic and concrete of all questions. All sciences develop their basic concepts and are concerned with their own foundations. Oftentimes, such foundations are a matter for philosophy, which, in the case of History as a science, for example, interprets historical entities with respect to their historicity, or, in the case of Nature, asks about the distinctive features of this area we call 'Nature'. But fundamental ontology is more fundamental still, in that it asks about the meaning of being in general and raises the question concerning the meaning of the being of all beings. This amounts to the *ontological* priority of the question of the sense of being.

To this, we need to add another priority, which corresponds to the second sense of 'fundamental'; this is what Heidegger calls the 'ontical' priority of the question of Being. It points to the way in which a distinctive being, 'Dasein', must serve as the point of departure and the absolute foundation for the investigation into the question concerning the sense of being. Why? Because the being of Dasein, and the fact that Dasein always moves itself within a certain understanding of its own being, is always implicated and thus presupposed in all the types of investigation and the sciences directed at the various aspects of the world. Therefore fundamental ontology, from which all other ontologies derive, must find its point of departure in the 'existential analytic' of Dasein.

M. de Beistegui

GADAMER, HANS-GEORG (1900–2002) German philosopher best known for his work in philosophical hermeneutics. Gadamer studied with the Marburg neo-Kantians and with Husserl and Heidegger, under whose direction he completed his *Habilitation* thesis. Gadamer's academic career was long and eventful, from 1933 to 1947 at Marburg and Leipzig (under successive National Socialist, Allied and Communist administrations) and then after 1947 at Heidelberg (in what was by then the Federal Republic of Germany ('West Germany')). After his retirement in 1970 Gadamer remained active in philosophy for a full thirty years, until shortly before his death, aged 102.

Throughout his work Gadamer weaves together two basic themes. The first, inspired by classical Greek philosophy, is that dialogue is essential to human understanding. The general lesson of Plato's dialogues, as Gadamer innovatively reads them, is that the meaning of something, as well as its truth, can only come out in the course of a conversation. There is no higher authority than the agreement of partners in dialogue, no 'absolute knowledge' that stands above the process of conversational exchange. Human understanding is thus necessarily mediated by an 'other' (the conversation partner) and is in principle incomplete (like a conversation, it has no natural terminus). The 'finitude' of understanding that follows from its dialogical, intersubjective character is a central principle of Gadamer's philosophy.

The second thought, which Gadamer takes from Heidegger, is that understanding is a primordial feature of human existence: we are, merely on account of being in the world, 'always already' engaged in tasks of understanding. Gadamer follows Heidegger's lead in claiming that understanding, and not some flow of ideas or series of mental representations, is ontologically basic. We do not first neutrally experience the world and then try to understand or interpret that experience; rather experience is from the beginning disclosive of a world that concerns us. Moreover, the world we encounter is shaped by a historically unfolding language, culture and traditions that provide the 'horizon' of our actual and possible experience. Human understanding thus displays 'historicity' and in this sense, too, finitude.

Gadamer thus argues against the idea that understanding can be secured simply by following the correct method. The philosophers of the Enlightenment – and many since – placed great weight on epistemology, or the theory of knowledge, because they thought that truth would only be revealed to inquirers who methodically abstracted from their concrete historical situation. It seemed imperative, then, to state explicitly what the objective method was, and to show how it might be applied universally. In Gadamer's view, such an approach is deeply misguided. It makes it hard to see that even the objective knowledge of the natural sciences has its roots in pre-reflective modes of lived understanding. And it sets up a false and alienating model of understanding in the human sciences. Gadamer's major work, *Truth and Method* (1960), sets out to liberate truth from its ensnarement in method.

His main strategy is to draw attention to the truth-disclosive role of the experience of art and of historical experience. If, in the manner of phenomenology, we attend closely to the experience of art, Gadamer claims, we find that it does not conform to the dominant 'aesthetic paradigm' according to which the art work qua art work elicits a subjective aesthetic pleasure. Rather, art at its best reveals a world in a manner that both resonates with and challenges the world of the recipient. The experience of art is thus properly speaking a mode of understanding. The work makes a claim on an addressee, but the validity of the claim is not independent of the involvement and concerns of the addressees themselves. It follows that, while no artwork is ever fully complete, it always invites completion through its various modes of manifestation and reception.

Gadamer argues for a similar way of thinking about history. The historian can seek to reconstruct or restore the original meaning of past texts and events. Historical understanding, on this model, is geared by the need to avoid the misunderstandings to which temporal distance makes us vulnerable. According to Gadamer, this was the way the German tradition of historical interpretation (that is, the hermeneutic tradition) from Schleiermacher to Dilthey understood its task. By contrast, Gadamer proposes a model of historical understanding as an integration of the past and present. To think of the historian's relation to her subject matter in this way is to transform a merely external relation to the past into an internal relation of involvement and participation: we move from mere consciousness of something from the past to a historical experience of our emplacement in an ongoing tradition. This is the crux of Gadamer's key notion of 'historically effected consciousness'.

The philosophical hermeneutics that Gadamer expounds is not, then, meant as a method to be followed in the interpretation of art and history, still less as a procedure for generating truth in the human sciences generally. His point is rather to retrieve a sense of the experience of understanding that we are in danger of forgetting through an obsession with methodological propriety. Gadamer's lack of concern for questions of interpretive validity and accountability has prompted critics to accuse him of forfeiting critical standards, a charge made easier to make by Gadamer's provocative, reactionary-sounding talk of rehabilitating the notions of authority and tradition. Defenders of Gadamer, on the other hand, can point to the theory of practical reason he draws from Aristotle's *Nicomachean Ethics*, an account that goes a long way to vitiating the appearance of irrationalism.

Besides *Truth and Method*, Gadamer has written a huge number of shorter works including important interpretations of Greek and German philosophy; exchanges with contemporaries such as Habermas, Apel and Derrida; and reflections on science, medicine, philosophical ethics, religion and modern poetry (especially Celan). His intellectual autobiography, *Philosophical Apprenticeships* (1977), contains personal recollections of many of the key figures in twentieth-century continental philosophy.

N. Smith

See also: dialogism; Hermeneutics; Language

GELASSENHEIT ('letting-be') A concept inherited from German mysticism, and from Meister Eckhart in particular, which captures Heidegger's later thought, as expressed in the 1959 essay of the same name. Heidegger asks whether we are a defenceless and perplexed victim at the mercy of the irresistible superior power of technology. Is 'calculative thinking', or technoscience, the only possible modality of thought in the age of technology? Or is there room for another modality of thought and another response to the age and its demands? The question is one of knowing whether we can develop a free relation to technology, that is accept it, use it and at the same time contain it, or whether we are destined to becoming technologised animals, enslaved to the power of calculation and planning? Heidegger suggests that there is another way, one that consists of a letting-go of technology and a letting-be of the world in 'meditative thinking'. This attitude signifies the possibility of dwelling in the world in a completely different way. At issue, for Heidegger, is the possibility of saving the (much threatened) essence of the human as 'ek-sistence', of releasing thought for it, of allowing ourselves to be drawn into the Open as such by letting-go of the technological and calculative environment that has become our familiar world. *Gelassenheit* is an especially difficult idea to grasp, as trying to do so is something of a performative contradiction: how can one grasp the idea of not grasping? How can one represent the idea of not representing?

M. de Beistegui

GENDER A term introduced within 'second-wave' feminism, especially liberal and Marxist feminism, to refer to the socially constituted dimension of sexual difference. From the inception of the concept within Anglophone feminism and through the 1970s and 1980s, gender was differentiated from sex. While 'sex' (female and male) was reserved for denoting biological and other bodily markers of sexual difference, gender (feminine and masculine) came to denote behavioural identity or psychological make-up. Gender, it is argued, is, unlike sex, socially constituted in two senses: in the sense that characteristics are deemed feminine or masculine according to social convention and, more strongly, in the sense that these social conceptions of femininity and masculinity inform the socialisation of females and males such that they conform to those gendered identities. Gender categories usually imply reference to the basic descriptors 'activity' and 'passivity', where femininity is equated with passivity and masculinity with activity and sometimes with aggressivity. More broadly, gender refers to all non-physical, socially determined attributes associated with womanhood and manhood. This concept of gender has undergone revision since the 1980s as a consequence of feminist critiques of the distinction between (biological) sex and (social) gender and through the development of conceptions of human being and the social constitution of identity and sexual difference that do not hold to the related distinctions between body and psychology and between nature and culture.

The point of distinguishing gender from sex has been to work against the essentialism apparent in characterisations of sexual difference that have justified the social subordination of women. The essentialism that feminist theory targets is any claim that men and women have different essences that are a-historical, a-social, and immutable; that such essential natural differences between the sexes manifest themselves in differences in aptitude for different social roles; and that, as these differences are based on essence, they cannot or should not be altered. With the advent of the concept of gender, this essentialism could be challenged for the way it illegitimately assumes a causal relation between biology or nature, on the one hand, and behavioural or social identity on the other. By distinguishing gender from sex and by positing an arbitrary rather than necessary relation between sex and gender, feminists could then argue against any essential gender differences that provide the basis of social discrimination. After all, there are 'feminine' men and 'masculine' women (a formula for the arbitrary relation between sex and gender that has played a central role in the emergence of the idea of 'transgender' since the 1970s). The argument for sexual equality based on the concept of gender begins from the proposition that current differences in gender identity are due to the operation of discriminatory practices effecting asymmetrical socialisation. But, as gender is socially constituted, it, unlike sex, is mutable. Social and economic equality would flow from the resocialisation of women, or from the resocialisation of men and women, where the outcome of resocialisation would be androgynous or gender neutral identity.

While this idea of gender has played a pivotal role in arguments advancing the status of women in Western democracies, it is considered conceptually problematic and has undergone criticism and revision since the 1980s. One problem with the concept as it has been used in arguments for sexual equality is the way that achievement of equality between the sexes has been tied to achieving gender sameness or neutrality. This, as feminists such as Irigaray point out, repeats a 'phallocentric' convention in the conceptualisation of sexual difference that defines woman in terms of man, as either the same as man (and therefore deserving of equal status) or a lack. Given this phallocentrism, is gender sameness desirable or even possible? Critics also point to the way that the political goal of gender neutrality eschews differences between women (particularly racial and ethnic differences) that also contribute to the formation of social identity and have provided the basis for discrimination.

Two kinds of analyses of sexual difference have emerged within continental philosophy that address these criticisms and that have thereby added a degree of complexity to the concept of gender. The first focuses on the social production of meaning and value, pointing to the relational, historically contingent but structurally asymmetrical feature of the concepts 'masculine' and 'feminine' and 'male' and 'female'. Building on the Hegelian idea that identity arises from a relation to difference and the Saussurean idea that, in language, meaning arises through differences between terms rather than adhering to terms themselves, feminist theorists, such as Cixous, argue that the meaning and value of 'masculinity' (and 'male') arises from a systematic (although not necessarily intentional) denigration of the 'feminine' and women ('Sorties', *The Newly Born Woman*, 1975). This phallocentrism of Western discourse is so endemic that other asymmetric dichotomies (such as active/passive, rational/irrational, reason/passion, culture/nature) are reducible to the oppositions man/woman and masculine/feminine. Genevieve Lloyd (in *The Man of Reason*, 1984) has demonstrated, for example, how ideals of Reason in the history of philosophy are male in the sense that they have been built upon the exclusion of the feminine and that 'femininity itself has been partly constituted through such a process of exclusion'. Such analyses of gender at the level of symbolic production suggest that the political goal of gender neutrality through resocialisation obscures, rather than redresses, the way that sexual discrimination operates discursively. The conviction that arguments for equality between the sexes should be accompanied by ongoing critique of the phallocentrism of dichotomous thought, rather than the goal of erasing gender differences, grounds deconstructive feminism.

The second (and related) kind of analysis driving revisions to the idea of gender is critical of the distinction between sex and gender. The distinction itself is a feature of the body/mind dualism inherent in the political ontology from which the idea of gender emerged. Moira Gatens points out in her 'Critique of the Sex/Gender Distinction' (1983, reprinted in *Imaginary Bodies*, 1996) that ignoring the role of the sex of the body in the social constitution of gender difference not only eschews the ways that male and female bodies (and their manifest behaviours) are socially evaluated differently (and usually in a phallocentric manner), but also how sexed bodies are lived differently ('masculine' women are not the same, symbolically or experientially, as 'masculine' men). The political problem for feminism then is not so much that masculinity is privileged over a feminine gender identity as male bodies are privileged over female bodies. Rather than reverting to an essentialism that posits a causal relation between biological sex and gender, such critics develop ontologies that understand gender as socially constituted but necessarily embodied. Accounting for the corporeal dimension of gender identity formation allows consideration of how other bodily markers, such as those of race, impact on the social constitution, expression and experience of identity. Together with deconstructive feminism, such corporeal feminism has modified the idea of gender to include sex (such that gender difference and sexual difference are often used interchangeably) and to advance the proposition that sexed identity formation is material, social, dynamic and multifarious.

R. Diprose

See also: Corporeal Feminism; Embodiment; essentialism; Feminism

GENEALOGY The method of inquiry developed by Nietzsche for the purpose of disclosing 'the origin of our moral prejudices'. In his influential book, *On the Genealogy of Morals* (1887), Nietzsche maintained that every morality is founded on certain 'prejudices' (or unsupported presuppositions) and that a reckoning of these 'prejudices' would reveal the historical conditions under which the morality in question has evolved. As a genealogist of morals, he was particularly concerned to document the natural origins of human values and, so, to link the practice of morality to the survival and flourishing of certain forms of life.

In addition to compiling a descriptive typology of extant moralities, Nietzsche also judged particular moralities, most notably Christian morality, to be inimical to the advance of Western civilisation. He identified the asceticism promoted by Christianity as especially harmful to the cultivation of those singular, heroic figures who alone warrant the future of humankind. He furthermore interpreted the currency and influence of Christian morality as symptomatic of the decay of European culture and of the decline more generally of the human species.

Nietzsche's genealogical method was indebted to the predecessor investigations conducted by the 'English [*sic*] psychologists', including Hume, Carlyle, Spencer, Huxley, Buckle and Bagehot. While appreciative of their efforts to trace morality to its roots in natural human sentiments, he was sharply critical of their ahistorical approach. In their hands, he complained, the inquiry into the natural history of morality devolved into little more than a clumsy pretext for confirming the superiority of 'English' customs and manners. Alternatively, Nietzsche sought to locate the origins of contemporary bourgeois morality in its *other*, in that which it most vehemently rejects and disowns. He consequently documented a lineage that is both familiar *and* unknown (or repressed), incorporating into it all of the values, wishes, impulses and activities that have been collectively identified as 'evil', 'inhuman' and 'barbaric'.

The most famous of Nietzsche's genealogical hypotheses centres on his claim that contemporary bourgeois morality is in fact descended from a *slave morality*, which in turn arose only in reaction to a dominant, predecessor morality that favoured *noble* and *masterly* types. He consequently traced the 'origin of our moral prejudices' to what he calls the 'slave revolt in morality', by means of which the slaves effectively disempowered their oppressors and founded an arena in which they could feel themselves victorious. Claiming to prefer the suffering imposed on them by the evil nobles, the slaves identified their suffering as a mark of their surpassing 'goodness'. That their 'victory' was psychological rather than physical, imaginary rather than real, did not diminish the feeling of power they derived from their 'revolt' against the nobles.

Although the material conditions of slavery have largely disappeared from modern Europe, contemporary bourgeois morality bears the unmistakable imprint of its servile origins. We moderns continue to associate goodness with suffering and evil with spontaneous self-assertion and gratuitous self-enjoyment. What makes us unique within the lineage of the slave morality is that we have fully assumed the role and duties of our own oppressors. We moderns require minimal external surveillance because we rely pre-reflectively on conscience and guilt to police the expression of our natural, animal instincts. Nietzsche thus identifies our experience of guilt as the defining characteristic of contemporary bourgeois morality.

Nietzsche's attention to the experience of guilt also accounts for the generally pessimistic tone of *On the Genealogy of Morals* and the larger cultural diagnosis it advances. While indisputably valuable to human-kind as an instrument of adaptation and survival, the psychological mechanism of guilt has now exhausted its usefulness to the species. We now deny ourselves spontaneous expressions of self-assertion only at the expense of our own future. If humankind does not wean itself from its reliance on guilt, he warned, then the likely fate of the species will be its capitulation to the 'will-to-nothingness', that is the will never to will again.

Nietzsche's genealogical method was taken up and adapted by Foucault. Early in his career, Foucault developed an 'archaeological' approach that allowed him to identify historical periods of epistemic convergence across related sciences and disciplines. Within any such period of epistemic convergence, he discovered, the various discursive practices of science shared a common structure and expressed significant agreement on the general conditions and criteria of truth, knowledge and certainty. As an 'archaeologist of knowledge', Foucault was also concerned to chart the transformations, and eventual disintegration, of epistemic coherence within the discursive practices of science. In *The Order of Things* (1966), for example, Foucault documented the epistemic disintegration of the Classical Age and the subsequent dawning of the Age of Man.

Later in his career, Foucault developed a 'genealogical' approach that enabled him to investigate the intricate power relations that inform discursive practices. As a genealogist, he documented the shifting relationships between power and knowledge within particular discursive practices, and he illuminated the resulting fluctuations in the exclusionary power of these practices. He was especially concerned to conduct genealogical investigations of those discursive practices responsible for enforcing the institutionalised definitions of madness, criminality and sexual deviancy.

Foucault continued to refine his genealogical approach in the 'ethical' writings from the final period of his career. These writings focused on the historical processes of 'subjectivation', through and by means of which human beings are transformed into subjects invested with circumscribed powers and limited capacities for self-legislation. The twofold aim of these investigations was to expose the hidden power interests that are served by various techniques of subjectivation; and to reveal the uniquely productive opportunities made available (if not apparent) to various subjects. In the writings from this period of his career, Foucault was particularly concerned to illuminate the techniques of subjectivation deployed by 'biopower', which mobilises social resources under the pretext of attending to the care of the species and the health of individual human beings.

The historical production of healthy, responsible subjects has most recently contributed to the identification of sexuality as the arena in which subjects may discover the truth about themselves – albeit only by means of familiar, juridical techniques of experimentation, introspection and self-reporting. The goal of sexual 'liberation' thus establishes sexuality as the nexus of personal 'truth', but only at the expense of making subjects ever more dependent on those scientific 'experts' who are ever-ready to judge 'deviant' behaviours against established norms of health and responsibility.

D. Conway

GENERAL STRIKE, SOCIAL MYTH OF THE Sorel's most significant theoretical innovation in revolutionary political theory. As defined in *Reflections on Violence* (1908), this myth is not a distortion of truth, but rather 'a body of images capable of evoking instinctively all the sentiments which correspond to the different manifestations of the war undertaken by Socialism against modern society'. Indeed it is 'the myth in which Socialism is wholly comprised'. In Sorel's interpretation such myths have been the driving impulse behind all great historical movements like early Christianity and the French Revolution. Marx's theory of proletarian revolution, although originally intended to be 'scientific' in the objective sense, is not to be interpreted literally, as this leads to the superstitious positivistic dogma of which the Second International socialists are guilty. Rather it is the symbolic aspect that constitutes what is definitive in Marx's work. As such, Marx, who never consciously dealt in myths, nevertheless sets up the framework that Sorel argues constitutes the 'catastrophic myth' most suited to industrial capitalist society. This myth must be constantly maintained and reinforced in working-class consciousness if there is to be a successful revolutionary struggle because, as Sorel puts it:

> There is only one force which can produce today that enthusiasm without whose co-operation no morality is possible, and that is the force resulting from the idea of the general strike, *which* constantly rejuvenated by . . . proletarian violence produces an entirely epic state of mind, and at the same time bends all the energies of the mind to that condition necessary to the . . . creation of the ethics of the producers.

W. McNeish

GEOGRAPHY The study of the interaction of humans and the earth. The academic discipline of geography is populated by an array of subfields stretching from the physical sciences (climatology, biogeography) through the social sciences (cultural ecology, political geography, urban geography) to the humanities (philosophy of geography and certain new approaches to traditionally social scientific subdisciplines). Despite the historical presence of a few radical geographers (Élisée Reclus, Peter Kropotkin), the modern discipline as a whole, from the 1800s until the 1980s, was heavily dominated by descriptive and explanatory approaches quite distant from continental philosophy and divorced even from such foundational thinkers as Marx and Heidegger. Geographers felt they had little need of 'high theory', and sought the 'truth' of the earth, space, places and landscapes through direct observations; if necessary, these were bolstered by statistical data. Geographers in favour with the state were strong forces for imperialism, while reactionaries (for example, the 'Berkeley School' under Carl Sauer) avoided political and social theories altogether and went 'directly to the landscape'.

Eventually, openings were created in geography that, by the 1970s, began to allow continental thought to filter in. The positivist revolution in Western science spurred geography's 'quantitative revolution', which, largely in the service of the state, threatened in the 1960s to smother other currents. However, it was the sensitivity, albeit atheoretical, which geographers had to the landscape (*Landschaft, paysage*) that helped extract human geography from the positivist trap. Without the benefit of social theory, geographers had been 'reading the landscape' and otherwise trying to make sense of it for a long time, so in the 1970s Marxism (fostered in journals such as *Antipode* and *Hérodote*) and a 'soft' phenomenology (Yi-Fu Tuan's 'topophilia' borrowed from Bachelard) began to attract disaffected refugees from the quantitative revolution. The protest movements of the 1960s also galvanised a generation of radical geographers who over the following decades remained at the cutting edge of social theoretical projects within geography, and were moderately successful in communicating to other disciplines the importance of space and place.

In the 1980s, Anglo-American geographers and their counterparts in Germany, France, Scandinavia, Quebec and other bulwarks of Western geography began to comb the works of Foucault, Barthes, Derrida and others for geographic inspiration, and as more works appeared in translation, the 'postmodern' current emerged as a viable realm of geographic investigation, crosscutting human geography's subdisciplines. Foucault's 1976 'Questions on Geography' interview in *Hérodote* (reprinted in *Power/Knowledge*, 1980) galvanised the Anglo-American 'postmodernists', now becoming aware that continental thinkers addressed geographical questions in their writings, even if, as in the case of Foucault, space and place were hardly their main concerns.

The first sustained engagement between Anglo-American geography and continental philosophy emerged in the 'landscape-as-text' paradigm that became known as the 'new cultural geography'. Geographers such as James Duncan and Trevor Barnes, following on the heels of literary criticism's fascination with structuralist and poststructuralist semiotics, proclaimed that landscapes, long proclaimed the 'basic units' of geographical analysis, were actually and always assembled and reassembled texts extracted from geohistorical discourses, contentious but open to interpretation in the manner of Barthes, Ricoeur and Foucault. By the late 1980s, there was also an 'iconography of landscape', slightly more traditionalist, championed by scholars such as

Denis Cosgrove and Stephen Daniels, while David Seamons's and Robert Mugerauer's phenomenologies of place drew from the late Heidegger.

The mid-1990s saw a shift from landscape-as-text to a wider and more nuanced appropriation of continental thought. The appearance of Lefebvre's *Production of Space* in English translation (1974), with its pretension to a spatial metaphilosophy, became a central inspiration for materialists of all stripes. With this work, geographers interested in social theory now had a source for spatial investigations that instigated a veritable explosion of creativity, and 'postmodern' as well as structuralist geographers began to characterise multitudinous spaces in terms not only of their texts and structures but also of their emancipatory or oppressive possibilities. Edward Casey's *The Fate of Place* (1997) was a rare example of a philosopher drawing inspiration from geography, thus providing geographers with a renewed sense of the importance of the key concept of 'place'.

By the late 1990s, numerous currents of continental thought were sweeping through academic geography. Reading of the 'French feminists' as well as Anglo-American feminists brought about the widespread incorporation of gender into the discipline, while sensitivity to the body replaced landscape-as-text orthodoxy; scholars studying corporeality, embodiment and the gendering of spaces turned to the work of Merleau-Ponty, Butler and 'performativity' theory. Meanwhile, postcolonialism, influenced heavily by Foucault and Edward Said, became popular. Overall, by the end of the millennium a wide spectrum of geographers had become intimately engaged with continental thought. There remained, however, strong divisions between Marxist-related theories and poststructuralism in geography. David Harvey, for example, perhaps the social theoretical geographer best known outside the discipline, continued on a Marxist track, while cultural ecology and political ecology (hybrids of anthropology, geography and so forth) moved only warily toward poststructuralist approaches.

Physical geography and cartography yielded little to continental theory. However, Brian Harley's essay 'Deconstructing the Map' (*Cartographica*, 1989) shook cartography to its roots, for he asserted that maps needed to be understood as power-saturated texts embedded in discourses rather than 'objective' graphic representations of 'reality'. His voice pervades the University of Chicago's magisterial *History of Cartography* project (based at the University of Wisconsin). Nonetheless, the exploding subfield of Geographic Information Science had by the early 2000s only begun to engage non-orthodox modes of spatial representation. Physical geography (climate science, for example) had scant engagement with continental thought, on the one hand because it was predominantly based on quantitative and often positivistic science, and on the other because few social theoretical geographers considered the physical world as accessible to inquiry outside the bounds of discourse (considering 'nature' to be solely socially constructed). However, the ontology of Deleuze and Guattari (particularly in *A Thousand Plateaus*, 1980) may help to mend this rift, because their 'geophilosophy', which philosophers such as Manuel DeLanda have interpreted as inspired by 'complexity theory' (the dynamics of self-organising systems), offers the promise of providing a common framework for physical and human geographical projects.

Meanwhile, into the new millennium, 'postmodernism', as continental philosophy has generally been pigeonholed by 'traditional' geographers (and by many structuralists), continues to be viewed suspiciously, largely due to its threat to destabilise meanings and throw dearly held spatial ontologies into disarray. In the background looms the challenge 'postmodernism' poses to that ever-present neo-imperialist, globalist geography bankrolled by the state and the corporation.

In conclusion, while continental thought has thus far remained a marginal influence on the discipline of Western geography as a whole, it has helped spawn myriad new approaches to traditional questions that with time will doubtless become 'mainstream'. Meanwhile, the work of geographers is being increasingly incorporated into social theory in other disciplines, and considerations of space, perhaps geography's dominant quandary, are now rarely absent from the contents of social theoretical journals.

M. Bonta

GERMAN IDEALISM The philosophy developed in the immediately post-Kantian era in Germany by Fichte, Schelling, Hegel and their associates. Their works are now subject to a thorough-going reinterpretation that has done much to clarify the philosophical sense and importance of their views. Assimilating 'German idealism' to textbook versions of Berkeley's idealism is a grotesque historical anachronism, as is the simplistic idea that the German idealists simply 'radicalised' Kant's transcendental idealism by dropping the notoriously problematic 'thing in itself'. Instead, it has become apparent that the importance of both Spinozism and Platonism in the development of absolute idealism cannot be overestimated. The publication of Kant's critical philosophy stimulated a torrent of philosophical activity, both defending traditional views (such as Hume's or Leibniz's) and developing radically new views. The German Idealists were among the most radical of philosophical innovators in the response to Kant.

Fichte. The first of the German Idealists to achieve philosophical fame was Fichte, who, on Kant's advice, published anonymously his dissertation, *Attempt at a Critique of All Revelation* (1792). This preceded by a year Kant's own *Religion within the Limits of Reason Alone*, and readers initially assumed that the *Attempt* was in fact the work of Kant. When Kant subsequently announced that the book was very good, though it was by Fichte, the latter immediately became a philosophical star. However, due to perceived problems in Kant's Critical philosophy, Fichte soon claimed in his *Wissenschaftslehre* (*Doctrine of Knowledge*, 1794) to distinguish the spirit from the letter of Kant's views, and claimed to develop that spirit beyond Kant's monumental achievement. Kant immediately revoked his approval, rejecting any distinction between the letter and the spirit of his critical philosophy. Nevertheless, Fichte's philosophical star continued to soar.

Three alleged problems in Kant's philosophy were particularly important historically. Friedrich Heinrich Jacobi charged that it is not possible to enter Kant's philosophical system without accepting Kant's notorious 'thing in itself', though it is equally impossible to stay within Kant's system while accepting the 'thing in itself'. Solomon Maimon charged, in effect, that Hume's error theory of our belief in physical objects (that we imagine rather than perceive any such objects) was at least as satisfactory as Kant's 'empirical realism', and that the mind–body problem lodged itself at the core of Kant's critical theory of knowledge in the allegedly incomprehensible 'interaction' between causally determined sensibility and spontaneously judging understanding. Additionally, no one understood Kant's basis for claiming that his crucial Table of Judgements, and hence his Table of Categories, was complete.

To overcome these difficulties, and to preserve and extend the spirit of Kant's philosophy, Fichte proposed to outdo Descartes, by accounting for and justifying transcendentally our entire experience – of ourselves, of others and of the world – on a single first principle: 'I am I'. This is a deeply challenging undertaking; hence many of Fichte's writings are highly exploratory, and their precise interpretation remains disputed. Kant allowed self-knowledge only of our empirical aspects, though he ascribed freedom to our noumenal aspect, to reason itself. Fichte sought to avoid problems common to the modern 'new way of ideas' by attending, not to our ideas as either objects or facts, but rather to our conscious *acts* through which alone we can represent anything. Representation itself is possible only through our possible and actual acts of relating ourselves to, and distinguishing ourselves from, both our conscious states and their objects. According to Fichte, intellectual intuition enables us to know *that* we are active intellects, though it provides no insight into how we are active, nor does it provide insight into any alleged 'absolute'. Fichte's fundamental focus on our acts gave philosophical primacy to human agency; theoretical (cognitive) reason is rooted in practical (active) reason. Fichte takes it as fundamental that we are finite beings who exist within and are limited by an external reality, which gives us the 'matter' of our sensations. He argued that proof of the existence of the external world derives from our moral obligations: we can only be obligated to do something if there is something we can change within a context in which we can act. Because we are morally obligated, there must be a natural world in which we can execute our obligations. Practical reason also enables us to justify certain basic moral and religious truths that cannot be justified by theoretical reason; the moral ideas of God, immortality and providence are justified only as goals for our moral action. Following Kant, Fichte held that all of our creative action must comply with universal and necessary rational norms; his voluntarism remained fully within Enlightenment universalism. In Fichte's hands, transcendental analysis specifies the conditions required to act in the empirical world in accord with fundamental principles of morals and natural laws of justice (*jus*).

The primacy Fichte gives to practical reason also provides his ultimate response to Maimon's Humean scepticism. As finite beings, we are limited by and acted on by the external world, which provides among other things the sensory material for knowledge. However, reason demands that we achieve full autonomy and independence. We can achieve this only by developing full control over nature. Full control belongs to God alone, but we are obligated to achieve such control so far as we are able, and so far as we do this, we also produce genuine knowledge of nature. In developing this view, Fichte was indebted to Francis Bacon, and indeed to some suggestions by his sceptical opponent Maimon. Scepticism, according to Fichte, results from a faulty contemplative model of knowledge.

More fully, Fichte argues as follows for the reality of the natural world. Each of us first knows ourself through our drives, which we act on and whose satisfaction or dissatisfaction we can feel, for example, through pleasure or pain. That and what one feels is not up to oneself. Although one can chose whether or how to satisfy various drives, exactly how or whether our drives can be satisfied is independent of our free choice. In these ways, each of us incorporates both freedom and nature. Yet nature within each of us requires nature outside of us, too, for only in this way can any of one's acts have any definite form, order of execution or effectiveness. Nature within each of us and nature outside of us are similar in that they are causally structured independently of one's free choice, though they also mutually condition each other. Hence they must be two parts or aspects of one whole, which is nature itself, within which our own individual human nature(s) are parts. Precisely because the world does not automatically conform to anyone's immediate wants or desires, it must be independent of ourselves and especially of our freedom. Hence the external world exists.

Influenced by Rousseau's account of *amour-propre*, Fichte first developed the issue of mutual recognition (*Anerkennung*) in his *Foundations of Natural Right* (1795–6). This idea was adopted by Friedrich Schleiermacher and William von Humboldt, then by Hegel, and continues to gain philosophical importance. Note first that Fichte offers an argument for the existence of other minds that parallels his practical argument for the existence of the natural world: we are morally obligated to act, and all moral obligations are at least in part other-regarding. Thus we could not be morally obligated at all if there were no others by whom we are obligated. Thus other free rational agents exist. Mutual recognition, however, develops this idea much further.

The core idea of mutual recognition is that one cannot be conscious of oneself as a free rational agent unless one is recognised by others as a free and rational agent. Because this is true of each of us, it equally requires that each of us recognise the free rational agency of others in order to be aware of oneself as a free rational agent. A free, autonomous agent is one who acts and chooses to act on principles that acknowledge and respect the like freedom and autonomy of all other agents. Hence *being* a free, autonomous rational agent requires recognising, and being recognised by, other free, autonomous rational agents. Fichte develops this idea both in the context of education and in the context of individual rights; it makes the basic equality and reciprocity among subjects that is fundamental to modern political and philosophical thought into the fundamental principle of philosophy itself, because philosophical thought is the thought of free rational agents, and the analysis of free rational agency is Fichte's basis for developing and justifying all the rest of his philosophical system.

Fichte's philosophy is very insightful, but also difficult and obscure. Thus it is no surprise that many of his contemporaries doubted that he had avoided subjective idealism, and many thought he was committed to subjective idealism either explicitly or implicitly. The founders of 'Absolute Idealism' thought Fichte's basic error was to accept Kant's starting point, the analysis of rational self-consciousness and its necessary 'transcendental' preconditions. Instead, the absolute idealists thought that Fichte's alleged subjectivism could be corrected, while preserving and improving upon the best insights of Kant's critical philosophy, by taking nature much more seriously. The most basic or fundamental philosophical and ontological principle must be something 'absolute', that is something *neither* subjective nor objective, something from which the subjective and the objective devolve, or within which they develop. Though the term 'absolute idealism' is most closely associated with Schelling and Hegel, the view was first developed by some philosophically savvy romantic authors, primarily Friedrich Hölderlin, Friedrich von Hardenberg (Novalis) and Friedrich Schlegel.

Schelling. Already as a master's student at the seminary (*Stift*) in Tübingen, Schelling began corresponding with Fichte, which in Schelling's eyes soon became collaborative. The collaborative aspect of their correspondence soon collapsed, once Schelling insisted that transcendental philosophy (essentially Kantian-Fichtean critical epistemology) required its proper complement, philosophy of nature (*Naturphilosophie*), for which Fichte's philosophy had no place at all. Schelling's new 'absolute' idealism (no longer Kantian-Fichtean 'critical' idealism) required two equally important demonstrations: the object of knowledge and action must be 'deduced' from the subject; and vice versa, the subject of knowledge must be 'deduced' from the object, that is nature, where to 'deduce' (following Kant) means to account for and to justify.

One key aim of *Naturphilosophie* was to resolve the mind–body problem. Descartes generated this problem by defining 'mind' and 'matter' in ways that made their interaction completely mysterious: if 'matter' is inactive extended substance, while 'mind' is non-extended thinking (hence active) substance, how can they possibly communicate or interact at all? Descartes' appeal to the pineal gland convinced no one, though it took the sharp wits and questioning of Princess Elizabeth of Bohemia to extract Descartes' confession of philosophical defeat on this count. Absolute idealists followed Kant's lead that the 'substance' of which the mind is made is really peripheral to the key question: What does the mind do? What functions does the mind perform, and how does it perform them? Descartes' anti-Aristotelian innovation really lay in reconceiving the body as nothing but dead, mechanically functioning extension. A key aim of *Naturphilosophie* was to demonstrate that, although many physical phenomena are merely mechanical, natural phenomena include a vast array of more complex forms of organisation which cannot be explained by or reduced to mere mechanism. In this way, *Naturphilosophie* developed the first versions of what is now called 'emergentism'.

According to emergence theories, the behaviour of a natural system or organism is a function of both its structural organisation and the material of its components. Obviously, no physical system can behave in ways that exceed the limits of its material limits. However, with proper organisation a physical system can perform functions that cannot be defined in terms of, nor 'reduced to', the merely physical capacities of the matter of which it is composed. Long derided by reductionist philosophers, the principles of emergentism are fundamental to the well-established philosophy of biology, and in philosophy of mind they are now supplanting (generally vacuous) appeals to 'supervenience', a logically sophisticated form of co-variance that involves dualism of descriptions or perhaps even of properties while rejecting substance dualisms. Despite widespread earlier scorn, the principles of emergentism are now for the most part considered philosophically legitimate.

Where Aristotle appealed to different kinds of 'soul', with differing degrees of sophistication, to account for the behaviour of various natural, including biological and human phenomena, advocates of *Naturphilosophie* appealed instead to different kinds and degrees of systematic organisation of matter to account for such phenomena. In this way, *Naturphilosophie* sought to establish a hierarchy of levels and kinds of organisation, beginning with mere matter, in which each level formed the necessary precondition for the subsequent, more sophisticated level. If mere matter was subject to Newtonian laws of motion, Newton's system of the world (astronomy) required, and assumed, a complex set of bodies, namely our planetary system, the complex motions of whose members, the individual planets and the sun, it could then explain. Furthermore, this astronomical system provides certain material preconditions for organic phenomena, including light and a viable temperature range, as well as special minerals and proto-organic compounds. However, organic life properly speaking requires a degree of organisation that cannot be explained by those material preconditions alone. Within the vast organic realm, thinkers in the school of *Naturphilosopie* further distinguished the various kinds and degrees of organisation that typify vegetable and animal forms of life, and argued that our commonalities with our primate relatives are as important to our affective self-awareness and our rational agency as are our more complex capacities for feeling, thought and action. Schelling called these levels of organisation 'Potenzen', drawing on the connotations of a term that equally means a dynamic potential and a mathematical power (exponent).

Schelling was truly a wunderkind. By his mid-twenties he had devised six distinct systems of philosophy. When just twenty-three, he was appointed Professor of Philosophy at Jena, on Goethe's recommendation. His views proved to be extremely fruitful for the development of biological science in the nineteenth century, for he made it legitimate to conceive organic functions as constitutive of biological systems rather than as mere heuristic devices for trying to grapple with what must be intrinsically mechanical organisations (as Kant had insisted). However, this scientific fruitfulness does not much reflect on the philosophical soundness of Schelling's views. For their purposes, biologists only needed the key idea just mentioned, just as Faraday only needed the basic idea of Kant's dynamic theory of matter (that 'matter' could consist of active forces rather than dead massy 'stuff'), conveyed to him by Coleridge, for the development of his electrostatic field theory. Schelling was a visionary, and many have felt he was often uncritical about the philosophical underpinnings of his views. In part this is reflected in his appeal to quasi-rational 'intuitions' of the absolute as such. A standard problem confronting all forms of intuitionism (outside purely formal domains of logic or mathematics) is providing any criterion to distinguish between the following, cognitively quite distinct situations: intuiting something as it is, and thus knowing that and what it is, versus being convinced that one intuits something as it is, and thus being certain that one knows that and what it is. Presumably, these two circumstances should only occur together. However, nothing in the resources of intuitionism can guarantee that they do, or that they can be known by us only to co-occur.

Initially, Schelling and his junior partner Hegel thought these sceptical issues only infected the 'finite' or limited thought of the (Kantian) understanding, which only provided conditional knowledge of causally conditioned individual phenomena. The 'absolute' is unconditioned because it contains all finite, limited, conditioned phenomena within it, and it is grasped in intellectual intuition of the 'ideas' that structure it. The term 'idea' extended Kant's technical sense of the term, in which it contrasts with 'concept' and transcends our inherently partial experience, in a highly Platonist direction, so that 'ideas' are fundamental structures of reality as such, or 'the absolute'. Schelling thought that the intellectual intuitionism invoked by absolute idealism simply transcended the sceptical problematic.

Hegel. G. E. Schultze challenged this presumption with his brilliant anonymous parody of absolute idealism, 'Aphorisms on the Absolute' (1803). In response, Schelling clamed that Hegel had already settled this issue in his early essay, 'The Relation of Scepticism to Philosophy' (1801). Hegel recognised that Schultze was right, that like any other philosophical view, especially any philosophical account of knowledge, absolute idealism, too, must either solve or avoid Sextus Empiricus' 'Dilemma of the Criterion' by answering the question: how can any standards of justification be established, when the very standards of justification are fundamentally disputed, while avoiding dogmatism, question-begging (*petitio principii*), infinite regress, ungrounded assumption or just plain error? Hegel made Sextus' Dilemma into the central methodological and epistemological problem to be solved in his *Phenomenology of Spirit*.

By 1802, Hegel had already recognised that Kant's critical achievement could not be taken for granted, because Kant in fact failed to justify causal judgements. The *Critique of Pure Reason* only considers the general causal principle, that every event has a cause. The problem is that Kant's principles of causal judgement about spatio-temporal events (in the 'Analogies of Experience') require the specific causal principle that every physical event has an external physical cause. Kant only identified and defended this principle in his *Foundations*, though Kant himself soon realised that his justification of it there fails utterly. Hegel also recognised that Kant's *Metaphysical Foundations of Natural Science* failed to establish the basic terms of Kant's dynamic theory of matter, in which matter as such consists in counterbalanced basic forces of attraction and repulsion. Kant's dynamic theory of matter was the point of departure for Schelling's *Naturphilosophie*, which unwittingly exhibits the failure of Kant's dynamic theory of matter to foreclose, as Kant intended it to, on unbridled speculation about the physical microstructure of material beings – a vice Kant urged against contemporaneous corpuscular theories of matter. Finally, Hegel also recognised that Schelling abused Kant's heuristic use of structural analogies among natural phenomena (central to Kant's 'Critique of Teleological Judgement', the first part of the *Critique of Judgement*), not because Schelling sought to convert Kant's heuristic principles into constitutive ones for our knowledge of nature, but because Schelling persistently mistook analogies for identities. (This error is especially evident in Schelling's seminal 'Universal Deduction of the Dynamic Process', 1800.) Thus while Hegel adopted many of the aims and aspirations of absolute idealism, and especially of its component *Naturphilosophie*, from Schelling, Hegel clearly recognised the need to develop his philosophical principles much more carefully and rigorously than Schelling did, and with much greater epistemological sophistication than Schelling had.

K. Westphal

GERMAN ROMANTICISM One of the first romantic movements in Europe, and distinct from later forms of Romanticism, it is often called early or Jena Romanticism, achieving its peak during the 1790s. Principal figures associated with the movement include the brothers Friedrich and August Wilhelm von Schlegel, Caroline Schlegel-Schelling, Dorothea Schlegel, Novalis, Schelling, Schleiermacher, Ludwig Tieck and W. H. Wackenroder. Many of their writings were published in the *Athenaeum* journal.

The German Romantics did not have a clear or unified programme, but they were concerned with a set of issues arising from Kantian transcendental philosophy and German Idealism, Fichte in particular. These issues included: (1) the inability to achieve an experience of a transcendental subject; (2) the distinction between noumenon and phenomenon; and (3) the claim that key features of the world of experience are shaped or conditioned by the subject of knowledge. These themes, taken together, suggested to the Romantics that the empirical world had a non-ultimate, even illusory character. The last theme in particular – the claim that experience is in part shaped by the requirements of the knowing subject – suggested to them that the world can be viewed as produced or created. Consequently, the Romantics tended to view the world in analogy (at least) with artistic production.

However, the Romantics generally agreed that the subject, as well as the conditions of artistic production, is not present to experience. They reacted to this absence in different ways: from quasi-mysticism to a fascination with the occluded past to theories of author-less production. This last in particular provided a provocative set of insights about the manner in which language is not fully under authorial control.

The Romantics experimented with devices such as the fragment, fairy tale and collective writing to interrupt conventional theories of authorship and to indicate transcendence, loss of unity and the (merely) produced and non-ultimate status of the work of art/reality. They made ample use of irony for this reason as well, and irony became a signature device of the moment. They often thematised the notion of incompletion or loss more positively, in terms of infinite progress (terms borrowed, in part, from Fichte's philosophy); in a famous self-definition of German Romanticism, F. Schlegel writes: 'Romantic poesy is a progressive, universal poesy . . . The romantic kind of poesy is still in the state of becoming; that, in fact, is its real essence: that it should forever be becoming and never be perfected' (from *Athenaeum Fragments*, 1798).

German Romanticism is known at least as much for its literary criticism as for any literary output. Their notion of literary criticism was largely inspired by Kant's critical philosophy; as critical philosophy reflects on the conditions of knowing, literature can be self-reflective too and contain its own theory. Twentieth-century philosophers such as Benjamin, Blanchot, Lacoue-Labarthe and Nancy have demonstrated how the resulting conception of literature as self-reflective and theoretically adept continues to influence both the theory and production of literature to this day.

J. Norman

GESTELL ('enframing') A Heideggerian term, developed in 'The Question Concerning Technology' (1954), for the 'essence of technology', understood as a mode of revealing or truth. The revealing that rules in modern technology is a challenging (*Herausfordern*), which puts to nature the demand that it supply energy that can be extracted and stored as such. As a result, everything is ordered to stand by, to be immediately on hand and indeed to stand there so that it may be on call for a further ordering. Whatever is ordered about in this way has its own way of standing: it is the standing-reserve (*Bestand*). This is the way in which things stand or unfold in the age of technology: no longer as an object (*Gegenstand*), but as that which stands by and so is held in reserve. The sense of the human itself has changed: man is no longer a subject, but the one being upon whom falls the challenge to order and exploit the energies of nature. 'Gestell' means the coming together of man and nature in technology, the specific constellation man-being in which we find ourselves. 'Enframing' (or the 'set-up') means the gathering ('*ge-*') of that setting-upon (*stellen*) that sets upon man, that is challenges him forth, to reveal the real, in the mode of ordering, as standing-reserve. It means that way of revealing – as producing and presenting (*Her- und Dar-stellen*) – that dominates in the essence of modern technology, and that is itself nothing technological.

M. de Beistegui

GIFT (*don*) (1) One of the most persistent examples of the aporias whose analysis Derrida has made indispensable to philosophical inquiry. The gift was first thematised in *Glas* (1974), but its workings are already implicit in *Of Grammatology* and *Writing and Difference* (1967). It comes back into focus in the 1990s with *Given Time*, where Derrida refers to the way Mauss analyses the potlatch in *Essay on the Gift* (1925) as well as to the bilingual pun in which the German word for poison is *Gift*. In *The Gift of Death* it is related to sacrifice, the secret and responsibility.

For there to be such a thing as a gift in the true sense of the word – Derrida does not presume that there is – one would have to be able to give without knowing one was giving. Anything less than that involves an economic calculation (expecting something in return) and relies rather on a system of exchange: 'For there to be a gift, there must be no reciprocity, return, exchange, countergift, or debt. If the other gives me back or owes me . . . there will not have been a gift' (*Given Time*). The notion of a radically unconscious or absolutely forgetful giver calls into question traditional conceptions of agency and of subjectivity, and by extension basic concepts of ontology and epistemology. Irreducible to a concept, to a philosophical category or to discursive logic, the gift would instead represent the opening to a type of non-knowledge or thinking of the impossible that, far from preventing thinking, makes it possible.

D. Wills

GIFT (2) A term redefined by Jean-Luc Marion in *Being Given* (1997), to answer Derrida's challenge in *Given Time*. Marion redefines the gift by employing a 'triple epoché', that is, the triple bracketing out of the giver (in the case of an absent or dead giver), the givee (in the case of an anonymous recipient) and even the objectivity of the gift (in the cases of giving power, oneself in a relationship or one's word). The gift is thus reduced only to givenness, but even so it is still possible to give. Marion offers concrete examples where givenness defies the understanding of the gift on the basis of an economy of exchanges or causation without, however, eradicating the possibility of giving.

J. Manoussakis

GIRARD, RENÉ (1923–) Literary critic, anthropologist of religion and Christian philosopher of history in a spirit reminiscent of Augustine and Pascal. Though born and educated in France, Girard has spent his entire academic career in the United States. A pre-eminent theorist of violence and the origins of religion, Girard's melancholy insight stresses the inevitable violence of human desire, the productivity of violence in generating culture, and its ultimate mortality, its incapacity to sustain order. In *Violence and the Sacred* (1972) he offers a powerful explanation of the genesis of myth and society through 'mimetic desire' and 'scapegoat' mechanisms of sacrifice. Social desire is reciprocally imitative, but this produces envy, jealousy and rage. A cipher of the destructive power of imitation appears in the mythic fear in primitive communities of twins, look-a-likes, monsters and so forth, which evinces the terrifying spectre of mimetic contagion – the unbridled spread of violence and breakdown of distinctions set off by uncontrolled reciprocity. Original communities, without settled institutions, had recourse only to scapegoating to protect them from chaos. Communal violence seized on a victim whose scandal to the community grew in proportion to the inability to defend himself or herself, directing violence away from the community itself. By the same token, the target of communal anger acquired a salvific quality in death. Ritualised as sacrifice, this intimates a violent mechanism that conceals and transfigures itself, to produce order, institutions and cultural myths. The 'sacred' is the generative difference, arbitrary but effective and self-confirming, between 'good' and 'bad' violence, in rituals and prohibitions structuring human reciprocity, limiting the potential for violence.

Girard then elaborated an apocalyptic theory of history in *Things Hidden Since the Foundation of the World* (1978). The Christian Gospels set in motion a process by which society is deprived of the most effective means of order it has ever known, by fully revealing the hidden violence and sacrificial mechanisms of culture in the perfect innocence of the ultimate victim, Christ. For all its injustice – its arbitrary hierarchy – sacrificial order is a great accomplishment of history, not less humane than modern regimes which live off its borrowed capital. It is vulnerable, though, to a weakening over time (its success undermines it) and to the catastrophic exposé of its secret by the Cross. Demythologisation unleashes vast creative energies of rivalry in the modern world, but also a violence threatening to spiral out of control. Modern 'progress' owes its success, paradoxically, to the effect of the Bible, but it is not an unmixed blessing. Destruction of sacrificial order sets the stage for a vast sacrificial crisis, possibly global and signifying the 'end of history'. Demythologisation does not immediately lead to a lessening of sacrificial tensions but to their desperate increase, evidenced in the ideological fanaticisms of the last century. Violence loses the effectiveness it had – as myth – to contain violence. National and global society loses the wherewithal to contain destructive antagonisms. The only solution to this crisis is renunciation of violence as a means of social order, in effect universal conversion to Christianity, in spirit if not in the letter.

S. Gardner

See also: mimetic desire; scapegoat

GOVERNMENTALITY A concept typically used by Foucauldian scholars to encompass the formal aspects of governance associated with states and institutions in liberal democracies and the informal forms of power associated with discipline and self-discipline. Governmentality denotes relationships between power, knowledge and discipline that move away from coercion and techniques of rational control by the state and/or other institutions towards a more indeterminate relationship between self-discipline and the regulatory processes through which self-discipline occurs.

Governmentality differs from concepts such as social control or domination because it arises in a context of liberal citizenship and emphasises the individual as an active agent exercising choice and free will. Individuals are not coerced by the state to behave according to norms it establishes. On the contrary, governmentality refers to the ways in which individuals are encouraged to observe and monitor their own behaviour through 'self-correction to norms'. In liberal or neo-liberal states, such conduct is associated with lifestyle choices which individuals are expected and encouraged to reflexively make through self-examination, as explored by N. Rose in *Governing the Soul: The Shaping of the Private Self* (1990). As such, governmentality ties the abstract individual of liberal citizenship to 'technologies of the self' that develop self-discipline in line with formal models or norms against which individuals can be assessed or assess themselves.

Experts and expert knowledge are crucial to establishing and measuring the boundaries of conduct, which become guides for self-regulation by individuals. Thus, governmentality refers to the relationship between how conduct is defined and encouraged by the state and institutions and how individuals conduct themselves. It emphasises the relationship between the agency of individuals and the self-conduct engendered through agency (self-subjection) and the regulatory contexts in which they are situated (social regulation).

The concept of governmentality is increasingly used in conjunction with analysis of the actions taken by states to protect citizens from risks associated with late modern society. Much of this protection takes the form of population surveillance in relation to health, the environment and education. For instance, through public health and health promotion practices individuals are encouraged to take responsibility for their own health by considering themselves to be 'at risk' in various ways and comply with state policies to address these risks. However, the uncertainties surrounding many risks mean that knowledge becomes politicised and open to scrutiny in ways that challenge the rationality of the forms of conduct established by the state and its institutions.

For some commentators the concept of governmentality and the lighter mode of liberal governance that it implies places too much emphasis on the autonomous individual and his/her ability to reflexively construct a self. However, ideas about duty and obligation are not redundant within the concept of governmentality. While individuals are 'free' to make 'choices' within the neo-liberal state, the state continues to set the parameters and contexts in which such choices are exercised, and which may make it difficult for individuals to exercise some choices without incurring penalities or sanctions.

A. Howson

GRAMSCI, ANTONIO (1891–1937) Italian philosopher, Marxist theoretician and founder of the Italian Communist Party. Gramsci produced a series of important writings between 1929 and 1935 while imprisoned in fascist jails. Gramsci's trial prosecutor had demanded: 'We must prevent this brain from functioning for twenty years'. Partly due to Gramsci's resort to Aesopian language to pass the prison censor, the *Prison Notebooks* have become a matter of constant and partisan reinterpretation since their Italian publication in the 1940s.

Influenced by Croce's historicism, Gramsci repudiated fatalistic versions of positivistic Marxism, where history was propelled forward by law-like economic forces. For Gramsci the 1917 Bolshevik Revolution represented a 'revolution against *Capital*', expressing all that was 'invigorating, immanent' in Marx's own thought. Gramsci dubbed Marxism the 'philosophy of praxis', and adopted Romain Rolland's aphorism: 'Pessimism of the intellect, optimism of the will'. Gramsci advocated a form of Bolshevism adapted to Italian conditions in the 'Lyons Theses' of 1926.

Italy underwent tumultuous political and industrial upheaval during the 'two red years', 1919–20, followed by fascist reaction and Mussolini's seizure of power in 1922. The 2,848 pages of the *Prison Notebooks* represented Gramsci's efforts to comprehend these developments. Gramsci settled on three principal topics: '(1st) Italian history of the nineteenth century, with special reference to the formation and evolution of intellectual groups; (2nd) The theory of history and historiography; (3rd) Americanism and Fordism'. A long sweep of Italian history, from the Roman Republic to the Risorgimento of the 1860s, was developed to determine in Crocean fashion the historical forces shaping the construction of the unified State and the shared life of the 'people-nation'. Carried through by 'traditional' cosmopolitan intellectuals, the Risorgimento was a 'passive revolution' from above; 'passive', because the process of national unification failed to involve the peasantry. As a construct above civil society the Italian state proved vulnerable to fascist reaction at moments of crisis.

Gramsci drew on Hegel's concept of 'civil society' to show the impossibility of the Bolshevik Revolution being replayed in liberal democracies. Gramsci refused to counterpose state and civil society against each other, stressing their mutual interdependency. In liberal democracies a kind of 'spontaneous' consent is generated out of the 'complex structure' of myriad voluntary and private institutions, clubs, associations, groups. 'In the East the State was everything, civil society was primordial and gelatinous; in the West, there was a proper relation between State and civil society, and when the State trembled a sturdy structure of civil society was at once revealed.' In conditions of a vibrant civil society and hegemonic rule, a political organisation, what Gramsci, following Machiavelli, termed 'the Modern Prince', is needed to acquire broad hegemonic leadership of the 'collective, national-popular will'.

Even in the difficult circumstances of imprisonment Gramsci proved alert to the problems and possibilities of the most historical recent developments. What he termed 'Fordism' in the rationalisation of production was complemented by further rationalisation of civil society, 'Americanism'. Americanism was not exceptional but 'an organic extension and an intensification of European civilisation'. Fordism had 'not yet posed', let alone resolved, 'the fundamental question of hegemony'. A new balance of force and persuasion was thus necessary to create 'a new type of man' where 'the whole life of the nation revolves around production'.

A. Law

See also: hegemony; Marxism

GUATTARI, FÉLIX (1930–92) French activist-intellectual and key figure in the materialist critique of psychiatry as well as a collaborator with Deleuze in a remarkable series of works. Trained as a psychoanalyst under Lacan, Guattari practised privately and also worked at Clinique de la Borde where, with the clinic's founder Jean Oury, he developed the principles of institutional analysis, including the treatment of psychotics, for whom traditional psychoanalysis had been of little help. Guattari was active in the European anti-psychiatry movement and was an instigator of 'schizoanalysis', a renegade form of analysis which was based on a critique of the Freudian, Lacanian and Kleinian principles of Oedipus, linguistic structure and partial objects, and aimed at developing a notion of the unconscious beyond perso-nological, familial, structural, universal and mythical coordinates.

In *Psychanalyse et transversalité* (1972), Guattari exposed the limits of the psychoanalytic concept of the unconscious by retheorising its immersion in the social and historical field. By critically analysing the organisational textures of radical groups, Guattari discovered a dein-dividuated subject, understood as a 'collective assemblage' of hetero-geneous components – particular arrangements of habits, desires and the like – freed from abstract overdeterminations such as race and gender. A theory of groups inspired by Sartre's *Critique of Dialectical Reason* emerged from this period of Guattari's work, distinguishing between subject groups (actively exploring self-defined projects) and subjugated groups (passively receiving directions), each affecting the relations of their members to social processes and shaping the potential for subject formation and for revolution.

L'inconscient machinique (1979) developed schizoanalysis as a prac-tical, detailed semiotics, a politically progressive and provisional transformation of situational power relations. Eschewing neutrality, the analyst's micropolitical task is to discern in a particular assemblage the potential of a given component to mutate, and to explore the effects of its passages in and between assemblages, producing and extracting 'singularities' – irreducibly idiosyncratic arrangements – by undoing alienations, stratifications and redundancies. *Cartographies schizoana-lytiques* (1989) and *Chaosmosis* (1995) furthered this work, elaborating non-representational maps of the self-engendering processes of sub-jectification, pragmatically attending to the specific ways in which singularities come together.

Internationally recognised for his collaborations with Deleuze on *Anti-Oedipus* (1972), *Kafka* (1986), *A Thousand Plateaus* (1980) and *What Is Philosophy?* (1991), Guattari also theorised a new vision of progressive politics with Antonio Negri in *New Spaces of Liberty* (1990) and, in the early 1980s with Eric Alliez, laid the intellectual foundation for anti-globalisation struggles, gauging the limits of the integration of production and information in neo-liberal capitalism.

G. *Genosko*

See also: Cybernetics; transversality

HABERMAS, JÜRGEN (1929–) German philosopher widely considered to be the most influential contemporary representative of the critical social theory associated with the Frankfurt School. His capacious knowledge – ranging from linguistics, psychology and social and political science to literature, law, history, theology and philosophy – is reflected in his prolific publication record, which includes *The Structural Transformation of the Public Sphere* (1962), *Knowledge and Human Interests* (1968), *Legitimation Crisis* (1973), *The Theory of Communicative Action: Volumes One and Two* (1981), *The Philosophical Discourse of Modernity* (1985), and *Between Facts and Norms* (1993). In addition to his academic acclaim, he has made his mark as one of Germany's most significant public intellectuals, evidenced by his courageous defence of student activists in the 1960s and peaceful anti-nuke demonstrators in the 1970s. After debating revisionist historians of the Third Reich in the 1980s, he turned his attention to injustices perpetrated on immigrants, guest workers, refugees and former East Germans in the process of German unification in the 1990s. Recently he has contributed to debates on economic globalisation and on global politics in the 'post-9/11' era.

The defining feature of the philosophy of Habermas is his reformulation of critical theory. Since its official inception in the 1930s, critical theory had been proclaimed as a unique synthesis of social science and philosophy oriented toward the rational enlightenment of social agents and their subsequent emancipation from domination and oppression, both psychological and physical. However, by the 1940s the leading exponents of critical theory – most notably Horkheimer and Adorno – had come to doubt the viability of this programme. In their opinion, rational enlightenment invariably leads to moral scepticism, which in turn propels the uncontested hegemony of scientific and technological reasoning. So truncated, rationality becomes increasingly identified with prediction and control in service to domination. The subsequent conclusion drawn by critical theorists could not be less encouraging for collective social action aimed at emancipation: any sources of critical resistance that remain do so solely from within the interior recesses of the reflective individual's pre-rational aesthetic imagination.

Habermas rejects the starkly apolitical and irrationalist sentiments implied in this conclusion. Was it not, after all, hatred of the Enlightenment that motivated fascism, and was it not lack of collective political resistance that enabled it to triumph? Responding to what he perceived to be fascist tendencies in postwar Germany, Habermas set about transforming the philosophical paradigm that led first-generation critical theorists to their fateful conclusion. That paradigm defined knowledge and action principally in terms of a lone conscious subject acting upon a field of material objects. So construed, rational knowledge and action take the form of instrumental knowledge, that is the efficient discovery of means for achieving pre-given ends. For Habermas, this paradigm of rationality derives from a more basic one that is rooted not in subjective consciousness but intersubjective communication. In short, individual consciousness, knowledge and action are conditioned by a prior process of socialisation, understood as the learning of roles, values, categories of meaning and significant (his)stories by means of communicative interaction between parent and child.

Not only is instrumental activity and knowledge informed by shared categories of substance, space, time and natural kinds that have been acquired through communicative learning, but at some point in the evolution of scientific knowledge these categories themselves are critically evaluated in argumentative speech. Significantly, Habermas maintains that argumentative speech, or discourse, implicates a non-instrumental, communicative type of rationality. More precisely, communicative rationality consists in the concerted effort to reach impartial and unconstrained agreement over contested claims. Agreement is impartial and unconstrained, however, only to the extent that all persons affected by the disputed claim are included in the conversation, and everyone has equal chances to speak, free from internal (ideological) and external pressures. Habermas thus concludes that universal freedom and justice are implicit in the very communicative rationality towards which all communicative interaction aspires.

Contrary to the conclusion reached by his predecessors, rational enlightenment does not undermine faith in moral values like freedom and justice but rather embodies them – so long as it is properly understood to embrace first and foremost rational discussion. Indeed, rational discussion is not only the principal ideal underlying scientific inquiry: it is also the principal ideal underlying democracy. Accordingly, following Habermas's lead, contemporary critical theory has shifted away from its original Marxian focus on economic oppression under capitalism to a more liberal concern regarding legal and political domination. This does not mean that the original focus has entirely dropped out of Habermas's theory. Some of his most enduring insights concern the way in which capitalism threatens democracy. In *Legitimation Crisis*, for instance, he argued that the principal contradiction of the welfare state – using public revenue to sustain capitalist growth while simultaneously compensating the victims of such growth – can be successfully managed only by encouraging depoliticised masses oriented toward private consumption to defer uncritically to directives issued by appointed technological-administrative elites. In the *Theory of Communicative Action*, he observed how areas of domestic and public life oriented toward socialisation and critical discussion had become increasingly 'colonised' by more instrumental and functional forms of rationality associated with the marketplace and legal bureaucracy. More recently, he has deftly analysed the tension between neo-liberal policies associated with globalisation and the capacity of liberal democracies to control their economic destinies and provide education, health and welfare services to their citizens.

D. Ingram

See also: Critical Theory; discourse ethics; Enlightenment; Epistemology; ideal speech situation; universal pragmatics

HABITUS A term employed by Bourdieu for the batteries of dispositions that generate human action. These subconscious, bodily structures resemble skills or practical senses ('business sense', 'moral sense', 'a sense for the game'). In postulating them, Bourdieu transcended the prior theoretical either-or that held that action either results from subjective will or is necessitated by objective structures.

People acquire a habitus in learning to carry on the practices about them. Since for Bourdieu habitus is directly lodged in the body, he called this acquisition process, which is largely wordless and non-overt, 'bodily pedagogy'. Habitus is such, moreover, that the actions it generates perpetuate both the practices in which it is acquired and the social domains in which those practices transpire, in particular the objective structures of those domains (for example, the distribution of capital). These actions, however, do not simply repeat the actions that were encountered in learning contexts. Habitus generates actions – possibly innovative actions – that are sensible in and appropriate to actors' current situations. Still, absent external intervention, habitus nearly guarantees the perpetuation of the practices in which it is acquired. Since (1) people are not, and cannot directly be, aware of habitus and (2) thought and motivation are likewise products of habitus, people cannot obviously intervene consciously in the habitus-practice circle.

Bourdieu questioned whether it is possible to have a theory that explains habitus. Nonetheless, he took steps toward developing a logic of practice that made explicit how the habitus selects actions, as in *The Logic of Practice* (1980).

T. Schatzki

HAECCEITY A term coined by the medieval theologian Duns Scotus to denote the property of being an individual, adapted by Deleuze and Guattari in *A Thousand Plateaus* (1980) as a principle of individuation different from and prior to the individuation of subjects, things and formed substances.

For Scotus, haecceity or 'thisness' is the property of an individual that distinguishes it from any other individual, even from one that shares all its properties. This idea of difference cannot be captured by familiar hierarchy-based 'tree' schemes like Aristotle's. Such schemes individuate entities on the basis of properties that are in principle shared, clustering individuals into classes and so on. By contrast, Deleuze develops a 'flat' ontology in which individuals are primary, and can send out connections in any direction regardless of hierarchy.

Deleuze explains haecceity in several ways. First, in *Difference and Repetition* (1968), he argues for the primacy of a spatio-temporal intuition of something over its position in a conceptual hierarchy. Second, in *A Thousand Plateaus* (1980), he emphasises the importance of quantitative measures like longitude and latitude (although these are not to be understood in a normal geographical sense, but more like the spatial thresholds on an egg developing into an embryo). Lastly, he points to the semiotics of events: the uniqueness of tropical storms is not captured by a catalogue of their properties, but by the fact that they receive a proper name. This practice is common when new scientific discoveries are made and given proper names as unique designations, as in the 'Doppler effect'.

A. Welchman

HARAWAY, DONNA (1944–) American feminist philosopher of science and technology, whose work has been highly influential on philosophical, literary and social studies of technology, nature, the body and identity; her ideas have reached artists, fiction writers, activists and theorists far beyond the academic world.

Haraway's most influential text is 'A Cyborg Manifesto: Science, Technology, and Twentieth Century Feminism in the Late Twentieth Century', which first appeared in *Socialist Review* in 1985 and was republished in her 1991 book of essays, *Simians, Cyborgs and Women:*

the Reinvention of Nature. In common with much of her work, this text is a radical, ambitious and rigorous onslaught on received ideas about the boundaries between the natural and the artificial, the human and the animal, the organic and the machine. Written at a time when new technologies were being uncritically promoted or opposed, Haraway's 'Cyborg Manifesto' opened up a new standpoint from which it was possible to see technological developments challenging many of the boundaries and certainties it was more commonly assumed to uphold.

While much feminist theory had perceived science and technology as means of dominating nature and reinforcing social inequalities, Haraway used the figure of the cyborg – the cybernetic organism – as a radical means of contesting the construction of identities. Exploring the ways in which women have themselves been constructed by a complex of social, technological, biological and economic discourses and processes, Haraway pursued the ways in which all fixed notions of identity are subverted by the emergence, both metaphorical and actual, of the overtly constructed cyborg. The increasing difficulty of drawing fixed lines between humans, machines and the networks they compose gave Haraway the opportunity to demonstrate the malleability of all the many binaries and boundaries on which modern conceptions of the world have relied.

Haraway's manifesto made an unprecedented challenge to both social constructionist feminist ideas and the 'earthy' feminisms of the 1970s, and paved the way for the cyberfeminist ideas of the 1990s. In the scope of themes and its imaginative style, it made a radical departure from many scholarly conventions too: the manifesto employs both rigorous argument and playful satire, and draws on both scientific sources and the work of science fiction writers such as Octavia Butler. Haraway's closing declaration – 'I'd rather be a cyborg than a goddess' – inspired a wave of innovative thinking about the implications of technological developments for the ways in which nature, gender, sexuality, race and identities of all kinds are conceptualised and experienced.

These concerns are developed throughout Haraway's work. In 1990, she published *Primate Visions: Gender, Race and Nature in the World of Modern Science*, a history and analysis of primatology, as well as an ambitious critique of relations between humans and animals and the prejudices inherent in their study. In several of her essays, her critiques of the boundaries which have been established between humans, each other and the rest of the world are developed in relation to her studies of viruses and immunology; in her third major text, *Modest_Witness@Second_Millennium: FemaleMan$^©$_Meets_OncoMouse$^™$:*

Feminism and Technoscience (1997), she explores them in the context of developments in genetic engineering and biotechnology.

S. Plant

See also: Technology, Philosophy of

HARDING, SANDRA *See* Feminist Epistemology

HARTMANN, NIKOLAI (1882–1950) Latvian-born German philosopher whose thought can be loosely situated in the space between neo-Kantianism and Husserl. Hartmann was educated in St. Petersburg and then in Marburg, where he studied with Hermann Cohen and Paul Natorp; he later taught in Marburg, Cologne, Berlin and Göttingen.

Beginning in neo-Kantianism, Hartmann later developed his own position, on the basis of which, thinking that the age of systems was over, he believed that philosophy needed to concentrate on problems. Unlike many other philosophers, he saw philosophy as yielding only probability, not certainty. In his first important work on epistemology, *Basic Principles of a Metaphysics of Knowledge* (1921), he broke with neo-Kantianism in founding a critical ontology based on epistemological realism. In giving up idealism, he also gave up the generally Kantian view that reality is dependent on subjective, albeit transcendental, acts. Rather, for Hartmann, philosophy is concerned with the problems of being as well as understanding the irrational or enigmatic. His critical realism belonged to so-called new metaphysics.

With respect to previous ontologies, Hartmann innovates in holding that the world is neither wholly knowable nor wholly unknowable, and categories that hold for one level of being can not unreflectively be applied to other ontological levels. Philosophical realism is based on the intelligibility of being under the conditions of human experience. Like the neo-Kantian Emil Lask, Hartmann sees reality in itself as beyond cognition while holding that no categorial approach can avoid being confronted with the irrational. Like Martin Heidegger, he was influenced by the German phenomenologist Marx Scheler and concerned with ontology. Unlike Heidegger, he was concerned with beings, not being as such. Hartmann understands traditional metaphysics as seeking a priori knowledge that, after Kant, is no longer possible. Contemporary ontology can only be a posteriori, hence based on and indissociable from the limits of experience.

Hartmann identifies four levels of being: the inorganic, the organic, the psychic and the spiritual. He distinguishes two categorial levels: basic categories that apply to all levels of being and level-specific categories that apply only to one or more ontological levels. Denying that being as such is spiritual, Hartmann sees Hegel's error as holding that the spiritual categories apply even to the lowest levels of being. In denying that the lower categories of being apply automatically to higher levels, he opposes social Darwinism. The categories of being cannot be deduced from knowledge, since we cannot know how human knowledge relates to objective being. They must be derived from the sciences and other experiences with no pretence to agree with the mind-independent world. In Hartmann's realist ontology, reality is divided into various levels of being, each with its own categories.

In his important three-volume study of ethics (*Ethik*, 1932), which builds on Scheler, Hartmann develops a non-formal but objective system of values with only ideal being, which are intuitable and function as guides for action. Values are not all equal, but are arranged hierarchically and interrelated; we do not construct but only recognise them. As an ontologist, Hartmann was overshadowed by his more famous contemporary Heidegger. One of his strongest influences is on the social ontology of Lukács.

T. Rockmore

HEGEL, G. W. F. (1770–1831) German philosopher most commonly associated with 'Absolute Idealism'. Recent scholarship has revolutionised our understanding of the philosophical sense and importance of Hegel's views. Long associated with unbridled speculation, obscurantism and totalitarianism, Hegel can now be seen as the Aristotle of the modern world. Synoptic in scope, Hegel's philosophy is challenging both in style and substance.

Hegel's readers often worsen their plight by assimilating Hegel's views to familiar positions, while failing to recognise ways in which, and the often great extent to which, Hegel criticised and sought to replace familiar dichotomies underlying those positions. For example, Hegel's first book, *The Phenomenology of Spirit* (1807), concerns the development of 'absolute knowledge'. The phrase 'absolute knowledge' is syntactically ambiguous. In the first paragraph of the Introduction to the *Phenomenology*, Hegel explains that the relevant sense of 'absolute' is 'whatever in truth is', or whatever ultimately there is. Hence the *Phenomenology* is concerned with showing that and how we actually know whatever in truth is. Too often his readers take 'absolute' adverbially, to modify how we know whatever we may know. This assimilates Hegel's epistemology to the Cartesian tradition Hegel sought, with Kant, to supplant, and occludes Hegel's aim to develop a pragmatic, fallibilist account of human knowledge. Those who recognise the pragmatic dimensions of Hegel's theory of knowledge typically assume that pragmatism and fallibilism are incompatible with realism. Hegel, however, sought to show how a sober fallibilist account of justification is consistent with a realist, 'correspondence' analysis of the nature of truth. This may appear incompatible with 'idealism', while Hegel avows idealism. A 'Remark' to the second edition of Hegel's *Science of Logic* (1812, rev. edn 1831) explains this misunderstood view: something is 'ideal' if it is not ultimately real, in the sense that it does not contain the ground of its own being or existence. Accordingly, something's causal dependencies are so many ways in which its being or characteristics depend on other things or events. Dependence on human minds is only an insignificant sub-species of causal dependency in Hegel's ontology. Hegel's 'idealism' is a kind of ontological holism that stresses the causal interdependence of objects and events, along with what Hegel regarded as constitutive contrasts among their characteristics. Hence Hegel's idealism is, as he says, entirely consistent with realism about the objects of human knowledge, namely that they exist and are whatever they are, regardless of what we may think, believe or say about them.

The Phenomenology of Spirit. Hegel's philosophy is comprehensive and systematic. Hegel presented its parts in distinct books, which may be taken in order, beginning with the *Phenomenology of Spirit* (1807). Philosophical controversy was rife when Hegel began philosophising in the era we now call that of 'German Idealism', thus raising the issue: how can any philosophy show itself to be justified when basic standards of justification are themselves disputed? Accordingly, in the middle of the Introduction to the *Phenomenology* Hegel posed Sextus Empiricus' 'Dilemma of the Criterion': how can criteria of truth be established without dogmatism, vicious circularity or infinite regress? Hegel is the only philosopher to solve this problem. Hegel justifies his own philosophical views only through the strictly internal critique of all relevant opposed views. Though his claim to completeness is controversial, Hegel fulfilled his stringent justificatory requirements astonishingly well. Hegel's internal critique goes beyond *reductio ad absurdum* refutations. Hegel's phenomenological method is constructive because it considers philosophical principles as they can be used by a representative 'form of consciousness' to grasp and grapple with the intended domain of those principles. One commentator adroitly noted: 'The full strength of Hegel's position is appreciated only when it is understood that he is arguing that bad theory makes for bad practice, and that the bad practice shows up the logical difficulties of the theory'. These logical difficulties are revealed in part by relevant phenomena that cannot be accounted for by the express principles held by the form of consciousness in question; the process of revealing such failure is what Hegel called 'dialectic'.

Key points of Hegel's epistemology in the *Phenomenology* include the following: empirical knowledge requires conjoint sensation and conceptual classification of particular objects or events; our conceptual and linguistic resources are historically and socially transmitted, assessed and revised; epistemic justification is pragmatic and fallible; justification (whether cognitive or practical) involves constructive self- and mutual criticism; and knowledge requires truth and involves a correspondence analysis of truth. Hegel defends realism in epistemology through a transcendental argument for mental content externalism. 'Mental content externalism' holds that the content of some 'mental' contents are, or can only be specified in terms of, objects or events in one's environment; Hegel's transcendental argument aims to show that unless some of our key 'mental' contents were external to our minds, we could not be self-consciously aware of any mental contents at all.

Hegel is the first philosopher to recognise that a sober social and historical account of human knowledge is consistent with realism. Hegel's social theory of knowledge is based on his social ontology, which he called 'spirit'. Henry Harris (*Hegel's Ladder*, 2 vols, 1997) contends that the *Phenomenology* contains Hegel's genuine philosophy of history. One important aspect of his philosophy of history pertains to his account of epistemic justification. Hegel's main reason for designating Attic Greek culture as 'immediate spirit' is that, for example, neither Antigone nor Creon can justify their key principles; they can only assert them. Hegel aims to reconcile the deeply felt and held communal basis found in ancient Greek culture within our modern, highly individualistic, rationalistic and often critical culture. He does this in part by arguing that no principle, whether cognitive or practical, can be justified apart from its ongoing use and critical scrutiny by all concerned parties.

Hegel is a staunch defender of rational autonomy because it is crucial to our individual and to our collective life: nothing counts as a ground or reason for action, or for knowledge, unless its sufficiency is assessed and affirmed in someone's judgement. Correlatively, anyone's judgement on such matters is subject to self-critical and mutual assessment; individual autonomy is necessary but only collective autonomy (which all autonomous individuals constitute) suffices for rational justification. He defends rational autonomy by arguing that the relevant alternative accounts of justification (such as natural law, royal edict, positivism, intuitionism, hedonism or utilitarianism) have been tried in various phases of our cultural history, and have not provided adequate principles or methods of justification. This, Hegel argues, is true of the various individualist accounts of reason considered in 'Self-Consciousness' and 'Reason'; and it is true of the various forms of collectivism and individualism considered in 'Spirit'. (The quoted terms name the second, third and fourth main sections of Hegel's *Phenomenology*.) Constructive mutual assessment of principles is necessary in part due to the sociological 'law of unintended consequences', that the same kind of act performed by a group of people can have quite different results than were anticipated. In cognition, collective autonomy is sufficient for justification only because it functions on the basis of our generally reliable neurophysiology and psychology of perception.

Up to this point, Hegel develops and defends his position for the philosophically wise. 'Religion' (section five of the *Phenomenology*) takes a different tack. Here Hegel attempts to construct a historical narrative of the history and content of religion, from Zoroastrianism up to a reconstructed Christianity he calls 'Manifest Religion'. The first principle of Hegel's holistic metaphysics is: posit no transcendent entities. Accordingly, Hegel interprets transcendent religious deities as human projections. However, rather than debunk them, Hegel interprets these projections as expressing profound human needs and aspirations, including the needs for humility, grace and forgiveness regarding our justificatory oversights and errors – our fallibility, whether cognitive or practical. These, too, are fundamental for constructive self- and mutual criticism, and thus for genuinely rational justification. Achieving this mutual recognition among rational agents who assess themselves and others *is* the advent of 'absolute spirit'. This point is reached for Hegel's philosophical readers at the very end of 'Spirit'. Hegel's historical narration of Religion is intended to bring the non-philosophical public to this same recognition, at least at an allegorical level: 'God is attainable in pure speculative knowledge alone and is only in that knowledge, and is only that knowledge itself [*sic*]'.

Hegel begins the *Phenomenology* by identifying 'the absolute' as 'whatever in truth is'. The *Phenomenology* closes, in 'Absolute Knowledge' (section six), with the thoroughly if fallibly justified claims that we do have knowledge of 'whatever in truth is'; that we know the natural, cultural and historical world as it is; and that our genuine knowledge of the world is a collective, historical achievement. We also now recognise that we are individual participants within our communal 'spirit', and that through our communities we play crucial roles in achieving and recognising the achievement of 'absolute spirit': Hegel claims to show that we have finally arrived at an adequate account of justification that enables us to justify our claims to know 'what in truth is', and to justify sound principles of action (moral, social and legal norms), where all of this is due to mature, autonomous rational judgement, both individually and collectively. These principles are fundamental to human knowledge, and also to human freedom, both in theory and in practice. In retrospect, we can, Hegel contends, understand that this is and has been the historical *telos* of world history. This marks the advent of 'absolute spirit' as both substance and subject: through our knowledge of the world, the world-whole to which we belong achieves knowledge of itself.

The *Science of Logic* **and the** *Encyclopaedia.* Attaining this standpoint of 'absolute knowledge' enables us to engage Hegel's *Science of Logic*. Hegel's *Logic* is a successor to Kant's 'Transcendental Logic', a study of the fundamental cognitive significance and roles of our most basic categories and principles of judgement. It is as much a study in cognitive semantics as it is a theory of judgement and a metaphysics. Metaphysics pertains to Hegel's *Logic* because he sought to determine what must be the fundamental structure of the world, such that it can be known by us at all. Although Russell objected that Hegel conflated 'the "is" of identity' and 'the "is" of predication', Hegel deliberately assumed this conflation only in order to argue by *reductio ad absurdum* that predication is distinct from identity. Hegel's *Logic* first considers a variety of what may be called 'single-tiered' concepts required to characterise whatever is, such as 'being', 'quality', 'quantity' and 'measure'. Hegel contends that specifying and understanding these concepts leads to a host of 'two-tiered' concepts, likewise required to characterise whatever is, such as 'essence', 'ground', 'appearance' and 'manifestation'. One key concern is to show how proper use of these concepts generates no cognitively opaque distinctions between what appears to us and what in fact exists. Hegel's *Logic* then considers our conceptual repertoire of concepts, judgements and inferences, including mechanical, chemical and teleological principles of explanation. It concludes by examining the 'idea', life, the idea of knowledge and the 'absolute idea'.

Hegel's moderate holism in ontology, semantics and justification requires systematic philosophy, for only a systematic and comprehensive philosophy can specify precisely the semantic, cognitive and ontological significance of concepts and principles, because these depend in part on their systematic integration within the whole of our conceptual repertoire, and on their systematic differentiation within their immediate sub-species and families of concepts or principles. This is one key point of Hegel's *Logic*. Hegel sought to exhibit this systematicity and thereby to specify as closely as possible the semantic, cognitive and ontological significance of our concepts and principles, in his *Encyclopaedia of Philosophical Sciences* (1817, 1827, 1830), which served as Hegel's lecture syllabus on the three parts of his philosophical system, Logic, Philosophy of Nature and Philosophy of Spirit.

Hegel's 'Philosophy of Nature' reconsiders mechanical, chemical and organic concepts and principles, in close connection with an astonishing range of concrete examples, covering terrestrial and celestial mechanics, cohesion, sound, heat, geology, and plant and animal organisms. Hegel was deeply versed in contemporaneous natural science; recent scholarship shows his views are a far cry from their common caricatures. For example, Hegel was mathematically sophisticated enough to have well-considered reasons for preferring certain schools of French analysis in physical mechanics.

The three parts of Hegel's 'Philosophy of Spirit' are 'subjective', 'objective' and 'absolute' spirit. Part one is most important; in it Hegel details his account of our individual physiological, psychological and rational capacities for thought, action and freedom. 'Anthropology' first considers our natural capacities for growth, feeling – including our affective sense of ourselves – and habit. A revised 'Phenomenology' examines our capacities for consciousness, self-consciousness and reason. Finally, 'Psychology' examines our capacities for knowledge, action and freedom. Part two, 'objective spirit', briefly summarises Hegel's social and political philosophy, elaborated in his *Philosophy of Right* (1821). Part three, 'absolute spirit', briefly sketches three topics of Hegel's lecture cycles in Berlin on 'absolute spirit': art, religion and philosophy.

Hegel's *Philosophy of Right* integrates fundamental insights from Aristotle, Kant and Scottish political economy. Wrongly condemned as a historicist, Hegel succinctly refuted the principle of the historical school of jurisprudence: tracing a present law or institution back to its historical origin voids its justification, because those historical conditions no longer obtain. Hegel expressly followed Montesquieu, whose *Spirit of the Laws* (1748) showed that legal institutions are justified only by how well they function within their social-institutional context. Though Hegel states that individuals are related to the social order 'as accidents to substance', he conversely holds that 'substance is the totality of its accidents'. In brief, 'substance' exists only through and as its 'accidents'. Hegel holds that it is rational for individuals to 'conform to the universal', because universal principles are only valid if sufficient justifying reasons for them can be offered to all interested or affected

parties, without appeal to any other antecedent norms. Hegel's republicanism is thus rooted directly in this fundamental principle of rational
justification. Hegel's criteria of justification develop and extend precisely the kind of 'constructivism' recently identified in Kant's views by
Onora O'Neill.

Hegel argues that the substance of many of our most important
legitimate moral and legal principles are rooted in our economic
activities. Though it cannot generate legitimate principles *ex nihilo*,
individual moral reflection is crucial for understanding, assessing and
acting on the basis of those principles. Legitimate law codifies,
promulgates and protects those social and economic patterns of activity
that are crucial for securing and facilitating individual freedom of
action. Hegel advocated a professional civil service to handle affairs of
state, including legislation, though he insisted that it function under the
scrutiny of a constitutional monarch and a public well-informed by
their political representatives. The *Philosophy of Right* closes by briefly
sketching Hegel's philosophy of world history.

Hegel's lectures on world history, art, religion and philosophy are
classics of Western literature. Though history is a 'slaughter bench', it
is nevertheless possible to discern the slow but cumulative historical
growth of knowledge, reason and freedom. Hegel developed a sophisticated account of aesthetic judgement based on detailed comparative
knowledge of a vast array of historical media, styles and genre. His
lectures on religion elaborate the views Hegel first sketches in the
Phenomenology. His lectures on philosophy established the history of
philosophy as a philosophical discipline.

K. Westphal

See also: absolute; *Aufhebung*; contradiction (1); constitution; Death;
despair; dialectic; German Idealism; Idea (2); organism; Reason (2);
Repetition; Spirit; Time; Truth

HEGEMONY A term used by Gramsci in his *Prison Notebooks* to refer
to the process by which a dominant class maintains its rule through
ideological, moral and intellectual leadership. A class can be said to
merely 'dominate' antagonistic social groups when it resorts to open or
veiled coercion through state power to impose its will. It can be said to
be 'hegemonic' when it also provides 'intellectual and moral leadership'
over allied groups in civil society. Hegemony thus involves ideologically transcending narrow sectional interests and advancing universally
acceptable notions while maintaining class rule. Among subordinate
social groups a struggle for hegemonic leadership ensues during 'a crisis
of authority'. As Gramsci puts it:

If the ruling class has lost its consensus, i.e. is no longer leading but only 'dominant', exercising coercive force alone, this means precisely that the great masses have become detached from their traditional ideologies, and no longer believe what they used to believe previously, etc. The crisis consists precisely in the fact that the old is dying and the new cannot be born; in this interregnum a great variety of morbid symptoms appear.

The idea of hegemony almost became hegemonic itself in the 1980s in various political projects for 'historic blocs' associated with the 'post-Marxism' of Ernesto Laclau and Chantal Mouffe, and in the disciplinary claims of Cultural Studies.

A. Law

HEIDEGGER, MARTIN (1889–1976) German philosopher with a profound impact on existentialism, phenomenology, aesthetics, philosophy of technology and many other fields. Heidegger is without doubt one of the most important figures in all of continental philosophy.

The philosophical earthquake produced by Heidegger's thought can be summarised in the following points: first, the entire history of philosophy is based on the forgetfulness of the most decisive of questions, the question concerning being; second, the task of philosophy is to make explicit what, up until then, was always presupposed and never questioned, namely the fact that we understand our own being, as well as the being of things around us, on the basis of time. Hence the title of his masterpiece, *Being and Time* (1927). Time is the key to understanding the question upon which philosophy has always stumbled and never been able to tackle adequately. This unity of time and being will never be called into question, although it will be transformed substantially by the late essay 'Time and Being' (1962). The way in which ontology can overcome its traditional shortcomings is by becoming fundamental and phenomenological (*see* Phenomenology).

The early work. Initially (circa 1920), Heidegger seeks to develop an adequate interpretation and an anthropological comprehension of the Christian conscience. This task implies that he distance himself from the dogmatic tradition of the Church, which had shaped his mind so profoundly, and from its dominant Neo-Thomism. In a way that is nothing short of revolutionary, and much inspired by Husserlian phenomenology, Heidegger returns to Aristotle to address his philosophical concern. In turning to Aristotle, however, Heidegger does not seek to return philosophy to a past doctrine, or to study it as a merely historical object. On the contrary: he is looking to develop a *radical* problematic on the basis of philosophy's main preoccupations at the time. These have to do with an interpretation of the phenomenon of 'life'. What came to be known as the 'philosophy of life' (*Lebensphilosophie*) understood itself to be philosophising not about life, but from life itself: it is life itself that philosophises. As philosophy, it seeks to be an organ of that life, and is concerned with the possibility of clarifying life. In doing so, it strives to enhance life, to open up new modalities and figures of life. It does not wish only to discover which values are valid; it is daring enough to wish to create new values. It asks not about the usefulness of knowledge but about its creative potential; life is richer than any theory. Although Nietzsche, Bergson and Scheler can be seen as promoters of this type of philosophy, each in a different way, it is perhaps Dilthey with whom Heidegger has the most in common. For life, Dilthey argues, is the fundamental *fact* that must be the starting point of philosophy. It is what is known from within, and that behind which one cannot go back: it cannot be brought before the judgement seat of reason. These are words that resonate with Heidegger's early phenomenological interpretations of Aristotle, in which he develops the fundamental traits of a philosophical and phenomenological anthropology. Although not explicitly ontological, Heidegger's analyses pave the way for his subsequent inquiry into the question of the sense of being.

Heidegger finds in Aristotle a description of the basic phenomenon of human life, namely facticity. By facticity, we must understand that the human being (or 'Dasein') is essentially open: open-onto or exposed to something (*das Aussein-auf-etwas*). The being of who we are is characterised by this irreducible structure of openness and exposedness. For Heidegger, of the entire tradition it is Aristotle who poses the question of what it means 'to be' for the human Dasein (*psyche*) in the most clear and systematic manner; Husserl's concept of intentionality, which designates the central and irreducible structure of human consciousness, is a rediscovery of a phenomenon first revealed by Aristotle. The phenomenon of intentional life, or existence, involves the 'world' as its object, or, in Husserlian terminology, its 'correlate'. Yet this world is itself there, present, and 'worlds', only to the extent that the human Dasein uncovers or unveils it. To be, for the world, means to be present (this is the sense of being as presence, or *parousia*), yet the presence of the present is directly a function of the being of the human Dasein as unveiling. The phenomenon that underlies and sustains the essential openness or exposedness of the human Dasein is that of uncovering, or 'disclosing'. To be, for the human Dasein, or factical life, means to disclose.

Disclosedness, Heidegger argues, is the fundamental sense of truth as *aletheia* in Ancient Greek thought.

The question of the sense of being. The question that progressively finds its way through Heidegger's interpretations of Aristotle and his systematic reading of Husserl's *Logical Investigations* (1900–1), is that concerning the meaning or sense (*Sinn*) of being (*Sein*). In his *Metaphysics*, Aristotle raised a question that was to become seminal for an entire tradition after him, from medieval scholasticism to Hegel and beyond: if things can be said to be (*einai*) in many ways (those ways that came to be gathered in a list or table of 'categories'), if the word 'being' (*to on*) applies to beings in many different ways, and so itself has different senses, is there one, unifying sense beneath them all? Is 'being' merely equivocal, a mere homonym, or is it univocal, and so a kind of synonym? The answer that Aristotle provided, and that Heidegger was to find insufficient, pointed to presence (*parousia*) as the implicit, underlying sense of being: to be always amounts to being present. The question, however, is one to know whether this understanding of being as presence, which the tradition took for granted, does not presuppose the dimension of the present, and so of time itself, as its deeper, hidden sense. Is time not the key to understanding the sense of being? But, assuming that we can say what time consists in – an attempt previously always frustrated – should we understand the present as the point at which time originates? Or is it possible that, contrary to our most stubborn conception, and possibly our own intuition, the present is itself only the outcome of a complex temporal process, the tip of the iceberg, as it were?

In pursuing these questions, *Being and Time* (1927) establishes time as the sense of being. How does Heidegger understand 'sense'? As the horizon, or the limit, on the basis of which we 'understand' the world in which we live. This means that time operates as the transcendental horizon, or the necessary condition under which beings can take on their various significations. Time, to speak Kant's language, is the a priori. Yet, contrary to what Kant argued, this a priori, on the basis of which we gain our understanding of the world, does not depend on some cognitive faculty, normally referred to as the understanding (*Verstand*), or as reason (*Vernunft*), or as both. In fact, it is neither a faculty, nor a straightforward representation. Rather, this understanding is a function of life itself, or, to be more precise, of existence (Dasein). We 'understand' the world, things, events, phenomena, as well as others within it, simply by virtue of the fact that we exist, that is by virtue of the fact that we are existent beings. There is no being, no essence of humanity outside this world of things that surrounds us and which we find meaningful. There is no inner self, no essence outside existence. This idea became the point of departure for existentialism. But other beings, such as animals, or objects, do they not exist too? Not in Heidegger's sense. For to exist, Heidegger claims, is to be in the world. And being-in-the-world is the distinctive trait of human beings. But what does being-in-the-world mean? It means, Heidegger claims, to be outside oneself, amid things, in such a way that the question regarding *who* we are can only be answered by looking at *how* we are in the world, how we comport ourselves in it, how it matters to us, how things and others affect us. This presupposes that we describe existence in its average, ordinary way of being, and reveal the way in which we understand our world. It presupposes that we describe the way in which, from the start and always, we move ourselves within an average, implicit understanding of our being, that of things, and that of other existent beings. When I call up a friend in a state of excitement, when I get into my car and drive to work, when I am bored, when I look at a landscape, each time, I understand my world – my world is this understanding of it – in a way that does not involve any theoretical activity, but that is immediate and intuitive.

Such is Heidegger's radical gesture of desubjectivising. But if we are nothing outside this outside, if we are this pure ex-istence, or this being out there in the world, do we not run the risk of losing ourselves, of dissolving into pure exteriority? This would indeed be the case, were it not for the fact that our openness to the world itself and as such, which we experience in limit phenomena (or 'moods') such as anxiety, boredom and perhaps others, were not itself based on a possibility of a radical closure, namely death. In a world of possibilities, death is the most primordial, the most radical and the defining possibility: it is the horizon against which we exist, it is, paradoxically, where we come from, it is the background against which the world unfolds. Were it not for death, or, more specifically, for our being-towards death, there would be no existence, no world (in this 'rich' sense of the word), but mere matter. Our being would be no different from that of a stone or bacteria. From the realisation of the essential finitude of human existence and the decisive role it plays in opening up the world for us (as well as threatening to close it down: the two are mutually dependent), comes the further realisation that the sense of our being is temporal and specifically futural. We are beings that are projected into the future from the start, and it is because we are so oriented that our world is a world of possibilities. It is because we are so oriented that our world is one in which we can be this or that, do this or that. Our freedom is itself a function of our finitude. And our freedom to do good and bad – indeed, our very sense of good and evil – is itself a function of our being as existents. Ethics stems from ontology, a challenge to which Levinas will respond by claiming exactly the inverse, that ethics is 'first philosophy'.

So: our having a world, our understanding of our own being, of the being of other things, and of that of others, stems not from our ability to produce representations of them or to match an intuition of them with an innate concept or idea built into the structure of subjectivity, but from our essentially futural, temporal being. The future is the primary temporal dimension, or, as Heidegger prefers to call it, the primary 'ecstasis' (existence is ecstatic, that is always out there, ahead of itself). But it is not the only one. Co-extensive with the future is the past, or, as Heidegger calls it, the fact that we are a being that *is* in the mode of having-been, that we not only relate to the future, but also to the past, in the present itself. In other words, there is always more to the present situation than the present itself. In presence, in the presence of a moment, of a thing, of a person, there is, folded as it were, invisible, yet always at work, the future, as well as the past. The present, so often taken for granted, is actually a complex construction, and in fact the result of the way in which, at any given time, future and past come together. Philosophy, Heidegger claims, has always under-stood being as presence, the being of things, of the world, in terms of presence. What is, is what's present. In other words, it's always understood being on the basis of time. But it never understood time adequately. Why? Because – as Augustine beautifully illustrated in his *Confessions* – it always insisted on beginning with the present, on denying any reality to the time that was not the present. For Heidegger, it is exactly the other way around.

The transformation of the question. Heidegger had already achieved a phenomenal amount (much of which we are still trying to assimilate today). Yet his project remained incomplete so long as the openness, or the clearing for which the word 'being' stood, remained bound up with traces of subjectivity and anthropocentrism – so long, that is, as the 'sense' or the 'truth' of being as time was to be found in a distinctly human finitude and not in being itself. In other words, Heidegger's radical desubjectivising needed to be pushed still further. Could this horizon, on the basis of which being unfolds, could this 'sense', on the basis of which presence opens up, be discovered in being itself, and not simply in the being of the human? And would this entail a debunking of time as such a horizon? These questions led to a radical revision and transformation of the question. More specifically, it led to a displacement of the question, a shift of the burden of proof, as it were, from Dasein, as the existent being, to being itself. This is a project that begins to be carried out in 'On the Essence of Truth' (1930) as well as in a number of lecture courses and texts throughout the 1930s, the most experimental and fascinating of them all being perhaps *Contributions to Philosophy. From Ereignis* (written 1936–8, published 1989).

Two decisive traits emerge from the work of that period: time is now understood as history. But this history is not that of humanity. It is the history of being, within which the human finds its own being. In other words, the being of the human being is reinterpreted within the context of that history. Heidegger understands history (*Geschichte*) not as a chronological succession of events that can be linked causally, but as sending (*Schicken*) and destiny (*Geschick*). What does this mean? That being destines itself to the human, and that the destiny of the human is played out in the way in which it responds to this sending. (Thus, in a way, after having reworked Kantian and Husserlian subjectivity, Heidegger now found himself compelled to rework Hegel's thematising of historical difference in categorial structures, though without the latter's sense of 'spiritual' development.) The co-belonging of man and being Heidegger calls *Ereignis*. This word indicates the reciprocal and mutual event of appropriation between man and being. Man can respond to what is sent to him either by turning away from it, either, that is, by closing down the space opened up by this sending, or he can respond to it by opening itself to it, by taking it up and safekeeping it. The former response, Heidegger argues, is the one dominant in Western history, and especially in Western philosophy, which has become science and technology. Philosophy, science and technology, which stand for the advance of rationality, are distinct ways of responding to this call. The problem is, they are concerned not with being itself, with the truth of being, but with beings, and with the way in which they can be represented, ordered, measured, calculated in advanced, in short 'understood' in a very distinct sense. This mode of understanding, Heidegger argues, has led to the destruction of the earth, the occultation of truth as *aletheia*, or to what he calls technological nihilism. But, Heidegger argues, there are other modes of understanding the world and ourselves, modes that amount to a reversal of the rationalist-technological trend. According to this mode, the human can understand itself on the basis of its belonging to the earth, and not the other way around. Another relation to nature, and truth, is possible, which Heidegger sees in certain works of art ('The Origin of the Work of Art,' 1935), and most notably in Hölderlin's poetry (*Hölderlin's Hymns 'Germanien' and 'Der Rhein'*, 1934, and *Hölderlin's Hymn, 'The Ister'*, 1942). In his later work, Heidegger will understand language as the one decisive space in which our relation to being is played out: either as mere commodity, as an instrument of communication, and ultimately as cybernetics; or as poetry, and by that we need to understand the possibility of relating to the earth as the place in which we dwell and to which we belong.

M. de Beistegui

See also: aletheia; anxiety; attunement (*Befindlichkeit*); authenticity (*Eigentlichkeit*); Dasein; Death; disclosedness/resolute disclosedness (*Erschlossenheit/Entschlossenheit*); 'earth and world'; Ecocriticism; Ek-sistence; Environmental Philosophy; *Ereignis*; Ethics; existential analytic; Existentialism; four-fold; fundamental ontology; *Gelassenheit* (letting-be); *Gestell* (enframing); Hermeneutics; historicity; hylomorphism; Memory; Metaphysics; moment of vision (2); Nature, Philosophy of; ontological difference; onto-theo-logy; 'the nothing'; Repetition; Space; Subject; Technology, Philosophy of; Thought; thrownness; Time; Truth; worldhood

HERDER, JOHANN GOTTFRIED (1744–1803) German philosopher and critic whose organicist views on nature and language influenced Kant (whose *Critique of Judgement* was in part a response to Herder's anti-mechanism), Goethe, Novalis, Schelling, Hegel, Schleiermacher and Dilthey. Herder studied at the University of Königsberg in the early 1760s, where he was taught by Kant (then in his 'pre-critical' period) and by Johann Georg Hamann, a founder of the *Sturm und Drang* ('Storm and Stress') movement; his two professors remained key interlocutors for him throughout his life. Herder never occupied a university position himself, however: he worked first as a school teacher in Riga, and then, after a period travelling in France as a Lutheran pastor, he settled in Weimar in a clerical post obtained with the support of Goethe, a long-standing friend. Herder wrote prolifically from a young age, in a colourful quasi-conversational style that reflected his conviction that philosophy at its best connects with the people, and with the whole personality, not just professional philosophers. His most famous works include *Fragments on Recent German Literature* (1767), *Treatise on the Origin of Language* (1772), *On the Knowledge and Sensation of the Human Soul* (1778), *Ideas for a Philosophy of History of Humanity* (1784–91), *God, Some Conversations* (1787) and *Letters for the Advancement of Humanity* (1793–7).

Herder was a pioneer of what has been called the 'expressivist' revolution in German thought. His aim was to provide an account of the natural origins of distinctive human powers, and so their continuity with forces at play in the rest of nature, in a way that was consistent with the spontaneity and diversity through which these capacities were expressed across human cultures. This required, in his view, the complementary working out of an organic, non-mechanistic conception of nature and a genuinely historical approach to the human world. In his account of language, for instance, Herder rejected the idea that language may have some supernatural or divine origin. At the same time, he argued that human language, while natural, is different in kind from the modes of communication that exist between other animals. Through language, human beings realise their capacity for 'reflection' or self-awareness. But for Herder, while possession of this capacity sets human beings apart from other animals, there is no single legitimate way in which it naturally develops. On the contrary, for Herder languages and cultures are marked by irreducible plurality, having evolved under diverse natural and historical conditions. Herder was a sharp critic of the ethnocentric tendency among Enlightenment historians to understand and judge other cultures by the standards of their own, a tendency he linked to European imperialism. Moreover, for Herder human plurality was a sign of vitality and insight rather than corruption or confusion. And although, in his political writings, he was an advocate of cultural nationalism, he saw this not as an alternative to democracy but as the form self-rule takes under the historical conditions of modernity.

N. Smith

HERMENEUTICS The science or art of interpretation, but also a particular tradition of continental philosophy, the main figures in which are Schleiermacher, Dilthey, Heidegger, Gadamer and Ricoeur. This tradition is only partly concerned, in fact, with the detail of interpretative technique. Of greater interest to it is the philosophical significance of the very act of interpretation, especially as that feeds into epistemology, theories of meaning and conceptions of human subjectivity.

Hermeneutics can be characterised in epistemological terms as pluralist and anti-foundationalist. It is pluralist in so far as it recognises the existence of many legitimate ways of knowing, whether or not they possess the formalisable precision of logic and mathematics or the predictive power of the modern natural sciences. While mindful of the achievements of natural science, hermeneutics questions the widespread modern assumption that this is the only genuine knowledge there is. The arts, humanities and social sciences have an epistemic dignity of their own, and much hermeneutic philosophy is aimed at clarifying and where necessary 'retrieving' the claim to truth they rightfully possess.

Hermeneutics is also an anti-foundationalist philosophy in that it repudiates the project of grounding knowledge in some indubitable, self-justifying acquaintance with things. On the hermeneutic view, there is no unmediated access to reality, no transparent disclosure of self or world. There is disagreement within the hermeneutic tradition about the source of this non-transparency. For example, some (Schleiermacher and Frank) ascribe it to the structure of reflection, others (Husserl, Gadamer and Habermas) to the non-thematisable cultural horizons that provide the background for all specific knowledge claims. But all hermeneutic thought is at odds with philosophical outlooks that assume or aspire towards an absolute standpoint, that is, a standpoint outside of history. Hermeneutics thus embraces the 'historicity' and 'finitude' of human understanding.

On account of its pluralism and anti-foundationalism, hermeneutics is routinely said to lack critical bite. But this charge usually presupposes the availability of an ahistorical, 'universalist' critical standpoint which is difficult to sustain, and it ignores the potential for critical reflection that hermeneutics itself unleashes. Hermeneutic theorists such as Gadamer and Charles Taylor, for instance, have developed a model of practical reason based on lucid self-interpretation. According to this model (which draws heavily on Aristotle's *Nicomachean Ethics*), practical reason is a matter of interpreting the values that define a subject's identity. Whether the subject is an individual person or a collective agent (such as a nation), hermeneutic reflection begins with a historically inherited conception of the good but it never ends with exactly the same conception. Self–interpretations are inherently open to criticism, improvement and transformation. The contrast with other self-interpretations plays a crucial role in this learning process, in a manner suggested by Gadamer's notion of a 'fusion of horizons'.

How wide, then, is the scope of hermeneutic reflection? This was the topic of an important debate between Gadamer, Habermas and Ricoeur. Habermas argued that discourses oriented towards 'emancipation', such as psychoanalysis and Marxism, departed in crucial ways from the logic of interpretation. They involved theoretically mediated modes of reflection that could penetrate through the masks of ideology and false consciousness. Habermas has also argued, this time more against Taylor, that hermeneutic self-clarification does not exhaust the possibilities of practical reason, since there are universal standards of right or justice to which practical reasoners can and sometimes must appeal. To the extent that this move requires an emphatic distinction between the right and the good, however, it is vulnerable to a range of hermeneutic counter-objections.

Much philosophy in the hermeneutic tradition is concerned with language and the 'linguisticality' of human beings. There is no single theory of meaning to which all hermeneutic philosophers subscribe, but generally they are hostile to the 'realist' view that meaning is 'ready-made' in the world and that the essence of language is to name independently existing objects (be they 'inner' pre-linguistic thoughts or items in the 'external' world). As well as rejecting this kind of realism, hermeneutics opposes nominalism. For hermeneutics, meaning is as little an 'effect' of arbitrary systems of signs as it is the product of a subject's will. The central thesis of the hermeneutic view, which derives from Herder, is that language, far from being an instrument at the disposal of the thinking and acting subject, is the medium through which thought and action comes to expression (and so comes to be). In asserting this proposition, hermeneutics does not deny that language has real representative or communicative powers, as some postmodern theories rashly do. The claim is rather that representation and communication presuppose a prior capacity for expression. Since the expressive power of language is most palpable not in everyday communication or scientific theorising but in works of art, art typically provides the point of departure for hermeneutic theories of meaning.

But if there is agreement within the hermeneutic tradition about the importance of the expressive power of language, there is disagreement about how to characterise it. In Schleiermacher's romantic hermeneutics the role of the individual subject in the production and reproduction of meaning is emphasised, though it is not a role that allows the subject to stand outside of language or to make its expressive powers transparent to itself. By contrast, Gadamer, whose thinking on language was strongly influenced by Heidegger's later work, assigns a subordinate role to the individual. For Gadamer, the expressive power of 'bringing forth' and 'making manifest' in language belongs to intersubjectively constituted traditions, shared forms of life that in a sense 'speak through' the individual subject. Gadamer puts forward this view as a corrective to the 'subjectivism' he thinks has dominated Western philosophy since the Enlightenment. More recently, Manfred Frank has challenged the Heidegger/Gadamer line from a standpoint sympathetic to Schleiermacher, while Paul Ricoeur and Charles Taylor have tried to show that the critique of subjectivism need not conflict with the claims of the individual creative imagination.

N. Smith

HETEROGLOSSIA/MONOGLOSSIA Central terms in Mikhail Bakhtin's linguistic philosophy. In *The Dialogic Imagination* (1975) and *Problems of Dostoevsky's Poetics* (1929 and 1972), Bakhtin postulates that the linguistic community is enmeshed in a continual struggle between two tendencies, 'monoglossia' and 'heteroglossia'. Bakhtin associates monoglossia with the development of a 'unitary master language', which aids socio-political as well as cultural centralisation. This master language is not a system of abstract categories; rather it is a 'world-view' ensuring mutual understanding in all spheres of ideological life. Examples of monoglossic master languages would be: a national language; a lingua franca of diplomacy or international meetings; the literary language of a culture; mathematics, logic and other idioms of calculation; and Orwell's 'Newspeak' in the novel *1984*.

'Heteroglossia', on the other hand, names the stratification of social languages and the ongoing development of generational, professional and other forms of social differentiation. The centrifugal movement of heteroglossia stands in constant tension with the centripetal and homogenising movement of monoglossia. Bakhtin sometimes uses the term 'dialogised heteroglossia' to refer to hybridisation – the struggle among and mixture of socio-linguistic points of view – and, more particularly, to the permanent resistance of heteroglossia to monoglossia. As one example of this more specific meaning, Bakhtin points to the struggle for audibility by the lower social-economic groups of the Renaissance period in Europe against the hegemony of the language of the officials and upper classes. This struggle includes parody – the debunking citation or hybridisation of the official language within the polemics and colloquial forms of speech of the lower social-economic groups.

F. Evans

HETEROTOPIA A medical term taken up by Foucault in his 1967 lecture 'Of Other Spaces'. A heterotopia is not a fiction constructed to criticise the present, but a real place in which normal social structuring is simultaneously represented, contested and inverted. The principal heterotopias are sites for rites of passage (boarding schools, military camps) and for deviant groups (prisons, psychiatric hospitals, retirement homes), but there are also sites for sanctioned transgression (brothels, carnivals); sites where time flows differently (cemeteries, the indefinite time of the museum or library); and sites that provide miniatures of ordinary society (ships, hotels, intentional communes). Heterotopias link persons from widely different locations, and entry typically involves a special passage or permission. Heterotopias disrupt simple rootedness and standard modern social dichotomies such as leisure/work, private/public, family/social and culture/function.

Heterotopias show that despite the disciplinary efforts of power we no longer live in a homogeneous space. Structures and counter-structures coexist as sites that cannot be superimposed into a total order, even as they function together and need one another. Foucault's list of heterotopias itself refuses to come together into any homogeneous concept. Foucault's complex usage of his term has been criticised for demanding too total a self-reflection on society in the heterotopias while underestimating the contested nature of ordinary social places. After Foucault the term has been used by others to discuss counter-sites that reflect totalising social structures while staging transgression and affirming otherness.

D. Kolb

HISTORICAL MATERIALISM The basic social and historical theory of Marxism. According to Engels:

> The term 'historical materialism' . . . designate[s] that view of the course of history which seeks the ultimate cause . . . of all important historic events in the economic development of society, in the changes in the modes of production and exchange, in the consequent division of society into distinct classes, and in the struggles of these classes against one another. (Engels, *Socialism: Utopian and Scientific*, Introduction to the English edition 1892).

The essentials of this theory are first set out explicitly by Marx and Engels in *The German Ideology* (1845). It receives its 'canonical' formulation in Marx's 'Preface' to *A Contribution to a Critique of Political Economy* (1859), in which Marx analyses social formations into an economic 'foundation' or 'base' upon which arises a political and ideological 'superstructure'. Historical change is caused by contradictions within the base between developing 'productive forces' and existing 'relations of production'. These conflicts give rise to class struggle and to increasingly severe economic crises. Revolutionary change eventually results. Societies thus pass through a series of progressive stages: 'the Asiatic, ancient, feudal and modern bourgeois modes of production'. According to Marx, the bourgeois mode of production (capitalism) is 'the last' antagonistic social form. It is destined to give way to a communist society free of antagonistic classes.

These ideas have been the subject of much discussion in the history of Marxism. The 'base-superstructure' model is criticised as a form of 'economism' or technological determinism, most influentially in recent years in Althusser and Balibar, *Reading Capital* (1971); it is defended in Cohen, *Karl Marx's Theory of History* (1978).

S. Sayers

HISTORICITY (*Geschichtlichkeit*) A term which for Heidegger in *Being and Time* characterises the essentially historical nature of Dasein. This means that Dasein does not exist *in* history, as in some temporal dimension that would be independent from it, but is, or exists, historically; history is a feature of Dasein's being. The science we normally call history (*Historie*), which is concerned with clarifying events and establishing links between them so as to provide a coherent account of the past, is itself a function of the historicity (*Geschichtlichkeit*) of human life, which the existential analytic is to clarify. The historicity of Dasein, and so the fact that Dasein 'has' a history, is a function of the fact that, as an essentially temporal process, Dasein is constantly relating to itself as this being that has been, and the having been of which stems from Dasein's relation to itself as always to come, or as futural. It is only because Dasein is temporal in this existential, ecstatic and finite sense that it is 'historical'. It is as 'thrown' that Dasein has a heritage. But it is really as being-towards-death that Dasein becomes *free* for this heritage, and for the most historically decisive possibilities contained therein. It is only as being-towards-death that Dasein becomes its own fate (*Schiksal*): in choosing itself, or in deciding itself for what is most its own, Dasein opens up its own past, and reveals its possibilities, on the basis of itself. The way in which such decisions come to be made, and a history constituted, at the level of a people, Heidegger calls 'destiny' (*Geschick*).

M. de Beistegui

HORKHEIMER, MAX (1895–1973) German philosopher, founder of the Frankfurt School of Critical Theory. Horkheimer's life is bonded in a very special way with the city of Frankfurt. At the newly founded University of Frankfurt, he completed his course of studies with a thesis and dissertation on Kant's *Critique of Judgement*. In 1931, he became director of the Institute for Social Research in Frankfurt and the editor of the *Zeitschrift für Sozialforschung*, a journal where the foundational essays of Critical Theory appeared for the first time. Starting from the early 1930s, papers by Adorno, Marcuse, Benjamin, Erich Fromm and Horkheimer made the *Zeitschrift* one of the most innovative interdisciplinary publications ever.

In all these roles, Horkheimer formulated, both institutionally and theoretically, the project of Critical Theory: the recasting of Marx's legacy in light of the integration between new fields of empirical inquiry – ethnology, anthropology and psychoanalysis are just examples – and traditional philosophical reflection. For example, the social concept of domination can be studied alongside the psychological notions of repression and internalisation: in *Authority and the Family* (1936), written in collaboration with Fromm and Marcuse, Horkheimer foregrounds the link between the structure of individual personality, the impact of ideology and the dimension of labour, which entails social and economic production. As Hitler rose to power, Horkheimer moved the Institute first to Geneva then to Paris and finally to New York. After the Second World War, he re-established the Institute in Frankfurt, serving as Rector of the University from 1951 to 1953.

In an article entitled 'Traditional and Critical Theory', Horkheimer distinguishes between the critical theory of society, which examines historical processes in terms of pathologically alienated social relations, and the traditional theory of society, which looks at the same processes as a set of neutral facts, as in the practice of positivist sociology. While the traditional theory of society is aimed at reaching a description of social phenomena, critical theory is oriented toward action. The interdependence between theory and practice is one of the defining traits of Horkheimer's philosophy and will remain the most distinctive feature of Critical Theory.

With *Dialectic of Enlightenment* (1947), co-authored with Adorno, Horkheimer begins a pessimistic turn that will accompany him in his later works, including the *Eclipse of Reason* (1967). In both books, Horkheimer offers a critique of modernity in the form of an indictment of instrumental rationality. While in its narrow definition instrumental rationality refers to the calculation of relating means to ends, its broader understanding includes the unexamined approval of the scientific method as the only form of objective thinking. Horkheimer suggests that throughout history myth, religion and philosophy used to embody objective reason, which, in modernity, has been progressively 'eclipsed' by subjective reason. Obviously, critical thinking cannot resume the old paradigms of objectivity; but it cannot succumb to instrumentality as the only safe ground either. Here is where, next to Kant as the 'critical' philosopher par excellence, Schopenhauer becomes for the late Horkheimer a conspicuous figure. The contemplation of the definitive character of human suffering in a meaningless universe maintains, for him, an absolute value, for no future society can forget or erase the victims of history. However, human suffering is also the ground of compassion and solidarity, of the exercise of critique in the name of the other, which constitute the very core of Horkheimer's ethical sensibility.

G. Borradori

See also: Cinema; Critical Theory; dialectic of enlightenment; Enlightenment

HOSPITALITY An aporia developed in the work of Derrida and functioning in company with forgiveness (*pardon*), thereby giving particular ethical and political focus to the gift. The term draws on the diverse derivations of the Latin *hostis*, 'host', 'guest' and 'enemy'. Derrida argues that hospitality is always conditional, since unconditional hospitality would mean leaving the door permanently open to whomever or whatever were to arrive totally unannounced, and allowing them to enter without even asking who or what they were. One of the most determinant factors conditioning hospitality is identity – the possibility of distinguishing between friend and enemy (even if one accepts to harbour an enemy), but also the basis upon which citizenship, language, privacy, property and sovereignty, even the human itself, are determined – and hence the idea of unconditional hospitality necessarily raises questions for identity and for political apparatuses of control of it, all the way from the home to the state and international conventions. Derrida's activism, in conjunction with the Parliament of Writers and the Cities of Asylum programme, as well as with various anti-racist and pro-immigrant causes, falls within the ambit of this line of questioning.

Derrida often refers, as a form of challenge or resistance to the traditional concept of hospitality, to the figure of the *Marrano*, or else to the *arrivant absolu* or 'absolute arriver' (not reducible to a person) who, as he puts it in *Aporias*, 'does not simply cross a threshold. Such an *arrivant* affects the very experience of the threshold, whose possibility he [/it] brings to light before one even knows there has been an invitation, a call, a nomination, a promise'.

D. Wills

HUMBOLDT, WILHELM VON (1767–1835) German linguist, political and cultural philosopher, and founder of the Humboldt University of Berlin. In addition to his academic pursuits, Humboldt was also a Prussian reformer and statesman with a variety of important missions, including, most notably, taking part in the Prussian delegation to the Congress of Vienna (1814–15) which helped Europe recover from the Napoleonic Wars. Humboldt is noted for his historical and holistic approach to language, which 'makes infinite employment of finite means'. He characterised human languages as organic wholes and rule-governed systems that express the uniqueness and genius of a people and include possibilities for transformation and individuation. For Chomsky, Humboldt's position comes closest to his own generative linguistics. Humboldt also wrote about aesthetics, poetry, education, history and political philosophy. His work is distinguished by a romantic humanism oriented toward the creative freedom and self-realisation of the individual. The ancient Greeks provided a classical model of achieving harmony and balance in relation to a multiplicity of conflicting forces. His *On the Limits of State Action* (1810), an important source for Mill's *On Liberty*, is an argument for expanding civil rights and liberties while radically limiting state power. He argued that freedom and the greatest possible variety of situations was the basis of education and self-cultivation (*Bildung*) as well as a virtuous and flourishing society. He attempted to put these views into practice as a political and educational reformer; his educational reforms continue to influence the structure of universities to this day.

E. Nelson

HUSSERL, EDMUND (1859–1938) Founder of the 'phenomenological movement' and one of the most influential philosophers of the twentieth century in the continental tradition. Husserl produced seminal studies in the philosophy of arithmetic, logic and psychology, together with an attempt to establish a methodological foundation for philosophy as rigorous science. Major thinkers who have defined their thought in terms of an (often critical) appropriation of his thought include Martin Heidegger, Maurice Merleau-Ponty, Emmanuel Levinas and Jacques Derrida.

Husserl's major works include four introductions to phenomenology published during his lifetime, *Ideas Pertaining to a Pure Phenomenology and a Phenomenological Philosophy* (1913), *Formal and Transcendental Logic* (1929), *Cartesian Meditations* (1931) and *The Crisis of European Sciences and Transcendental Phenomenology* (1936), along with two earlier works, *Philosophy of Arithmetic* (1891) and *Logical Investigations* (1900–1), whose titles are indicative of their contents. Husserl's philosophical legacy also includes over 40,000 pages of research manuscripts and lecture notes, which are in the process of being edited and published with thirty-five volumes having appeared to date.

Husserl's philosophy is both critical and foundational. It is critical in so far as he seeks to demonstrate that empirical, rational and socio-historical theories of knowledge are unable to account adequately for the basic concepts, categories and cognitive operations that are presupposed by any theory, including their own. His thought is foundational in so far as he seeks to provide an adequate account of these concepts, categories and cognitive operations by appealing to their genesis in experience, albeit an experience that has been methodically 'purified' in accordance with strictures established by his critical concerns. The two orientations proper to Husserl's thought find their unity in the method he invented to establish philosophy as rigorous science, which he named the 'phenomenological reduction'. It took Husserl almost two decades to invent this method (which he first mentioned in his lectures in 1906) and he spent the rest of his life using it to investigate the basic structures of logical and scientific (both natural and human) cognition, the experience of time as well as that of other people and other cultures, and finally the experience of history in a novel sense that includes the radical self-responsibility of the phenomenological philosopher for the destiny of rational humanity.

The story of Husserl's work before he invented the reduction is important, however, as it was the realisation of how his initial project failed that pointed him in the right direction. Husserl was initially trained in mathematics (receiving a Ph.D. with a dissertation on the theory of variation calculus in 1883) and his first major philosophical work, *Philosophy of Arithmetic*, attempted to provide an experiential foundation for both the basic concepts of arithmetic and algebra and for basic mathematical operations using these concepts. Husserl, like others working at that time in the field of mathematics, was concerned to clarify the conceptual status of mathematical numerals and symbols, including whether their reference and origin are mundane.

Husserl investigated their status by logical analysis, albeit an analysis assisted by a philosophical psychology, known then as 'descriptive psychology'. Husserl attempted to provide a foundation for mathematics by logically analysing the concept of number and, on the basis of the results of this analysis, clarifying its meaning by tracing its origin to psychological experience. His logical analyses initially led him to believe that there were actually two concepts of number at issue in mathematics, the first and more basic of which kept track of the amounts of any counted items whatever, and the second and more abstract of which dealt with sensibly perceptible signs (that is, mathematical symbols) that, somehow, indirectly referred to the more basic amounts of counted items.

Husserl's analyses led him from abstract concepts to psychological activities. With respect to the first concept of number, both the grouping of items to be counted as well as the determination of their specific amounts did not arise through either the abstract concepts of a 'group' (or 'multiplicity') or a 'number', but in the psychological activities of forming a group ('collective combination') and counting.

The concepts of a group and a number therefore were thought by Husserl to originate in these very activities, specifically in the inner perception (or reflection) upon the respective similarities of each act of collective combination with other such acts and of each act of counting with other such acts, similarities that, when they were in turn reflected upon, were thought to yield the concepts in question as concepts.

Moreover, Husserl initially thought that the object of the symbolic concept of number was the same as the object of these more basic numbers, namely the amounts of items collected in a multiplicity. He thought this because the inability of the mind to keep track of more than a dozen or so counted items seemed, in the cases of computations that have to deal with numbers greater than a dozen or so, to make it *logically* necessary that a system of calculating be devised that is capable of overcoming this mental limitation. Indeed, he initially thought that this is exactly what calculation with mathematical symbols accomplished, that is it substituted sensibly perceivable signs for the 'authentic' numbers at issue in amounts of a dozen or less, and it devised rules for manipulating these signs that produced the same (and therefore the correct) results as actually counting and computing with the more basic numbers.

However, Husserl eventually came to the realisation that not only could calculation with symbols yield correct results without referring, even indirectly, to authentic numbers, but that it was actually better off not referring to them, since such references only slowed down the process of calculation. In addition, he eventually came to the realisation that reflections upon the similarities of the psychological acts of collective combination and counting were unable to accomplish what he had initially thought they could, namely to account for the origin of the concepts of multiplicity and numbers, concepts whose objective meaning is lost, so Husserl realised, with this attempt to derive them from the subjective psychological experiences in which they are presented. These twin realisations led Husserl to abandon his attempt to provide the foundation of mathematics in a logical analysis assisted by descriptive psychology and instead to seek its basis in a 'pure' logic.

Husserl's notion of a pure logic grew out of his recognition that the concepts of multiplicity and number refer to any objects whatever, no matter what kind they are. Further, because of this, he realised that their very meaning as concepts cannot possibility be reduced to, or otherwise be understood to have their basis in, any of the objects or their kinds to which they, as concepts, refer, including individual human minds or the human mind per se. This conclusion gave Husserl the idea of an all-embracing science that would devote itself to investigating precisely the qualities that belong to what he called the 'formal category' of any object whatever. One of the first tasks Husserl set for this science, first called 'pure logic' and then 'formal ontology', was to establish how the pure (formal) categories and their relations are nevertheless related to psychological acts of cognition. Husserl was confronted with the problem of establishing this relation because he now recognised that such acts can no longer be understood, as he thought they could in the *Philosophy of Arithmetic*, as the originative source of the concepts to which they are also related.

Husserl's second major work, the *Logical Investigations*, attempted to solve this problem by showing that the psychological acts involved in theoretical cognition have a part that has its foundation in a structural whole that is *not* psychological. Husserl called this whole 'intentionality', by which he meant precisely the aspect of our psychological experience of cognition that, because it judges about pure (formal) categories and their relations, is no longer merely psychological in an empirical or subjective sense. The structural whole of intentionality was itself understood by Husserl to be comprised of parts, the major ones being 'acts' and 'objects': the acts of cognitive judgement that are involved in pure logic, including the expression of these acts in propositional meanings, and the pure (formal) categories and their relations that are the 'objects' of these acts and meaning expressions. Indeed, it was precisely the discovery that cognitive experience includes a psychological dimension that does not have as its object sensible things, but instead the categories and their relations that are responsible for the objective meaning of sensible things (and any other kind of thing), that Husserl characterised as the 'breakthrough' to a new science he called 'phenomenology'. As its names implies, this science seeks to extract the 'Logos' – the pure logic – from what shows up – that is, phenomena – in experience.

Subsequent to his breakthrough, Husserl soon realised that the intentional structure found in cognition extended to any kind of act, whether cognitive, emotive, evaluative, perceptual, aesthetic, religious and so on. In other words, Husserl discovered that the structural whole of intentionality was a part of any possible psychological act. In response to this discovery, he set about developing phenomenology as a science that would describe the structure of the intentionality of all the various types of psychological experience without recourse to the sort of causality that reigns in nature. For Husserl, this manner of investigation was prescribed to phenomenology because the mode of being belonging to intentionality was neither natural nor factual, but what he came to call 'phenomenological'. He referred to it thus in recognition of both (1) the non–contingent character of the 'essential' relationship of its parts to one another and to the whole of which they are parts and (2) the fact that, as 'phenomena', both the terms and the essentiality of this relationship are inseparable from the 'evidence' with which their mode of being shows up in experience. Moreover, the two major criteria that determined phenomenology as rigorous science, namely its investigation of the essence of experience and the grounding of this investigation in evidence, have for Husserl their basis in these two aspects of intentionality's mode of being.

Husserl's self-understanding of phenomenology as the science proper to (the essential mode of the being of) the psychological part of experience that belongs to the structural whole of intentionality, however, underwent a major revision in his next major work, *Ideas I*. What precipitated this revision was Husserl's realisation that so long as phenomenology, as the science of the essential mode of being proper to intentionality, understood the part of experience that the structural whole of intentionality contained to be psychological, phenomenology could not properly be established (in a foundational manner) as an essential – in contrast to a natural – science. And it could not be so established for the simple reason that the psyche, in addition to having a part that belongs to the structural whole of intentionality, also has a part that belongs to material nature. Thus Husserl realised that in order to investigate, in the most fundamental way proper to its non–natural mode of being, the structural whole of intentionality in terms of the essential relations between its parts, he had to find a way to secure access to it that no longer considered it and its parts to be a part of psychological experience.

Husserl found this way by developing – in a manner suited to phenomenology's goal of becoming the rigorous science of essential rather than natural being – a characteristic of the acts of reflection in which phenomenological cognition takes place. Specifically, he developed the characteristic of philosophical reflection that in Descartes' famous method of doubt involves the suspension of the belief in the independence (from the cogito) of the existence of what it is that shows up to reflection. Husserl focused his cognitive concern on precisely the moment in which the belief in the independent existence of something is neutralised in such reflection; but instead of pretending that it does not exist (as in Descartes' method) Husserl prescribed for his method that its existence merely be 'put out of play' or 'bracketed'. Husserl called the development of reflection along these lines the 'phenomenological epoché' and he argued that when it is performed, the content of what was previously believed to exist independently of the cogito is not disregarded (as in Cartesian doubt) but rather 'reduced' to a phenomenon that is manifest in the sphere of the cogito's intentional awareness. Husserl denominated such awareness or consciousness and the subjectivity to which it belongs, respectively, 'transcendental consciousnesses' and 'transcendental subjectivity', and the 'reduction' to it following the epoché the 'phenomenological reduction' – or, more precisely, the 'transcendental phenomenological reduction'.

After such a bracketing, the part of experience contained by the structural whole of intentionality is no longer understood by Husserl to be an aspect of the natural world. He has thus put out of play what he called the 'natural attitude', that is the uncritical acceptance of the truth of the belief in the cogito-independent existence of things that characterises psychological experience. Rather, this experience, as well as intentionality itself, now came to assume for Husserl the status of 'transcendental' phenomena; in other words, they assume the status of neutralised contents of phenomena. They retain the same sense as before the reduction, but they are now available for study without having to believe that they issue from the independent existence of the material world. From this point on, the cognitive goal of phenomenology for Husserl became the investigation of the essential structures of the transcendentally reduced content of whatever is experienced in the natural attitude. Husserl designates the mode of coming to awareness of the evidential experience proper to phenomena as their 'constitution' and its investigation as 'constitutional analysis'. Husserl's writings published during his lifetime investigated the constitution of the experience of perception, time, nature, spirit, the person, the 'lived-body', logical and scientific cognition, the alter ego and, in his last published writing, *The Crisis of European Sciences and Transcendental Phenomenology*, the special role that the phenomenological philosopher's self-responsible relation to history and to living tradition plays in the rational resolution of the 'crisis' that a scientific project increasingly out of touch with lived experience falls into. In addition to these topics, Husserl's posthumously published writings also investigated the constitution of the experience of foreign cultures, values, emotions, community, intersubjectivity and many other things, among them smoking (mostly Cuban) cigars.

B. Hopkins

See also: eidetic reduction; Epistemology; epoché; intersubjectivity; Memory; naturalising phenomenology; phenomenological reflection; Phenomenology; Repetition; Space; Time; transcendental ego (2)

HYBRIDITY A term in postcolonial theory associated especially with the work of literary theorist Homi K. Bhabha. By speaking of the 'hybrid' identities of those human subjects shaped by the postcolonial situation, Bhabha and others aim to challenge the notion of stable essences and fixed dichotomies, such as 'Western' vs. 'non-Western' and 'colonizer vs. native'. The emphasis on hybridity in late-twentieth-century theories of cultural identity contrasts with the rhetoric typical of the mid-century, when intellectuals speaking for colonised peoples, in their projects of resistance, liberation and nation-formation, tended to posit enduring ethnic and racial essences. For instance, the notion of *négritude*, promoted in the mid-century by Aimé Césaire and Léopold Senghor, asserts that there is a sharp difference between the basic mentalities of Europeans and Africans (in Senghor's words, 'Emotion is black as reason is Hellenic'). The concept of hybridity complicates and deconstructs all such oppositions based on determinate cultural identities. This deconstruction works both ways: just as there is no 'pure' native culture to which a people might return following its liberation from colonialism, so the culture of the West is continually reshaped by its contact with formerly colonised territories and peoples. The celebration of hybridity and related concepts such as 'border-crossing' and 'migration' has been attacked by Marxist and other politically-oriented critics who regard the concept as symptomatic of an affluent Western-educated Third World intelligentsia's abandonment of hope for national autonomy in formerly colonised states.

G. Stone

HYLOMORPHISM The doctrine that the order displayed by material systems is due to the form projected in advance of production by an external producer, a form which organises what would otherwise be chaotic or passive matter.

In *Basic Problems of Phenomenology* Heidegger describes the architect's vision of form (*eidos*) as a drive beyond the flow of moments to a constantly present appearance. For Heidegger, the 'metaphysics of presence' thence arises through the unthematised transfer of this sense of being to all regions of beings.

In *A Thousand Plateaus* Deleuze and Guattari pick up the critique of hylomorphism in the work of Gilbert Simondon and follow him in developing a non-hylomorphic or 'artisanal' theory of production. In this theory, forms are developed by artisans out of suggested potentials of matter rather than being dreamed up by architects and then imposed on passive matter. In artisanal production, the artisan must therefore 'surrender' to matter, that is follow its potentials by attending to its implicit forms and then devise operations that bring forth those potentials to actualise the desired properties.

Deleuze and Guattari also follow Simondon in analysing the political significance of hylomorphism. For Simondon, hylomorphism is 'a socialised representation of work', the viewpoint of a master commanding slave labour. For Deleuze and Guattari, hylomorphism also has an important political dimension, as a hylomorphic representation of a body politic resonates with fascist desire, in which the leader comes from on high to rescue his people from chaos by his imposition of order.

J. Protevi

HYPPOLITE, JEAN (1907–68) French philosopher with enormous influence both as a Hegel scholar and as the teacher of Derrida, Deleuze and Foucault. Hyppolite had an illustrious university career: professor at Strasbourg in 1945; at the Sorbonne in 1949; director of the École Normale Supérieure in 1954; and finally, the chair at the Collège de France in 'Histoire des systèmes' from 1963 until his death.

Hyppolite became famous as the French translator of Hegel's *Phenomenology of Spirit* (1941); he then produced a commentary, *Genesis and Structure of Hegel's Phenomenology of Spirit* (1947). In many essays, Hyppolite recounts the French reception of Hegel. The French reception had first been formed by Jean Wahl, but during the 1930s it was especially influenced by the humanistic reading Kojève produced, which oriented the philosophies of Sartre and the early Merleau-Ponty. Hyppolite, however, tried to show that Hegel goes beyond the human. This claim becomes most evident in Hyppolite's 1952 *Logic and Existence*, a book that sets up the philosophies of Derrida, Deleuze and Foucault. Indeed, in his inaugural address to the Collège de France in 1970, Foucault, who was then assuming the chair vacated by Hyppolite's death, says that '*Logic and Existence* established all the problems that are ours'.

Logic and Existence makes three basic claims. First, Hyppolite tries to show that Hegel's philosophy is a logic, in the literal sense of the word a *logos*: language. If we start from language, we can see that Hegel's philosophy attempts to reconstruct the genesis from sensible (experience) to sense (or essence). But second, again, if we start from language, we can see that Hegel's thought 'completes immanence', as Hyppolite says. This claim means that Hegel, like Nietzsche, is an anti-Platonist; there is no second world of ideas or essences behind the first sensible one; there is only sense. In this second claim, Hyppolite returns to his earlier commentary on the *Phenomenology*. There he had claimed that the most difficult idea in Hegel's thought was the difference between essence and appearance, that is the difference within immanence itself. Hyppolite's discussion in Part II of *Logic and Existence* of the problem of difference in Hegel sets up the entire philosophy of difference that will arise in France in the 1960s. This difference within immanence brings us to the third and final claim Hyppolite makes in *Logic and Existence*: Hegel is not a humanist because sense (which has now replaced the old metaphysical concept of essence) is indeed different from man. Hegel therefore is trying to think not man but 'across' man, and through this anti-humanism Hyppolite's reading broke decisively with that of Kojève. Again, to quote Foucault, because of these three claims, Hyppolite showed 'us all the ways that it was possible to escape from Hegel but also that Hegel always is waiting for us beyond the exit'.

L. Lawlor

IDEA (1) In the 'Transcendental Dialectic' of the *Critique of Pure Reason* Kant distinguishes 'ideas' or 'pure concepts of reason' from the categories or 'pure concepts of the understanding'. While the categories of the understanding are applied to the objects of possible experience, the ideas of reason refer to an 'absolute totality of experience' which cannot itself be an object of experience. Indeed, it is the tendency of reason to view its ideas as if they corresponded to objects that is exposed in the dialectical inferences of the 'Transcendental Dialectic'. Refusing the traditional options of regarding the ideas as either existing beyond spatio-temporal experience or being in some way abstracted from it, Kant derives the ideas from the form of the syllogism. For him, the syllogism consists in relating the object of the conclusion to a universal condition stated in the major premise. By accepting only three forms of relation between major premise and conclusion – the categorical relation of substance and accident, the hypothetical relation of cause and effect, and the disjunctive relation of community – Kant is able to identify three major forms of idea or universal syntheses. The first is the synthesis of unconditioned subject as substance, the second the synthesis of members of a series and the third the synthesis of parts into a whole. These are then identified in the soul, world and God with their sciences of psychology, cosmology and theology.

The 'Transcendental Dialectic' criticises the approach to these ideas as if they were objects of possible experience, their use as 'constitutive principles'. Instead the ideas are restricted to serving as guides for the orientation of the understanding with respect to totality, that is they have a 'regulative use'. This understanding of the theoretical ideas is carried over to the practical ideas or postulates of the *Critique of Practical Reason* – immortality (soul), freedom (world) and God. These are not objects of knowledge but are postulated in order to help orient the will towards the highest good. Similarly, the aesthetic ideas of the *Critique of Judgement* are not constitutive but functional, serving to stimulate the harmony of understanding and intuition that contributes to the feeling of pleasure.

H. Caygill

IDEA (2) Post-Kantian German idealists were dissatisfied with Kant's apparent cleft between the phenomenal world of physical appearances and the noumenal world of 'things in themselves'. Kant's 'concepts' pertain to the phenomenal realm, whereas 'ideas' pertain to the unconditioned noumenal realm, to totalities or norms which in principle cannot be presented in our (inherently limited) perceptual experience. Nevertheless, Kant held that these ideas can and must guide our empirical inquiry and moral behaviour. German idealists tended to regard Kant's noumenal realm as genuine or ultimate reality. Schelling greatly extended Kant's view that great works of art can express transcendent 'ideas' in the form of 'aesthetic ideas'. Schelling held that visionary artists, like some philosophers, are endowed with 'intuitive' intellects, which directly grasp reality as it is, and that we can share such insights by experiencing works of art. Schelling's ontology borrowed from Plato the view that the fundamental structures of reality are 'ideas', which Schelling held could be grasped by 'intellectual intuition'.

By 1804 Hegel had rejected intuitionism in all forms. In his mature philosophy Hegel gave the term 'idea' a highly non-Kantian use, to designate the worldly instantiation of the conceptual structure articulated in his *Logic* and exhibited *in concreto* in his *Philosophy of Nature* and *Philosophy of Spirit*, Parts Two and Three of the *Encyclopaedia of Philosophical Sciences*.

When Husserl titled his first distinctive work in phenomenology, *Ideas on a Pure Phenomenology and on a Phenomenological Philosophy*, these Kantian and post-Kantian uses of 'idea' had fallen into neglect. Hence Husserl could use 'idea' in a more traditional vein, concerning how we conceive or represent something.

K. Westphal

IDEA (3) In *Difference and Repetition* Deleuze – following Salomon Maimon in his post–Kantian return to Leibniz – attempted to take the Kantian critical project to its conclusion by formulating a purely *immanent* theory of ideas, using the mathematical theory of differential equations as his model. As with Kant, Deleuzean Ideas condition the empirical realm by providing it with a principle of determination while not corresponding to any empirical object, but for Deleuze what is conditioned is not merely possible experience, but material reality. Ideas for Deleuze are virtual multiplicities of differential elements, differential relations and singular points that structure the genesis of material systems, which are said to be actualisations of these purely differential Ideas. In addition then to his radicalisation of Kant, Deleuze attempted to 'overturn' Platonism by placing Ideas within the world – albeit as virtual structures – even as he resuscitated the importance of the theory of Ideas.

D. Smith

IDEAL SPEECH SITUATION A concept introduced by Apel and Habermas to indicate the necessary features that any purely rational form of communication would have. The concept is closely related to their attempt to develop a discourse ethics. In their opinion, ethical deliberations are binding only to the extent that they approximate the conditions of ideal speech. The ideal speech situation serves to distinguish the notion of rational persuasion or true conviction from mere rhetorical compulsion or manipulated assent. We can only be convinced of the rightness or truth of a belief that has been backed up with the best arguments. But we cannot know with any reliability whether a given argument is the best argument unless we know the full range of competing arguments and are assured that these arguments have been optimally presented and most charitably received. The only way to effectively promote this knowledge is by ensuring that the discussion in question includes all persons who might have a say regarding the matter in dispute and by ensuring that they have equal chances to present and rebut arguments, free from external and internal (ideological) constraint. So construed, the ideal speech situation models a just form of social interaction that approximates a purely rational community, at least in so far as the interlocutors have suspended all motives save that of trying to reach an impartial consensus based on the best arguments. As a model of justice, the ideal speech situation can never be fully implemented. Nor should it be. However, it does provide a standard for critically evaluating the justice and rationality of real-life deliberations that constitute the heart and soul of democratic life.

D. Ingram

IDEAL TYPE A term introduced into the sociological lexicon by Max Weber, who defined it as a mental construct developed to serve a heuristic purpose by allowing empirical reality to be measured against it. The ideal does not refer to a normative value preference, but rather is to be contrasted to the real. The ideal type is not found in the empirical world, but rather is a concept developed by distilling from the real what is construed to be a pristine if exaggerated description of the phenomenon, whether that phenomenon involves characteristic features of human agency or aspects of social structure. Thus it derives from the empirical world, but is not found in it. Weber's discussion of the central defining elements of bureaucracy offers a good example of what he meant. The ideal type of a modern bureaucracy includes the following elements: a hierarchy of authority, governance by written rules, full-time salaried officials hired on the basis of formal credentials and separated from ownership of the organisation, and a clear-cut division of labour. On the basis of such a definition, concrete examples of bureaucracy can not only be measured against the ideal type, but also compared to one another. Indeed, one of the key functions of the ideal type is to make comparative sociology possible. Given their derivation, ideal types are necessarily historically contingent, so that when the gap between ideal and real becomes too pronounced, it becomes necessary to revise or reformulate the type.

P. Kivisto

IDEOLOGICAL STATE APPARATUSES A term introduced by Althusser to designate the practical realisation of social norms within a state that, together, serve to sustain and reproduce that society and its modes of production. Althusser wanted the concept to correct the naive theory of ideology found in Marx and Engels's *The German Ideology* (1846) and to complement Lenin's discussion of 'Repressive State Apparatuses' detailed in *The State and Revolution* (1917). Departing from the theses that humans always live in ideology, that ideology is a material practice and that ideology is one way in which social and economic systems reproduce themselves, Althusser argued that institutions such as the family, schools and the church as well as ethics, aesthetics and law all serve to 'realise ideology'. Ideological state apparatuses do so by prescribing the roles through which people understand themselves and thus delimiting the ways in which they are able to conceive of and perform possible actions. In North America, for example, schools, churches, the judiciary and 'common sense' may all indicate that a subject is free and responsible for her own actions. Recognising herself as such a subject, the individual tends to act as though her fate were her own and 'freely' enters into the roles that society needs her to assume. Thus, whereas repressive state apparatuses such as armies and police limit by violence any changes to the mode of production or threats to the dominant ideology, ideological state apparatuses work by means of misrecognition to ensure the reproduction of the social order.

W. Lewis

IDEOLOGY A set of ideas, beliefs, attitudes and so on which shape the understanding (or misunderstanding) of the world, usually of the social and political world, and which serve to explain and justify specific institutions and/or practices. The term was first used by Destutt de Tracy (*Eléments d'idéologie*, 1796), but in a different sense. Its modern usage derives from Marx and Engels in *The German Ideology* (1845). However, the term has come to be used very widely and variously in social theory and in political and popular discourse. The term is usually used to suggest that ideas arise from, and give conscious or unconscious expression to, a particular social or political perspective. Two different usages prevail, with opposite implications. For some, ideology is a critical, even pejorative, notion which equates ideology with false or mistaken beliefs or attitudes. Others use the term neutrally to emphasise the social origins and causes of both true and false ideas and attitudes. The term plays a central role in Marxism and much modern social and political theory. There has been an enduring and unresolved controversy about which of these senses is to be preferred.

S. Sayers

IL Y A ('there is') A term first employed in Blanchot's novel *Aminadab* and taken up by Levinas in *Existence and Existents* to indicate the positive horror of being. Reacting against the Heideggerian claim that anxiety arises primarily in our relation to death and finitude, Levinas suggests that there is an equal horror in the positive fact that *there is* being and that even nothingness in some sense *is*. Levinas describes the *il y a* as an anonymous existing devoid of determinate beings or existents and thus devoid of meaning. His early works describe existence as having a tragic character in so far as the subject is chained to its own being, and thus always threatened with the overwhelming absurdity of the *il y a*. The desire for an exit from being and the impossibility of any escape are central problems driving Levinas's later development of the ethical or social relationship as a relation which produces a plurality within being, a transcendence within and of immanence. The *il y a* is revived in late sections of *Otherwise than*

Being or Beyond Essence in a more positive sense that links the over-whelming of sense by nonsense with the overwhelming of the Said by an ethical Saying.

D. *Perpich*

IMAGINARY ORDER That which, in Lacan's theory, replaces Freud's ego agency. Its contents are the 'signifieds', that is significa-tions and representations produced by the ego processes of identifica-tion and projection on the objects of the world. As such, it is always built between two poles, the ego itself and its mirror-image, the other (little *o*).

The imaginary order is in charge of actualising repression; it has to be assimilated to what has been known before psychoanalysis as 'reality', which is grasped by Lacan as an imaginary construct. Hence, imaginary reality has to be differentiated in principle from the Real, which is the locus of meaning and truth as opposed to significations belonging to and consisting in the imaginary order. The imaginary order is subordinated to the Symbolic order, the Other (capital *O*), by an absolute determinism: the chain of signifiers is the determinant that will organise the signifieds and representations carried by the imagin-ary order. Early on, Lacan defined the orders as mathematical sets. The imaginary order would be the set comprising all the representations of an individual as he or she shares them with his or her group, community, ethnicity, nation, etc. As such, the imaginary order defines a subject's particularity, through which he identifies himself as *part* of a group.

The notion of the imaginary does not make sense per se, but only in relationship to the other sets distinguished by Lacan, the Real and the Symbolic order, and only in the mapping out of their respective positioning in the 'topology of the subject'.

A. *Leupin*

IMMANENCE The state of being within. Immanence and transcen-dence are relative concepts, defined in relation to each other, most often in three contexts.

(1) In post-Cartesian philosophy, immanence usually refers to the sphere of the subject, while transcendence refers to that which transcends the field of consciousness immanent to the subject, such as the 'external word' or 'others'. The problems posed by this form of transcendence have been explored in Husserl's fifth *Cartesian Meditation*; in the theme of 'Being-with-Others' in Sartre's *Being and Nothingness*; and in Levinas's philosophy of alterity in *Totality*

and Infinity. Within the subjectivist tradition, a different, and perhaps more profound, formulation of the problem of transcendence was presented by Sartre in his article 'The Transcendence of the Ego': when one says that the field of consciousness is immanent to a transcendental subject, one is already erecting the subject itself as an element of transcendence that goes beyond the flux of experience. Sartre thus pushed for a conception of an *impersonal* transcendental field, without an ego or self, much like William James's notion of a 'pure flux of consciousness'.

(2) In the domain of ontology, immanence refers to that which lies within the field of being, whereas transcendence refers to that which is 'beyond' or 'higher than' or 'superior to' Being. The traditional concepts of ontological transcendence would include the 'Good' in Plato, the 'One' in Plotinus and the 'God' of the Christian tradition. In the *Critique of Pure Reason*, Kant gave the distinction an explicit epistemological orientation: 'We shall entitle the principles whose application is confined entirely within the limits of possible experience, *immanent*, and those, on the other hand, which profess to pass beyond these limits, *transcendent*'. The aim of Kant's transcendental philosophy was to critique those transcendent Ideas that went beyond the limits of possible experience, especially the ideas of the Soul, the World and God which in traditional metaphysics are said to constitute objects adequate to those ideas. Kantian Ideas receive a sort of transcendent use, however, when they are said to regulate our practical experience, that is to orient our moral behaviour.

(3) Today, the term 'immanence' is often associated with the work of Deleuze, who attempts a philosophy of 'pure' immanence by exploring, via a 'transcendental empiricism', a virtual field that is no longer immanent to a subject, transcendental or otherwise, nor is composed of Platonic or Kantian Ideas, but is instead composed of purely differential Ideas or 'multiplicities'. The virtual field is immanent in the sense of being non-supernatural, being immanent in the world – or at least in the material processes of the world which are structured by differential Ideas or multiplicities – without being immanent to a higher unity.

D. Smith

IMMANENT CRITIQUE A method of reading deriving from Hegelian and Marxist dialectics. Beginning with a thorough account of a targeted philosophy's own structure, an immanent critique displays the contradictions that philosophy produces from its own standpoint. The goal of immanent critique is not to invalidate the initial theory logically so much as to overcome it by revealing how its internal weaknesses and inconsistencies help to create utopian potential: immanent critique reveals the means by which a philosophy produces its own alternatives. Hegel's dialectical passage from sense consciousness to self-consciousness in *Phenomenology* is often cited as a good example of this process.

In its Marxist incarnation, immanent critique typically provides a historical treatment of previously static or metaphysical philosophical themes. The critique reveals the dialectical flux of these themes and is associated with slogans such as the 'withering away of the state' or the fetishism of the commodity. Marx's analysis of capitalism in *Capital* is grounded in immanent critique, because it reveals the structure and history of capitalist logic rather than beginning from an alternate set of principles as a transcendent critique might do.

Compared to deconstruction or poststructuralist analysis, immanent critique is more insistently utopian, while compared to ideology critique, immanent critique is more focused on the methods and rhetoric of argumentation. Prominent twentieth- and twenty-first-century practitioners of immanent critique include Adorno, Benjamin, Irigaray, Jameson and Simmel.

C. Irr

IMMATERIAL LABOUR The new modality of production undertaken by the socialised worker in the period of the real subsumption of labour under capital, according to Antonio Negri and his collaborators, most importantly Michael Hardt and Maurizio Lazzarato. The term refers not to any dematerialisation or disembodiment of the labouring subject him/herself, but rather to the dematerialisation of the product. Immaterial labour produces commodities that are primarily intellectual, affective or communicational by means of processes that are themselves primarily intellectual, affective or communicational. It comprises technical or scientific research and application such as computer programming, product design or marketing, but also decentralised manual production facilitated by computerised communications networks, as well as caring labour such as nursing, hosting or personal service work. Common to all these cases is an immediate sociality of productive cooperation in which physical distance or isolation is not a limiting factor. Rather than identifying a wholly new essential category or stratum of labour, this concept cuts across both traditional and more recent divisions of labour to provide an organisational basis for the emerging political collectivity and agent that Negri and Hardt call the multitude.

T. Murphy

INCLINATION (*Neigung*) A concept in Kant's critical moral philosophy which forms the counterpart to duty, and which is grounded in the world of sense which duty 'proudly rejects'. Inclinations form the subjective, material, plural and partial counterparts to the objective, intelligible, unified and complete status of duty. They express the dependence of the human 'faculty of desire' on sensation, which entails that they are born of need and respond to need. Just as duty is attributed to the divine of humanity, so are inclinations to the animal – the inclinations respond to different, partial stimuli from the environment, and not to the unified and universal moral law. For this reason they express the 'heteronomy' of the will as opposed the autonomy expressed in duty – through them, action is determined by the object rather than by the law. Due to their partiality they cannot serve as principles for moral judgement, and indeed are often conceived as antithetical to morality. Kant's accounts of the inclinations remained consistent across the *Groundwork for the Metaphysics of Morals* and *Critique of Practical Reason* and, always in the shadow of duty, were never subjected to full and sympathetic analysis. Criticism of Kant's moral philosophy, however, largely consisted in a re-evaluation of the inclinations, considered in their own right and not solely as the inverse of duty.

H. Caygill

INESSENTIAL OTHER A key term for Beauvoir, whose *The Second Sex* describes Hegel's master/slave dialectic through the categories of the Subject and the Other. The Subject is the absolute, while the Other is the inessential. Beauvoir then distinguishes the dialectic of oppression between Subjects and Others who were othered through historical events and those othered by the circumstances of women's oppression. In the first case the antagonism is clear. Here, the Other calls on the resources of a common history and a shared exploited situation to assert their subjectivity and demand recognition and reciprocity. The situation of women is like that of the Other in this: while men identify themselves as the absolute human type, the essential, the subject, women are defined relative to men; they are the inessential, inadequate other. Unlike the Other, however, women are unable to identify the origin of their otherness and call on the bond of a shared history. Dispersed among the world of men, they do not identify with each other. They lack the solidarity and resources of the Other for organising themselves into a we that demands equality. Further, their conflict with men is ambiguous. According to Beauvoir, who here borrows a term from Heidegger, women and men exist in a 'primordial *Mitsein*' (being with) so that there is a unique bond between this Subject and Other. In contesting their status as inessential, women must discover their 'we' and take account of the *Mitsein*. The category of the Inessential Other designates the unique situation of women as the ambiguous Other of men. Unlike the Other of the master/slave dialectic, women are not positioned to rebel. As Inessential Others, women's routes to subjectivity and recognition cannot follow the Hegelian script.

D. Bergoffen

INFINITY Levinas borrows the form, though not the content, of Descartes' 'idea of infinity' to express the possibility of being in a relation with a being (here, the Other) that exceeds one's grasp not just provisionally or contingently but necessarily and in principle. In having the idea of infinity, the Cartesian ego has a thought which could not have come from itself and in which the reality of what is thought is not simply greater than the reality contained in the idea, but is immeasurably distant from it because it is the reality of God as compared to the reality of our idea of God. In an analogous manner, Levinas claims that in the relation to the other person, I am in relation to a being whose reality is infinitely distant from my own, without that distance destroying the relation, and without the relation overcoming or negating that distance. Levinas uses the idea of infinity to make comprehensible what, by definition, cannot be comprehended, namely the absolute alterity of the Other. This relation, in which the ego 'thinks more than it thinks,' at every moment shatters the framework of a would-be totalising system in which thought and being are united in an all-encompassing whole. It bears emphasising that although the term 'infinity' seems to connote a relation to the other characterised by distance, height and abstraction, as deformalised or concretised in the relation to the face of the Other, this term indicates a relation with a being in all his or her concrete, irreducible singularity.

D. Perpich

INFORMATION BOMB A term coined by Paul Virilio for the situation in which the interactivity enabled by increasingly dense networks of information and communications technologies threatens humankind with the possibility not of a local but a global accident.

In *The Information Bomb* (1999) Virilio explains his techno-dystopian vision of interactivity as a new kind of weapons system inaugurated by the arrival of technoscience, cyberwar, the Internet and global society's new-found capacity to hurl itself into real time. In *Virilio Live*

(2001) the German media theorist Friedrich A. Kittler and Virilio explore Einstein's original analysis of the information bomb before expanding on a number of ideas designed to avert the destruction they ascribe to the proliferation of interactivity. One such idea is that resistance against the global society of real time is not only fertile but also able to challenge those techno-utopians of the network society that aspire to inflict interactivity on everyone. By hindering the propagation of interactivity, then, informational insurgents such as Virilio and Kittler seek to impede the social consequences of the immediacy of action and information exchange on the deprived and the frail.

In addition, Virilio and Kittler adhere to Einstein in their investigation into the military and socio-economic significance of the information bomb. For the information bomb, like the atomic bomb before it, incorporates comparable dangers to that of a Chernobyl-like disaster, with potentially harmful repercussions for social life, including computerised manufacturing, pervasive structural unemployment, rising industrial concentration and the centralisation of corporate decision-making.

J. Armitage

INTELLECTUAL INTUITION A term most associated with German Idealism, although its concept appears in the 'divided line' passage of Plato's *Republic*, where it refers to a direct apprehension of the forms, a seeing not through the eyes, but through the understanding. Something similar is given in mathematical intuition. When we 'see', for instance, what a circle is, we clearly understand that it is something different from its visual representation. Even so, mathematical intuition is not identical with intellectual intuition, for it relies on a definition and thus reveals a merely postulated form of truth. Even when, as in Kant, the mathematical is not regarded as a conceptual construction, but as pure intuition of space and time, it remains improper to speak of intellectual intuition as such. Space and time are not Platonic forms; for Kant they are not 'noumenal', but are instead frameworks for organising phenomenal experience. In contrast, intellectual intuition purports to lay bare the truth itself, beyond all hypothesis, unveiled by sensual representation or any kind of predicative determination. While Kant raises the possibility of intellectual intuition only in order to deny it, the first edition of the *Critique of Pure Reason* does suggest that the imagination has the ability to create the very intuitions that it apprehends. It is this view that enables Fichte and Schelling to distinguish themselves from an older tradition that regards intellectual intuition (what Spinoza calls the intellectual love of God) as an act of self-annihilation or self-submersion in the Absolute. The idea that the mind can actively create the very form that it apprehends presents the positive idea of intellectual intuition as a self-realisation, an awakening, as it were, of an 'infinite' self within the finite self.

The capacity for such an awakening is the distinguishing mark of the philosopher, even though in an unconscious way it lies hidden within any being who can say 'I'. The I represents being that is real only in so far as it is thought. What the philosopher alone realises is that the unconditional nature of such self-positing is ultimately possible only for that 'One' which gathers all things together into the unity of being. I may have the impression of being self-sufficient enough to be the ground of my own awareness, but a refined act of intellectual intuition will make it clear that the 'unconditioned' or 'absolute' is what ultimately grounds all awareness, whether it is yours or mine. This involves more than the passive realisation that 'I am only to the degree that the absolute is in me', for it implies that 'I really am only to the degree that I become that absolute'.

Because the absolute is not a thing apart from its self-positing activity, there is no point in time in which this project of becoming absolute can be completed. For Schelling, as for Fichte, it is an infinite task. They differ in so far as Schelling remains close enough to Spinoza to use the language of self-annihilation; the project demands that we remove ourselves so that something else – nature, art or God – can speak through us. For Fichte, on the other hand, there is no 'something else'. The entire project is inscribed within a knowledge that belongs to the finite subject even as it elevates that subject toward infinity.

J. Lawrence

INTENSIVE DIFFERENCE A concept which plays an important role in the philosophy of Deleuze, notably in *Difference and Repetition*. Extensive differences, such as length, area or volume, are intrinsically divisible. A volume of matter divided into two equal halves produces two volumes, each having half the extent of the original one. Intensive differences, by contrast, refer to properties such as temperature or pressure that cannot be so divided. If a volume of water whose temperature is 90 is divided in half, the result is two volumes at the original temperature, and not two volumes at 45. However, the important property of intensity is not that it is indivisible, but that it is a property that cannot be divided without involving a change in kind. The temperature of a volume of water, for instance, can be 'divided' by heating the container from below, causing a temperature difference between the top and the bottom. In so doing, however, we change the system qualitatively; moreover, if the temperature reaches a certain intensity, the system will undergo a 'phase transition', losing symmetry and changing its dynamics, entering into a periodic pattern of motion called 'convection'. Drawing on these kinds of analyses, Deleuze will assign a transcendental status to the intensive: intensity, he argues, constitutes the 'genetic' condition of extensive space. The status of intensive differences in Deleuze's philosophy, along with their relationship to the concept of the virtual, has been explicated in detail by Manuel DeLanda in his *Intensive Science and Virtual Philosophy* (2002). 'The metric space we inhabit', he explains, 'emerges from a nonmetric continuum through a cascade of broken symmetries'. Deleuze, for his part, revived the notion of intensity from the physics of the Middle Ages, where it had a status that was eventually forgotten in seventeenth-century thought, which gave a prominence to extensive space.

D. Smith

INTENTIONALITY A term associated in its modern usage with phenomenology, which uses it to designate the essentially relational aspect of consciousness. Nineteenth-century neo-Thomism was the background to Brentano's reintroduction of the Scholastic term 'intention' into modern philosophy. He conceived it (not entirely in accord with Thomistic understanding) as a kind of 'mental inexistence' of the objects of consciousness; scholars disagree as to its exact sense in Brentano, although they agree on its being conditioned by Brentano's commitment to a realistic metaphysics. Above all, however, the term is central to the work of Husserl, who, after studying with Brentano, launched his phenomenology as a philosophic inquiry into the fundamental intentionality of consciousness; Husserl continued to transform and deepen its meaning from his first elaboration in *Logical Investigations* (1900–1) through virtually the entire span of his work.

Husserl departs from Brentano's explication of intentionality in trying to define a genus for the psychological that radically sets it apart from previous philosophic categories. The self-description of consciousness generated by careful reflection cannot make use of any natural category: consciousness is not a thing or substance of any kind. It is, moreover, intrinsically intentional, that is it only functions as always consciousness of something, with no interposition of a representation separating mind and object. It is important to emphasise that despite Husserl's choice of the word 'act' for an instance of intentional consciousness – a choice which he warns against misinterpreting (*Logical Investigations*, 5th Investigation Ch. 2) – intentionality is neither a relation between substances nor an action exercised between beings. This intentional 'act' is, he asserts, an intentional 'experience', not a 'psychic action', a claim backed up by his word for 'experience', *Erlebnis* ('living through'): intentional experience is living through a temporal duration, however small or large, in a 'multi-modal' (aesthetic, kinaesthetic, affective) engagement in an entire situation.

Intentionality, then, is the aspect of this plenum wherein the specifics of something experienced – whether in perception, or in recollection or imagination, or in disciplined cognition or reflective thought – become manifest in clear intuitional givenness. Intentionality is the particularity of experiencing wherein the one that experiences 'takes up' or 'takes in' something of something else that nonetheless remains in and of that something else. The problem, however, lies in analysing this multi-modal 'plenum' and the 'particularity' of its going-on so as to grasp how it all works; analyses of intentionality consist largely in detailing the constituents and processes of this going-on.

The tendency in philosophy in the past has been to locate this going-on entirely within the substance of the perceiver, in the 'soul', 'mind' or 'intellect'. But this presupposes one of the primary things that intentional experience is supposed to yield, namely knowledge of our world in terms of the outside around us and the inside within us. What is needed instead is an inquiry that recognises intentional experience as primary. To do this we need to stop interpreting the primary situation in terms of some item that comes to show within it, that is we need to stop interpreting intentional experience in terms of particulars of the world which the intentional situation itself allows us to experience. This inquiry is what Husserl took up after his *Logical Investigations*, in what is known as his 'transcendental turn', presented in classic form in his *Ideas pertaining to a Pure Phenomenology and to a Phenomenological Philosophy, First Book*. The complex analysis of 'noetic' and 'noematic' structures of intentionality has been endlessly explicated and criticised, especially in regard to the role of the 'phenomenological epoché' whereby one sets aside all presuppositions and ontological commitments in order to pay attention to the elements and working of intentional experience. Most disconcerting to many readers of *Ideas I* has been the seeming absolutising of 'conscious being', in the sense of the immanence of consciousness to itself. In *Ideas I*, the going-on of the plenum of intentional experiencing wherein this or that feature of the world is grasped as 'within' consciousness is described in terms of features that seem to be no more than constituents of a human mind as such. This is then named 'transcendental subjectivity', as if by this terminological sleight of hand the ultimate something that brings this whole plenum into realisation is thus fully disclosed. But closer reading shows that throughout the analysis Husserl tries to counter this understanding: intentional experience is not something I as a human individual do, it is something that goes on within me as the very opening of my being out to what is beyond my individual being. The 'psychic' or the 'psychological' about me is not something within, but precisely this opening out to everything, even while leaving both me and objects I experience as distinct in our respective being. Yet I can find this going-on nowhere else but within myself, even if it is precisely the opening out of this 'within', so that, strictly speaking, I am my own experiencing precisely in that it is not enclosed within itself. I live through this experiencing precisely to the extent that there is more to me than myself, even if this 'more' is hard to define.

This, then, is intentionality, as a living through, as an *Erlebnis*, that consists in going out of myself in remaining myself. And this is the point of a 'transcendental analysis' such as Husserl attempts in *Ideas I* and develops further in later works. To understand intentionality fully, then, one has to look at these later efforts of his, as well as at the work of his successor in Freiburg, Martin Heidegger, despite all the conflict and contrast scholars see between their respective projects. For in one sense Heidegger's designation of the 'there' of the world (which is constitutively intrinsic to *Dasein*) as the 'openness' of being (*Being and Time*) is in effect the core of intentionality, if one considers intention-ality as the particularity of someone's experiential opening out to something else in its own being.

R. Bruzina

INTERPELLATION A term introduced by Althusser to designate the act of recognition by which individuals are subjectified. Insisting that individuals are always already ideological subjects as well as subject to ideology, Althusser proposed this account of subject formation in the essay 'Ideology and Ideological State Apparatuses' (1970). Building upon, but also critical of, psychoanalytic and Western Marxist accounts of the self, holding that individuals are constituted though an encounter with an 'outside' power, Althusser maintains that an individual is (or becomes) a subject only in the act of recognising itself as a subject when 'interpellated' or called out to by an other. At its simplest, this act can be as straightforward as responding with a wave to someone who hails from across a crowded room. By responding to this interpellation, you have recognised that you are the subject called. Choosing to enter the women's toilet rather than the men's to relieve yourself would also be an instance of subjectification by interpellation: you choose that door which is made for you when you recognise yourself in the sign on the lavatory door. The fact that which door to choose is obvious to most if not all subjects would be, for Althusser, proof that individuals are always already subjectified and that ideology has a place for them as a gendered subject. Put more generally, subjects are always ready to recognise themselves in and through the categories that ideology provides for them and which they instantiate by their recognition of themselves as being a certain kind of person and not another.

W. Lewis

INTERSUBJECTIVITY The term used in Husserlian phenomenology to refer to the way subjects, both before and after the transcendental reduction or epoché, always appear as one among an indeterminate number of subjects, as well as the way such subjects appear as 'other'.

The Husserlian investigation of the 'other' focuses on the manner in which the ego of the other subject is constituted in the experience of the ego that is given in phenomenological reflection. Husserl devised a special reduction in order to conduct this investigation, namely the reduction to the reflected ego's sphere of 'ownness'. This reduction performs an epoché directed to the naturally given world, in order to isolate and then trace from within phenomenological reflection the emergence of the sense as 'other' that belongs to the reflectively given subject's experience of the subjects among which it is given.

The emergence of the sense as 'other' of such subjects, according to Husserl's analysis, involves three fundamentally invariant structures. The first of these is the inseparability of the subject of reflection's ego from its 'lived' body, which is something that is revealed subsequent to the reduction to its sphere of ownness. The 'lived body' means the body as it is experienced by the reflected ego prior to its perception as a physical object among other physical objects. The second fundamentally invariant structure is what he calls 'pairing', which articulates the inseparable bond of the reflected ego's sphere of ownness with the body of the other, which is experienced by the reflected ego not as a physical body but as the body that belongs to the lived experience of another. Finally, there is the fundamental and invariant structure of 'analogical apperception', which according to Husserl is the phenomenon that accounts for the givenness of the paired lived body of the other *as* the *other's* lived body. The ego of the other is not given as a reflected ego in the reflecting ego's sphere of ownness, but only as an ego that, mutatis mutandis, is related to its own lived body as the reflected ego is related to its lived body. Because of this, the other or alter ego cannot be accurately described as an object of perception. Nevertheless, the alter ego, as alter ego, is still given in some sense, namely as the ego that is not given directly but indirectly. Specifically, the alter ego is given as the ego that, *like* and therefore analogous to the ego that is directly given in phenomenological experience, belongs to its own lived body as this reflected ego belongs to its own lived body. Consequently, what is phenomenologically at issue here is not the direct perception of the alter ego but its indirect apperception.

B. Hopkins

INTUITION For Bergson, intuition represents a way of knowing which differs from, but complements, intelligence. Intelligence is analytic by nature, and thus perfectly adapted to knowledge of matter which is itself, as Bergson argues, discrete. Duration, life, evolution and so on, are all continuous, however, and so require a different mode of knowing if they are to be understood as adequately as intelligence understands matter. This mode of knowing is intuition. Where intelligence takes a perspective external to the object it seeks to know, intuition seeks an internal perspective, and it is from such a perspective that it is able to attain absolute knowledge, that is knowledge of the whole. For example, where intelligence, standing outside of movement, seeks to analyse the movement of a hand into its constituent parts, which can thereby be represented by a series of points plotted as a curve on a graph, intuition experiences the undivided act as a whole. From the perspective of intelligence, the account of movement would be confronted with the task of explaining how the infinity of parts combine. From the perspective of intuition, however, the task confronted is that of explaining the constraints or obstacles which impede movement. But framed in this way, it becomes apparent that the former task requires metaphysical speculation in the worst sense, whereas the latter requires no such speculation, relying as it does solely on empirical facts. Intuition thus forms a method which enables traditional philosophical problems to be recast in a form which allows for genuine solution.

R. Durie

IRIGARAY, LUCE (1930–) Belgian-born linguist, philosopher and psychoanalyst, now living in France and one of the leading figures of so-called French feminism.

Critique of sameness. Irigaray describes herself as a theorist of 'sexual difference' rather than as a 'feminist', in order to distinguish her project from the egalitarian premises and goals of other feminisms, such as the liberal feminism of the nineteenth and early twentieth centuries and the existential feminism of Simone de Beauvoir. For Irigaray, both of these feminisms argue that men and women are fundamentally the same in order to debunk the hierarchical claims concerning sexual difference in the history of Western discourses and politics. Liberal feminism relies on the modern concepts of subjectivity, rationality, right and so on, while Beauvoir provides an existential account of 'human subjectivity' as a dialectic between transcendence and facticity. The source of women's oppression, for Beauvoir, is men's alignment of themselves with transcendence and women with facticity, thereby historically and socially legitimating women's oppression and making women's existential situation difficult. Irigaray's disagreement with these feminisms, however, does not mean that she seeks to maintain inequality, but rather that there is a socio-cultural need to emphasise difference over sameness. Irigaray provocatively claims that not only does feminism rely on the category of sameness, but also that the various historical articulations of sexual difference themselves rely on sameness; in doing so Irigaray demonstrates a logic of 'same-ing' within the metaphysical reflections on sexual difference that establishes difference as relativity. For Irigaray, the difference that traditionally marks women as other than men is a difference of negation, and she seeks to recast sexual difference such that it refuses the traditional notion of difference as other-than. Negative difference maintains a delineation of the feminine in terms of the masculine, and historically, this movement has been covered over through pretensions to universality, objectivity and neutrality.

Aristotle's definition of 'the human being' can be seen as an example of the negative difference Irigaray opposes. In the *Politics* Aristotle defines the human being according to three separate but harmonious features: a nutritive, appetitive aspect, which outlines the human being's necessary, material existence composed of eating, desire and so on, and a twofold rational aspect in which the human being has the capacities to obey reason, on the one hand, and to actively reason, on the other. This definition appears universal and objective, but as we look further we find qualifications. Women's nature, by which Aristotle seems to mean Greek women, is defined in accordance with the three features, but the features are not harmonious. For Aristotle, women's emotional nature overpowers the capacity to obey reason. Natural slaves are defined according to the absence of the capacity to reason actively, and (Greek, male) children are thought to have all three capacities, but in undeveloped, immature form. Aristotle thereby argues that 'masters' (in the form of husbands, slave owners and fathers) are needed in order to supplement the lack inherent in these other natures. These other natures are demarcated as different according to their difference from the primary term, 'human being', and no account is sought that would suspend the false pretension to universality that results in the privileging of the Greek adult male. Further, because these other natures are delineated according to their difference from a primary term, marked by completion rather than lack, otherness is ultimately relativised according to the same. In this sense, difference is concealed and hidden.

Irigaray's early reading strategy in relation to such an example is a practice in mimesis. By repeating the claims of the texts, by literally rewriting them under the sign of her own signature, Irigaray performs a disruption of the claims to universality, objectivity and neutrality. By parodying the philosopher's claims, Irigaray's writing demonstrates the partiality of the 'neutral' claim and shows that philosophy's 'other' is essential to the establishment of a unitary, coherent philosophical system; that is, she is excluded from full human status at the same time as she is enclosed in the system as a subordinate member. The excluding/enclosing movement with regards to the feminine makes the feminine the unthought ground of Western philosophy. This is also practically visible in the formation of patriarchal communities in which women provide the nutritive ground of the home that makes possible the space and time of (men's) reflection.

Irigaray's work first gained attention in the Anglophone world in the mid-1980s. Her mimetic strategy and insistence on the term 'sexual difference' initially provoked much feminist disapproval, as her work was received by many as fundamentally essentialist. However, the work of feminists working in the continental tradition quickly provided the focused analyses that corrected this reception. Elizabeth Grosz's *Sexual Subversions* (1989), Margaret Whitford's *Philosophy in the Feminine* (1991) and Tina Chanter's *Ethics of Eros: Irigaray's Rewriting of the Philosophers* (1995) are essential to this correction. Irigaray's conception of sexual difference and her rethinking of corporeality are irreducible to given, metaphysical essences. Rather, Irigaray's rigorous attention to history and language seeks to rethink the imaginary and symbolic space and potentiality of sexual difference. Her work is intimately bound up with the history of philosophy, as the medium in which her thought takes place.

Stages. Irigaray divides her work according to three stages. Mimicry, as a concern for the dissolution of the masculine subject, exemplifies the earliest stage of Irigaray's work. Her doctoral thesis, *Speculum of the Other Woman* (1974), and *This Sex Which Is Not One*

(1977) are representative of this stage. In *Speculum*, Irigaray claims that 'any theory of the subject has always been appropriated by the "masculine"'. Tracking the discursive constitution of the subject in Western philosophy and its culmination in psychoanalysis from Plato to Freud, Irigaray's early work has been widely influential in establishing feminist reading strategies of historical texts, but has also assured her status as a controversial figure. She was removed from her teaching position at the École Freudienne by Lacan for teaching some of the ideas in *Speculum*, but her dismissal only raised feminist interest. Mimesis, as a critical strategy, forces the text to confront its own lie and thereby opens a new discursive, imaginary space for the thinking of another subject without pretension to universalist or naturalist categories. One of the most memorable attempts to undo the singular subject can be seen in *This Sex* where Irigaray references a non-reducible multiplicity and fluidity of feminine sexuality that refuses the account provided by Western philosophy, thereby experientially undoing the privilege of the singular phallus as a model of feminine sexuality. The outcome of the early persistence on 'fluidity' in Irigaray's work can be seen in her subsequent project regarding the elemental, which includes *Marine Love of Friedrich Nietzsche* (1980), *Elementary Passions* (1982) and *The Forgetting of Air in Martin Heidegger* (1983). She seeks to recover the exclusion of the feminine from its conflation with nature in the history of metaphysics, and thereby open the space for reimagining feminine subjectivity and a sexuate dynamism of materiality as the medium of an intersubjective relation of sexual difference, both of which, respectively, are representative of the next two stages of her work.

The second stage of Irigaray's work is the attempt to reimagine a feminine subjectivity, as can be seen most forcefully in *Sexes and Genealogies* (1987), a text heavily influenced by Lacan. For Irigaray, genealogy has always been figured according to a triadic structure. Even the Oedipus triangle of psychoanalysis goes back at least to the Tragic Age of ancient Greece. The triangle of genealogy is composed of mother, father and child, but the mother's position within genealogy only serves as a point of historical movement between father and son. The mother/daughter genealogy is essentially lost. Irigaray stresses the necessity of reconfiguring the mother/daughter relationship at a concrete level so that a new subject, a specifically feminine subjectivity, can be imagined and historically produced. For Irigaray, as long as the triadic structure governs the mother/daughter relationship, no positive space for a distinctly feminine subjectivity is possible. Further, Irigaray's insistence on female genealogy is also thought necessary as a starting point for overcoming women's estrangement from one another. Women's relationships are diagnosed as disaffected in their service to male genealogies so that change at the concrete familial level is indispensable to change at a political or global level.

The third and current stage of Irigaray's work seeks to construct an intersubjectivity of sexual difference, marking a strong turn toward linguistic patterns and politics in relationship to sexual difference. The insight that drives the positive political moment of Irigaray's thought can be seen in *I Love to You* (1992). There, Irigaray demonstrates the relationship between law and sexual difference, where law is thought to precede and condition sexual difference. For Irigaray, if sexual difference is a futural idea that can be realised, it requires certain changes in law. Irigaray does not essentialise sexual difference and then seek to provide laws in accordance with it, as modern political theory theorises a 'contract'. Rather, Irigaray claims that nothing can be said of the modern concept of nature, other than that we know that it is 'at least two'. Irigaray prefers to speak of *genres* (types, kinds) of being and *phusis*, a Greek term that signals, for Irigaray, the manner in which something appears or manifests itself and the conditions of one's birth, and not what the term 'nature' has come to mean for modern philosophy and science. Irigaray's attempt to initiate the realisation of sexual difference has brought her under the critical scrutiny of other feminists for the provision of a content to the ambiguous term 'sexual difference', particularly those who are supporters of her earlier work as the performance of a critique that gains its movement from a formal principle of sexual difference. In *I Love to You* Irigaray claims that the notion of 'sexual difference' always harboured the possibility of a realisation (and thereby a content). Nevertheless, the universality of her latest project is a call for some feminist scepticism, for it subordinates other forms of difference to sexual difference as that which serves to correct all historical forms of social domination.

Though Irigaray provides seemingly clear-cut distinctions that mark the movement of her thought, any coherent 'methodology' according to these stages or to her work in total is difficult to identify. Her close, mimetic readings of historical texts most often require the critical appropriation of a certain text's own method. In this sense, Irigaray's 'method' in some ways is the dissolution of any grand methodology. Her readings, however, should not be understood as 'critique' in the mere negative sense. Irigaray carefully chooses the figures with whom she enters into dialogue. Though limitations and exclusions are revealed, so too are imaginary possibilities. Her textual reading becomes inextricably bound to the history of the text itself, as its own rewriting and rethinking of sexual difference, and this is essential to any discussion of a possible 'Irigarayan method'. However, there are philosophical affiliations that influence her reading strategies and theorisation of sexual difference throughout her work. Irigaray's strategy of thinking by means of historical texts should be situated within the philosophical landscape of twentieth-century theory. Derrida's reading of the history of philosophy as governed by a privileging of presence and unity in its production of meaning and truth has been particularly influential in Irigaray's conceptualisation of language and history as phallogocentric. Irigaray's 'method', understood as a disruptive, textual practice that is simultaneously a theorisation of sexual difference, takes seriously the sense in which historical linguistic practices outline the situation of thinking and experience. Lacanian psychoanalysis is also essential to this enterprise. Lacan provides an account of the exclusion of the feminine in subject formation and demonstrates the lack of a feminine subject position within language. Yet, against Lacan, Irigaray insists on the historical dimension of psychoanalysis as itself a phallogocentric discourse subject to deconstruction. Irigaray's challenge to phallogocentrism reimagines the body as an imaginary body, subject to a necessary phantasmatic existence, but one that does not dispense with the elemental ground of corporeality. Indeed, it is with reference to this corporeality within phallogocentric discourse that sexual difference gains new imaginary and symbolic representation and the possibility of a distinctly feminine subject position within language is opened.

Irigaray's readings. All of Irigaray's work can be understood as the attempt to open the space of enunciation to further differentiation. Nevertheless, as Irigaray's thinking is inextricably linked to the thinkers she reads, her work cannot be understood outside of those readings. Three specific readings directly influence Irigaray's thinking of history and the question of sexual difference, those of Freud, Heidegger and Levinas.

The necessity of Irigaray's close affiliation with historical texts, as the process by which sexual difference is theorised, must be understood within her relationship to Heidegger, specifically his diagnosis of the history of metaphysics and its culmination in modern technological society, as well as the rethinking of 'thinking' itself in such an age as the attempt to recover what has gone missing in the philosophical tradition. Heidegger's influence on Irigaray is not limited to *The Forgetting of Air in Martin Heidegger*, but begins much earlier, for Irigaray's understanding and theorisation of 'sexual difference' is intimately connected to Heidegger's understanding of the history of being. For Heidegger, every age has essentially one question which must be answered. Whereas for Heidegger it is the question of the sense of being, for Irigaray, ours is the question of sexual difference. Through her dialogue with Heidegger, Irigaray rethinks being as sexuate and corporeal. Irigaray follows Heidegger's phenomenological ontology mimetically and pushes his thought in directions that would have been quite unfamiliar to Heidegger himself, but in directions that critically open the possibility of the thought of sexual difference. For Irigaray, Heidegger forgets the materiality that is the medium of sexual difference and makes possible his thought.

In her readings and appropriations of Freud, Irigaray feels psychoanalysis offers insight into the sexuate nature of discourse itself, though this essential insight is commonly neglected in psychoanalysis's own self-reflection. *Speculum* and *This Sex* offer a conceptualisation of psychoanalysis according to sexual difference, history and culture, which concomitantly fuels a critique of psychoanalysis's own self-understanding. For Irigaray, psychoanalysis is precisely the death of universalism, including the universality of its own discourse. However, psychoanalysis is an essential discourse in that it is the only discourse that thematises sexual difference in subject constitution. Once historicised and its conditions of emergence delineated, psychoanalysis proves an indispensable discourse for re-evaluating one's relationship to the history of philosophy. Furthermore, psychoanalysis proves a fruitful ally in its insistence on the role of language in subject formation, which marks the preconditions for entrance into the imaginary and symbolic space of self-positing through sexual difference.

Finally, Irigaray's articulation of sexual difference as an alterity that exceeds binary oppositions is greatly influenced by the work of Emmanuel Levinas. In *Time and the Other* (1947) Levinas claims that sexual difference is the model figure of alterity. Whereas Beauvoir responded that Levinas was just one more philosopher who associated women with otherness, Irigaray takes this claim up in a positive direction in order to think a difference that exceeds the sameness of egalitarian feminist positions. She uses this claim against the later Levinas of *Totality and Infinity* (1961) in order to demonstrate that feminine being is precisely not an alterity in Levinas's work. For Irigaray, sexual difference is a difference that repudiates not only concepts, but also refuses to show itself as a phenomenon that can be described phenomenologically. Irigaray thereby, with Levinas, breaks with phenomenology at this point, but she also breaks with Levinas at the same point in so far as she seeks to demonstrate what remains hidden in Levinas's own critique of phenomenology: 'sexual

difference'. Nonetheless, to further her theorisation of sexual difference in the history of metaphysics, Irigaray appropriates psychoanalytic discourse in order to articulate more fully the originary
experiences that underwrite that history. Irigaray interestingly trans-
poses the work of Freud, Heidegger and Levinas onto one another in
order to strategically think the history of sexual difference in the West
as an originary matricide. This is one example of the sense in which her
thought is bound to the history of discourse and its fate, and how her
critical reading strategies have opened a unique position within the
diversity of feminist thought.

S. Keltner

See also: Death; essentialism; Feminism; jouissance; mimesis; phallogocentrism; Poststructuralism; Time

ITERABILITY A Derridean term that suggests that every repetition
involves a difference, a decontextualisation and a recontextualisation.
This can be understood most clearly in the case of language, where the
units of sound that one uses are not invented but taken from a common
pool, yet each time they are used a different sense is produced. Even the
simplest and strictest repetition, because it is not instantaneous,
involves at least a temporal difference and so is not an exact repetition
but creates a different context. To emphasise these points, Derrida uses
the word 'iterability' because it is derived from the Sanskrit *itara* or
'other', via Latin *iter*, 'again'.

Iterability also implies a break, a *différance*, with respect to the origin
of an utterance for if a speaker is required to express herself in a
language that exists independently of her, she cannot express herself in
any pure or intact sense, but has to, as it were, take what she wants to
express outside of herself and into the play of a language that functions
beyond her control. Derrida is most explicit concerning iterability in
his analysis of Austin's speech act theory and in the debate with John
Searle that followed.

D. Wills

JAMES, WILLIAM (1842–1910) American philosopher and psycholo-
gist. Widely influential for his later work developing and popularising
American Pragmatism and as author of 'The Will to Believe' and *The
Varieties of Religious Experience* (1902), James has also been an early

and continuing source of phenomenological inspiration, particularly through key insights concerning the 'stream of thought', horizonality and 'the fringe', the lived body, the self and intersubjectivity.

James was always highly sceptical of elaborate a priori systems and metaphysical presuppositions, preferring to offer 'introspective' descriptions which could be validated through emergent consensus. In his early masterpiece, *The Principles of Psychology* (1890), James sharply criticised received views, particularly empiricism's obsession with stable images and its temporal and mental atomism, and offered instead an account of thought as always personal, ever-changing, 'sensibly continuous', directed towards apparently independent objects, and selectively attentive to objects we have been 'taught to discern'.

In thus emphasising how consciousness 'deals with objects independent of itself', and can knowingly 'intend' the 'same' in and through the shifting 'mental stream', James went well beyond Brentano towards understanding intentionality as a 'mental act' aiming at a transcendent object. Though this 'act' is not yet productive in Husserl's sense of 'constitution' – nor is his description of the present as 'no knife-edge but a saddle-back' with a 'certain breadth' or duration, a 'rearward- and forward-looking end', as detailed as the latter's account of protention and retention in inner time consciousness – James's early work is widely seen as crucially influencing classical phenomenology.

In fact, however, James would likely have resisted the 'pure seeing' of eidetic analysis, preferring what William Earle termed 'peri-phenomenology', attending to 'what has every chance of being lost sight of'. Thought, for James, is always underway, and what is most vital for philosophy is the 'direction' manifest in the transitive movements, leadings-on and feelings of tendency in which it 'lives' – in its 'flight' rather than its 'perchings'. Thus James's pivotal notion of 'the fringe' names not merely a dimly-attended-to horizon of not-yet-actualised objects, but a contextual 'aura' or 'halo' of propulsive directional vectors unfolding into felt affinities, and so thoughts, inclination and connections being born and 'on the fly'.

This awakening to the temporally projective penumbral fringe informed James's pragmatic theory of truth as 'worthwhile leadings', and ultimately involved not just a rejection of discrete sensations but mentalism itself and the subject–object opposition. Already in his early search for 'the self', he had found only bodily processes and activities, shot through with lines of direction, on the periphery of awareness; by *Essays in Radical Empiricism* (1912), the self was 'the whole field, with all those indefinitely radiating subconscious possibilities of increase that we can only feel'. Here it is no longer mind but reality itself that is recognised as 'processes', in Whitehead's sense: a conflux of directional flows and affective lines of force vying and mixing with one another in a radical pluralism; the flux of existence itself, directly encountered; a cohesion of self and world as they are mutually implicated and intertwined.

R. Switzer

JAMESON, FREDRIC (1934–) American literary theorist and the leading Marxist cultural critic in the United States. Influenced by Hegel and Adorno, Jameson's writings wed an account of the major developments in twentieth-century European philosophy to a broad historical analysis of capitalism to produce dialectical readings of first-, second- and third-world cultural politics. Jameson's basic project has been a materialist 'periodisation' of global cultures; he correlates the major periods of literary and artistic culture – realism, modernism and postmodernism – to transformations in the economy, from industrialisation to the global (or 'late') capitalism of the twenty-first century. According to Jameson's theory, as the totality of a culture fused with economy expands, its internal relations change and the potential of high culture to act as a critical subject atrophies, while utopian impulses disperse across a wider field.

Jameson's work of the 1960s and 1970s establishes the theoretical grounds for his project. *Sartre* (1961) and *Wyndham Lewis* (1979) find a radical politics in the form and matter of texts, thus shifting Marxist criticism from a fixation on ideological content to questions of style, especially the stylistic effects of reification and commodification. Extending this account of literary modernism to core texts of critical theory, *The Prison House of Language* (1972) and *Marxism and Form* (1971) present strong readings of structuralism and the Frankfurt School respectively, arguing that an understanding of the phenomenological tradition should be grounded in reflection on its concrete situation. With the Frankfurt School in particular (see *Late Marxism*, 1990 and *Brecht and Method*, 1998), Jameson consistently demonstrates how historical analysis helps make potentially outdated hypotheses useful for analysis of contemporary culture.

In *The Political Unconscious* (1981), *Seeds of Time* (1994) and the essays in *Ideologies of Theory* (1988), Jameson's theses on periodisation are stated most forcefully. Presenting an influential critique of Althusserian structuralism, *Political Unconscious* defends and applies a Hegelian (and indirectly Spinozist) concept of 'expressive totality' to intensive readings of literary genre, revealing in each the unconscious class politics organising its horizon. In all these works, Jameson's slogan 'always historicise' complements analysis of the deep synchronic structures diagrammed in the semiotic rectangles of A. J. Greimas – a crucial tool in Jameson's ideology critique.

The fruits of this method for an ontology of the present have appeared in Jameson's work since the mid-1980s. The enormously influential *Postmodernism* (1991) treats a wide array of cultural production as evidence of a postmodern style that expresses culture's integration with economy in late capitalism. A more particular account of filmic aesthetics and genres as sites for reading the emergence of new global relations appears in *The Geopolitical Aesthetic* (1992) and *Signatures of the Visible* (1990). The role of the concept (as opposed to the more linguistic 'word' or 'text") in this new ontology is reiterated in *The Cultures of Globalisation* (1998) and *A Singular Modernity* (2002). Altogether, Jameson's periodising has led him to stress the historical contradictions and transformations that have produced a seemingly seamless culture of capitalism.

C. Irr

See also: immanent critique; Literary Theory; Postmodernism

JASPERS, KARL (1883–1969) German psychologist and philosopher, active in existential psychology and philosophy and as well as intercultural philosophy, philosophy of communication and religion, and liberal political philosophy. According to Arendt, his former student, Jaspers' philosophy is especially relevant for how it 'detyrannises' thinking.

Jaspers was born in Oldenburg, studied medicine and began work in 1909 at a psychiatric hospital in Heidelberg. Increasingly uneasy with the study and treatment of mental illness, Jaspers strove to understand it in new and more appropriate ways by subjecting to critique the diagnostic criteria and methods of clinical psychiatry. He published an article in 1910 on paranoia in which he used a biographical approach to understanding patients as well as including their own first-person perspective. The influential two-volume work *General Psychopathology* (1913) systematically developed his insights into mental illness and its treatment, critiqued the therapeutic consequences of determinism and scientism, and analysed symptoms according to their form instead of their content. Jaspers became increasingly interested in philosophy and published *Psychology of World Views* (1919) in which he explored the psychological and philosophical aspects of world-views as possible attitudes toward and expressions of life.

Jaspers was deeply influenced by Kantian ethics, the concrete individualism of Kierkegaard and Nietzsche, and Weber's interpretive methodology. In 1922 Jaspers became professor of philosophy in Heidelberg. During this period, Jaspers developed *Existenzphilosophie* as a philosophy of concrete human existence concerned with the margins, limits and breakdowns of human experience and with possibilities of transcendence. These early works were important for the young Heidegger who adopted and radically transformed some of the insights of Jaspers, such as the notion of limit-situation (*Grenzsituation*). Jaspers systematically articulated his views of philosophy and its history in his three-volume magnum opus *Philosophy* (1932). In this work, he developed the notion of the 'encompassing' (*das Umgreifende*) as the intersection of facticity and transcendence, the finitude and infinity of human existence, and as its inexhaustible and indefinite context and horizon.

For Jaspers, transcendence and the encompassing intrinsically defy objectification. In *Philosophy and Existence* (1938), Jaspers explored how existence indicates the experience of freedom as concrete possibility. This experience of transcendence constitutes the individual's authenticity in becoming aware of the encompassing through exposure to limit-situations such as suffering, conflict, guilt, chance and death. Jaspers' *Philosophical Faith* (1948) demonstrates the inherent difference between philosophical and religious faith and how they both reflect different modes of grasping existence in the context of the encompassing. Jaspers would later systematically develop his account of the encompassing and its 'ciphers' in his contribution to philosophy of religion, *Philosophical Faith and Revelation* (1962). Ciphers are traces of the infinite in the finite, the sacred in the profane and the ineffable in language. These ciphers cannot be coherently systematised, since they are infinitely multiple and even conflict. As such, they potentially disrupt both mythology and demythologisation, as Jaspers argued against Rudolf Bultmann. This philosophy of ciphers influenced the early Ricoeur.

Jaspers' early contribution to politics, *The Spiritual Situation of the Time* (1931), emphasised individual freedom and authenticity in the face of the alienation of mass society. Jaspers and his Jewish wife were increasingly marginalised and threatened under National Socialism. He lost his chair and was prevented from teaching. They retreated from public life and decided to commit suicide if arrested. Allowed to leave for Switzerland in 1942, he refused since his wife was not permitted to travel. After the War, Jaspers helped found the journal *Transformation*, argued for the denazification of German institutions and published his best known political work, *The Question of German Guilt* (1946), which discussed German guilt for the Holocaust and its consequences for any German future. Although he actively contributed to postwar debates about German war-crimes and possibilities for democracy, he became professor of philosophy at the University of Basel in Switzerland in 1948. Jaspers continued his political engagement by writing extensively about the threats to human freedom posed by modern science and technology, nuclear warfare and contemporary political and economic structures.

Jaspers grounded his political philosophy in his philosophy of communication, which stresses individuality and diversity connected through dialogue. The significance of individuation as self-transcendence shifts in Jaspers' later thought as the emphasis turns from the alterity of experience in limit-situations to that of the other in communication. Both involve an inherent openness that entails an irreducible and productive insecurity in the relationship of self and other. This openness of communication indicates possibilities for humanity, rationality and a humane political order. The ethical is already present in the very act of communication and ethics as the realisation of the 'unreserved readiness for communication' and the commitment to open and unlimited communication which is the ideal of reason itself. Although Habermas incorporated some of these theses into his theory of communicative action, communication is not primarily rational or formal for Jaspers, since it inherently involves all aspects of human existence. Communication is restrictive and coercive unless it is open to all modes of communication in their multiplicity. It thus presupposes not only an unlimited willingness to communicate but a genuine openness to the possibility of being transformed by the other in a concrete encounter. Jaspers accordingly articulated communication as the possibility of individuation through the socialisation of solidarity. It is precisely in solidarity for the other that I am individuated.

Communication unfolds through solitude and union, love and struggle, and reaches its height in loving struggle, which indicates the possibility of solidarity without identity, agreement without totality, because it is a struggle for the truth of existence. Loving struggle has the recognition of the other as its condition and unfolds through the give and take of questioning and being questioned. Communication as loving struggle is thus the openness of a questioning that involves more than universal validity claims in bringing all of the content and particularity of *Existenz* into dialogue 'existence to existence'.

E. *Nelson*

See also: Existentialism; *Lebensphilosophie*; limit situation

JEWISH PHILOSOPHY A hybrid combining non-philosophical forms of Jewish thought (Bible, rabbinic Midrash and Talmud, kabbalah) and Western philosophy (Greek philosophy, German Idealism, French 'existentialism' and postmodernism, American pragmatism). Made possible by the common human root that is at the centre of all inquiry and translation, the relationship is profoundly allergic to rigid distinctions between Athens and Jerusalem, reason and revelation, knowledge and faith, freedom and constraint, universal and particular. Neither completely identical to nor radically distinct from each other, Jewish thought and Western philosophy have historically shared broad areas of consonance, despite the often sharp points of dissonance that define the difference between them. Jewish philosophy constitutes the attempt to mediate this relationship. It brings a Hebrew key, a non-philosophical corpus of thought, to the intersection between God, world and human subjectivity. Jewish philosophy thus secures revelation and its practice on a rational or semi-rational basis, even as it leads reason up to its limit, where it overlaps into the imagination.

Notwithstanding the case of Philo of Alexandria, Jewish philosophy, as well as opposition to it, first flowered alongside the work of Al-Farabi, Ibn Sina (Avicenna), Ibn Rushd (Averroes) and Al-Ghazali. The canon of medieval Jewish philosophy is dominated by Saadia Gaon (*Beliefs and Opinions*, 933), Abraham ibn Daud (*Exalted Faith*, 1168), Moses Maimonides (the monumental *Guide of the Perplexed*, c.1190) and Gersonides (*Wars of the Lord*, 1329). The work of medieval Jewish philosophy goes beyond scholastic arguments as to the existence of God, namely the cosmological argument and the argument from design founded upon neo-Aristotelean physics and metaphysics. Of more interest is the exploration of prophecy, language and law, particularly as they relate to Scripture and its philosophical hermeneutic. Rooted in divine wisdom, law provides the indispensable platform from which to understand the world of physical creation, to follow the order of causation back to its first purpose, the highest telos of which is the intellectual love of God, a God whose most simple and perfect essence is one that no finite conception can ever comprehend. On the ultimate limit of human reason, the proponents and critics of philosophy were of one mind. With its seat in divine will, it was love that compelled the philosophical resistance to philosophy on the part of critics of philosophy such as Judah Halevy (*The Kuzari*, 1140), Hasdai Crescas (*The Light of the Lord*, 1410) and Nachmanides (1194–c.1270). A God who can love, namely God's particular love and special providence for the Jewish people and its Torah, upturns Greek metaphysical theology in which God stands as the most recondite object of its own intellection.

Modern Jewish philosophy belongs to that moment in the history of philosophy when the perfect order presupposed by medieval philosophy has forever collapsed, when the human world is radically reorganised around forms of human consciousness (reason, spirit, will). In impugning the abiding rationality of post-biblical Judaism, Spinoza laid down the gauntlet, not just to Jewish philosophy, but to modern Judaism writ large in his *Theological-Political Treatise* (1670). With Spinoza, Moses Mendelssohn's *Jerusalem* (1783) reduced revelation to law and political ethics, not philosophical truth, the comprehension of which was universal and thus not limited to any one scriptural tradition. But for Mendelssohn, the ceremonial law is a 'living script', a sublime propaedeutic to philosophical truth. More aggressive commitments to Judaism and to traditional forms of Jewish thought inform twentieth-century Jewish philosophy. For Hermann Cohen (*Religion of Reason*, 1919), prophetic Judaism is the quintessential religion of reason. The temporal stabilisation of human subjectivity is the effect of individual, moral piety as it grows out of social ethics. Rejecting the emphasis placed by Cohen on reason, Martin Buber (*I and Thou*, 1923) and Franz Rosenzweig (*The Star of Redemption*, 1921) root human existence in a revelation that is prior to reason. Their own turn to the Hebrew Bible, Jewish mystical traditions and medieval Hebrew poetry reflect a self-conscious decision to open philosophy to forms of non-philosophical and anti-metaphysical thought that are the analogue to human sensation and symbolic expression. Revelation and redemption, intersubjectivity and dialogue, are the common key points on the basis of which not just Buber and Rosenzweig but also Cohen veer off from the philosophical trajectories set by Kant, Hegel and Nietzsche, trajectories upon which nonetheless their own work depends.

The particular problematic that bedevils Jewish philosophy, both medieval and modern, reflects the sociology of knowledge as defined by the minority status of a diasporic people. In his pioneering *Philosophies of Judaism* (1973), Julius Guttman argued that philosophy was never indigenous to Judaism:

> The Jewish people did not begin to philosophise because of an irresistible urge to do so. They received philosophy from outside sources and the history of Jewish philosophy is a history of successive absorptions of foreign ideas which were then transformed and adapted according to specific Jewish points of view.

But if philosophical forms of elite cultural expression are never 'indigenous' to Judaism, neither were they ever native to Greek myth,

Christianity and Islam. Philosophical expression belongs to intellectual lexicons that are in one sense broader and in one sense narrower than the religious cultures that their practitioners inhabit. Such forms transcend particular religious traditions, but those who master them belong to very small circles. Guttman's thesis therefore rests on a historical claim that is impossible to substantiate. We have no idea what 'irresistible urges' may or may not have compelled Jewish people to philosophise at any given moment.

Viewed sequentially, 'specific Jewish points of view' predate the Persian, Hellenistic, Islamic, European and American philosophical, aesthetic and political cultures that have stamped the Jewish people from one moment to the next. Yet at various historical junctures, these impress Judaism so powerfully that the 'urge' they represent seems elemental to Jewish thought and culture. The logical order displayed by the Mishna's redactor, a grandly baroque style in seventeenth-century synagogue design, and the passion for social justice in the twentieth century are not simply 'alien' points of view adapted to Judaism. The same holds true of philosophy: the blinding vision of God's perfection in medieval philosophy or the intersubjective interplay established by correlation and dialogue in modern Jewish thought are both anticipated in Jewish culture. As such, chronological priority does not reflect logical priority or establish value. Logically and axiologically, if not historically, neither Judaism nor its other in art, philosophy and social thought subsist one after the other. Instead, they might be said to assume inchoate form, all at once and at the same time, one next to and inside each other. The history of Jewish philosophy from Philo onwards is the discontinuous history of one such exposure.

Z. Braiterman

JONAS, HANS (1903–93) German philosopher with a profound impact on environmental philosophy. Jonas was one of the remarkable group of Jewish students of Heidegger (including Levinas, Arendt, Marcuse and Karl Löwith) who eventually distinguished themselves as significant thinkers in their own right. Jonas's dissertation (co-directed by Heidegger and the theologian Rudolf Bultmann) was a highly acclaimed study of Gnosticism in late antiquity. In 1933, faced with the crisis of Nazism, Jonas emigrated first to London and then to Palestine. At the outset of the Second World War he enlisted in the British Army's Jewish Brigade, serving for five years as a soldier on the front lines and participating in the liberation of Germany in 1945. After returning to Palestine, Jonas fought for Israel in the 1948 Arab-Israeli

War. He then emigrated to Canada and finally to New York, where he taught philosophy at the New School for Social Research from 1955 until his retirement in 1976.

Reflecting back, late in life, on his intellectual development, Jonas would remark that his personal experience as a soldier profoundly altered his philosophical perspective, compelling him to overcome the mind–body, man–nature dualism inherent in the idealist tradition. He came to recognise that humans are embodied beings and thus not radically other than the rest of the earth's organisms. This 'ecological' stance is apparent in his two major books of philosophy, *The Phenomenon of Life: Toward a Philosophical Biology* (1966) and *The Imperative of Responsibility: In Search of an Ethics for the Technological Age* (1979). In the former book, he applies the tools of existentialist phenomenology to all living organisms, thus broadening the realm of freedom, subjectivity and meaning: these are not uniquely human qualities, and nature is not merely the realm of dead, meaningless, mechanically determined or uncaring matter. The freedom of self-making (the 'care' or concern for one's own existence) touted by existentialism as uniquely human is in fact the very principle of life itself, manifest in the event of metabolism, in which the organism shows itself as freely self-transforming. The latter book, which was a best-seller in Germany and the 'Bible' of the German Green Party in the 1980s, argues that modern humankind's unprecedented technological power, with which for the first time we have become capable of truly altering the natural world as well as the human species, necessitates the formulation of a new ground for ethics. Whereas all previous ethics were essentially concerned with the present generation, the new ethics must be essentially concerned with the welfare of future generations. Since humans tend to be swayed by short-term self-interest, the new ethical imperative may well need to be implemented through a rhetoric of fear and a politics of deception.

By the time Jonas published the completed version of *The Gnostic Religion* (a work which remains the classic in its field) in 1955, he had come to regard Heidegger's *Being and Time* as a pernicious mode of Gnostic dualism that contributes to the estrangement between humans and the natural world. He is also severely critical of Heidegger's later writings, which he sees as marked by a false humility that masks 'the most enormous hubris in the whole history of thought'. Anticipating a critique of Heidegger that would become commonplace in the latter decades of the twentieth century, Jonas regards Heideggerian existentialism as a purely formalist 'decisionism' devoid of ethical content or norms. Jonas, for his part, attempts to ground ethics in 'the very nature of things', reintroducing humankind to its role as a lead player in a cosmic biological project.

G. Stone

See also: Environmental Philosophy

JOUISSANCE A technical term in Lacanian psychoanalysis for which no proper English equivalent exists. It can be translated by 'pleasure' or 'enjoyment', but the French term connotes an orgasmic pleasure not translatable into English. It is thereby generally left untranslated. Lacan relates the term to the place of the feminine, which he claims exceeds the phallic economy of discourse.

Lacan's term is taken up in French feminism as a strategy for thinking the place of the feminine beyond the economy of phallogo-centrism. Feminine *jouissance* is suppressed in and by a masculine imaginary and symbolic, but it is also the site at which the phallic economy of discourse is challenged by the dissolution of traditional linguistic and conceptual borders in a blissful pleasure that refuses to take note of its prohibition. For Irigaray, feminine *jouissance* exceeds the singularity, unity and location of masculine *jouissance*. Irigaray imagines feminine sexuality as heterogeneous, fluid and an excess that refuses phallic representation. Kristeva relates the problem of *jouissance* to the symbolic representation of motherhood and insists that the traditional absorption of the feminine by the image of the mother disallows the experience of feminine pleasure. For Kristeva, the *jouissance* of the mother needs to be represented in the cultural imaginary in order to open the place of the feminine. Cixous speaks of the *jouissance* of the poetic word. For Cixous, the pleasure of the text is related to the dissolution of the boundaries of the traditional subject and the gathering together of infinite, imaginary possibility.

S. Keltner

KANT, IMMANUEL (1724–1804) Prussian philosopher whose celebrated series of works in critical philosophy, and the transcendental method they employ, are, on most accounts, credited with being the origin of what we now call the tradition of continental philosophy.

Early training and first works. Kant's philosophical education, which took place as did all the events of his life in the Baltic port city of Königsberg, was shaped by the contemporary controversies surrounding the philosophy of Christian Wolff, whose rationalist system – deeply indebted to Leibniz – was vehemently attacked from both religious (Pietist) and a scientific (Newtonian) perspectives. Kant's first, privately published work – *Thoughts on the True Estimation of Living Forces* (1746) – is a metaphysically motivated meditation on the concept of force, whose character had been the subject of dispute between Newton and Leibniz and their followers. Between 1748 and 1754 Kant worked as a private tutor, publishing newspaper articles on popular science while also satisfying the formal requirements necessary to pursue an academic career at the University of Königsberg. He attained his licence to teach in 1755 with a dissertation *A New Exposition of the First Principles of Metaphysics*, and in the same year published the extraordinary *Universal Natural History and the Theory of the Heavens*, at once a work of popular science and an unrestrained contribution to speculative cosmology. Apart from the 1756 disputation *Physical Monadology* his writings for the rest of the decade were largely pamphlets advertising his lecture courses as a *Privatdozent* to potential students. Among these are some of his most important early writings including 'A New Doctrine of Motion and Rest' (1758) and 'The False Subtlety of the Four Syllogistic Figures' (1762).

During the 1760s Kant continued to teach as a *Privatdozent* and to work as a librarian in Königsberg Castle. He was not to be appointed to the Professorship of Logic and Metaphysics until 1770. Nevertheless, this was for him an extremely prolific decade, when he produced most of what are now known collectively as the 'pre-critical' writings. At this time Kant was preoccupied with the issue of 'false subtlety' or the scholastic retreat from common sense into a world of unreal definitions and distinctions. 'False subtlety' was evident not only in traditional philosophy, but also in the 'dream castles' of such moderns as Christian Wolff. Kant regarded it as a danger to sound judgement and common sense and to be resisted from within philosophy. Accordingly, in 1762 he resisted the 'false subtlety' of the syllogistic figures of scholastic logic and in 1763 turned his attention to the false subtlety of the arguments for the existence of God in *The Only Possible Argument in Support of a Demonstration of the Existence of God* (1763). He divided the theological arguments into the 'ontological' and 'cosmological' proofs' – the former departing from rational, the latter from empirical concepts – in order to show the 'artificial' character of their argumentation. He has not yet reached the position of his later critical philosophy – namely that no argument can prove the existence of God – but the sceptical direction of his argument is already firmly established. 'False subtlety' in moral philosophy is criticised in the Berlin

Academy Prize Essay 'Inquiry concerning the Distinctness of the Principles of Natural Theology and Morality' (1764) and in the same year diagnosed as a form of mental illness in 'Essay on the Diseases of the Head'.

In the mid-1760s Kant published two of his most unusual writings – *Observations on the Feeling of the Beautiful and the Sublime* (1764) and *Dreams of a Spirit Seer Elucidated by Dreams of Metaphysics* (1766). The former comprises a number of aesthetic and anthropological reflections inspired by Edmund Burke and deeply influenced, as are most of Kant's works of this decade, by Rousseau. The object of the reflections is the concept of feeling and its role in experience and character. While the aesthetic categories of the beautiful and the sublime organise the contents of the reflections, it is not primarily a work in aesthetics, although some of its ideas would be further developed in the *Critique of Judgement* (1790). The *Dreams of a Spirit Seer* also anticipates the critical philosophy with its attack on the delusional 'false subtleties' of metaphysics. Ostensibly a critique of the Swedish physiologist and mystic Emmanuel Swedenborg, it takes his accounts of visions and cosmic mystical flights as an occasion to criticise the fantasies of metaphysics, including the rational metaphysics of Christian Wolff.

The 'silent decade'. With his appointment to a Professorship at Königsberg in 1770 Kant embarked on a decade of teaching and academic administration that has become legendary as his 'silent decade'. While it is true that he published very little during this period, his innovative lecture courses and his sustained and intense private reflections contributed to the emergence of the critical philosophy of the 1780s. On the eve of his temporary retreat from the public sphere Kant published his remarkable Inaugural Dissertation *On the Form and Principles of the Sensible and Intelligible World* (1770), at once a summation of his work to date and a programmatic statement of what was to come. Proceeding from the definition of 'world' as a synthetic whole, Kant inquires into its matter and form before proposing a novel definition of form as involving the problem of coordination of contents (matter or substance). This leads him first to a distinction between the sensible and the intelligible and then to one between sensible and intelligible principles of coordination. Here Kant introduces the 'transcendental distinction' between sensibility and conceptuality that will be axiomatic for the critical philosophy. The 'transcendental distinction' allows Kant to distance himself from Leibniz – for whom there was a continuum between sensibility and concepts, the former being a 'confused' expression of the latter – and empiricists such as

Locke who derived concepts from the reflection upon sensible experience.

Not only the basic argument of the Dissertation, but also many of its details and innovations in vocabulary, anticipate the critical philosophy. The second section introduces the distinction between *phenomenon* and *noumenon*, along with a first statement of Kant's concept of experience and the character of the 'concepts of the understanding'. His views on the origins of the latter are also consistent with the critical philosophy: concepts are acquired rather than innate, but not acquired as Locke would have by means of reflection upon sensibility but by means of an act of abstraction from the laws of the mind that only become evident in an act of experience. The dissertation cites concepts such as possibility, existence, necessity, substance, cause (namely the three critical categories of modality and two of the categories of relation) along with their opposites or correlates. The *Critique of Pure Reason* will propose a more elaborate and 'complete' account of these in the 'Table of Categories'.

Perhaps the most radical step in the Dissertation is represented by Kant's presentation of space and time as the forms of sensibility. Space and time are identified as subjective intuitions prior to experience, even though it is only through experience that their work of coordinating sensible objects becomes visible. The implications of these views are extensively analysed in the 'Transcendental Aesthetic' of the *Critique of Pure Reason*. The dissertation ends with some reflections on the method of determining what belongs to the sensibility and to the understanding, and the consequences of their confusion. While the critical analysis of 'subreptive principles' that confuse sensibility and conceptuality is not the same as the critique of dialectical syllogisms developed in the 'Transcendental Dialectic' of the *Critique of Pure Reason*, the illusory character of subreptive principles in many ways provides a model for the later critical analysis of dialectical inference.

The critical philosophy. In the decade from 1781 Kant published the three works that define the critical philosophy: *Critique of Pure Reason* (1781, with a revised second edition in 1787), *Critique of Practical Reason* (1787) and *Critique of Judgement* (1790). Accompanying these books – which achieved a still incomplete revolution in philosophy – were three shorter texts: an outline of the argument of the first critique for didactic purposes, *Prolegomena to Any Future Metaphysics that would Present itself as a Science* (1783); a first formulation of the critical position in moral philosophy in the *Groundwork of the Metaphysics of Morals* (1785); and a critical exposition of natural science focused on the concept of force in the *Metaphysical Foundations* *of Natural Science* (1785). Kant also published a number of important essays during this decade which, while not directly related to the *critiques* nevertheless form an integral part of the emerging critical philosophy. These include the justly celebrated 'Answer to the Question: "What is Enlightenment'" (1784), 'Conjectural Beginnings of the Human Race' (1786) and 'What does "Orientation in Thinking" Mean?' (1786).

The revolutionary ambition of the critical philosophy was immediately appreciated by Kant's contemporaries, although there was considerable debate as to its precise significance. Already in the 1780s works of criticism and explication began to be published; some hostile contributions, above all that of Eberhard, even provoked Kant to clarify some of his positions, as in the extremely defensive 'On a New Discovery, which Makes All New Critiques of Pure Reason Unnecessary Because of an Older One' (1790) (namely, that of Leibniz). The debate initiated by his contemporaries has continued for over two centuries and shows little sign of abating. There are, however, by now considerable grounds for consensus regarding Kant's intentions and mode of argumentation in the critical philosophy.

The basic object of philosophical scrutiny in the three critiques is the form adopted by judgement when applied to diverse fields of objects and actions. The critical philosophy seeks to justify acts of judgement by means of a demarcation of the limits of legitimate judgement. Each of the three critiques presents an Analytic of judgement that determines the character of legitimate judgements, then a Dialectic that criticises illegitimate forms of judgement and inference, and finally a methodology that determines how to present a system of such judgements as a science. The *Critique of Pure Reason* scrutinises metaphysical judgements, limiting their legitimacy to objects of experience in space and time; the *Critique of Practical Reason* considers moral judgements and limits their legitimacy to those motivated solely by duty, while the *Critique of Judgement* considers aesthetic and teleological judgements, providing complex and perhaps still not fully understood conditions for their legitimate use.

While sharing this general structure, the content of the three critiques nevertheless differ widely in style and direction of argument. The structure of the *Critique of Pure Reason* is governed by the critique of the Wolffian division of metaphysics into the science of being as such (ontology) and the sciences of particular regions of being (God, the World and the Soul). The Analytic of the first critique – which Kant conceived as a replacement for ontology – is informed by a tension between respecting the transcendental distinction between sensibility and understanding and proving the possibility of legitimate judgements that combine the form and the content of both. Concepts and intuitions are a priori – not derived from experience but providing its condition – but nevertheless need to combine to form experience. The synthetic a priori judgement thus adds an element derived from conceptuality to sensible experience, while the analytic of principles analyses concepts in a spatio-temporal setting. The Transcendental Dialectic, on the other hand, seeks to contain the exorbitant tendency of human reason to think beyond the limits of spatio-temporal experience, to call the objects of those thoughts 'God', the 'Cosmos' and the 'Soul' and to reason of them in the metaphysical sciences of theology, cosmology and psychology. The concerns of the second critique differ considerably from those of the first: here Kant seeks to ground moral judgements not in the 'heteronomous principles' associated with sensible feeling, but in the autonomous principles derived from duty. The third critique again pursues a different strategy of argument, disclosing the aporetic or undecidable character of aesthetic judgements of taste in the first, and delimiting a space for the legitimate use of teleological judgement in the second part of the book.

Later works. In the decade following the publication of the critiques Kant continued to be extremely active. The Revolution in France and the increasing pressure on the Enlightenment in Prussia following the death of Frederick the Great in 1786 was reflected in the censorship applied to Kant for his writings on religion (his *Religion within the Limits of Reason Alone* was published in 1792). Writings such as *Perpetual Peace* (1795) point to the emergence of political concerns in Kant's writings, always present but now clearly accentuated. Kant also published the full elaboration of his practical philosophy – *The Metaphysics of Morals* – in 1797 drawing on his lectures in practical philosophy. The decade also saw the publication of texts based on Kant's lectures by his followers, above all the innovative *Anthropology from a Pragmatic Point of View* (1798), but also the lectures on logic in 1800, physical geography in 1802 and pedagogy in 1803.

While most of the writings of the 1790s may be considered as defences, applications or elaborations of critical positions – such as the *Conflict of the Faculties* (1798) and *On the Progress of Metaphysics since Leibniz and Wolff* (written 1790 and published posthumously 1804) it is by no means clear that the 1790s constituted little more than an extension of the 'critical decade' of the 1780s. This is apparent above all in the controversial notes that make up the manuscript of a projected late work on science and metaphysics that after many vicissitudes was published in the 1930s as the *Opus Postumum*. This text shows Kant willing to revisit and revise many of the achievements of his critical philosophy and to develop his thought in response to the work of the younger generation of philosophers such as Fichte and Schelling.

By the time of Kant's death in 1804 the critical philosophy was not only attracting criticism but also being used as the occasion for the formulation of new directions in philosophy. The work of Fichte, Schelling and Hegel emerges directly from an engagement with Kant, and announced a season of Kantian philosophy which in spite of occasional eclipses and renewals has yet to pass. The critique of Kant remained central to the thought of late nineteenth- and twentieth-century philosophers, from Nietzsche to Husserl, Heidegger, Lukács and more recently Arendt and Lyotard. And alongside philosophers who have received inspiration from Kant's work to formulate their own thought there continues a sophisticated tradition of exegesis of the Kantian corpus, still growing with the addition of previously unpublished lecture transcripts and the comprehensive projects for the translation of his work.

H. Caygill

See also: aesthetic judgement; categorial imperative; Critique; deduction; duty; Enlightenment; Immanence; inclination; Idea (1); Metaphysics; organism; Reason (1); sensibility; synthetic a priori judgement; teleological judgment; Time; Transcendental Analytic; Transcendental Dialectic; Transcendental Unity of Apperception; Truth; Understanding (1); vitalism

KELLER, EVELYN FOX (1936–) American historian and philosopher of science, known for her early work on gender and science and her later work on philosophy of biology. Keller trained as a scientist, earning a doctorate in theoretical physics and molecular biology from Harvard in 1963. She then worked for several years as a mathematical biologist but became disenchanted with scientific practice in the American academy and began anew as a historian and philosopher of science in the mid-1970s.

Keller's work is marked not only by a scrupulous attention to the details of scientific knowledge production – what has been discovered – but also by an equally scrupulous reconstruction of the social, political, economic and gendered contexts of scientific work – how things are discovered . Keller's critique of scientific practice does not champion a distinctive 'feminine' way of doing science, but tries to unlock the potentials for scientific practice shackled by unexamined commitments to patriarchal and hierarchical social systems.

Among the most binding of those shackles is the search for the 'master molecule', an isolated and transcendent command centre whose unidirectional commands account for the order of an otherwise chaotic or passive material. Against all such hylomorphism – which has been consistently gendered in Western culture and science (the active command centre figured as masculine and the passive or chaotic matter figured as feminine) – Keller points us to the study of the morpho-genetic patterns of complex interactive systems, that is to processes of immanent self-organisation across multiple levels. The critique of hylomorphism, then, in the context of molecular biology, is also the critique of reductionism, the idea that biological form can be fully accounted for by the 'information' contained in a genetic blue-print.

After several important articles on 'gender and science' in the late 1970s and early 1980s, Keller's first book was a biographical study of the biologist Barbara McClintock and her 'feeling for the organism', published in 1983. In addition to the criticism of masculinised science, we can also see the critique of reductionism, as Keller details McClin-tock's attention to the level of the organism as well as to the genetic level.

In *Reflections on Gender and Science* (1984), Keller produces a decisive interpretation of Bacon's desire to subjugate nature, in which is visible the deep-seated masculinist orientation of modern science. Hugely controversial, *Reflections* was often misread as supporting a feminine science, but this misreading only reinforces the gender binary which is Keller's object of critique.

By the time of *Secrets of Life/Secrets of Death* (1992) Keller had begun to re-examine her positions with regard to much contempora-neous feminist work in philosophy of science. Her mature position results in a twofold warning against both naive positivism and naive social constructivism: (1) instead of looking for the 'laws' of nature we should look to the 'capacities' of nature; and (2) instead of dissolving nature into culture we should look to the 'constraints and opportu-nities' nature provides for our engagement with it.

Keller's last three books, *Refiguring Life: Metaphors of Twentieth-Century Biology* (1995), *Century of the Gene* (2000) and *Making Sense of Life* (2002) focus on three intersections in twentieth-century science: (1) genetics and embryology; (2) physics and biology; (3) cybernetics and molecular biology. Keller's thick reconstructions bring into play social, economic and political contexts as she tracks the multiple 'models, metaphors, and machines' by means of which scientists have sought to explain biological development. What comes to the fore in all these works, but particularly in the last one, is the question of knowledge production in biology, especially with regard to the different roles played by mathematics and experiment.

J. Protevi

KIERKEGAARD, SØREN (1813–55) Danish religious writer who never regarded himself as a philosopher, although many of his works engage with key issues in philosophy and he came to exert a decisive influence on the course of twentieth-century continental philosophy. He is often chiefly remembered for his polemic with Hegel, especially in his *Concluding Unscientific Postscript* (1846). Accusing the Hegelians of absorbing themselves in a world of pure thought and forgetting their own real-life existence, he drew a series of sharp contrasts between thought and existence; possibility and actuality; objectivity and subjectivity; the speculative and the ethical; the perspectives of world-historical generality ('the race') and the individual; and between disinterestedness and the interest or passion of a subject who is always confronted with the demands of choosing himself in one or other concrete situation.

Many of his objections to Hegelianism applied also to Romantic idealism. In his dissertation *The Concept of Irony* (1841), Kierkegaard had allied himself with the Hegelians in depicting the Romantics as using idealism to justify their cult of ironic detachment and irresponsibility. Even here, however, there were hints that the same critique might be extended to other forms of idealism. The problem, as Kierkegaard saw it, was that precisely the movement of abstraction that enables us to form universal ideas makes it difficult to relate these ideas back to life. Whereas Hegel claimed that intensifying Cartesian doubt until it became an all-embracing despair enabled him to overcome Descartes' dualism, Kierkegaard believed that once one accepted doubt as a point of departure it was impossible to return to solid ground. This was above all pressing in relation to ethical and religious issues such as marriage, guilt, death and the possibility of eternal life.

What is striking about Kierkegaard is not the formal objections he raised but the style of his critique. In attacking Romantic versions of idealism he produced novel-like works such as *Either-Or* (1843), *Repetition* (1844) and *Stages on Life's Way* (1846) in which he exposed the impossibility of basing life on aesthetic values. These works contained a dazzling array of aphorisms, writings about art (such as a review of Mozart's *Don Giovanni*), novellas and many passages of shimmering prose. When it came to Hegel, he employed irony and humour in undermining the serious demeanour of the systematic philosophers, who, as Kierkegaard saw them, suffered from absent-mindedness, constructing great palaces of thought while living in tumbledown shacks.

Kierkegaard's work was not merely negative, however, as he also attempted to show how the self might extract itself from the delusions of philosophy and aestheticism and fulfil its potential freedom. This freedom was disclosed through such phenomena as anxiety (*The Concept of Anxiety*, 1844), concern, patience and suffering (explored in his many religious discourses), and despair (*The Sickness unto Death*, 1849). Time is always important to Kierkegaard, who sees the 'moment of vision' as offering a point at which the flux of time is intersected by the eternal. Through freely embracing what is revealed in such a moment, the self develops a quality of existential self-relation that, in its deepest forms, leads it to realise its dependence on God. Much of this Kierkegaardian psychology was incorporated into Heidegger's *Being and Time* (1927) and subsequent existential thought, though without Kierkegaard's religious motivation.

Religion was in fact Kierkegaard's driving interest. Already in *Fear and Trembling* (1843) he portrayed the religious hero as someone who, relying on God alone, might find himself called to transgress not only local customs but even universal moral rules in a 'teleological suspension of the ethical' – as when Abraham was called to sacrifice his son, an act that ethics must regard as murder. Abraham's faith was faith in the power of the absurd. In an analogous way, God's self-revelation in the Incarnation of the God-man Jesus Christ will necessarily appear to human reason as a paradox, since reason cannot accept the identity of such contrary predicates as 'God' and 'an individual human being'. Reason finds the claims of faith to be an 'offence' and a 'stumbling-block'. Faith in the paradox of the incarnation demands a leap, an act for which adequate grounds can never be given.

If this confrontational view of the relationship between God and humanity points to his Lutheran background, with its emphasis on sin and the limitations of reason, Kierkegaard did not simply confront his contemporaries in the manner of a reforming prophet. Instead he sought to deploy what he called 'indirect communication', accepting his interlocutors' premises only to show their incoherence and their need for a higher-level religious resolution. Thus he wrote aesthetic books to counter aestheticism and used philosophy to undermine philosophy. He even allowed himself to appear as a scoundrel in order to further the cause of the ethical. His model for this procedure was Socrates, who was, apart from Christianity itself, the most constant influence on his work. Many times he described his own task as analogous to Socrates' maieutic pedagogy, helping his auditors to distinguish between what they knew and what they didn't know (but thought they did). The use of pseudonyms, as well as the irony, humour and dialogical character of such indirect communication, has contributed to the recent interest in Kierkegaard among those concerned with the frontier between literature and philosophy.

If Kierkegaard's reputation has remained distinctly sombre ('the melancholy Dane'), it should be stressed that although there are many dark tones in his religiosity, he wrote important and beautiful treatises on love (*Works of Love*, 1847, a work that is attracting increasing interest from moral philosophers) and the religious life (several collections of 'upbuilding' or 'Christian' discourses), and much that is, simply, hilarious. He has suffered more than most from woeful misreadings, due either to commentators' inadequate access to the Danish sources or to their refusal to note Kierkegaard's cautions concerning the complex architectonics of his authorial practice(s). His indirect method has often led to him being seen as representing positions that his work is precisely directed to opposing. But as Kierkegaard insisted, each reader must judge for themselves.

G. Pattison

See also: absurdity (1); anxiety (1); despair; leap; moment of vision (1); Religion, Philosophy of; Repetition; teleological suspension of the ethical

KOFMAN, SARAH (1934–94) French philosopher best known for her readings of Nietzsche and Freud, her examination of the position of women in the Western tradition, and her writing on the Holocaust. Kofman's books typically undertake close readings of works by important male, Western thinkers, uncovering their blind spots and unconscious investments. Her work is aligned with the critical perspectives of deconstruction and psychoanalysis, though it does not unreservedly follow any theory or methodology. In works such as *Aberrations: le devenir-femme d'Auguste Comte* (1978), devoted to the founder of positivism, Kofman builds on psychoanalysis by drawing attention to the drives, desires and constructions of sexual identity woven into all philosophical systems. Like Derrida, Kofman attempts to dismantle binary oppositions, notably the opposition between text and life as well as gendered polarities such as the intelligible and the sensible. Her philosophical style has been described as playful and impertinent, a kind of poking-holes in the great systems of Western thought that reflects her self-conscious position as a woman reading its great masters.

The Enigma of Woman: Woman in Freud's Writings (1980) examines Freud's representation of woman as a mystery or enigma that waits to be unveiled. This analysis shifts between several levels of interpretation, at times offering a Freudian analysis of Freud, at others underscoring the heterogeneous, unstable economy of Freud's writing on the feminine. This influential study drew the attention of an international group of feminist theorists to Kofman's work. Unlike some of her contemporaries, however, Kofman never embraced the idea of a specifically feminine writing. Her contribution to feminism consists rather in a sustained reflection on the question of woman in philosophy and in her own philosophical work.

If Kofman's work on Freud helped to generate a new interest in psychoanalysis among philosophers and literary critics, the series of books that she devoted to Nietzsche contributed to growth, in the 1970s and 1980s, of a body of critical writing that bridges the traditional divide between philosophy and literature. Her groundbreaking *Nietzsche and Metaphor* (1972) offers an epistemological analysis of Nietzsche's demonstration of the intimate relationship between concept and metaphor. *Nietzsche and the Scene of Philosophy* (1979) examines Nietzsche's claim that logic, notably the Aristotelian principle of non-contradiction, fulfils a human need for order in the universe. Developing this argument, Kofman suggests that logic acts as a form of catharsis. In *Explosion I: of Nietzsche's 'Ecce Homo'* (1992) and *Explosion II: les enfants de Nietzsche* (1993), Kofman examines the radical exploration, in *Ecce Homo*, of the unstable boundary between life and literature, sanity and madness.

In *Smothered Words* (1987) Kofman explores the representation of the Holocaust in literature and philosophy, with a focus on the contributions of Maurice Blanchot and Robert Antelme. In this work she also addresses for the first time the death of her father, a Polish-born rabbi, in Auschwitz. In a short autobiographical work, *Rue Ordener, Rue Labat* (1994), she returns to this subject. This text relates both the deportation of her father and her own traumatic experience as a Jewish child in occupied Paris. Shortly before the publication of this autobiographical work, Kofman, who had long suffered from ill health and anxiety, took her own life.

M. Dobie

See also: Death; Feminism

KOJÈVE, ALEXANDRE (1902–68) Russian-born French philosopher, noteworthy for his anthropological reading of Hegel which influenced French thinkers for decades, and for his thoughts on the 'end of history', which some think have acquired new relevance with the collapse of the Soviet Union and the end of the Cold War. After the Russian Revolution, Kojève studied in Russia and then for a number of years in Germany, where he wrote a dissertation under the direction of Karl Jaspers. He later emigrated to France, where he became a citizen and changed his name from its Russian original to that by which he is now known. When his friend, Alexandre Koyré, was obliged to give up his course on Hegel's philosophy of religion at the École Pratique des Hautes Études, with only the summer to prepare Kojève stepped into the breach with a seminar on Hegel's *Phenomenology of Spirit*, which lasted from 1933 until 1939.

Kojève's now-famous seminar had a mesmerising effect on his students, which included such future leaders of French intellectual life as the poets Raymond Queneau and André Breton; the psychoanalyst Jacques Lacan; the philosophers Georges Bataille, Pierre Klossowski, Alexandre Koyré, Gaston Fessard, Jean Desanti and Eric Weil; and the sociologists Raymond Aron and Aron Gurwitsch. Without personal ambition, Kojève later became a French civil servant, confining his work on philosophy to his leisure time. His course on Hegel, which was transcribed and later edited for publication by Queneau, only appeared in 1947 as *Introduction to the Reading of Hegel. Lectures on the Phenomenology of Spirit.*

French Hegel studies really began again at the end of 1920s with the work of Jean Wahl. With Jean Hyppolite, author of an important commentary on the *Phenomenology*, Kojève is generally regarded as one of the two most important French Hegel specialists. Unlike Hyppolite, who offers a careful, reliable, scholarly exposition of Hegel, Kojève provides not an exposition but rather a highly original, unorthodox, often arbitrary, but unquestionably brilliant and very influential reading of the *Phenomenology*. There is an evident disparity between Hegel's text and Kojève's reading of that text, in that, like Feuerbach and Lukács – the other singularly important Marxist Hegelian – Kojève proposes an anthropological reading. Kojève's approach was anachronistic in two ways. First, he adopts a strongly Marxist interpretation, albeit one which, unlike that of Lukács, was entirely unconcerned with Marxist orthodoxy. Second, Kojève brings a Heideggerian inflection to his reading of Hegel's view of death. In general terms, Kojève reads the *Phenomenology* as a description of human existence from an anti-religious and atheist perspective, including a critique of the extension of dialectic to nature and an anti-dialectical view of method as basically the same in Husserl and Hegel. An instance of his own view he attributes to Hegel is the idea of the end of history in Napoleon, which Kojève amends to find in Stalin.

Kojève's thought of the 'end of history' is ambivalent. On the one hand, the enormous productivity unleashed by capitalism, coupled with enlightened redistribution policies, produce a realm of peace and freedom from want. On the other hand, those who live in such a world, happy as they are with sports, play, art and so forth, have lost the power of the negative, that striving and struggle which has always defined the human. With the end of history, then, we have also reached the 'death of man'.

T. Rockmore

KRISTEVA, JULIA (1940–) Bulgarian-born philosopher, living in Paris and writing in French on psychoanalysis, semiotics and other topics. Taking up the question 'Why do we speak?' in all of its ambiguities, Kristeva addresses the relationships of meaning to language, meaning to life and language to life. In fact, Kristeva's most famous contribution to language theory, the distinction between the symbolic and the semiotic elements of signification, speaks to these questions in a revolutionary way, opening pathways rather than resigning us to an impasse.

Kristeva maintains that all signification is composed of two elements, the symbolic and the semiotic. The symbolic element governs what philosophers might think of as referential meaning. That is, the symbolic is the element of signification that sets up the structures by which signs operate; it is the structure or grammar that governs the ways in which signs can refer. The semiotic element, on the other hand, is the organisation of drives in language. It is associated with rhythms and tones that are meaningful parts of language and yet do not represent or signify something. In *Revolution in Poetic Language* (1974), Kristeva maintains that rhythms and tones do not represent bodily drives; rather bodily drives are discharged through rhythms and tones. In *New Maladies of the Soul* (1993), she discusses different ways of representing that are not linguistic in a traditional sense. There, Kristeva says that the meaning of the semiotic element of language is 'translinguistic' or 'nonlinguistic'; she explains this by describing these semiotic elements as irreducible to language because they 'turn toward language even though they are irreducible to its grammatical and logical structures'. This is to say, they are irreducible to the symbolic element of language, the domain of position and judgement associated with the grammar or structure of language that enables it to signify something.

The dialectical oscillation between the semiotic and the symbolic is what makes signification possible. Without the symbolic element of signification, we have only sounds or delirious babble. But without the semiotic element of signification, signification would be empty and we would not speak, for the semiotic provides the motivation for engaging in signifying processes. We have a bodily need to communicate and the symbolic provides the structure necessary to communicate; both elements are essential to signification, and it is the tension between them that makes signification dynamic. The semiotic both motivates signification and threatens the symbolic element. The semiotic provides the movement or negativity and the symbolic provides the stasis or stability that keeps signification both dynamic and structured.

While the symbolic element gives signification its meaning in the strict sense of reference, the semiotic element gives signification 'meaning' in a broader sense. That is, the semiotic element makes symbols matter; by discharging drive force in symbols, it makes them significant in the sense of 'important', carrying weight. Even though the semiotic challenges meaning in the strict sense, meaning in the terms of the symbolic, it gives symbols their meaning for our lives. Signification makes our lives meaningful, in both senses of meaning – signifying something and having significance – through its symbolic and semiotic elements. The interdependence of the symbolic and semiotic elements of signification guarantees a relationship between language and life, signification and experience; the interdependence between the symbolic and semiotic guarantees a relationship between body (*soma*) and soul (*psyche*).

By insisting that the language expresses bodily drives through its semiotic element, Kristeva's articulation of the relationship between language and the body circumvents the traditional problems of representation. The tones and rhythms of language, the materiality of language, is bodily. Kristeva's theory addresses the problem of the relationship between language and bodily experience by postulating that, through the semiotic element, bodily drives manifest themselves in language. Instead of lamenting what is lost, absent or impossible in language, Kristeva marvels at this other realm that makes its way into language. The force of language is living drive force transferred into language. Signification is like a transfusion of the living body into language. This is why psychoanalysis can be effective; the analyst can diagnose the active drive force as it is manifest in the analysand's language. Language is not cut off from the body. And, while, for Kristeva, bodily drives involve a type of violence, negation or force, this process does not merely necessitate sacrifice and loss. The drives are not sacrificed to signification; rather bodily drives are an essential semiotic element of signification.

In *Tales of Love* (1983), Kristeva identifies meaning – both the meaning of language and of life – with love. She describes the contemporary melancholic or borderline personality as a child with no adequate images of a loving mother or a loving father. Kristeva suggests that (in the West) Christianity has traditionally provided images of a loving mother and a loving father, as problematic as those images might be. But, with contemporary suspicions of religion, she seems to ask, where can we find images of loving mothers and fathers? And, without images of loving mothers and fathers, how can we love ourselves?

For Kristeva, love provides the support for fragmented meanings and fragmented subjectivities; love provides the support to reconnect words and affects. She says that 'love is something spoken, and it is only that'. Our lives have meaning for us, we have a sense of ourselves, through the narratives which we prepare to tell others about our experience. Even if we do not tell our stories, we live our experience through the stories that we construct in order to 'tell ourselves' to another, a loved one. As we wander through our days, an event takes on its significance in the narrative that we construct for an imaginary conversation with a loved one as we are living it. The living body is a loving body, and the loving body is a speaking body. Without love we are nothing but walking corpses. Love is essential to the living body and it is essential in bringing the living body to life in language.

K. Oliver

See also: abjection; Cosmopolitanism; Death; Feminism; Poststructuralism; the semiotic; Time

L

LACAN, JACQUES (1901–81) French psychiatrist and psychoanalyst, who redefined Freud's work in the *Écrits* (1966), the *Autres écrits* (2001) and 26 *Seminars* held between 1953 and 1979. Lacan's output is characterised by its conceptual coherence and by the huge body of knowledge put to work: philosophy (Plato, Aristotle, Descartes, Kant, Hegel, Marx, Kierkegaard, Heidegger, Wittgenstein, Koyré, Kojève, Popper); logic (Aristotle, Boole, Hittinka); mathematics and topology (Gödel, Moebius, Cantor); linguistics (Saussure); game theory; literature (Sophocles, Jaufré Rudel, Arnaut Daniel and courtly love,

Shakespeare, Sade, Claudel, Gide, Duras); religion (Judaism, Christianity); mythology and art – no field of human endeavour is left untouched by Lacan.

Lacan's formidable contribution to the practice of psychoanalysis will not be treated here. Instead we will consider the following two points as those most relevant to philosophy: (1) a (pre-) ontology of the subject arrived at via the elaboration and refinement of Freud's theories, which he submits to a logical and mathematical formalisation, in order to ensure their pertinence and transmissibility; (2) an epistemology in which psychoanalysis operates as a reflective link repositioning the humanities and hard sciences, a repositioning that results in an ethics of singularity.

Lacan's (pre-) ontology of the subject is deeply rooted in a medieval philosophical controversy, the quarrel of universals, where he positions himself squarely on the realists' side. With a caveat against any idealism still lingering on either side of the quarrel, he posits his own brand of materialism: matter, in his theory, will be language, 'the signifier transcended into language'. Boole, Tarski and Saussure, among others, have shown this linguistic matter susceptible to a mathematical and logical formalisation. Lacan will go one step beyond towards topology and the theory of knots and strings. Signifying matter therefore organises the underlying structure of Lacan's symbolic-real axis (the axis of the signifier and the unconscious) and can be rigorously, up to a point, formalised.

As a matter of fact, for Lacan, language, contrary to what it was for medieval thought, is not a projection of an internal soul or thought onto the world, a representation of something that pre-exists it, but is a material exteriority that obeys its own laws and thus structures the human subject and the vision this subject has of the world. This allows him to position himself outside the entire Western philosophical tradition (for which a self-transparent consciousness is an almost insuperable tenet) and to map out, as far as possible, the logic of the unconscious as a place ('another stage', as Freud would say) where 'something' thinks. The unified thinking subject thus gives way to a split subject, divided between conscious and unconscious thinking, and mastered in part by the signifying chain hidden in the unconscious.

In return, the philosophical tradition and the different world-views it promotes are reread as instances of a forgetting or repressing of unconscious thinking. However, the unconscious resists a complete formalisation, be it mathematical or topological: this defines it as an impossible real, beyond any possible representation. Indeed, because of Gödel's incompleteness theorem (in sciences), and because of the existence of an unrepresentable unconscious (in humanities), no attempt at a totalising representation of reality is possible: as he says in *Radiophonie* (1970), 'Nothing is whole'. Any world-view (including philosophy) that falls prey to the seduction of totalisation proposes an imaginary structure that represses the real unconscious. This situates Lacan, as he claims in *Seminar XI* (1964), in a pre-ontology; the impossible unconscious is neither a being nor a non-being, but an interdicted being, whose existence differentiates the psychoanalytic view from philosophy's (in particular the Presocratics and Heidegger).

Lacan's epistemology substitutes for the question, 'is psychoanalysis a science?' another one, 'what would be a science that would include psychoanalysis?' Going beyond the seemingly irreducibility of science and humanities, Lacan unifies them around a void, which conjoins matter's and the unconscious's ultimate resistance to formalisation. Indeed, Lacan's enlightening of science by psychoanalysis, and vice-versa, constitutes the cornerstone of a general epistemology that avoids the trap of a metaphorisation of science itself. Lacan uses scientific tools like topology and knots and strings theory according to their own principles, even if he submits them to a special use that is hard to comprehend for mathematicians and even harder for humanists. Although it is 'general', Lacan's epistemology will not be a totalising one, because of our representations' inherent incompleteness. Seen through the prism of psychoanalysis, science appears as the ultimate symbolic repression: 'Science is the abolition of the subject'. This repression that cannot be held in check because there is no internal reason for its possible entropy: its expansion is limitless, as is the universe it inhabits.

This does not mean that Lacan takes refuge in a desperate irrationalism. Quite to the contrary, he uses science's tools to map out where resistance is possible. Hence his recourse, outside of science (there is no ethics of science in itself), to an ethics of desire in *Seminar VII, The ethics of psychoanalysis* (1959–60). We may call it an 'ethics of singularity', since Lacan calls on individuals not to make any concession about their own desire, in order to hold in check the increasing demands of the superego and the symbolic order, of which science is an integral part. This ethics is at the same time entirely logical (it is the only form the subject can oppose to its own abolition by science) and paradoxical: how can we not make concession about our desire, if, according to Lacan, it is unconscious, therefore impossible to incarnate in an image? How can we resist the expansion of the superego if it is also beyond the reach of our consciousness?

The answer to these questions, for the psychoanalyst, and perhaps for all of us, is to take subjects one by one, and always stress the ability of singular analysands to finally tolerate what is a structural lack of figuration for the unconscious core of our being. As far as the broader society is concerned, Lacanian ethics may be summarised as a word of caution about the repression of singular desires by the agglomeration of individuals as numbers in a set (the probability calculation of life insurance is here a good example), lest these desires reappear under the wildest, most phantasmatic and most aggressive forms of the return of the repressed.

A. Leupin

See also: anti-philosophy; imaginary order; real; Structuralism; subject, topology of; symbolic order

LANGUAGE One of the central topics of both the continental and analytic traditions of philosophy in the twentieth century. This pre-occupation with language is often called the 'linguistic turn'; we will focus on four of its aspects, which all emerge at the turn of the century in different parts of the West. (1) The 'analytic tradition', in its purest form, focuses on the conceptual analysis of ordinary language, and flourished in Great Britain, the United States and other parts of the Anglophone world, finding its roots in the writings of a German, Frege, a contemporary of Husserl and a major influence on Wittgenstein and Austin. (2) At the time Frege was writing, German hermeneutics was being refreshed by Dilthey; this impetus was to increase in the hands of Heidegger and find its most explicit form in the writings of Heidegger's student Gadamer. (3) In French-speaking Geneva, structural linguistics was developing in the hands of Saussure, a contemporary of both Frege and Dilthey. (4) In the United States, James and Peirce produced what has come to be called 'pragmatism'. These four strands developed throughout the twentieth century, sometimes independently and sometimes in concert; in addition, their geographical contours are quite complex.

As suggested, the origins of each of the philosophical approaches to language can be indexed to a particular country. Hermeneutics, for instance, is primarily of German origin. Its modern incarnation dates back to Schleiermacher and the era of German Romanticism. The history of German hermeneutics, from Schleiermacher to Gadamer, might be summed up as the move from the search for a method for the interpretation of historical texts (originally religious texts) to philosophical hermeneutics, where the hermeneutic task gains, initially in the hands of Heidegger, fundamental philosophical significance. It does so, in brief, because what follows from Heidegger's reading of Kant's First

Critique in *Kant and the Problem of Metaphysics* (1929) is the centrality
to philosophy of the understanding of being and being's self understanding; in Heidegger's own words, 'language is the house of being'.
However, it was Gadamer who produced the classic twentieth-century
text in German philosophical hermeneutics: *Truth and Method* (1975).
Gadamer, in one sense, turns Schleiermacher on his head by employing
hermeneutic understanding in the service of a critique of the very
notion of 'method'. Some of the most influential work in late twentieth-
century hermeneutics has come not from Germany, however, but from
France, from Ricoeur. There are subtle differences between the
hermeneutics of Gadamer and Ricoeur; while the latter shows the
influence of structural linguistics and psychoanalysis, Gadamer is very
much a Heideggerian, focusing on questions of ontology.

Structural linguistics is based on the writings of Saussure, whose
approach to linguistics has been influential not only in philosophy and
linguistics but in twentieth-century anthropology (Lévi-Strauss), in
the 'history of systems of thought' (early Foucault), in political
philosophy (Althusser) and in psychoanalysis (Lacan). However, it
is in the hands of the poststructuralists that French linguistic philosophy has gained fame and infamy in equal measure. Poststructuralism
is most readily identified with the work of (the later) Foucault,
Deleuze, Kristeva, Irigaray and Derrida, the last of whose work has
been probably the most controversial in implication and reception.

Derrida's corpus is vast, and one might say of varying quality.
However, it would take a hard-nosed cynic (of which there are plenty in
the academies of Britain and the United States) to deny the brilliance
with which, in his first major work *Speech and Phenomena* (1967), he
deconstructs Husserl's theory of signs. We might also mention in this
context *Limited Inc* (1977, 1988), Derrida's response to criticisms
offered by the American philosopher John Searle on the former's
work on the speech act theory of Austin. Finally, there is also an
encounter with Gadamer (*Dialogue and Deconstruction: The Gadamer-
Derrida Encounter*, 1989), in which the relative emphases of philosophical hermeneutics and (Derrida's) poststructuralism are made clear
in the centrality the former gives to conversation and the latter to the
written text. Derrida seeks to deconstruct the 'philosophy of presence',
whereby one might, for example, in the case of linguistic meaning,
reduce meaning to the intentions of the author, to an interpretation of
the intended recipient or to the context of authorship or reading of the
text. Derrida seeks to keep in play all aspects that contribute to
meaning, including an opening to the unforeseeable nature of future
contexts, thus disrupting attempts to offer reductionist accounts –

accounts that rely on just one aspect. Derrida, therefore, moves beyond structuralism in refusing to replace 'presence' with 'structure', but rather keeping all aspects in play.

The other two strands – American pragmatism and the Anglophone analytic philosophy stemming from the work of the Austrian logician Frege – have had complex geographical itineraries. In Germany there has been a burgeoning interest in Peirce, where both Habermas and Apel have both employed his work in the context of their own work in 'discourse ethics'. The appeal of Peirce's work seems to be based on (and often explicitly linked to) a worry that Heideggerian/Gadamerian philosophical hermeneutics and Derridean/Foucauldian poststructuralism (and for that matter Wittgensteinian approaches) are politically conservative in their implications for moral, political and social philosophy. It is questionable whether this diagnosis does more than demonstrate a lack of understanding; however, this approach is influential, at least through its employment and application in the social sciences, and thus is of more than passing note.

In France the contemporary philosophical landscape is also quite complex, for there we find little mainstream interest in its 'own' poststructuralist tradition and instead a growing interest in what they would call 'Anglo-Saxon' philosophers such as Frege, Quine and Davidson; Wittgensteinian approaches to philosophy are also important, following the work of Jacques Bouveresse. Thus while it serves an initial heuristic purpose to see the different strands discussed above as indexed to different countries, it only serves to do so in terms of their genesis. When it comes to their genealogy things become more complex. Just as there are many philosophers in France who would keenly distance themselves from 'native' poststructuralism, there are many in Germany who wish to do the same from what they see as the conservatism inherent to home-grown philosophical hermeneutics.

P. Hutchinson

LATOUR, BRUNO (1947–) French philosopher and pioneering Science and Technology Studies figure, whose influences include Deleuze and Serres. Spanning the philosophy, history, sociology and the anthropology of science, his research extends to topics as varied as microbial biology, religion, aesthetics, urban planning and the judicial system. Some of the technical terms he uses ('black box', 'hybrid' and 'quasi-object') have found their way into the philosophical lexicon.

Latour appeals to the image of a software designer to depict his writings as compatible with one another, although not subsumable into a unified field of thought. In *Chasing Technoscience: Matrix for Materiality* (2003), he notes that he is what Annemarie Mol calls an 'empirical philosopher', someone who inquires into time, space and agency by way of fieldwork and case studies. He characterises this research programme as 'experimental metaphysics', claiming it is a non-reductive style of inquiry that allows analysts to suspend modern concepts, such as nature and culture, to see how actors build their worlds in ways that defy modern categorisation. Latour's most explicit dialogue with philosophy can be found in *We Have Never Been Modern* (1993) and *Pandora's Hope*: *Essays on the Reality of Science Studies* (1999).

In Latour's early writing, scientific culture is examined anthropologically. He turns scientists into objects of study in order to discover what they actually do, as opposed to what they and traditional theorists claim they do. In *Laboratory Life: the Social Construction of Scientific Facts* (1979), co-authored with Steve Woolgar, he provides what some consider the first detailed study of the daily activities of scientists in their natural habitat. He highlights the collaborative/competitive dimensions of science, focuses upon its reliance on networks and forms of rhetoric, and shows how scientific facts become established through the entwined engagement of humans and non-humans. Latour became critical of the human-centred research trajectory found in the 'sociology of scientific knowledge' (SSK), embraced and ultimately abandoned Actor-Network Theory (ANT), and became best known for his extended meditations on materiality. In *Science and Action: How to Follow Scientists and Engineers through Society* (1987), he characterises the main products of a scientific laboratory – preprints, graphs, traces, photographs, published papers – as 'inscriptions'. By differentiating between science in-action and ready-made science, Latour analyses published scientific results and then works backwards towards appeals to nature. He inverts the traditional image of science, showing how 'trials of strength' underlie scientific facts, and postulates that nature is not a transcendent substance but the effect generated by the process of research and controversy. In *The Pasteurisation of France* (1988) he uses a modified and radicalised semiotics to symmetrically describe humans, including Louis Pasteur, and non-humans, including microbes, as 'actants' who are formed together through negotiated processes of co-constitution. While Latour's endorsement of symmetry has come under criticism from a number of fronts, his network of allies seems to be ever-expanding.

E. Selinger

See also: Actor-Network Theory; Epistemology; quasi-object

LEAP A drastic change of being with little or no rational justification. 'Leap of faith' is an expression associated with Kierkegaard, although not actually used by him. The idea of a leap is nevertheless important to Kierkegaard. In the *Philosophical Fragments* (1843) he argues that faith cannot be derived from a series of progressive approximations, as in the figure of the sorites. In relation to other forms of consciousness, faith requires a *metabasis in allo genos*, a change to another genus, higher than that of reason. This requires a deliberate leap. The same may be said of sin. In *The Concept of Anxiety* (1844), anxiety is depicted as a neutral state from which either sin or faith may emerge. Either will come into being as a leap, an act of freedom that cannot be deduced or inferred from the preceding state.

Heidegger will also use the term at key points of his later philosophy. Modern philosophy, he claimed, is dominated by the paradigm of scientific-technological knowledge. In *What Calls for Thinking?* (1954) he claims that to think otherwise than in the mode of science-technology we must leap into an immediate awareness of things as they are, such as a tree in blossom. The leap is not into an 'other' world but onto the ground on which we already are. Heideggerian hermeneutics also calls for something similar to a leap. If we wish to understand the earliest Greek philosophers, we must leap out of our language and hear their words in Greek. The leap thus becomes the presupposition of a new beginning of philosophy after science and metaphysics.

G. Pattison

LE DOEUFF, MICHELE (1948–) French philosopher with major contributions to feminism, epistemology and the way we view the tradition of Western philosophy. Her first major work is *The Philosophical Imaginary* (1980), in which she shows how philosophy defines itself by its rejection of certain forms of thinking as 'off limits', being derived from less elevated sources. Discourse in images, one of these outcasts, may be dispatched upstream to a source in a 'primitive soul', a 'child within us'. Or it may be consigned 'downstream', in order to explain why philosophy is never properly received. Le Doeuff shows this process at work in recent philosophy and traces the problem back to philosophy's classical origins. She develops a new use of terms familiar in recent French philosophy: the image as a point of tension, the 'imaginary' of a discourse, the historical 'detour', 'intertextuality', the disruption of 'genre' by a 'nomadic' rationality.

In a monograph attached to her translation (with Margaret Llasera) of Francis Bacon's *New Atlantis*, Le Doeuff developed her 'critical epistemology'. In *Hipparchia's Choice* (1989), she criticised the epistemology and ethics of existentialism, while exhibiting the creative use made of it by Beauvoir in *The Second Sex*. Rather than a single theory to replace postmodernist reactions to phenomenology and to Marxism, Le Doeuff creates forms of rigorous philosophy that nevertheless do not close an issue, but require the reader to resume the action. Producing philosophy through its history, she responds to the dilemma that either one is bound to 'get the classical authors wrong' or else that it is only the modern commentator who knows what the classical author was really saying. Philosophy becomes 'neither a monument nor an effect which is blind to its origins . . . but *an effort to shift thinking from one state to another*'.

Her work in the early 1990s focused on how research by women is buried, and on philosophical and popular receptions of scientific ideas. In *The Sex of Knowing* (1998), Le Doeuff continued to expose the strategies by which women's research and ideas continue, are overlooked or disenfranchised. At the same time Le Doeuff opposes vigorously the 'imaginary' of a special feminine way of knowing that 'masculine' knowledge cannot recognise. Le Doeuff cuts across prejudices of both the analytic and the poststructuralist traditions. Reason is liberating rather than oppressive; the idea of reason as 'masculine' is a male fantasy. Also, in rejecting a dichotomy between reasoning and thinking in images she exhibits the variety of forms of reason. She has created new forms of philosophical writing, making important contributions to our understanding of the self, the possibility of a philosophical ethics and the relation of women to knowledge.

M. Deutscher

See also: critical epistemology; Feminist Rereadings of the Tradition; particularism; philosophical imaginary

LEBENSPHILOSOPHIE (Life-philosophy) A term retrospectively applied to a diverse set of thinkers – Bergson, Dilthey, Nietzsche, Simmel and even William James – who were seen as affirming the concreteness, irrationality and passion of life in protest against nineteenth-century rationalism and positivism and its bland faith in progress. This term was often connected with *Weltanschauungsphilosophie* (world-view philosophy), which was disparagingly said to express an attitude about life rather than a reasoned position. *Lebensphilosophie* was used positively to describe a new more concrete way of philosophising by Max Scheler and polemically as a designation for irrationality and relativism by Heinrich Rickert. Husserl's polemical essay 'Philosophy as a Rigorous Science' (1911) should be read in this context

Lebensphilosophie has roots in the pantheistic and vitalistic reactions to the growth of the modern natural sciences in thinkers as diverse as Giordano Bruno, the Cambridge Platonists, Spinoza and Leibniz. As a philosophical reflection on nature and life, which both used and was in tension with the natural sciences, it took further impetus from the reflective account of nature developed in Kant's *Critique of Judgement* and the philosophy of nature of Rousseau, Goethe, the Romantics, Schopenhauer and the German Idealists, especially Schelling. Nineteenth-century *Lebensphilosophie* should be distinguished from (1) vitalism, which sought to re-establish a traditional teleological account of nature through scientific and other means, and (2) Darwinism, which rejected not only teleology in nature but also the possibility of a philosophy of nature outside of the natural sciences.

Notwithstanding their retrospective labelling as avatars of *Lebensphilosophie*, Bergson, Dilthey, Nietzsche and Simmel were not influenced by one another and had radically different philosophical methodologies and concerns. Although they all pursued questions of life and nature in response to the dominant scientism and the debates between Darwinism and vitalism in biology, they did not leave behind a common message or school. Even the accusation of 'irrationalism' is contestable. For example, Nietzsche did not naively oppose the Apollonian and Dionysian but his thought, a genealogy in the service of life, used both. Bergson and Dilthey, on the other hand, both developed methodologically sophisticated approaches to the question of concrete life, the former through intuition and the latter through a historically informed hermeneutics of socially embodied life. Simmel also connected life-philosophy and social scientific research.

Lebensphilosophie became a fashionable and quickly worn-out term after the end of the First World War, when it was given a vitalistic and even racist direction. It was employed by thinkers such as Oswald Spengler who developed neo-conservative and culturally pessimistic critiques of the decline of the vitality of the West in its growing modernity, rationality and technology. This popularised and vulgarised *Lebensphilosophie* is part of the context for the emergence of European fascism.

Philosophers influenced by Dilthey continued to use the term constructively: Georg Misch, for example, in his neglected but significant work *Lebensphilosophie und Phänomenologie* (1929), discussed Heidegger's relation to Dilthey and life-philosophy. Yet the term faded with the National Socialist assumption of power and has since been primarily used as a historical designation. Even so, *Lebensphilosophie* has often been a highly contentious and contested word. After the Second World War, Lukács argued in his polemical work *The*

Destruction of Reason that irrational and decisionistic life-philosophy constitutes a direct line from Schelling through Nietzsche and Heidegger to Hitler, an argument modified by Habermas to include recent French philosophy in his *Philosophical Discourse of Modernity*.

The legacy of *Lebensphilosophie* has been significant and widespread. In Germany, for instance, the early Heidegger positively engaged the thought of Dilthey and often that of his colleague York von Wartenburg, although by the late 1930s Heidegger, in response to the popularised use of the word and biologistic and racist interpretations of Nietzsche, had come to interpret *Lebensphilosophie* polemically as another form of metaphysical domination, the making of life into a present-at-hand resource for manipulation. In France, Merleau-Ponty and Levinas critically engaged Bergson, while Deleuze productively revived issues of life and nature by engaging and transforming the life-philosophy of Nietzsche and Bergson.

E. Nelson

LEFEBVRE, HENRI (1901–91) French sociologist, historian and philosopher renowned for *The Production of Space* (1974) which influenced spatial theories in several disciplines. Lefebvre's work engaged, critiqued and influenced surrealists, existentialists, communists and the Situationists, as well as theorists and practitioners of urban studies and architecture. Focused on everyday life, the body and lived experience, and antipathic toward capitalism and the state, he was a trenchant critic of Bauhaus, Le Corbusier, Fascism, consumerism and globalisation. He evolved from staunch Marxist to steadfast critic of the French Communist Party (which eventually banished him), and ultimately became an important figure in the events of May 1968. Throughout his career, Lefebvre was not only anti-modernist but also wary of structuralism. He distrusted any homogenising and dogmatic system (the last sentence of *Production* reads 'And we are concerned with nothing that even remotely resembles a system'), and kept his distance from totalising semiological and poststructuralist projects as well.

In his mature works, Lefebvre uses an array of techniques to construct a 'metaphilosophy' that situates space with its attendant concepts and practices at the epicentre of human existence. To Lefebvre, all social space, at all scales of consideration, is produced. (Meanwhile, the unproduced, creative spaces of 'nature' are trapped within the complexly interwoven grids that constitute social reality; hence they are beyond our recapture.) Lefebvre's metaphilosophy seeks to create awareness of social space as produced by the state and by capitalism, and he calls repeatedly for the recovery of 'authentic' spaces that neither commodify nor oppress, yet that are not simply 'leisure spaces' set aside for workers. His is an activist project: we need to construct new or retooled pathways, buildings, living spaces, communal gathering-places and other concrete works that express and bring forth the truth of spaces as much as we need to reconceptualise lived space. Otherwise, capitalism and the 'logic' of markets (with all the force of the state behind them) will create 'true space' that turns us all into labourer-consumers and the world into pure resource.

Lefebvre's theory of space sets forth three principles or modes of production: 'spatial practice', 'representations of space' and 'representational space'. (1) Spatial practice is what people – the enactors of social space – do. Though this may seem obvious, it is a considerable conceptual leap for those who assume that space (as a container) precedes activities in space. Spatial practice is ordered, hence spaces take on order, through (2) representations of space, the plans established by social bodies with the power to create blueprints for the world, thus establishing and defining what 'true space' is. In the West, these representations of space have tended to exclude the spatial practices of workers, privileging instead the conceptions of priests, mathematicians, architects, composers, artists, economists and so forth. A prime example is the invention of perspective in landscape painting, with the consequent 'true space' that such paintings engendered in the world. Societies are thus said to inhabit (3) representational spaces that contain and are produced by spatial codes that change over time. The representational spaces of everyday life are produced by contemporary spatial codes, fragments of discarded codes, and echoes of revolutionary codes (such as those of May 1968). The complex mixtures of spatial codes allow experiments that may return spaces to the control of humanised, anti-capitalist, everyday spatial practice.

M. Bonta

See also: Geography; Space

LEFORT, CLAUDE (1924–) French philosopher and post-Marxist political theorist, and frequent commentator on the work of Merleau-Ponty, who was his teacher at the *lycée*. Lefort also wrote a major work on Machiavelli entitled *Le Travail de l'Oeuvre Machiavel*, which contains the key to Lefort's political philosophy. That someone who was once a Marxist would be attracted to Machiavelli is not anomalous, since the Florentine saw the class conflict between the grandee and the people as essential. But, unlike Marx, Machiavelli did not envision a resolution of this conflict. Lefort's interpretation of Machiavelli is novel in a number of respects. He does not interpret *The Prince* as a work written under the pressure of events, or as its author's attempt to get a job with the Medicis. Nor does he interpret it as a manual on governance, and unlike Leo Strauss, he does not view it as a 'teaching of evil'. Most importantly, Lefort does not present Machiavelli as the founder of empirical political science. He views him rather as the first thinker to have elaborated a distinctively modern political theory, that is a theory not dependent on religion or metaphysics, but also not positivistic. The symbolic exchange between the prince and the people, to the disadvantage of the grandee, generates the image of the prince, which is to say a transcendence of the political relative to social conflict.

After the Second World War, Lefort joined the French Trotskyite movement, which shows that although he was a Marxist, he was never fascinated with the USSR. He broke with Trotskyism over the issue of the nature of the Soviet Union. While the Trotskyite considered it a 'worker's state' with a 'bureaucratic deformation', Lefort saw it as a new type of social formation characterised by the dominance of a bureaucratic class. After his break with the Trotskyites, he formed a group called *Socialisme ou Barbarie* with Cornelius Castoriadis and a few others to pursue an independent leftist vision. Eventually Lefort came to view the USSR not only in terms of a real oppression of the masses by a bureaucratic class, but also as the phantasmatic attempt of the leader to incarnate the body of the people. This analysis converges with Lefort's reading of Machiavelli, for whom the transcendence of the image of the prince frees the political stage for conflict. Whenever, by contrast, the image of the leader incarnates the people, political conflict is excluded, since all opposition must be presented as coming from the 'outside', as instigated by 'enemies of the people': the mad, the Jews and so forth. As early as 1956 Lefort detected signs of a fatal instability in the USSR; excluding as illegitimate all conflict, it had repressed a fundamental dimension of any possible society.

In Lefort's novel conception, modern democracy does not instantiate principles taken from the Enlightenment or elsewhere but is the determinate negation of medieval monarchy. Following Kantorowitz, Lefort sees monarchy as the secularisation of the mystical body of Christ, whereby the king, by the doubling of his body (body of nature and body of grace), is the intersection of the earthly and the supersensible. In monarchy the king's natural body figures as the image of the unity of the realm and his second body, the body of grace, is linked to God; legitimacy is then viewed as descending from a transcendent God.

In democratic revolutions the king is killed, both his body of nature and his body of grace. The figure of the king is effaced, but the place that it occupied is not. Legitimacy descends no longer from God but from the people; however, the 'identity of the people' is always indefinite. Thus it cannot occupy the place of power made vacant by the death of a king. This place remains, but it remains as an empty place. In Lefort's conception of modern democracy, the markers which connected the society to the supersensible have been effaced, and with them the sense of certainty that premodern society experienced. For Lefort, democracy is not simply a form of government; rather it is a way of life in which everything is subject to question and all legitimacy is attained discursively and provisionally. Thus totalitarianism is a counter-revolution against the uncertainty of democracy. Totalitarianism attempts to fill the empty place, to reincarnate the being of the people in the body of the leader; this body, however, does not refer to any transcendence but saturates the social space, thereby excluding conflict, killing politics itself along with all would-be adversaries.

B. Flynn

See also: Socialisme ou Barbarie

LENIN, V. I. (1870–1924) Russian revolutionary leader and political thinker. The leader of the Bolshevik Party and of the Russian Revolution of October 1917, Lenin is the most influential Marxist political leader and theorist after Marx and Engels. Founding figure of twentieth-century communism, he is revered and reviled as such; his version of Marxist theory and his organisational principles were adopted by official Communist Parties throughout the world under the title of Marxism-Leninism. This, it is claimed, is merely a development and systematisation of Marxism. Its main components are dialectical and historical materialism.

Politically, Lenin insisted that communism, as a revolutionary movement, needed to be led by a disciplined and centrally organised Party. He extended the Marxist analysis of capitalism to cover the development of imperialism (*Imperialism: The Highest Stage of Capitalism*, 1916). He clarified and developed the Marxist analysis of the state in socialist society (*State and Revolution*, 1917). His ideas, embodied in the international communist movement, have had an unprecedented impact on modern political life.

Lenin's main purely philosophical work is *Materialism and Empirio-Criticism* (1907), written, after only a few months study of philosophy, to combat the influence of positivist and neo-Kantian ideas in the Bolshevik Party. This stridently polemical work puts forward a simple version of the reflection theory of knowledge and a mechanistic sort of materialism. It defends the view that there is an objective world independent of consciousness and that our knowledge is a reflection of it. Though this theory is stated with decisive clarity, it is not fully worked out or defended against familiar philosophical difficulties raised by Berkeley, Kant and other philosophers. Lenin returned to philosophy during the First World War, when he studied and made extensive notes, which are published in Volume 38 of his *Collected Works*, on Hegel's *Science of Logic* and other works. In these he appears to correct his earlier mechanistic approach and to develop an illuminating understanding of Hegelian dialectic. His philosophical and political legacy has continued to be the subject of a great deal of controversy. It is rejected as naive by writers such as Acton, *The Illusion of the Epoch* (1955), but defended equally vigorously by Althusser, *Lenin and Philosophy* (1971).

S. Sayers

See also: Marxism

LEVINAS, EMMANUEL (1906–95) Lithuanian-born philosopher of Jewish heritage who became one of the most celebrated thinkers of postwar France by developing a philosophy of 'radical alterity' with important ethical implications. During the Second World War, Levinas's Lithuanian family was killed by the Nazis; only his wife and daughter survived in hiding in France. He has said that the presentiment and memory of the Nazi horror dominates his personal and intellectual biography.

Levinas's first book, *The Theory of Intuition in Husserl's Phenomenology* (1931), and several early essays on Heidegger played a significant role in introducing phenomenology into France. Levinas reports being attracted to phenomenology's account of the movement of thought which went well beyond traditional accounts of induction, deduction or dialectic. Phenomenology returned thought to its 'forgotten horizons', passing from an abstract object back to the intentional structures of lived experience (for example, to the perceiving or remembering of the object and to the component parts thereof) and then to the wider horizons in which such intentional structures were situated (including, for example, an account of their relation to affective moods and practical comportments and to historically embedded cultural and linguistic formations). To give an account of meaning, for phenomenology, was to give an account of this rich complex of affairs. As this description suggests, Levinas held that the principal innovations of Heidegger's thought were anticipated by Husserl's phenomenology and represented its full flowering.

Levinas invokes this return to the forgotten horizons of experience in describing the method of his first major work, *Totality and Infinity* (1961). He largely accepts the phenomenological account of intentional consciousness, but argues that intentionality 'lives from' an experience that it does not suspect and that cannot be reduced to an intention, namely the ethical relation to the other person. Intentionality, understood formally as the intrinsic directedness of consciousness toward objects, is lived concretely as the ego's appropriation of the world around it. To be an ego or subjectivity is not to be an unchanging substance with the formal identity of A = A; it consists in a dynamic movement of self-identification, in which everything that is distinguished from the self (even aspects of itself) is, upon being so distinguished, thus found to be a moment of the self's own consciousness and is thereby reabsorbed into its identity as a thinker and possessor.

The only being that cannot be so absorbed, Levinas argues, is the other person (*l'Autrui*). This other is not other in the sense of the relative alterity of things, but is an absolute other who resists the ego's appropriative grasp with a resistance that is not physical, but ethical. The formal structure (though not the content) of this relation to absolute alterity is given by the Cartesian 'idea of infinity', read as a figure for the non-adequation of thought to the object it thinks. This non-adequation does not represent the failure of thought, but indicates a positive relation to that which exceeds or shatters the framing structures of intentionality. The idea of infinity is 'deformalised' or 'concretised' in the notion of the relation to the face of the other, which Levinas describes as an unsurpassable relation to the particular and personal, that is as a relation to the other where she is not conceived as *this* or *that* but is encountered as a wholly unique and singular being.

Totality and Infinity thus defends the thesis that the face of the other calls into question the naive spontaneity and freedom of the ego – its appropriative mode of existing in the world – and calls the ego to the work of re-establishing freedom in a manner compatible with justice. The ethical relationship thus precedes ontology and politics because it is the moment in which the ego is called to institute the sorts of rational deliberation and comparison necessary for epistemological and social and political critique.

Similar themes are pursued in *Otherwise Than Being or Beyond Essence* (1974), with some important changes and innovations. Whereas the earlier work described subjectivity primarily in terms of its separation from the other and its mode of being 'at home' in the world, and thus struggled to develop an account of how the other can be encountered without being absorbed into the ego's identity in the same way as a thing, Levinas's later work reinterprets subjectivity in a manner that sees the unicity and identity of the 'I' as due to its relation to the other. In a reinterpretation of sensibility, criticising models which reduce it to a form of passive reception, Levinas argues that the 'I' is bound to others through proximity and contact even before or in the very processes by which it is bound to its own body. The body is interpreted non-reductively in this text as the site of the ethical encounter: skin serves as a privileged figure of the manner in which the body is simultaneously that which protects me or encloses me in a 'site' and that through which I am exposed and vulnerable to the other, in contact with the other even as I am constituted as self-same whole. To have one's *ipseity* constituted in relation to an other is again concretised, as in *Totality and Infinity*, in terms of an infinite responsibility to the other person. This is, Levinas says, the responsibility of a 'hostage' who is responsible even to the point of being responsible for the other's responsibilities. The exorbitance of this responsibility is tamed only through the move from ethics to politics, from the unique perspective of the I–Other relationship to a universal perspective that includes all the others or 'third parties'. Two other innovations of this text deserve special mention. One is Levinas's distinction between 'the Saying and the Said'. The other is the method of the book which Levinas describes as hyperbolic. Expressions such as 'a saying without a said' or a 'passivity more passive than passivity' are not just rhetorical excesses but a method of pushing concepts to an extreme limit at which they break free of their customary significations and make new meanings available.

It is an understatement to say that the texts of the Jewish tradition, the Torah and Talmud, are an important source for Levinas's philosophical thinking. While Levinas denied that these texts served as an extrinsic authority for his philosophical position, he stressed repeatedly that Western culture in his eyes had a double origin in Greek philosophy and in the Biblical Talmudic traditions. The relation of these two sources and of the two halves of Levinas's thought – on the one side, his philosophical writings (sketched above) and, on the other, his Talmudic commentaries and essays on contemporary Jewish cultural and educational issues – is one of the most interesting problems bequeathed to us by the Levinasian corpus.

D. Perpich

See also: Death; Ethics; face; *il y a*; infinity; 'the Saying and the Said'; Subject; Time; totality

LÉVI-STRAUSS, CLAUDE *See* Structuralism

LIMIT-SITUATION (*Grenzsituation*) A central concept of Jaspers' philosophy, taken up and transformed by the early Heidegger in his account of anxiety in the face of one's own death and, more generally, uncanniness. For both thinkers, limit-situations move one from everyday indifference to insecurity in placing the self and its meanings into question. They are the disruptions of experience that potentially cannot be avoided, escaped or changed in an easy way. They cannot be avoided or mastered and yet call for a response.

For Jaspers, limit-situations are the 'breakdowns' and 'breakthroughs' which jolt one out of natural existence in being exposed to forced labour, old-age, illness and accident as well as death. They can disclose either the nothingness or the being of the world, but they indicate the possibility of transcendence precisely in their facticity. As his thought developed, Jaspers emphasised the centrality of limit-situations and communication as demanding individuation as self-transcendence. For Jaspers, it is only this alterity of experience in limit-situations and the alterity of the other in communication that enables the individual to be and become who he or she is.

Extreme experience or limit-situations are also, in different contexts and for different reasons, critical concepts for Bataille – for whom they are often linked to eroticism – and for Foucault, especially in his early study of the history of madness. In *A Thousand Plateaus*, Deleuze and Guattari advocate prudence with such extreme experience in order to experiment with social and somatic body composition.

E. Nelson

LINES OF FLIGHT An expression central to the philosophy of Deleuze and Guattari and their politics of becoming, indicating transformations and differentiations that are always possible because no system can ever circumscribe its elements to the point of preventing their escape. The more a system attempts to stave off change, the more it creates lines for escape. In *A Thousand Plateaus* Deleuze and Guattari identify three lines which, in their co-imbrication, provide the mobile configuration of individuals and groups: (1) a molar line – divided into segments of stable identity (such as gender or race), whereupon exclusive disjunctions prevail (either/or, but not both); (2) a molecular line – hospitable to inclusive disjunctions (either/or, and both), whereupon real transformations take place; and (3) the line of death (the line of becoming imperceptible) – whereupon the vestiges of identity that survive the second line tend to become even less visible.

Lines of flight pre-exist the individuals and groups that flee along their trajectories; they pre-exist as virtual tendencies. But individuals and groups must trace them, thereby assisting in the actualisation of the virtual. Deleuze and Guattari warn against the dangers inherent in all three lines and counsel prudence about them: the entropic death of the exclusive disjunctions; the micro-fascisms of the process of molecular-isation; and the war of self-abolition and destruction, endemic in the line of death. The task of schizoanalysis is to discover the actual lines of flight of individuals or groups, to point out their blockages and to warn against the dangers inhabiting these blockages.

C. Boundas

LINGIS, ALPHONSO (1933–) American philosopher, traveller and teacher, whose radical reformulation of the style and content of philosophical writing has earned him wide praise as the most original and, to many, most important thinker in American continental philosophy. Translator of Levinas and Merleau-Ponty, Lingis has authored ten books and scores of articles, by turns tightly reasoned and lucidly sensual; books such as *Libido* (1985), *Phenomenological Explanations* (1986), *Deathbound Subjectivity* (1989), and *The Impera-tive* (1998) abound in concise, rigorous argumentation, while in other works, such as *Excesses* (1983) *Abuses* (1994), and *Dangerous Emotions* (2000), the meticulous analysis is augmented and illustrated with passages of rare descriptive and evocative power. Lingis's writing encompasses philosophical anthropology and travelogue; explorations of literature (Mishima, Tournier) and post-psychoanalytic theory (Lyotard, Lacan, Deleuze and Guattari); and sustained dialogues with major figures such as Kant, Nietzsche, Husserl, Heidegger and Foucault. Rebelling against anonymous ideality and unnatural barriers of the body-subject or subjugated body, his dominant work constitutes a profoundly redrawn phenomenology of self-other-world.

Deeper than the layout of things on which our projects are dia-grammed, Lingis argues, there is also immersion in the elemental (luminosity, sonority, a clearing upon the supporting earth, atmo-sphere, warmth, the night); enjoyment, as sensual 'movement of involution' into this plenum; the sensory levels, in terms of which things take form, objects as salient and as sensible, which only then mesh with the pathways of our practical worlds. The elements, the levels and the sensuous things, as also the ends ordering the environing fields, function as directives, indeed as perceptual imperatives.

Before language as interchange of signs and the face as a surface of signs there is also, Lingis writes, the vivacity of 'the light in someone's eyes'; beneath the rational and discursive community is another community that demands that I 'expose myself to the one with whom I have nothing in common, the stranger'. The others are experienced bodily, in terms of inner diagrams of motility; affectively, as 'surges and tumults' in the fields of emotional force; erotically, as 'surfaces of excitation', as I 'seep into' the saturating, languorous fever of desire; and ethically, with the imperative to moral respect and responsibility, through an immediate affective sense of the susceptibility and suffering, the neediness and destitution of the other, as 'an arrest put on my hedonism'.

For Lingis, language is not first or fundamentally a means of identification, a commerce of ideal content and coded information, but contestation and consecration via 'sovereign words', words of joy and of lamentation. Language arises out of elemental sonority, the animal cry and murmur, and remains rooted in this affective materiality. Laughter or weeping, blessing or cursing, Lingis argues, communicate not a message but a surge of sensuality, a tone, a carnal energy or rhythm; it is only in these outcries and stirrings, the noise of life, that the other as such, and our own singularity, can be heard, and that we can be there for others, to suffer alongside the downtrodden and oppressed, and the dying, when words fail.

R. Switzer

LITERARY THEORY The reflection on methods of interpreting aesthetic and cultural works. Following the advent of structuralism and poststructuralism, a new literary theory gradually replaced earlier methods of formalist criticism and literary history, so that the dominant ways of interpreting literary works shifted from either close reading ('New Criticism') or a focus on the intentionality of authors to a systematic analysis of the various contexts (social, semiotic, political or ideological) of the work. Such a move was prefigured by Wellek and Warren, who, in *Theory of Literature* (1942), argued that every literary-critical practice must presuppose a theory of literature, even if this is narrowly defined as a set of critical terms or preliminary concepts that condition the act of interpretation. The distinction between theory and criticism occurs, therefore, when the critic analyses the formal object of interpretation by referring to the underlying semiotic and cultural processes in which the object (or 'text') is embedded.

This epistemological shift was first announced in Barthes' writings of the early 1970s ('From Work to Text'; 'The Death of the Author') in which the guiding question that determines the act of interpretation is no longer 'what does it mean?' but rather, 'how does it work or function?' Barthes and other structuralist critics such as Todorov, Rifaterre and Gennette sought instead to reveal the discontinuous and often contradictory nature of literary representation by analysing the multiple codes that inform the historical meaning of texts, and which determine the meaning of literature as a special region of semiotic activity. As a consequence of this new orientation, structuralists often departed from the traditional role of literary criticism, the interpretation of individual works and their authors, and instead began to investigate the nature of literary discourse and its semiotic systems. The structures found in literary and cultural texts could thus be analysed to reveal the relationship between the expressed values of cultural works and the underlying or primary structures of politics, economy, ideology and history.

Whereas structuralist methods of interpretation concentrated on classification, the creation of new taxonomies, and advocated a study of the underlying elements of literary discourse, later poststructuralist theories of interpretation eschewed scientific description in favour of a more 'decentred' or strategic engagement with Western traditions of knowledge and culture. The evolution of literary theory in poststructuralism can be roughly divided following two dominant trends which persisted through the 1980s and early 1990s. According to the first trend, the primary goal of literary theory was to break with the idea of literary representation as a natural reflection of cultural values and norms. Proponents of this view, often associated with the 'deconstructive' writings of Derrida and de Man, often privileged the function of literature itself as an artificial or highly reflexive form of representation through which language itself is unmasked as historically and ideologically motivated. The second trend was comprised by those theorists and literary critics, including Marxist, feminist and postcolonial critics, who saw this critical or rhetorical approach to literary representation, including the criticism of its dominant historical institutions and canon formation, as only a first stage in the discovery of other regions of expression and potential political subjectivities which had been repressed or exiled to the margins of the historical representation of literary and cultural works.

As a result of both these trends, the object of traditional literary interpretation became increasingly multifaceted. This change can be illustrated in three areas: (1) the 'object' of literary study has been expanded to include other discursive forms and other media (including film and popular culture) under expanded notions of 'textuality' and cultural criticism; (2) postcolonial literatures, canon-formation and minority aesthetics have become topics of debate; (3) literary and cultural critics have embraced an explicit political and interventionist stance.

As these three areas of theoretical inquiry have evolved through the end of the 1990s, however, the term 'literary theory' might appear today as a misnomer in the sense that the object of theory no longer takes literature as its sole object of concern, but has come to be applied to other regions of culture (including forms of popular culture) and to broader concerns of historical representation and political subjectivity. This can either be understood as a corrective to the increasing fragmentation of postmodern societies, as Jameson has argued, or as a symptom of further compartmentalisation and specialisation.

In *The Postmodern Condition*, Lyotard argued that in the human sciences the validity of any theory is ultimately tested (or legitimated) by the consistency and coherence of its own 'language game' and that the proper medium of experimentation in the human sciences is discourse and, more specifically, narrative. In one sense, this could account for the peculiar temporal or historical rhythm of certain theories which, for a period of time, gain prominence as an author-itative description of cultural processes that determine the meaning of individual works, but which over an ensuing period are gradually changed through experimentation by which the theory is tested and constantly debated. Rather than judging the consistency of its repre-sentation with an external object, therefore, theoretical knowledge concerns an object that is not a simple datum, but rather a structure or process. In other words, the consistency of truth in theory is the internal coherence of theoretical discourse itself, whose referent is not outside or opposed to its representation, but rather becomes the description of a genetic system, historical process or form of causality, and which can be made to account for seemingly remote phenomena it brings together in its representation of the meaning of the cultural work.

G. Lambert

LLEWELYN, JOHN (1931–) One of the leading practitioners of continental philosophy in the United Kingdom. Along with Robert Bernasconi and David Farrell Krell (Essex), and David Wood (War-wick), Llewelyn (Edinburgh) helped establish the serious study of Husserl, Heidegger, Derrida and Levinas during the 1980s. Llewelyn read French Language and Literature at the University College of Wales, Aberystwyth, and remains committed to both the Welsh language and the causes of the people of Wales. He subsequently read Philosophy at the Universities of Edinburgh and Oxford, gaining a grounding in the analytic philosophy of language dominant in the UK during the 1950s and 1960s. He served with the Royal Air Force and had posts with the French Air Force and in Germany, before beginning to teach philosophy at the University of New England, Australia, after which he returned to Edinburgh, where he has since remained.

In 1985 Llewelyn published *Beyond Metaphysics? The Hermeneutic Circle in Contemporary Continental Philosophy* and *Derrida on the Threshold of Sense*. Both studies are primarily exegetical. The former considers Heidegger's distinctive formulation of the hermeneutic circle, in which he argues that scientific knowledge presupposes 'pre-scientific' structures (or 'fore-structures') of understanding which he calls 'existentials'. Llewelyn's formidable knowledge of continental philosophy is apparent from the succeeding chapters in which he discusses whether a series of thinkers – including Husserl, Sartre, Bachelard, Gadamer, Merleau-Ponty, Saussure, Levi-Strauss, Ricoeur, Derrida and Levinas – manage to go 'beyond metaphysics' towards Heidegger's fundamental ontology. The latter book was one of a series of 'introductions' to Derrida that appeared in the mid-1980s, though in retrospect, Llewelyn's was the text that engaged with Derrida's work in the most nuanced fashion. This is in part because of Llewelyn's knowledge of the history of philosophy, but also due to his remarkable style, in which Hegel and Derrida's shared liking for multilingual philosophical punning is intertwined with a grammatical dexterity enabling complex or aporetic notions to be addressed with wit, precision and illumination.

If it is, in the final analysis, the voices of Levinas and Derrida which have resonated most forcefully in Llewelyn's work (in particular *Appositions of Jacques Derrida and Emmanuel Levinas*, 2002), two abiding themes have characterised his philosophical interests. The first is that of the imagination, 'singular but not single', a manifoldness which, by way of bringing Kant and Levinas face to face, Llewelyn nicknames *The HypoCritical Imagination* (2000). The second theme is that of ethical responsibility, again derived primarily from Levinas, but going beyond Levinas in Llewelyn's insistent posing of the question of the possibility, and necessity, of an ethical responsibility towards animals, and towards the earth, which is not simply the environing world within which we find ourselves (most notably in *The Middle Voice of Ecological Conscience*, 1991 and *Seeing Through God: A Geophenomenology*, 2004). Llewelyn's own embodiment of ethical responsibility would be attested to by the legion of philosophers who have been fortunate enough to be the recipients of his generosity, and in his own long-term commitment to training guide dogs for the blind.

R. Durie

LOGOCENTRISM Derrida's term for the emphasis, in Western philosophy, on a metaphysics of presence, particularly as that plays out through the idea of the (spoken) word, *logos*, as truth, originating in a subject conceived of as conscious and present-to-itself. Logocentrism also borrows such forms as phonocentrism, ethnocentrism, phallocentrism, or as what Heidegger referred to as onto-theo-logy, which Derrida seeks to displace through a 'grammatology' informed by (arche-)writing.

In his analysis of logocentrism Derrida most often returns to the way in which writing, from Plato to Saussure, is consistently conceived of as subordinate to speech and even accused of being the corruption of true speech, or at least a fall into an exteriority that betrays meaning and allows for error and misunderstanding. He shows how, upon examination, speech cannot be structurally distinguished from writing on those terms, that speech is also derivative, that it likewise relies on language as an 'exterior' system, that it similarly allows for a rupture to transpire between what is thought and what is said, thereby introducing absence and the irreducible possibility of non-truth.

What allows logocentrism to continue to function, in spite of what a variety of thinkers themselves reveal, however unwittingly, as its logical inconsistencies, is the unexamined recourse to a system of presence-focused metaphysics whereby those inconsistencies are occluded or reabsorbed by an ultimate (source of) truth that is able to contain and preserve the *logos* as intact yet at the same time deliver it (still intact) to thought, to meaning, to language and to the real world.

D. Wills

LUKÁCS, GYORGY (GEORG) (1885–1971) Hungarian philosopher, literary theorist and leading Communist. Influenced by contemporary philosophers like Dilthey, Husserl, Lask, Simmel and Weber, the young Lukács constructed a tragic world-view in literary and aesthetic studies such as *Soul and Form* (1910), *Aesthetic Culture* (1913) and *The Theory of the Novel* (1916). Lukács began to reject neo-Kantianism by 1911 and in 1918 made the transition from ethical anti-capitalism to Marxist revolutionary. Lukács thereafter produced the seminal work of twentieth-century Marxist philosophy, *History and Class Consciousness* (1923).

Enthused by the proximity of revolutions in Russia and Germany,

Lukács departed sharply from vulgar, positivistic materialism in *History and Class Consciousness*, bringing Marxism closer to contemporary European philosophy. Its influence extended to Bloch, Mannheim, Adorno, Horkheimer, Benjamin, Korsch, Sartre, Lefebvre, Merleau-Ponty and Marcuse. It has also been fiercely criticised by both sympathetic thinkers like Meszaros as well as defenders of orthodoxy like Zinoviev. It was later repudiated in the 1930s by Lukács himself, who went on to produce such major studies as *The Historical Novel* (1937), *The Young Hegel* (1938) and *Towards an Ontology of Social Being* (1971).

In *History and Class Consciousness* Lukács dialectically transcended 'the antinomies of bourgeois thought' by reworking German Idealism through a symptomatic rereading of Marx. For Lukács, revolutionary praxis transcends the antinomies of contemplative thought, replacing the formal possibility of the moral 'ought' with the objective possibility of the historical process itself. Lukács found the 'practical essence' of Marxism in its dialectical conception of totality as a concrete process and notoriously claimed that even if Marxism was falsified empirically its dialectical method would still remain capable of bearing further development.

The central preoccupation of Lukács was the objective possibility of proletarian revolution under conditions of capitalist reification. If reification obscures the social character of commodity relations how might a subject emerge to overthrow exploitation? Lukács saw the proletariat in Hegelian terms as 'the identical subject-object' of commodity society because it occupies a unique standpoint that allows capitalism to be grasped as a totality. Wage labourers can become self-conscious of themselves as special sorts of commodities that put into motion and make possible the entire commodity system as both its cause and its presupposition.

Perhaps the most contentious aspect of *History and Class Consciousness* has been the notion of *zugerechnet*, or 'ascribed' class consciousness. Lukács 'infers' consciousness to a shared class position rather than as an 'empirically-given' individual consciousness: 'By relating consciousness to the whole of society it becomes possible to infer the thoughts and feelings which men would have in a particular situation if they were *able* to assess both it and the interests arising from it in their impact on immediate action and on the whole structure of society.' Some critics like Althusser took this to be 'an idealist and voluntarist interpretation of Marxism as the exclusive product and expression of proletarian practice'. Others saw it in terms of a rationalistic denial of empirical or psychological consciousness. From a Lukácsian perspective, such critiques reproduced the unmediated antimonies that Lukács himself criticised – on the one side formal abstractions and on the other empiricist reductions – and neglected 'the higher reality' of total development beyond empirical 'facts' or theoretical schema.

A. Law

See also: Marxism; reification

LYOTARD, JEAN-FRANÇOIS (1925–98) French philosopher, perhaps the greatest philosophical essayist of his generation. He experimented with styles and ideas in order to do justice to a series of deep-rooted philosophical, ethical and political problems. From his earliest essays on the Algerian war of independence for the journal *Socialisme ou barbarie* (1956–63) to the last posthumous essays on Augustine, Lyotard's writing vibrates with love for the productive energies of lives – and with anger against the structures that consume this liberating power.

Through a series of collected articles – *Driftworks* (1973), *The Inhuman* (1988), *Political Writings* (1993) and *Postmodern Fables* (1993) – and three major books – *Discours, figure* (1971), *Libidinal Economy* (1974) and *The Differend* (1983) – Lyotard combines innovation at the level of philosophical style, a wide appreciation of art and a sense of the contemporary importance of the history of philosophy. This fusion allows him to go beyond the detachment and possible sterility of theory while still maintaining its synthetic and analytical capacities. A radical philosopher, Lyotard constantly goes beyond established modes of presentation and interpretation in order to respond to wrongs and to injustice. This radicalism has been widely missed, partly due to an inability of school philosophers to adapt to the subtlety of his thought (where thought must not be confused with ideas, but rather followed through feelings and structures).

For instance, his influential work on the postmodern in, for example, *The Postmodern Condition* (1979), *The Inhuman* and *Postmodern Fables*, has been dogged by the lazy confusion of a diagnosis of the postmodern condition with a resignation to it. For Lyotard, the postmodern condition occurs with the death of grand narratives. These are over-arching accounts of historical development and progress. When they fail, the different forms of thought and practices that they articulated are thrown into a state of naked competition. The narratives provide rules for resolving conflicts and for judging between claims. Without such rules we are left with competing language games with different, irreducible, stakes and internal logics. This does not mean that Lyotard thinks that the rules were just. On the contrary, while writing on

Algeria – and ever since – he has stressed the necessary failure and violence of totalising narratives.

Capitalism has evolved alongside these narratives and has taken over their mantle as ultimate arbiter. According to Lyotard, capital works with the most flexible rules for making decisions between different claims and projects. In *The Differend*, he describes this power of arbitration as the goal of gaining time in exchanging capital. Any conflict will be resolved according to which decision gains time, in the sense of increasing the flow of capital. This gives capital great adaptability, since its goals are empty (it does not matter what you do, but whether it gains time). But capital also rides over differences and conflicts, by claiming that gaining time must be the ultimate goal and that all sides of a conflict can be measured in terms of capital and time.

Lyotard's description of the fragmented postmodern condition and its articulation by capital and liberal democracy is not approving. On the contrary, the whole point of Lyotard's work is to give voice to that which has been excluded by this alliance. Where he differs from most contemporary commentators is on the difficulty of the task. How can we do justice to that which has been excluded without wholly reincorporating it into the system of capital – without giving it a fixed value and a place in the grand scheme of gaining time or making profits?

In *The Differend* and subsequent texts, his answer is to testify to the differend, that is, to irresolvable conflicts and to those who have been silenced in them. But doesn't that involve resolving the conflict – at least in the sense where an explanation of a difference bridges it in terms of our understanding? This is the greatest challenge of Lyotard's essays: how do we give voice to something without betraying it as something that cannot and must not be fully expressed? He uses the beautiful phrase of 'presenting the unpresentable' to describe the problem.

Lyotard's essays present the unpresentable by using styles, artworks and philosophy to trigger and describe affects or feelings while at the same time drawing up philosophical concepts. In the work around the differend, this feeling is the sublime, drawn from Kant. That which cannot be captured by capital or the understanding is signalled by a simultaneous attraction and repulsion, by a combination of pleasure and pain. We feel that something ought to be represented, but at the same time cannot be. The feeling is therefore a barrier to overarching rules and systems. *Here lies something beyond your measures and equivalences.*

This explains the importance of art, and in particular avant-garde art, for Lyotard. The avant-garde is in a constant battle to adapt against the reduction of difference to orthodoxy. We must struggle for the shock that draws us to the value of life against the rationalisations that make life into a successful system or structure. In *Libidinal Economy*, he describes this relation in terms of the dissimulation of intensity in structures. Feelings or intensities are hidden in structures and must be hidden in them, in order to give them energy and to stop them becoming fixed and exclusive.

The two key phrases of libidinal economy are therefore 'Our politics is of flight, primarily, like our style' and 'We must be good conductors of intensities'. They mean that a libidinal politics is about challenging orthodoxies, fixed definitions and rules. This is done by releasing the hidden feelings at work within any structure, by conducting intensities. But that politics itself must avoid becoming fixed: hence its flight. It is because intensities must somehow be outside any structure that this politics must also be actively passive, in the sense of allowing ourselves to conduct feelings, rather than identifying them. An identified and valued intensity or feeling is already compromised within a structure. All of Lyotard's works are attempts to renew thought by inviting new feelings into what we take as given and as known. They do this for what must always lie beyond representation, as the most precious value of life.

J. Williams

See also: differend; Literary Theory; Postmodernism; Poststructuralism

MACINTYRE, ALASDAIR (1929–) Scots-Irish philosopher who lived and worked in England before emigrating to America in 1970. In his first book, *Marxism: An Interpretation* (1953, reissued in 1968 as *Marxism and Christianity*, with a second edition in 1995), MacIntyre presented Marxism as the most powerful secular expression of the radical social hopes that were once embodied in Christianity. At the same time, he argued that both Marxism and Christianity lacked the resources for undertaking a thoroughgoing critique of capitalism and its main ideology, liberalism. Subsequent work on the nature of the human sciences – for example, *The Unconscious* (1958) – and the history of philosophical ethics (*A Short History of Ethics*, 1966) reinforced MacIntyre's misgivings about Marxism. But it was only with the publication of *After Virtue* (1981) that MacIntyre's alternative to Marxism became clear: that an understanding and effective critique of the morals of modernity, such as it has them, requires the adoption of an Aristotelian point of view.

Central to this point of view is a concept of the virtues. The virtues are qualities human beings require in order to flourish both as members of social practices and in their individual lives as a whole. But modern moral culture, MacIntyre argued, has all but lost its grip on what it means to be virtuous, a fact that, in MacIntyre's view, merely reflects the exclusion of the common good from modern politics and the compartmentalisation of life imposed by the labour market and state bureaucracy. For MacIntyre, it is only to be expected that morality should seem subjective and arbitrary to the denizens of modernity, since in the modern world morality lacks grounding in concrete social practices and ongoing traditions of practical rationality. MacIntyre thus agreed with Nietzsche that 'the Enlightenment project' of justifying modern morality was a failure. Nietzsche's mistake, according to MacIntyre, lay in generalising this conclusion to all morality, in wrongly taking for granted the obsolescence of the Aristotelian paradigm of the virtues.

In the two books that followed *After Virtue* – *Whose Justice? Which Rationality?* (1988) and *Three Rival Versions of Moral Inquiry* (1990) – MacIntyre developed a theory of practical reason that emphasised the role of narrative, history and tradition. The rationality of a moral standpoint, MacIntyre argued, is inseparable from the rationality of the tradition in which it is embedded, which in turn is intelligible only through its history, including the history of its encounters with rival traditions. This can be seen to countenance relativism but MacIntyre repudiates that interpretation of his view. In *Dependent Rational Animals* (1999), MacIntyre broke new ground in arguing that a tradition's claim to allegiance must in part be a function of the recognition it gives to human animality. MacIntyre points out that an animal-like vulnerability to injury and dependence on others is a pervasive feature of the human condition – in infancy, old age and in periods of disability – and he suggests ways in which the virtues of 'acknowledged dependence' might be both comprehended philosophically and sustained politically.

N. Smith

MARCEL, GABRIEL (1889–1973) French philosopher, dramatist, critic and musician. Although he preferred the title 'Neo-Socratic', Marcel is known as a Christian existentialist. His philosophy of the mystery of being turns to lived existence in the hopes of breaking away from the modern Cartesian world view of mechanised nature, and leads to the focus and emphasis on the depth of mystery at the heart of human existence. The mystery of being is developed in terms of his celebrated themes of presence, recollection and second reflection, creative fidelity, participation, charity, hope and faith.

For Marcel existence as mystery is irreducible to any problematical treatment. It is not a problem before me to be solved but, rather, a mystery which involves me in such a way that I cannot abstract myself from it. Further, it entails a reflecting 'I' that is precisely 'what' – or better, 'who' – is being reflected upon. On this level there is an ontological exigency at the heart of human existence that should prevent it from closing itself off into the problematic and the objective. It is on this level that the 'thou' is encountered in a presence that bespeaks availability (*disponibilité*) for the other person. In contrast, the unavailable person is not 'really' there for the other but, rather, maintains a certain closedness and distraction toward something else.

With the recollective move in second reflection to existence as mystery, Marcel has turned toward the fullness of existence that eludes first reflection and which is irreducible to it. Thus, in this critique of the primacy of objectivity, Marcel has overcome the primacy of epistemology, and at once found its source. But what is more important for him is the affirmation that existence is not only given, but is also giving. Existence as giving encompasses creativity, which must be considered the central motif of Marcel's whole philosophy of the mystery of being. This insight grew as he concentrated more on the relations among his philosophical thought, his dramatic work and his musical compositions.

Second reflection is an immediate, but blind intuition, which is not mediated by thought or conceptual knowledge, thus reminding us of the notions of reflective judgement and aesthetic experience in Kant's *Critique of Judgement*. However, this intuition can be made the focus of conceptual analysis, which is where reflection begins, but not without a loss of immediacy. This is the place of imaginative presentation at work in positive constructions operating in drama and in narrative. This place in secondary reflection of interpretation and productive imagination at the heart of Marcel's philosophy of mystery makes his thought quite relevant to philosophy for the twenty-first century, in which the interpretation of the role of the imagination, paralleling its various developments during the several decades after Kant, is so central.

P. Bourgeois

MARCUSE, HERBERT (1898–1979) German philosopher, a prominent member of the early Frankfurt School of critical theory and later famous as the chief philosophical spokesman for the New Left student movement in the 1960s. Marcuse began his revolutionary career as a young socialist in the Berlin Soldier's Council (1919–20). After finishing his doctoral thesis, *The German Novel about the Artist* (1922), he went on to study with both Husserl and Heidegger before joining the Frankfurt School in 1933. Shortly thereafter he followed his colleagues in exile in the United States, where he worked for the Office of Strategic Services during the Second World War and later taught at Columbia University, Brandeis University and the University of California, San Diego. Among his most important works are *Hegel's Ontology* (1932), *Reason and Revolution* (1941), *Eros and Civilisation* (1955), *One-Dimensional Man* (1964), *Counter-Revolution and Revolt* (1972) and *The Aesthetic Dimension* (1979).

From the outset of his career, Marcuse sought to fuse the humanistic writings of the early (Hegelian) Marx with the historically oriented existentialism of Heidegger (and later Sartre). In the 1950s he turned to Freud's theory of instincts to highlight the biological core of revolutionary praxis. Not surprisingly, his existential predilection led him to repudiate the economic determinism of orthodox Marxism. Eventually he attacked Soviet-styled bureaucratic socialism, which together with Western-styled 'state monopoly capitalism' he accused of being totalitarian.

Marcuse regarded revolution less in economic and political terms than in cultural ones. In his opinion, the abolition of capitalism and the establishment of democratic control over the means of production were only the beginning of a deeper biological revolution. The virtual elimination of scarcity through automation – for Marcuse a real possibility given the current development of science and technology – would make possible the total emancipation of the senses. Erotic energy would be diverted away from the false need to consume and produce at excessive, wasteful levels; the need to dominate nature would be replaced by a 'new science and technology' aimed at pacifying life, thereby making possible the liberation of nature and humanity from their own destructive violence while realising their aesthetic potentials. Utopia would thus ultimately consist in the reconciliation of humanity and nature.

Perhaps Marcuse's most enduring contribution to social thought was his notion of 'repressive desublimation', or the manipulation of sexual liberation in reinforcing a repressive regime of consumption and production. Other well-known and related concepts introduced by him included 'surplus repression' and 'repressive tolerance'. Capitalism, he argued, entailed 'surplus repression' in its demand that production and consumption expand beyond levels necessary for human fulfilment; liberal democracy was said by him to tolerate mildly critical points of view, but only on condition that they be made 'safe' for the system by suppressing any radical critique of it.

D. Ingram

See also: Critical Theory; Marxism; repressive desublimation

MARION, JEAN-LUC (1946–) French philosopher with a major impact on phenomenology and continental philosophy of religion. Marion entered the French intellectual scene in 1975 with the publication of his thesis on Descartes, which led to him being hailed as one of the foremost authorities in the field. In the Anglophone world he became well known with the 1991 translation of his *God Without Being* (published in French in 1982).

Marion's work can be divided into phenomenological and theological investigations (although the latter are never explicitly declared as such). The former discuss the revelation ('r') of phenomena, while the latter are concerned with the phenomenon of revelation ('R'). The relation between the two is both complex and intriguing. The revelation of phenomena invokes the possibility of a phenomenon to appear (*Offenbarkeit*). The phenomenon of revelation, on the other hand, refers to the historical and thus actual phenomenon of Christian and Christic revelation (*Offenbarung*). It immediately becomes evident that the latter needs and presupposes the former; the Christian revelation ('R'), to the extent that is a revelation, is actualised only through the possibility offered by phenomenality ('r') and it is, therefore, a revelation to the second degree or, better yet, the square of a revelation ($R = r^2$). But this is not all. For Marion, God's presence is occasioned by His withdrawal, the absence that follows Nietzsche's death of God, the 'distance' of the title in *The Idol and Distance* (1977). The appearance, however, of a phenomenon, of any phenomenon, can only take place in this very distance, in this space opened up by the withdrawal of the divine and because of it. The phenomenon of revelation, therefore, ultimately conditions the revelation of the phenomena ($R > r$).

This interplay repeats itself on another level. Marion's thought is to be situated at the much-discussed end of metaphysics, a metaphysics whose constitution is, after Heidegger, onto-theological. Wishing to safeguard the irreducibility of the absolute (be it God or the other) vis-à-vis categories of the subject, Marion envisaged a God disentangled from ontology (*God Without Being*), soon to be complemented by a Self equally without being (*Being Given*, 1997). More precisely, liberating God from the metaphysical (read conceptual) impediments that were imposed on Him by the tradition emancipates the human self from the restraint of subjectivism. The latter is achieved thanks to what Marion calls the third reduction, the reduction to given-ness, prior to Husserl's reduction to the transcendental and Heidegger's reduction to the existential. The self is given when the I of consciousness gives itself up to what is given in the appearance of the phenomenon – receiving, thereby, itself back as gift: not as an I any more, but as a Me. This process is structured around three moments: (1) given-ness, that which allows and enables (2) the giving (appearing) of (3) the given (the phenomenon). All three instances are captured by 'donation', the term Marion uses to translate Husserl's *Gegebenheit*. Certain types of phenomena (such as the event, the flesh, the idol and the icon) are paradigmatic of both the abundance and the irreducibility of donation (*In Excess*, 2001).

J. Manoussakis

See *also*: gift (2); onto-theo-logy; Religion, Philosophy of; saturated phenomenon

MARKEDNESS A term in linguistics and semiotics often employed in deconstructionist analysis of texts and practices. The concept of markedness, introduced by the Russian linguist Roman Jakobson, can be applied to both the signifiers and the signifieds of a paradigmatic opposition (such as male/female). Paired signifiers consist of an un-marked form (in this case, the word 'male') and a marked form (in this case the word 'female'). The marked signifier is distinguished by some special semiotic feature (in this linguistic example the addition of an initial fe-). Within some texts the marked term may even be suppressed as an 'absent signifier'. Similarly, the two signifieds may be valorised – accorded different values. The marked concept (typically listed as second in familiar pairings) is presented as 'different' or even (im-plicitly) negative. The unmarked concept is typically dominant (for example, statistically within a text or corpus) and therefore seems to be neutral, normal and 'natural'. Derrida demonstrated that within the oppositional logic of binarism neither of the terms (or concepts) makes sense without the other. This is what he calls 'the logic of supple-mentarity': the 'secondary' term which is represented as 'marginal' and external is in fact constitutive of the 'primary' term and essential to it. The concept of markedness can be applied more broadly: whether in textual or social practices, the choice of a marked form 'makes a statement'. Where a text deviates from conventional expectations it is marked. Conventional or over-coded text (which follows a fairly predictable formula) is unmarked whereas unconventional or under-coded text is marked.

D. Chandler

MARX, KARL HEINRICH (1818–83) German social theorist, philosopher and revolutionary. The most influential theorist of socialism, Marx came from a Jewish family which converted to Christianity so that his father could continue a successful career as a lawyer in the face of Prussia's anti-Jewish laws. Marx studied law and philosophy at the Universities of Bonn and Berlin at a time when German intellectual life was dominated by Hegel's philosophy. In Berlin Marx joined the radical, 'left Hegelian' movement, which included Feuerbach, Stirner, Bruno Bauer and others. Denied the prospect of an academic career because of his radical views, he took up journalism; he was briefly editor of the *Rheinische Zeitung* until it was suppressed. In 1843 he moved to Paris where he made contact with French socialists and began a lifelong collaboration with Engels. In Paris he started another radical journal but this too was soon suppressed. In 1847 Marx and Engels were among the founders of the Communist League, a tiny revolutionary group for which they wrote the *Communist Manifesto* (1848). In 1848, a year of revolutionary upheaval throughout Europe, Marx was in Cologne where he again briefly edited a radical newspaper. After the failure of the 1848 revolution, he was expelled from Germany. He made his way to London, where he remained in exile for the rest of his life.

In London, he lived in considerable poverty, supported by occasional journalism and regular financial help from Engels. His main energies were devoted to producing a systematic theory of capitalist society, based on a huge mass of material gathered from his studies in the British Museum Library. Although the defeats of 1848 were a major setback for the communist movement, Marx stayed active and was a founding member of the International Working Men's Association (the 'First International') in 1864. In 1871 the Paris Commune was established in the aftermath of the Franco-Prussian war and then bloodily suppressed. Marx analyses these events in *The Civil War in France* (1871). In the last decade of his life Marx's health worsened and his output declined. However, he produced an important critique of the programme of the German socialist party, *Critique of the Gotha Programme* (1875, published 1891). This work gives Marx's fullest account of future socialist society, a subject about which Marx says remarkably little.

Marx's earliest writings are devoted to the critique of Hegel's philosophy from a left Hegelian, radical humanist perspective, influenced particularly by Feuerbach. However, he soon came to appreciate that legal, political and social forces have their roots in material and economic conditions. Engels had been moving towards similar conclusions. The two collaborated on a number of works in which they criticised the idealism of their left Hegelian contemporaries, including *The Holy Family* (1844) and *The German Ideology* (1845, first published in full 1932). These works contain the first expressions of the 'materialist theory of history', the theory which, Marx later said, thenceforth served as the 'guiding thread' for his studies. History and social philosophy prior to Marx had focused predominantly on the actions of rulers. The materialist theory of history, by contrast, is founded on the proposition that people have inescapable physical needs and hence that the material and economic side of human life is primary and basic. Some, such as Althusser in *For Marx* (1965), argue that there is a fundamental distinction between Marx's early Hegelian and 'philosophical' writings and his later 'scientific' work. However, this claim is questioned by many others who hold that although Marx's thought develops and changes with his increasing focus on economics and history, there is no radical discontinuity in his thought; philosophical and Hegelian themes continue throughout.

Marx analysed the historical and political lessons of the 1848 revolutions in France in two influential works, *The Class Struggles in France* (1850) and *The Eighteenth Brumaire of Louis Bonaparte* (1852). The theory of capitalism that Marx was developing first appeared in a preliminary form in *A Contribution to the Critique of Political Economy* (1859). However, this work is best known for its celebrated Preface in which Marx outlines his basic theoretical assumptions. This brief passage is commonly taken to be the authoritative statement of the principles of historical materialism. According to it, every society is founded on certain 'productive forces' (workers, tools, machinery) which are necessarily associated with specific 'relations of production' (economic and property relations). Together these constitute the material 'base' of society, upon which arises a 'superstructure' of political and legal institutions, and ideological forms (art, religion, philosophy and so on). Historical development occurs because conflicts develop within the economic base of society. These conflicts give rise eventually to economic crisis and social revolution. History is divided into a series of stages or modes of production: ancient slave society, feudalism and capitalism. But capitalism is not the end of the story. Through the development of conflicts inherent to it, it will bring about its own downfall and give rise to a new socialist mode of production.

Marx's systematic account of capitalist society is embodied in his major theoretical work, *Capital* (three volumes, 1867–94). The first volume appeared in 1867; volumes two (1885) and three (1894) were assembled by Engels after the death of Marx from the latter's drafts. Manuscript notes for a fourth volume dealing with the theories of previous political economists (Adam Smith, Ricardo and others) were later edited by Karl Kautsky and published as *Theories of Surplus Value* (three volumes, 1905–10). Marx's London work also resulted in a number of lengthy manuscripts which were only published long after his death, the most influential of which has been the *Grundrisse*, written in 1857–8 (first published 1953, English translation 1973).

Marx regarded himself as a social scientist whose primary aim was to understand the workings of existing capitalist society. He rejected as 'utopian' visions of socialism based on ethical ideas. His concept of socialism, he insists, is not a mere ideal but rather the predicted outcome of developments evident in present, capitalist, society. Nevertheless, there is clearly a visionary dimension to Marx's thought which has been a potent influence in the modern world. By the time of his death in 1883, socialism was emerging as a major political force throughout the industrial world. In the course of the next 100 years it was to have an unparalleled impact on world history, making Marx one of the most influential thinkers the world has ever known. By the 1980s more than one-third of the world's population was ruled by regimes claiming allegiance to Marx's ideas.

Since then, however, following the collapse of Soviet communism in 1989, the influence of Marxism has declined dramatically. Some, such as Francis Fukuyama in *The End of History* (1989), say that Marx's prediction of a historical stage beyond capitalism has been refuted, and that Marxism as a political force is now dead. Given the continuing crises in the capitalist world, that is questionable. Although many aspects of Marx's theory have been disproved and others need to be fundamentally revised, Marxism remains the most comprehensive and powerful theory for understanding and explaining capitalist society. It also continues to serve as a source of hope and inspiration for all those who believe that a better form of human life is possible.

S. Sayers

See also: alienation (1); contradiction (2); dialectical materialism; historical materialism; ideology; Marxism

MARXISM The system of thought created by Marx, providing the main theoretical basis for modern socialism and communism. The term is often also taken to include the work of Marx's lifelong collaborator, Engels, and by extension, the ideas of Marx's subsequent followers. The term was first employed by Marx's opponents in the socialist movement during the 1870s and 1880s. Neither Marx nor Engels used it. Indeed, Engels reports that Marx once claimed 'all I know is that I am not a "Marxist" '. Towards the end of Engels's life, however, the term began to be used by the followers as well as opponents of Marx, and this usage rapidly gained acceptance.

Marxism has had an unprecedented impact on modern life. In the century or so after Marx's death it grew into a movement of world-historical proportions. It was adapted to new conditions, extended into new areas of inquiry, and developed in a variety of intellectual contexts. In the process a profusion of different forms of Marxism emerged. There have been distinctive traditions of Marxism in Russia, China, Cuba, France, Italy, Germany and elsewhere, each containing a diversity of schools, tendencies and theories. Moreover, there have been numerous attempts to combine Marxism with other major schools of thought, giving rise to neo-Kantian, existentialist, psychoanalytic, structuralist and other interpretations of Marxism.

Thus, while a dictionary definition is relatively uncontroversial, problems arise when the attempt is made to be more specific. What did Marx really say? Who are his genuine followers? There are a number of different ways of answering these questions, none without problems. Marxism may be defined in terms of an essential core of social and economic theory, but it resists such systematisation. Thus Lenin insists that Marxism must develop and change if it is 'to keep pace with life'. Others try to specify Marxism in terms of its dialectical and materialist method. According to Lukács, in *History and Class Consciousness*, 'orthodox Marxism is not the belief in this or that thesis . . . orthodoxy refers exclusively to method'. Others have looked upon the active, political commitment of Marxism to the cause of the working class and to socialism as its defining feature.

Marxism is thus divided into different, often conflicting, tendencies, none of which can unproblematically claim to be the sole 'true' heirs of Marx. Some writers argue that there is no longer a single theory of Marxism and that we must talk instead of 'Marxisms' in the plural. Others maintain that Marxism should be seen as a concrete and complex historical tradition which contains within it many different schools and theories. However, such views do not ultimately escape the problems of distinguishing between Marxism (or Marxisms) and non-Marxism. If anyone who is called a 'Marxist' is regarded as ipso facto a Marxist, then the identity of Marxism becomes arbitrary; otherwise the problem remains.

Marx's thought. Marx's initial formation was as a member of the radical 'left Hegelian' movement which emerged in Germany after Hegel's death in 1831 and which contributed to the ferment of ideas leading up to the revolutions of 1848. However, Marx soon came to appreciate that legal and political matters have their roots in material and economic conditions. Engels was reaching similar conclusions and the two collaborated in a number of works attacking their left Hegelian contemporaries for their idealism in *The Holy Family* (1844) and *The German Ideology* (1845). From these works emerged the 'materialist theory of history', the theory which, Marx says, then served as the 'guiding thread' for his thought.

The materialist theory of history starts from the proposition that human beings are creatures of need, and hence that the material side of human life is primary and basic. This may seem obvious to the point of triviality, but history and social theory prior to Marx had focused on the actions of rulers and paid virtually no attention to economic developments. According to Marx, every society is composed of certain 'productive forces' (tools, machinery and labour to operate them) with which are associated particular social 'relations of production' (property, economic relations, division of labour). These together constitute the material 'base' of society, upon which arises a 'superstructure' of political and legal institutions, and ideological forms (art, religion and philosophy). At any given historical period the relations of production provide the framework for economic development. The developing forces of production give rise to increasing conflict with the existing relations of production and these conflicts are reflected as class struggles. 'From forms of development of the productive forces these relations turn into their fetters. Then begins an epoch of social revolution in which social relations and the entire immense superstructure is transformed' (*A Contribution to the Critique of Political Economy*, Preface, 1859). Marx divides history into a sequence of different epochs or modes of production: ancient slave-based society, feudalism and capitalism.

Economic development creates not only new goods but also new forms of social relation and new classes. The proletariat (industrial working class) is a specific product of capitalism. Marx and Engels trace its development in the brilliant opening chapter of the *Communist Manifesto* (1848). They show how the process of industrialisation concentrates working people in factories and cities and how, as a result, the working class develops from being an unorganised and unconscious mass (a class 'in-itself') to being an organised and conscious political force, a class 'for itself', a force which, Marx believed, is ultimately destined to be the 'gravedigger' of capitalism and to inaugurate a new mode of production, socialism.

According to Marx, all societies are divided into competing classes, defined structurally and economically in terms of their relationship to the means of production. The bourgeoisie are the owners, and the proletariat the non-owners, of the means of production. Marx believed that capitalist society was increasingly becoming polarised into 'two great opposed camps' of bourgeois and proletarians. Actual historical development has not borne this out, at least in advanced industrial societies; though it may be argued that such a polarisation has occurred on an international scale. The character of the social classes of industrial society has changed considerably since Marx wrote in the middle of the nineteenth century, and there has been much debate about whether they can still be understood in Marxist terms. Nevertheless, an understanding of society in terms of social class is now an indispensable element of modern social thought.

Marx believed that capitalism would inevitably lead to increasing class polarisation and conflict. Through its own inherent processes it is destined to give rise ultimately to its own dissolution, to crisis and revolution which will result in a socialist society. The conquest of political power by the working class will involve, in the first instance, the creation of a socialist state, a state in which the working class is the ruling class and which functions in the interests of the working class. In this way the 'dictatorship of the proletariat' will replace the 'dictatorship of the bourgeoisie'. By these phrases Marx does not mean that such states have a dictatorial political form, but rather that they rule in the interests of a particular class. The 'dictatorship of the proletariat' is, however, only the 'first phase' of post-capitalist development. Its main purpose is to abolish the private ownership of the means of production, and hence the social and economic basis of class divisions. Moreover, Marx believed that the advent of socialist relations of production would unfetter the productive forces and give rise to great economic development. As the material basis of class divisions is dissolved, class differences will gradually disappear, and with them, the need for the state as an instrument of class rule and as a distinct coercive force.

In the higher stage of full communism, the state is destined ultimately to 'wither away', as Engels puts it. Marx describes his vision of communist society as follows.

In a higher phase of communist society, after the enslaving subordination of the individual to the division of labour, and therewith also the antithesis of mental and physical labour has vanished; after labour has become not only a means of life but life's prime want; after the productive forces have also increased with the all-round development of the individual, and all the springs of cooperative wealth flow more abundantly, only then can the narrow horizon of bourgeois right be crossed in its entirety and society inscribe on its banners: from each according to his ability, to each according to his needs! ('Critique of the Gotha Programme', 1875)

Marx rejects 'utopian' and ethical ideas of socialism in favour of what he claims to be an objective and 'scientific' account. Socialism, he insists, is not an ideal, it is the real predicted tendency of capitalist development. Nevertheless, there is clearly a visionary and 'utopian' dimension to Marx's thought, which has inspired socialists ever since and which has been one of the most potent moral ideals of the modern world.

Marxism after Marx. A notable feature of Marx's thought is its systematic unity and philosophical depth. However, Marx never found the time to present his philosophy in an extended or systematic fashion. It was left to others to articulate the underlying method and wider implications of Marx's outlook. In the first place, this task fell to Engels. In a series of works written towards the end of his life, Engels began the process of making explicit the philosophy of Marxism – later to be called 'dialectical materialism' – and developing Marxism into a comprehensive world-view: *Origin of the Family* (1884), *Ludwig Feuerbach and the End of Classical German Philosophy* (1886) and *Anti-Dühring* (1878). These works have exerted a great influence on the subsequent development of Marxism.

The process of systematising Marx's thought and extending it to new areas was continued by the first generation of Marx's followers (Kautsky, Plekhanov). During this period, furthermore, serious doctrinal disputes arose for the first time within Marxism. Eduard Bernstein argued that historical and economic developments had invalidated important aspects of Marx's theory, including the theory of value, the intensification of the class struggle and the inevitability of revolutions in capitalist societies. He also criticised Marx's philosophy on the basis of neo-Kantian ethical ideas. Bernstein's 'revisionism' gave expression to a current of thought which has had a continuing influence, particularly among non-Marxist socialists; it also provoked critical responses from Kautsky, Luxemburg and Lenin.

The First World War marked a watershed in the development of Marxism. Its onset brought about the collapse of the international socialist movement (Second International); its end saw the triumph of the Bolshevik Revolution in Russia under Lenin's leadership and the creation of the first Marxist state, followed by the formation of communist parties in many other countries and their unification in the Third International.

Lenin was a leader of extraordinary determination and decisiveness, and a thinker of great tenacity, clarity and vision. Apart from Marx and Engels, no other figure has had a comparable impact upon the history of Marxism. His most important contributions may be summarised as follows. He insisted upon the centrality of class struggle and the role of the proletariat, even in the relatively backward conditions that prevailed in Russia. He revitalised Marxism as a revolutionary philosophy and formulated principles of political organisation which were widely adopted by communist parties. He extended Marx's analysis of capitalism to the conditions of imperialism, which he conceived as the 'highest' and final stage of capitalism. In his account of imperialism, he emphasised the conflicts between the capitalist powers and the uneven character of capitalist development. Moreover, he realised the extended possibilities for revolutionary activity which were thus created. He clarified and extended Marx's account of the state and, in his final works, he began to grapple with the problems of creating a socialist society in the Soviet Union.

With the triumph of the revolution in Russia, there was a great flowering of Marxism in many different areas. There was also an explosion of Marxist influence in the arts (Eisenstein, Prokofiev, Mayakovsky and others). Beyond the Soviet Union, there were major contributions from the Hungarian philosopher Lukács and the Italian Gramsci. Lenin's contribution to Marxism was first called 'Leninism' by his successor, Stalin. Stalin was not an innovative thinker. He reduced Lenin's ideas to a simplified and lifeless doctrinal system, but due to the centralised organisation of the world communist movement, his writings served to define orthodox Marxism from the end of the 1920s until his death in 1953 and beyond. Nevertheless, oppositional tendencies emerged. Nicolai Bukharin was an important critic of Stalin's economic policies before his arrest and execution. The most significant movement of political opposition was led by Leon Trotsky after his expulsion from the Soviet Union in 1929. Trotsky's main theoretical divergences from Soviet Marxism concern questions of the revolutionary process and the nature of Soviet society, which he characterised as a 'degenerated' workers' state. After Stalin's death in 1953 a cautious process of liberalisation began, but soon faltered. Critical and oppositional voices were stifled or driven into exile (Ilyenkov, Kolakowski, Bahro). Soviet Marxism stagnated.

In China during this period Marxism developed very differently. The Chinese communist victory in 1949 under the leadership of Mao Zedong greatly extended the influence of Marxism. Mao developed a distinctive form of Marxism, especially in political and military theory and philosophy. During the 1960s and early 1970s Mao's ideas provided an alternative model and inspiration for many Marxists. However, the chaos and destruction of the 'Cultural Revolution' (1966–76) led eventually to a questioning of them, not least in China itself, and to a decline in their influence internationally. Other revolutionary movements in the Third World have also led to distinctive contributions to Marxism.

In Western Europe, by contrast, Marxism developed in a context of relatively stable, prosperous and non-revolutionary conditions. In France, it had a particularly important impact on intellectual life in the middle years of the twentieth century through the work of such thinkers as Sartre and Althusser. In Germany, there have been notable Marxist thinkers such as Korsch and Bloch, as well as others who drew on Marxism, including members of the Frankfurt School (Adorno, Horkheimer, Marcuse). In Italy, too, Marxism played an important role in intellectual life (Gramsci, Della Volpe, Colletti). In the English-speaking world there was influential Marxist work, particularly in history (E. P. Thompson, Hill, Hobsbawm) and in economic theory (Dobb, J. Robinson, Sweezy). A school of Marxism using the methods of analytical philosophy, 'analytical Marxism', flourished briefly (Cohen, Elster). Marxism has infused the work of many modern writers and artists (Brecht, Picasso, Mayakovsky, Eisenstein, Aragon, Rivera and others).

Marxism today. The *Communist Manifesto* opens with the bold words, 'a spectre is haunting Europe, the spectre of communism'. At the time they were written, these words were an expression of hope rather than a description of reality. The Communist League, for which the Manifesto was written, was only a tiny group of activists. Hardly had the Manifesto been published than the revolutionary hopes it expressed were dashed as the revolutions of 1848 were defeated. The Communist League was smashed, its members hounded and persecuted. The 'spectre of communism' had, to all appearances, been extinguished and the bold vision of the Manifesto refuted.

Gradually but steadily, however, the revolutionary socialist movement reorganised and re-emerged. In 1864, the International Working

Men's Association, the 'First International', was founded with Marx as its Secretary and leading thinker. By 1883, the year of Marx's death, Marx's ideas were influential throughout the industrial world. The spectre had returned. During the next 100 years, history itself seemed to be confirming the main outlines of Marx's thought. Communism became a 'spectre' that haunted not only Europe but the whole world. At its apogee more than one-third of the world's population was ruled by governments claiming to be 'Marxist'.

With the collapse of Soviet and Eastern European communism in 1989, however, the seeming demise of Marxism has been sudden. Some say that Marxism is now dead and that its prediction of a historical stage beyond capitalism is an illusion. For these thinkers, capitalism and liberal democracy are the highest possible stages of social development, the 'end of history'. Given the continuing crises and conflicts in the capitalist world, such complacency is questionable. Many aspects of Marxism have indeed been refuted by historical developments, and others require fundamental rethinking. Nevertheless, Marxism still constitutes perhaps the most comprehensive and powerful theory for understanding and explaining the capitalist world and a continuing source of inspiration for all those who believe in the possibility of a better society in the future.

S. Sayers

MATERIALISM The ontological doctrine that only matter exists, although there are as many kinds of materialism as there are conceptions of matter. The main problematic of materialist thinking is how to account for phenomena that are more complex than the base conception of matter; one of its persistent difficulties is overcoming critics who use an impoverished conception of matter inherited from non-materialist systems of thought.

Western philosophy started out materialist: many of the pre-Socratics thought in terms of elements, and thereby introduced a significant and long-lived theme according to which complexes of objects are thought in terms of the composition of material components. Canonical here is Democritus, who argued that there must be a primary element, an *atom*, not capable of further decomposition, out of which everything else is constructed. Epicurus and his Roman expositor Lucretius took up the atomic theory of Democritus and attempted to think through a further problematic: how is organisation possible? The result was the idea of a *clinamen* or swerve that makes atoms deviate randomly from their paths and which is the origin of all organisation. These specific ideas had a profound impact on the work of Michel Serres. But the problematic is very general. An idealist philosophy can account for form, complexity and organisation by appealing to non-material entities (like Plato's forms). This option – in any event question-begging – is not open to materialism, which must live up to the challenge of showing how organisation can be produced materially.

Christianity was deeply hostile to materialism, and its social and intellectual hegemony was marked by a regression in the development of materialist ideas. The modern conception of matter was therefore created largely by non-materialists such as Descartes. Impressed by the outstanding success of the mathematical sciences, Descartes sought to return to something like view Democritus held. This he refined by restricting the properties of matter to those capable of extensive measurement: the primary qualities of size, shape, motion and position that could be modelled by the new mathematics.

Descartes' conception of matter is described as 'mechanical' because it asserts that motion can only be transferred through the physical proximity of particles, an idea based on the predominant technology of the time. Because he was not a materialist, however, Descartes was under no pressure to generate a conception of matter adequate to explain everything. Indeed he thought materialist explanations had a well-defined limit, and could not account for complex phenomena like human language. One of the problems posed for subsequent materialism is that reliance on this Cartesian formulation of matter leaves complexity inexplicable.

The radical Jacobin atheist materialists in revolutionary France, for instance figures like de la Mettrie and even Sade, espoused a materialism obtained essentially by guillotining the spiritual elements off Cartesianism. While the connections they made between Christian theology, the arbitrary political authoritarianism of the *ancien régime* and ontological dualism are provoking, their claim that everything must be particles in motion was unsupported by argument.

Other early modern European figures, however, did make progress away from a Cartesian conception of matter. Although he did not call himself a materialist, Spinoza nevertheless developed a monist ontology in which there is only one substance. Consequently no distinction can be made between God, humans and nature. This rejection of substance dualism allowed Spinoza, in another important move, to establish a pluralism of powers according to which all objects, including humans, are endowed with a variety of capacities.

Kant's transcendental idealism is the matrix of modern European thought. Its basic insight is to distinguish between a still recognisably

Cartesian conception of empirical objects and things as they are in themselves. Kant did not see empirical objects as primary, but rather as the product of an intensive process of structuring by transcendental forms operating on sensory input derived from unknown things-in-themselves. Transcendental idealism decomposed historically in two ways, both of which led to materialist philosophies, although of very different kinds. Eliminating things-in-themselves produced the absolute idealist stream of nineteenth-century German thought, culminating in Hegel; Marx formulated his materialism by inverting Hegel's idealism. Eliminating transcendental forms as primary, however, led to a deepened kind of materialism, liberated from the mechanical definition of matter. Schopenhauer developed this idea first, regarding things-in-themselves as a more fundamental kind of matter, active and capable of giving rise to new forms. On an analogy with human volition, he called this matter 'will'.

This idea of a form-producing, transcendental matter has been extremely influential on contemporary European materialism. Schopenhauer's conception of the (material) will decisively shaped Nietzsche's thought of the will-to-power. The notion of power in Nietzsche is not too distant from Spinoza, but in conjunction with the Schopenhauerian will, it takes seriously and critically the problem of how organisation can arise. The problematic raised by Epicurus receives its first proper answer here. These ideas were taken up, sometimes indirectly, by a number of figures in twentieth-century French thought, first by Bataille and later by Lyotard, Deleuze and Guattari. The latter movement might be called libidinal materialism because all three thinkers generalise a conception of psychic energy, or libido in Freudian terminology, into an ontological notion of the transcendental unconscious. The libidinal materialists depersonalised Freud's conception of libido, taking it back, philosophically, to its nineteenth-century roots in Schopenhauer and Nietzsche.

In the United States and Britain, the term materialism is largely restricted to the doctrine in philosophy of mind that mental phenomena are reducible to or somehow based in material phenomena, understood as exactly those described by the natural sciences. Critics of this doctrine point out that this splits reality along precisely Cartesian lines, duplicating the position of the eighteenth-century French materialists. Thus some contemporary philosophers and cognitive scientists, following the lead of Hubert Dreyfus and Francisco Varela, now use resources from the European phenomenological tradition to problematise these Cartesian presuppositions.

The European tradition of materialist thought itself, however philosophically sophisticated it may be, has not yet generated much dialogue with contemporary science. This may be changing, though, especially by those following Manuel DeLanda's engagement with Deleuze, the libidinal materialist who in any case took scientific issues most seriously.

A. Welchman

MATHEMATICS, PHILOSOPHY OF That branch of philosophical reflection dealing with the nature of thinking, argumentation and truth as these pertain to mathematics, as well as with the nature of mathematics itself. Leaving this last (difficult) question aside, the history of the philosophy of mathematics may be seen as having proceeded along two main lines of development, unavoidably interactive but distinct nevertheless, and each with important consequences for continental philosophy: (1) the investigation of the foundational concepts of mathematics, and (2) the exploration of a certain structure or architecture of mathematical concepts in general.

The first type of philosophy of mathematics focuses on primitive foundational concepts, such as numbers, and on the nature of mathematical argument as based on these concepts. (The term 'primitive' refers here to that from which everything else is derived in a given domain. The great nineteenth-century German mathematician Leopold Kronecker captured, and maximally extended, this sense of the 'primitive' by his famous statement that 'God created the whole numbers, everything else is the work of man'.) The central concern of most contemporary philosophy of mathematics of this sort is set theory, introduced by Georg Cantor in the late nineteenth century. Set theory defines its 'primitives' in terms of 'sets', as collections of previously given 'objects' (of whatever kind) and it also notes the property of a given object of belonging or not belonging to a given set. Thus, the number 2 belongs to the set of integer numbers, while ½, being a fraction, does not. It belongs to the set of rational numbers, which would, however, exclude $\sqrt{2}$, since it cannot be represented as a fraction. Such numbers would form the set of irrationals, which combined with all rationals form the set of real numbers, which may be represented as a set of points on a straight line – or so it appears, since this claim, linked to what is known as Cantor's continuum problem ('how many points are there on a straight line'?), leads to considerable complications. David Hilbert, one of the greatest mathematicians of the last century, called set theory a paradise from which (he hoped) mathematicians will never allow themselves to be exiled, a hope eventually destroyed by Kurt Gödel's findings, discussed below. During the last decades, the so-called category and topos theories entered the field as well; while institutionally relatively marginal, this development is significant conceptually, not least by relating the two forms of philosophy of mathematics here considered.

The second form of philosophy of mathematics focuses on identifying a structure or architecture of mathematical concepts in general, including the way in which such concepts shape practices in any given area of mathematics. Accordingly, this concern now pertains less to primitive foundational ones, such as numbers or sets, than to complex mathematical entities such as groups in algebra, manifolds in topology or infinite dimensional spaces in functional analysis (all of which, of course, may also be seen as sets). The focus on the fundamental architecture of such concepts – as well as the very activity of inventing these concepts – is formally similar to that activity which, according to Deleuze and Guattari in *What is Philosophy?* (1991), defines philosophy. In other words, although mathematics and philosophy are different disciplines, this aspect of mathematics may be seen as essentially philosophical in Deleuze and Guattari's sense: an activity of inventing, building, new concepts and thinking about their nature and structure, in this case, as they shape our practice of mathematics and our understanding of its nature.

While this aspect of mathematics as conceptual creation has been less significant for, if not outright bypassed by, mainstream philosophy of mathematics, it has been crucial to the practice of mathematics and to the thought of most great mathematicians on the nature of mathematics and its practice. Hence, one might indeed better speak of mathematical philosophy here than of philosophy of mathematics. It is somewhat ironic, then, although with a certain historical and conceptual logic, that the work of Alexandre Grothendieck in algebraic geometry – motivated by this second type of philosophical practice and thought in mathematics and resulting in the invention of topos theory – proves to have an essential role in the foundational issues arising from set theory. Although too technical to be explained here, Grothendieck's concept of 'topos' is arguably the most general concept of space that we have in mathematics and, indeed, in all thought, for the concepts of topos and 'category' are more general or more 'primitive' than the concept of set, as all three are articulated in Grothendieck's scheme.

Both forms of philosophy of mathematics – identification of primitives and construction of concepts – have significant implications for recent continental thought. Some aspects of both may indeed be seen as forms of non-classical thought, just as relativity and quantum theory are in physics, or evolutionary theory and genetics are in biology.

Arguably the most significant implications of the first aspect concern the role Gödel's findings on the undecidability and incompleteness of (most) formal systems play in the work of Derrida and his followers. Gödel demonstrated, first, that any rigorous formal system of axioms and rules of procedure in mathematics, large enough to contain arithmetic and free of contradiction, would contain undecidable propositions, that is propositions that are neither provable nor disprovable by means of that system. This is known as Gödel's first theorem. Gödel's second theorem then showed that the very proposition of the consistency of the system in question is itself undecidable. In other words, if the system is consistent, this consistency can never be rigorously demonstrated. It is possible, however, that the system will, one day, be proven to be inconsistent, to contain a contradiction.

It is not possible to discuss here the significance and implications of these momentous findings for mathematics itself, philosophy or culture, although these ideas have been widely circulated (and sometimes abused). We can show, however, that the role of these ideas in Derrida's work, especially *Dissemination* (1972), is considerable. Indeed, in some respects, Derrida's deconstruction may be seen as a theory and practice of philosophical undecidability and incompleteness, by analogy (qualified but crucial) with Gödel's undecidability and incompleteness in mathematical logic. It may be argued that, on Derrida's quasi-Gödelian deconstruction, philosophy can never make all of its propositions – perhaps any of its propositions – or the determination of its field as philosophy, decidable, or any of its systems complete.

In terms of the second aspect, that of conceptual creation involving a certain interplay between mathematical and philosophical concepts, we can point to the ways in which topological concepts are used in Lacan and Deleuze, in the latter case influenced by the ideas of Bernhard Riemann (1826–66), a powerful presence in *A Thousand Plateaus* (1980) and the Cinema books of the mid-1980s. Riemann was one of the foremost philosophical thinkers in mathematics and one of the creators of the discipline of topology, dealing with the mathematics of space. Indeed, for Riemann, mathematics, in its essential nature and in its practice, was defined by (mathematical) concepts rather than by sets. So it is then interesting to note that while set theory ruled mathematics from Cantor on, it is Grothendieck's work in topos theory – inspired by Riemann – that offers us a new form of mathematics and, one might argue, a new philosophy of space. Although the work of both Lacan and Deleuze engages a broad spectrum of mathematical conceptuality – including Deleuze's interest in the theory of differential equations and especially its notion of singularity – it may best be seen as the investigation of the philosophical (and of course psychoanalytic) nature of spatiality, as a form of philosophical topology. This aspect of their work has had a major (although sometimes unperceived) influence on and significance for contemporary philosophical thinking of spatiality, which indeed largely defined its own thinking as a thinking of space in general and of 'postmodern' space in particular.

A. Plotnitsky

MEMORY Discussions of memory in continental philosophy may be grouped around four axes: the epistemological (Husserl); the hermeneutic (Heidegger, Gadamer, Ricoeur); the ontological (Merleau-Ponty, Bergson, Derrida, Deleuze); and the ethical (Ricoeur, Derrida, Levinas, Lyotard).

Husserl's descriptive phenomenology takes up memory in the context of time-consciousness. After an initial distinction between retention and recollection, the issue becomes whether or not reproductive consciousness may share in the clarity of presence and the trustworthiness of simple retention. Despite the fact that Husserl's usual integrity is manifested in his continuous hesitations and self-corrections, his notion of time, based on the (contradictory) configuration of a continuum of now-points, and his relentless effort to ground phenomenology on incontrovertible evidence, dictate his (unconvincing) attempt to guarantee the objectivity of memory through the self-givenness of each part of a recollection at a discrete point of time in the past.

Heidegger lifts memory out of the narrow epistemological concerns of Husserl and assigns to it the epochal task of hearkening to the call of Being and witnessing its withdrawal, through the many traces of an oblivion marked by the massive and usurping presence of beings. He calls the kind of memory that will be equal to this task 'futural recollection' (*zukunftiges Erinnerung*), signalling thereby the need to reactivate, hermeneutically, possibilities worthy of the future of a Dasein that wants to be interpellated by Being. Gadamer (incidentally) and Ricoeur (intentionally), without abandoning the hermeneutic task that Heidegger conceived, proceeded to show how memory may be connected with the ontic concerns of epistemologically inclined scientists. In their work, hermeneutic memory is the never ending process by means of which the 'prejudices', that is the presuppositions of the one who wants to remember and be remembered, get progressively (yet asymptotically) refined and aligned with that which calls us to memory.

Following a different route, Merleau-Ponty repositioned memory from the quest for phenomenological evidence to ontological ambiguity. Memory is for him neither conservation nor construction; neither is it contrary to forgetting. Just like Heidegger before him, Merleau-Ponty also argued that memory is in the intersection of anamnesis (remembrance) and lēthē (oblivion). He concluded that severing the traditional linkage of memory to representation was the only way to achieve fidelity to the ambiguity of memory (its activity and passivity). He then tied memory to his notions of the lived body and flesh. It is thus wrong to conceive of memory as a 'mental activity'; it is in the world of our lived body that we find our past.

Derrida's discussions of memory are bound up with his notions of *différance* and trace; it is difference between forces which permit memory. In line with Husserl's notion of originary delay, Derrida argues that there is never full, original experience, never full presence; the so-called 'first'experience is already repeated, rehearsed and echoed in memory – a memory of traces. Trace is a simulacrum of presence by means of which the present becomes the trace of a trace. 'Arche-trace' and 'originary trace' are Derrida's chosen terms, meant to deconstruct origin and continuity. To be sure, such deconstructive moves do not show that memory is impossible. On the contrary, the desire to construct memorial archives is endless. Derrida's deferral and dissemination of the memorandum are meant to problematise the faulty foundation of presence. Radicalising Heidegger's futurist recollection, Derrida's later work centres on a future anterior recollection of a messianic memory that is far removed from the Husserlian quest for a memory that would be capable veridically of retracing the arrow of time.

In Bergson's *Time and Free Will, Matter and Memory* and *Duration and Simultaneity*, the reality of time has found its most ardent proponent. Time is not an affair of psychology; it is a question of ontology. Memories are not conserved in the brain as in a container; they are acts, which can be facilitated or inhibited by our habits. Bergson distinguishes between three kinds of memory: habit memory; representational memory; and pure (virtual) memory. It is clear, however, that only the third kind of memory deserves to be called memory. Habit serves as a base for the operations of true memory. As for representational memory, actualised in an image, it differs in kind from pure memory because to picture and to remember are not the same thing. From such premises, Bergson concludes that duration and pure memory are coextensive, but he concedes that without memory, in the restricted sense of recollection, there is still duration. Given the co-extensiveness of duration and pure memory, a memory which cannot actualise itself is not lost. The past does not cease to exist;

rather, it may cease to be useful and to be active. Bergson admitted innumerable layers of past, coexisting with one another, as well as multiple presents to the extent that each present is contingent on which past is connected with it. Memory relates between all these levels of the past, performing the operations of selectivity and interpretation required for each layer of past. To the extent that past and present are co-extensive, Bergsonism understands time as the contemporaneity of past with the present rather than a succession of nows.

Building on Bergson's intuition of duration, but also on Kierkegaard's repetition and Nietzsche's eternal return, Deleuze in *Difference and Repetition* distinguished between the memory/repetition of the past which enslaves and degrades – repetition of the same – and the other memory/repetition – repetition of difference – which goes against the generality of habit and the particularity of memory. Instead of being mere recollection, this repetition, being a task of freedom, is the one that makes a difference. This memory/repetition that makes a difference is not attained by will power alone. But to the extent that there is effort involved in remaining open to the possibility of repetition, Deleuze's theory of memory/repetition links ontology and ethics together: repetition is itself the test that selects worlds; we get, however, the world that we deserve.

The ethics of memory are discussed by Ricoeur in the context of his work on time and narrative, by Levinas in the context of his championing ethics as first philosophy, and by Derrida and Lyotard in the context of the duty of bearing witness. Memories are not only subjective, but as sedimented in institutions and cultures form who we can be. Shared narratives are constitutive of identity, and the realisation that identity is fundamentally narrative in character (and thus never innocent) makes us sensitive to the indeterminacy at the root of one's collective memory. For Levinas, time and memory are situated between the two injunctions: 'thou shall not kill', which addresses the self from the depths of an immemorial past – a past that has never been a present – and the 'à dieu' that releases the other to a messianic future. In this way, time and memory shed the 'virility' of the 'I can' and find themselves beyond the eternal opposition of efficacy and inefficacy. Pursuing demands that can be traced back to Merleau-Ponty for a memory without representation, and giving these demands an ethical turn, Lyotard argued that only 'phrasing' remains as an ethical and political duty, that is, the creation of a chain of 'testimonies' by witnesses who testify to the impossibility of representing horror and the silence of the dead.

C. *Boundas*

MERLEAU-PONTY, MAURICE (1908–61) French phenomenologist and theorist of embodiment; not only one of the greatest philosophers of the twentieth century, he is also the hinge linking Bergson, Husserl and Heidegger to Derrida, Deleuze and Foucault.

Merleau-Ponty was involved in many of the crucial events in the history of twentieth-century French philosophy. Shortly after completing his first thesis, *The Structure of Behaviour*, in 1938, he travelled to the then just-established Husserl Archives in Leuven, Belgium, where he was able to read many of Husserl's late texts, such as the second volume of *Ideas*, which contains Husserl's descriptions of the lived-body. The Archives also authorised him to take copies of certain manuscripts back to Paris in order to found the Husserl archives in Paris, which still reside at the École Normale Supérieure. During the occupation, Merleau-Ponty was active in the French Resistance, but he was also in the process of finishing his main thesis, the *Phenomenology of Perception*, one of the central texts of 'French Existentialism'. After the war, he founded, with Sartre, the journal *Les Temps Modernes*, and in 1952 he was elected to the Collège de France, at the age of 44. During the early 1950s, his friendship with Sartre and Beauvoir ends due to differences concerning politics and communism; Merleau-Ponty's publication of *Adventures of the Dialectic* (1955) marks this rupture. In 1960, he published *Signs*, a collection of his own essays, and, in 1961, a long essay on art and vision called 'Eye and Mind'. He died suddenly of a heart attack at his desk in Paris while in the process of writing a new major work, *The Visible and the Invisible*, which was published by his friend and former student, Claude Lefort, in 1964. Although incomplete, *The Visible and the Invisible* has exerted continuous influence over recent thought.

Merleau-Ponty always criticises what he calls in *The Visible and the Invisible* 'high-altitude or surveying thought'. What most generally characterises surveying thought is abstraction from existence – hence Merleau-Ponty's commitment to existentialism – or abstraction from experience. From the beginning of his career to the end, Merleau-Ponty criticises science for being abstract in this way, for explaining behaviour through one-to-one correspondences of stimulus and response found only in the experimental situation of the laboratory. More specifically, he tries to show that, whenever science tries to give a realist, causal or mechanistic explanation, it ends up supporting itself by means of an idealist, spontaneous or vitalistic explanation. Merleau-Ponty calls this shifting back and forth between contradictory positions – positions which end up being identical since neither provides an adequate explanation of behaviour – 'bad equivocity' or 'bad ambiguity' or 'bad dialectic'. By means of this criticism of science, we can see that Merleau-Ponty's thought is critical of all dualistic endeavours, and this rejection of dualism is why Merleau-Ponty is, as his career progresses, increasingly critical of Sartre's 'dialectic of being and nothingness'. Merleau-Ponty is resolutely anti-Cartesian, opposed to any sort of dual-substance metaphysics.

For Merleau-Ponty, we find good dialectic or good ambiguity when we return to the 'lived world'; here Merleau-Ponty appropriates Husserlian phenomenology. Merleau-Ponty's project consists in describing the phenomena of the world just as they are given to us or lived by us. But Merleau-Ponty is more than a phenomenologist. While Merleau-Ponty always remains close to Husserl's thought, he still sees in phenomenology the problems of dualism; we find this criticism in Merleau-Ponty's Preface to the *Phenomenology of Perception*. For Merleau-Ponty, Husserlian phenomenology is a modern version of Cartesianism. There is a bad dialectic in Husserl in so far as he wants to make a 'me' be the foundation for all knowledge, and then tries to explain the 'me' by means of an 'us' (by means of intersubjectivity).

Because of this criticism of phenomenology, Merleau-Ponty's return to the lived-world consists in a pre-reflective, anonymous, nearly unconscious level of experience. Most importantly, it is a return to tacit experience. Therefore, for Merleau-Ponty, the lived-world is first of all silent; it is the world of vision. Although Merleau-Ponty is famous for his descriptions of the lived body, the flesh, the touching-touched relation, his starting point is always the eyes. Most simply, we have to say that seeing something occurs by means of a differentiation between the figure and the background. There is in vision, as Merleau-Ponty will say in *The Visible and the Invisible*, a divergence or hiatus, 'un écart'. Merleau-Ponty always describes this divergence in two ways. On the one hand, vision is a specific kind of form or structure or sense, or, most precisely, a specific kind of whole. While Merleau-Ponty explicitly cites Gestalt psychology as his source for the concept of form (a Gestalt), it is clear that Bergson is his inspiration. In Merleau-Ponty, a whole is an indecomposable unity of internal, reciprocal determinations. This means that that if one of the parts changes, then the whole changes; conversely, if all the parts change, but still maintain the same relations among them, then the whole does not change.

For Merleau-Ponty, then, the whole is not the sum of its parts. There is no atomism of parts – parts are conceptually abstracted out of the whole – and no external parts (no *partes extra partes*). Since the differentiation in vision never results in external parts, since it never completely destroys the unity of the whole, the whole is always ambiguous or equivocal; this is the 'good ambiguity', in which the differentiated parts are never identical or contradictory. On the other hand, in so far as we can make this difference in the whole or in the field of vision, we learn a 'general aptitude' for discernment. Merleau-Ponty says that when a child starts to differentiate between colours, he or she is not learning each colour independently of the others; rather, the child is learning how to distinguish nuances. In 1952, in 'Indirect Language and the Voices of Silence', Merleau-Ponty will describe children's learning of language in the same way. One does not learn vocabulary; one learns a general aptitude for distinguishing sounds. The general aptitude is the power to make more differences, more variations and more expressions. This power to express is why we have to call Merleau-Ponty's thought 'expressionism'.

But we must also notice that in such an expressionism we have passed from silence to speech, indeed to creative speech, to what Merleau-Ponty would call 'speaking speech'. It in this passage that Merleau-Ponty will appropriate Heidegger's thought, especially Heidegger's reflections on history. For Merleau-Ponty, this general aptitude is a principle, an origin, or an 'arche'. In fact, Merleau-Ponty also characterises his thought as an 'archeology'. The general aptitude institutes a field in which we can work and which we can investigate; it therefore institutes a history or a tradition. For instance, Merleau-Ponty thinks that the cave paintings found in the south of France at the beginning of the twentieth century instituted the art of painting, in so far as those cave painters learned the general aptitude for drawing the world, for painting it, for saying it and writing it. In other words, by combining the two descriptions, we can say that this silent, general aptitude contained potentially the whole of what can be vocally expressed about the world. This general aptitude – which is an origin – and this whole – in which parts are indecomposably interwoven with other parts – is what Merleau-Ponty, in *The Visible and the Invisible*, calls the chiasm.

The idea of the chiasm (the X) – the interlacing or the folding together of parts which are nevertheless differentiated – also determines Merleau-Ponty's political thought. In his political writings, Merleau-Ponty never advocates an ideal for political action; the advocacy of a utopia (as we find in Marx and in Marxism) would be a form of 'high-altitude thinking'. For Merleau-Ponty, values and ends are always situated, always in the world. The ruling power and the subjects ruled are indecomposably interwoven. Given this chiasm of ruling and ruled, what is required for political action, according to Merleau-Ponty, is 'political virtue'. Political virtue, in Merleau-Ponty, is a means of living with others, that is it consists in, at once, not deciding according to others because then the ruling power would be contemptible, and not governing in isolation since governing in isolation is not authority. Therefore political virtue would be a general aptitude for expressing power in institutions that would create indefinitely more possibilities for living.

L. Lawlor

See also: chiasm; Embodiment; flesh; Gender; Memory; Psychology

METAPHYSICS A term which has been given a wide set of definitions, though in its first application, to certain books of Aristotle, it had no definition at all. The twelve books 'On Things After the Physics' (*tôn meta ta physika*) were, according to scholarly legend, merely a group of treatises which the ancient editors did not know where to place, and so simply slipped them in after the *Physics*.

In fact there is a thematic unity to (most of) Aristotle's *Metaphysics*, and it is one which indeed places it 'beyond physics'. For physics, on Aristotle's definition, concerns beings which have a principle of motion and rest within themselves, that is all material beings. The various treatises that come 'after' the *Physics* concern beings which do not have such principles, either because they do not move at all (and so cannot be at rest), or because their motions are entirely from outside (as is the case with words discussed in book V).

Metaphysics can thus be considered as the investigation of timeless entities, and since this is the foundation of more concrete investigations, Aristotle called it 'first philosophy'. Leibniz makes clear the moral and political significance of that priority when he writes in the *New Essays*: 'Metaphysics relates to true moral philosophy as theory to practice. That is because of the dependence on the doctrine of substances in general of that knowledge about spirits – and especially about God and the soul – which gives to justice and to virtue their proper extent.' This grounding function whereby metaphysics supports certain fixed concepts of 'justice' and 'virtue' will become the target of continental philosophy's critical work.

In modern times, as Heidegger has argued, epistemology became philosophically basic; what had previously been regarded as different orders of being were accordingly reconceptualised as objects of special sorts of knowing ('The Age of the World Picture', 1938). What now distinguished metaphysics from physics was not the kind of objects it studied, but the kind of knowledge it claimed to afford. Thus, for Kant in the *Critique of Pure Reason*, metaphysics claimed to give us knowledge which could not come from experience. The objects of this knowledge could be beings which change, such as souls, ghosts and angels. The important thing about them was that they could not be known empirically, which meant, for Kant, that they could not be known at all. Metaphysics was thus for Kant a cognitively spurious discipline. However, it had moral uses, because the things that make us good, our freedom, our souls, our immortality and even God himself, are supposed to be outside of experience. They are morally necessary intellectual fictions, and fully justified as such.

At this point, philosophy divided into two groups, both of which were critical of metaphysics but which defined it in the two different ways noted above. One group remained with Kant's epistemological definition of metaphysics; it tolerated appeals to an atemporal realm, so long as that realm was treated in strictly epistemological terms, i.e. as containing the 'laws' of logic. Those laws themselves were either grounded in some form of non-empirical intuition into logical structure (Husserl, Russell) or were simply viewed as stipulations or conventions justified by their success in guiding science (Carnap, Quine). The way was left to continue metaphysics, one which did not so much deny as disregard the moral dimension accorded to it by Kant.

The other, 'continental' approach is latent in Hegel and was decisively launched by Nietzsche ('On Truth and Lies in an Extramoral Sense') and Heidegger (*Being and Time*). It returns to the more ancient view of metaphysics as the study of unchanging or atemporal beings, and rejects it as such. In this perspective, metaphysics is not merely a cognitive mistake but has serious ethical and political consequences, for as the articulation of the atemporal realm it necessarily underlies and makes possible all attempts to impose an unchanging order on human affairs. In continental philosophy, then, the critique of metaphysics has become a part of critical theory in general. Thus, to mention only three great thinkers of recent French philosophy, Derrida attacks atemporal approaches as exemplifying the 'privileging of presence', that is, the idea that something can be 'summed up (*résumée*) in some absolute simultaneity or instantaneity' ('Force and Signification', 1967); Foucault attacks the unities and continuities posited by traditional history in the name of discontinuity and rupture (*The Archaeology of Knowledge*); and Deleuze attempts to think beyond identity by means of a thought of 'difference in itself' (*Difference and Repetition*).

Metaphysics as the focus upon presence or atemporality thus figures within continental philosophy primarily as an object of critique; it is not a field which could be redefined and carried forward. Nor is it merely a wrongheaded direction for philosophy, a set of fallacies to be exposed and eliminated through philosophical argumentation. Rather, in its downgrading of the temporal dimension in favour of what is taken to be permanent, it is an ideological warrant for static oppression and for manifold resulting injustices.

J. McCumber

METAPOLITICS A term used by both Badiou and Rancière in their political writings, with opposite meanings. For Badiou, politics is one of the four domains where truths are possible, alongside art, science and love. As philosophy is the articulation of truths that are effectively produced elsewhere, the programme of a 'political philosophy' leads to a negation of politics. The philosophy of politics must be more modestly described as metapolitical. Rancière agrees with Badiou that classical and contemporary political philosophies proceed to expel the political out of politics. Both believe that the rise of political philosophy as an academic discipline is one of the symptoms of the death of real, that is antagonistic and egalitarian, politics in contemporary societies. In Rancière's work, however, metapolitics designates only one of the three ideal-typical models, next to Platonic archipolitics and Aristotelian parapolitics, with which philosophy attempts to conjure the scandal immanent in the political axiom. This scandal is the assertion of the radical equality of all speaking beings that undermines all master discourses, including philosophy. Rancière's metapolitics refers to the Marxian thesis that the truth of politics is to be found in the social, and is always irretrievably lost in the institutions and language of democracy. This casts a deadly suspicion over all democratic struggles. Ironically, by projecting the truth of politics in an ideal situation where the whole sum of social parts and interests are to be reconciled, Marxist metapolitics announce the end of politics achieved in liberal post-democracy.

J.-P. Deranty

MIMESIS ('imitation') A Greek term used by Irigaray as the name for a reading strategy that subverts masculinist texts by imitating their claims. Plato and Aristotle use 'mimesis' to speak of the representation of one thing by another, particularly in the work of art. Though the term is now considered an outmoded way to speak about art, it has considerable use in feminist circles.

Irigaray employs a mimetic strategy for reading historical texts to counter the way women have been subordinated to the 'outside' of essentially masculine discourse. The (male) subject position of enunciation establishes itself as self, idea, spirit, consciousness by exiling the feminine to the border of discourse as otherness, matter, nature, unconsciousness. To establish a subject position for women within the imaginary and symbolic realms of 'phallogocentrism' requires more than a simple act of recognition, since one cannot simply step outside of meanings into which one is born. Rather, we must seek a new relationship to discourse itself. Irigaray thus rethinks her relationship to discourse by miming the discourses of philosophers. Irigaray speaks the very language she is excluded from, turning the muteness of otherness, matter, nature, unconsciousness into a disruptive performance of the impossibility of a (female) subject position within language.

Irigaray's appropriation of masculinist imaginary and symbolic representations of the feminine has caused some feminist critics to charge her with essentialism. However, Irigaray's mimetic strategy calls essentialism into question by its performance of a repetition that overflows the very meaning of that which it repeats.

S. Keltner

MIMETIC DESIRE The core theoretical concept of René Girard in *Deceit, Desire, and the Novel* (1961), it describes unconscious mechanisms of imitation revealed by great novelists underneath the agonised pretensions of romantic 'spontaneity' or freedom. Girard then broadened it into a 'fundamental anthropology' to explain the origins of culture and religion. What is original in Girard's theory is that mimesis, as an interpersonal relation (not a metaphysical or aesthetic one), is a source of violence, though one that is potentially creative, if only within limits. Human beings imitate each other not only outwardly but inwardly, in their emotional lives as in their behaviour. Desires must be learned, objects acquired from others by imitation; desire does not naturally know how or what to desire. It is 'triangular', mediated by a model whose example suggests what is desirable. Reciprocal imitation of desires, though, entails rivalry, conflict and violence if unchecked. Beings who acquire objects by imitating each other become rivals and enemies if they desire the same things, and also because they may become fascinated and obsessed with each other. A charismatic model for desire might become its object, and an obstacle, even an enemy, just because he or she is a model. Modern romantic desire illustrates this propensity for moral or psychological master–slave relations, an internalised violence leading to moral, psychological or physical self-destruction. The violence of mimetic desire is productive if channelled cathartically, as in ancient sacrificial systems and (more ambiguously) in the creative rivalries of modern economies.

S. Gardner

MINOR LITERATURE A term employed by Deleuze and Guattari to designate a style of writing that transforms 'major literature' (those works which form unities and establish standards, producing a norm for a people or nation) by challenging its established codes and canons. Derived from their reading of Kafka, for Deleuze and Guattari minor literature is neither determined on the basis of numbers nor on the mere presence of dissidence. Rather, the analysis of minor literature follows from Deleuze and Guattari's notion that language does not essentially communicate information but, by means of 'order words', triggers habitual behaviour within a social 'assemblage'. Bypassing and experimenting with these order words are the tasks of minor literature; in doing so, nothing in minor literature escapes the political and everything takes on a collective value. Minor writers thus shun the ideology that celebrates the greatness of individual authors. Instead they opt for anonymity and engage in fabulation, as they attempt to conjure up a people that do not yet exist rather than reinforce the habits of a nationalised people. By their experimentation with language minor authors look to bring out the 'passwords' and the lines of flight (or lines of continuous variation and modulation) that inhabit language, so they can transform dominant and canonic language from within. 'Making language stutter', one of Deleuze and Guattari's own 'passwords', means engaging in an intensive use of language beyond the symbolic and the signifying, in order to take language to its limit, to reveal its outer side, its rhythms, painting and music, and thereby free it as a field of experimentation for the production of new bodies, new habits, indeed, a 'new earth' as they call for in both *A Thousand Plateaus* and *What is Philosophy?*

C. Boundas

MODERNITY A contested value within continental philosophy designating social practices of rationalisation, in which traditional ways and values are judged according to their efficiency in reaching individual and social goals that do not need traditional justifications. No given value or way of life is to be accepted without scrutiny. The modern expectation is that everything can be changed, that things should be different from what they have been, and that this change will continue beyond the present.

The proponents of modernisation promise that it will liberate us from brute forces of nature, oppressive social powers and the alien within our psyches, bringing us self-reliance through reason and dispelling illusion and superstition in a self-authorising and self-transparent manner. So it seems to be the final and culminating stance towards the world, society and ourselves. It is not just another particular traditional mode of living, with its own individualistic values. It is what we get when we remove all traditional modes of living, a degree zero of bare humanity. So modernisation seems to be a universal process, a development beyond any fixed set of values, rather than the imposition of a particular set of Western values.

Modernity is said to begin at different times. Self-announced modern painting begins in the second half of the nineteenth century, modern architecture in the early twentieth century, modern political institutions in the eighteenth century, modern economic systems at various times from the Renaissance onward. Modern philosophy is usually said to begin with Descartes in the sixteenth century, though some have traced its precursors earlier to Nicholas of Cusa and Giordano Bruno.

Modern philosophy's first emblem is Descartes' refusal to accept anything merely because of authority or history, his search for individual certainty and his ambition to make us 'the masters and possessors of nature'. Its second emblem is the dispute between Hobbes and Locke over a civil commonwealth based on the consent of its citizens. Its third is the programme of the Enlightenment to bring the triumph of reason over superstition and of human nature over oppressive social systems. Its fourth is Hume's scepticism about knowledge even as he affirms the Enlightenment's moral and political goals. Then comes Kant's redefinition of philosophy's task as the self-analysis of knowledge, with the modern goal of moral autonomy and self-legislation. This is picked up and broadened in the German Romantics and in Hegel and other nineteenth-century philosophers, and developed anew in Husserl's projects of rational grounding, in neo-Kantian efforts at rational analysis and in many movements of analytic philosophy.

The most common popular reaction against modernity is a forced return to tradition in the name of some political or religious fundamentalism, and in philosophy there are anti-modern movements that try to reassert traditional values and authorities. But more common in philosophy is the attempt to show that the definition of modernity given by any one thinker is not the final word. Champions of modernity claim to have understood the process within which historical constructions of knowledge and value happen, and further that this process can be described in formal terms devoid of historical content. Self-confident moderns seldom ask whether their formal processes and empty selves could be masks over something deeper, a neglect that critics of modernity such as Schopenhauer, Nietzsche and Heidegger find ludicrous. Others such as Derrida, Foucault and Deleuze affirm, in their own way, the modern goals of freedom and justice while refusing their equation with any programme of rationalisation or any idea of transparent and dominating selfhood. All these thinkers try to show that modernity is located within a context and made possible by processes that modernity cannot describe. If so, then the standard modern dualities (self/other, private/public, form/content, individual/ community) cannot be taken as the last word.

In continental philosophy modernity then becomes a contested topic. Debates often centre on the relevance today of Enlightenment values, and on whether rationality and freedom stand together or in conflict. Few, aside from Nietzsche wearing some of his masks, dispute the goals of freedom and self-responsibility, but there is little agreement about what they mean and how they should be achieved. Some Marxists and feminists see modernity as an oppressive era tied to capitalism and patriarchy. Others, such as Habermas, affirm modernity as an unfinished project to realise Enlightenment goals; the problems of modernity are said to stem from their so far incomplete realisation in inadequate economic and political structures. Still others, such as Lyotard, see an open-ended movement in which so-called postmodernity is only a deeper version of modernity.

D. Kolb

MOMENT OF VISION (1) The Danish *Øjeblikket* means literally 'the glance of the eye', and as both the temporal and visionary elements are crucial to its Kierkegaardian meaning, it is rendered 'moment of vision'. Its background is the New Testament idea of the 'fullness of time' (*kairos*) in which alone the Messiah could come, thus filling the emptiness of human, historical time with divine meaning. Kierkegaard uses it to emphasise the significance of the historical moment in Christianity, as opposed to Platonism (and idealism generally). He also applies it to the individual, whose anxious struggle for meaning is continuously threatened by time, with its message that all things must pass and end in death. This situation invites despair, but despair can be defeated if the individual learns through anxious concern to find trans-temporal meaning ('the eternal') in the moment. This is reflected in the virtues of patience and hope as well as in faith in the moment of the incarnation.

G. Pattison

MOMENT OF VISION (2) The German word for 'moment of vision', *Augenblick* (more literally, the 'glance of the eye'), is used by Heidegger in *Being and Time* to designate the authentic present, that is the present situation as disclosed on the basis of the ecstatic nature of the temporality of existence. Da-sein, as the there of being, is essentially a clearing, or a making present – in other words, a temporal phenomenon. But the temporality of time is not rooted in the present understood in terms of the 'now', or as what is happening right now. It is not made of a succession of present moments. Rather, the present, as a present situation, is opened up as a result of the fact that Dasein is at once the being that always has been, or the being that 'I am-as-having-been', and the being that is always coming towards itself, or ahead of itself. The present situation of existence, then, is a function of existence's irreducible having-been-ness (which must not be mistaken for its mere past, as something that is 'no longer') and futurity (which must not be mistaken for something that is merely 'not yet'). It is only as a result of the specific transformation, or conversion, of Dasein in the phenomenon of 'resolute disclosedness' that ever so briefly existence envisages the present as Augenblick. Then, and only then, is the present understood as an 'ecstasis', a standing-outside-oneself (alongside those of having-been-ness and futurity), and not as a mere point on a continuous line.

M. de Beistegui

MULTIPLICITY A term used in contemporary philosophy to designate the multiple as a substantive, rather than as a predicate. The multiple as predicate generates a set of philosophical problems under the rubric of 'the one and the many' (a thing is one or multiple, one and multiple, and so on). With multiplicity, or the multiple as substantive, the question of the relation between the predicates one/multiple is replaced by the question of distinguishing between types of multiplicities. A typological difference between substantive multiplicities, in short, is substituted for the dialectical opposition of the one and the multiple.

Several thinkers stand out in the contemporary development of a philosophy of multiplicity. The term itself, 'multiplicity' (*Manigfaltigkeit*), owes its provenance to the German mathematician G. F. B. Riemann (1826–66). In his *Habilitationschrift* (1859) on foundational geometry, Riemann argued that the axioms of traditional geometry remain grounded in assumptions about space as we ordinarily experience it. Geometry should rather begin from general notions of 'multiply extended magnitudes', what we now know as 'n-dimensional spaces'. Such magnitudes can be either continuous or discrete. In contradistinction to sets, no other quality determines a multiplicity, so the multiplicity is not unified by any principle transcending it. Discrete multiplicities contain the principle of their own measurement relations, whereas there is no internal potential for quantification of comparisons in continuous multiplicities, so this principle has to be introduced into the multiplicity.

In *Time and Free Will*, Bergson applies this distinction to differentiate between the multiplicities of time (or duration) and space. The former is continuous, and since it contains no internal principle of quantifiable measurement, is characterised as qualitative. Thus, whenever time is rendered measurable in philosophy, a quantitative principle from the discrete multiplicity of spatiality is introduced into temporality. This fundamentally alters the nature of the temporal multiplicity, meaning metaphysics fails to grasp time's true nature. Bergson further argues that many problems in metaphysics need to be recast in genuinely temporal rather than spatial terms to overcome traditional philosophical errors stemming from the intellectual tendency to render phenomena spatial and hence measurable.

Edmund Husserl, in his *Philosophy of Arithmetic*, noted that certain sensory perceptions (for example, that of a flock of birds) present multiplicities that are irreducible to numerical multiplicities, since they lack any explicit colligation: he called them 'implied' multiplicities with 'quasi-qualitative characteristics' or 'figural factors'.

Current discussions of the theory of multiplicities, however, have tended to focus on the work of Deleuze and Badiou. In *Difference and Repetition*, Deleuze attempted to present an explicit formalisation of virtual multiplicities in terms of three conditions, borrowed from the model of the calculus: (1) their elements are merely determinable, having neither identity, form, signification or function in themselves; (2) the elements nonetheless receive a reciprocal determination in the differential relation; and (3) the values of these relations determine a distribution of singularities, which constitute the multiplicity as a virtual and problematic field which is progressively determined and resolved. Deleuze has insisted on distinguishing between problematics (virtual multiplicities) and axiomatics (numerical multiplicities or sets): while the path of science is to reduce the former to the latter, virtual multiplicities nonetheless maintain an irreducible ontological status.

Badiou, by contrast, in *Being and Event* (1988), argued, against Deleuze, that (1) the theory of multiplicities is exhausted in axiomatic set theory, and hence that virtual multiplicities do not exist (all multiplicities are discrete); and (2) that axiomatic set theory is the discourse of ontology itself, the theory of 'being as being'. For Badiou, what remains undecidable or indiscernible from the ontological viewpoint of axiomatic set theory (ontology) is the 'event', which marks the infinite excess of an inconsistent multiplicity over the consistent sets of a situation. Lacking any ontological status, the event in Badiou is linked to a rigorous conception of subjectivity, the subject being the sole instance capable of 'naming' the event and maintaining a fidelity to it through the declaration of an axiom. Badiou summarised his criticisms in *Deleuze: The Clamour of Being* (1997), and the debate between the two positions remains a lively one.

R. Durie and D. Smith

MULTITUDE The supranational collective political subject emerging from the conditions of contemporary globalisation or Empire in the political philosophy of Michael Hardt, Antonio Negri and their collaborators, most importantly Paolo Virno. They draw the term from Spinoza's political writings and deploy it in opposition to the traditional nationalist/imperialist conception of the people. The people is the product of a double operation of (mis)representation: first, the imaginary construction of an essentialised racial identity defined against external or subordinated racial groups, especially colonised peoples; and second, the ideological erasure of internal class, gender or ethnic differentiations among the people so that one sub-group, for example the white male bourgeoisie, can claim to represent the whole nation and govern in the people's name by means of immutable state institutions. Since the concept of the people is a product of the nation-state and not the prior logical basis for it, it has no validity and offers no leverage for collective resistance at the supranational level of Empire. The multitude, conversely, is not a monolithic and exclusionary essence but an inclusive multiplicity, an open set of heterogeneous and irreducible singularities that operates not through fixed national institutions but through the protean processes of constituent power. The multitude's intermittent but ongoing political project is the constitution of a global, denationalised, non-representational radical democracy, and one of the crucial subjective positions in this project is the socialised worker of immaterial labour.

T. Murphy

NANCY, JEAN-LUC (1940–) French philosopher whose thought, while in close proximity with the deconstructive thought of Jacques Derrida, is marked by a clear originality. A good bit of Nancy's early work was pursued in collaboration with Philippe Lacoue-Labarthe, who went on to write several interesting works in the area marked by the intersection of the thought of Derrida and Heidegger. Nancy's first book with Lacoue-Labarthe was *The Title of the Letter* (1973), a short but dense essay on Lacan's 'Agency of the Letter in the Unconscious' in which the authors undertake to expose the metaphysical underpinnings of Lacan's theory; their reading was praised by Lacan (in *Seminar XX*), albeit begrudgingly. Nancy soon published several solo essays, also of a deconstructive nature, each bearing on a key figure or movement in the history of philosophy: Hegel, Descartes, Heidegger, Kant and, with Lacoue-Labarthe, German Idealism.

In 1980 Nancy and Lacoue-Labarthe founded the Centre de Recherches Philosophiques sur le Politique (Centre for Philosophical Research on the Political); from the work of this group emerged two works on political philosophy: *Rejouer le Politique* (1981) and *Le Retrait du Politique* (1983; translated as *Retreating the Political*, 1997). The decisive work, however, which set the tone for the rest of Nancy's career, was *The Inoperative Community* (1983). Nancy here attempts, inspired in large part by Bataille, to conceive community outside traditional concepts like the individual and the group. In a decisive gesture, Nancy distinguishes our being-in-common from commonality, so that to be in-common no longer means sharing a commonality or identity. Rather, the 'in' of 'in-common' does not mark an essential identity, but a relation of differences. That way, being in-common no longer means sharing a sameness, a substantial identity, a phantasm of oneness with all of its catastrophic political implications; rather, 'we' share an 'inoperative' community, an absence of commonality, in a word we share a difference or our non-identity, 'our' differences. This is why Nancy focuses on the term 'partage', which in French retains the senses of both a sharing and a division. Community is then a tear, which is connected precisely through those tears and gaps. Nancy summarises his position as follows: 'The community that becomes a single thing (body, mind, fatherland, Leader . . .) necessarily loses the in of being-in-common. Or, it loses the with or the together that defines it. It yields its being-together to a being of togetherness. The truth of community, on the contrary, resides in the withdrawal of such a being.'

Nancy pursues this work on community in *La comparution* (1991) by focusing on the nature of the 'with' in our being-with, while moving away from the language of 'community', which still recalls too much the common and a logic of unity. Thus, in *Being Singular Plural* (1996), he elaborates a logic of the 'with' by which the with is said to distribute singularities which themselves are nothing outside of the with which communicates them to other singularities. There lies the non-essential structure of being-with, the singular/plural structure of existence.

Finally, Nancy develops an important thought of our finite existence, radically devoid of any theological background and justification, also devoid of a grounding in a subject, 'subsisting' only in the with where it happens, each time singularly, and each time plurally. This opens onto a renewed thought of freedom, of free existence, developed in *The Experience of Freedom* (1988); it also opens onto a renewed thought of democracy and political sovereignty elaborated in *A Finite Thought* (1990), *The Sense of the World* (1993), and *La création du monde ou la mondialisation* (2002). Several essays on art also elaborate on this ungrounded making of the sense of the world (the world itself being nothing other than this making): *Les muses* (1994), *La naissance des seins* (1997), *Le regard du portrait* (2000), and *Visitation* (2001). A long-awaited multi-volume work on 'The Deconstruction of Christianity' is forthcoming in 2005. Nancy thus displays an extraordinary creativity, all the more impressive since he has gone through serious health difficulties – a heart transplant and cancer – an experience of which he writes movingly in *L'intrus* (2000).

F. Raffoul

NARRATIVE VOICE, THE A term by which Blanchot referred to the possibility of saying without showing, and thus of escaping the forms of conscious subjectivity that always intervene within narrative, turning it into a temporal continuity of that very subjectivity. Even in cases in which writers try to distance themselves from their own presence in the narrative such a presence can still be discerned. Two cases in point that Blanchot mentions in his essay 'The Narrative Voice' are Flaubert and Henry James. Even though Flaubert was looking for a certain 'impersonality' in *Madame Bovary* he nevertheless 'affirmed the validity of the narrative mode: to tell is to show'. In James's *Ambassadors* the impersonal forces of the narrative assume in the end a privileged point of view. In both cases 'the primacy of an individual consciousness' is maintained. In contrast to that, the narrative voice is the effect of the self-distancing of the I from itself, its passage from the first person (*je*) to the third person (*il*) subjective pronoun, which, being nobody's voice, becomes the voice of the neutral 'it'. This voice that tells without representing does not represent 'characters'. Characters become 'bearers of speech' whose subjective coherence is substituted by their falling into a 'relation of self-nonidentification'. The neutral voice and the absence of characters make of the narrative what Blanchot called a *récit* – a strange and 'perverse', distant and reserved recounting of absolute oblivion, from which the subjectivity capable of remembering and narrating has vanished.

B. Arsić

NATALITY A technical term introduced by Arendt to capture the distinctive capacity of human action to initiate new beginnings. The concept owes much to Arendt's lifelong obsession with modernity and political revolutions, although she herself traces it back to ancient Greek and early Christian notions of freedom. Early Christian thinkers like Paul and Augustine were among the first to articulate the inner conflict of the will with itself and the capacity of the will to radically choose a new beginning in the form of religious conversion or spiritual rebirth. The distinctly modern idea of breaking with the political past later informs modern revolutionary thought, which seeks to found new constitutions of freedom on the basis of free consent rather than traditional authority. The political meaning of natality, however, descends more directly from the Greek notion of action (*archein* = to begin or initiate). Here Arendt stresses the utter unpredictability of unique actions that draw their very meaning and identity from the sheer distinctiveness of individual actors. For the Greeks, the unpredictable and agonal display of personality in the public political sphere sharply contrasts with the ordinary and commonplace routines of economic life in the domestic sphere. Aside from its Greek and early Christian genealogy, the concept of natality also strongly resonates with contemporary existentialist themes, most notably Heidegger's conception of the sheer contingency of human beings who find themselves inserted into a world not of their own making and who must carry the burden of freely remaking themselves over and over again, that is of giving their life fresh meaning.

D. Ingram

NATURALISING PHENOMENOLOGY A phrase that refers to the attempt to integrate first-person phenomenological descriptions with third-person natural science. This integration would allow phenomenological insights to enlighten or constrain the cognitive sciences just as it would encourage natural scientists to take first-person experience seriously.

For some phenomenologists, however, naturalising phenomenology is a controversial proposal. Husserl's transcendental phenomenology is understood to be opposed to naturalistic explanations and to methodologically exclude (by phenomenological reduction) such explanations. Thus any attempt to integrate phenomenological descriptions with naturalistic explanation is like trying to create, in Husserl's phrase, 'wooden iron'. These phenomenologists argue that objective discoveries in the cognitive sciences cannot constrain phenomenology since any change of understanding we may gain about the objective facts concerning brain function or behaviour will not change what our experience is like. If our experience is describable as 'X', the fact that the brain events that correspond to it are discovered to be ABC rather than CDE will not change the experience.

Others are not so negative about the project, however, and argue that the attempt to naturalise phenomenology is not an attempt to revise or reformulate the phenomenological project, but is rather simply an attempt to use the first-person methods, or the important results, of phenomenological investigations to inform the cognitive sciences about the experiences that they are attempting to explain. Jean Petitot, Francisco Varela, Bernard Pachoud, Jean-Michel Roy and others in the volume *Naturalising Phenomenology* (1999) argue that Husserl's anti-naturalist orientation was motivated by an obsolete understanding of mathematics (namely, his belief that a geometrical or mathematical descriptive eidetics is impossible), and that phenomenological results can be integrated into a scientific explanatory framework by employing advanced mathematical models (including dynamical systems theory) to show how every phenomenal property is continuous with properties explained by the natural sciences.

There are, however, other ways to move forward on naturalising phenomenology. A team of scientists led by Francisco Varela used the method of phenomenological reduction in experimental brain science, specifically in brain imaging studies, in order to provide an additional level of control on experiential reports, to identify correlations between brain activity and structural features of consciousness, and to make the results more precisely tuned to the subjects' actual experience. Others have proposed that insights developed in strict phenomenological investigations can be used to inform experimental design in the cognitive sciences. A complement to this approach can be found in Merleau-Ponty's attempt to use phenomenology to guide the interpretation of scientific results, as in *Phenomenology of Perception*. These are different ways in which phenomenology may be able to constrain work in the cognitive sciences, and in that way integrate first-person experience with objective accounts.

Just as some phenomenologists argue against scientific constraints on phenomenology, however, some cognitive scientists and philosophers of mind reject the idea that phenomenology can constrain the

scientific investigation of consciousness. They claim that phenomenology is simply a form of introspection, and that first-person reports are
not to be trusted; for these thinkers, the task is to neutralise phenomenology rather than naturalise it. Specifically, they attempt to neutralise or reduce first-person descriptions of experience to third-person
data. Dennett's notion of 'heterophenomenology', as advanced in
Consciousness Explained (1991), is a good example. Following a hetero-
phenomenological procedure, introspective reports of experimental
subjects are not taken at face value, but treated as narrative texts
open to interpretation informed by other more objective measures. In
this approach, scientific objective measures always take precedence
over any experiential report.

Proponents of naturalising phenomenology thus walk a thin line
between defenders of pure phenomenology, on the one side, and critics
of phenomenology on the other. For discussion of these different
viewpoints, see Anthony Jack and Andreas Roepstorff (eds), *Trusting
the Subject?* (2003).

S. Gallagher

NATURE, PHILOSOPHY OF Philosophical reflection on nature – at
least in the West – can be said to begin when the Ionians hypothesised
an intelligible principle subtending the incessant, phenomenal flux of
sensible reality. They named this principle *phusis*, from the Greek
phuo-, *phuein*, referring to the growth, becoming and generation (and
also to the decline, degeneration and death) immanent to and the cause
of the cosmos. The early Greeks thus conceived of a living nature, and
their *phusis* is translated later by their Latin heirs as *nascor*, to be born,
to live, from which our modern word 'nature' is derived. The observation of natural phenomena ('physics') led these natural philosophers to replace the mythical explanation of the world with a reflection
on the hidden causes (Heraclitus: 'Nature likes to hide itself') that lay
beyond what was available to sense ('metaphysics') and that govern all
phenomenal life. Whether these causes are the elements (Empedocles,
anticipating Deleuze, named them *rhizomata*, the roots that sustain
life), or the *apeiron*, the unlimited, nature is understood as a blind
productivity acting in and sustaining the cosmos and as the principle of
all natural phenomena.

From this vitalistic conception, the Greeks derived ethical and
political principles, constituting a philosophical naturalism of which
Plato was the first great critic. For Plato, the productive 'forces' of
nature (*ananke* and *eros* – 'necessity' and 'desire') must be guided by
the superior principle of the soul or *psuchē*, because the cosmic order

cannot be the result of mere chance; rather, the true 'nature' and cause of the world is its transcendent, intelligible idea (*eidos*). Aristotle criticises the Platonic *eidē* as metaphysical, arguing that Nature is the substance or essence (*ousia*) of beings that contain within themselves their principle of movement and the cause that directs them to the end (*telos*) of their becoming, thus introducing the idea of finalism or teleology (later revived by Kant) into the philosophy of nature. The different natural sciences are constructed on the basis of this definition as a general branch of philosophy, second only to metaphysics: natural science studies the essence and causality of natural beings. But this natural essentialism will also have important ethico-political implications, as are clear from Aristotle's remarks on 'the nature' of women and slaves, important contributions to the history of Western misogyny and racism.

Within the continental philosophical tradition, Heidegger is perhaps the foremost reader of Greek *phusis* and its conceptual transformations. His readings of the Greeks, together with those comprising his critical history of being, and with his own work on 'earth and world', constitute a trend in the continental philosophy of nature that we may call 'autochthontology', the logos of the autochthonous or 'earth-born'. Heidegger's efforts, and the resources of the phenomenological tradition more generally, have also been brought to bear on environmental issues in order both to resist the anthropocentric and naturalistic assumptions of ecological science; this 'eco-phenomenology' offers a new approach to nature, the natural world and environmental ethics.

It is noteworthy that the idea of Nature, and the sciences that refer to it, are instituted only when the work of reflection transcends the naive attitude of living in accord with Nature, that is when thought 'denaturalises' its object. There can be no conception of a 'nature-in-itself' that is not always already a product of reflection, of discourse or, more generally, of a culture, precisely because every concept of nature is constructed by external observers, recognising neither that they participate in the object they describe, nor that their own situation is already marked by history and culture. Every 'philosophy of nature' must therefore be understood as a discursive production or as a cultural history of representations that shape the operative concepts of a civilisation, with implications for science, politics and ethics, which themselves reciprocally continue to construct their object ('nature') in order to legitimate their discursive authority. The Ionian institution of the idea of Nature thus also institutes a scientifico-philosophical tradition stretching from Parmenides to phenomenology, from Thales to the theory of quantum mechanics, and a critical 'reading' of this tradition is also a dominant theme in the continental approach to the philosophy of nature.

One such reading is offered by Merleau-Ponty. When the theoretical attitude determines nature as an object of thought, the task of scientific and philosophical discourse becomes the full determination of this object. This objectification or desire for a complete 'ontology of the object' reaches a fevered pitch at the dawn of the Modern period. For Descartes, the only indubitable reality is the essential nature of the cogito (*res cogitans*), while natural, material existence (the body and its irrational natural inclinations) is devalued in virtue of its negativity and its continuous diremption. Only the intellectual idea of the body and of external nature (*res extensa*) can be known, because, as extension in space, bodies are measurable and can be translated into the ideal and intelligible, permanent and positive language of mathematics and geometry (Galileo: the book of nature is written in geometrical figures), the principles of which can be derived from the cogito. The objective ontology thus dominates the tradition through the strategic devaluation of an 'ontology of the existent'. The living Nature of the Greeks is replaced by a system of physical laws and mathemes, and a double death blow is delivered when, first, Descartes argues that extended nature operates as a mechanical system, and when, second, Newton conceives of inert matter affected by external forces. Goethe, Schelling and the Romantics react strongly against this conception of 'dead', inert nature and the instrumentalisation of reason by reasserting a notion of Nature as living dynamism, seeking to overcome the metaphysical dualism of the external orders of subject and object by underlining our own belongingness to nature (the implications of which will be more fully theorised by quantum mechanics). For Merleau-Ponty, the Western philosophico-scientific tradition is structured by the tension between these two ontologies, and he interrogates the repressive strategies deployed by the tradition in order both to disrupt objectivism and to determine whether contemporary scientific discourse remains tributary to (or corrects the false postulates of) objectivism, or if it discloses a new, implicit but unthematised ontology of nature. The goal of such a reading is not to gainsay the contributions of science, but rather to let the philosophical and scientific research of nature inform one another, in order to articulate a non-objectivist conception of nature that more closely conforms to our experience of the world.

Critically reading the concept of nature as a product of discursive practices has allowed for the emergence of a philosophical anti-naturalism, with significant implications for contemporary feminism, critical race theory and queer theory. When Beauvoir asserted in *The Second Sex* that 'one is not born a woman, but rather, becomes one', she at once delivered a sharp blow to the biological essentialism inaugurated by Aristotle and recognised that the subject is 'constructed' by the complex interplay of social structures that operate directly on the body. DuBois, influenced by his reading of Hegel and Marx, had already taken a step in this direction when, against Kant, he recognised that 'race' was a product of a common historical and cultural experience. Beauvoir and Fanon demonstrate that the biological 'fact' of one's sex or 'the fact of blackness' does not determine the moral value of the person; rather, embodied facticity contributes to how one experiences a world always already structured by oppressors who deploy an essentialism in order to maintain their own power and privilege. While attacking this essentialism is 'the work of liberation', Beauvoir is sometimes criticised for not subjecting the concept of nature itself to radical examination. Her heirs (Guillaumin, Delphy, Irigaray) show that the idea of nature on which dangerous essentialisms depends is a product of racist, sexist and phallogocentric ideologies that inform scientific discourse and cultural practice in order to define 'the natural' as normative. Foucault's work in general extends and radicalises this anti-essentialism by analysing the historical operations of discourse and power; his work on human sexuality, the body and biopower have likewise had important political and social consequences by liberating them from their traditional, naturalistic framework.

Perhaps the most radically innovative continental approach to the philosophy of nature is articulated by Deleuze (sometimes with his colleague Guattari), and can be characterised as an anti-humanist biophilosophy. Seeking to dissolve the privilege that human being has enjoyed since the advent of Kantian humanism and to undermine every received scientifico-philosophical orthodoxy, Deleuze argues (against the Aristotelian-Kantian definition, and inspired by Nietzsche, Bergson and others) that the organism is a 'machinic' assemblage of multiplicities that deploys various technics of complexification and symbiotic integration in order to create new forms. This means, first, that species do not only evolve in linear, genetic, teleological descent but also through a 'rhizomatic' becoming, that is transversal alliances of heterogeneous terms whose plural, symbiotic and machinic functionings (or technics) constitute an open-ended 'unity'. Second, it implies that 'artifice is fully a part of nature,' thus collapsing the classic distinctions (human/machine, organic/inorganic, phusis/technē) on which old, anthropocentric narratives like humanism are grounded. Deleuze's biophilosophy is not a postmodern philosophy of nature, but rather challenges us to think, in a radically and rigorously un-Kantian manner, 'beyond the human', a challenge with disconcerting implications for any epistemology attempting to ground knowledge in a subject.

R. Vallier

NEGATIVE DIALECTICS A term coined by Adorno for a process of thinking akin to Hegel's 'determinate negation', in which the meaning of concepts is shown to be immanently and determinately related to that from which such concepts are distinguished – most fundamentally the material world itself. For Adorno, negative dialectics does not constitute consciousness and/or being as such but is rather a mode of 'second reflection' on form(s) of reason constituted in the course of the historical effort to dominate nature. Negative dialectics maps out the mutual implication and antagonisms within a series of conceptual 'extremes': subject and object, concept and thing, history and nature. At the same time, it resists the temptation to 'freeze' these extremes as ontological firsts, or to order them as terms in a developing synthesis. Negative dialectics is thus 'the logic of the wrong state of things'. As both the product of – and a form of resistance to – the history that structures thought and practice, it is the practice needed for one to think non-identity while still under the spell of identity thinking. Negative dialectics opens the hesitant possibility for thinking otherwise, for thinking in the form of 'constellations' of concepts that cognise determinate objects by means of a field of conceptual antagonisms, without reducing them to that field. Negative dialectics thus embodies the sense of a debt to the 'object' that suffers under the domination of identity-thinking as well as the possibility of 'reconciliation' in which the thought no longer dominates nature.

M. Bray

NEGATIVE PHILOSOPHY The term Schelling uses late in his career to indicate the limit of rational metaphysics, which is 'negative' in the sense that it can only develop the logical implications of our concepts and is incapable of penetrating to actual existence. Because concepts do have logical implications, Schelling understands them as denoting an order of pure possibility (he calls his own version of negative philosophy a theory of 'potencies'). An example of what he has in mind is the ontological proof of the existence of God. While Schelling agrees that the concept of God entails his necessary existence, he denies that existence therefore flows from the concept. He says that what the argument really demonstrates is that if God happens to exist, then He is that being that exists by necessity. It is in some sense logical to reply that some being must exist, in so far as the alternative, non-being, is precisely what by definition cannot be. The problem, however, is that if in fact there were nothing, then the logical itself would have no power and authority. Being is in this sense prior to logic. Schelling cites Aristotle and Hegel as having offered the most complete examples of negative philosophy. He criticises Hegel, however, for failing to understand the impossibility of a logical transition from the Logic to nature and existence. Had he seen the impossibility of the transition, he would have followed Schelling in holding negative and positive philosophy apart.

J. Lawrence

NEGRI, ANTONIO (1933–) Italian philosopher and political activist whose work on the modern state, revolutionary subjectivity and globalisation has played a major role in the renewal of Marxism and materialism over the past thirty years. Negri is best known for his studies of Marx, Spinoza and the contemporary form of transnational governance he and Michael Hardt call Empire. Negri's career can be divided into three overlapping periods, each defined by its focus on a fundamental problem: from 1958 to 1970, the modern capitalist state and its philosophical legitimation; from 1968 to 1979, new forms of collective subjectivity and their organisation into political agents; from 1979 to the present, ontological alternatives to the modern dialectical conception of sovereignty that has given rise to global capitalism.

Negri's early writings as a philosopher of law examine the juridical foundations of the modern capitalist state as they emerge in the works of Hegel, Kant and Max Weber, as well as the metaphysical legitimation of the state that Negri finds in Descartes' rationalism. While publishing these scholarly works, Negri was also active in factory workers' organisations, and his focus gradually shifted from critical analyses of the state to the phenomenology of contemporary labour and its political organisation. He helped found and lead two major groups of the Italian extra-parliamentary left, *Potere Operaio* (Workers' Power) and *Autonomia* (Autonomy), and his experience as an activist led him to theorise a shift in the subjectivity of labour from the mass worker of the trade unions and traditional socialist parties to the new socialised worker who was not centred in the factory, with its ethnic and gender norms, but dispersed across networks of generalised sociality and communication. Much of his work in the 1970s was collaborative and concerned with theorising a form of political organisation for socialised workers that would enable them to struggle against the conditions of the real subsumption of society within capital.

In April 1979 Negri was arrested on politically motivated charges of terrorism and imprisoned for over four years before coming to trial. In the midst of his trial he was elected to the Italian parliament and freed, but when his immunity was lifted he sought refuge in France where he lived until 1997. During and after his incarceration, Negri's philosophy turned from questions of organisation to questions of ontology. Like Deleuze, he found in Spinoza a non-dialectical alternative to the dominant dialectical theories of power, and later traced the vicissitudes of this conception of constituent power through modern history. His collaboration with Michael Hardt, which began in the 1990s, culminated in their controversial model of Empire, the decentred structure of global control and exploitation that they derive from Foucault's conception of biopolitics. Empire subordinates nation-states as tools to manage the transnational flows of capital, commodities and workers that define its hegemony, but it is not subject to national control or delegated democratic oversight and can only be contested by the supranational collective subject Hardt and Negri call the multitude.

T. Murphy

See also: constituent/constituted power; Empire; immaterial labour; multitude; real subsumption; socialised worker

NEGRITUDE A political and aesthetic movement founded by Aimé Césaire (1913–), Léopold Senghor (1906–1991) and others in the Francophone world of the 1930s, it came to play a key role in anti-colonial struggles. It was, in its earlier times, characterised by Marxist dialectics that questioned racism and by poetic imagery that celebrated and searched for a black or African way of being human, a black or African ontology. In the middle of the twentieth century as the struggle of political independence in the colonies intensified, negritude became a political myth in the hands of champions of black affirmation.

Influenced by a number of thinkers such as the Jesuit philosopher-priest Teilhard de Chardin, who asserted that the inequality but complementarity of the races is in fact a superior form of equality, Senghor created his own mythical version of negritude. He sought to define a way of being black and knowing the world that is qualitatively different from, and is supposed to act symbiotically with, the white man's ontology and epistemology in producing a new all-encompassing humanity/humanism and a new 'Universal Civilisation'. These differences, Senghor asserts in *The Spirit of Civilisation or the Laws of African Negro* (1956), are exemplified by the fact that White/European reason is analytical, working through 'utilisation', whereas Negro/ African reason is intuitive, working through 'participation'. It follows that Senghor's *On African Socialism* (1964) is a political attempt to realise the symbiosis of these mythical differences through the integration of Marx and Engel's European-based socialism and Senghor's African-based negritude.

In *The African Experience in Literature and Ideology* (1981), Abiola Irele situates negritude in the broad historical context of a larger movement of black cultural nationalism, which dates back to the earliest encounters of Africans with European domination. He asserts that it is 'a version, a distinctive current, of the same cultural nationalism expressed in different ways among black people and at various times in their reactions against white dominions'. The coining of the term *négritude* in Césaire's *Notebook of a Return to the Native Land* (1939) acknowledges this historical dimension in alluding to the Haitian Revolution: 'Haiti, where negritude first stood up and declared it believed in its humanity'. The same broad historical and geographical scope is evident in Senghor's *Negritude: Humanism of the Twentieth Century* (1970) where he claims that 'Negritude is nothing more or less than what some English-speaking Africans have called the African Personality. It is not different from the "black personality" discovered and proclaimed by the American New Negro Movement.'

In *Pan-Africanism* (1962), Colin Legum uses a dialectical definition of negritude, based on Sartre's Hegelian assertion that negritude poetry is an anti-racist racism, to assert that as an antithesis of the thesis of white supremacy, this poetry can make it possible for racism to find an ultimate synthesis in a common humanity without racism. This possibility, he claims, is evident in the following stanza from Cesaire's *Four Poems* (1948): 'You know my world-wide love, know it is not hatred against other races that turns me into the cultivator of this one race'. This quest for a new synthesis, for humanity beyond racial privilege, is also evident in Senghor's *On African Socialism* where he insists that we need to 'be careful to remember that man is "the whole man and all men." '

C. Chachage

NEO-KANTIANISM A series of philosophical movements in the late nineteenth and early twentieth centuries advocating a 'return to Kant'. Of these, only the Marburg School and the Southwest or Baden School, centred mainly in Heidelberg, strictly adhered to the 'trancendental method' of analysing the conditions for knowing and willing as the only way of providing a firm foundation to both philosophy and science. These two schools were also the only ones that maintained their force and influence into the first three decades of the twentieth century, coming to an end in the late 1930s in the National Socialist suppression of movements having 'Jewish elements'.

One of the main features of both these schools is their striking amplification of Kant's idealism; for they repudiate his idea of the 'thing in itself', that is they deny a register of reality lying beyond experience. Moreover, they also contend that only the capacity of explicit conceptualisation gives something the clear knowability that makes it an object; for the neo-Kantians, intellectual judgement is the factor determining knowledge, with experiential, 'intuitional' givenness – as sheer determinability – providing nothing of a positive kind. At the same time, they were not subjective idealists in the classical, psychological sense; they did not place reality inside the mind of some actual individual human being. Instead, judgement as such, in its non-individual, non-empirical (non-experiential) validity, is the 'realm' of true knowing. Thus knowing is not a matter of psychology, much less of some metaphysically ethereal substance termed 'spiritual'. It is simply a matter of judgement as propositional truth, even if this might be termed 'consciousness pure and simple'.

There is a difference, however, between Marburg and Baden on how this was worked out. In Marburg, for example, Hermann Cohen emphasised the purely logical character of judgement and truth, seeing mathematical operations as the paradigm of generating content in cognition, in particular in mathematical physics (*Logik der reinen Erkenntnis*, 1902). Succeeding Cohen, Paul Natorp wished to find a mediating role for psychology between formalistic judgement and experienced reality, even if the 'psyche' had no role in originating cognitive content (*Allgemeine Psychologie nach kritischer Methode*, 1912). His proposal for this was to cast the psychological as the correlational system of subject and object, thus giving categorical characterisation to a realm that provides neither pure judgemental form nor the naturalistic structure of beings. Finally, Ernst Cassirer, after initial work on the formalism of judgement (*Substance and Function*, 1910), developed further the generative role of 'pure consciousness' in the productive richness of symbolism (*Philosophy of Symbolic Forms*, 1923–9).

In Baden the study of history by German scholars was heavily influential. In fact the founder of the Baden school was an eminent historian of philosophy, Wilhelm Windelband. Not surprisingly, considering the prominence of culture in this kind of interest, the Baden neo-Kantians focused on value; for them, the grounds of validity lie in axiological laws. There is, in other words, a non-rational element at play in determining judgements, not simply logical formality. Thus for Windelband three classes of value confer validity, those pertaining to truth, to morality and to beauty, although one should note his adding the class of the religious to these. Heinrich Rickert, Windelband's successor at Heidelberg, worked out the way these kinds of value come together in subjective functioning: those of truth pertaining to judgements about the constitutive features of objects, and those of morality and beauty pertaining to judgements about cultural matters. In other words, Baden neo-Kantians emphasised the objects of the human sciences (*Geisteswissenschaften*) rather than those of the natural sciences (*Naturwissenschaften*).

Neo-Kantianism of both varieties offered a significant context for a philosophical movement sometimes taken to be little different from it, but which was indeed distinct: the phenomenology of Husserl, especially with his 'transcendental turn' in *Ideas I* (1913). Indeed, the intellectual strength of neo-Kantianism was an encouragement to Husserl to renew and deepen his study of Kant, but the fact remains that phenomenology is not a branch of neo-Kantianism, since Husserl insisted that intuition of the evident was the ground of truth. Nevertheless, there were cordial and even fruitful relations between Husserl and both Natorp and Rickert. Indeed, by leaving Freiburg in 1916 to succeed Windelband in Heidelberg, Rickert opened the way for Husserl to be given the chair of philosophy there, and supported his candidacy. Equally notable, and highly regarded by nearly everyone, was the work of Emil Lask whose seminal work *Die Logik der Philosophie und die Kategorienlehre* (1911) investigated pre-theoretical sources of meaning and value. Lask located these in the primordial relationship of the unity of meaning and form underlying both logical validity or judgement and a subject's individual experience. In this he indicated the way towards a rapprochement of neo-Kantianism with phenomenology, but unfortunately the ultimate fruit of Lask's burgeoning work would never be realised owing to his death in the First World War.

In no small part owing to the force of approaches that took issue with the primacy and sufficiency of the purely transcendental – approaches such as Husserl's phenomenology, Heidegger's fundamental ontology, life-philosophies and philosophies of existence – neo-Kantianism began to lose favour between the two world wars. After the second of these there were virtually no neo-Kantians still active, with the exception of Cassirer, whose work, in keeping with the loss of favour on the part of neo-Kantianism, was read perhaps more for his emphasising the importance of the symbolic than for his theoretical position.

R. Bruzina

NEO-THOMISM a movement in modern philosophical and theological thought deriving its inspiration from Thomas Aquinas. Strictly speaking, 'Thomism' refers to the intellectual approach, in both philosophy and theology, of Aquinas, an approach which includes a metaphysics of causes; a world-view of natures with their activities; a presence of Trinitarian grace harmoniously interacting in human life; and an Incarnation not only in Jesus but in sacraments and people. The term has often also been used to refer to the history of Aquinas' thought in all the various interpretations given by individuals, religious orders or schools over the centuries. In this sense, we can distinguish four periods of Thomism: the first two centuries after his death; the Thomisms of the sixteenth century; Thomist neo-scholasticism from 1860 to 1960; and recent decades. While 'neo-Thomism' can also mean the reawakening of interest in Aquinas's philosophy seen in the sixteenth century, we will concentrate on the latter two periods.

After 1850, church authorities and Catholic philosophers came to view modern pantheism, relativism and subjectivism as dangerous, and to counter them they turned to the objectivity and realism of Aristotle and Aquinas. This 'Third Thomism' is often what is meant by the term 'neo-Thomism'. It is important to realise that just as Aquinas's theology was only one scholasticism in the diversity of the thirteenth century, so neo-Thomism is one direction within the neo-scholastic revival which after 1850 provided an encompassing current for Catholic intellectual movements for the following century.

Thomism in the twentieth century developed a variety of directions, and after 1900 institutes and journals devoted to his thought multiplied. Here we find expositors of the text alone, disciples of a particular school in a religious order like that of the Dominicans or professors at universities like Louvain. Much of scholastic revival at that time was interested in logic and metaphysics and did not present in much depth Aquinas's theology: his fundamental approach of Trinitarian grace and active personality was repressed by a conviction that his thought was a Christian apologetic of syllogisms or a perennial ontology. In the early twentieth century, however, gifted scholars, such as Martin Grabmann and Étienne Gilson reconstructed the historical context of Aquinas's work, even as some philosophers and theologians were intent upon finding positive ways to relate Thomistic thought to modern philosophy. Those historical, transcendental and theological interpretations and applications of Aquinas' theology approach him as both a historical figure and a contemporary intellectual inspiration. Among the many important Thomists of the recent century one might mention Reginald Garrigou-Lagrange, who composed defences of philosophy and commentaries on the *Summa Theologiae*; Jacques Maritain, who pursued an eclectic Thomism to address art, science and society; historians like Gilson and M.-D. Chenu; thinkers such as Joseph Maréchal, Pierre Rousselot, Erich Przywara, J. B. Lotz, Gustav Siewerth and Bernard Lonergan, who all worked to develop Thomist treatments of the dynamics of knowing and being; and theologians active in the decades before and after Second Vatican Council, such as Henri de Lubac, Yves Congar, Karl Rahner and Edward Schillebeeckx, who gained a wide audience for their theological works.

With the Second Vatican Council the worldwide neo-scholastic monopoly in the Catholic Church collapsed after 1965, and so Aquinas's influence was reduced. The action of the Council, however, gave Thomist theology the opportunity to return to its basic principles; by doing so, and by fostering historical research and theological creativity, Thomism continued in new forms. In 1974, the 700th anniversary of his death, a new interest in Aquinas was manifest in congresses, multi-volume collections, computer indices and centres of Thomistic studies. New issues were found in medical ethics; the theology of church as communion, sacraments and liturgy; Christian virtues and spirituality; and human dignity and destiny. These themes and still others are apparent in the major studies of recent decades by thinkers such as Walter Principe, Ghislain Lafont, Albert Patfoort, Otto Pesch, Ulrich Horst, S. T. Bonino and Jean-Pierre Torrell. Their works are a crown and a conclusion to the vast research into Aquinas's thought done in the twentieth century.

T. O'Meara

NIETZSCHE, FRIEDRICH WILHELM (1844–1900) German-born philosopher and classical scholar, a critic of modernity with a powerful impact on the development of twentieth-century thought, particularly French poststructuralism, but also extending to classical scholarship, literary criticism, political theory and psychoanalysis.

Life. The son and grandson of Lutheran ministers, Nietzsche studied classical philology with such brilliant success that in 1869 he was appointed to the Chair in Classical Philology at the University of Basel in Switzerland, despite not yet having completed his doctorate. Nietzsche's tenure at Basel was interrupted by military service (as a medical orderly in the Franco-Prussian War), bouts of illness and a growing sense of disenchantment with the field of classical philology. While posted at Basel, he published a number of books and essays, including *The Birth of Tragedy from the Spirit of Music* (1872), the four *Untimely Meditations* (1873–6) and *Human, All-Too-Human* (1878). Although now widely read and acclaimed by scholars, *The Birth of Tragedy* initially received unfavourable reviews from many influential scholars of classical philology. This negative response, which Nietzsche surely anticipated and perhaps provoked, cemented his decision to distance himself from the academic practice of classical philology. Citing poor health, he resigned his University appointment in 1879.

Granted a modest pension from the Swiss government, Nietzsche spent the remainder of his sane life cultivating a nomadic existence. In this period of fertile errancy, he penned *Daybreak* (1881), *The Gay Science* (1882), *Thus Spoke Zarathustra* (1883–5), *Beyond Good and Evil* (1886), *On the Genealogy of Morals* (1887) and a number of new prefaces, appendices, poems and other materials. In 1888, his final year of sanity, he wrote *The Case of Wagner*, *Twilight of the Idols* (published in 1889), *The Antichrist* (published in 1895), *Nietzsche contra Wagner* (published in 1895) and *Ecce Homo* (published in 1908).

In January of 1889, Nietzsche's productive career ended abruptly as madness enveloped him. After a brief period of institutionalisation in Jena, he returned with his mother to her Naumburg home. They were soon joined there by his sister, Elisabeth Förster-Nietzsche, the opportunistic widow of a prominent Aryan supremacist. Upon returning to Germany from a failed colonial adventure in Paraguay, Elisabeth promptly set out to capitalise on her brother's growing reputation. She fostered a cult-like enthusiasm for his books and teachings, oversaw the founding of the Nietzsche Archive, and eventually convinced their mother to cede to her (and a cousin) the trusteeship of Nietzsche's writings. After their mother died in 1897, Elisabeth moved her brother and the Archive to Weimar, where she redoubled her efforts to exploit his growing fame and influence.

Nietzsche finally died on 25 August 1900. His reward for a lifetime of anti-Christian iconoclasm was a traditional Protestant burial. Following his death, Elisabeth oversaw renovations of the Nietzsche Archive, from which she launched her aggressive campaign to promote international interest in her late brother's philosophy. Early in the new century, she produced a two-volume biography of Nietzsche, an edited collection of his works and an edition of his unpublished notes and drafts entitled *The Will to Power*. While in the process of steering her brother's teachings into ever closer conformity with her own (strongly nationalistic) convictions, she offered his reputation and legacy to admirers like Mussolini and Hitler. Elisabeth died in Weimar in 1935. Her lavish, state-sponsored funeral was attended by the Führer himself.

Works. Nietzsche's most influential book was *Thus Spoke Zarathustra*, which was published in four parts over the period 1883–5. Although originally envisioned as a tripartite work culminating in the central character's lyric expression of his love for eternity, Zarathustra also includes a parodic fourth part that places into question the larger aims and perceived accomplishments of the book. The central character, modelled loosely on the Persian prophet Zoroaster, is best known for his peripatetic teaching of the *Übermensch* ('Overman') which has been widely received as conveying Nietzsche's post-moral, post-theistic human ideal. Over the course of his travels, however, Zarathustra is routinely frustrated by his failure to disseminate this novel teaching to his disciples. Convinced that the problem lies solely with his obtuse auditors, he experiments with various forms of address and presents tailored renditions of his teaching to an array of different audiences. These experiments are punctuated by his occasional retreats to, and returns from, the solitude of his mountaintop retreat, where he reflects on his pedagogical successes and develops his plans for an improved rapport with his auditors.

Zarathustra remains dissatisfied with his disciples until the very end of Part IV, when he interprets an enigmatic 'sign' as proof that his ideal companions (whom he describes as his 'children') will soon appear. He promptly banishes the 'higher men' whom he has attracted throughout Part IV, thereby disowning the apparent progress they have made together – including, in 'The Drunken Song', their collaborative embrace of eternity. Although he sets out in the final scene of the book to greet his 'children', the eventuality of this meeting is not confirmed by the narrator. For all we know, in fact, Zarathustra never identifies, much less corrects for, his own share in the communicative failures that have beset his pedagogy. He may be no more successful in his quest to meet his 'children' than in any of his previous attempts to forge enduring relationships with his auditors and disciples.

Nietzsche may have meant for the ambiguous, open-ended conclusion of Zarathustra to depict the nihilism that, in his opinion, defines the late modern condition. Nihilism manifests itself most obviously, he believed, in the crisis of will that afflicts agents in late modernity and renders them irresolute. Unable either to embrace or to refuse the redemptive wisdom that Zarathustra wishes to dispense, his auditors frustrate his efforts to bring about the desired transformation in them. His own share in the nihilism of late modernity is reflected in his ongoing struggles to transform himself into the teacher he presumes to be.

The crisis of European nihilism is most powerfully conveyed by Nietzsche's famous image of the 'death of God', by means of which he intended to convey an epistemic (rather than a theological) truth about late modernity. Although God no longer serves as a credible guarantor of human meaning, we late moderns are as yet powerless to accept or to renounce the redemption that only God could provide. We simply know too much to invest our wholehearted belief in God (or Truth, or Beauty). But we are also not yet resolved to take our rightful place at the recently vacated centre of the cosmos. This paralysing sense of ambivalence indicates to Nietzsche that that we are as yet ill-prepared to receive the ideas and teachings that would facilitate our transition to the post-moral, post-theistic epoch that he envisions. If a Zarathustra were to appear among us, that is, we would be no more receptive to his teachings than were the various auditors who alternately mocked, idolised and ignored him.

Zarathustra's failure to measure his own limitations, as well as those of his auditors, thus obliged Nietzsche to articulate an effective response to the problem of nihilism. Toward this end, he devoted his post-Zarathustran writings to the task of cultivating a sympathetic readership for his Zarathustra. In *Beyond Good and Evil* (1886), he endeavoured to expose the illusions, fictions and prejudices that have arrested the progress of philosophy and science thus far. He thus offered a sustained criticism of the metaphysical oppositions on which philosophers have typically relied for their normative evaluations, recommending instead a more nuanced appreciation for the (non-oppositional) differences that obtain between varying perspectives, shades and gradations. Having exposed the prejudices at work in contemporary philosophy and science, he proceeded to interpret the currency of these prejudices as symptomatic of the decline and disintegration of European culture. The recommended emigration 'beyond good and evil' would happily coincide, he believed, with the renewal of a distinctly European culture.

In *On the Genealogy of Morals*, Nietzsche advanced his widely influential hypothesis that contemporary Christian morality is descended from an ancient slave morality. The servile pedigree of contemporary Christian morality is apparent, he believed, in its promotion of suffering and inwardness, its praise for the virtues of passivity and concomitant disdain for the virtues of activity, its opposition of 'good' to 'evil', its allegiance to the ascetic ideal and its orientation to reward (and revenge) in a promised afterlife. What is most characteristic of contemporary morality, however, is its reliance on guilt to ensure ethical behaviour.

Nietzsche accounts for the feeling of guilt as nothing more than the pain of the 'bad conscience', which all human beings suffer simply by virtue of being civilised. The benefits of civilisation, he conjectures, are secured only on the strength of the non-negotiable ban it imposes on spontaneous, outward displays of animal vitality. To be civilised simply means that one is obliged to suffer the inward discharge of one's animal drives and impulses. Rather than acknowledge this brute fact of civilised existence, however, contemporary Christian morality instead blames 'guilty' individuals for their experience of discomfort. According to this interpretation, guilty parties suffer because they deserve to suffer, because their very being is faulted beyond repair. This interpretation of the pain of the 'bad conscience' is ingenious, Nietzsche concedes, for it makes our suffering meaningful and charges us with the impossible task of atoning for our guilt. At the same time, however, the cost of securing meaning for our suffering has become prohibitively high. Our reliance on guilt has involved us in a protracted (and escalating) assault on our own affects, which has in turn restricted our capacity to will. As we come to require ever more exotic goals to activate our weakened wills, we verge precariously upon the 'will to nothingness', which Nietzsche identifies as the will never to will again.

In the following year, 1888, Nietzsche produced several short books that collectively essay his summary critique of modernity and its signature institutions. In these books, he elaborates on his earlier account of European nihilism and advances his diagnosis of late modernity as a decadent epoch. The crisis of will that he earlier associated with the onset of nihilism is presented in these books as symptomatic of a much larger (and inevitable) process of cultural decay. It is the decay of European culture, he conjectures, that explains the rise of the projects in terms of which modernity tends to define itself, including democracy, liberalism, science, progress, cosmopolitanism, feminism and secularism. While questions remain about his prescriptions, if any, for treating the decadence he diagnoses, these books present a deeply sceptical appraisal of the generative and regenerative resources available to late modernity. He goes so far as to suggest that the best course of action may be to assist the failing projects of modernity in their decline and accelerate their dissolution.

Influence. Nietzsche's influence today is multifarious and far-reaching. Five such influences are especially worth noting.

1. His first book, *The Birth of Tragedy*, is now widely read and cited, especially for its ingenious pairing of Dionysus and Apollo as the patron deities of Attic tragedy and as the twin impulses responsible for the health of a tragic culture. *The Birth of Tragedy* is also influential for its heterodox exposé of Socrates as a hyper-rational enemy of tragedy and tragic culture. In general, Nietzsche is acclaimed not only for his unique appreciation of Attic tragedy, but also for his renewed attention to the relevance of ancient Greek culture for modern scholars and leaders.

2. The psychological insights that informed *The Birth of Tragedy* were later expanded to support Nietzsche's pioneering research in the field of depth psychology. In sharp contrast to the models of subjectivity delivered, respectively, by the Enlightenment and German Idealism, Nietzsche located the core of human agency in the pre-reflective operation of unconscious drives and impulses. He thus treated human psychology as a complicated instance of animal psychology, which, as he understood it, is based on the pursuit of optimal conditions under which an organism may discharge its native stores of animal vitality. Every animal wishes above all else to attain a maximal feeling of power, and all of human psychology can be derived from this simple, naturalistic principle of explanation. Consciousness, he opined, was a feeble organ of relatively recent emergence; our over-reliance on it is largely responsible for the myriad discontents of modern life. In this respect and others, Nietzsche is profitably read alongside Freud.

3. Nietzsche is also influential for his attention to the personal and rhetorical dimensions of philosophy. Well known for his own cultivation of multiple styles, tropes and personae, he possessed a keen, critical eye for the subjective inflections of philosophical discourse. Declaring every great philosophy to be an 'involuntary memoir and confession' on the part of its author, he sought to isolate the personal 'prejudices' lurking behind seemingly impersonal philosophical pronouncements. His attention to the personal and rhetorical dimensions of philosophy is furthermore consistent with the larger, expressivist sympathies of his own philosophising. He prized above all else the capacity for spontaneous self-assertion, whether in himself or others. He regularly urged his readers toward lives of greater urgency, passion and authenticity, and he praised as exemplary those rare individuals who asserted themselves in defiance of prevailing norms and conventions. His influence on the philosophical and literary traditions of existentialism is well known, and this influence largely derives from his irrepressible affirmation of human self-assertion.

4. Nietzsche's influence on the development of French thought in the

twentieth century was profound and perhaps the most important of any German thinker. Starting with Bataille and Klossowski, and reaching a peak with the poststructuralists (including Foucault, Derrida and Deleuze), the French read Nietzsche as furnishing the rudiments of a 'philosophy of difference' that would be non-dialectical and hence enable an 'escape', or at least a certain distance, however envisioned, from Hegel. In addition, many noteworthy French feminists, among them Kofman and Irigaray, found Nietzsche to be both critical and exemplary of the masculinist prejudices that continue to inform the dominant paradigms and discourse of Western philosophy.

5. Finally, Nietzsche remains influential for his sweeping critique of European modernity. Flatly rejecting the familiar modernist narratives of growth, progress, amelioration and maturation, he diagnosed European modernity as irreversibly decadent. He exposed its signature institutions and projects as unmitigated failures, and he disclosed with considerable prescience its growing thirst for blood (including its own). He also lamented the disintegration of a distinctly European culture and concomitant rise of squabbling nation-states bent on imperial expansion. His criticisms were so penetrating, and his diagnoses so astute, that they cannot be ignored by aspiring champions of modern ideals. Even a full century after his death, Nietzsche stands as the most formidable critic of European modernity.

D. Conway

See also: active forgetting; bad conscience; Embodiment; eternal recurrence; Ethics; Genealogy; nihilism; Overman (*Übermensch*); Psychology; Repetition; *ressentiment*; revaluation of all values; self-overcoming; slave revolt in morality; Time; will-to-power; will-to-truth

NIHILISM Nietzsche's term for the general condition in which human beings find themselves unable to invest resolute belief in anything, including (or especially) the authority of God (or any other putatively transcendent value). In such a condition, human beings can find no causes or tasks whose pursuit promises to engage the will and thereby secure an affective attachment to life itself. In the shadow of nihilism, in fact, life itself ceases to be meaningful, and human beings turn ever more aggressively toward ascetic practices of self-destruction. Bereft of a goal whose pursuit might justify the suffering attendant to the human condition, human beings will inevitably commit themselves to the goal of self-annihilation. According to Nietzsche, the persistence of nihilism thus signals the advent of the 'will-to-nothingness', which he identifies as the will never to will again.

D. Conway

NOMADOLOGY An investigation led by Deleuze and Guattari in *A Thousand Plateaus* to discover those in a position to stand against the State's capturing forces. While the paradigm or most intense plateau of nomadism is the steppe nomads of Central Asia, nomadism is not limited to these people, but instead involves any minor, transformative force (of life, politics, thought, artistic creation) capable of escaping the sedentarity and stratification so dear to majorities. Nomads, unlike migrants, have territories, but, having portable roots, they reterritorialise upon the line and the trajectory of their deterritorialisation. In other words, nomads most feel at home while on the move; their habit is the capacity of changing habits. The subject matter of their 'knowledge' (that derived from the 'nomad sciences') is the behaviour of material and force, rather than the matter and form of hierarchical and hylomorphic sedentary sciences. The singular, not the universal or the essence, is their objective. Deleuze and Guattari hypothesise that nomads (or nomadic tendencies) have the ability to ward off the encroaching forces of sedentary society. In fact, they are the inventors of the war machine: of all that is required in people and machines to 'make the steppe grow' and to trace the lines of flight of their nomadic trajectory. The state wages war in order to conserve its integrative power; nomads wage war because their lines of flight are blocked and their deterritorialisation prevented.

C. Boundas

NORMALISATION Foucault's name for networks of power and knowledge that manage people through surveillance and examination in accordance with developmental norms. Foucault contrasts normalising power with forms of social control that operate with reference to law. When the power of law is brought to bear on a situation, we establish a set of facts about a past event, judge whether a particular person obeyed the law and exact punishment as payment for disobedience. By contrast, when the power of the norm is brought to bear, we characterise a person's present state as either in accord with the norm or deviating from it, project that person's future development in relation to the norm, and take steps to alter his or her developmental course to bring him or her into compliance with the norm at some future time. Thus, whereas the law is only invoked when there is an infraction, normalisation operates continuously. Normalisation assumes that people are inherently developmental, that development can be measured against statistical calculations of populations and that developmental trajectories are malleable. It tends to homogenise populations by bringing individuals into compliance with valued norms, but it also individualises by identifying some persons as life-long deviants. Often, especially in institutions such as hospitals, reformatories and schools, persons who are assigned identities based on their degrees of deviation from norms internalise those identities. In this way, we can say that normalisation creates deviants. The existence of such deviants can then be used as justification for increased surveillance and control over entire populations, further extending normalising power networks.

L. McWhorter

NOTHING, THE (*das Nichts*) In one of his most notorious claims, Heidegger tells us in 'What is Metaphysics?' (1929) that metaphysics (or philosophy) alone can take the nothing seriously. In fact, it takes it so seriously as to make it its own theme. All the other sciences are concerned with a specific thing or object and, as such, view any talk about the nothing as empty speculation and a waste of time. But metaphysics insists that the nothing, while itself not a single thing or a specific set of things, cannot be dismissed as a mere illusion. In fact, Heidegger understands the possibility of metaphysics itself as a rigorous investigation rooted in existence itself, and so, as the science whose object is presupposed in all other sciences, as emerging from the positive encounter with the nothing in anxiety. While for the most part engaged in practical dealings, and at times in theoretical dealings, existence occasionally experiences the withdrawal and seeming dissolution of all things. Certain dispositions or attunements such as anxiety or boredom reveal our situation in the world as such, that is existence as being-in-the-world. It is only when faced with 'nothing' that we are faced with ourselves. It is only from within the experience of the nothing that we can understand ourselves as the being that is disclosed – and so destined – to that which, in excess of all things, nonetheless makes the manifestation of things possible, or as 'ek-sistence'.

M. de Beistegui

ONTOLOGICAL DIFFERENCE For Heidegger, the difference, or the distinction, between being and beings, which fundamental ontology is to thematise systematically, and which the philosophical tradition presupposed, while never being able to envisage it as such. A clear exposition of Heidegger's view can be found in *Basic Problems of Phenomenology*, a 1928 lecture course first published in 1976.

The ontological difference is a distinction that 'is there' (*ist da*), latent as it were, in Dasein and its existence, albeit never explicitly. It is a distinction that exists, and not simply a distinction that we make. It is a real, actual or existent distinction, and not a formal or theoretical one. Existence itself is the performing of this distinction. This means that existence opens up a difference – the difference between the presence and manifestation of things and the horizon from out of which they become manifest, namely time. A being (say, a table) must be distinguished from its being, which is not an essence, in the sense of an Idea, an eidos or a quiddity. An idea is a representation of that thing, its image. Yet the being of a thing, as it is given in experience, differs from its concept. For the most part, the being of the table is not encountered through the question: what is a table? It is encountered as something I need to write on, or something I can put my bags on, or even something I can hide under. In other words, we encounter beings contextually. The being of beings is always contextual, that is always a function of the meaning, possibilities and general disposition or attunement in which I find myself when facing the table.

Between the ontological and the ontical, there is a relation of grounding: the ontological indicates the basic structures of existence, which sustain and enable Dasein in its everyday existence. They reveal how beings are granted with their being. As such, however, they are never revealed to Dasein. They can only be revealed in a philosophical analysis, and through a phenomenological examination of Dasein's comportment. Dasein is (or exists) this difference, and for that reason it remains obscure to Dasein. This distinction between a being, and the being of that thing, on the basis of which that thing comes to be, or manifests itself in a certain way, leads to a number of further distinctions: ontological and ontical, existential and existentiell. The ontological or existential level always points to those structures underlying existence, such as existentiality, facticity and falling. The ontical or existentiell level points to the level of experience at which existence is played out.

M. de Beistegui

ONTO-THEO-LOGY Heidegger's term for the presence-focused understanding of being (*Sein*) to which, in his eyes, the entire metaphysical tradition (from Plato to Nietzsche) is pledged ('The Onto-theo-logical Constitution of Metaphysics', 1957). The ontotheological understanding of being is based on the ambiguity of the Greek word for 'being' (*to on*), which, grammatically, is a participle. That means that it can be understood either as a noun (the being) or as a verb (to be). Taken in its nominal sense, *to on* would indicate the beings in general (hence an onto-logy). Taken in its verbal meaning, it would point towards the ground and cause of all beings qua God as supreme being (hence a theo-logy). To allow a thought of being as such, Heidegger proposed what he called the 'ontological difference'.

Both Derrida and Marion responded in their own unique ways to Heidegger's criticism of onto-theo-logy, the former by *différance*, which remains irreducible to onto-theo-logy, and the latter by positing a *God Without Being*. Furthermore, Derrida's work problematised the -logos suffix in onto-theo-logy (as much as in ontology and theology) in his critique of logocentrism and the metaphysics of presence (*Writing and Difference* and *Dissemination*).

J. Manoussakis

ORDER-WORD (*mot d'ordre*) An expression borrowed by Deleuze and Guattari in *A Thousand Plateaus* from Elias Canetti (*Crowds and Power*), in order to designate the function of language as the establishment of collective order. The primary function of language, according to Deleuze and Guattari, is not the exchange of information or the establishment of communication, for language is not made to be believed but to be obeyed; before becoming the affair of linguistics, language is the affair of politics. Order-words are thus issued from a 'collective assemblage of enunciation', the habits of speech of a social collective. Order-words secure the transmission of indirect discourse and the imposition of a collective order, what 'they say' as well as that which 'should be done'. At first sight, an order-word is reminiscent of Austin's performative utterances, where saying is doing, and Deleuze and Guattari acknowledge the initial similarity. But the order-word is not the function of a single category of statements as it is with Austin; nor are order-words linguistic entities. Their performative function is better explained by means of the Stoic doctrine of incorporeal transformations. 'Guilty', said by the judge to the defendant, is an incorporeal transformation, even though it is said of bodies, their actions and their passions. An order-word thus effectuates a change in social status; in doing so it intervenes in a 'machinic assemblage of bodies' or set of social institutions with which it is in 'reciprocal presupposition'. Vocabulary, syntax and semantics vary as order-words change. Behind order-words, responsible for blockages and stratification, one finds 'passwords' that facilitate the trajectory of lines of flight and the deterritorialisation of those who flee along with them.

C. Boundas

ORGANISM A term designating biological individuality and the object of two key debates in continental philosophy.

The first debate bears on the question of whether special concepts – such as teleology, self-regulation and functional differentiation – are necessary to account for individual living things and whether these concepts are commensurate with the foundations of our scientific knowledge. In Kant's *Critique of Judgement*, it is argued that our knowledge of organisms ('natural purposes') can only be regulative or problematic, since the type of recursive causality they suggest lies beyond the purview of determinative judgement, which brings a particular under an already established genus; reflective judgement, in contrast, establishes the genus in its very operation. Some contemporary approaches, such as autopoiesis, have attempted to dispel these limitations on our cognition of organisms by providing mechanistic or non-teleological models of the living.

The second debate – also arising out of Kant, but with roots going back to Plato's *Timaeus* and Renaissance thought – concerns the extent to which the organism as a developing and functionally differentiated totality can be considered as a symbol of reason or thinking. Such a vision is arguably forwarded by Hegel's *Phenomenology of Spirit*, in which the concept of reason realises itself by analogy with the manner in which the plan of an organism unfolds in its development, maintaining a dynamic unity throughout its history. In *Difference and Repetition*, Deleuze counters this organic image of thought by thinking the organism itself as an actualisation neither contained nor prefigured in the 'idea' of the organism, and further, in his work with Guattari, by viewing the task of thinking as the creation of a non-totalisable 'body without organs'.

A. Toscano

ORIENTALISM A term which in the eighteenth and nineteenth centuries referred to what we now call 'Middle Eastern Studies' or 'Near Eastern Studies' but which, following the influence of Edward Said's 1978 book *Orientalism* (regarded by some as postcolonial theory's founding text), now refers to the process by which, in the name of the disinterested pursuit of knowledge, European and American scholarship has produced distorted or stereotyped representations of non-Western peoples and cultures. Said adapts Foucault's analysis of the complicity between knowledge and power so that it pertains not only to the way modern Western societies control, discipline and regulate their own subjects but also to the West's domination of non-Western societies. 'Orientalism' thus signifies the constellation of Western academic and cultural discursive practices which, while presenting themselves as objective science, are in fact an integral element of the West's imperialist, colonialist and neo-colonialist enterprise. For Said, the 'oriental' as portrayed in Occidental scholarship bears little or no relation to reality; such scholarship does not disclose the truth concerning its object but rather produces it. One should note that Said's critique of Orientalism was anticipated, in many of its main points, by the Egyptian philosopher Anouar Abdel-Malek, who argues in his 1963 article 'Orientalism in Crisis' that the West has only been able to conceive of the Orient as 'stamped with . . . a constitutive otherness, of an essentialist character . . . non-active, non-autonomous, non-sovereign with regard to itself.'

G. Stone

ORTEGA Y GASSET, JOSÉ (1883–1955) Spanish philosopher associated tangentially with the existentialist movement. After studies at Madrid University and in Germany, Ortega played a very important role in the modernisation of academic philosophy in the Spanish speaking world. He founded the *Revista de Occidente*, a leading intellectual journal, and was party to the translation of many of the leading German philosophers of the 1920s. Until the Spanish Civil War Ortega had a large lay readership in Spain, while after the war his pupils played an important role in Latin American universities. Because of his republican activities, Ortega lived in exile from 1936 until after the Second World War.

One can divide his philosophical work into two periods. In the first period he develops a theory of truth and perspective drawing both on Nietzsche and Husserl, as is exemplified in *Meditations on Quixote* (1914) and *The Modern Theme* (1923). The second period opens with *What Is Philosophy?* (1929) and reveals the importance of the reception of Heidegger's *Being and Time* (1927), which moves Ortega to formulate a theory of life largely implicit in his previous work and practice.

For Ortega, 'I am I and my circumstance' is the systematic starting point of an attempt to understand oneself in one's historical setting. *Man and Crisis* (1933) provides the framework for the application of Ortega's concept of historical reason. His previous work on perspectivism is developed by attending to the concepts of belief and vocation. By 'belief' he understands the unconscious assumptions that allow all representation of reality; a cultural crisis ensues whenever inherited beliefs no longer hold sway. With the concept of 'vocation' Ortega wishes to offer an understanding of the human that stresses self-understanding over that of external motivation. Though his

understanding of philosophical method brings him close to existentialism, he would recognise in individual practice a form of logic, *razón
vital*, which is at variance with extreme forms of existentialism which
affirm the sheer gratuity of human action. In his later work, Ortega
develops this concept of historical reason in studies on human
activities like hunting (1942), biographical sketches like the series
on Goethe (1932), and the reconstruction of Western intellectual
development as in his work on Leibniz and the origin of philosophy
(1947).

Ortega is also known for his defence of abstract art in *The Dehumanisation of Art* (1925) and for his political philosophy. *The Revolt of
the Masses* (1930) is his major contribution, though both *Invertebrate
Spain* (1921) and *Man and People* (1949) are among his most accomplished works. *The Revolt of the Masses* analyses the construction of
'mass society', composed of faceless, anonymous, replaceable men, and
its relation to fascism and communism. In doing so he anticipates many
of the postwar analyses of Arendt. He also presented a positive image of
a united Europe.

J. de Salas

OVERDETERMINATION A term developed by Althusser for the
constitution of a subject (be it an individual, a class or a state) by a
multiplicity of specific and real differences not reducible to a single
essence or cause. In the essay 'Contradiction and Overdetermination'
(1962) Althusser takes off from the Freudian notion that the dream
image is 'overdetermined' by the many unconscious impulses and
events which it comes to represent. In the social realm, the uneven
development of the economic sphere, like the 'drives' in psychoanalysis, is the real or essential which produces diverse phenomena
such as mores, social hierarchies, language, law and ideology. These
phenomena come together and are focused and reflected in an individual subject who is said to be overdetermined by them and whose
subjectivity can be said to consist of the ensemble of contradictions it
embodies. For example, a state is overdetermined inasmuch as it
'focuses' and represents the contradictory expressions of both its
internal and external uneven development. Thus the individual contradiction that is a State is made actual by its industries, by its dominant
ideology, by its religion and by all the other things that constitute its
past and sustain its present. It is also, however, made actual by its place
in the world context in terms of what it dominates and what dominates
it. Since Althusser's original formulation, many continental social
philosophers have embraced the concept of overdetermination but

have rejected its appeal to a material economic real that is, in the last instance, determinative of all subjects.

W. Lewis

OVERMAN (*Übermensch*) The signature teaching of Nietzsche's Zarathustra and, to a lesser degree, of Nietzsche himself. In *Thus Spoke Zarathustra* (1883–5), the central character presents his teaching of 'the overman' as both an alternative and an antidote to the moral and religious ideals that have prevailed over the rise and development of Western civilisation. Whereas these ideals have collectively demeaned humankind, teaching us to despise our finitude and frailty, the overman is a celebration of humankind as it is, including what is most powerful and unique about us. Zarathustra's teaching of the overman is therefore meant to promote a life of self-possession, self-mastery and self-sufficiency, wherein human beings lay unmitigated claim to their passions, creativity and sexuality.

The teaching of the overman is inextricably linked to Zarathustra's (and Nietzsche's) pronouncement of the 'death of God', by which they mean to convey the erosion of theological authority that is specific to late European modernity. With God out of the picture, or so Zarathustra believes, humankind may finally take its rightful place at the value-positing centre of the cosmos. Unencumbered by the crushing weight of religious tradition and theological prejudice, humankind may finally renounce its reliance on superstition and accede to full maturity as a species. The 'death of God' thus furnishes the historical context for Zarathustra's teaching of 'the overman', which heralds the advent of human beings who are prepared to serve as guarantors of their own value and meaning.

While undeniably popular, even notoriously so in the century following its initial presentation, Zarathustra's teaching of the overman remains somewhat elusive. Some critics insist that Zarathustra manages, despite his best intentions, to present this teaching as yet another ideal of transcendence, which simply reproduces the unwanted dependency of humankind on an external source of meaning and recognition. Other critics believe that Zarathustra and Nietzsche accept too readily their roles as prophets of the overman, thereby presenting a teaching that is dangerously vague and devoid of specific content.

In evaluating this teaching, we might do well to bear in mind that Zarathustra himself was largely unsuccessful in promulgating it to his various audiences. By his own account, Nietzsche too felt largely misunderstood as a champion of this teaching. Although both were quick to blame this failing on others (Zarathustra's obtuse auditors,

Nietzsche's inept readers), their respective presentations of this teaching may also be responsible for the controversies that continue to surround it. Part of the problem here can be traced to the historical and psychological gulf that separates the 'death of God' from the advent of the overman. For although we are no longer prepared to invest our resolute belief in the saving power of God, we are also unprepared to forego the redemptive meaning that God supposedly could provide. In other words, although God is 'dead' we are not yet prepared to live as the teaching of the overman prescribes. So long as we experience ourselves as needing the redemption that only God could provide, we will continue to distrust ourselves and seek external meaning and recognition. The advent of the overman thus appears to require the 'death' not only of God, but also of the misanthropy whence God was born.

D. Conway

PANOPTICON The name Jeremy Bentham gave to his architectural design for a new kind of prison, a penitentiary where law-breakers could be kept under surveillance and supervision while they reflected on their errors and became rehabilitated for future participation in society. The Panopticon was so named because it maximised the visibility of the prisoners. Each prisoner was to be kept in a small cell on the outer ring of a circular building. Walls between the cells were solid, but the back and front were merely barred, allowing for the prisoner to be backlit and thus visible at all times to a guard posted in a centre tower. Consequently, the Panopticon was economical; one single guard could 'see all', that is could keep watch over scores of inmates simultaneously, thus minimising the cost of running the facility. In fact, since the central observation post could consist of a tower with small slits for windows, it would be possible to dispense with guards altogether as long as prisoners still believed they were being watched. Foucault analyses the Panopticon in *Discipline and Punish*. He sees it as a herald and an emblem of a new kind of institutional power, one based not on direct intimidation and brute force but rather on constant surveillance and rigid disciplinary management of people's time and self-presentation, a kind of power that grew and became dominant in Western society in the two centuries since Bentham's invention, although with some modification now that dispersed databases can track behaviour in open society outside explicit institutions.

L. McWhorter

PARADIGM AND SYNTAGM Terms used by structuralist semioticians in formal textual analysis. The term 'paradigmatic' was introduced by the Russian linguist Roman Jakobson (1896–1982); Saussure used the term 'associative'. On the syntagmatic plane we find combinations ('this–*and*–this–*and*–this', as in the sentence, 'the man cried'), while on the paradigmatic plane we find selection ('this–*or*–this–*or*–this', as in the replacement of the last word in the previous sample sentence with 'died' or 'sang').

Moving beyond language, Barthes outlined the paradigmatic and syntagmatic elements of the 'garment system'. The paradigmatic elements are the items which cannot be worn at the same time on the same part of the body (such as hats, trousers, shoes). The syntagmatic dimension is the juxtaposition of different elements at the same time in a complete ensemble from hat to shoes. Syntagmatic relationships exist both between signifiers and between signifieds. Relationships between signifiers can be either sequential (as in film and television narrative sequences) or spatial (as in the 'composition' of a painting, photograph or filmic shot). Relationships between signifieds are conceptual relationships.

The 'value' of a sign is determined by both its paradigmatic and its syntagmatic relations. The use of one signifier (a particular word or a garment) rather than another from the same paradigm set (adjectives or hats) shapes the preferred meaning of a text. So too would the placing of one signifier above, below, before or after another (a syntagmatic relation). Syntagms and paradigms provide a structural context within which signs make sense; they are the structural forms through which signs are organised into codes.

Structuralist textual analysis explores both paradigmatic and syntagmatic relations. Paradigmatic analysis seeks to identify the 'underlying' paradigms within the 'deep' or 'hidden' structure of a text or practice. Jakobson built on Saussure's differential model of sign systems, proposing that texts are bound together by a system of binary oppositions, such as male/female and mind/body. Lévi-Strauss noted that such linkages become aligned in some texts and codes so that additional 'vertical' relationships (male/mind, female/body) acquire apparent links of their own. Barthes applied the 'commutation test' to structural analysis based on a purely phonetic version derived from Jakobson. In Barthes's version the analyst focuses on a particular signifier in a text and seeks to identify which changes to this signifier would make sense (for example, white for black) and what the differing (positive and negative) connotations might be, in the process classifying the relevant paradigm sets on which the text draws and the codes to which these belong (for example, colour symbolism). The same process enables the text to be divided into minimal significant units, after which the syntagmatic relations between them can be identified. Syntagmatic analysis seeks to establish the 'surface structure' of a text and the relationships between its parts. The study of syntagmatic relations reveals the conventions or 'rules of combination' underlying the production and interpretation of texts.

D. Chandler

PARASITE A border or 'supplement' phenomenon referred to by Derrida in order to underscore the way in which a system is constantly redefined by both adding to and feeding off itself. The parasite also serves to relate seemingly local questions of linguistics and philosophical signification to the coding functions that traverse various fields of knowledge, from law to the biological sciences. Reference is also made to the complex functioning of the virus – it is not for nothing that the same word is borrowed from biology to be applied to what invades computer programs or information systems from within – and to auto-immunity. Derrida has stated that 'deconstruction is always a discourse about the parasite' ('The Rhetoric of Drugs' in *Points*) and also that 'the virus will have been the only object of my work' ('Circumfession' in *Jacques Derrida*).

In Derrida's terms the parasite is therefore less something that attaches itself like a foreign body on the outside and then comes to invade its host than a structural phenomenon. A virus is something that occurs within a system as the impossibility, for that system, of successfully delimiting itself. In fact the system, or a category such as a genre, cannot define itself and determine its integrity without also installing the law of its own contamination. Its internal necessity requires that it negotiate with what is supposed to reside outside of it.

D. Wills

PARTI COMMUNISTE FRANÇAIS or **PCF** (French Communist Party) An explicitly Marxist-Leninist political party that during its eight-decade existence has exerted considerable influence on French politics, culture and thought. Born of a split between socialists favouring parliamentary tactics and those endorsing revolution as the best means for accomplishing socialist ends, the PCF organised itself in 1920 as a 'party not like the others'. Though it can and did do things just like other political parties (adopt platforms, run candidates, influence policy and so on), it was first and foremost constituted as the avant-garde expression of the revolutionary will of the proletariat. As such and for its first sixty years, the PCF saw itself as the vehicle by and through which the communist revolution would occur. Consecrated to this end, the PCF did not feel itself bound to the laws and practices of the French state except when these were amenable to its own initiatives. This tense relationship to the Republic was exacerbated by the Party's long-standing identification with the Soviet Union as that state which represented and enabled the possibility of any and all successful communist revolutions. Due to this identification, from 1920 until the coup against Gorbachev in 1991, PCF policy was heavily influenced by Moscow. Despite the sometimes bewildering policy moves that this alignment demanded, the PCF at certain moments enjoyed great political influence and popular support. For the most part, these times of greatest popularity coincided with a liberalisation of the Party's Marxist-Leninist hardline, a strategy that usually forbade it from participating in left coalitions lest its pure revolutionary role be compromised.

Though popular support for the French Communist Party came and went in cycles, support for and identification with the PCF on the part of the French intelligentsia was one of its most enduring features. Even during periods of orthodoxy when petit-bourgeois intellectuals and their ideas were not welcome in the Party, the PCF played a large role in the intellectual imagination; for many a thinker and artist, communism represented the most radical overturning of the present order of things and thoughts imaginable. For this reason, the Party attracted not only cultural critics and philosophers but also poets, artists, mathematicians and biologists. Prior to the Second World War, among the most prominent of these were Romain Rolland, René Maublanc, André Breton, Georges Politzer and Henri Lefebvre. After the Second World War, and in the wake of the PCF's heroic role during the resistance, some affiliation with the Communist Party or with Marxism became almost the norm for French intellectuals. This was as true for artists like Picasso as it was for thinkers like Lévi-Strauss, Sartre and Althusser. This engagement continued for many even after the revelations in 1956 of Stalinist atrocities. It was only in the 1970s and following electoral reversals and the abandonment of a Leninist platform by the PCF that intellectuals defected in droves. Searching for alternatives to Marxism in neo-liberalism and poststructuralism, these defectors are now among the most prominent political philosophers

working in France today and include Bernard-Henri Levy, Alain
Badiou and Jacques Rancière.

                                                                    W. Lewis

  See also: French Maoism

PARTICULARISM A term designating Michèle Le Doeuff's study of
  what specific philosophers have said, and her critique of them in
  relation to the social conditions in which they wrote. A feminist critic of
  the historical tendency to erase or overlook the intellectual work of
  women, Le Doeuff investigates what specific women have achieved,
  and the circumstances that have muted or 'disinherited' their legacy.
  Critical, nevertheless, of any lament for a lost or suppressed specifically
  'feminine' voice or writing, associated with 'intuition' rather than
  'reason', she shows how at various stages in the history of philosophy
  and science, intuition has been regarded as man's highest form of
  understanding. Women's 'lack' was seen as an absence of such deep
  understanding, as if women only mime men's intellectual 'intuition'.

  Against Descartes' extreme scepticism, Le Doeuff favours Francis
  Bacon's alertness to our tendency to err about what common practice
  presents as 'obvious'. For instance, that an intellectual woman is a
  'bluestocking' is uttered as a truism. Yet what it implies, that learned
  women thus lose libido, is easily refuted empirically. Placing a term
  within its social practice is vital. 'Bluestocking' works as a 'cast-off'
  phrase, originally coined by English Tories to derogate *men* who, when
  gathering for intellectual discussion, dressed more casually than 'gen-
  tlemen' should. 'There is no closure of discourse', she writes, 'discourse
  only being a compromise . . . between what it is legitimate to say, what
  one would like to argue, and what one is forced to recognise.'

                                                                M. Deutscher

PATOČKA, JAN (1907–77) Czech philosopher, the leading phenomenologist and political philosopher of Central Europe in the twentieth
  century. A student of Husserl in the 1930s, Patočka's phenomenologically derived philosophy of history and concept of 'living in truth'
  inspired a generation of Central European dissidents, most notably
  Václav Havel. Patočka died in 1977 of a brain haemorrhage after arrest
  and interrogation by Czechoslovak secret police for his activity as
  spokesperson, with Havel, on behalf of Charter 77. Patočka's philosophy attempts to bridge the gap between the subjectivist phenomenology of Husserl and the existentialist ontology of Heidegger. His
  engagement with Heidegger leads him to augment a fundamentally
  phenomenological perspective with an analysis of the ontological

structures inherent to human being. Patočka calls his approach a 'phenomenological philosophy', and intends by it a philosophy that is adequate to our self-understanding as well as to our concrete existence in history and in society.

In his most original treatise, *Body, Community, Language, World* (1968), Patočka postulates a phenomenology of three hierarchical movements to human existence: an instinctive-affective movement of acceptance; a second movement of self-sustenance, self-projection and work; and a third movement of 'truth' in which explicit recognition of our non-indifference to being allows us to 'break free' of the bondage of the first two movements and bestow closure and meaning upon them. The third movement represents a life of awareness, in relation to the world 'as a whole' and therefore to our most intrinsically human possibility: the possibility to transcend the pull of objectivity and to live freely.

With *Plato and Europe* (1973), a collection of lectures first published as *samizdat* (underground writings), Patočka responds to the Husserlian call (in *Crisis*) for a phenomenological rediscovery of the 'spirit' of European rationality; he locates this spirit in classical Greek philosophy understood not as metaphysics, but rather in light of the anti-metaphysical insights of Heideggerian thought. He characterises Platonic philosophy as fundamentally a struggle against decline and a recognition of human freedom: it is a process, he writes, of 'caring for the soul'. Care for the soul, in turn, reveals itself 'in the ontological-cosmological representation of reality' as a 'theory of motion'. The soul is not a metaphysical entity, it is rather 'an indicator' of the main 'arteries' of our being, arteries which can lead us either toward a legitimate growth in being or towards decline and a loss of being.

Patočka's most widely recognised work is his *Heretical Essays in the Philosophy of History* (1975), in which he analyses history and politics in terms of the ontological content of human activity, the primary characteristics of which are freedom and a recognition of problematicity. Patočka's political thought links the third movement of life – 'living in truth' – to the recognition of human historicity and a Socratic willingness to 'shake' the objectivist myths on which the polis is founded, to act both freely and ethically even in the face of heavy sacrifice. Patočka declared, with these *Essays*, a 'solidarity of the shaken' that lent support to persecuted anti-communist dissidents throughout Eastern Europe.

E. Findlay

PEIRCE, CHARLES SANDERS *See* Pragmatism, Semiotics

PERFORMATIVITY The notion that one's identity is actualised through the accomplishment of certain performances and does not pre-exist these actions. While the notion of performativity has been taken up by many thinkers in the continental tradition, among them Butler, Derrida and Foucault, the term 'performative' emerges as well in the work of analytic philosopher J. L. Austin to indicate a doing that constitutes a being. In this sense, performativity must be differentiated from performance. Performance presupposes a subject, while the idea of performativity is meant to combat the very notion of the subject, stressing instead the ways in which subjectivity is constituted in particular historic moments as the effect of certain linguistic or cultural acts. Hence to say that identity is performative is not to say that the performance masks a more foundational subject that assumes or performs certain roles. It is rather to claim performativity as that aspect of discourse that has the power to actualise what it names or connotes. The performative model of identity undermines the belief that there is a static agent that prefigures the performance of certain acts. Understood in this way, identity is not the expression of some core 'inner' self but is rather the retroactive effect of our actions. Such an understanding of subject contests the notion that there is a thinking self that precedes and remains unchanged through action. As such, the notion of performativity might be read as a challenge to the moral, social and political relations of modernity.

A. Murphy

PHALLOGOCENTRISM A term which associates the 'phallus' with the *logos* in order to account for the privileging of the masculine in discourse and culture. The Greek *logos* can be roughly translated as 'word', 'speech', 'knowledge', 'account', or 'reason'. Derrida uses the term 'logocentrism' to describe the organisation of language, meaning and truth according to a logic of presence in which being is present to the subject and representable by language. It is the dominant logic of the history of Western metaphysics by which difference is excluded in favour of identity. The term 'phallus' pervades psychoanalytic theory. It is used interchangeably with 'penis' by Freud as the privileged organ that differentiates the sexes. Lacan, however, distinguishes between the phallus and the penis. The penis refers to the biological organ, but 'phallus' is irreducible to biology and instead denotes the imaginary and symbolic function the penis takes on in language, fantasy and subject constitution.

In 'phallogocentrism', or more simply 'phallocentrism', the 'phallus' occupies the place of the *logos*. French feminism has made use of this term in order to challenge the hierarchical organisation of sexual difference in and by a patriarchal imaginary and symbolic in which the phallus takes centre stage. A phallogocentric economy represents the feminine, most often through negation, only in subordination to the (normative) male subject and never in and for itself. Female *jouissance* has become a privileged site for disrupting the patriarchal organisation of language and society and for opening a new discursive space for reimagining new cultural forms and subjectivities.

S. Keltner

PHARMAKON A Greek word picked up by Derrida in a discussion of Plato's treatment of writing, in the *Phaedrus*, as 'bad' memory and therefore a poison, but also as a necessary remedy for forgetfulness, with the Greek word doing double duty for both opposing senses. Indeed, different translations decide on one side or the other, or somewhere in between (e.g. 'drug'), according to context ('Plato's Pharmacy' in *Dissemination*). Derrida's analysis shows how ambivalence towards writing derives not only from its being a substitute for memory but also from its being a 'dead' technological version of living speech and the 'bastard' offspring of royal and paternal truth.

The word 'pharmakon' appears in various versions of a list that Derrida refers to as a 'chain of substitutions', which by definition 'has no taxonomical closure' and 'even less . . . constitute[s] a lexicon'. They are 'undecidables . . . unities of simulacrum, "false" verbal properties' (*Positions*), each of which qualifies and modifies the sense of the last. Other members of the list are dissemination, differance, supplement, hymen, gram, reserve, incision, spacing, blank, margin-mark-march/step, *écriture* (writing), trace, *entame* (broaching/breaching), parergon. They are hinge-words (*brisure*, 'hinge/break' is another of them) through which meaning breaks on one side or the other, or on both sides at once, and they are sometimes used, as if symptomatically, by a thinker whose text Derrida is analysing, to condense, occlude or otherwise deal with a complication in the logic that 'cannot' be faced explicitly because that would mean calling the whole metaphysical tradition or thinking itself into question. On other occasions Derrida himself coins the hinge-word in order to point to a similar conundrum.

D. Wills

PHENOMENOLOGICAL REFLECTION The process by which Husserlian phenomenologists isolate that which is purely immanent to experience. Phenomenological reflection is thus radically distinguished from 'inner' perception or 'inner' reflection. The basis of this distinction is the different character of that upon which each type of reflection focuses. In the case of reflection understood as 'inner' perception, what is focused upon is characterised as an inner object, the interiority of which is determined ontologically on the basis of its contradistinction to the 'outer' objects perceived in 'external' perception. The interiority of what is focused upon by phenomenological reflection, in contrast, is determined experientially, namely as what is inseparable and therefore immanent in the reflected to the regard that reflects it. Hence, the *experience* proper to the perception of both inner and outer objects is something that is focused upon in phenomenological reflection.

B. Hopkins

PHENOMENOLOGY The name for what began as a movement within European philosophy at the beginning of the twentieth century, expanded into a worldwide school of philosophy by the middle of the twentieth century, and now, in the early years of the twenty-first century, after a slow and steady decline, has degenerated into a mode of philosophy generally associated with a subdiscipline of the contemporarily more prevalent style of philosophising known as 'continental philosophy'. Originally envisioned by its founder, Husserl, as a philosophy whose method and basic principles were sufficiently cogent to warrant the designations 'rigorous science' and 'first philosophy', phenomenology has come to be understood as a method for describing subjective or first person experiences – such as perceptions, emotions, valuations – in a manner that supplements and sometimes even eclipses the current natural scientific knowledge of what is characterised as the 'objective' correlates or (in some cases) bases of these experiences.

Husserl presents phenomenology as a philosophical programme of research into a novel region of being, variously described as 'phenomenological being' or 'intentional being'. Intentional being, or more simply, 'intentionality', is characterised as a dimension of experience that has cognitive precedence over all natural and social scientific cognition and ontological precedence over all the regions of worldly being, including the psychological being of the human. Because, however, intentionality is methodically accessed through reflection, and because, moreover, reflection is unmediated in comparison with external perception and therefore in some sense appropriately characterised as an 'inner' perception, intentionality bears a superficial resemblance to what since the seventeenth century has been known as 'inner experience' and classified as a psychological reality. To counteract the misunderstanding of intentionality as a psychological reality (a misunderstanding which is an understandable consequence of this resemblance), Husserl articulated two indispensable methodological procedures for securing philosophical access to it: the phenomenological and transcendental phenomenological reductions and the eidetic reduction. The first reductions function to exclude systematically from phenomenological reflection all cognitive and ontological appeals, respectively, to transcendent objects and the transcendent being of the world as bases for cognition and meaning formation. The second functions to precipitate out from phenomenologically reduced reflection individual instances of intentionality and therefore to highlight what is intentionally invariant. The invariant structures of intentionality are termed 'essences' or 'eide' by Husserl. They are so termed in order to forestall their confusion with the psychologically internal and therefore representational 'ideas' that are inseparable from the metaphysics and epistemologies of both the empirical and idealistic traditions in modern philosophy.

The cognitive and ontological priority of intentionality is revealed in the 'descriptive' modality of phenomenological cognition, by which Husserl understands its reference to the invariant structures of intentionality. This reference is mediated by a special or technical language made such by its continual purification from all cognitive appeals to empirical principles – such as 'causality' – and all ontological appeals to transcendent principles – such as 'being', 'mind' and 'bodies'. Husserl describes the fundamental essence of intentionality as 'the consciousness of something', and uses the Cartesian term 'cogito' to designate it. This essence is further described as having two dimensions that are both distinct and inseparable, namely the 'directedness toward' or 'noesis' and the object to which this directedness is directed, the 'noema'. Each of these dimensions of intentionality, in turn, is described as having two modalities, one of which is thematic and the other non-thematic. Moreover, both the noesis and noema are descriptively revealed as structured by temporality and as therefore having phenomenologically temporal essences, characterised respectively as time consciousness and temporality.

Phenomenological cognition, being both experientially unmediated and oriented descriptively to what is prior to all cognition and being, therefore has as its domain of research the 'a priori' of intentionality. As a consequence of the immediate and descriptive character of phenomenological cognition, the objects of phenomenological research are characterised as the 'things themselves'. What is meant by this expression is above all the direct and therefore intuitive apprehension of what – in its priority to cognition and ontological meaning –

functions as the condition of possibility for both the knowledge and being of that which is, no matter what kind of knowledge or being is at stake.

The history and development of phenomenology subsequent to Husserl's formulation of it can be characterised as a succession of fundamental critiques directed at his formulation of the cognitive and ontological priority of intentionality. These critiques, significantly, are made on the basis of arguments that recognise and indeed grant the philosophical pre-eminence of phenomenology's guiding principle of striving to achieve access to the 'things themselves' in an unmediated manner, that is in a manner devoid of the appeal to empirical and ontological transcendencies. In concert with these critiques, new dimensions and domains of phenomenological problems were discovered and investigated by both their original authors and by succeeding generations of phenomenologists.

In what is arguably the most original and enduring critique of Husserl's formulation of phenomenology, Heidegger took issue with both Husserl's characterisation of the fundamentality of intentionality and his understanding of the meaning of being that guides this characterisation. Regarding the former, Heidegger presented analyses intended to show that a more original phenomenon underlies intentionality, and that it does so in a manner that at once renders it a derivative phenomenon while also making it possible as a phenomenon. Heidegger characterised this more original phenomenon as human existence. He articulated its basic structure in terms of the finitude proper to the opacity of its comprehension of what it means to exist as a being whose ultimate possibility is simultaneously its impossibility. Regarding Heidegger's critique of the sense of being that guides Husserl's characterisation of intentionality, he maintains that this sense is manifest in the modern identification of what being is with its being known by consciousness. Moreover, Heidegger presents analyses of human existence that purport to show the fundamental question that concerns it is also the fundamental question that concerns philosophy, namely the question of the sense of being over all. Because this sense is something that Heidegger thinks, strictly speaking, cannot be known, he formulated his phenomenological method as an analysis of human existence and a hermeneutic (interpretation) of the sense proper to both the being of this existence and to the being over all that shows up in its understanding of itself and the world.

Merleau-Ponty's critique of Husserl's phenomenology, or, perhaps better, his critical appropriation of it, has set the tone for much of its reception in postwar France. Like Heidegger, Merleau-Ponty takes issue with the fundamentality of Husserl's characterisation of intentionality. However, unlike Heidegger's attempt to establish the phenomenological priority of an ontological mode of understanding and a hermeneutical methodology, Merleau-Ponty's engagement with Husserl's phenomenology presents a series of investigations designed to explore pre-cognitive dimensions of the cogito either overlooked or undeveloped in Husserl's investigations. To this end, in addition to the technical employment of language, Merleau-Ponty experimented with other media to describe and elicit the phenomena with which he was concerned, including poetic metaphors and the paintings of European artists. Proceeding in this manner, he mapped a dimension of the pre- and indeed non-cognitive cogito that he termed the 'tacit' cogito, the most distinguishing feature of which is not structural but tactile. The tactility of the tacit cogito, as a function of its priority to cognition, is something that Merleau-Ponty attempted to access by attending to the pre-reflective awareness that he sought to show is inseparable from the body as it is lived, and thus prior to its apprehension and experience as an extended body among other extended bodies and objects. The most basic phenomenon of this awareness of the body as lived is characterised by Merleau-Ponty as the 'flesh'. With this term he attempted to both describe and elicit the phenomenality of the phenomenal at the precise but ever elusive moment of its appearance from out of an invisible but nevertheless functional web of sense and non-sense, a web that is the insuperable condition for the relationality of all relations and the linguisticality of all language.

We will conclude with a brief discussion of the movement to 'naturalise phenomenology', that is to render it useful to cognitive science. In this project the commitment to the philosophical and scientific priority of phenomenology's 'descriptive' mode of cognition is forgotten. Husserl, Heidegger and Merleau-Ponty all recognised the insuperable gulf separating phenomenological description from the activities of the modern sciences rooted in (or derivative of) modern (formalised) mathematics. For them, a mathematical object's very meaning as a mode of formal objectivity precludes in principle its significance as a tool for describing the fundamentally non-formal modes of experience and encounters with objects that defines phenomenology as a science of phenomena.

The editors of the essay collection *Naturalising Phenomenology* (1999) try to overcome such anti-naturalism by claiming it stems from Husserl's 'having mistaken certain contingent limitations of the mathematical and material sciences of his time for absolute ones' (42). To naturalise phenomenology, for these thinkers, is to attempt a 'qualitative physics of phenomenological morphologies'; should such a 'pheno-physics' be successful, they claim, it would demonstrate that 'what Husserl called "inexact morphological essences", essences foreign to fundamental classical physics, are indeed amenable to a physical account, provided that we rely upon the qualitative macrophysics of complex systems (and no longer on the microphysics of elementary systems)' (55).

It must be said that this approach produces strongly negative reactions from those phenomenologists who insist that Husserl's anti-naturalism was principled rather than contingent upon the mathematics of his day. For them, even a 'qualitative physics' will still violate the injunction to respect the absolute ontological difference between formalised and non-formalised modes of being. This judgement, of course, does not address the possibility that something useful or interesting may arise from the project of naturalising phenomenology for the purposes of advancing scientific knowledge in the fields of cognitive science. But it does suggest to the classical phenomenologist that naturalising phenomenology amounts to the obliteration of philosophy itself as a mode of cognition independent of – let alone more fundamental than – modern science.

B. Hopkins

See also: naturalising phenomenology

PHILOSOPHICAL IMAGINARY A term introduced by Michèle Le Doeuff in *The Philosophical Imaginary* (1980), to be read as a noun rather than an adjective, that is as the domain of a work of philosophy, by analogy with the fictional world of a novel. A philosophy creates its 'imaginary' both by the use of specific images that lend credibility to the issues with which it cannot deal (the theory's 'neuralgic points'), and by a system of producing a variety of tropes. For instance, Sartre's *Being and Nothingness* embeds particular arguments within specific images such as walking on the edge of a precipice or looking for someone in a café. Beyond this, its basic terms of *being-in-itself* and *being-for-itself* generate a system of imagery in relation to sexual and other bodily perceptions.

Le Doeuff has also investigated the imaginary of utopias and of epic poetry. Philosophy defines itself as against stories, myths, fables and poetry, but incorporates them and is incorporated by them. Thus philosophical discourse wears a 'shameful face' in relation to its inveterate making of images, preferring to pretend that these are mere ornaments or aids to the uninitiated reader – devices to be replaced by argument. Le Doeuff's approach seeks to exhibit this division between philosophy's practice and its ideal. It is important to emphasise that the imaginary is not beyond reason. Like argument, and the use of specific images, any one imaginary is subject to critical scrutiny.

M. Deutscher

PLATEAU A term whose social, non-geographic use was coined by Gregory Bateson in his study of Balinese culture and extended by Deleuze and Gauttari in their *A Thousand Plateaus* (1980). Bateson showed that in Balinese practice, affective interactions like sexual games or hostile arguments have a quite different structure than in the West. Balinese tend to achieve a degree of intensity that is then maintained over a period of time. The full interaction will traverse a series of these sustained plateaus, which may increase or decrease in intensity without any well-defined end point. In the West, by contrast, such interactions follow a typical pattern of crescendo followed by a climax that terminates the interaction through a violent discharge of affect. Climactic discharge is transcendent because the nature of the whole interaction is defined by a goal that is exterior to it. The components of such a system are deduced from the central goal, branching off from it as if from the trunk of a tree. Indeed Deleuze and Guattari contrast plateaus with tree-like or arborescent systems.

Plateaus, on the other hand, are immanent, or self-maintaining systems, forming a series with other terms like 'rhizome', which is 'composed' of plateaus. Significantly, Deleuze and Guattari use plateaus as the principle of organisation for their text, so that the components do not develop linearly, like chapters towards a conclusion, but rather plot different levels of intensity, connected to each other in unexpected and subterranean ways. Consequently, the authors claim they may be read in any order, but many readers have found this to be an exaggeration.

A. Welchman

PLAY IMPULSE (*Spieltrieb*) The drive toward beauty and humanity described by Schiller in *On the Aesthetic Education of Man*. Schiller's play impulse or play drive functions like the imagination (*Einbildungskraft*) in Kant's and Fichte's philosophies. According to Schiller, there are three basic drives toward human personality: sense, reason and play. The play drive equalises the divergent powers of the other two, producing harmony in the mind, Schiller's idea of Beauty, and a vision of freedom, Schiller's hope for moral society.

For Schiller, the play impulse is the highest phase in the development of the imagination. Borrowing from Kant's *Critique of Judgement*, he calls imagination's movement 'free play', but qualifies it as 'material' or 'aesthetic', according to the individual's development. As long as individuals are primarily in a state of sensuousness, imagination's movement is 'material play', a happy engagement with the abundance of physical existence. As individuals discover ornament, taking a delight in the appearances of things for their own sake, imagination becomes 'aesthetic play', a 'contemplation of the Beautiful' as 'a happy midway point between law and exigency', where sense meets ideals and 'living shape' emerges.

Like Kant and Fichte in their epistemological and moral projects, Schiller understands imagination to be a synthesising and productive power. However, while they are concerned with its power to secure the foundations of knowledge, Schiller sees it producing Beauty, a revelation of humanity to humanity. In this way, he makes aesthetic play central to the attainment of morality.

M. Robinson

POSITIVE PHILOSOPHY A term which for Schelling indicates thought which is grounded in a revelation that extends beyond what can be disclosed by reason. At the same time, it is philosophical only in so far as it is posited by negative (or purely rational) philosophy. This takes place when reason grasps its own final limit: the very rationality of reason requires that something first must be. This priority of existence over essence has to become apparent before we are able to become open to revelation. In very simple terms, the project of deduction must be silenced, if we are ever to learn how to listen. Schelling sometimes referred to such listening as the 'ecstasy of reason', which enables one to grasp the difference between the purely conceptual and its actually existent correlate, for instance the difference between non-being and actual matter or between the idea of humanity (nature awakened into spirit) and this fallen being that I myself happen to be. Recognition of this difference transforms the potencies of negative philosophy into the living gods of mythology. Positive philosophy is the historical account of the life of those gods, their entanglement in nature, and their final release into a sphere of pure luminosity. The account is historical (and positive) to the degree that whatever has proven itself to be could also conceivably not have been. It rests on the notion that the world itself is a free (but by no means an arbitrary) creation of God.

J. Lawrence

POSITIVISM A philosophical system created by Auguste Comte, who expressed its main tenets in the *Cours de philosophie positive* (1830–42) and the *Système de politique positive* (1851–4). Positivism considered as valid only the areas of knowledge to which the positive, that is scientific, method was applied. It insisted on the need to make observations of real, concrete phenomena and to use these facts to create scientific laws that explained how, not why, phenomena operated. These descriptive laws had to express the spatial and temporal relationships of phenomena in terms that were as certain and precise as possible. However, Comte's positivism should not be confused with empiricism, which he believed advocated the accumulation of facts for their own sakes without any attempt at fruitful generalisations or rational predictions about the future. To him, scientific investigation rested on the use of both induction and deduction, included rationalism as well as experimentation, and required the use of imagination. Observations of phenomena could be indirect and facts could not be observed or connected without first formulating a theory. Scientific laws themselves were provisional, because all knowledge was relative. The only absolute was that there was no absolute. In addition, positivism should not be equated with scientism. Comte argued against using the sciences to satisfy humankind's love of power and conquest, and he rejected all utopias based on the rule of scientists, whose tendencies toward specialisation made them narrow-minded, egoistic and indifferent to social welfare. Positivism was not value-free, as is often thought to be the case. Its purpose was to facilitate useful, constructive action that improved the human condition and furthered progress.

M. Pickering

POSTCOLONIAL THEORY A term used to name the interdisciplinary field which, drawing on literary criticism and theory, philosophy, psychoanalysis, history, anthropology, politics and economics, treats the whole phenomenon of colonialism and its aftermath. Although the field does not offer a single theory of colonialism, it is marked by an impulse to generalise concerning such issues as the role of language, literature and culture in supporting or resisting European and American domination of the Third World, the influence of colonisation on the formation of personal and cultural identities, and the relative merits or demerits of discourses of nationalism. Emerging in the mid-1980s as a branch of poststructural (above all, Foucauldian and Derridean) literary theory which aimed to extend the critique of the Western tradition into a critique of Western hegemony over the non-West, by the end of the 1990s it had become one of the chief humanistic interpretive paradigms in Anglophone universities throughout the world. This tremendous success amounts to a perhaps belated acknowledgement of the immense effect that colonialist imperialism has had in constituting present-day historical situations and subjectivities. But this same success also raises some doubts. Is it possible that, rather than enabling critique or resistance, the legitimation of postcolonial theory at the heart of the Western academy in fact operates to contain, domesticate and defuse it? Does the popularity of the postcolonial research paradigm allow the West a channel for an ostentatious display of self-critique which does little or nothing to alter the fundamental reality of Western hegemony?

The prefix 'post' in the term 'postcolonial' is not meant to signify that the era of colonialism has ended. Rather, there is common consensus that Western imperialism still persists, now operating through the less perceptible mechanisms of global capitalism rather than through direct political rule by nation-states over subject territories (this persistence is referred to as 'neo-colonialism'). Nor does the 'post' mean that the theory in question is limited to considering the period following the liberation of formerly colonised nations from Western control. Rather, the object of study includes the entire period of relations between colonisers and colonised, from the initial encounter to the present day. Although most work in the field has pertained to the cultural effects of British, French and American imperialism of the nineteenth and twentieth centuries, the postcolonial approach has been applied to other historical periods. It has also been extended to include analysis of the discursive structures by which indigenous peoples and minorities within Western nations are marginalised and disempowered. Some understand the term 'postcolonial' in a particular sense, as naming a certain pervasive global condition of late twentieth-century culture and thought.

While the genealogy of postcolonial theory as a discipline is usually traced back to the rise to prominence of the literary theorists Edward Said, Gayatri Spivak and Homi K. Bhabha (Said's 1978 book *Orientalism* is often regarded as the discipline's founding text), these Anglophone scholars would themselves acknowledge the importance of an earlier Francophone tradition which, although not called 'postcolonial theory', shared many of the same concerns. This tradition includes the two primary proponents of *négritude*, the poet-politicians Aimé Césaire and Léopold Senghor; Octave Mannoni, a colonial administrator in French-ruled Madagascar, whose 1950 book *Psychologie de la colonisation* (much criticised for its claim that the Malagasy suffer from a primitive 'dependency complex') offers the important insight that colonisation is a matter of psychology as well as physical coercion; Albert Memmi, a Tunisian novelist and literary critic whose 1957 book *The Colonizer and the Colonized* offers a rich analysis of colonialism's debilitating effects on both those who dominate and those who are dominated; and above all the psychiatrist-turned-revolutionary Frantz Fanon, celebrated both for his 1952 book *Black Skin, White Masks* (notable for its critique of Freudian psychoanalysis's pretensions to universality) and his 1961 book *The Wretched of the Earth*, in which, radicalised by his participation in the Algerian War of Independence, he moved away from a concern for solidarity through racial identity toward a more internationalist profession of faith in the emancipatory violence of the peasant class.

It should be noted that Jean-Paul Sartre, who wrote the preface to *The Wretched of the Earth* and who earlier had actively promoted the poetry of *négritude*, was in the 1950s and 1960s very much engaged in what we would now call 'postcolonial criticism.' The example of Sartre helps us see, retrospectively, that the mainstream of the post-Second World War French intellectual tradition was working in directions consonant with postcolonial theory. A central aim of Claude Lévi-Strauss's highly influential Structural Anthropology was to deny that the abstract logical discourse of the modern West can be termed an intellectual 'advance' over the thinking of those peoples sometimes called 'primitive'. When in 1948 he was elected to the chair of 'Religions of Primitive Peoples' at the École Pratique des Hautes Études, Lévi-Strauss quickly changed its name to the chair of 'Religions of Peoples without Writing Systems'. Robert Young, noting the North African provenance or involvement of many of the most important French intellectuals (Camus, Althusser, Derrida, Cixous were all born in Algeria; Lyotard and Bourdieu lived there in the 1950s and became critics of French rule; Foucault wrote *The Archaeology of Knowledge* while living in Tunisia) suggests that it would not be inaccurate to rechristen French poststructuralism 'Franco-Maghrebian theory', indicating that the poststructuralist critique of Enlightenment Reason was in part a response to the continuing spectacle of France's colonialist domination of its 'possessions' in North Africa and elsewhere.

Not all of those who aim to liberate third world nations, indigenous peoples and minorities from the grasp of Western imperialist powers agree that bringing to bear poststructuralist understandings of language and textuality or concepts from Lacanian psychoanalysis on issues concerning colonisation is a good thing. Marxist-oriented critics have charged that 'textualising' the West's exploitation of the non-West deflects attention away from the actual material basis of that exploitation. The poststructural penchant for rendering issues complex and for eschewing 'grand narratives' discourages clear explanations of economic injustice, perhaps allowing those who are truly responsible to evade detection. Postcolonial theory's celebration of cosmopolitanism, hybridity, diaspora and migrancy may well be a sign of its complicity with late twentieth-century global capitalism, which has operated through disseminating rather than concentrating its forces of production. The border-crossing and globe-trotting postcolonial intellectual, proclaiming that notions such as national identity are outmoded, may not really represent the local political aspirations of those for whom he or she claims to speak. Postcolonial criticism's tendency to dwell on the heterogeneous construction of individual identities may in fact hinder the accomplishment of collective social movements.

G. Stone

POSTDEMOCRACY A term coined by Rancière in *Disagreement* (1995) to characterise liberal democracy after the fall of totalitarian states. For Rancière, democracy is not a form of government or a modality of social life but the other name of politics. He defines politics as the polemical interruption of the hierarchical, inegalitarian principle structuring the social, in the name of the radical equality of anyone with anyone. Politics thus defined challenges the sociological, functionalist perspective on the community that considers it as the total summation of its diverse and unequal parts and functions. It also challenges classical and contemporary political philosophy that sees the political as the emanation of the social. Instead, politics relies on the postulation of a *demos*, a community of equals, immanent to the social order but incommensurable with it. Postdemocracy replaces the *demos* constitutive of democracy, and thus of politics, with a community fully identical with itself, and reformulates social conflicts as problems between already constituted partners and interest groups, to be solved technocratically with a view to finding a compromise or consensus. Two important symptoms of the apolitical nature of contemporary democracy are the replacement of conflictual democratic disagreements by the consensual notion of public opinion, in which the community is supposed to present itself exhaustively, and the juridification of social life, where the law, by becoming ever more adapted to social evolution, is supposed to express in its own medium the community's self-identity.

J.-P. Deranty

POSTMODERNISM A concept with a number of different references, it has been used to describe the stylistic or formal elements of an artistic or cultural work (as in 'postmodern' literature or architecture), to signal a particular set of philosophical, intellectual or epistemological allegiances, positions and strategies, or, most generally of all, as a periodising concept akin to 'postmodernity'. Drawing together these diverse usages is a shared sense of a decisive break or rupture with, or reconfiguration of, the practices of 'modernism', a term encompassing a diverse range of experimental literary, artistic and intellectual movements, generally agreed to have extended from the late-nineteenth century through the Second World War and reaching its highpoint in the 1910s and 1920s, and/or the cultures of 'modernity', a more sweeping term referring to the Western and European values, practices and institutions that begin to emerge in the sixteenth century and become dominant in the nineteenth and twentieth centuries.

The first uses of the term *postmodernismo* appear in Spanish language literary debates of the 1930s. The term then resurfaces in the Anglo-American context in the 1950s in the work of such figures as the historian Arnold Toynbee, the poet Charles Olson, the sociologist C. Wright Mills and the literary critic Irving Howe. Although the term would appear periodically throughout the next two decades, it would not be until the publication of a series of seminal works in the late 1970s and early 1980s that 'postmodernism' would take on a new centrality in the intellectual debates in a wide range of disciplines. Among the most significant of these works are Charles Jencks's *The Language of Post-modern Architecture* (1977), Jean-François Lyotard's *The Postmodern Condition* (1979), and Fredric Jameson's 1984 essay 'Postmodernism, or, the cultural logic of late capitalism'.

Each of these interventions also exemplifies one of the three uses of postmodernism outlined earlier. Jencks describes postmodern architecture in terms that would later be applied to other artistic practices, as for example in Linda Hutcheon's *A Poetics of Postmodernism* (1988). On the one hand, postmodernism is characterised by a rejection of the abstraction, cold formalism, elitism and utopian transformative pretensions of the modernism of such figures as Le Corbusier or Mies Van der Rohe. On the other, it is distinguished by an embracing of the vernacular; by an eclectic and ironic playfulness, a willingness to draw upon and incorporate elements of the historical past; and by a collapsing of the distinction between the high and the low. Jencks also argues that these works deploy a form of 'double coding', and thereby simultaneously appeal to both a broad popular and an elite audience.

Lyotard defines postmodernism 'as incredulity toward metanarratives'. The more ambitious scope of Lyotard's work is evident from this opening declaration. These metanarratives (*grand récits*) are the foundational stories of Western philosophical modernity: 'the dialectics of Spirit, the hermeneutics of meaning, the emancipation of the rational or working subject, or the creation of wealth'. These also include such legitimating notions as Enlightenment rationality, universal progress and the objectivity of science, and political and intellectual programmes such as those of Marxism and psychoanalysis. These stories are often described as 'totalising' – and in the final line of the English translation of his book, Lyotard declares 'Let us wage a war on totality', since totalities present themselves as universal and applicable to all peoples at all times and places; moreover, there is sometimes suggested a short line between their totalising drives and the political totalitarianisms that had such a dramatic effect on the course of the last century. In postmodernism, on the other hand, which Lyotard crucially restricts to 'knowledge in the most highly developed societies', we see a proliferation of local knowledges and a turn toward a plurality of 'language games', each deploying a range of rhetorical and argumentative strategies and each aimed at a specific end.

Lyotard's work has led to the identification as postmodern of a diverse range of philosophical trends, often assembled under the vague umbrella of 'poststructuralism', including the work of such thinkers as Jacques Derrida and Michel Foucault, who also engage in a critique of the foundational texts, stories and assumptions of Western modernity. Moreover, such critical engagement with the fundamental values of modernity has been extended by figures such as Judith Butler and Gayatri Spivak into gender, sexuality and postcolonial identities. However, such a project is not without its critics. Perhaps the best known is Jürgen Habermas, who decries what he sees as the conservative anarchic turn of postmodern thought and calls for a resumption of the 'unfinished project' of modernity.

Jameson's analysis of postmodernism begins by accepting the premises of Jencks, Lyotard and a number of other thinkers including Jean Baudrillard and Henri Lefebvre. Jameson argues that beginning in the early 1970s we have witnessed the emergence of postmodernism in literary and cultural production, in philosophy and in everyday life. Its central features include the collapse of critical distance, the waning of affect, the weakening of our sense of historicity, the dissolution of the centred subject, the collapse of the referent, the rise of micro- and small group politics, and a new centrality of the image and information technologies. Moreover, Jameson notes that in postmodernism the modern 'semi-autonomy' of the aesthetic, something codified in the work of Immanuel Kant, as well as the modernist dichotomy of high and mass culture, have come to an end.

Jameson's analysis differs from that of many of his predecessors, however, in that his is 'a historical rather than a merely stylistic one', as he attempts to grasp the postmodern as 'the cultural dominant of the logic of late capitalism'. In his essay, as well as the later book of the same title (1991), Jameson draws extensively upon Ernest Mandel's masterpiece of political economic theory, *Late Capitalism* (1972), for an explanation of the material transformations that lie at the root of postmodern cultural productions. Jameson argues that postmodernism represents a transformation within rather than a full break with capitalist modernity, an insight developed in a different fashion in David Harvey's *The Condition of Postmodernity* (1989), and in fact corresponds to Mandel's third stage of 'post-industrial' or 'multi-national capitalism' (realism and modernism being the cultural correlates of Mandel's two earlier stages). Jameson describes this as the 'purest form of capital yet to have emerged', marked by a 'new and historically original penetration and colonisation of Nature and the Unconscious: that is, the destruction of the precapitalist Third World agriculture by the Green Revolution, and the rise of the media and the advertising industry'. And yet, while Jameson does claim a new global nature for the uniquely spatialised culture of postmodernism, his original analysis remains almost exclusively on the particular cultural productions of the United States, 'which is justified only to the degree that it was the brief "American century" (1945–73) that constituted the hothouse, or forcing ground of the new system, while the development of the cultural forms of postmodernism may be said to be the first specifically North American global style'. With this, Jameson leaves open the possibility that the postmodern will in fact be 'lived' differently in other locations within a now unified global totality – an insight he develops in more depth in his subsequent discussions of postmodernism in *The Geopolitical Aesthetic* (1992), *The Seeds of Time* (1994) and *The Cultural Turn* (1998). Since its original publication, Jameson's essay has become a touchstone in not only discussions of postmodernism but of contemporary culture more generally.

There has in recent years been a waning of the centrality of the concept of postmodernism, as it is subsumed on the one hand into discussions of globalisation, and as it is displaced, on the other, by what we might call the 'post-postmodernism' of such thinkers as Alain Badiou, Michael Hardt and Antonio Negri, and Slavoj Žižek. While all are attentive to the central lessons of postmodern and poststructuralist thought, their work is distinctive in that it marks a return to many of the categories stigmatised by postmodernism, including totality, universalism and truth. All challenge as well any postmodern declaration of the 'end of history', as they once again put on the table the project of a human liberation from the grasp of global capitalism.

P. Wegner

POSTSTRUCTURALISM The North American name of a way of theorising and a style of writing which, beginning in France in the 1950s, gained prominence in the 1960s and 1970s, and was then transplanted to the rest of the world. Prominent contributors to this intellectual movement include Barthes, Baudrillard, Cixous, Deleuze, Derrida, Foucault, Guattari, Irigaray, Kofman, Kristeva, Lacan, Lyotard, Levinas and Nancy in France; de Man and the Yale deconstructionists in the United States; and Agamben in Italy.

The advent of poststructuralism was brought about by the convergence of a variety of intellectual, social, political and cultural factors. Among the most notable intellectual factors were a turn against the ahistorical nature of classical structuralism; a dissatisfaction with then-current attempts at a Marx-Freud synthesis; and a strong anti-Hegelian current which targeted both the programme of absolute knowledge and the role of the negative and of dialectical thought in attaining that standpoint, as well as a vision of a society that, thanks to the state, was destined to become reconciled and transparent. In the process of re-examining Saussure and the structuralists, the diacritical nature of the sign was not challenged (signs remain differential values, receiving their identity in the system of sign-relations to which they belong); retained also – with different variations – are the arbitrariness of the sign, the decentredness of the subject, the constructivist function of language and theory, as well as the notions of non-presence, the remainder and the undecidable.

Difference and différance. Poststructuralism is opposed to using 'the one and the many' as a fundamental concept since the sort of difference that results is a totalising one. Rather, three major poststructuralists think we should conceive differentiation as a process through which identities arise. In search of this alternative, Deleuze and Derrida developed separate strategies for the articulation of a theory of difference in itself, while Foucault developed an 'archaeology' and a 'genealogy'. What these discourses share is the dislike of totalised or closed systems. Heterotopias substitute themselves for utopias, and centers give way to dissemination and lines of flight; paradoxes and aporias replace the concept; the fold occupies the place of linearity and its telos; presence, as the matrix of time, is denounced because it renders any account of temporality impossible; and the subject is seen as constructed by practices within a field of social relations. Deleuze,

Derrida and Foucault agree that the traditional way of conceiving identity as prior to difference leads to conceptual, ethical and political dead ends. But their itineraries to different/ciation (Deleuze), *différance* (Derrida) or 'the outside' (Foucault) diverge significantly.

The border between Deleuze and Derrida is located between the virtual tendencies of Deleuze and the differential signs/undecidable aporias of Derrida. For Deleuze, tendencies and signs belong to different levels of sensibility, imagination and intelligibility. Tendencies are essential to Deleuze's philosophy of becoming, with its Bergsonian inspiration. In order to safeguard the continuity of becoming and to prevent the reduction of temporal sequences to sets of discrete moments, this ontology requires the distinction between intensity and extension. Tendencies are on the side of intensity, and transformation goes from (actual) states of affairs to (virtual) tendencies and back to changed (actual) states of affairs. Tendencies are the outside of the actual and the search for the virtual is a search for tendencies that offer the conditions for experimentation and creation – tendencies to transform speech and writing, tendencies to make language itself stutter, that is tendencies to deterritorialise the forces of deferral/reproduction and tendencies to hijack language for the sake of those who do not yet have it.

Signs, on the other hand, along with their traces and the traces of their traces, are essential to Derrida, who launches his theory of difference by continuing and radicalising Heidegger's view of language as the house of being. Deconstruction – a name for his strategy that Derrida accepted rather begrudgingly – followed initially from the premises of his grammatology. Grammatology, having contested the primacy and the alleged transparency of the voice of the logocentric tradition, and having salvaged writing from its detractors, insisted on the function of the interval, the space and the trace in the constitution of sense. Later on, Derrida's deconstruction will capitalise on the aporetic character of concepts that have been essential to the traditional image of thought.

Deleuze's ontology and Derrida's grammatology denounce the fact that difference in itself has become invisible under layers of theory with progressivist and continuist assumptions. Foucault scrutinises these assumptions and challenges their grip upon the human sciences. With his 'archaeologies', Foucault analyses the limits of the discourse of the human sciences, investigating the constitution and succession of their theories and their practices; with his 'genealogies', Foucault investigates the relation between power and the putative truth of subjectivity-constituting discourses. Archaeology uncovers the 'historical a priori' or *episteme* of a society at a given time – an a priori which, like the structuralist sign, is in itself arbitrary and yet can be reconstructed as a posteriori necessary. Historical a priori *epistemes* represent the limits of the visible and the sayable of a given period. As for the power/knowledge nexus investigated by genealogy, it maintains its a priori arbitrariness. To think otherwise and to try to be otherwise would be unthinkable, if it were not for this arbitrariness. In his studies of the medical gaze, the asylum and madness, discipline and governmentality, Foucault shows that the change of *epistemes* is not due to subjects, but rather to solicitations whose origins we cannot understand, although we can reconstitute analytically their historical a priori. Nevertheless, in folding the forces of the outside, in making themselves the sites of the sayable and the visible, individuals subject themselves to these forces and give themselves a style. The subject, therefore, for Foucault, is an after-effect of folding and of ethical self-fashioning.

The demise of grand narratives and the sprouting of lines of flight. In the 1960s Habermas speculated that the inability of modern states to generate and sustain myths and ideologies of self-legitimation may be a more promising reason for their crises than the economic crashes predicted by Marx. The poststructuralist response in the 1970s, led by Lyotard, was that the grand Western metanarratives had delegitimised themselves and that there was no reason to be nostalgic about them. Politics should rather be concerned with the ominous counter-tendency of postmodern societies to favour a climate of performativity which valorises the ability to serve efficiently the imperatives of the decision-makers. To prevent a performativity-driven closing of horizons and the ensuing injustice against the plural, Lyotard appealed to what he took to be the modern scientific paradigm, with its openness to experimentation, the plural and the paralogic. Lyotard called then for activists to unleash short stories, to learn from the equitable distribution of narratival roles in traditional narratives and to respect the justice of equal time for all stories, not in the name of truth, but for their intrinsic interest. This call to arms gained in depth through Lyotard's fascination with the sublime. In the Kantian metanarrative, the sublime is what, in the absence of categories and concepts capable of encompassing it, humbles the understanding and, at the same time, issues a demand that the imagination find a way to grasp it – safeguarding all along the honour of the unrepresentable. The link between the unrepresentable sublime and the political became, in the sequence, more clear when Lyotard restated and clarified his reason (the differend) and his strategy (phrasing) behind his politics of dissonance: we are confronted with a differend each time that we have no rules for the subsumption of different claims under one concept. The problem, then, is one of justice without criteria, where the political must bear witness to the impossibility of a judgement that would decide the dispute. Only the phrasing of the unspeakable is in this case left as our political duty. To phrase is to create a syntagm where every new phrase corrects a virtual tort, and assists in the emergence of affects, which Lyotard places *hors-phrase*. The expression of the differend becomes a goal for philosophy more urgent than the resolution of conflicts.

Poststructuralist feminism. To the extent that poststructuralism is the quest for difference in itself, any political agenda bent on reversing gender hierarchy, or merely on championing gender equality, can be seen as ultimately regressive, even if strategically necessary in the short term. With regard to the rigorous emphasis on difference, then, the writings of Irigaray, Cixous and Kristeva are poststructuralist.

The quest by Irigaray for new ways of thinking the feminine, the demand for a new imaginary and a new symbolic by women and for women, her reference to women in the metonymy of the 'two lips, without suture' and her advocacy of sexuate rights and of female *jouissance* would have reinscribed gender dualism if it were not for the fact that Irigaray's point is that the reversal of the gender polarity shows decisively that woman is not self-identical. And the same goes for the demand by Irigaray and Cixous for a new speech and a new writing (*écriture féminine*) made against the fact that the generation of discourse is always sexuate and that to speak is never neutral. Whether designated as mimicry of the dominant patriarchal discourse that would make possible, through a playful repetition, the cover-up of a possible operation of the feminine in language; or whether anticipated as a new, disruptive, tactile and fluid style – this *parler femme* (speaking [as] woman) is meant to challenge the dominant discursive mechanism for the sake of the plural and the multiple. Finally, Kristeva is resolutely poststructuralist when, even as she acknowledges the results of the 'women's' movement, at the same time refuses to admit that sexual difference is fundamental; what is fundamental for her is difference. She is poststructuralist when she thinks of the subject as a subject-in-process/in trial; she is also close to it when she champions an ethic between love and transgression (she calls it 'herethic' and takes it to be based on *jouissance*, an alternative to the juridical models that presuppose autonomous subjects who relate to each other through the force of law), despite the fact that her models for this ethic (poetry, maternity and psychoanalysis) may not be as rigorously differential as they might be.

C. Boundas

POTENCY A term that for Schelling, much the same as for Aristotle, signifies an active capacity rather than a logical possibility. In his early philosophy of nature the term describes how the original tension between expansion and contraction recurs in the chemical and life processes, but each time in a higher manifestation or 'power'. In his subsequent system of identity, he began to reduce the potencies to a mathematical formula, detailing the movement from A^0 through B to A^2 and A^3, whereby 'A' is identical with real being (or expansion) and 'B' with its negation (or contraction). Despite the fact that Hegel caricatured such formulas in the *Phenomenology of Spirit*, Schelling spent the next four and a half decades of his life in a tireless search for a completed theory. In the philosophy of identity, he thought consistently in terms of magnetic polarity (where the opposing force is present in either of the poles). His goal was to make clear that the sum of opposing and dynamic forces constitutes a point of identity that reconciles all opposition. With the *Ages of the World*, he articulated a more profound conception of potency that began with the realisation that a Parmenides-like Absolute Identity, while reflecting the view from eternity, is useless as a tool for comprehending finitude. The relationship to potency must characterise eternity itself: finitude becomes an attribute of God.

J. Lawrence

POUR-SOI/EN-SOI ('for-itself / in-itself') A distinction fundamental to the system of ontology Sartre develops in *Being and Nothingness* (1946). Although the terminology is inherited from the German idealists (*für-sich/an-sich*), particularly Hegel, Sartre uses it in a new way, rejecting the idealist belief that reality is essentially spiritual, in favour of a highly anthropocentric form of realism according to which the world as we know it is basically material but at the same time thoroughly shaped by free human actions.

In his Introduction to *Being and Nothingness*, 'The Pursuit of Being', Sartre employs Husserl's technique of phenomenological description to attempt to establish the real existence of the *en-soi*, being-in-itself, about which he concludes that all we can say is that it is, it is what it is, and it is in itself. As part of the extended analysis leading to this seemingly unexciting outcome, he offers an 'ontological proof' of *l'être-en-soi* by way of countering traditional ontological proofs of the existence of God. Sartre then attempts, through an exploration of the 'negativities' that pervade our experience, to establish the existence of a region of being radically different from the *en-soi*, which he calls being-for-itself, *l'être-pour-soi*. This *pour-soi* is nothing in itself; it is non-substantial (unlike Descartes' *ego*), totally free and the source of all meaning in the world. Since the *pour-soi* cannot exist detached but is always embodied and enmeshed in real, concrete situations, or what Sartre calls 'facticity', human reality must be understood as an always-contingent conjuncture of *pour-soi* and *en-soi*.

W. McBride

POWER In its primary sense, the capacity of something to be or to do or to become something. This metaphysical concept of power as capacity has assumed more or less relational forms, from Plato's characterisation of the power of a thing in terms of its capacity to affect or be affected by other things to Nietzsche's characterisation of power as that which is expressed by any activity whatsoever. Since the capacities of any given body will be determined by the environment in which it operates, it is implausible to suggest an absolute distinction between a relational and a non-relational sense of power: all bodies will have particular capacities only in relation to a given set of background circumstances. Nevertheless, when these are relatively stable and unlikely to change, we can speak of the power of a body, so long as we bear in mind that this may change as a result of changes external to and independent of the body concerned.

Political theory is interested in the power exercised by human beings, and by institutional or collective bodies which are the products of human agency. As a result, theorists such as Arendt focus on political power and seek to emphasise its consensual basis by defining it in terms of the ability of a group to achieve its collective ends through cooperation. Others define power as it is exercised in social relations more broadly so as to include relationships involving violence or sanctions as well as cooperative relations. In this context, a distinction is often drawn between the power of a particular agent understood in the primary sense above (power to) and the power which an agent is capable of exercising over other agents (power over). 'Power over' is exercised by individual or collective human bodies when they act upon each other's actions. In these terms, when the actions of one party A succeed in modifying the field of possible actions of another B, we can say that A has exercised power over B.

Since one important way to increase one's power is to acquire power over the capacities of others, power as capacity and 'power over' are intimately related in practice. Thus Hobbes begins *Leviathan* with a general conception of the power of a man as 'his present means to obtain some future apparent good' before going on to list the various ways in which one person gains power over the power of others. These include the possession of servants or friends upon whose resources one can draw, or the possession of wealth in so far as this is a means to procure both servants and friends. As James Mill commented, 'The grand instrument for attaining what a man likes is the actions of other men'.

In itself, the exercise of power over others is an inescapable feature of social interaction and a normatively neutral activity neither to be applauded nor denigrated. However, political theorists frequently import an implicit normative content into their concepts of power. Thus, by defining power in terms of means to obtain some future apparent good, Hobbes narrows the exercise of power to include only those actions which aim at some benefit for the agent concerned. Another widespread approach associates the exercise of power over others with action that harms them or adversely impacts upon their interests in some way. Thus, in criticising behaviourist definitions of power in terms of causing agents to act or not act in ways they might otherwise do so, Stephen Lukes in *Power: A Radical View* (1974) argues that A exercises power over B when A affects B in a manner contrary to B's interests. Not only does this definition commit him to a prior account of the interests of those on whom power is exercised, it cannot then identify as the exercise of power paternalistic actions which are not adverse to those interests. Nor can it distinguish the exercise of power from unintended actions which cause harm to the interests of an agent. Thomas Wartenberg's *The Forms of Power* (1990) offers a more comprehensive definition of the power that social agents exercise over each other in suggesting that 'A has power over B if and only if A strategically constrains B's action-environment'. It follows from this definition that the exercise of power over others will not always imply effective modification of their actions. Indeed, it is only in particular circumstances that A can be sure of achieving a desired effect on the actions of B. The history of efforts to achieve this result is the history of techniques of government, where 'to govern . . . is to structure the possible field of action of others', as Foucault puts it in 'The Subject and Power'. Only when the possibility of effective resistance has been removed does the power relation between two subjects of power become unilateral and one-sided such that A can reliably control or direct the conduct of B. When this occurs a state of domination is established.

Systems of domination often enable some to extract a benefit from the activity of others: economic exploitation in all its forms, from slavery through to the system of extraction of surplus value which Marx identified as the secret of capital, depends upon such systems of domination. The sexual division of labour in many societies embodies another such system of domination. Such systems establish asymmetrical and impersonal power relations between particular classes or castes of people. However, it is not essential to the concept of domination that it should be detrimental to the interests of the dominated party: the relation of parents to children, teachers to pupils or political authorities to citizens may involve domination in the interests of those subject to it. In this sense, the government of others may be aimed at the increase of their capacities for self-government or self-direction as well as at the extraction of some benefit from the use of their capacities. If, as Foucault suggests, social relations are indissociable from power relations, then the critical task is not the abandonment or the removal of power relations. Rather, it is to identify and dismantle forms of exploitation and to transform existing techniques of government so that they also serve to enhance or increase the power of those governed.

P. Patton

PRAGMATISM The name of a philosophical tendency – a loose association of thinkers whose specific doctrines differ in important ways – which emerged in the United States at the beginning of the twentieth century. In the 1940s it became unfashionable to profess pragmatism, but in the 1980s the tendency underwent a revival in a form often referred to as neo-pragmatism. This leader of this revival, Richard Rorty, suggests commonalities between some of the landmark thinkers of the pragmatist and continental traditions, namely Dewey and Heidegger.

'Pragmatism' was introduced by Charles Sanders Peirce for the doctrine that 'the meaning of a *concept* . . . lies in the manner in which it could *conceivably* modify purposive action'. The term, and the notion, began to collect adherents when it was used (with acknowledgement to Peirce) in a widely publicised lecture given in 1898 by William James (1842–1910). James recommended his friend's doctrine as particularly useful for clarifying philosophical concepts and problems. In James' *Pragmatism* (1907), its application resulted in classifying truth as a moral notion: 'the true is the name of whatever proves itself to be good in the way of belief'.

Peirce approved neither of James's treatment of truth nor of what he identified as the results of James's sympathy for nominalism and 'ultra-sensationalist psychology'. Peirce had identified truth as the limit of an indefinitely continued process of scientifically conducted inquiry, and as there would be true general statements in this limit, Peirce reckoned he was committed to 'Scholastic realism'. His thought, moreover, had been shaped by the close study of Kant; he chose to label his concern with practical consequences 'pragmatic' rather than 'practical' because in Kant *praktich*, as opposed to *pragmatich*, belonged to moral philosophy. James, on the other hand, was deeply sympathetic to British Empiricism, including its nominalistic metaphysics, and he treated Kant with disdain.

What united Peirce and James, along with other prominent early pragmatists such as John Dewey and George Herbert Mead, was their stress on the purposive nature of cognition. Whether trying to understand concepts or the possibility of knowledge, philosophy must recognise that humans always represent the world in order to further purposes shaped by their biological and social natures. Dewey's own word for his position, before it was swept up into pragmatism, was 'instrumentalism', but unlike later doctrines identified as 'instrumentalism', Dewey's allowed that the discovery and adoption of new means (the fruits of 'inquiry') typically reconstituted the ends that had stimulated inquiry.

Dewey had been prompted by reading James's *Principles of Psychology* (1890) to a biologically framed conception of human cognition; he followed Peirce in thinking of human beliefs and desires as dispositional (as 'habits') and he held that results of successful inquiry were modifications in our dispositions of response so that our dealings with the environment could proceed smoothly. Under the influence of his friend and one-time colleague George Herbert Mead, he came to appreciate and to stress the importance of the social dimension of inquiry. By the end of its first phase pragmatism was responding to the basis of the criticism later levelled specifically against Peirce by Habermas in *Knowledge and Human Interests* (1968) that in relying on 'the community of inquiry' Peirce had paid too little attention to the conditions of the possibility of intersubjectivity. Pragmatist philosophers, however, moved too far from Kant and became too naturalistic in outlook for them to have much interest in the transcendental investigation that Habermas was calling for.

The understanding of pragmatism as held together by belief in the purposive nature of cognition allows the term to be applied far from its American home. Mark Okrent in *Heidegger's Pragmatism* (1988) characterises Heidegger's early work as 'an extended argument designed to show that no self-consciousness is possible unless Dasein is being-in-the-world, an agent actively working on and with things to achieve self-defined ends'. The chief architect of the recent revival of pragmatism, Richard Rorty, also suggests that Dewey and Heidegger share a common vision of the predicament of Western philosophy in the early twentieth century, but recommend very different remedies.

Rorty explicitly distances his new pragmatism from Peirce and the Kantian legacy. In Rorty's *Consequences of Pragmatism*, Peirce's efforts to establish a theory of signs (his 'Semiology') are dismissed as at best ill-conceived anticipations of the 'linguistic turn' taken by analytic philosophy. In following analytic philosophy around this turn his own pragmatism is, Rorty contends, superior to earlier versions of the tendency and superior to contemporary alternative philosophical positions to the extent that it makes clear how we can, and why we should, dispense with impossible aspirations and empty pretensions. Rorty applauds James's account of truth, holding that it is the denial that truth has an essence and should be understood as the denial that a theory of truth is possible. (To those analytic philosophers who regard the culmination of the 'linguistic turn' as centred on formal theories of truth, this is a very paradoxical claim.)

Rorty is also closer to James in explicitly espousing nominalism, although Rorty's writings focus more attention on Dewey. Dewey did indeed urge that philosophy should give up using the notion of truth (in favour of 'warranted assertibility') and should abandon any belief in a deep metaphysical divide between facts and values – another thesis advocated by the new pragmatism. But Dewey retains, in Rorty's view, a number of Peircean elements that need to be purged, in particular the belief that natural science provides a model of how inquiry should be conducted. Rorty's version of pragmatism holds that 'there are no constraints on inquiry save conversational ones', that is only those 'provided by the remarks of our fellow-inquirers'. Although he acknowledged that inquiry was historically situated, Dewey clung to the belief that its techniques could be improved through experience and one might on that basis identify constraints other than conversational agreement as well as grounds to criticise an inquiry as inadequate.

J. Tiles

PRINCIPLE OF HOPE *See* Bloch, Ernst

PROBLEMATIC A term developed by Canguilhem and Bachelard to designate a system of interrelated concepts that define the possibility of what can be thought at any specific historical moment. Somewhat independently, they advanced the thesis that scientific knowledge finds its truth status not by dint of external verification but by the degree that it conforms internally to the unarticulated and unconscious rules by which specific scientific disciplines are constituted. By using a method of historical analysis that pays close attention both to that which is included and that which is excluded from a science's practice, both philosophers argued that these rules can be articulated. Made explicit, these rules and their relations constitute a science's problematic. Once identified, the problematic can then be used to explain why some thoughts are thinkable in an era (such as that of voids in nature) and others are not. In the early 1960s, this concept and method of interpretation was extended by Althusser and other structuralist thinkers (including Foucault, who preferred the term *episteme*) in order to give an account of the origin and transformation of knowledge that did not include in it any rational or necessary logic of development. Since then, the notion has been widely adopted by social theorists from diverse disciplines. With this adoption, the term has lost some of its technical meaning and now seems to designate the diverse historical influences that, taken together, occasion the creation of a specific text.

W. Lewis

PROJECT A term used by Beauvoir for the temporality, the engagement with the world and the relationship to others of the freedom through which we bring value and meaning into being. In embracing a project, I declare that the world lacks a meaning which it ought to have. I transcend myself toward a future where that value is realised. Propelling me toward that future, my present choices engage the past, either discovering that it provides resources for the future (in which case I affirm the continuity of the temporal flow) or finding that it is an obstacle to the future (in which case I rebel against it and announce the rupture of time). Valid projects can neither be solipsistic nor dictatorial. Declaring that the 'me–others' relationship is as fundamental as the 'subject–object' one, Beauvoir argues that I cannot legitimately assert my freedom without simultaneously affirming the freedom of others. She ties the idea of the just project to the concept of the appeal. The unjust project imposes my will on others. The just one appeals to the freedom of others to take up my cause. Neither just nor unjust projects are absolute. Both are grounded in the vicissitudes of freedom. They may be sustained but they will not be static. If they endure it will be through choices (mine and others') that transform and change them. They may not be sustained. This failure that lies at the heart of the project is, for Beauvoir, a source of joy rather than despair. It preserves the possibility of bringing new values and meanings to the world by situating us within the horizon of an always open future.

D. Bergoffen

PSYCHOLOGY 'The science of mind' which attempts to provide a deeper understanding of that which is closest to us: our thinking, perceiving, desiring, willing, remembering, imagining, self-conscious acts and their base – if any – in our 'self'. Although we could start with systematic studies of these activities that go as far back as ancient times, contemporary psychology, and continental philosophy's relation to it, has its roots most firmly in the seventeenth and eighteenth centuries and the psychological inquiries of rationalists such as Descartes and Kant and empiricists such as Locke, Berkeley and Hume.

A main issue of this early period in psychology concerned 'nativism'. Descartes and Kant argued that sensory experience must be supplemented by innate or a priori mental structures in order to account for perception and other psychic activities. Descartes used the example of a melting piece of wax in order to show that we judge rather than see that bodies remain numerically the same throughout changes in their sensory qualities. Because all the melting wax's sensory qualities change, Descartes reasoned that we must infer rather than sensorily experience its temporal continuity; further, this inference must rest upon the innate idea that extension is the unchanging essence of physical bodies. Kant argued in turn that space and time are a priori forms of sensory experience and that therefore the mind is responsible even for the spatial and temporal properties of sensory qualities and objects.

In contrast, the empiricists took the adage 'seeing is believing' literally and claimed that all ideas are derived completely from sensory experience. These sensory experiences, or 'impressions' in Hume's terminology, were linked together by three 'laws of association': resemblance, spatial and temporal contiguity, and cause and effect. On this view, no innate ideas are necessary in order to explain perception and our other mental activities.

Although rationalism and empiricism provided self-consistent but conflicting responses to the issue of nativism, each plagued future psychology with difficult problems. Descartes assigned thinking as the essence of mental substance and extension as the essence of physical substance. This mind–body dualism initiated the 'mind–body problem': how could two things so radically different from one another interact causally? Moreover, Descartes thought that we immediately experience only our mental representations (sensations or ideas) of things in the world – the contents of our minds – and not the things themselves. Although at least Hume's empiricism avoided both of these problems, it bequeathed to psychology the method of introspectively analysing ideas in terms of their constituent impressions and the three laws of association that led to their original combination. This entailed that at least one of the variables in any psychological experiment was a 'private' mental event and thus unfortunately inaccessible to inter-subjective scrutiny, for example one's colour experience in response to a measurable wavelength of light.

Although psychology continued to favour empiricism over the rationalist and nativist tradition, it replaced introspectionism with behaviourism and thus with a psychology in which both independent and dependent variables are intersubjectively observable and measur-able. Initially developed by the Russian psychologist Ivan Pavlov (1849–1936) as well as by E. L. Thorndike (1874–1949) and John B. Watson (1878–1958) of the United States, behaviourism was soon dominated by B. F. Skinner (*Science and Human Behaviour*, 1953) and his 'operant conditioning' paradigm. According to this stridently anti-metaphysical view, a person is no more than a repertoire of measurable behaviours reinforced by environmental stimuli. Behaviourism dis-placed its chief competitor from Europe, Gestalt psychology, and reigned supreme in the United States for the first three-quarters of the twentieth century, until Chomsky ('Review of Skinner's *Verbal Behaviour*', 1959) convincingly argued that language acquisition re-quires an innate 'universal grammar' to intervene between environ-mental stimuli (verbal sounds) and the child's response to them.

With this development, cognitive psychology and cognitive science began to displace behaviourism as the leading paradigm for a science of the mind. In order not to fall back into introspectionism, cognitive psychologists use the experimental method and computer simulation in order to validate their claims concerning the cognitive processes that mediate between stimuli and behavioural responses. On the basis of these techniques, they might show, for example, that the visual array of the previous sentence provides inputs to a mental lexicon. These inputs are then matched with, and understood because of, the corresponding words and their meanings contained in the lexicon. Although the word 'mental' is used here, this approach avoids Descartes' mind–body problem. Just as the software of a computer designates particular functions of the computer's hardware, so the cognitive or computa-tional processes of the 'mind' refer to functions of the brain. Thus everything that takes place is the function of a physical process and does not imply the existence of an ontologically distinct mental realm.

However, the same computational functions can be realised in different kinds of physical 'tokens', for example a computer as well as a brain. By understanding the causal role of these computational or 'functional types' in relation to one another (for example, the visual inputs in relation to the lexicon), many cognitive psychologists feel that they can provide us with a characterisation of mental activity that is irreducible to and makes minimal mention of neurophysiology while still declaring that all tokens are physical.

Two alternatives to these paradigms are phenomenological and Nietzschean-inspired psychology. Of the phenomenologists, Merleau-Ponty provides the most systematic treatment of psychology. His investigation of perception in *Phenomenology of Perception* (1945), based in phenomenology and Gestalt psychology, shows perception to be the continual realisation of the tacit meaning of the situations in which we find ourselves. More specifically, perception is a 'dialogue' between a subject and an object: the subject draws together the meaning diffused throughout the object, and the object simultaneously pulls together the intentions of the subject in its direction. This dialogue establishes around the subject and object a world 'horizon' that reflects the bodily schema of the subject, provides the subject with a setting and calls upon the subject to realise more fully the meaning or further possibilities of the object. Because the subject and object are both initially somewhat indeterminate and are involved in a process of temporarily becoming a more determinate version of themselves through their current dialogue, perception is as much the creation as it is the discovery of its object.

Nietzsche treats the self and society as an interplay of many 'value-creating forces' and is the precursor of two other important trends in psychology. His emphasis upon the unconscious status of many of these value-creating powers in relation to the individual, and on the relative unimportance of consciousness, influenced psychoanalytic psychology, as both Freud and Jung acknowledged. On the other hand, his valorisation of 'perspectivism' (as opposed to neutral knowledge) and heterogeneity (as opposed to essences) has inspired Lacan (*Ecrits*, 1966), Deleuze and Guattari (*Anti-Oedipus*, 1972), Kenneth J. Gergen (*The Saturated Self and Dilemmas of Identity in Contemporary Life*, 1991) and other philosophers and psychologists who are thought of as postmodernists or poststructuralists.

F. Evans

QUANTUM MECHANICS A scientific field inaugurated in 1900 by Max Planck's discovery that radiation, such as light, previously believed to be a continuous, wave-like, phenomenon in all circumstances, can, under certain conditions, have a discontinuous or quantum character. The limit at which this discontinuity appears is defined by the frequency of the radiation and a universal constant of a very small magnitude, h, Planck's constant, one of the most fundamental constants in physics. Planck's discovery and related developments transformed physics and our sense of the limits of our knowledge, scientific and philosophical, and its claims upon nature and mind. The transformation took a while, as did a more adequate understanding of quantum phenomena themselves.

First of all, both radiation, such as light – wave-like according to the classical view – and particles, such as electrons, may manifest their existence, if not themselves, in both wave-like and particle-like phenomena under different circumstances, in conflict with the classical view. At the same time, it does not appear possible to ever observe both types of phenomena together. On the one hand, this circumstance appeared to make the situation paradoxical. What are, ultimately, quantum entities: particles or waves? How does one combine such incompatible features as properties of the same objects? On the other hand, the situation suggested, especially to Niels Bohr, a way out of the paradox: since such incompatible observational effects are always mutually exclusive and can never be simultaneously observed, the paradox in fact disappears, although, as explained below, at a price of suspending any possible knowledge concerning quantum objects themselves and their behaviour. Bohr called the mutual exclusivity 'complementarity', which eventually came to designate Bohr's overall interpretation of quantum mechanics, arguably the best known and yet still one of the most controversial.

It took more than two decades to sort out the initial complexities that arose from Planck's discovery, by means of quantum mechanics, introduced in 1925–6 by Werner Heisenberg and Erwin Schrödinger in two different but mathematically equivalent versions, and developed in the work of Max Born, Pasqual Jordan, Paul Dirac and (primarily in terms of interpretation) by Bohr. Quantum mechanics is *analogous in functioning* to Newtonian mechanics, but *different in its epistemological character*, specifically as concerns the possibility of a realist and causal description of quantum objects and processes. Quantum mechanics is able to predict in statistical terms (and no theory can do better) the outcome of certain individual events, such as collisions between particles and a photographic screen, but it appears unable to describe the motion of quantum objects in a manner analogous to classical physics. In short, it can *predict* the outcome of the experiments in question but does not appear to (and in certain interpretations, such as Bohr's, strictly does not) describe the behaviour of physical objects in the way classical physics would, say, the motion of a planet around the sun. Nor would it predict in the same way either. For it makes chance an irreducible part of the theory even in dealing with individual, rather than only collective, behaviour, as would be the case in classical statistical physics, such as the kinetic theory of gases.

The majority of even the most resilient critics, Einstein and Schrödinger among them, acknowledged that quantum mechanics brought with it considerable improvements as concerns the predictive capacity of quantum theory. What bothered these critics was a deficiency of the explanatory-descriptive capacity of the theory with respect to quantum objects themselves, as just explained – the apparently uncircumventable lack of causality and realism of the theory. By contrast, Bohr, Heisenberg and other founders of quantum mechanics saw these features, captured in Bohr's interpretation and its avatars (often assembled under the rubric of the 'Copenhagen interpretation'), as ensuring the consistency of the theory and its effectiveness as the mathematical science of nature.

Controversy has continued to surround quantum mechanics and its developments, such as quantum field theory, which provides what is currently known as the standard model of nature at its ultimate microscopic level. The controversy has also led to a proliferation of new interpretations of quantum mechanics, and further debates and controversies concerning them. No end appears to be in sight. On the other hand, beyond an extraordinary role quantum theory played in physics itself, this history has also led to a philosophical rethinking of the nature of our knowledge and thinking. The philosophy of quantum theory served as a major source and, conversely, absorbed numerous philosophical ideas from elsewhere. While the conceptuality and epistemology of quantum theory could be traced to such earlier figures as David Hume and Immanuel Kant, it exhibits its greatest affinities with postmodernist thought, as developed from Nietzsche on, in the work of Georges Bataille, Jacques Lacan, Maurice Blanchot, Jacques Derrida and Paul de Man. It may indeed be expected that further developments of quantum physics will reveal still greater, as yet unexpected, complexities of both nature and mind. Indeed, we may need all the complexity of quantum theory to be able to think either mind or nature – and both of them as reflected in quantum theory.

A. Plotnitsky

QUASI-OBJECT A classificatory term in Science and Technology Studies often used in conjunction with 'quasi-subject', designating a conceptual interstice. Whereas modern epistemologists tend to treat 'nature' and 'society' as binary oppositions that are in need of dialectical reconciliation, a quasi-object simultaneously designates a source of agency that bypasses the duality of immanence-transcendence and fabricated-discovered.

In *The Parasite* (1980) Serres characterises the ferret in a children's game as a quasi-object. The identity of the child who is caught with the ferret changes as he or she becomes distinguished from the others by becoming 'it'. This specific example suggests Serres's general point, namely that in order to understand distinctive human relations and identities it is necessary to: (1) analyse the entwined series of displacements and transformations that have historically occurred between humans and material entities, and (2) avoid reducing the principal terms of this analysis into analytically or pragmatically separable subjects and objects.

Under the influence of Serres's book *Statues* (1987), Latour in *We Have Never Been Modern* (1991) discusses the quasi-object in ontological terms in order to distinguish and assess modern, postmodern and non-modern perspectives. Latour contends that because the identity of modern Western industrialised society is founded upon an epistemology of 'mediation' and 'purification', it is riddled with representational paradoxes that have impeded both natural and social scientists. He appeals to the quasi-object in order to examine how politics, science, technology and nature are mixed, and to explain why the two-culture view (the split between the sciences and the humanities) needs to be re-examined.

E. Selinger

QUEER THEORY A theoretical movement primarily located in the humanities and arts (especially literary, art and film criticism, cultural studies, and history) and to some extent in social science disciplines such as anthropology. Although Butler's 1990 book *Gender Trouble* was subsequently incorporated into the body of works considered part of the movement, Queer Theory made its official debut with the summer 1991 issue of *differences: A Journal of Feminist Cultural Studies*. The term was coined by Teresa de Lauretis in her article 'Queer Theory, Lesbian and Gay Studies: An Introduction'.

From the beginning, Queer Theory sought to distinguish itself from Gay and Lesbian Studies by critiquing the idea that sexual identities are fixed, stable and completely representable in language and liberal politics. In her 1993 book *Epistemology of the Closet*, literary critic and theorist Eve Kosofsky Sedgwick pointed out that terms such as 'heterosexual' (which supposedly names a normal, naturally given state of being) are actually dependent for their meaning on what they attempt to exclude as abnormal or unnatural, for example 'homosexual'. Thus such identity terms are neither simple and accurate representations of phenomena in the natural world nor fully self-contained concepts, and, therefore, the stability of what they purport to signify is at best seriously questionable. Queer Theorists often contend, following Butler (who roots some of her analysis in Austin's speech act theory), that identities – primarily gender identities but sexual identities and other sorts of identities as well – are not best conceived of and analysed as characteristics of human bodies or personalities but rather as 'performances' in which human beings (usually without much deliberative thought) continually engage. This 'performative' analysis of gender and sexuality emphasises the malleability of such identities (Butler's now famous examples include drag performances) but also their dependence upon the power relations and social and historical contexts in which gender and sexuality occur. While it is true and very important that gender and sexuality have not remained the same through historical changes and across regional divides and are, therefore, vulnerable to political action and intellectual critique, it is equally true that they are not under the control of individual subjects who might reform them through personal acts of will.

Clearly this sort of analysis tends to undermine political movements based on fixed identities. Since some feminist activists, gay and lesbian activists and others have maintained that their movements are viable only as long as individuals 'identify' as female, gay, lesbian and so on, and that calls for civil rights and legal protections depend upon general recognition of various groups' status as immutable minorities, the advent of Queer Theory created some anxiety and conflict within feminist and sexual liberation movements. Many gay and lesbian theorists and activists feared that Queer Theory, with its notion of performativity, would play into the hands of radical right-wing critics of gay and lesbian rights, because it seemed to allege that homosexual people could simply stop acting like homosexuals and act like (and therefore *be*) heterosexuals instead. However, activist groups such as

Queer Nation, founded in New York City in 1990, insisted that political movements for radical change do not require belief in essential identities or, indeed, in any historically stable gender and sexual identities at all, and that political change does not depend upon convincing the radical right that homosexuals cannot be otherwise than they are.

These activists, who first began to disavow identity politics by calling themselves 'queer' rather than 'homosexual' or 'lesbian' or 'gay', often looked to the work of Foucault for inspiration and insight, both into the history of sexuality and sexual identities and into the nature of power, as David Halperin notes in *Saint Foucault: Towards a Gay Hagiography* (1995). In *The History of Sexuality, Volume One* (1976), Foucault claims that sexual identities are products of nine-teenth-century medical discourses and governmental politics. These identities took shape in networks of power and knowledge and from the beginning functioned in many respects to trap individuals within those networks, the better to manage and exploit them. Thus, while any formation of power might serve as a site of political reversal – in other words, while it is always possible that those who are labelled pejora-tively might appropriate their label as a means of uniting and fighting their exploiters – the notion of sexual identity is extremely dangerous and must be thoroughly critiqued and possibly displaced or even abandoned. Foucault's ideas – both those in *The History of Sexuality, Volume One* and those in two later books, *The Use of Pleasure* (1984) and *The Care of the Self* (1984) – helped to shape Queer Theory by lending historical and philosophical support to the emerging queer theoretical critique of liberal representational politics and culture and to queer theory's arguments regarding the historical and performative nature of gender and sexuality.

Queer Theorists (such as Lauretis and Butler, in particular) have also been influenced to varying degrees by Lacanian psychoanalysis, especially by Lacan's idea that human subjective unity is based on misrecognition of the unified mirror image of the body as an accurate representation of a truly unified self. Lacan insisted that the self is inescapably 'split', dependent for its sense of self-sameness and self-containment on what is outside it (that is, other selves, its own reflected image, and so on). This idea, too, lends weight to queer theoretical critiques of identity politics. The use of psychoanalytic theory is controversial among Queer Theorists, however, because of psychoanalysis's historical involvement with the medical discourses that established sexual identities in the first place and because of psychological institutions' complicity (in fact often their leading role) in the oppression of non-heterosexual people since the nineteenth century.

Other important influences on some Queer Theorists include the feminist theoretical work of Irigaray, Kristeva and Monique Wittig and the Marxist theory of subject formation through interpolation developed by Althusser. William B. Turner provides a history and analysis of the movement and its antecedents in *A Genealogy of Queer Theory* (2000).

L. McWhorter

R

RACE THEORY One of the most influential areas of work in recent continental philosophy, especially in the United States, it seeks to analyse the historical, social, political and economic conditions for the use of 'race' as a concept and practice.

'Race' is a polyvalent category. It has been used to describe a religious group (the Jews), a national group (the Nazi's idea of the German people), a linguistic group (the Ibo), a political economic class (India's Aryan castes), an ethnic or ethnographic identity (Enoch Powell's idea of the English), a cohort of alleles (in population studies), and a universal (the 'human race'). It is because 'race' can be used to explain anything and everything that some writers have argued that the idea is conceptually fictive or empty. On this view, then, race is only a powerful illusion. But it is not only the status of the concept of 'race' that has been put into question; one also wants to investigate the historical conditions under which the concept of race emerges. For example, in philosophy, the birth of the idea that humans belong to different 'races', or the becoming aware that race is a philosophical problem, are historical events. The historical element requires that we distinguish between three different conceptions of race: the religio- or metaphysico-mythical, the scientific and the critical. Each conception has consequences for understanding our ideas about racial difference and race relations.

The myth of race. Geographical isolation allows self-absorbed ethnic groups to think that, beyond their own borders and the security of their own way of life, nothing short of social and metaphysical disorder abounds. Such active 'ignorance' about the 'outside' world, combined with the limited epistemic and emotional security afforded by the ignorance, functions to render the outsider a hostile 'other'.

Images are formed of the other as extra-human or even extra-terres-
trial, as simultaneously like and unlike 'us'. In antiquity, Herodotus
was a master of the genre; in his *History* he taught the Greeks about
Antipodes, 'men on the opposite side of the earth' who are either 'dog-
headed' or entirely 'headless'. Likewise, Pliny led Europeans to believe
in 'foreigners' who lived where 'the sun rises when it sets on us',
'walked with their feet opposite ours' and, tellingly, 'have no names'. In
The Monstrous Races in Medieval Art and Thought (2000), John Block
Friedman shows how the other 'races' of the medieval mind always
existed in places far away, nameless places, or places whose names
evoked mystery: India, Ethiopia or Cathay. Even as greater geographical and historical consciousness developed with modern voyages of
'discovery', the other remained, in the secular Christian imagination,
peoples in regions normatively situated as nearly unreachable: the Far
North, the Far East, the New World or the Dark Continent.

The mythological ordering of the cosmos as our world and their
chaos is reproduced within the group. Skin colour, hair texture or some
other visible particular becomes fantastically coded in a language meant
to justify established social, economic or political relations. In the
Hindu caste system, for example, Brahmins are coded White, the
Kshatriyas Red, the Vaishyas Yellow, and the Shudras Black. The
order and hierarchy may vary, but in whatever order, the categories
claim to describe 'nature', both material and moral. As the female is
opposed to the male, the day to the night, the right hand to the left, or
the hetero- to the homosexual, social relations are constructed in
binaries and essentialised in a hierarchy of values and norms presumed
guaranteed by natural law.

This is why for Sartre or Beauvoir to ask about the 'race' or 'sex' of
another is never a neutral question, for in the question one already
supposes oneself a judge on the scope of freedom of the other. The
'facts' of colour or sex as we know them are indeed always facts-as-
interpreted. The race and gender of an individual or group emerges as
productions in social encounters – from what Frantz Fanon and Stuart
Hall call the racial-sexual 'look', for example. Because race and gender
are social signs of struggles about freedom, other people could, indeed,
be 'hell' for the racially stereotyped. As Fanon recounted in *Black Skin,
White Masks* (1952): 'You are in a bar in Rouen or Strasbourg, and you
have the misfortune to be spotted by an old drunk. He sits down at your
table right away. "You, African? Dakar, Rufisque, whorehouses,
dames, coffee, mangoes, bananas". You stand up and leave, and your
farewell is a torrent of abuse'.

The modern science of race. As late as 1653, in a schema developed by the Dutch mapmaker Georg Hornius and included in an atlas published by the house of Jan Jansson, there is a tripartite division of human species, a sort of racial geography: the Yellow Semites, the Black Hamites, and the White Japhetites. This geographical spirit in raciology slowly matured, leading, eighty years later, to Linnaeus's work in natural history. In *Systema naturae* (1735), Linnaeus posited 'Homo' as a stem branching world-wide into four races. Claiming to refine Hortius's system by greater empirical observation, Linnaeus classified the Asian as Yellow, the American Indian as Red, the African as Black, and the European as White. Each racial type was explicitly assigned, in categorical terms, corresponding physical, cultural, moral and temperamental contents.

One can recognise in the Linnaean system the persistence of the ancient anthropological doctrine of the 'humours'. For the Greeks and Romans, the so-called four Galenic humours were medical facts, so that Linnaeus and, later, Kant's *Anthropology* (1798) tried to map anatomical 'racial' differences (eye and skin colours, hair textures and so on) first onto moral and mental dispositions and then to what were considered biologically determined bodily fluid types, namely: yellow bile, black bile, phlegm and blood (the Sanguine). Archaic as it is, the Linnaean taxonomy remains, to date, the most influential in biologistic thought. In many parts of the world, including the United States, the Linnaean system, nearly unchanged, also informs the basic categories the state uses, in policy matters, to categorise racial identities. Even after the end of the 1990s, when it became possible for US citizens to self-identify as belonging to more than one of Linnaeus's four races, the basic divisions across which one makes this subjective choice remain, as of today, Linnaean.

A critical theory of race. 'Race' is not a concept used in contemporary biology. In June 2000, J. Craig Venter, the first to complete a draft of the human genome sequence, stated: 'The concept of race has no genetic or scientific basis'. This statement was based on the fact that humans share 99.9 per cent of their genome with one another. If the human genome is made up of about 3 billion nucleotides, strung together in a specific order along the chromosomes, then all but 00.01 per cent are identical from one person to another, no matter the person's race, ethnicity, continent of origin or economic and social status. To the 00.01 per cent genes suspected to code for variations like skin colour or hair texture, no other biologically significant function could be attributed.

We cannot therefore scientifically justify, on the basis of genetic profiles, any moral ascriptions or any claims to knowledge about

behaviour traits allegedly linked to physical characteristics such as skin
or eye colour or hair texture. Because our modern racial attitudes are
still largely based on myth and stereotype, we should remember that
there are more genetic variations within what we normally identify as a
racial group (brown, yellow, red, black or white) than across them. In
fact, the most common variants in our 3 billion genomic nucleotides are
single nucleotide polymorphisms (SNP). But SNPs usually occur in
regions where the nucleotides are known to be doing nothing. It is not
just that the SNPs do not have any known racial function; they are not
known to have any biological functions at all.

In 1998, the American Anthropological Association took a public
stand on the matter: the idea of 'race', it declared, is a social invention.
But the invented character of race does not diminish its social potency.
Along with whatever cognitive utility race stories give our societies (as
shorthand for categorisation of peoples, as religious, ethnic, national or
class self-identifications), the idea or ideas of race have also produced a
variety of practical consequences – consequences that range from the
benevolent through the benign to the pernicious, from self-esteem and
group solidarity through everyday racial discrimination to genocide.
Because racial beliefs fuse behaviour and physical features together in
the public mind, and impede development of better explanations of both
biological variations and cultural behaviour, 'race' erroneously implies
that human behaviour and physical feature are both genetically determined. Far from denying the cultural, social, political or economic
salience of race-consciousness, twenty-first-century anthropology denies the biological foundation of race precisely because it wants to better
understand race's real foundations in social relations and in history.

A post-racial future. The most serviceable theory of race must
thus remain the one proposed in contemporary social and political
theories. From Georg Simmel through Robert Park to Sartre and
Fanon, in sociology as in philosophy, one has come to think of race as
'racialism' (the belief or ideology that segregates individuals or groups
into 'races') or as racism (prejudice against a person or group segre-
gated from others in the name of 'race'). Although the concept 'race'
may be physically arbitrary or even materially empty, in racialism and
racism, however, the word 'race' retains its normative or ideological
force, and enforces this normativity or ideology wherever there is the
social will to do so by those who also have the power to enforce their
racial will. Where such will to race triumphs, it distorts social relation,
and we call the social totality raciofascism or racial supremacy. Thus,
for Park, 'race' is a name for 'relations that exist between individuals
conscious of racial differences'.

In *Race in Another America: The Significance of Skin Color in Brazil* (2004) Edward E. Telles notes the current consensus in sociology: 'race is a social construction'. 'Race', he argues, 'exists only because of racist ideologies'. Beliefs in the existence of races are therefore embedded in social practices, giving the social and cultural concept a great influence on social organisation. It is this sociological and cultural reality of race – the normative system of racial beliefs – that current theoretical projects in philosophy, critical legal studies and sociologies of race try to illuminate. The critical projects are necessary because the non-existent or weak biological basis of race has not yet diminished race's extremely strong sociological and cultural strength. In addition, because of the supreme social and linguistic manipulability of the term 'race', the idea of race changes and adapts itself successfully in diverse environments where there may exist a will to racial discrimination. A 'white' person in Brazil or Jamaica may be 'black' in the United States; a 'white' person in the United States may be 'coloured' in South Africa; a 'white' South African may be 'brown' in Brazil; and so forth. To transcend race through critical understanding is thus to unmask its claims to normative legitimacy and to contain the damaging and unjust effects of its social currency.

E. C. Eze

RANCIÈRE, JACQUES (1940–) French philosopher and political theorist. The great coherence in Rancière's multidirectional work stems from his fundamental intuition: equality is not a value or a goal, but a necessary presupposition of theory. In remaining faithful to the axiom of equality, Rancière conducts cultural revolution within theory.

In Rancière's first period he devoted himself to social and political questions. After a promising contribution to *Reading Capital* (1965), Rancière separated from Althusserianism and philosophy. As *Althusser's Lesson* (1974) and *The Philosopher and His Poor* (1983) explain, he broke with them because of the equality principle, which repudiates the division of labour between intellectual and manual work, a division on which the entire history of philosophy is based, and that can be traced even in the emancipatory theories of Marx, Sartre and Bourdieu. To overcome this division, Rimbaud's 'logical revolts' became a programmatic necessity that Rancière takes up in the journal of the same title (reprinted in *Les scènes du peuple*, 2003), where, methodologically, the words and thoughts of workers are studied as equivalents in nature and value to those of recognised writers and philosophers. His research into 'the archives of the proletarian dreams' led to their conceptual recount in *The Nights of Labour* (1981) and the publication of the texts of major nineteenth-century proletarian philosophers.

In *The Ignorant Schoolmaster* (1987), Rancière reconstructs Joseph Jacotot's pedagogy of emancipation, based on the principle of the equal intelligence of all human beings. The encounter with Jacotot pushed Rancière to systematise his thoughts in a political treatise, *Disagreement* (1995). In it, he opposes the functionalist ordering of social reality, *la police*, and its disruption in politics, *la politique*. Social logic is based on hierarchy and domination; it excludes some individuals by making them invisible and inaudible, even though it needs their existence to establish a social hierarchy. When this *tort* (both an ontological 'twist' and an ethical wrong) becomes challenged in action, true politics emerge in the interruption of social inequality by its immanent egalitarian dimension.

Rancière essentially links his aesthetics to his politics. Political disagreement questions the *partage* (sharing/partitioning) *du sensible*: how the social perception of reality partitions what is equally shared. Politics are fundamentally aesthetic since they propose a new perception of the common, where unseen subjects, things and problems suddenly become perceptible (*Le partage du sensible*, 2000). When we examine the historical path of political aesthetics, we see that, since the modern democratic revolutions which collapsed social hierarchies, artists have abandoned the representative system of the arts, which was based on rules for properly linking genres, themes and styles of representation. Artists imbued with such a democratic aesthetic, however, produce their own 'twist': with romanticism, they liberate the symbolic power of all things, defying the conventional rules of discourse. The symbolic principle, however, is contradicted by a principle of indifference: style and language are indifferent to their object, pointing to an 'aesthetic unconscious' that denies the artist the ability to ever find a language adequate to the world's expressivity (*La parole muette*, 1998; *L'inconscient esthétique*, 2001). Rancière's later texts on literature (*Mallarmé*, 1996; *La chair des mots*, 1998), cinema and the visual arts (*La fable cinématographique*, 2001; *Le destin des images*, 2003; *Malaise dans l'esthétique*, 2004), explore the contradictions that the democratic axiom applied to the arts imposes on aesthetics.

J.-P. Deranty

See also: disagreement; metapolitics; postdemocracy

RATIONALISATION A term developed by Max Weber for a long-term socio-historical process, linked inextricably to the rise of capitalist industrial societies, whereby social life is shaped by methods designed to enhance systematisation, calculation, efficiency and control. The master theme shaping Weber's social thought, it has become a central concept in sociological analysis, with theorists applying and amplifying it in various ways to postmodern conditions. Rationalisation is a process that should not be equated with rationality per se, for it can promote at the same time rationality and irrationality. Thus the rationalisation of industrial production can be rational in so far as profits are enhanced, but from the point of view of the worker or the environment, the consequences of rationalisation can be irrational. The impact of rationalisation on social institutions, particularly the economic and political, takes the form of the modern bureaucratic organisation, which Weber depicted as over time coming to resemble an 'iron cage'. In terms of belief systems, rationalisation contributes to the disen-chantment of the world, which in terms of religion means the advance of secularisation. Weber saw rationalisation as increasingly penetrating all spheres of social and cultural life, including aesthetics, ethics and science. This thesis has been taken up by members of the Frankfurt School, from its founders, Horkheimer and Adorno, to Habermas and more indirectly by figures such as Foucault and Bourdieu.

P. Kivisto

REAL That which replaces Freud's unconscious in Lacan's theory. It is the locus of singularity, defined as an interdicted being that escapes any formalisation and representation: it is impossible (to represent) and cannot be called an *order*, as are the Symbolic and the Imaginary. As such, it overlaps with the real in science, which the incompleteness of our mathematical representations prevents us from knowing in its totality.

Escaping any formalisation, the Real is the set where truth, meaning and sense are to be. We have only partial access to the Real, through lapses, dreams, and bungled actions: 'The unconscious is to not remember what one knows' ('La méprise du sujet supposé savoir', *Autres Écrits*, 2001). Hence, 'Truth can be told only in half, because, beyond this half said, there is nothing to say. (. . .) Here, in con-sequence, discourse disappears. We don't speak about what is unutter-able' (*Seminar XVII*, 1969–70).

If we follow Lacan in grasping femininity as an existence without representation, the ultimate meaning of the Real is that that there is no sexual rapport, that is it is impossible to write a logical rapport between man and woman, since one side will always lack an adequate signifier to represent itself. This notion does not make sense per se, but only in relationship to the other sets distinguished by Lacan, the Imaginary order and the Symbolic order, and only in the mapping out of their respective positioning in the 'topology of the subject'.

A. Leupin

REAL SUBSUMPTION Marx's term for the complete subjection of society to capitalist relations of production, taken up by Negri to define and dissect globalisation and its chief cultural symptom, postmodernism. Real subsumption succeeds formal subsumption, in which capitalist relations exercise hegemony over society at the highest levels but do not penetrate into all individual forms of production and remake them along rationalised industrial lines. European imperialism of the nineteenth century is an example of formal subsumption: agents of national capital controlled the large-scale extraction of wealth from their colonies, but did not necessarily impose changes in the indigenous methods of agricultural or artisanal production that generated the wealth. Under real subsumption, however, even those forms of indigenous production are reorganised according to capitalist models of efficiency, and thus capital's hegemony reaches into and transforms every productive situation or relationship. The logic and structure of the factory spread throughout society, making all activities directly productive in immediately capitalist terms. This key characteristic of real subsumption distinguishes Empire, the governing structure of contemporary globalisation, from traditional imperialism: capital no longer uses one central, metropolitan nation-state to control other peripheral, colonised ones, but instead treats all nation-states as interchangeable frameworks for global production. Postmodernism, as Negri sees it, is the mystified artistic and cultural expression of the new collective subjects, such as the socialised worker, who have emerged from the transition to real subsumption that has been underway since 1968, but who have not yet developed an adequate form of political expression.

T. Murphy

REASON (*Vernunft*) (1) In Kant's topography of the faculties, that which comprises with the understanding the 'higher faculty' as opposed to the 'lower faculty' of the sensibility. However, it also differs considerably from the understanding. Both of the higher faculties are characterised by their 'capacity of judgement' but while the work of the understanding is limited to discrete spatio-temporal appearance, reason ranges beyond all limits in pursuit of a unity based on the total syntheses expressed in the ideas. The freedom of pure reason to pursue totality leads to the tangled inferences of the paralogisms, antinomies and ideals that become the main objects of Kant's critique.

Kant regards the epistemological function of reason within the organisation of the faculties from two distinct standpoints. In the one, sensibility offers a manifold that is unified by the concepts of the understanding, that in their turn are unified into a system by the ideas of reason. In the other, the spontaneity of reason makes visible objects, determines the rules of the understanding which are then applied to objects in space and time. On the whole, the *Critique of Pure Reason* observes the first standpoint, although the latter is present and becomes increasingly prominent in the *Opus postumum* where the account of knowledge departs from the spontaneity of reason and not from the receptivity of intuition. The independence of reason from spatio-temporal limits gives it an important role in Kant's practical philosophy; free from the claims of heteronomy, it becomes the source of moral obligation.

H. Caygill

REASON (2) Hegel modified Kant's contrast between 'reason' and 'understanding'. Hegel viewed understanding much as Kant did, as our capacity to make various determinate cognitive judgements about particular phenomena. Most importantly, Hegel ascribed to 'understanding' our capacity to identify something's specific features by discriminating and isolating them; 'understanding' is essentially analytical, and is crucial to the development of knowledge, especially in natural science. Hegel also held that understanding is not sufficient for knowledge, because knowledge also requires correctly reintegrating the distinct analytical factors identified by understanding. This synthetic activity Hegel ascribed to 'reason'. Hegel retained Kant's association of 'reason' with 'the unconditioned', though Hegel radically reinterprets this latter. According to Kant, no unconditioned totality can be given in experience; hence it is necessarily transcendent. Hegel's ontological holism instead entails that the only 'unconditioned totality' is the world-whole itself, which we can know in principle and of which we know much, both in outline and in detail, by systematically integrating (and continuing to extend) our knowledge of the world so far as we can.

K. Westphal

REIFICATION A concept developed by Lukács in *History and Class Consciousness* (1923) to describe the condition of subjectivity in capitalism. In forming his concept, Lukács brought themes from Weber, Simmel and Ferdinand Tonnies about the trajectory of modernity into his emerging Marxist theory of revolutionary subjectivity.

Marx himself had made few explicit references to reification. For Marx, commodity fetishism is the form of alienation specific to bourgeois society. Commodities are qualitatively different objects that are exchanged through the medium of the money-commodity as if equivalent to each other. They appear as fantastic 'thing-like objects' possessing autonomous 'magical powers'. Social relations, as Marx put it, assume the form of 'material relations between persons, and social relations between things'.

For Lukács, the concept of reification, rather than that of fetishism, better expresses the structure of a society founded upon universal commodity exchange. Reification is 'only an illusion' but it is also a necessary one. In so far as human functions are transformed into a commodity, self-objectification, atomisation and estrangement are already presupposed by the abstract, quantitative mode of calculability inscribed within the commodity structure. Consciousness thus both reifies and is reified by the commodity structure. By means of his concept of reification Lukács thus undermines the vaunted explanatory position within Western Marxism of 'false consciousness' and ideology.

A. Law

RELIGION, PHILOSOPHY OF In the continental tradition, religion and the question of God have often been an integral part of philosophy. Whether theistic or atheistic, intellectual movements such as phenomenology, hermeneutics, existentialism, structuralism and poststructuralism have all engaged in various ways with questions of ultimacy, transcendence and alterity. Two of the foremost thinkers in this dialogue are Kierkegaard and Heidegger, the former emphasising faith over reason and the latter giving precedence to thought over faith. Both, however, draw from a Paulian tradition, although they interpret it differently. To that extent, a proper understanding of continental philosophy of religion presupposes some familiarity with the ways major thinkers of this tradition reopen and reinterpret old debates (ancient and medieval).

Some of the early thinkers in the history of western philosophy were also saints and Church Fathers (Augustine, Anselm, Aquinas), and some later continental thinkers received early training in seminaries (Kant, Hegel, Nietzsche, Heidegger). Perhaps the conversation between theology and philosophy then goes much farther than one would suspect, so much so that 'philosophy of religion' can arguably be said to be a pleonasm: must not any philosophy worth its salt ultimately deal with questions of transcendence? Such a view was reflected most succinctly in John Scotus Eriugena's maxim, 'True religion is true philosophy and, conversely, true philosophy is true religion'.

However, this loving relationship between philosophy and religion was not always uncontested. Already since medieval times the question as to what extent philosophy can be allowed to contaminate revelation and vice versa was crystallised in the formula *aut fides aut ratio*, either faith (religion) or reason (philosophy). The two were seen as incompatible with each other; their incompatibility was primarily judged on the grounds of reason, on which philosophy was supposed to firmly stand and which religion was supposed to lack. This debate goes as far back as Paul's *Letters*, where 'the wisdom of this world' is branded as 'folly' (I Cor. 3:19). Two thousand years later, Heidegger returned the accusation. Since Christian philosophy has recourse to the Biblical narratives of a creator God, it could never raise the fundamental question of metaphysics – namely, 'why there is something, rather than nothing?' – therefore, it is not a philosophy at all. Heidegger, then, goes on to call this kind of thinking 'a round square and a misunderstanding' (*Introduction to Metaphysics*, 1935).

The opposition, however, between an irrational faith dependent on Revelation and an independent and rational thinking seeking knowledge is not as uncomplicated as it appears. In the long history of philosophy there are many cases that would allow for a quite different story. Let us take, for example, Paul and Heidegger again. Both men have significantly helped in removing reason from its imperial throne: Paul declared in First *Corinthians* the Gospel he was preaching to be 'a stumbling block to the Jews and to the Greeks *foolishness*' and went as far as to characterise himself as a '*fool* for Christ's sake'. Heidegger, on the other hand, in his unceasing critique of grounds (*Grund* in German can mean both 'ground' but also 'reason') had disqualified reason as the sole foundation of philosophical thinking. More tellingly, perhaps, Nietzsche's evangelist of the death of God (a proclamation that can also open the way to a new, non-conceptual understanding of God) was a madman who sought God (*The Gay Science*, 1882). In the end, a genealogy of madness could show that irrationality permeates both camps (that of philosophy and of religion) and is perhaps one of the elements, as Plato argues in his *Phaedrus*, which unites rather than separates them.

With the advent of phenomenology, all normative questions about theistic claims – for example, the debate about the existence of God – are bracketed or suspended for the sake of a different and arguably more meaningful set of questions: Could God be given to consciousness as a phenomenon? What kind of phenomena are religious experiences?

What sort of phenomenological methodology is needed in order to describe them? In recent years, the question of God has assumed such important dimensions that Dominique Janicaud writes of a 'theological turn' in phenomenology.

In its existential trajectory, phenomenology, following Kierkegaard and Levinas, would embrace Pascal's distinction between the God of the Philosophers and the God of Abraham, Isaac and Jacob, giving precedence to the latter over the former. Such a gesture indicates a move away from metaphysics towards a God that surpasses the old categories of omnipresence, omniscience and omnipotence. Contemporary French thought (Jean-Luc Marion, Michel Henry and Jean-Louis Chrétien) has offered us some exemplary cases of such thinking. Marion, in particular, has greatly contributed to the formation of a non-metaphysical thinking of God. First, by following Heidegger's critique of ontotheology by which he freed God from any ontological burden (*God Without Being*, 1982); more recently, by recovering the notion of giveness in Husserl (*Being Given*, 1997); and finally, by developing his own insights on the 'saturated phenomenon' (*In Excess*, 2001).

In its hermeneutical trajectory, phenomenology, following Heidegger and Ricoeur, would exercise both a hermeneutics of suspicion and a hermeneutics of affirmation. Under the hermeneutical movement one should classify John Caputo (radical hermeneutics) and Richard Kearney (diacritical hermeneutics). Caputo should be credited with the revival of continental philosophy of religion in North America. Besides being the chief exponent of deconstruction's implications for religion (*The Prayers and Tears of Jacques Derrida*, 1997), his thought and a series of conferences at Villanova and now Syracuse universities have been of tremendous significance in explicating Derrida's 'turn to religion', represented by a series of works, most notably 'How to Avoid Speaking' (1987), '*Khora*' (1987), *Circumfession* (1990), *The Gift of Death* (1992) and 'Faith and Reason' (1992). Caputo's *Radical Hermeneutics* (1987) led him to a novel, post-metaphysical understanding of religion 'without religion' (*On Religion*, 2001), signalling with this paradox the undecidable mystery of God – 'an infinite questionability' that is, at the same time, 'endlessly questionable'. Kearney's diacritical hermeneutics, on the other hand, attempt to steer a middle path between Romantic hermeneutics (Schleirmacher) which retrieve and reappropriate God as presence and radical hermeneutics (Derrida, Caputo) which elevates alterity to the status of undecidable sublimity. This debate has already made its mark as one of the most challenging directions of continental thought.

J. Manoussakis

REPETITION A concept central to a variety of works in the continental tradition, though one that has tended to be overlooked by commentators and historians, perhaps in part because of the diversity of its semantic history. Yet all of the thinkers who bring repetition into play, whatever its specific form, do so because this enigmatic category, which braids together identity and difference, is indispensable to their accounts of experience.

Hegel's thought stands at the origin of the history of the concept of repetition, even though the word (or rather its German equivalent, *Wiederholung*) is uncommon in his works and not part of his technical vocabulary. In the *Phenomenology of Spirit*, Hegel describes the dialectical development of experience as driven by 'determinate negation' and 'sublation' (*Aufhebung*), that is the process by which consciousness evaluates its self-understanding in order to correct itself and proceed toward an understanding of the absolute. Across the different shapes of consciousness, in all possible forms of self-deception and illusion, in all the calamities that afflict spirit, reason is revealed in the self-corrective drive towards the unconditioned concept of thought thinking itself as its object. Philosophy, then, or the 'science of the experience of consciousness' demonstrates how identity and non-identity commingle in the production of self-knowledge. In this sense, philosophy is repetition, or as Hegel himself puts it, 'recollection' (*Erinnerung*): the progressive recapitulation of how the 'realm of spirit' produces itself.

In reaction to this understanding of recollection, Kierkegaard challenges Hegel on precisely this issue of dialectical movement in the book entitled *Repetition*: 'modern [that is, Hegelian] philosophy makes no movement; as a rule it makes only a commotion, and if it makes any movement at all, it is always within immanence, whereas repetition [*Gjentagelsen*] is and remains a transcendence'. In later works, particularly the *Concluding Unscientific Postscript to 'Philosophical Fragments'*, he stresses that the dialectic only serves to adumbrate the possibility of Christian faith, which confounds the self-knowing subject. In short, the Hegelian dialectic must be supplemented by a remedial (and ultimately self-annihilating) dialectic whereby the believing Christian 'believes Christianity against the understanding and here uses the understanding – in order to see to it that he believes against the understanding'. Repetition is thus an answer to the despair and disappointments of existence; it is a recovery of the self in a religious key, where the emphasis is on a faith 'by virtue of the absurd' that transcends the bounds of reason, in effect abandoning philosophy for the promise of eternal happiness.

Husserl marks a return to reason in the first half of the twentieth century. For him, the concept of repetition (*Wiederholung*) is central to the process whereby ideal objects (words, intentional content, mathematical theorems) are constituted and perpetuated. But there are different kinds of ideality. For example, while words are ideal objects that remain identical in being repeated, they also remain tied to the contingent contexts (cultural, linguistic, temporal, biological) of which they are inevitably a part. On the other hand, a mathematical theorem can be repeated (reaffirmed) in a total 'coincidence of identity' from one instantiation to the next, irrespective of the person, language, culture and so on, that attend the instantiation. In this way, the truths of science legitimately lay claim to supra-temporal status, not because they are eternally true in some Platonic sense, but because they can be repeatedly confirmed independently of the accidents of history and culture. Moreover, to repeat an ideal object such as a theorem signals the possibility of 'reactivating' the chains of evidence and reasoning that justify and found the entire history of science. For Husserl, repeatability is therefore an index of ideality and one of the chief criteria for rigorous science.

Repetition is also central to Heidegger's unfinished masterwork, *Being and Time*, which relies on the concept in a threefold manner. First, in his existential interpretation of Dasein (human existence), Heidegger makes explicit how we are constituted by repetition (*Wiederholung*): I relate to my possibilities by 'handing them down to myself' or by repeating (retrieving, appropriating) the possibilities implicit in my past in order to realise what I have not yet become. Second, repetition is just as essential to the project of 'destroying' the history of ontology, announced in the introduction to *Being and Time*. By destruction, Heidegger means the dismantling of centuries of misunderstanding and prejudice in the service of a repetition or retrieval of the fundamental questions that solicit thought. Third, these first two forms of repetition were meant to work together in a third form of repetition, that of *Being and Time* itself, which in its completed form would have offered the reader a restatement (again, a repetition, *Wiederholung*) of the question of being, of what it is *to be*.

Nietzsche's doctrine of eternal recurrence (*die ewige Wiederkunft* or *Wiederkehr*) is perhaps the most discussed form of repetition in the history of post-Kantian European thought, though in many ways it is quite alien to the lineage of thinkers just presented. Introduced briefly in *The Gay Science*, eternal recurrence swiftly becomes the 'basic idea' of *Thus Spoke Zarathustra*. For Nietzsche, the lack and impossibility of unchanging or eternally true values is coupled with a view of life defined only as 'that *which must overcome itself again and again*' in the perpetual struggle of the will to power of every being. But eternal recurrence is not merely the waxing and waning of force pitted against force in nature and human affairs; it is also the only possible standard for value creation. Hence the question 'Do you desire this once more and innumerable times more?' (*The Gay Science*) is an imperative that conditions human action: the authority of values must be rooted in the fact that they are an expression of life understood as the will to power constantly renewing itself.

Freud too speaks of repetition, or more specifically of a 'repetition compulsion' (*Wiederholungszwang*). The compulsion to repeat manifests itself most clearly in infantile play and in the neurotic obligation to repeat, instead of remembering, a painful or traumatic experience. In *Beyond the Pleasure Principle*, he describes psychoanalysis as an attempt to 'loosen' the unconscious repressed that is responsible for the compulsion so as to transform the repetition into memory. But the compulsion to repeat also leads Freud to propose an interpretation of drives in terms of an 'urge inherent in organic life to restore an earlier state of things'. In this way, the repetition compulsion points towards a restorative repetition that characterises all drives, which in turn leads Freud to the hypothesis of a death drive.

Inspired by problems emerging from the history of philosophy and psychoanalysis, Deleuze's *Difference and Repetition* sets out in search of a 'superior "positive" principle' of repetition in order to account for how conceptual identity can be disrupted or 'blocked' by various forms of 'difference without a concept'. In this sense, repetition in the first instance is the counterpart to generality. However, this form of repetition is explicable only by way of a more vital form of repetition, one that brings difference into play dynamically instead of regarding it as epiphenomenal to identity. Ultimately, this leads Deleuze to what he calls an '*ungrounding* repetition' (*une répétition d*'effondement) or an '*ontological* repetition', which he finds at work in Nietzsche's doctrine of eternal recurrence, interpreted as the return of that which differs and forever marks identity. In this manner, Deleuze undertakes a critique of traditional models of conceptuality and representation.

Derrida too inherits much from the tradition in his treatment of repetition, and deploys a number of concepts to adumbrate what he understands by it: iterability, supplementarity, *différance* and many others. In effect, he proposes a model of experience that controverts the claim that meaning and knowledge are founded on any discrete or positive presence or principle (some original, evident givenness, whether of some entity, an original meaning, a value or a metaphysical category). Thus in *Margins of Philosophy*, Derrida argues instead for the claim that 'there is no experience of *pure* presence, but only chains of differential marks'. On the one hand, the repeatability of language (its 'iterability', *itérabilité*) allows and moreover requires that words and meanings be infinitely transferable into new contexts ('chains of differential marks'). But on the other hand, this very iterability frustrates the expectation that meaning should somehow be guaranteed or underpinned in an absolute sense, for example by an ultimate self-evidence or authority of one kind or another. However, contrary to how Derrida is sometimes read, this does not mean that we cannot say what we mean and mean what we say. It is rather a call to understand experience as an economy in which difference, not identity, is determining.

I. Macdonald

See also: simulacrum

REPRESSIVE DESUBLIMATION A term introduced by Marcuse to explain how the freedom much touted by apologists of modern capitalism is in fact illusory and even repressive. The concept descends from Freud's notion of sublimation. According to Freud, individuals' desires to immediately gratify their sexual drives must be inhibited if they are to survive together. Rather than totally suppress these desires, which would be equally detrimental to their survival, society finds secondary outlets for their expression (so called 'substitute gratifications'). In other words, sexual drives are diverted away from explicit procreative activity (their primary object) and rechannelled toward familial love and group solidarity, productive labour and cultural and artistic creativity. Such sublimation, Marcuse argued, need not be as repressive as Freud himself thought and can actually serve to liberate the individual from the narrow demands of the body and prepare the way for fuller physical and spiritual self-realisation. By contrast, desublimation – or the uninhibited expression of desire – can be truly repressive. For example, Marcuse noted that the sexual liberation of the 1960s and 1970s not only caused people to define their sexuality narrowly – in terms of genital sex rather than sensuality, sensitivity and love – but also led them to view it as a kind of social imperative and even physical obsession. The preoccupation with looking and being sexy was repressive in a further sense, in that sexiness itself became identified with hedonistic consumption, which in turn could only be satisfied by working longer hours. Significantly, Marcuse later observed that other highly touted freedoms – such as free speech – could also be repressive, as when so-called 'open' debates regarding public policies exclude minority points of view or require their expression in ways favouring the dominant point of view.

D. Ingram

RESPONSIBILITY For Derrida, an aporia that defines the relation to the other and so is the necessary opening to ethical behaviour. It is discussed especially in *The Gift of Death* through an analysis of the Czech philosopher Patočka and a reading of Kierkegaard's text on Abraham's sacrifice of Isaac. Reference is also made to Heidegger and to Levinas.

For ethics to be of any consequence, to prevent it from being the sententious mouthing of platitudes with which history is replete, for it to respond to the overwhelming urgencies of the current situation of humanity, not to mention other animals, Derrida insists that it respond to and wrestle with the impossible fact, or infinitely singular tautology, that every other is every (bit), or wholly other (*tout autre est tout autre*). Responsibility thus implies a response, both an answering for (oneself) and an answering to (the other). From its very origin responsibility is therefore divided within and against itself. This becomes all the more explicit via the fact that in responding to one other, one is always, to some irreducible extent, neglecting all the other others. For example, in choosing to respond to God's call, to answer to some ultimate responsibility, Abraham had to deceive and turn his back on his family and prepare to sacrifice his son; to be both responsible and irresponsible. Derrida therefore also relates responsibility, in another type of self-division or seeming self-contradiction, to forms of secrecy, mystery, heresy or dissidence.

D. Wills

RESSENTIMENT The term Nietzsche uses to describe the signature affect of the 'slave' type, a 'feeling-again', an inability to forget perceived slights emanating from a hostile 'other'. (Rather than attempt to translate the term into German, he retains the original French word.) *Ressentiment* thus names the propensity of the 'slave' type to repudiate everything that it is not, as a means of generating affect and distracting itself from its lack of an integrated identity. In practical terms, *ressentiment* is directed not at what the 'slave' type covets for itself and schemes to possess, but at what it wishes for the other *not* to have and enjoy. *Ressentiment* is thus presented by Nietzsche as a destructive, corrosive affect, which enlivens the 'slave' only through the deprivation of others and the general levelling of cultural forms.

Whereas the 'noble' type immediately affirms itself and naturally extends this affirmation to everything and everyone related to it, the 'slave' type inverts this process and begins with a repudiation of everything outside itself. The 'slave' type can deem itself 'good' only derivatively, and only on the strength of its putative difference from everything outside it. Because the 'slave' type has no coherent self to affirm, moreover, it is utterly reliant on its enabling fantasy of a hostile external world. Without such a fantasy, the 'slave' would be obliged to confront its ongoing failure to constitute itself as a being worthy of direct, unmediated affirmation.

In order to secure the permanence of the hostility it locates in the external world, and thereby ensure the intensity of its enabling *ressentiment*, the 'slave' type executes what Nietzsche calls the 'slave revolt in morality'. The creative genius behind the 'slave revolt in morality' lies in the insistence of the 'slaves' that they *prefer* the conditions of oppression imposed upon them by the 'nobles'. Their 'goodness' is established, the 'slaves' propose, on the strength of their suffering, which they claim to affirm even though they are powerless to refuse it in any event. By means of its expressions of *ressentiment*, the 'slave' type thus derives power from powerlessness and thereby turns the tables on its 'noble' oppressors. If the 'slave' is to remain empowered, of course, the 'slave revolt in morality' must continue indefinitely. This means that the 'slave' type can never give up its *ressentiment* or work toward the rehabilitation of the supposedly hostile extenal world.

D. Conway

REVALUATION OF ALL VALUES (*Umwertung aller Werte*) Nietzsche's term for his signal, supposedly epochal contribution to Western morality. For several millennia, he maintains, the dominant religious and moral traditions of Western civilisation have succeeded in promulgating ascetic, anti-affective values, which have placed human beings at odds with themselves and estranged them from their natural environment. As an expression of these values, Western civilisation has promoted ideals of human flourishing that trade extensively on the 'goodness' associated with suffering, guilt, self-deprivation and self-contempt.

While indirectly productive of the art, politics and culture that define the glory of Western civilisation, the reign of these ideals has exacted from humankind a nearly mortal toll. Centuries of self-inflicted aggression have so thoroughly wearied the species that Nietzsche now fears for its future. He describes the historical situation of late modernity in terms of the advent of the 'will-to-nothingness', which he identifies as the (nihilistic) will never to will again. He consequently proposes to initiate a 'revaluation of all values' as a means of preventing or at least postponing the advent of the will-to-nothingness.

As envisioned by Nietzsche, the revaluation of all values would accomplish, first of all, a critical exposé of the ascetic, anti-affective values that have sustained the metaphysical systems of Western religion and philosophy. The 'highest' values of our civilisation would be exposed as life-denying and, so, conducive to nihilism. Second, a revaluation of all values would reassign the highest value to what is most real: the body and its affects, the earth and the cosmos understood as will-to-power. Accordingly, the lowest value would be assigned to those (nihilistic) values that heretofore were deemed highest. Third, Nietzsche also means for the revaluation of values to transform the very source and provenance of our values and systems of evaluation. Humankind will no longer orient its future toward values that reflect (and perpetuate) conditions of lack, deprivation or defect, but instead will enshrine values that express conditions of surfeit, overfulness, and wealth. The precise target of Nietzsche's envisioned revaluation of values is Christian morality, which has succeeded in denaturing human beings and setting them at odds against themselves. For his own part, he is hopeful that he can steer contemporary Christian morality into a direct confrontation with the hypocrisy and prejudice on which it rests. Doing so, he believes, will contribute to the self-overcoming of Christian morality and the inauguration of the post-moral epoch of human history.

Revaluation of All Values is also the title Nietzsche proposed for his ill-fated *Hauptwerk*, of which he completed only the Preface and 'First Book' (which we know as *The Antichrist*, 1888). He concludes this book by pronouncing on Christianity a summary 'curse', which he apparently hoped would play a decisive role in precipitating the destruction of Christian morality.

D. Conway

RHIZOME In botanical terminology, a tuber or bulb that reproduces by sending out shoots that consolidate into a new plant. The term is adapted by Deleuze and Guattari in *A Thousand Plateaus* to denote a network where any node can immediately connect with any other node, in contrast with tree-like organisational models. In the latter there is a central trunk with branches, each of which may also have branches, terminating in leaves: connectivity is thus limited by the structure of the tree, so that, for instance, leaf nodes are connected with each other only through a branch operating at a higher level. Examples that

Deleuze and Guattari use are those of the genealogical tree of evolution and the standard breakdown of a sentence into its constituents in linguistics. The evolutionary tree becomes rhizomatic when genetic code is directly transplanted from one species (leaf node) to another without mediation by a connecting branch as in viruses and in what Lynn Margulis calls 'symbiogenesis'. Genetic engineering techniques can also now forge new transversal connections that convert the tree into a network, but an important property of a rhizome is that it doesn't need this sort of intervention from an outside source.

In the case of linguistics, Deleuze and Guattari argue that language becomes a rhizome when words are made to connect with extra-linguistic, and especially socio-political phenomena; in other words, when linguistics becomes pragmatics. This illustrates a second important property of a rhizome: it changes nature when it expands the number of its connections, as when we move from language to politics. Indeed at a philosophical level a rhizome is nothing except its connections, which construct what they connect.

A. Welchman

RICOEUR, PAUL (1913–) The French philosopher most closely associated with philosophical hermeneutics. After publishing commentaries on Husserl, Marcel and Jaspers (prepared while a prisoner of war), Ricoeur rose to prominence in France with a series of studies on the human will: *The Voluntary and the Involuntary* (1950), and the two-volume *Finitude and Culpability* (1960). The image of the subject that emerges from these works – as embodied, historically situated and fallible – remains in the background of all Ricoeur's writings. Another enduring theme that makes its first appearance here is the need for interpretation in thinking about human existence. Analysis of the will raises the issue of the meaning of evil, but this meaning is not something that can be accessed directly by self-reflection. Rather it is mediated by symbols which, because they simultaneously reveal and conceal meaning, are subject to multiple and conflicting interpretations. The semantic 'surplus' of symbols, and the conflict of interpretations they engender, was investigated further in Ricoeur's next major work, *Freud and Philosophy* (1965). Ricoeur's study of Freud reinforced his conviction that the self-understanding promised by previous philosophy (especially phenomenology) could only be delivered by way of a 'hermeneutic detour', that is through the systematic interpretation of signs, symbols and texts.

Ricoeur's project thus led him to engage with the Structuralist theories of meaning then dominant in France, as well as Anglo-American philosophy of language. While attentive to the insights provided by these approaches, Ricoeur was dissatisfied with their treatment of the key question of semantic innovation, that is the processes by which meaning is created. Ricoeur's alternative account, based on the role of imagination in the operations of metaphor and narrative, is laid out in *The Rule of Metaphor* (1975) and the three-volume *Time and Narrative* (1983–5). Ricoeur's approach is distinctive partly on account of the emphasis it places on the 'referential' dimension of the creative work, which he interprets in terms of the disclosure of inhabitable worlds. In this way imagination is linked to the potential for action. However, it is just as important, in Ricoeur's view, that this potential be informed by a critical consciousness. In a number of works – for instance *From Text to Action* (1986) – Ricoeur has sought to formulate the need for, basis of and limits to a critique of ideology. For this reason Ricoeur's project is felicitously described as a 'critical hermeneutics'.

In the two decades that followed his work on Freud, Ricoeur's influence had been more marked in the English-speaking world than in his native France, but this changed with the publication of *Oneself as Another* (1990). This book returned to the themes of existential finitude and otherness that Ricoeur had explored, albeit in a different fashion, in his early work. *The Just* (1995) collects writings in moral and political philosophy (which Ricoeur endearingly calls his 'little ethics') and *Thinking Biblically* (1998) contains exercises in biblical exegesis. Ricoeur has provided lucid and informative accounts of his intellectual development in a number of essays and extended interviews, of which *Critique and Conviction* (1998) is exemplary.

N. Smith

See also: Hermeneutics

ROMANTIC IRONY A literary device used by writers of the German Romantic movement and by Friedrich Schlegel in particular. While retaining the basic meaning of a self-conscious, self-reflexive, linguistic self-undermining, irony took on broader philosophical significance for the Romantics. This is in part because Romanticism developed in tandem with German Idealism, and so the notions of reflectivity and self-consciousness were heavily philosophically charged. Kant had demonstrated that the subject of consciousness could not be aware of itself qua unified, temporally extended subject. Knowledge of a unified self could only be gleaned from the unity of experience. Romantic irony can be seen as a literary extension of this idea, the text reflecting on itself to demonstrate the absence of an organising principle located in some god-like author-subject.

Moreover, the self-undermining character of irony, the fact that it simultaneously asserts and withdraws assent, was considered emblematic of literature in general, which asserts truths in the form of fiction. As such, irony represents a moment of theoretical self-reflection on the part of the text, which calls attention to its own problematic status. The Romantics used irony not just to emphasise the artificial character of literature, but of language as well. Moreover, their writings suggest a significance beyond these limited realms, that irony calls attention to the constructed, non-ultimate status of the world around us. The romantic notion of irony remained influential after the demise of the German Romantic movement, influencing authors such as Paul DeMan.

J. Norman

RORTY, RICHARD MCKAY (1931–) American philosopher, leading figure in the revival of pragmatism, and one of the most important of those trained in the analytic tradition who nonetheless self-consciously incorporate continental thinkers into their work. More than anyone Rorty has been responsible for reanimating the term 'pragmatism' following its relegation in the 1940s to being merely a subject in the history of philosophy. Rorty claims to have advanced beyond the old pragmatism by incorporating into it insights generated by analytic philosophy of language. The results of doing so may be summarised under headings drawn from the title of Rorty's 1989 book, *Contingency, Irony and Solidarity*.

Contingency, which earlier pragmatists held to be a real feature of the physical world, is a reason not only for Rorty to deny that there is a privileged way to represent the world but for him to urge that we abandon altogether the idea that language functions as representation. Instead he urges us to use, as far as it will work, the Wittgensteinian analogy between tools and vocabularies. Not only language but our selves and our communities are products of contingent circumstances. Where earlier pragmatists might have joined Rorty in denying antecedent existence to self, community and the best way to cope with the world, none would have been comfortable with the suggestion that we can do no more than express individual preferences (which are conditioned of course by the contingencies of our historical context) in response to diverse realisations of character, forms of society or ways of understanding.

Earlier pragmatists were fallibilists, denying that they or anyone else were in a position to claim certainty, but feeling nevertheless entitled to confidence in beliefs and tastes formed in the crucible of argument and criticism. Rorty favours the stance of 'ironists', who, aware of diverse alternatives, are beset with radical and continuing doubts about the vocabularies they use, and have confidence neither that argument can confirm or remove those doubts nor that their linguistic practices are in closer touch with reality than competing vocabularies. Earlier pragmatists would have agreed that moral progress lies in the direction of greater human solidarity (a more inclusive sense of 'we') but not have embraced the relative validity of this commitment.

Rorty's 'ideally liberal polity' is one whose culture's heroes are not warriors, saints or scientists but 'strong poets', that is people who use words as they have never been used before and persuade especially the young to adopt this pattern of linguistic behaviour and to find appropriate compatible new forms of non-linguistic behaviour. It is their efforts in this respect that qualify Dewey, Wittgenstein and Heidegger as Rorty's consistent choice for the greats of twentieth-century philosophy. If, Rorty suggests, we followed the lead of any one of them, philosophy would become something hardly recognisable – certainly less argumentative, less obsessed with validation, legitimisation and justification, and located within very different institutional boundaries.

J. Tiles

See also: Pragmatism

ROSENZWEIG, FRANZ (1886–1929) German philosopher and religious thinker in the Judaic tradition, and a member of the first generation of twentieth-century thinkers who came to reject the legacy of German Idealism and abstract thought. In the case of Rosenzweig, revelation provided the key upon which to do so. By revelation, he took his cue from the biblical Song of Songs ('Love is stronger than death') to intend the empty form of divine–human eros. On the one hand, his thought embodies what he was to call a form of 'New Thinking', a type of thinking that eschews the contemplation of timeless essences divorced from the rhythms of speech in relation to silence and from everyday life in relation to death. Eternity is planted into cyclical patterns of time (biological procreation and the cultic calendars of Judaism and Christianity). On the other hand, the human discourse of love mirrors an eternity that stands outside the course of time as normally perceived, that is, outside linear time. For Rosenzweig, the human subject is typified neither by the atemporal reason of Kant nor by the historical Spirit thematised by Hegel. The human person is a soul whose temporal horizon is ripped open by the uncanny event of revelation, the alterity of God's active and redeeming presence by which the world is quickened.

At once physical and metaphysical, the amalgamation of visible and invisible elements contributes to the structure of Rosenzweig's greatest work, *The Star of Redemption* (1921), in which truth is multi-form. At first, the 'elements' of God, world and [man] constitute autonomous components, each irreducible to the other, each unable to exhaust reality. Terrified by death, the human subject inhabits a broken proto-cosmos of self-enclosed fragments symbolised by Mt Olympus, the Greek polis, classical sculpture, and tragic theatre. The 'course' through which the silent elements open out to each other is made real by the acoustic media of creation, revelation and redemption. Parallel to epic, lyric and dramatic speech, their language intensifies spiritual life by rendering it into the invisible shape of poetry. The forms of Jewish and Christian cults form constellations in a meta-cosmos, in which all six points – God, world, 'man', creation, revelation and redemption – assemble into an integrated star-shaped *Gestalt*. The visible manifestation of God's face – the imperative to love HIM, a palpable image of absolute truth – confronts the soul at the ecstatic anticipation of death's border and ushers it back into life.

For all the efforts made to break from the legacy of Hegel, Rosenzweig's masterpiece remains a structurally closed-in system that but reinscribes a more complex version of totality. Essayistic in character, his later work makes a more profound break from the philosophical tradition. After translating the medieval poet Judah Halevy alongside an extensive, running commentary and an important essay on translation-theory, Rosenzweig worked with Martin Buber on a new and idiosyncratic German-language translation of the Hebrew Bible. The translation pays scrupulous attention to the rhythm and word choice of the original Hebrew; it thereby uses the language of revelation to stretch German, the intended target language, and with it modern culture. Essays by the two authors about the translation were collected under separate cover, recently translated into English as *Scripture and Translation*. In addition, Rosenzweig wrote important essays on Jewish law and education. Thematically, they are all of one piece. Language plays a premium role, highlighting the interdependence between philosophical content and literary and ritual form.

Z. Braiterman

See also: Jewish Philosophy

RUSSIAN EXISTENTIALISM A nineteenth- and twentieth-century movement, flavoured by Eastern Orthodoxy's 1,700-year-old tradition of Platonism, and by a cultural tradition in which distinctions between lay thinkers and professional theologians and philosophers has long been blurred.

The first figure that should be mentioned is Ivan Vasilyevich Kireevsky (1806–56), the son of an Anglophile aristocrat. He met Hegel and Schelling and published a Western-looking journal *The European* in 1831–2 (repressed by imperial order). His philosophical orientation changed shortly after his marriage in 1834 to Natalia Petrovna Arbeneva, a pious young woman who convinced him that everything worthwhile in Schelling was contained in the writings of the Greek Fathers of the Church. Kireevsky studied the Fathers, and in 'On the Necessity and Possibility of New Principles in Philosophy' (1856) used them as the source of the 'new principles' that he hoped would displace the Hegelian-Schellingian system, which he construed as holding that reason is the highest instrument of cognition. He instead called for an organic, holistic way of philosophising, one that seeks truth beyond reason configured as the logical connections between abstract objects, and thus one that focuses on feeling and aesthetic experience as signposts on the path toward truth.

Fyodor Mikhailovich Dostoyevsky (1821–81) wrote no philosophical treatises, but in the popular mind is considered a founder of Russian Existentialism. A novelist, his work offers the kind of aphoristic, unsystematic wisdom that would become synonymous with existential philosophies everywhere. Moreover, Dostoyevsky was the de facto inventor of the multi-voiced, or 'polyphonic', novel. In his fictional world, no single vision – not even that of the narrator – holds authority over any other. This polyphony reflects three important aspects of Dostoevsky's existential world-view: that human reason looks in vain for God's finger directing the universe He has created, that the choice between living as a god-man or a slave-man is not determined, and that in the final analysis it is better to love life than to understand the meaning of life.

Existentialist strains in Russian thought continued to develop during the 'Silver Age' in Russia (from 1893 to the eve of the First World War), and in Czechoslovakia, France and the United States after the Bolshevik Revolution. The new generation included professional religious philosophers such as Sergei Bulgakov (1871–1944), Nikolai Aleksandrovich Berdyaev (1874–1948), Nikolai Onufrievich Lossky (1903–58) and Sergei Aleksandrovich Levitzky (1908–83). Some common tendencies are apparent in their thought. In ontology, they hold that humans are born with a divine spark burning dimly within, a spark that may flourish in an atmosphere of freedom and creative action, or which might just as easily be lost under a tide of material goods and bourgeois values (Berdyaev). Lossky's epistemology reaches back through Kireevsky to the Fathers; he stresses 'intuitivism', the notion that the epistemological relation between knower and the known is not solely causal, that the object exists immanently in the knower's consciousness via 'intuition' or 'contemplation'. The Russian existentialists are strongest in ethics, where they explore the problems of freedom and creativity as a means of achieving 'godmanhood' (Berdyaev), examine the events of the twentieth century against a notion of the transcendental development of evil (Levitzky), and establish the theoretical basis for the programme of social justice, industrial and agricultural economics and Christian ethics that would emerge in the late twentieth century in Poland as the Solidarity movement.

L. Stanton

RUSSIAN PHILOSOPHY Since the fifteenth century, Russian civilisation has been based on the self-understanding that as the 'third Rome' and successor to the Byzantine empire, it represented not only the authentic perpetuation of ancient civilisation, but also the bridging of East and West, as symbolised by the double-headed eagle facing in both directions – an emblem also appropriated from Byzantium. Russian philosophy, like Russian culture as a whole, has with few exceptions assumed the task of identifying binary oppositions and in one way or another uniting them: East and West; idealism and materialism; nature and culture; understanding reality and transforming it; salvation through the Byzantine notion of deification (*theosis*) versus salvation through politics and revolution; noetic intuition contrasted with discursive rationality.

Russian philosophical thought has exhibited this synthetic tendency in its styles and approaches, and Russia's most important thinkers have, more often than not, been just as much writers and critics (Dostoevsky, Tolstoy, Bakhtin), social-political theorists (Kropotkin, Bakunin, Lenin, Kojève) or priests and theologians (Solovyov, Bulgakov, Florensky) as they were philosophers in any narrowly professional sense. Even those such as N. O. Lossky and Berdyaev who had careers primarily as professional philosophers displayed in their philosophical work an ongoing preoccupation with art, politics and religion that would be seen as unusual in Western Europe; Berdyaev himself referred to Dostoevsky as 'Russia's greatest metaphysician'! This impulse toward unity has made German Idealism (and above all, Schelling) especially influential among Russian thinkers, and it can well be argued that rather than terminating with Hegelian thought, the final chapters of German Idealism were written in Cyrillic. Thus, in the nineteenth-century debate – perhaps Russia's first philosophical controversy – between the Slavophiles (such as Kireyevsky and Khomiakov) who emphasised Orthodox Christianity and the Eastern orientation of Russia, and the Westernisers (such as Chaadaev, Belinsky and Hertzen) who felt that Russia needed to appropriate more fully the fruits of the Enlightenment, the difference between the two sides was typically one of emphasis and degree, and both sides took their bearings from their counterparts in Germany, with the former more sympathetic with Schelling and the latter with Feuerbach. Even with the rise of Marxist thought in the twentieth century, and intertwined with the soberly materialistic Prometheanism of Lenin and Plekhanov, the writer Gorky revived and reworked (with the help of Feuerbach and Nietzsche) the coordinate Orthodox thoughts of deified humanity and transfigured cosmos into an exuberantly religious vision of a deified humanity living in harmony within a paradisiacal nature.

The study of Russian philosophy today is beginning to respect its cultural and historical integrity rather than seeing it solely through Western concepts and concerns such as Marxism and Existentialism. For example, the work of Dostoevsky is beginning to be read as forming a structured whole (not unlike Kierkegaard's authorship) that provides an alternative analysis and diagnosis of nihilism to that undertaken in the West by Nietzsche. And the 'Russian Religious Renaissance' or 'Silver Age' of the early twentieth century, proceeding from Soloviev and centred on figures such as Sergei Bulgakov and Pavel Florensky, with its key notions of Divine Humanity and Cosmic Sophia, is becoming recognised as the more authentically classic age of Russian philosophy than the dialectical materialism that historically supplanted and suppressed it.

B. Foltz

SAID, EDWARD (1936–2003) *See* orientalism; Postcolonial Theory

SALLIS, JOHN (1938–) American philosopher and one of the leading proponents of continental philosophy in the United States since the mid-1960s. An important teacher, author and editor (he was the founding editor of *Research in Phenomenology* in 1970), Sallis's earliest work concerned fundamental problems in traditional phenomenology

(Husserl, Merleau-Ponty, Heidegger), especially with regard to the limits of phenomenology. At the same time, Sallis has always exhibited a preoccupation with the thought of Nietzsche, culminating in the 1991 publication of *Crossings: Nietzsche and the Space of Tragedy*. Here, Sallis submits to analysis Nietzsche's *The Birth of Tragedy* and shows the presence of the presumably more sophisticated, later Nietzsche through the theme of the crossing of the Apollonian and Dionysian and then a recrossing by the music-practising Socrates.

With the publication of *Being and Logos: The Way of Platonic Dialogue* in 1975 it became apparent that Sallis's relation to phenomenology was inspired first and foremost by Heidegger's encounter with the history of philosophy. *Being and Logos* is a patient reading of six Platonic dialogues (*Apology*, *Meno*, *Phaedrus*, *Cratylus*, *Republic* and *Sophist*) with special attention to what gets shown and how it gets shown with respect to the limits that are enacted as conditions of showing. This attention problematises the relation between showing – in all its multiple forms, such as the city, wisdom, *logos* – and its conditions. The attention given to the many aspects of the Platonic dialogue (character, drama, myth) in 1975 is performed with even greater mastery twenty-four years later with the publication of *Chorology*, an extended meditation on the figure of χώρα in Plato's *Timaeus*, which is also concerned with limits, in this case the limits and very possibility of philosophy. A further encounter with the thought of Plato will soon be published under the title of *Platonic Legacies*, a text that will also take into account other writers, among them Nietzsche, Heidegger, Arendt and Derrida.

Sallis has also directed his attention to German Idealism and aesthetics, in *The Gathering of Reason* (1980), and *Spacings – of Reason and Imagination in the Texts of Kant, Fichte, Hegel* (1987). What joins these two texts together, aside from their respective concern for German Idealism, is the imagination. It is the imagination that also guides Sallis through his writings on aesthetics, notably *Stone* (1994) and *Shades – of Painting at the Limit* (1998). *The Gathering of Reason* takes as its point of departure Heidegger's discussion of the Kantian imagination in *Kant and the Problem of Metaphysics*, and then further situates the imagination in the other two critiques and the *Anthropology*. The culmination of these two concerns (German Idealism and aesthetics) results in Sallis's most independent, thought-provoking work to date, *Force of Imagination: The Sense of the Elemental* (2000), a systematic examination of the imagination that, at the same time, defies all previous notions of system. Over and again, depending on the issue at hand (sense, image, time, nature, tragedy), Sallis exhibits the role played by imagination in all modes of showing, a role that, in turn, concerns the play of showing in all self-showing.

J. Powell

SARTRE, JEAN-PAUL (1905–80) French philosopher, novelist, playwright and political activist, arguably the best-known continental philosopher of the mid-twentieth century. Sartre was the writer thought best to epitomise existentialism as both a literary and a philosophical movement, and for many years was the editor of an intellectual journal, *Les Temps Modernes*, that was politically identified with a portion of the non-Communist Left. Le Havre, where he taught philosophy in a *lycée* from 1931 to 1936, became the gloomy model for Bouville ('Mudville'), the setting of his first novel, *Nausea* (1938, originally entitled *Melancolia*), which introduced a number of central themes of later existentialism through the experiences of its protagonist, Roquentin. In particular, Roquentin's climactic meditation on a chestnut tree root in a park produces a recognition of the contingency of all that exists and a sense that he, along with everyone and everything else, is superfluous (*de trop*). The effect of this is ultimately liberating.

Meanwhile, Sartre had absorbed some fundamental techniques and ideas of Husserl's phenomenology during a year (1933–4) spent at the French Institute of Berlin. It was the time of the Nazis' rise to power, but Sartre still had very little political consciousness. In the ensuing years, he published *Imagination: A Psychological Critique* (1936) and a sequel, *Psychology of the Imagination* (1940), which review and critique alternative theories and advance a view, somewhat reliant on Husserl, stressing the unreality of images and sharply contrasting imagination with perception. The influence of Descartes' *ego cogito* as subjective starting-point for philosophical reflection is evident here, but at the same time Sartre strongly criticises Descartes' assertion that the ego must be conceived of as a substance with fixed properties. Sartre then brought this critical standpoint to bear on Husserl's own work, *Cartesian Meditations* (first presented as lectures at the Sorbonne in 1929), in an important essay, 'The Transcendence of the Ego' (1937). Here, Sartre deplores Husserl's introduction of a 'transcendental ego' into his philosophy, fearing that it leads to idealism and weakens the realist stance that Sartre considers the great achievement of phenomenology. Sartre insists that the 'self' is always a mutable construct, whether created by myself or by others, rather than an independent entity that defines who I am.

Six years later, having been called to military service, then imprisoned along with much of the rest of the French Army during the so-called 'phony war', and then having returned to Paris under the German Occupation, Sartre published his masterpiece, *Being and Nothingness* (1943). During the same period he had acquired further literary acclaim through his collection of short stories, *The Wall* (1939); published *The Emotions: Outline of a Theory* (1939), which treats emotions as sorts of magical incantations; written lengthy notebooks and much personal correspondence to Simone de Beauvoir (published posthumously) and others; and engaged in extensive reading. Included in the latter category was Heidegger's *Being and Time* (1927), which thenceforth constituted another important influence on his thinking, especially in *Being and Nothingness*, a systematic defence of human freedom as the source of all value and meaning. Using the juxtaposed pair, *pour-soi/en-soi* (for itself/in-itself), as the basic building blocks of his system, Sartre sets out to describe human beings as always in time, projected toward the future, and concretely situated in the world. Some of the most memorable phenomenological descriptions in this long work, including discussions of love, masochism and sadism, occur in the section dealing with the 'third ontological dimension', being-for-others (*l'être-pour-autrui*).

From the standpoint of his later philosophy this treatment of others was, while not false, too purely dyadic in nature, insufficiently attuned to the complexities of human social collectivities. Spurred by political concerns, notably opposition to colonialism and to American as well as Soviet dominance of the world in the Cold War era, Sartre's developing interest in social and political philosophy resulted in the publication first of *Search for a Method* (1957) and later of the massive *Critique of Dialectical Reason*, Volume I (1960), in which *Search for a Method* is included as a prefatory essay. Sartre had come to believe that Marxism was the dominant philosophical world-view of the time, but that in its official or 'orthodox' Communist Party version it had ceased to pay attention to the human individual. The sought-for 'method' would correct this inadequacy as well as the complementary inadequacies of Freudian psychoanalysis and behavioural psychology. In the published portion of the *Critique* proper, subtitled 'Theory of Practical Wholes', Sartre develops terminology that is new though not incompatible with the basic notions of *Being and Nothingness*, depicting the dialectical interplay of free human *praxis* with inert matter under conditions of scarcity (think, for example, of the traditional farmer battling nature to eke out subsistence), which produces passive forms of human social organisation to which Sartre gives the name 'seriality'. Under certain conditions, however, human freedom may reassert itself as revolutionary and active in the form of what Sartre calls, simply, 'the group':

the local residents who, under perceived threat of extermination by Royal troops, captured the Bastille in 1789 are his prime illustration.

Disillusioned by Soviet inflexibility and, as a final straw, by Soviet intervention in Czechoslovakia in 1968, Sartre made common cause with some of the French students in revolt in that same year and became more radicalised. At the same time he worked to complete the three volumes of over 2,000 pages that constitute *The Family Idiot* (1971, 1972), a study of Gustave Flaubert which attempts to answer, by illustration, the initial question of *Search for a Method*, 'What can we know about a man, today?' – for example, Flaubert. This last great work of Sartre's incorporates many of his ideas from his earliest work on imagination onward, and reflects his lifelong effort to bring philosophy and literature together in his novels, in his plays, in his plea for a politically committed literature, *What Is Literature?* (1947), in his *Saint Genet, Actor and Martyr* (1952), and in his self-deprecating autobiography about his earliest years, *Words* (1963).

W. McBride

See also: alienation (2); anxiety (3); bad faith (1); despair; Existentialism; *pour-soi/en-soi*

SATURATED PHENOMENON A notion developed by Marion in *Being Given* (1997) and *In Excess* (2001) on the basis of his phenomenological investigations into the following questions: could we speak of phenomena of 'things' that, strictly speaking, do not appear? Should we accept that the horizon of phenomenology overlaps and coincides with that of phenomenality? Are there certain phenomena excluded from phenomenology on the basis of their failing to produce enough intuition?

Based on the conviction that phenomenology ought to exclude only exclusion – that is, that it should pay attention to all phenomena, even those most difficult to attend to – Marion takes the decisive step of inverting the Husserlian model and thus envisaging a phenomenon saturated with intuition, an intuition that exceeds and overwhelms any intention. Later he gives a more detailed definition, using Kantian terms, of what we should expect a saturated phenomenon to be: 'it will therefore be *invisible* according to quantity, *unbearable* according to quality, *absolute* according to relation, and *incapable* of being looked at according to modality'. From this description one might expect a saturated phenomenon to be a rather rare and radical experience. On the contrary, in *In Excess*, Marion shows that such familiar categories of phenomena as the event, the flesh, the idol and the icon are all satisfying the conditions of the saturated phenomenon. The phenomenon of revelation is exceptional in that it recapitulates at once all four kinds of phenomenological saturation.

J. Manoussakis

SAUSSURE, FERDINAND DE (1857–1913) Swiss founder of modern linguistics, who provided the linguistic model which inspired the European structuralists. Saussure's *Course in General Linguistics* was first published posthumously in 1916 from student notes on his courses (1906–11). Although the words 'structure' and 'structuralism' are not mentioned, the *Course* is the source of much of the terminology of structuralism. It is here that Saussure envisaged the establishment of 'semiology' as 'a science which studies the role of signs as part of social life'. It was left to later scholars to study the social use of signs, however. To Saussure (and to most subsequent structuralists) what mattered most were the underlying structures and rules of the semiotic system as a whole (*langue*) rather than specific performances or practices which were merely instances of its use (*parole*). Furthermore, Saussure prioritised studying such a system synchronically (as it exists as a relatively stable system during a certain period) rather than diachronically (studying its evolution).

Saussure offered a dyadic model of the sign – in contrast to the triadic model of Peirce. Focusing on linguistic signs (in particular spoken words), Saussure defined a sign as composed of a *signifiant* ('signifier' or 'sound pattern') and a *signifié* ('signified' or 'concept'). Subsequent commentators now commonly interpret the signifier as the material (or physical) form of the sign – as something which can be seen, heard, touched, smelled or tasted. Unlike Peirce, Saussure 'brackets the referent': excluding direct reference to a world beyond the sign system. Saussure's conception of meaning was purely structural and relational rather than referential — signs refer primarily to each other. These functional relations are of two kinds: syntagmatic (concerning positioning) and 'associative' (concerning substitution), the latter now called 'paradigmatic' in accordance with the usage of the Russian linguist Roman Jakobson. Saussure distinguished the value of a sign from its signification or referential meaning. Even those words in different languages which have equivalent referential meanings have different values since they belong to different networks of associations.

Saussure stressed the arbitrariness of the link between the linguistic signifier and the signified. There is no inherent, essential, transparent, self-evident or natural connection between the signifier and the signified – between the sound (or shape) of a word and the concept to which it refers. The Saussurean model, with its emphasis on internal structures within a sign system and on the arbitrariness of the sign, can be seen as consonant with the stance that language does not 'reflect' reality but rather constructs it. Taking this together with its asocial and ahistorical focus on *langue* and synchronicity, the Saussurean model has been criticised as idealist.

There are two English translations of Saussure (Baskin, 1959, and Harris, 1983) though the latter substitutes 'signal' and 'signification' for what are still invariably known as the signifier and the signified.

D. Chandler

See also: codes; Semiotics; sign; signifier and signified; Structuralism

SAYING AND THE SAID, THE (*le Dire et le Dit*) A distinction developed primarily in Levinas's *Otherwise Than Being or Beyond Essence* between two features characteristic of language. As 'the Said' (*le Dit*), language consists of a system of signs and meaning is produced (in accordance with Saussure's model) by means of the position of each term in relation to all the others. The Said captures the dimension of language primarily geared toward the communication of a content. Language is not exhausted by this constative function, however, since every Said is said *to someone*. This dimension in which an interlocutor is invoked or addressed prior to being constituted as the theme of discourse is what Levinas calls 'the Saying' (*le Dire*). In keeping with Levinas's broader claim that the ethical relationship represents an inversion of the structures of intentionality, the Saying captures the moment in which the Other is addressed before being the object of a possible representation. Moreover, in the Saying, the ego is exposed to the Other before constituting her as an object for consciousness; this exposure is constitutive of the meaning of ethical subjectivity. All language – whether oral, written or the silent discourse of the self with itself – contains both a Saying and a Said. All language, then, is ethical address. Methodologically, Levinas faces the problem of how to state this non-constative Saying, since any discourse on Saying makes of it precisely something Said. In response to this problem, Levinas speaks of a reduction by which the Said is unsaid and a new Saying produced.

D. Perpich

SCAPEGOAT A term designating the arbitrary target of individual and collective violence in the religious anthropology of René Girard (*The Scapegoat*, 1982). The classic instance is in primitive communities ritualised as sacrifice. Communities fall prey to internal disturbances threatening to destroy them if they lack institutions or have only weak ones, as in early epochs of history. To restore order, or to protect themselves from future disorder, they typically relieve violence or pent-up anger on a marginal victim unable to retaliate. The success of this catharsis confers on it a miraculous quality, as if the victim were superhuman. The mechanism of violence works because it conceals itself, generating a myth. The victim who prior to immolation appeared as the evil cause of a plague (plague being a mythic recollection of an event of social chaos), is now revealed in death to be a protective deity. He must be kept happy by periodic offerings of substitute victims, who, when immolated, reveal the god. Commonly, the scapegoat is identified with the indigent, deformed, insane and so on, and this happens often enough. But in *Job, the Victim of his People* (1985) Girard stresses that scapegoating seises equally upon the exceptional, rich, important or high. In later periods, scapegoating may assume conscious or semi-conscious form, as in modern ideology or anti-Semitism, a desperate attempt to restore the efficacy of sacrificial violence in a context where it has been effectively demythologised. Demonisation and deification are inseparable in mythical thought, as enemies are inflated to super-human proportions.

S. Gardner

SCHELER, MAX (1874–1928) German philosopher and significant contributor to phenomenology and the philosophy of social science. He is known for his value ethics, and as a founder of philosophical anthropology and the sociology of knowledge. Although he was considered a most impressive figure in 1920s Germany, he is not as well-known today. His writings were banned for over a decade by the Nazi party and he died at the height of his powers.

Scheler's mature work is usually divided into two periods. From 1913–22, his writings are influenced by his conversion to Catholicism as a young man, and by his critical engagement with Husserlean idealism. He was also attracted to the life-philosophies of Dilthey and Bergson. In his first major work, *Formalism in Ethics* (1913), Scheler develops an anti-Kantian view of values, according to which values exist objectively in a hierarchy, ranging from the lowest bodily values (pleasure–pain), to the higher life values (noble–ignoble), the spiritual values (beauty, justice, truth and their correlates), on up to the highest religious values (holy–unholy). This ranking of values is not rationally comprehended; rather it is sensed a priori by emotion and feeling. Moral actions, therefore, are not rational acts, but emotional inclinations toward values of higher rank (or lower, as the case may be). The phenomena of 'good' and 'evil' are not fixed objects; they are rather dependent upon values, which are felt characteristics of objects.

Scheler refers to his ethics as 'personalist', because the choice of moral values depends upon a person's emotional structure. A person is neither a rational ego, nor an object or substance; rather, a person is constituted by his or her actions.

Scheler's second period is marked by a move away from ethics and the conventions of Catholicism. Instead, he attempts both metaphysically and epistemologically to reconcile the two essential poles of being: the life-drive, called impulsion (*Drang*), and the uniquely human spirit (*Geist*). In *The Place of Man in Nature* (1928), he develops a philosophical anthropology in which the human is distinguished from other animals as that being which possesses spirit. Because of spirit, humans are open to experiencing the world in a unique way, namely as the object of consciousness. Scheler's philosophical anthropology informs his metaphysics. He maintains that reality itself is the tension between spirit and impulsion; therefore, even God must be infused with both. His effort to maintain the tension between impulsion and spirit, without lapsing into positivism, idealism or anthropocentrism, influenced the thought of Heidegger, Sartre, Merleau-Ponty and others.

Scheler presents his sociology of knowledge in *Society and the Forms of Knowledge* (1924–6) and *Cognition and Work* (1926). In these works, he discusses the three forms of knowledge: knowledge of salvation (religious knowledge), knowledge of essences (philosophical knowledge), and knowledge of control (scientific knowledge). Pragmatism is seen as valid, but only within the realm of scientific knowledge. Different types of societies value and aspire to different forms of knowledge, and thereby issue in subsequent, yet overlapping, eras in history.

L. Jennings

See also: Environmental Philosophy

SCHELLING, F. W. J. (**1775–1854**) German philosopher who collaborated with Hegel and Hölderlin at a young age to produce a highly original response to Kant and Fichte. Schelling emphasised the unconscious origins of the self, thus making possible a version of German Idealism rooted in something other than self-consciousness. In so doing he overcame subjective idealism from within, replacing it with a conception of a transreflexive Absolute which lies at the ground not only of all selves, but of all things. In a later series of works (between 1796 and 1801), he elaborated a philosophy of nature (*Naturphilosophie*) that restored the pantheism of Bruno and Spinoza, according to which nature is self-sufficient, requiring a constituting ground neither in a transcendent deity (as in Christian metaphysics) nor in the knowing subject (as for his contemporaries). Into a highly speculative physics that comprehends the universe as an organic whole caught between the forces of expansion and contraction, Schelling incorporated the empirical knowledge of the day. Against the mechanical (or clockwork) conception of the universe, Schelling's view was dynamic and anticipated contemporary 'complexity theory'. It restored, within a more modern context, the Aristotelian view that nature is 'potency' awakened into form and actuality. Despite important areas of confluence between the philosophy of nature and nineteenth-century natural science (Oersted, Faraday, Darwin), what distinguishes Schelling's speculative philosophy from the modern natural sciences is its reliance on a non-mathematical conception of form.

The philosophy of nature did not resolve the question of knowledge. Schelling set out to do so in the *System of Transcendental Idealism* (1800). He claimed that, because everything in nature becomes explicit in the evolution of human beings, it is possible to reverse directions and look at nature as if it were a human construction. On the basis of this insight, he set forth a theoretical philosophy that closely follows Fichte and Kant. Reality is knowable in so far as it is bound by a causality that, even as it reflects the determinate order of the understanding, excludes the possibility of free action. To know the world theoretically is to know the impossibility of changing it. In a second stage, Schelling takes up the contrasting position of practical philosophy, which culminates in the thesis that what can be known is the political world we actively shape. The third and final stage of the *System* radicalises the position of Kant's *Critique of Judgement*. Because artistic creation is an active shaping of what is simultaneously a necessary and objective endowment of nature, it involves a mode of knowing that, transcending both theoretical and practical reason, alone reaches the truth. Aesthetic intuition is the highest form of reason for it allows us consciously to create forms even as they are unconsciously given to us through inspiration. Philosophy completes itself in art and poetry.

The tension between the objective realm of nature and the subjective realm of human knowledge and activity prepared the way for Schelling's most deeply metaphysical phase, his system of identity, which aimed to disclose behind these two realms the Absolute as it exists 'in itself', that is before and apart from its entry into the subject–object dichotomy. This is the famous 'night in which all cows are black' that Hegel parodied in the Preface to the *Phenomenology of Spirit*. In Schelling's defence, it should be pointed out that his system, still a theory of potency, preserves the full dynamism of the philosophy of nature and of transcendental philosophy. It represents perhaps the final and most impressive blossoming of Neoplatonism, a tradition of thinking that, by way of Proclus and Plotinus, ultimately goes back to Plato and Parmenides, reconciling the deepest impulses of both rationalism and mysticism. Central to the entire project is what Schelling called 'intellectual intuition', an inner 'seeing' that reveals the very essence of the Absolute. What emerges from this phase of Schelling's career is the philosophical understanding of religion – and of the divinity that lies at its centre. Just as Schelling's early philosophy emphasised the inherent rationality and order of nature, the philosophy of identity (completed by 1806) is essentially a philosophy of light and understanding.

But darkness lay on the horizon. The identification of the Absolute with reason only serves to highlight the mysterious nature of the finite. Starting with the *Philosophical Inquiries into the Nature of Human Freedom* (1809), Schelling began to reconstitute his fundamental project in terms of such mystery. Human freedom, conceived as the possibility of choosing evil, has as its condition a dark and unruly side of nature that Schelling had hitherto ignored. It is a darkness, more-over, that we can make sense of only to the degree that it stands at the basis of the Absolute itself. Just as he once treated nature as describing the 'transcendental past' of human consciousness, he now viewed both nature and history as constituting what in God himself is 'past', but which forms the nightmare of our own present. Not only temporality, but pain and evil are internal conditions that God himself had to overcome in order to 'become' God. The language of the Absolute, the self-sufficient foundation of rational metaphysics, thereby gave way to the new and more religious language of God, whose divinity had to be disentangled from the dark inscrutability of his origin. Through spiritual clarification, the primal will slowly freed itself from its blind craving. From 1811 until 1820, Schelling unfolded the epochs within the life of God in what he envisioned as his main work, *The Ages of the World*. The project collapsed, leaving a long series of fragments, none of which were published until after his death. Although he had published a steady stream of works from 1794 to 1809, the following forty-five years were marked by a stark silence that gave testimony to the darkness that engulfed him.

Even so, he continued to write feverishly, careful to preserve his lectures for posterity. He sought in the history of mythology and revelation proof of the emergence of divinity from darkness. This is where he locates hope. Schelling balanced his early rationalism with his later yearning for historical transformation by distinguishing between 'negative philosophy' and 'positive philosophy'. By drawing a contrast between the philosophy of the concept and the philosophy of history and transformation, he anticipates Nietzsche and Heidegger just as fully as he looks back to Plato and Aristotle.

J. Lawrence

See also: Biology, Philosophy of; Environmental Philosophy; German Idealism; intellectual intuition; Nature, Philosophy of; negative philosophy; positive philosophy

SCHILLER, JOHANN CHRISTOPH FRIEDRICH (1759–1805)

German poet, dramatist and philosopher, best known in English-speaking philosophical circles for *On the Aesthetic Education of Man* (1795), which asks whether a cultivation of the beautiful – an aesthetic education – can serve the ideal of freedom that inspired the French Revolution.

Horrified by the excesses of the Terror conducted under the banner of reason, Schiller crafts his own idea of personal and social freedom by focusing upon beauty. In the *Aesthetic Education*, he contends that a cultivation of the beautiful provides the best route to the development of free, moral society. A beautiful work of art functions like a mirror, giving individuals a vision of their own freedom by allowing them to recognise or intuit the free interplay of their own intellectual and sensuous powers. This recognition, in turn, inspires one to seek with others the highest expression of society in the state.

Schiller's discussion of beauty in the *Aesthetic Education* provides an insightful and compelling entry to German Idealism, Romanticism and aesthetics. One of his main concerns is to capture the spirit of Kant's aesthetic, moral and theoretical project by overcoming the divide between sense and reason inherent in the moral law's subjugation of feeling and desire. Following Kant, Schiller maintains that humans are both sentient, physical beings, belonging to the realm of nature, and intellectual beings, belonging to the realm of ideas. Kant has reason define human personality, proposing that it dominate or control the sensuous. Schiller disagrees. He contends that the divergent impulses of sense and reason have equal claims on human personality. Indeed, an individual is not a whole human being unless these opposing forces relate to each other in an intimate and balanced way that preserves the validity, distinctiveness and freedom of each.

Taking up Kant's conception of the coordination of imagination and understanding in the third *Critique*, Schiller advocates the free play and harmony of sense and reason as a means to correct the divisiveness that he finds in the moral subject of the second *Critique*. He contends that the 'play impulse' – a reinterpretation of Kant's imagination – balances or equalises the sensuous and formal impulses, with the resulting equilibrium and tranquility being precisely that beauty of soul that leads to free, moral society.

The *Aesthetic Education* resonates with other ideas, figures and tastes of the time. It evokes Fichte's views of imagination and will, culture and dialectic. Wherever Kant is prominent, Rousseau is also at hand. Goethe makes several appearances in direct and implied references. A love of Greek art and culture, so prevalent in Schiller's day, permeates the letters, especially his discussion of Juno Ludovici. Schiller's idea of aesthetic play opens the door for Schelling, and later Nietzsche. And his view of art and conception of three stages of human development anticipate the philosophy of Hegel, and in a more distant way, the stage theory of Kierkegaard.

M. Robinson

SCHIZOANALYSIS A term coined by Deleuze and Guattari in *Anti-Oedipus* designating the practice associated with their critique of psychoanalysis. Deleuze and Guattari exhibit particular impatience with the insistence of classical psychoanalysis that desire always constrains us to occupy some position laid out by Freud in his rereading of the Oedipus story. Schizoanalysis goes further than this, however, rejecting any pre-Oedipal accounts as still dependent on Oedipus. Ultimately, schizoanalysis refuses to interpret or read desire at all, positioning desire instead in relation to an unconscious that produces rather than represents, that is more like a factory than a theatre.

Schizoanalysis also involves mobilising a politicised unconscious in the service of revolution by distinguishing between conscious and unconscious investments of desire. In doing so Deleuze and Guattari identify two pathological cases. One, typified by the influence of the French Communist Party, combined conscious revolutionary investments of desire with deeply reactionary unconscious ones (building a powerful and repressive state apparatus). The other, exhibited by the work of Proust, does the opposite: Proust's reactionary infatuation with aristocrats is dissolved by a revolutionary desire demolishing state-like unities, a desire all the more powerful for being unconscious.

In *A Thousand Plateaus* schizoanalysis becomes one in a series of near-synonymous terms culminating in 'pragmatics'. It thereby loses its specific relation to capitalism and psychoanalysis is no longer its primary object of critique. As the term suggests, however, Deleuze and Guattari are still thinking in terms of direct action rather than representation.

A. Welchman

SCHLEIERMACHER, FRIEDRICH (1768–1834) German philosopher and theologian who was one of the founders of modern hermeneutics. As a young man, Schleiermacher was part of the Romantic circle of poets and philosophers who lived in Berlin. He published aphorisms in the Schlegel brothers' literary journal *Athenaeum*, and at the urging of his Romantic friends wrote *On Religion: Speeches to Its Cultural Despisers* (1799). This work, which emphasised the significance of pre-conceptual, lived religious experience and the close relation between religion and art, became a key reference point in the major theological debates of the twentieth century. *On Religion* was followed by pieces advancing progressive views on the position of Jews and women, and in 1804 Schleiermacher published the first of many German translations of Plato, which are still used today. In 1809 Schleiermacher became Professor of Theology at Alexander von Humboldt's new University of Berlin, a position he held till his death in 1834. The lecture notes and manuscripts that date from this period contain the theories of interpretation and translation for which Schleiermacher is most famous.

One of Schleiermacher's innovations was to identify the need for a 'general hermeneutics', that is an account of the rules and techniques that must be followed wherever interpretation is required. This would encompass (and reform) the series of 'regional hermeneutics' developed by interpreters of legal, classical and biblical texts. But it would not stop there, Schleiermacher argued, because misunderstanding is spontaneously generated in all language use, which makes the hermeneutical task of avoiding or correcting misunderstanding ever present. In order to avoid misunderstanding, the interpreter of a text should be familiar with the non-linguistic context of the text and possess a grammatical knowledge of the text's language. In addition, however, the interpreter must reach a 'psychological' understanding of the author, since any author has to find a 'style' and to use linguistic rules as he or she sees fit. This introduces an element of indeterminacy into the meaning, which the interpreter is forced to guess at or 'divine'. Another source of indeterminacy is the relation between the parts of the text and the whole. The interpreter has to judge the meaning of particular sentences with a view to how they fit within the text as a whole, but the meaning of the whole is only revealed through an understanding of its parts. For

Schleiermacher, this circular movement between part and whole is an inescapable feature of reaching understanding.

Schleiermacher left an ambiguous legacy for the hermeneutic tradition. In *Truth and Method* – the most influential twentieth-century statement of philosophical hermeneutics – Gadamer embraced certain aspects of Schleiermacher's hermeneutics while repudiating its alleged tendency both to objectify and to 'psychologise' the meaning of a text. In Gadamer's view, Schleiermacher leaves the interpreter with the pointless (and impossible) task of reconstructing the author's original psychic life. Others – most notably Manfred Frank – reject Gadamer's interpretation and credit Schleiermacher the Romantic with deeper insights regarding the irreducible role of the individual in the creation and transmission of meaning.

N. Smith

SCHMITT, CARL (1888–1985) The most important German constitutional lawyer and legal theorist of the twentieth century, whose theories are philosophically relevant for their consideration of the historical and social conditions of law. Schmitt's work is strongly influenced by Catholicism, but it also finds other sources in European philosophy, notably Hobbes, and poetry. Beginning in 1933, Schmitt advanced his career with the support of the National Socialists, but in 1936 he was removed from all positions of power in higher education due to inner-party power struggles. Although intellectually isolated after the war, his importance in jurisprudence, theology and philosophy has steadily grown.

Three prewar works are especially noteworthy. In *Political Theology* (1922) Schmitt proposes that modern political concepts of the state are actually secularised theological concepts. In support of this claim, Schmitt refers to the Catholic theoreticians De Maistre, Bonald and Donoso Cortéz. For Schmitt, the most important concept of this kind is that of the sovereign, the one who decides that an emergency constitutes a state of exception (*Ausnahmezustand*). A genuine 'state of exception' is thus a pre- or extra-legal situation, where the rule of law must itself first be determined, that is be decided. The pre- or extra-legal situation, the state of exception, is itself first called forth through a decision; decision is thus the central action of sovereignty. Because Schmitt's political understanding is concentrated upon decision, he himself characterises it as decisionism.

The Concept of the Political (1927) is Schmitt's most influential text. He begins by noting that the concept of the state presupposes the concept of the political, which remains vague despite all the efforts of a long tradition of political theory. To remedy this lack of clarity, Schmitt introduces an ultimate political distinction, that between friend and foe. This distinction is immediately applied in the text. For Schmitt, the foe of the political, that is the foe of the state, is liberalism, which derives its categories from the spheres of ethics and business. In maintaining a private sphere and in upholding a doctrine of separation of powers, both of which make sovereignty unclear, liberalism knows no submission of the individual to the political, a refusal which thereby destabilises the latter.

In *Constitutional Doctrine* (1928) Schmitt presents the concept of the constitution in a fundamental and systematic manner. At the centre of this system stands the constitution of the civil state of law, that is democracy. According to the classical division of states, democracy is contrasted to monarchy and aristocracy. This work has exercised an important influence upon the understanding of state's rights in postwar Germany.

In Schmitt's postwar work *The Law of the Earth in the International Law of the Jus Publicum Europaeum* (1950) is most noteworthy. Here he investigates international law based upon the fundamental distinction between the seizure and control of land and of sea, in other words a fundamental distinction in regard to place and order. On the basis of this difference, Schmitt describes the demise of the old Eurocentric law of the earth as well as the rise of a new one. The old law rested upon the unity of earth and law, that is of place and order. The understanding of law for the European nations was linked to the type of boundaries found in their geographic location. The new law includes the ocean, which has no boundaries and no unity of space and law, in its understanding of law. For Schmitt the so-called Monroe Doctrine (1823) signifies the demise of the European law and the emergence of a new global power, the United States.

P. Trawny

See also: friend–foe relation; Sovereignty; state of exception

SCHOPENHAUER, ARTHUR (1788–1860) German philosopher who stretched Kant's system to its breaking point by identifying the thing-in-itself with an impersonal, eternally striving but goalless will. Schopenhauer was the first modern European thinker to put desire at the centre of philosophical concern.

In his main work, *The World as Will and Representation* (1818; much expanded second edition 1844), Schopenhauer begins by briskly recapitulating and simplifying Kant's theoretical philosophy. The empirically real world of objects in space and time and bound together in a causal nexus is transcendentally ideal; it is how things-in-them-selves must appear to us as subjects. This is the world considered as representation. But the world cannot be only representation because, as Schopenhauer points out rather dramatically, if it were, we would have no reason to take an interest in it. The fact that we care about the world shows that we are also a part of the world considered as will.

Schopenhauer often uses the phrase 'the freedom of the will', but with a very different meaning from usual: not that individuals can do what they want, but that the will, as the inner essence of things as they are in themselves, is free from the world of objects, from the forms of space, time and causation, from all that he describes as the principle of sufficient reason. It follows that the will is impersonal, non-spatial, atemporal and uncaused. Most importantly it follows that the will cannot have a goal, since that would presuppose a distinction between the subject of willing and the object or state of affairs to be willed. But the distinction between subject and object is the highest condition of the world as representation, and things as they are in themselves cannot be subordinated to the principles of representation.

Schopenhauer's famous pessimism is the logical conclusion of this argument: since willing has no object it can never be satisfied and permanent suffering is the condition of existence. The aesthetic and ethical aspects of Schopenhauer's philosophy are responses to this pessimism. Aesthetic experience aspires to a kind of cognition that is not ultimately subordinate to and guided by the will, but to a 'pure will-less knowing' disengaged momentarily from the tragic fate of desire. Similarly, the ethical section with which the work closes proposes the only possible cure: ceasing to will at all. Although Schopenhauer is consistently atheistic and materialist in outlook, these pages shade off into an account of holiness that converges not with the stern imperatives of German pietism, but rather with what Schopenhauer took to be Buddhist quiet-ism. (Schopenhauer was one of the first European intellectuals to read and think about Asian philosophy; although what he says about it must always be seen as limited by the materials available to him.)

Schopenhauer is often seen as merely a transmission wheel between Kant's transcendental idealism and the work of Nietzsche, whose concept of the will-to-power was decisively shaped by Schopenhauer. This is not wrong, but it does tend to underestimate the originality of Schopenhauer's thought of the will and the extent of his impact on other areas: the novels of Hardy, the music of Wagner, the psychology of Freud and indeed the whole intellectual culture of *fin-de-siècle* Vienna.

A. Welchman

See also: Asian Philosophy; Materialism

SCIENCE WARS A cultural event of the mid-1990s, best seen as the most recent stage of the long-standing debate concerning what C. P. Snow famously defined in 1950s as the 'two cultures' – sciences and the humanities and social sciences. The 'Science Wars' events were triggered by the appearance of the book by the biologist Paul Gross and the mathematician Norman Levitt, *Higher Superstition: The Academic Left and Its Quarrels with Science* (1994) and then theoretical physicist Alan Sokal's hoax article published in the journal *Social Text* (1995). A subsequent book, *Impostures intellectueles* (1997), co-authored by Sokal and another theoretical physicist, Jean Bricmont, first published in France and then in England and the US as *Fashionable Nonsense: Postmodern Intellectuals' Abuse of Science* (1998), and hosts of related publications have expanded these debates both intellectually and politically. The proliferation of commentaries in scholarly or public domains, including the popular press in the United States and Europe, on and around 'Sokal's hoax' and then his and Bricmont's book has been staggering. The confrontation has both surface aspects (sometimes almost comic) and deep philosophical, cultural and political undercurrents. The latter reflect such essential subjects as the nature of scientific truth, or truth in general; the possibility of the interactions between different fields of human endeavour; the ethics and politics of academic discussion, and so forth.

The confrontation initially centred mostly on radical and controversial ideas and conceptual and metaphorical use (and, it was alleged, 'abuse') of mathematical and scientific theories found in the work of certain, primarily French, intellectuals associated with poststructuralism and postmodernism, such as Deleuze, Derrida, Lacan and Irigaray. Eventually certain controversial ideas of such scientific figures as Bohr and Heisenberg became targets as well.

The second focus of the confrontation, more prominent in the final stages of the Science Wars, was on the so-called constructivist studies of science, initiated by the work of such authors as Thomas Kuhn, Paul Feyerabend and Imre Lakatos, and developed along various lines during the last two decades. The constructivist studies of the role of gender in science had special significance and have been a subject of particularly intense Science War debates. Constructivist theories of science fundamentally question traditional ideas concerning scientific truth, rationality, objectivity and so forth, especially if seen as independent of the social and cultural conditions of their emergence. This part of the debate also led to some among the more significant discussions in and in the wake of Science Wars, which engaged more productively with what is indeed problematic in these new areas of the history and philosophy of science. Most of these discussions have been conducted by prominent mathematicians and scientists, on the one hand, and, on the other, leading representatives of the constructivist school, in particular Bruno Latour, in scientific journals such as *Nature* and *Physics Today*, and in *Social Studies of Science*.

The question that one might ask in the wake of the Science Wars is whether even the most radical postmodernist theories are radical enough to deal with what mathematics and science, or to begin with mind and nature, or, conversely, culture (including the 'two cultures'), confront us with.

A. Plotnitsky

SELF-OVERCOMING (*Selbstüberwindung*) Nietzsche's term for the process of immanent self-transformation in which all living beings necessarily participate. According to Nietzsche, living beings 'overcome' themselves by virtue of their native dynamism, which obliges them continuously to evolve novel incarnations. In its unrelenting struggles with external forces and alien entities, an organism is gradually, painfully, transformed into its 'other'. And although these transformations may often appear random, or even whimsical, their goal is in fact always the same: the unrelenting advance toward ever greater amplifications of disposable power. The irrepressible surge of life thus requires the continual obsolescence of formerly vital forms and the concomitant creation of new forms. This process furthermore ensures an appreciable degree of continuity and self-identity. Emerging forms of life always bear the imprint and history of predecessor forms. Thus the caterpillar becomes a butterfly, justice becomes mercy, the inveterate Wagnerian became an opponent of Wagner, and so on.

The process of self-overcoming is guided, Nietzsche believed, by none of the familiar teleological principles in vogue at the time, but by the simple, blind impulse for greater amplifications of power. In response to the Social Darwinists, most notably Spencer and Huxley, who identified self-preservation as the cardinal instinct of life and the primary goal of evolution, he insisted that the evolution of species and organisms aims only at the development of ever greater aggregates of power. To make this case, he often cited examples of self-transformation that placed the organisms in question at mortal risk; such developments, he believed, could hardly be explained by the primacy of an instinct for self-preservation. As an example of the 'squandering' involved in self-overcoming, he most frequently cites those great human beings who pursue superior expressions of power at their own expense.

Nietzsche's account of self-overcoming is not meant to be merely or narrowly descriptive, and he in fact avails himself of a distinctly normative application of this account. While all living beings overcome themselves, in accordance with the 'law of life', some do so at unusually propitious moments in world history. In particular, he notes, some human beings are historically situated such that their efforts to overcome themselves actually converge with, and contribute to, much larger processes of transformation. Most notably, he believed that his own labours of self-overcoming would contribute to the destruction of Christian morality, and he consequently attached a great deal of importance to his own efforts to become the 'other' of morality. He consequently presented himself as a 'destiny', for he believed that his seemingly quixotic attacks on contemporary Christian morality would precipitate a word-historical shift toward a post-moral epoch in the development of human history.

D. Conway

SEMIOTIC, THE A term by which Kristeva refers to the organisation of drives and their affective representations in language or any signifying system. Kristeva's use of the term is influenced by the study of semiotics as the science of signs developed by Charles Sanders Peirce (1839–1914) and by Ferdinand de Saussure in his ground-breaking *Course in General Linguistics* (1922). Peirce maintained that signifying systems could be studied through abstract observation to determine a logical structure that could be formalised. Saussure develops what he calls semiology from the Greek *sēmeîon* or sign. He describes semiology or the science of signs as part of social psychology that will show what constitutes signs and the laws that govern them. Kristeva is also influenced by Roland Barthes' applications of semiotics to various aspects of the human sciences in his 1966 *Elements of Semiology*.

Kristeva differentiates her notion of the semiotic element in language from semiotics as the science of signs. In French, semiotics takes the feminine article, *la sémiotique*; but Kristeva uses the masculine article, *le sémiotique*; to develop her notion of the semiotic element in language. She maintains that all forms of signification – language, art, dance and so on – are made up of two elements: the semiotic and the symbolic. The symbolic is associated with syntax, position and judgement, while the semiotic is associated with rhythm, tones, gestures and colour. While the symbolic gives signification referential meaning, the semiotic gives signification meaning for our lives by discharging drives into language.

K. Oliver

SEMIOTICS 'The study of signs' or 'the theory of signs'. Nowadays the term 'semiotics' is generally the preferred umbrella term for this field (at least in English), although the word 'semiology' is sometimes used, being derived from Saussure's coinage of *sémiologie* (from the Greek *sēmeîon*, a sign) to refer to 'a science which studies the role of signs as part of social life'. Saussure's use of the term *sémiologie* dates from 1894.

On occasion, 'semiology' is reserved for work emerging from the European structuralist tradition – such as that of the early Barthes; the Danish linguist Louis Hjelmslev, founder of the 'Copenhagen school'; Algirdas Greimas, founder of 'the Paris school'; the film theorist Christian Metz; Lévi-Strauss; and Lacan. Similarly, the term 'semiotics' is occasionally used to refer specifically to work which follows Peirce, for whom the field consisted of the 'formal doctrine of signs' (which he saw as closely related to logic). Peirce himself used the term *semiotic* (without an 's') as a noun to describe the field (originally in 1897), deriving it from its use by Locke. Those whose work is in the Peircean tradition include Charles William Morris, I. A. Richards, Charles K. Ogden and Thomas Sebeok. The Peircean and structuralist traditions are bridged by both the Russian linguist Roman Jakobson and the celebrated Italian writer Umberto Eco. A further distinction sometimes based on the Saussurean and Peircean legacies is the use of the term 'semiology' to refer to work concerned primarily with structuralist textual analysis and the term 'semiotics' to refer to more philosophically-oriented work. Beyond the most basic definition, there is considerable variation among leading semioticians as to what semiotics involves and even about core concepts – although the structuralist semioticians use the following key terms: sign, signifier, signified, paradigm, syntagm and code (albeit in varying definitions).

Semiotics has not become widely institutionalised as a formal academic discipline and it has not (yet) achieved the status of the 'science' which Saussure anticipated. It is still a relatively loosely defined critical practice rather than a fully-fledged analytical method or theory, and there is little sense of a unified enterprise building on cumulative research findings. Saussure's linguistic theories constituted a starting point for the development of various structuralist methodologies for analysing texts and social practices. These have been very widely employed in the analysis of many cultural phenomena. In an increasingly visual age, an important contribution of semiotics from Barthes onwards has been a concern with imagistic as well as linguistic signs, particularly in the context of advertising, photography and audio-visual media. However, in accord with Saussurean priorities, the structuralist focus has been on formal systems rather than on processes of use and production. Even Barthes, who argued that texts are codified to encourage a reading which favours the interests of the dominant class, confined his attention to the textual codes without fully engaging with the social context of interpretation. Such textual analysis has been so influential that it is quite common for naive critics of structuralist methods to dismiss the whole enterprise of semiotics, reductively equating the two.

Semiotic theory and practice have nevertheless continued to evolve – although not always in tandem. While Saussure envisaged the study of 'the role of signs as part of social life', it is only since the 1980s that practitioners of 'social semiotics' have sought to recover this focus in the study of 'signifying practices' in specific social contexts. That such research may show little resemblance to structuralist textual analysis does not make it any less semiotic, and it highlights the need to combine established semiotic methods with ethnographic and phenomenological approaches. Elsewhere, particularly in studies of advertising and television, the use of 'content analysis' alongside more familiar tools has broken the former tendency for semioticians to reject quantitative methods.

The assumptions of some post-Saussurean semioticians (such as Barthes and Eco) reflect a social constructionist epistemology according to which our sign systems (language and other media) play a major part in 'the social construction of reality', rather than simply 'reflecting reality'. We see only what are allowed to see by such sign systems which help to naturalise and reinforce particular framings of 'the way things are'. In contrast to Peirce, Saussure 'bracketed the referent' and emphasised the arbitrary relation between the signifier and the signified, and subsequent semoticians in this tradition emphasised mediating codes (even, in some cases, at the perceptual level). The Saussurean model thus offers a theoretical basis for social constructivism. Critics drawn towards realism (including orthodox Marxist historical materialists) tend to attack such stances as a form of idealism (which in the rhetoric of many postmodernist or poststructuralist inflections such as that of Derrida and Baudrillard is sometimes difficult to deny). However, constructivism need not involve any denial of external reality (nor need the Saussurean model itself). Constructivists insist that 'realities' are not limitless and unique to the individual as extreme idealists would argue; rather, they are the product of social definitions and as such far from equal in status. They are contested, and textual representations are thus 'sites of struggle'.

Some semioticians insist that their primary concern is to address the ideological issue of whose world-views prevail in society and how they are maintained and contested. If signs do not merely reflect reality but are involved in its construction then those who control the sign systems control the construction of reality. However, dominant as the constructivist stance is in European semiotics, even an unfashionably realist epistemology is not a disqualification from being a semiotician, since no single epistemology or ontology has succeeded in dominating the field of semiotics. Semiotics is thus itself no less a site of struggle than the domains which it seeks to investigate.

D. Chandler

SENGHOR, LÉOPOLD *See* African Philosophy; African Socialism; *négritude*

SENSE (*Sinn, sens*) Represents a prime example of what Hegel would feel was an exquisitely philosophical word, to the extent that it designates a variety of philosophical meanings which appear, at face value, to be contradictory. Thus, sense can designate the content of our sense experiences, but equally it can designate the meaning of a concept or expression. Thus the notion of sense already seems to bridge the chasm between intuition and understanding which Kant claimed was unbridgeable. In French, *sens* can also designate 'direction'. This complexity was exploited in Derrida's readings of Husserl. Husserl argued that language works by 'clothing' pre-expressive sense with a 'layer' of conceptual meaning, which is in turn the condition of possibility for such sense to be expressed within language. But, in 'Form and Meaning', Derrida highlights an ambiguity in Husserl's text between the notions of *Einbildung* and *Abbildung*, in order to ask whether meaning is a newly created form added to an absolutely formless sense, or whether sense already bears a trace of such form which is subsequently 'copied' by meaning. If the former, it appears impossible to account for how meaning is able to inform sense, but if the latter, it appears as if the distinction between sense and meaning evaporates. In either case, as Derrida suggests, the notion of sense seems to overflow that of meaning. In its very complexity, therefore, sense can be shown to open and determine the field of metaphysics, revealing why it remains the most philosophical of words.

R. Durie

SENSIBILITY (*Sinnlichkeit*) That faculty of human knowledge which, in Kant's critical philosophy, is receptive and yet not passive, as it possesses a formal element shaping the objects it presents. Throughout his work, Kant sought to distinguish his position from two other contemporary accounts of sensibility, Leibniz and Locke. For Leibniz, sensibility consisted in confused conceptual apprehension while for Locke it consisted in the registering of impressions upon a tabula rasa. Kant thus tried to develop an account of sensibility that neither subordinated it to conceptuality nor made it entirely a function of the impression of objects. His main statement is to be found in the 'Transcendental Aesthetic' that opens the *Critique of Pure Reason*. Sensibility and understanding are distinguished from each other as the 'two stems' of human knowledge, thus refusing any attempt to reduce sensibility and concepts to each other. To the understanding is assigned spontaneity and to sensibility receptivity, yet while receptive it is by no means passive. It too possesses a formal element which shapes the objects before it, although this differs from the formality proper to the concept.

In the 'Transcendental Aesthetic' Kant submits sensibility to the distinction of matter and form. The matter or 'appearance which corresponds to sensation' is coordinated by 'certain relations' which are not derived from it. These are the a priori forms of intuition, space and time. Kant insists that these are intuitions, that is, neither crypto-concepts nor mere abstractions from the matter of sensation. Space and time are not conceptual, since this would require objects to be subsumed under them, nor are they abstractions, since they are the conditions for the appearance of objects, not their consequence. For an appearance to enter sensibility it must be enveloped in the orders of space and time, namely the forms of intuition.

The formal element of sensibility is vital for Kant's concept of experience. While sensibility must be distinguished from the concep-tuality of the understanding, it cannot be so radically distinguished that it is excluded from all relations with it. Much of the Transcendental Analytic of the *Critique of Pure Reason* is dedicated to determining the conditions for the alignment of concept and intuition. This admission of the significance of sensibility to experience and knowledge differs considerably from its role in practical philosophy where, as a source of heteronomy, it serves only to distract from the call of duty.

H. Caygill

SERRES, MICHEL (1930–) French philosopher, well known for his work on the history of science, and a member of the Académie Française since 1990. Serres' career followed an unusual trajectory taking him from a naval academy to a chair in the philosophy of science. Among his works available in English are *Conversations on Science,*

Culture and Time (with Bruno Latour), *Genesis*, *The Parasite*, *The Natural Contract* and *Hermes: Literature, Science, Philosophy*.

The last of these is a selection of pieces from his five-volume French series. Hermes was a Greek god with many attributes; he was also the god who reassembled Zeus's body after it had been mutilated by the monster Typhon. And as Hermes Trismegistus he was the source of ancient wisdom whose works were revered by Renaissance natural philosophers and alchemists. In the *Hermes* series Serres attempts to reassemble, to weave back together, the domains of knowledge which the modern academic system has so fragmented. In combating this fragmentation, Serres insists that there can be no division between the sciences of man and nature, for man is a part of nature. Workers in the domains of literature, myth, history and the physical and human sciences thus need to communicate with one another.

The Natural Contract (1995) focuses on the extent to which humans can no longer afford to ignore the fact that they are part of a natural, global environmental system; therefore the human sciences can no longer concern themselves solely with human relations and the social contract but must include the natural world. More recently, Serres' long-standing emphasis on the significance of communication and its modes has led him to focus on the impact of the advent of the computer, the growth of the Internet and the transformation of humans and their social institutions that will follow. Just as the advent of print technology in Europe had a profound effect on religion, politics, education and the conception of knowledge, so too, Serres argues, computer technology – and the Internet in particular – cannot but bring about similarly profound changes on humans and their institutions. Specifically he has stressed the implications for education, the potentials of distance education and the need to reassess the roles of our educational institutions.

Serres' writing is provocative; its rhetorical devices are reminiscent of those of Francis Bacon: stylistically polished, highly literary, circling through themes from philosophy to science to mythology to literature, presenting challenging juxtapositions and images with the intent of starting dialogue, of prompting communication across the chasms created by disciplinary boundaries. This is philosophy as activity, not as system-building, even though methodologically Serres takes some leaves out of the structuralist's book; structural analogies and metaphors are not vehicles used to move us from one domain to another but are deployed as ways of suggesting underlying thematic unities.

M. Tiles

SEX AND SEXUALITY These are relatively recent philosophical issues. While sexual differences have been commented upon and used as metaphors by philosophers for more than two millennia, usually to the detriment of all things feminine, until the twentieth century sexuality rarely entered philosophical discussion. A notable exception is Plato's *Symposium*, where Socrates, following Diotima, suggests that love of a beautiful body is the first step toward philosophical love of the Beautiful itself. Generally, however, sexual intercourse and whatever pleasures, sentiments and niceties that might attend it have been considered animal functions with no bearing on rational inquiry.

In the nineteenth and twentieth centuries Western thinkers began to view sexuality as a region of distinctly human experience not necessarily limited or even related to the propagation of the species. Freud, among others, spoke of erotic pleasure as pervasive throughout the human life cycle from infancy to old age, thus detaching it from reproduction and incorporating it into the very processes that make us selves, language-users and disciplined subjects capable of rational thought. Hence by the mid-twentieth century, sexuality could not simply be renounced as medieval monks allegedly attempted to do; it was a permanent aspect of the social world. Therefore philosophers took it up, but primarily only as a set of problems for moral reasoning. Philosophers produced treatises and articles in applied ethics addressing issues such as marital fidelity, contraception and abortion, and homosexuality.

Feminist philosophers, who began to emerge in the late 1970s, insisted that sexuality be treated as a central issue not only in ethics – where they sought to broaden the questions raised – but also in such areas as philosophy of science and epistemology. Our attitudes and assumptions about sexuality deeply influence our understanding of reason itself, feminists argued. And certainly they influence how we understand human subjectivity, society and government, and even the natural world.

In the 1960s and 1970s a few historians and literary critics, sometimes informed by anthropological study or by feminist critique, began to suggest that sexuality, as a region of human experience, is historically variable; which activities count as sexual behaviour or what cultural symbols or practices carry sexual meanings differ dramatically through time. In other words, while sexual intercourse and similar behaviours might be natural, sexuality was socially constructed.

At an intersection between the disciplines of philosophy and history, Foucault's *The History of Sexuality, Volume One* appeared in French in 1976 and in English in 1978. Foucault argued that sexuality is not simply a socially constructed and thus historically variable set of interpretations of natural phenomena; sexuality is rather an historically singular event, a production of the last two centuries. There was no sexuality in the fourth or twelfth or sixteenth centuries. Western societies were differently organised and subjectivities – note the plural – were differently structured.

According to Foucault, sexuality is a *dispositif*, an apparatus of power that produces and maintains the social orders and types of subjectivity that characterise the industrial West. It is an outgrowth of normalisation and a tool of biopower. It came into existence, coalescing from disparate quarters, as a means of identifying individuals and managing populations at a state, corporate and institutional level. As a function of normalisation, the concept and apparatuses of sexuality enable, for example, classification of children according to developmental norms, and justify intervention in their growth, family dynamics, education and daily conduct when they evince either retardation or precocity of psychological or physiological development defined as sexual.

Foucault traces many of the mechanisms of surveillance and control over children and families to the eighteenth- and nineteenth-century wars on masturbation, in which officials persuaded parents and educators that children's lives were at stake if they were not constantly monitored and their genital pleasures carefully regulated. This attempt to stop masturbation was hardly more than a ruse of power, Foucault asserts, despite the sincerity of many physicians and other specialists; masturbation probably increased rather than decreased as discussion stimulated interest in it. However, the fear instilled in generations of parents enabled various professionals to establish themselves as authorities who could 'save' children's futures and safeguard the human resources of nations. The *dispositif* of sexuality also enabled authorities to identify sexual perverts (a category of subjectivity that did not exist before the advent of normalisation) and take steps to eliminate them from 'vulnerable' populations. As a function of biopower, Foucault claims, sexuality arose as authorities investigated reproductive practices – including contraception as well as 'sterile' pleasures – in the populations under their control so that they could regulate birth rates, manage disease, and attempt to control the 'quality' of each new generation of citizens and labourers. Officials persuaded parents of the importance of their responsibilities and convinced them of their need for authoritative advice and support. Effects of these efforts are especially notable for women; Foucault points out that women's bodies were 'hystericised': held to harbour a perpetual threat of sexual illness and so in need of constant self-monitoring and professional care.

All these strategies served to engender an enormous set of inter-locking mechanisms for maintaining surveillance over individuals and groups and for justifying all sorts of intrusions and interventions into what had before been seen as private familial life. These in turn produced new kinds of subjective experience, even new kinds of subjectivities. Eventually subjects in Western societies became thor-oughly sexualised beings dependent for a sense of self on sexual knowledges and power structures, Foucault says, thus offering a more political account of sexuality than even early feminists had (although in many respects his work is consonant with feminist critiques). Further-more, Foucault maintains, sex 'itself' is a product of sexuality, emer-ging as a concept within discourses that give account of the operations of sexuality.

As a result of all these developments, sex and sexuality are now philosophical issues, and not just in applied ethics but also in philo-sophy of science, political theory and epistemology. The ontological status of sex and sexuality are in question, as are their political effects and their influence on conceptions of truth, rationality and meaning.

L. McWhorter

SIGN Within contemporary semiotics, a meaningful unit which is interpreted by sign-users as 'standing for' something other than itself. Signs may take various physical forms such as spoken or written words, images, sounds, acts or objects. The physical form is sometimes known as the 'sign vehicle', although by most semioticians in the Saussurean and post-Saussurean tradition it is known as the 'signifier' – a more materialist usage than that of Saussure. The sign should not be equated with its physical form (a common casual usage); rather, sign vehicles become transformed into signs only when sign-users invest them with meaning with reference to a recognised code.

Saussure's model of the sign is dyadic – involving a combination of a signifier and a signified – whereas the main rival model, that of the Peirce, is triadic, explicitly featuring a referent, unlike Saussure's model. Sign systems with more than one level of structural 'articula-tion' (such as verbal language) include smaller units than the sign – minimal functional units which lack meaning in themselves, such as phonemes in speech or graphemes in writing. Such units are not signs in themselves. Analogical signs, such as oil paintings in an art gallery or gestures in face-to-face interaction, involve graded relationships on a continuum rather than discrete units, as is the case with digital signs.

D. Chandler

SIGNATURE For Derrida, an exceptional event of writing that proves the rule of signification in general, namely that any utterance is both singular and so tied to a specific context, and yet limitlessly repeatable in other contexts. For a signature is presumed to belong to its producer more than any other utterance, to be idiosyncratic, the singular and non-reproducible mark of authenticity. Yet a single signing would be neither recognisable nor acceptable as a signature; it would be some other event of language but without the institutional status of a signature. The signature functions only by being repeated, and thus opened to the irreducible possibility of being copied by whomsoever. The signature calls for counter*signing* – Derrida gives the example of the traveller's cheque – and at the same time invites counter*feiting*.

The signature is also a heterogeneous element (writing) within the space of the pictorial arts. It is, for example, of the same stuff or medium as the brushstrokes that produce a painting, and so belongs to the pictorial surface, but is treated as though it doesn't belong. In this way it works as a frame within the frame, the more or less illegible scrawl that forms an authenticating frame coming necessarily to be observed and read as part of the painting itself. In an analogous manner, in literary works the signature becomes a figure for the way in which the author, from the 'outside', puts himself 'into' what he writes, with the result that the proper name is disseminated as common noun in the work. Derrida has undertaken logical and systematic analyses of literary works as rewritings of the author's name within the text, as in *Signsponge*.

D. Wills

SIGNIFIER AND SIGNIFIED (*signifiant* and *signifié*) Terms that constitute the necessary and inseparable elements of a sign, according to Saussure. The 'signifier' is the 'sound pattern' and the 'signified' is the concept. Saussure emphasised the arbitrary, that is not intrinsic or 'natural', relationship between the (linguistic) signifier and signified. Working independently from Saussure, and going beyond purely verbal signs, Peirce stressed that such arbitrariness varied: from the radical arbitrariness of symbolicity, via perceived similarity in iconicity, we reach the direct causal connection of indexicality. Peirce's distinctions in this matter have been adopted by many semioticians whose framework is otherwise based largely on the Saussurean model.

Ostensibly, Saussure's account presented the signifier and the signified as wholly interdependent, neither pre-existing the other. Subsequent theorists applying Saussure's dyadic model have accorded ontological priority either to the signified or to the signifier. Realist epistemologies and 'common sense' tend to insist that the signified takes precedence over, and pre-exists, the signified: 'look after the sense', quipped Lewis Carroll, 'and the sounds will take care of themselves'. Derrida argued that dominant ideological discourse relies on the metaphysical illusion of a transcendent(al) signified, an ultimate referent at the heart of a signifying system which is portrayed as 'absolute and irreducible', stable, timeless and transparent – as if it were independent of and prior to that system. All other signifieds within that signifying system are subordinate to it. He noted that it is nevetheless subject to historical change, so that Neoplatonism focused on the One, Christianity on God, Romanticism on consciousness and so on. Without such a foundational term to provide closure for meaning, every signified functions as a signifier in an endless play of signification.

In more idealist epistemologies ontological priority is accorded to the signifier, thus reversing the commonsensical position. The argument that 'reality' or 'the world' is at least partly constructed by the language (and other media) we use insists on 'the primacy of the signifier' – suggesting that the signified is shaped by the signifier rather than vice versa. Poststructuralists such as the later Barthes, Derrida and Foucault developed this notion into a metaphysical presupposition of the priority of the signifier, but its roots can be found in Saussure and structuralism. Lévi-Strauss emphasised the primacy of the signifier, initially as a strategy for structural analysis in anthropology. In Saussure's model the signified is shown over the signifier (like the Marxist location of a political and cultural superstructure over a determining economic base). Lacan placed the signifier over the signified, reflecting his notion that the signified inevitably 'slips beneath' the signifier, resisting our attempts to delimit it. Some poststructuralists refer to an 'empty' or 'floating' signifier – variously defined as a signifier with a vague, highly variable, unspecifiable or non-existent signified. Such signifiers mean different things to different people: they may stand for many or even any signifieds; they may mean whatever their interpreters want them to mean. This suggests a radical disconnection between signifier and signified.

In Harris's translation of Saussure's *Course* (1983), note his substitution of 'signal' and 'signification' for what are still invariably known as the signifier and the signified.

D. Chandler

SIMMEL, GEORG (1858–1918) German sociologist and philosopher, seen today as a key theorist of modernity and a precursor to postmodern theory. Though his reputation has grown in recent decades, Simmel's place in the pantheon of classical figures in the formative period of sociology is far less secure than is that of Marx, Durkheim and Weber.

As a sociologist of modern culture, Simmel's thinking often appears as a reflection of what he understood to be a central defining trait of modernity – namely, its fragmentary character. Known primarily as an essayist, in his various writings he provided finely textured descriptions or snapshots of various social types, such as the stranger, the miser and the adventurer, as well as various types of social interaction, including exchange, conflict and sociability. Due to the focus on the fragmentary shards, the bits and pieces of contemporary social life, Simmel has often been viewed as a sociological miniaturist.

This assessment is a mistake, for he had a well-articulated macro-sociological theoretical framework that was developed in his magisterial and complex book, *The Philosophy of Money* (1907). Simmel defined his intention in this work as providing a complement to, rather than a critique of, historical materialism. Rather than being concerned with the economic factors that led to the emergence of a money economy, he was primarily interested in discerning the varied ways in which a society predicated on money transforms culture and patterns of social interaction. He sought to delineate the social psychology characteristic of a money economy, describing the various ways that it structures our internal and external lives.

Money, Simmel pointed out, possesses no value in itself, but functions as a tool to facilitate the exchange of goods and services. It is instrumental, abstract and impersonal, objectively being no more than a means to an end. In so far as this is the case, money promotes a rational orientation toward the world, though this rationality can become distorted for some individuals who treat money irrationally as an end in itself, such as in the cases of the miser and the spendthrift. By removing the emotional involvements from economic transactions, money makes it possible to expand considerably the range of one's trading partners by severing all-encompassing ties to primary groups. In so doing, it promotes an individualistic world-view. Money also encourages the individual to be future oriented, and thereby serves to undermine respect for and attachment to tradition. Money is Janus-faced: it is liberating but it also places a barrier between people and creates a heartless culture. Money thus underpins the ambiguities of the modern age.

The focus of Simmel's sociological studies was neither action nor structure, but instead social interaction. From his perspective, social structures are to be construed as crystallisations of interaction. Linked to his Kantian philosophical orientation, he took the calculative character of social interaction in modern economic conditions to be an indication of the growing disjuncture between the form and content of social life. This is what he had in mind when he wrote about the tragedy of culture.

P. Kivisto

SIMONDON, GILBERT (1924–89) French philosopher of technology and inspiration for Deleuze in *Difference and Repetition* and *Logic of Sense* as well as in his collaboration with Guattari, particularly in *A Thousand Plateaus*. Simondon's work focuses on the concept of individuation across ontological levels. His diverse explorations of individuation find a common source in his criticism of cybernetics and information theory, which he diagnoses as containing essentialist and hylomorphic presuppositions. All processes of individuation occur against a larger background of what Simondon calls the 'preindividual' and as temporary delimitations of the 'metastable' domain of potentiality.

In *Du mode d'existence des objets techniques* (1958), Simondon develops an ontogenetic account of the mode of existence of technical objects. The proximate inspiration for Simondon's philosophical treatment of technology was his dissatisfaction with the narrow focus of cybernetics on a specific type of machine (feedback mechanisms). Rather than opening onto a dynamic account of technology, cybernetics 'accepted what all theory of technology must refuse: a classification of technological objects conducted by means of established criteria and following genera and species'. In contrast to such essentialism, Simondon proposes to think the technical object as an evolutionary lineage or series. Like his teacher Canguilhem, Simondon's method involves the comparison of technical objects with biological processes. This method allows him to postulate a distinct mode of existence of technical objects between inanimate natural objects and human beings, what Bernard Stiegler has dubbed 'organised inorganic matter'. While technical objects undergo a process of evolution not entirely distinct from biological evolution, the process of concretisation driving evolution is different in the two cases: whereas natural objects like plants and animals are fully concretised, technical objects merely tend toward concreteness, and always retain a degree of abstraction.

In *L'individu et sa genèse physico-biologique* (1964) and *L'individuation psychique et collective* (1989), Simondon reworks information theory in order to describe individuation as an ontogenetic account of emergence in physical, biological, psychic and collective systems. Simondon reconceptualises traditional distinctions, including those of form and matter and of individual and milieu, in terms of information; only by conceiving these distinctions as processes of individuation can their reality be taken into account. Simondon begins his reconceptualisation by criticising the hylomorphic schema which has dominated thought about individuation from Aristotle onwards. In its place, Simondon offers the process of crystallisation as an example of individuation: by carrying out a proliferating series of communications to an amorphous substance, crystallisation gradually informs that substance, causing it to pass from a metastable to a stable state. Because the process of individuation takes place in each communication between each crystal and the metastable substance, it must precede the emergence of the individual. Simondon consequently proposes the model of crystallisation as a description of the process of individuation from the microscopic to the macroscopic, from the physical to the biological to the social. On this view, animate matter can be differentiated from inanimate matter by its capacity to sustain a certain degree of metastability that renders its individuation perpetual and necessarily incomplete.

It is regrettable that very little of Simondon's work has been translated into English, the notable exception being the Introduction to *L'individu*, which appears as 'The Genesis of the Individual' in *Zone 6: Incorporations* (1992).

M. Hansen

SIMULACRUM A term central to the French anti-Platonism of the 1960s; developed from reflections on Nietzsche and Heidegger, it concerns various ways of complicating the received notions of the relation of image and original. 'Simulacrum' is the Latin equivalent of the Greek *eidolon*. While both terms could be rendered in English as 'image', 'simulacrum' is based on the Latin verb *similare*, which means to be similar or to feign. It also has sense of 'likewise' or 'at the same time'; hence 'simul-taneous'. *Eidolon*, on the other hand, is etymologically connected to the term *eidos*, which itself comes from the verb *horao*, 'to see'. Thus an *eidolon* is something seen or the look of something. But, like 'simulacrum', the word 'eidolon' also suggests something feigned or false, like a phantasm; hence the English word 'idol'. Thus we find Plato in the *Republic* placing the poets third from the truth since they produce nothing but *eidola*, images of things, which are themselves images of the *eidē* or ideas or forms.

The philosophers associated with French anti-Platonism – Derrida,

Foucault and Deleuze – exploit all the resonances of these terms. But for them the most basic sense of 'simulacrum' is repetition. We can see this basic sense in three articles of the late 1960s which appear shortly thereafter in books: Deleuze's 'Renverser le platonisme' (included as an appendix to *Logic of Sense* under the title 'Plato and the Simulacrum'), Foucault's 'This is Not a Pipe', and Derrida's 'Plato's Pharmacy' (in *Dissemination*). In all three texts, anti-Platonism involves a reversal of the relation between image and original or between repetition and form or model. It thus involves a reversal of the sensible over the intelligible, the *eidola* over the *eidē*. That Plato placed the poets third from the truth shows us that in fact anti-Platonism concerned the status of the aesthetic in both of its senses, the sense of sensation and the sense of art. But with the simulacrum we have a paradoxical sensation. Thus all reflections on the simulacrum in the 1960s started with a paradox, the paradox of *répétition*. This French word means not only 'repetition', but also 'rehearsal'. Thus we could call this paradox 'the paradox of the theatre'.

To see the paradox, we must first think of technological reproduction. In technology, the model comes first and the repetitions or products come second. Moreover, all of the products must be identical repetitions of the model or form. But, in regard to a theatre rehearsal, which is indeed a repetition, a re-hearsal, we must ask ourselves what is repeated. The most obvious answer to this question is the performance. However, the performance comes after the rehearsal; it is a 'second'. Yet we call the performance a 'premiere', a 'first'. The paradox is that this 'first' is actually second and the 'second', the re-hearsal, is actually first. Even if we say that the rehearsal repeats the idea of the poet, we would not say – indeed the poet would not say – that the idea exists when it is in his or her head; the idea does not exist until it is realised in the performance. Again, the first is second and the second is first. Based in this paradox, the simulacrum is an 'original-less image'. Having no original, model or form, this repetition 'makes a difference'. Because in the theatre – in art – we have a repetition that makes a difference, we are inclined to see the same play performed many times; the performance is always powerful. This repetition is 'the power of the false'. For all three – Derrida, Deleuze and Foucault – this power produces the original and the truth.

Despite their similar stances to the paradox of *répétition*, our three philosophers develop different concepts of the simulacrum. Derrida argues in several texts from the late 1960s that writing is a supplement, meaning that it is something added onto speech, supplementing

speech. But why does speech need this supplement? Because speech
lacks persistence. But if speech lacks persistence, then it was never an
origin (since an origin must be something that persists). Where does the
persistence of speech then come from? Writing. The very thing that
looked to be added on – a 'second' – is actually a 'first'. It is a
simulacrum. For Derrida, this kind of simulacrum means that the
image always contaminates the original. In other words, even when we
have the most pure speech, writing is already there contaminating it.
Contamination is a concept of unity and continuity, mediation. If we
turn now to Deleuze, we see that his simulacrum is a concept of duality
and discontinuity. For Deleuze, since there is no original, there is no
mediation from one repetition to the next. Therefore each repetition
is 'different in itself'. Despite being a repetition, for Deleuze, each
repetition truly makes a difference. We can see the same structure in
Foucault, when he speaks of the statement (*l'énoncé*) in *The Archeology
of Knowledge* (1969). There he defines the statement as a material
repetition, which means that it is a simulacrum. But the statement's
repetition is such that it is not a kind of linguistic atom which would
remain the same in different contexts. Instead, we could have the same
sentence repeated identically – 'dreams fulfil desires' – but in Plato and
in Freud, it is two different statements.

With *répétition*, we have entered into a difficult kind of thinking.
Derrida's simulacrum is not a pure unity since it aims to include the
impure itself. Deleuze's simulacrum is not completely 'in itself' without mediation, since it is still a repetition. What is more difficult is that,
after the 1960s our three philosophers abandon the term 'simulacrum'.
Derrida's 'spectre' is not a simulacrum; Deleuze's 'concept' is not a
simulacrum; Foucault's 'writing of the self' is not a simulacrum. The
moment of anti-Platonism seems to have passed. Perhaps this abandonment indicates a kind of 'de-aesthetisation' of thought. Other
philosophers such as Baudrillard have used the term 'simulacrum'
in its traditional sense as a false image lacking all reality. But what we
must see here in the simulacrum is the paradox of *répétition*, the
paradox with which, always, thinking begins.

                                                                 L. Lawlor

See also: Repetition; simulation; Thought

SIMULATION A concept in which the 'real' is produced as an after-
effect by its supposed images, employed by Jean Baudrillard as the
principle of postmodern culture.

Simulacra and Simulation (1981) and *Simulations* (1983) contain
Baudrillard's orders of 'simulacra', his generic term for any relation of

original to copy in which the copy substitutes itself for the original from which it becomes thereby indistinguishable:

Law	Form	Sign	Machine	Period
1. natural	counterfeit	corrupt symbol	automaton	Renaissance
2. market	production	icon	robot	Industrial Revolution
3. structural	simulation	two-sided psychical	android	post-industrial
4. fractal	proliferation	metonym/index	virtual reality	Network Society

The first, counterfeit, order of simulacra, that of theatrical automata, emerges in the Renaissance with the emancipation of otherwise endogamous and cruel social relations and the becoming insecure of motivated signification. The second order arises with the Industrial Revolution, perfect for worker robots and serial signs of sameness subject to the market forces of fledgling capitalism; Baudrillard here adapts Benjamin's theses on 'mechanical reproduction'. The third order is post-industrial, in which mechanical reproduction is transcended; simulation is thus conceived strictly in terms of reproducibility, without any 'aura' left for the 'original'. Representation is commodified with the rise of signs without reference, a breeding ground for 'androids' controlled by matrices of codes; here we see Baudrillard's mockery of a society obsessed with genetic determinism. In *The Transparency of Evil* (1990) Baudrillard added a fourth order of aleatory dispersion by contiguity and viral metonymy, giving rise to the absorption of virtual media technologies by human beings without shadows; here Baudrillard mocks the mania for virtual reality.

The third order is the most influential. It is no longer possible to distinguish between signs and their objects, questions and answers, doubles and originals, because the terms in each of these pairs are equivalent to one another inasmuch as one has absorbed the other. This creates confusion. The entire edifice of representation in which images are yoked to a pre-imaged foundation falters. Instability reigns.

G. Genosko

See also: aura; simulacrum

SINGULARITY A term which tends to be used in two distinct manners in contemporary thought. (1) In classical logic, the notion of the 'singular' has long been understood in relation to the 'universal', just as the 'particular' has been understood in relation to the 'general'. The singular designates what is not 'difference', that which is non-relational. In relation to this tradition, certain thinkers, such as Alain Badiou, have formulated the notion of a 'singular universal'.

Negatively, it implies that every universal (especially in the political realm) is really a particularity that puts itself, ideologically, in the place of the universal. Positively, it means that the universality of emancipation, for example, can only come about through a singular 'event', that is through a singular break or rupture in the normal order: the true dimension of universality would emerge only when the 'normal' order of particularities is perturbed by the irruption of a singular event.

(2) In mathematics the concept of singularity is related to a somewhat different set of notions. First, the singular is distinguished from or opposed to the regular: the singular point is what escapes the regularity of the rule. Second, the theory of differential equations distinguishes between singularities that are remarkable and singularities that are not remarkable, that are ordinary. Geometrical figures, for instance, are a combination of singular and ordinary points (a square has four singular points).

In *Difference and Repetition* Gilles Deleuze made use of the theory of singularities in his ontology: one can say of any determination in general (a) that it is a multiplicity composed of singular and ordinary points; and (b) that such multiplicities are constructed through the formation of series from one singularity to another (unity is simply the effect of the functioning of the multiplicity). The singular points of physical systems, for instance, are their points of fusion, boiling, condensation; the singularities of psychic systems are their 'sensitive' points of tears and joy, sickness and health, hope and anxiety. Deleuze's theory of immanent Ideas is largely derived from the theory of singularities developed by Albert Lautmann. The concept of the singular, in both its logical and mathematical forms, is one of the most important conceptual innovations in contemporary continental philosophy.

D. Smith

SLAVE REVOLT IN MORALITY Nietzsche's term for the founding event in the history of a morality in which undeserved suffering is honoured as the primary index of one's 'goodness'. (He confirms in *Ecce Homo* that the founding event in question is none other than 'the birth of Christianity out of the spirit of *ressentiment*'.) As he explains in *On the Genealogy of Morals*, the 'slave morality' arose only in reaction to a historically prior morality that favoured 'noble' (or 'masterly') types. The 'noble' morality was predicated on the virtues of spontaneous self-assertion, uncompromising self-possession and outward displays of martial physicality. Noble types naturally and instinctively celebrate themselves (and everything pertaining or belonging to them) as 'good' (*gut*), while regarding everything and everyone else as 'bad' (*schlecht*). By way of contrast, slavish types always begin their evaluations with a denunciation of the hostile external world against which they must struggle. The slaves pronounce their masters 'evil' (*böse*), implying thereby that their masters are free to restrain their expressions of nobility and may be held accountable for failing to do so. Only as an afterthought do the slaves proclaim themselves 'good', and they do so only on the basis of the suffering they endure at the hands of their evil masters.

According to Nietzsche, the 'slave revolt in morality' occurred when the slaves claimed to *choose* the suffering inflicted on them by their noble captors. Suffering, they increasingly came to insist, was not their ineluctable lot in an amoral cosmos but a conscious preference they had cultivated in order to distinguish themselves from their evil masters. In addition to furnishing the slaves with a psychological defence against the suffering they would be obliged to endure in any event, the 'slave revolt in morality' also had the unintended effect of disarming the nobles, who gradually lost interest in causing suffering that was desired, even craved, by the slaves. By means of their 'revolt', the slaves were able to transform their unhappy, unchosen destiny into their crowning virtue. The 'slave revolt in morality' thus serves as the example *par excellence* of deriving power from powerlessness. It is also responsible for founding the slave morality and its various descendants, including contemporary Christian morality. This is why Nietzsche believes that his attack on Christian morality, if successful, will go a long way toward undoing the original 'slave revolt in morality'.

D. Conway

See also: ressentiment

SMOOTH/STRIATED SPACE Terms used by Deleuze and Guattari in *A Thousand Plateaus* to describe the social organisation of space, and then extended to describe social structures, systems of thought and art, and other kinds of order.

The model for striated space is a centrally controlled agricultural society such as existed in the river valleys of China and Mesopotamia. In the striated agricultural society, space is cut into portions tied to specific groups. People are tied to bits of land and particular social roles administered from a centre with a view of the whole and ordering it by these separations and assignments. People inhabit their assigned roles and locations, and do not transgress borders. Movement is subordinated to assigned points.

The model smooth space is the central Asian steppe inhabited by nomads. A smooth space lacks the divisions of striated space. The nomad does not own any land and is assigned nowhere. The nomad is located nowhere in particular and everywhere in the space, occupying the whole through lines of movement. In his wandering the nomad observes microenvironments and determines where best to pasture his animals and when to move on. Guidance comes from dispersed attention to the details of the locality and the feel of the moment, rather than from central decrees; points are established by movements.

Deleuze and Guattari emphasise that there are no pure cases of smooth or striated space, that all real spaces mix the two: the desert is always being organised; the State is always being transgressed in what they call 'lines of flight'.

D. Kolb

SOCIAL CONSTRUCTIVISM The theory that all forms of knowledge, or at least essential aspects of knowledge, are the consequence of socio-historical ideas and practices. Social constructivism arises as a response to essentialism in order to designate the irreducibility of history, society and culture to given, natural essences. In feminist theory, social constructivism relies on a distinction between sex as anatomical difference and gender as socio-cultural formation. The former is generally considered the arbitrary location of the latter. Though an essential term for the history of feminism in the English-speaking world, social construction has been criticised more recently for its neglect of the body. In social constructivism, materiality is conceived as an inert, passive and mute medium that simply receives arbitrary, cultural form. Thus 'corporeal feminism' has made a turn to rethinking corporeality dynamically. French feminism and philosophy are important in this enterprise. French feminism lacks a rigorous distinction between sex and gender; 'sexual difference' is rather understood as a complex *genre*. *Genre* is typically translated as type, kind or even sometimes gender, but these English equivalents lack the socio-historical sense of the term, which delineates a social group standing before the law. Further, attention to figures like Maurice Merleau-Ponty and Gilles Deleuze has opened a notion of bodily identity between essentialism and social construction that can account for the imaginary and socio-symbolic dimensions of corporeality without dispensing with a dynamic materialism. This has resulted in a more mature form of 'social constructivism' that takes seriously a more complex notion of materiality.

S. Keltner

SOCIALISED WORKER (*operaio sociale*) The term used by Antonio
Negri and his circle to define the new subjective composition of the
working class that arises in the period of the real subsumption of labour
under capital following 1968. For Negri, the modern forms of working-
class subjectivity are not fixed but historically evolving, and hence the
forms of political organisation appropriate to them must also evolve.
For example, early industrial production relied upon simple machines
that needed highly trained professional workers to operate and maintain them. Because of their skills, these workers stood at the top of the
organisational hierarchy within the factory, played the leading role in
union and soviet activity and expressed themselves politically through
the hierarchical vanguard party of the Leninist revolutionary tradition.
The party's hierarchical structure thus corresponded to the internal
hierarchy of the class. In response to this challenge, capital reorganised
production around more complex machines that no longer required
skilled operators, depriving the professional workers of their leverage
and the Leninist party of its prime movers. Out of the deskilling of the
professional workers emerged the mass workers of the mid-twentieth
century, whose undifferentiated internal structure expressed itself
politically through the mass trade unions and reformist left parties
of Europe and the US. Aggressive decentralisation of production
following 1968 dispersed the mass worker throughout society and
around the globe, shattering its political forms and giving rise to
the socialised workers of immaterial labour, whose collective subjectivity takes shape over communications networks and is still seeking an
effective political expression.

T. Murphy

SOCIALISME OU BARBARIE A political group and periodical in
France (1948/9–1965/6); they originated in alliance with the Trotskyite
Fourth International but soon developed their own completely post-
Marxist and anti-Soviet position. Its periodical (first issue March 1949)
was established by Cornelius Castoriadis (writing under pseudonyms
Pierre Chaulieu and Paul Cardan) and Claude Lefort, who earlier had
expressed similar opinions in their essay 'On the Regime and Against
the Defence of the USSR' (1946), which criticised the 'social layer' of
bureaucrats dominating Stalinist Soviet Union.

Despite its internal strife (leading to a split in 1958) and the uneasy
relationship between Castoriadis and Lefort, the group formed ideological alliances with important leftist organisations abroad such as
London Solidarity and later Philadelphia Solidarity (known as the
Johnson-Forrest Tendency). Issue 13 (1954) was dedicated to the East

German Revolt of June 1953 and the strikes of French workers; it analysed the nature of Communist parties as reactionary and totalitarian. Equally significant was issue 20 (1955) consisting mainly of discussions between Castoriadis, C. L. R. James and members of the group in France, leading to the co-authorship of *Facing Reality* (co-authored by James, Grace Lee and Castoriadis, 1958). After the Hungarian revolution of 1956, Castoriadis proceeded with a radical critique of Marxism.

The journal's central position was 'the self-activity and management of the working class'. Also important was the formation of Castoriadis's central thesis of 'bureaucratic capitalism' which led him to envisage a socialist organisation of society which would be based unconditionally on 'worker's management of production', on the political form of worker's councils and on 'the abolition of any separate managerial apparatus and the restitution of such an apparatus to the community of workers'. Despite low membership, the group and its journal exerted a deep influence on the 'generation of 68' in France and on the young Lyotard. The group disbanded officially in June 1967, its last periodical issue being issued in mid-1965; it was later recognised as the first post-Marxist theorisation of worker's experience and the empowerment project which could grow from it.

V. Karalis

SOREL, GEORGES (1847–1922) French social philosopher and pamphleteer, best known for *Reflections on Violence* (1908), where revolutionary 'violence' is theorised as the liberating other of the suppressing 'force' that holds the bourgeois political order in place. For the syndicalist Sorel of *Reflections*, only the conflict generated by the proletarian general strike could transform the prevailing rationalistic values of bourgeois society, which encourage mediocrity, decadence and corruption, into the 'heroic ethics of the producers' as embodied in instinct, creativity and poetry. When that which Sorel calls 'the social myth of the general strike' is maintained at the forefront of working-class minds, individual memories of past conflicts and aspirations for the future are bound together in a singular 'epic state of mind' to inspire collective action.

Although Sorel claimed to write 'in the spirit of Marx', his overwhelming concern, inherited largely from the anarchist tradition of Proudhon, was with the abstract notion of moral/ethical renewal as opposed to the concrete relations of production in an alternative socialist society. This concern with morality, coupled with a lifelong attempt to transpose Bergson's irrationalist and highly subjective philosophy of intuition into a social philosophy, led Sorel away from materialism to a peculiar form of vitalistic idealism which could just as easily appeal to the extreme right as to the left, and explains Sorel's extraordinary political vacillations as he sought for a mechanism of progressive moral/social change.

Sorel gave up his engineering career at age 45 in 1892 to embark on an intellectual odyssey whose eclecticism was to embrace almost every major radical philosophical and political school of thought of his time. By 1894 Sorel was a Marxist but was also beginning his association with Bergson's philosophy; by 1896 he was a follower of Vico and a socialist critical of the Second International, in 1898 a reformist syndicalist, in 1899 a Dreyfusard, and by 1904 he had become a revolutionary syndicalist in whose cause his most celebrated works were produced. However, after the French state's forcible suppression of the syndic- alist-inspired strike wave of 1906–9, Sorel became increasingly dis- illusioned with syndicalism and from 1910 to 1913 flirted with nationalism and anti-Semitism. After the First World War, Sorel was to express admiration for both Lenin's Bolshevism and, somewhat more tentatively, Mussolini's fascism. The latter, in an attempt to gain intellectual credibility, acknowledged Sorel as an important influence, the former dismissing him, however, as a 'notorious muddler'.

Alongside *Reflections*, Sorel's key works include *The Illusions of Progress* (1906), which anticipates a number of themes developed by later thinkers of the Frankfurt School, as well as those of contem- porary poststructuralists and postmodernists, in its unrelenting cri- tique of the positivistic faith in Enlightenment rationality and science to bring about human emancipation. *The Organisation of Democracy* (1906) and *The Decomposition of Marxism* (1908) offer powerful anarchist critiques of bourgeois democracy and parliamentary soci- alism respectively.

W. McNeish

See also: General Strike, Social Myth of

SOVEREIGNTY A concept which emerged in conjunction with the modern understanding of political authority as derived from a single, indivisible and incontrovertible source. The classical definition of sovereignty states that there is a final and absolute source of authority within a given political community. To describe sovereign power as a certain kind of authority is already to distinguish it from brute coercion. Sovereign authority implies the legitimate exercise of power, where legitimacy is typically derived from natural, divine or secular law. To say that sovereignty is characteristic of the final instance of legal or political authority implies that there is no higher source of legitimate power.

Sovereign power was not a feature of the medieval European political order, in which separate sources of spiritual and secular authority held sway over the same territory. Only with the effective collapse of the Holy Roman Empire in the aftermath of the Thirty Years War and the Peace of Wesphalia in 1648 did sovereign territorial states become the predominant form of political authority in Europe. Influential theorists such as Carl Schmitt have emphasised the theological origins of the concept, pointing out the analogy between political sovereignty and the unconstrained and authoritative will of God. However, a number of other developments in Renaissance political thought also contributed to the emergence of this concept. These included Machiavelli's argument that the duties and obligations of rulers were a function of the needs of a strong and well ordered state (*raison d'état*), Luther's strict separation of the realms of spiritual and secular authority, and a renewed understanding of the relation between a ruler and his territory along the lines of the Roman legal notion of property as *dominium* over which the owner exercised absolute control.

The term 'sovereignty' first played a significant role in Jean Bodin's *The Six Books of a Commonweal* (1576). In contrast to Machiavelli's conception of political power as *raison d'état* free from religious or customary constraints, Bodin viewed the political community as a unity of ruler and ruled which required a sovereign power for its very survival. Sovereignty was 'the absolute and perpetual power of a republic'. The sovereign alone had the power to declare war and peace and to make laws for the commonwealth. Although he viewed sovereign power as by definition indivisible, Bodin distinguished between the form of the state and the form of its government, which could be monarchical, aristocratic or democratic. While Bodin believed that the sovereign ought to respect natural and customary law, he recognised no right of resistance on the part of subjects or any role for their consent.

Writing in the aftermath of the English civil war, Hobbes agreed with Bodin that the fundamental purpose of political community was the preservation of order and the prevention of civil war. His *Leviathan* (1651) laid out an equally absolutist conception of political authority, albeit one founded in a social contract and exercised through an elected assembly. This conception of sovereign political power was subsequently democratised in the eighteenth century in Rousseau's conception of republican government. Although not an accurate description of the exercise of power within and between states, sovereignty remains a constitutive principle both of the forms of domestic legal order and of the international order.

Modern political communities have typically been territorial states, with the result that sovereignty is often defined as supreme authority within a given territory. However territoriality is not a necessary feature of sovereign power: Karl Renner proposed a constitutional structure in which non-territorial sovereign nations shared final authority with the territorial state.

The idea that sovereign territorial states are subordinated to no higher authority in turn implies that their internal affairs should not be subject to external interference and that they are free to enter into relations with other such states. Some theorists have sought to differentiate internal and external dimensions of sovereignty, according to whether the focus is on the ultimate source of authority within a political community or its independence in relation to other political communities. There is justification for this distinction in particular contexts: for example English common law enshrines the principle that 'acts of state' by the executive power in respect of foreign entities or territories are not subject to review by domestic courts. But the two dimensions of sovereignty are not without reciprocal and sometimes paradoxical effects, for example, when the external sovereign power of the state allows it to enter into treaties which have consequences for its internal sovereign power. The development of the European Union clearly exposes the tension between internal and external dimensions of sovereignty as member states have entered into treaties and agreements which impose contraints on both executive and judicial branches of their governments.

Bodin and Hobbes thought that sovereign power should be absolute and undivided in the sense that a single instance of authority exercised unrestricted scope over matters affecting the political community. However, there are many ways in which modern state power is divided and less than absolute. In democratic states legal and constitutional doctrine tends to locate sovereignty in the people, while the exercise of sovereign power is typically distributed among legislative, judicial and executive arms of government such that there is no single highest authority. Carl Schmitt, in *Poltical Theology* (1922), reacted against this feature of liberal democratic sovereignty by reverting to the early modern concept and suggesting that the true sovereign is that power capable of bringing about an exceptional state and suspending the rule of law or replacing one constitution with another.

Not only is the exercise of sovereignty divided among the institutions of modern liberal government, these are not always absolute:

internal authorities, such as sovereign Indigenous nations, may set limits to the scope of sovereign state power. Externally, more powerful states have often set limits to the autonomy of their weaker neighbours, while non-state international or transnational agencies such as the Catholic Church or the International Monetary Fund set a variety of limits to the authority of individual states. Although the United Nations explicitly endorses the autonomy of its member states, it also supports limits to state sovereignty in the form of treaties which protect individual human rights. Since the closing decade of the twentieth century, it has supported military intervention in order to enforce those rights, and established an International Criminal Court to judge offenders against human rights principles.

P. Patton

SPACE From the seventeenth into the twentieth centuries, philosophical discussions of space revolved around two oppositions: objective and subjective, and absolute and relational. Modern philosophers construed space either as a feature of the world that is independent of human beings and their minds (objective) or as something that minds or subjects of experience impose on empirical objects (subjective). Conceptions of objective space further differed on whether space is absolute or relational: a container or arena in which entities exist or a collection of relations among entities. It is distinctive of continental philosophy that it has largely forsaken these modern debates and focused on three other types of space: lived space, the space of intelligibility and social space.

Analyses of lived space are analyses of either the spatiality of continuous human life or the spaces in which people dwell. Most analyses of the first sort focus on human experience and action and are phenomenological in character, meaning that they elucidate human life by reference to lived experience of it. Prominent examples are Husserl, *Thing and Space: Lectures of 1907* (1970), Heidegger, *Being and Time* (1927), Merleau-Ponty, *Phenomenology of Perception* (1945), and Otto Bollnow, *Mensch und Raum* (1963). These accounts examine the spatiality of people's involvement in the world along with the therewith coordinated spatiality of the practical worlds in which people are involved. Heidegger, for instance, analysed the spatiality of involvement as: (1) the orientation of people's dealings with things; and (2) things being brought close in people's activities, in the sense of being available for and involved in those activities. He described the world's spatiality, meanwhile, as the regionalised places of the equipment people use, places which are coordinated with what people are up to when using this equipment. Merleau-Ponty subsequently inserted the body into this overall account, treating the spatiality of involvement as a bodily space understood as a matrix of habitual and possible actions and tying regions of places to the human body as the repository of abilities and habits.

Paradigmatic for the second type of analysis of lived space is Heidegger's essay 'Building Dwelling Thinking' (1952), in which he described the setting of human dwelling as arrays of activity paths and places, which are centred, not in human activity as in his earlier account, but on features of the built and natural environment in which human existence transpires. Other accounts of dwelling space are found in Bachelard, *The Poetics of Space* (1958), and Edward Casey, *Getting Back into Place* (1993). Bachelard, for example, joined phenomenology with psychoanalysis, psychology and literature to give a 'topoanalysis' of the places of intimate life. This topoanalysis, for which the house as a world of places is especially significant, explores human dwelling in these places while simultaneously examining the inner life as a place for images.

The second type of space examined by continental philosophers is the space of intelligibility. Heidegger conceived of a 'clearing' of being in which anything that is, including human existence, shows up. This clearing is a sort of openness (*Offene*), presupposed by and prior to all representation and determinateness. This clearing has been interpreted as a space of intelligibility: whatever is, shows up in the clearing intelligible as something. The idea of such a space as the overall place and horizon for entities and human existence has reappeared in much subsequent continental thought. Perhaps the most prominent version is Derrida's (*Of Grammatology*, 1967) notion of textuality as the 'scene of writing' (*scène de l'écriture*). Derrida departed from ordinary usage in construing writing as the articulation of intelligibility and a text as anything intelligible, i.e. anything that is. The scene of writing is the setting in which anything that is exists, and its basic action is 'spacing' (*espacement*). To be in this scene is to exist in a space of *différance* (*Margins of Philosophy*, 1972). This means that something's being both lies in its differences with other entities and is perpetually deferred, that is can never be fully articulated. Ernesto Laclau and Chantal Mouffe subsequently transformed Derrida's textuality into the 'field of discursivity' in which social orders – distinct arrangements of actions, things and words – coalesce (*Hegemony and Socialist Strategy*, 1985). The fact that as textual, that is in the field of differential discursivity, something's being is never fully determinate implies that social orders can never be stable. Other prominent appropriations of Heidegger's space of intelligibility are Charles Taylor's account of social reality as practices ('Interpretation and the Sciences of Man' 1971), and Charles Spinosa, Fernando Flores and Hubert Dreyfus's analysis of the worlds in which people act as 'disclosure spaces' (*Disclosing New Worlds*, 1997). A particularly innovative appropriation of Heidegger's clearing is Arendt's conception of the public sphere as a space of appearances that opens up among human beings amid a common world (*The Human Condition*, 1958). This public sphere is a space of visibility in which people appear to one another.

Continental philosophers have also contributed to the wider intellectual effort to conceptualise the spaces of social life. Indeed, many appropriations of Heidegger's clearing pursue this end. A further attempt to theorise social spaces is Foucault's notion of heterotopias ('Of Other Spaces', 1984): 'other' places, for example cemeteries, boarding houses and prisons, which contest and reverse familiar and prevalent social places. Foucault also pointedly observed both that space has a history ('Today the site has been substituted for extension which itself had replaced emplacement') and that the twentieth century was the epoch of space: of simultaneous, that is, interconnected sites. A final continental analysis of social space is Deleuze and Guattari's differentiation of smooth from striated space in *A Thousand Plateaus*. Whereas striated space is laid-out, mapped and controlled space, the type typical of state societies, smooth space, the space of nomads, is the space forged by continuous movement, which can burst out of and pass through and thereby undermine the grids of its striated counterpart. The overall space of social life results from clashes between them.

T. Schatzki

SPECTRALITY A notion developed by Derrida for thinking both the other side of thinking and the other side of life. The spectre cannot be thought within the parameters of scholarly knowledge (in *Hamlet*, Marcellus tells Horatio to speak to the ghost because 'thou art a Scholler'), nor of an ontology (Derrida calls instead for a 'hauntology') (*Spectres of Marx*). The spectre or ghost (*revenant*) is also what comes back from the other side in the sense of arriving as an event or promise, and what calls for a new theory of mourning. Derrida's reading of Marx is thus as much a return to a too hastily buried Marx for what he offers in the way of political or 'emancipatory promise', as it is a critique of a certain thematics of spectrality in Marx's work. Spectrality also follows from a line of questioning concerning 'spirit' (*Geist*) in Hegel ('The Pit and the Pyramid' in *Margins*, and *Glas*) and in Heidegger (*Of Spirit*). In the latter case it is especially a matter of coming to grips with the various hauntings of the political and of Nazism in his work.

Thanks to its undecidable existential status the spectre draws attention to urgent contemporary questions posed by technology and in particular by biotechnologies that redefine the borders between life and death. It also relates to so-called virtuality, and transformations as well as manipulations of information introduced by new media, which are understood most keenly in terms of the 'time' of those media and what they imply for the time and speed of reflection and debate.

D. *Wills*

SPEECH ACTS What people do when they communicate orally with one another, effecting through their words changes in the social environment. A catalogue of speech acts would include asserting, denying, commanding, advising, inviting, promising, apologising and thanking.

J. L. Austin (*How to Do Things with Words*, 1962) drew attention to the variety of speech acts in order to challenge what he perceived as a widespread assumption that 'the business of a (sentence) can only be to "describe some state of affairs", or to "state some fact", which it must do either truly of falsely'. Austin focused attention on 'performative utterances', through which one might, if the right conditions obtained, directly bring about changes in some institutional state of affairs. To say 'You're fired', might be to terminate someone's employment; to say 'I second', might place a motion before an assembly. Whether the termination of employment or the seconding of the motion are successfully completed does not depend on whether the words uttered truly describe some state of affairs.

The attention Austin gave to the conditions under which performative utterances could fail (his 'doctrine of the *Infelicities*') was criticised by Derrida ('Signature Event Context', in *Margins of Philosophy*, 1972) for relying on the possibility of 'ideal' speech situations rather than exploring how the risks of infelicities are bound up in the possibility of such acts. Derrida's criticisms touched off an acrimonious controversy with one of Austin's former students, John Searle. (See Searle, 'Reiterating the Differences', *Glyph*, 1977, and Derrida, *Limited Inc.*, 1988.)

Communicating is evidently a complex activity and to clarify the levels of actions involved, Austin distinguished the (locutionary) act of uttering words, the (illocutionary) act of what one does *in* uttering the words and the (perlocutionary) acts one performs *by* uttering the words. An officer may utter the words (locutionary act) 'The platoon will fall in at 1500 hours'. The illocutionary act is a command or imperative and through this act the officer causes (perlocutionary act) the members of the platoon to assemble at a certain time. The grammar of the words of the officer's locutionary act are such that it might function (in the mouth of a spy) as the illocutionary act of making a prediction, but grammar does not by itself determine the character of an illocutionary act.

It has been common to treat speech acts as the responsibility of a branch of philosophical linguistics known as pragmatics. Accounts of what make an utterance grammatical are assigned to 'syntactics'; accounts of representational content belong to 'semantics'; accounts of how conventions of use contribute to meaning are assigned to 'pragmatics'. When this distinction was introduced by Charles W. Morris in *Foundations of the Theory of Signs* (1938), it was assumed that pragmatics would be addressed after syntactics and semantics had been completed. Now a number of Anglophone theorists concur with Deleuze and Guattari in *A Thousand Plateaus* that 'it is impossible to define semantics, syntactics or even phonematics as scientific zones of language independent of *pragmatics*'.

J. Tiles

SPIRIT (*Geist*) A term most closely associated in continental philosophy with Hegel, who distinguished and integrated three aspects of 'spirit': 'subjective', 'objective' and 'absolute'. 'Subjective' spirit concerns the cognitive and practical physiology and psychology of individual human beings. 'Objective' spirit concerns the structure and functioning of extant communities. 'Absolute' spirit concerns the development of knowledge, freedom and human self-understanding over historical time, as expressed in art, religion and philosophy.

Hegel undercut the sterile debate between 'individualism' and 'holism' in social ontology by arguing for three theses. (1) Individual human beings are fundamentally social practitioners, in the sense that, though naturally and physiologically grounded, any and all specific aims, desires, abilities, along with all of one's conceptual and practical resources, are developed and literally customised by and within the culture and community in which one grows, matures and is educated. (2) In these regards, one's community strongly conditions one's character, behaviour and self-understanding, although it cannot fully determine it. One's community provides opportunities, resources, recommendations, permissions and prohibitions, although any individual can and must determine him- or herself how to respond to present circumstances, needs, aims and so on. (3) Furthermore, Hegel argued that individuals and their communities are mutually interdependent: there are no social practitioners without social practices for them to learn and engage in; nor are their social practices without social practitioners, without individuals who learn, engage in *and who modify* them according to their changing needs and circumstances (including information). Hegel's unique social ontology may be called 'moderate collectivism'; Marx referred to it as our 'species-being' (*Gattungswesen*). Both views are consistent with 'methodological individualism', the view that all social phenomena must be understood in terms of the behaviour and dispositions of individuals and their relations.

Hegel's understanding of the human community as 'spirit' was deeply indebted to Montesquieu's *The Spirit of the Laws* (1748), which showed how law as a living institution is thoroughly integrated into the structure and functioning of a community. 'Spirit' in this sense includes the aims and aspirations of a community along with its particular structure, activities and procedures; these aims and aspirations may be only implicit in particular acts or expressions, and are not reducible to any specific subset of acts or expressions.

In connection with 'absolute' spirit and the historical development of human self-understanding and freedom, Hegel identified the Attic Greek community as 'immediate' spirit, because they could not justify their basic norms and principles rationally, hence they could not rationally resolve conflicts among them. Even Periclean Athens was built on an unstable mix of customary and positive law; the conflict between these was dramatically expressed in Sophocles' *Antigone*. Hegel's *Phenomenology of Spirit* attempts to show, among other things, that combining Kant's constructivist account of norms and their justification with Scottish political economy enables us to achieve a properly reflective, rationally sophisticated 'mediated' spirit befitting our modern condition as genuinely rational, autonomous social agents; his *Philosophy of Right* attempts to show how these principles and practices are or can be instantiated in modern society. Hegel's great lecture cycles on 'absolute spirit' attempt to integrate and celebrate the highest aspirations of humanity, as expressed in their most profound forms as art, religion and philosophy.

K. Westphal

SPIVAK, GAYATRI *See* Postcolonial Theory

STATE OF EXCEPTION (*Ausnahmezustand*) The key concept in Carl Schmitt's theory of sovereignty, it designates a civil state of emergency which calls for extraordinary measures. The states of siege and war count as preparatory forms to the state of exception.

In Schmitt's *The Dictatorship* (1921), the institution of dictatorship, which first appeared in the Roman Republic, is conceived as a state of exception. This form of dominance is instituted when the existence of the state is put into question for political reasons, either internal or international. The dialectic of dictatorship consists in negating a norm of law that it precisely has to preserve. From this there results the possibility of distinguishing norms of law from the actualisation of law. The historical occasion for a consideration of the state of exception of dictatorship, for Schmitt, is based on article 48 of the Weimar constitution. According to this law, the *Reichspräsident* was authorised to proclaim a dictatorship in case of a danger to the republic. In fact, this article was increasingly used until 1933 and was involved in Hitler's seizure of power.

In Schmitt's *Political Theology* (1922), the state of exception is the index of sovereignty. As every type of mastery involves decision, the decision over the state of exception is a decision in an eminent sense. Normal law cannot conceive of the radical exception and thus cannot really determine when an exception is given and when one is not. An exception, upon which a state of exception must follow, is a danger to the existence of the state. If this state of affairs is entered into, then this indicates political sovereignty. The sovereign, the one who calls forth states of exception and ends them, thus stands just as much outside as inside of the order of law. The genuine state of exception is entered into where an order of law is first founded.

In *Homo Sacer* (1995), Giorgio Agamben continues Schmitt's theory of the relationship between sovereignty and the state of exception. Agamben starts from Schmitt's concept of sovereignty in order to interpret what he calls the 'biopolitical' phenomenon of the concentration camps. In Agamben's diagnosis of our time, the state of exception of the camp is to be understood not as an historical datum, but rather as the model for an epoch of biopolitics which opened with modernity.

P. Trawny

STRATIFICATION The process of laying down strata or layers, as in the formation of sedimentary rocks. In *A Thousand Plateaus*, Deleuze and Guattari generalise this process, treating strata as a very broad class of ordered hierarchical systems not only in the inorganic domain, but also in the organic and social domains, where they are particularly associated with bureaucratic state apparatuses.

Strata arise immanently out of the flow of matter, as a kind of thickening, and do not presuppose any kind of prior organisation, except other strata. Deleuze and Guattari therefore abandon the familiar dualism of form and matter, even for their explanation of strata as ordered hierarchical systems. Instead they distinguish between two articulations, one of content and the other of expression, each of which is produced by means of quite distinct formed substances. On the organic stratum for instance, an organism is composed of proteins, forms of content whose molecular substances are amino acids. The form of expression of an organism, however, is nucleic acid, itself composed out of quite different molecular substances, nucleotides. Content and expression are really distinct from each other and expression does not represent or resemble content; but the two are in reciprocal presupposition, a relation that allows for mutually reinforcing feedback of a runaway kind, producing unexpected de- and reformations. The possibilities of such destratification, although built into the strata because of their immanence to the flow of matter, are covered over or enveloped by the slow pace of change within strata.

A. Welchman

STRAUSS, LEO (1899–1973) German political philosopher, whose work has influenced conservative thought both inside and outside the academy, particularly in the neo-conservative movement in the United States from the 1970s to the present. He received his doctorate under Cassirer and thereafter studied with Husserl and Heidegger. At the end of the 1930s fleeing National Socialism, he settled in the United States where he enjoyed a very influential career at the University of Chicago.

His work, which he decisively understands as 'political philosophy' as distinct from 'political science', is based upon intensive interpretations of the texts of Plato, Maimonides, Machiavelli, Hobbes, Spinoza and Rousseau, among others, and is guided by a precisely articulated hermeneutic. Strauss insists that philosophy's ability to articulate the essence of the political must be maintained against the claims of religion, science and history.

In *Spinoza's Critique of Religion* (1930), Strauss interprets Spinoza's *Tractatus theologico-politicus* as the first systematic expression of a tradition that begins with Epicurus' critique of the gods. Strauss shows to what extent Spinoza's rational critique of revealed religion allows him to question the necessity of religion for the state. Here we see Strauss's interest in natural law, which forms a thematic structure of philosophy, religion, science and politics found in every one of Strauss's texts.

In *Philosophy and Law* (1935), Strauss opposes the medieval rationalism of Maimonides to the modern rationalism of Judaism. He wants to reconcile the strife which arose between Orthodoxy and the Enlightenment since the seventeenth and eighteenth centuries (specifically in regard to the inherent atheism of the latter). By means of a specific interpretation of the major work of Maimonides, *The Guide for the Perplexed*, Strauss proposes a legal grounding of philosophy upon the Torah and revelation, just as there is a philosophical grounding of law. In this sense, according to Strauss, it should be possible to understand revelation in light of Platonic politics.

In *Natural Law and History* (1953), Strauss presents a vehement plea for natural law in comparison to the relativism and even nihilism which Strauss detects in the modern social and historical sciences. Natural law is a universal norm of law for human life as such. By taking into account the natural goals of the rational animal, natural law pronounces what is right by nature, but it can only provide such a norm of law when it maintains its independence from all historical conditions (including the ethnological). Historicism, by contrast, proceeds from the idea that all known norms of law are built upon specific historical presuppositions. In order to ground natural law, then, we need a type of knowledge that excludes relativism. For Strauss, this knowledge is found in the classical tradition of political philosophy.

What is Political Philosophy? (1954), in fact, distinguishes political philosophy from political thought, theory, theology and science. Strauss provocatively claims that political philosophy, as the most unbiased and comprehensive perspective upon it, is the authentic way to think about the political. Beyond this, political philosophy distinguishes itself from political science in that it is not value-free. Political philosophy for Strauss is thus the attempt to know both the essence of the political and the true or good political order.

P. Trawny

STRUCTURALISM A multi-disciplinary movement that dominated the intellectual scene in France and other parts of Europe in the middle part of the twentieth century. During its heyday in the 1950s and 1960s, structuralism promised scientific rigour to disciplines whose status as sciences had not been firmly or unequivocally established: primarily anthropology, psychoanalysis, sociology, literary studies, history, political science and philosophy, or in short most of what we generally call the humanities and the social sciences. What united researchers and writers under the banner of structuralism was really the insight that much of human culture and experience can be understood in terms of complex systems of signs, ruled by simple terms and laws that generate meaning or values within a particular context: linguistic, social, literary and so on. Structuralism is for this reason usually associated with semiology, or the science of signs and signification.

The word 'semiology' came into currency with Saussure's *Course in General Linguistics* (1906–11, published in 1916). Saussure saw linguistics as but one branch (albeit the principal one) of semiology, a totally new scientific discipline that would have as its task to 'investigate the nature of signs and the laws governing them'. Because Saussure had defined language as 'a system of signs expressing ideas', the study of language could be related to other such systems, such as 'writing, the deaf-and-dumb alphabet, symbolic rites, forms of politeness, military signals, and so on'. However, because Saussure's main concern was linguistics, he only sketched the outlines of what semiological research should comprise, and instead focused his own investigations on the signs that make up language.

Saussure opposed language as a scientific object of study (*langue*) to language in its concrete manifestations (*parole*, speech) and to language as the product of physical and physiological processes; his aim was to separate what was essential from what was contingent or ancillary. He therefore reduced language to a system of signs that link sound patterns (signifiers) and concepts (signifieds) in a way that liberated language from the expressive will of the speaking subject. From this starting point, he discovered a number of invariants or principles that govern the production and employment of meaningful signs. Saussure's insights paved the way for two major developments in the genesis of structuralism: the structural linguistics of Roman Jakobson and Nikolai Trubetzkoy of the so-called Prague School, and the work of Lévi-Strauss, who adopted and adapted the structuralist method in anthropology.

Lévi-Strauss is often regarded as the founder of classical structuralism, for the simple reason that by taking up Saussure's suggestive remarks about semiology and by applying the ideas of structural linguistics, he saw that 'in *another order of reality*, kinship phenomena are of the *same type* as linguistic phenomena' (from 'Structural Analysis in Linguistics and in Anthropology', 1945). In other words, Lévi-Strauss claimed that kinship relations (and not *just* kinship relations) were structured like Saussure's systems of signs, whose units have value only in the coordination of their mutual differences.

Barthes ranks with Lévi-Strauss as one of the main progenitors of structuralism. Barthes elaborated a semiological understanding of signification that complements Saussure's, in an attempt to demystify the everyday mythological 'languages' of wrestling, advertising, astrology, food and other cultural phenomena (*Mythologies,* 1957). But in this, his approach was not merely that of a cultural commentator; he was also concerned to draw out the ideological and political implications of literary and cultural signification in order to debunk the prejudices of a complacent bourgeoisie. Barthes was also in large measure responsible for refining the structuralist critique of the speaking subject; his seminal essay on 'The Death of the Author' (1968) explores the ways in which the primacy of language in Saussure's sense plays itself out in literary production.

Drawing heavily on Saussure, Jakobson and Lévi-Strauss – as well as on Freud –Lacan also pursued the structuralist themes of the primordiality of language and the critique of the subject. More precisely, Lacan stressed the metaphorical and metonymical play of signifiers to show how 'psychoanalytic experience discovers the whole structure of language in the unconscious' ('The Agency of the Letter in the Unconscious, or Reason since Freud', 1957). According to Lacan, the unconscious operates on the principles of condensation (linked to metaphor) and displacement (linked to metonymy), which explain how signifieds tend to 'slide' in an analysand's discourse or in dreams. The task of psychoanalysis is therefore to understand how the unconscious works with signifiers in order to interpret the actions and pronouncements of the speaking subject according to laws which are not of the subject's making, but which are proper only to language.

Althusser adhered to the structuralist demand for scientific rigour in his attempt to develop a form of Marxism that could appeal to transhistorical invariants in order to secure its status as a true science of human society. To this end, Althusser proposed 'a theory of ideology *in general* in the sense that Freud presented a theory of the unconscious *in general*' ('Ideology and Ideological State Apparatuses', 1970), that is a concept of ideology that transcends history and explains how we represent to ourselves our relationship to real conditions of existence. Among the many consequences of Althusser's theory is that ideology 'interpellates' subjects in the sense that individuals become social subjects only through Ideological State Apparatuses (the political system, religion, schools, the family and so on). In other words, ideology is the structure that informs how we become complacent and controlled by the state: '*There are no subjects except by and for their subjection*'.

Foucault is often associated with the history of structuralism, though he regarded his work as having little of substance in common with the thinkers usually grouped under the rubric. Nevertheless, his work is an attempt to articulate 'the unconscious of knowledge', or the abstract laws and institutional power structures that govern the history of knowledge and science beyond the scope of the individual subject, in a way that recalls the structuralist derogation of the speaking subject. For the early Foucault, it is the modes of discourse that evolve in history that allow individuals to take on social functions; toward the end of his life, Foucault extended this concern to ethics and the 'care of the self'.

I. Macdonald

SUBJECT A term with a broad range of senses in continental philosophy, being at once a logical, grammatical, epistemological and metaphysical notion. However, some unity in meaning can be found by looking at the etymology of the term. 'Subject' can be traced back to the Latin *subjectum*, which means literally that which is thrown underneath: *sub-jectum*. It thus indicates an underlying support and basis, a foundation. The logical and grammatical sense of 'subject' is that which provides the basis for predication and thus that which in turn cannot be predicated of something else. Metaphysically, the term 'subject' is thus synonymous with the 'substantial', a ground and foundation. As such, the concept of the 'subject' is intrinsically connected with neither the 'I' nor the self.

However, in the modern Cartesian and post-Cartesian era, the 'I think' became the true substrate, as Descartes established in the first two of his 'meditations'. Hence the term 'subject' came to designate the thinking 'I' in so far as this self becomes the new foundation for philosophical reflection. For Descartes, the ego as subject is what is certain, and the external world was rendered problematic. Post-Cartesian thought endeavoured to resolve this problem, and one sees in Kant and Hegel the attempt to have the subject encompass much more than a mere 'inner' sphere, and instead determine the whole of reality. With Kant, the subject thus becomes transcendental, which means that the subject is now the condition of possibility of objectivity itself, and no longer problematically cut off from it. Eventually in German Idealism, and in Hegel particularly, the subject is absolutised so as to become the totality of all that is as absolute Spirit.

This radical overcoming of the limits of finite subjectivity paradoxically led to the collapse of the subject, as if its absolutising amounted to its cancellation. Hence after Hegel, in various thinkers and in different ways, one can observe how the subject underwent an astonishing undoing, to the point of only appearing as a fiction, an empty word, an imaginary vapour. In Nietzsche, the subject is denounced as a lie, as what falsely pretends to be an underlying substrate, and is characterised as a grammatical habit, a fiction and an imaginary cause. Whether as a theoretical subject, as the underlying unity of self, or as a practical subject, through the imaginary free will, Nietzsche denounces the illusory character of the subject. The subject belongs to that list of great errors such as the error of identity, permanence, thinghood, unity and so forth and is now to be analysed in its genealogical provenance.

One could claim that much of contemporary continental philosophy attempts to come to terms with this Nietzschean challenge, and that the elaborations on the subject have been ways of rethinking a subject in crisis – to redraw its limits, as it were. In this regard, we will pay particular attention to Heidegger's ontological deconstruction of the subject, the displacement of the subject in psychoanalysis, and Levinas's stress on the ethical dimension of the subject, though the question of the subject is also very important to Foucault, Deleuze, Derrida and all feminist thinkers.

Heidegger's entire thought is an attempt to think what he calls the event of being, in its distinction from beings. With respect to such an enterprise, the motif of subjectivity, with its reliance on an ontology of substance and power, first appears as an obstacle to be overcome. Heidegger thus undertakes a destruction or deconstruction of the subject in order to reveal a more primordial element, that of being itself in its advent and call. However, once the subject is deconstructed, it nevertheless remains that being, as Heidegger says, 'needs' humans for its givenness. The subject is thus overcome in order to let another form of humanity emerge, which Heidegger names Dasein. The term Dasein, Heidegger tells us, is the subject ontologically understood. The subject is only one particular interpretation of the human being, and not the most primordial. Ultimately for Heidegger, the subject characterises only a moment in the history of being and of humanity.

For Lacan, the Freudian revolution consists in decentring the subject, from the conscious ego to the unconscious subject, or 'subject of the unconscious'. In this way the conscious subject is destituted so as to reveal unconscious psychical processes ignored by the ego. It also consists in revealing the dependency of the subject on the significance of language that operates at an unconscious level; Lacan is thus interpreting Freud's primary processes in light of Saussurean linguistics. As a linguistic being, the speaking subject, according to Lacan, is essentially a spoken subject, a subject that comes to itself in and through language, as a pre-existing treasure. However, as a linguistic being, the Lacanian subject can only appear henceforth as represented by a signifier, and thus radically alienated from its being. We are for Lacan only signifiers, places or anchoring points of a meaning always shifting, operating in a place unbeknownst to us, and which does not belong to us.

Levinas reverses the modern tradition of wilful subjectivity as well as the tradition of intentionality one still finds in a certain phenomenology. In such a reversal, Levinas seeks to manifest the ethical status of subjectivity. What Levinas stresses is that the subject, far from being that masterful agency of power described by modern philosophy, is in fact subject-ed to a call of the other to which it must respond as obligated. The subject is thus destituted or de-posed by the other, and thrown in an ethical relation to that other. According to Levinas, the other is accessible through the phenomenon of 'the face' (which is not a perceptual phenomenon but the appearance of the vulnerability and nakedness of the other). Levinas is then led to describe subjectivity in terms inverse to that of the modern tradition of will and agency: the subject is a 'hostage of the other'; the subject is 'persecuted' by the other; the subject is in the 'accusative' and not in the nominative; the subject can never initiate but only respond; and so on. Levinas's thought presents us with a finite subject assigned to an infinite other to whom the subject is infinitely obligated. The subject, far from constituting a sphere of ownness, in fact reveals an essential expropriated belongingness to the other and to alterity. The subject is a structure of hospitality, a welcome of the other.

F. Raffoul

SUBJECT, TOPOLOGY OF A mathematical formalisation by means of which Lacan hoped to transmit his theory unencumbered by the interferences that always appear in human communication, since everything, in any given algorithm, is totally transmissible and not subject to the loss that occurs in communicating in common language. The latest stage of Lacan's formalisation deals with the way by which the different orders (Real, Symbolic order, Imaginary order) are organised in any given human subject. As a model, he borrows the Borromean knot from knot theory.

To best understand this model, it is necessary to redefine the sets that will be tied together to represent the structure of the subject:

R   (the Real) = There is . . . that is nothing more can be affirmed of the unconscious, since we only partially know its content.

S   (the Symbolic order) = There is difference, that is there is a set of signifiers, which define themselves only through their relative and negative difference to each other.

I   (the Imaginary order) = There is similarity, that is there are
    signifieds, defined by the intersubjective play of projections and
    identification; through this play we define our signifieds: our ego,
    our consciousness, our representations, 'reality'.

Once the three sets are defined, we can represent them, as in set theory,
by three circles. These three circles, in their turn, can be materialised
by strings. The human psyche can then be written in a particular
Borromean combination of the three sets ('Conférences et entretiens
dans des universités américaines', *Scilicet*, 6–7, 1976).

   There are only two minimal conditions for this representation to
work: (1) every set has to be defined by properties unique to it, and (2)
if one string is cut, all strings are loosened, that is each set is
indispensable to the existence of every other set.

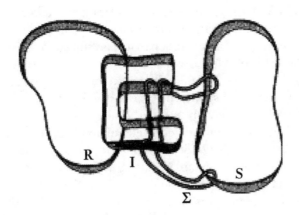

In this diagram: **R** = Real; **S** = Symbolic; **Σ** = Symptom; **I** =
Imaginary. To hold the three sets together, it is necessary to add a
fourth element: the symptom. The symptom is a signifier, more
precisely a metaphor, unthinkable outside a rhetoric of the unconscious, which produces the individual as a unique combination of the
three exigencies: 'The symptom is the peculiar notation of the human
dimension', Lacan states in the same text.

   For this last topology, Lacan claimed a particular status; stressing its
originality, he asserted that it was not a metaphor, a figuration or an
image but a real notation of the human psyche, the real being indexed
four times in the schema by the void: 'I am trying to constitute another
geometry, which would deal with the being of the chain. It has never,
never been done. This geometry is not imaginary; contrary to the one

of triangles, it is real; it is knots of strings' ('Séminaire de Caracas', 1980).

The fecundity and power of the Borromean representation of the subject can be best indicated by filling in the sets with a series of approximate synonyms and then establishing their respective relationships. For example, the set of the Real may comprise notions that are impossible to represent fully: truth, meaning, desire, femininity, God and singularity; the Imaginary set includes signifieds, representations ('reality') and particularities shared by a group of human beings; and the Symbolic set contains signifiers, the laws (of language, of society) and conceptual generalities. This is, however, only an indication of possibilities that cannot be developed in this space.

A. Leupin

SUPPLEMENT One of Derrida's 'undecidables' that concentrates on the way in which a system or structural arrangement fails, in spite of its attempts, to satisfactorily enclose itself. A supplement – the dictionary is a good example – is an addition that is presumed to remain within the ambit or orbit of what it is added to (a particular language), but it necessarily enlarges and alters that orbit and so in a sense redirects or supplants what it is supposed to be controlled by.

In French a single verb, *suppléer*, conveys both 'to supplement' and 'to supplant'. Supplementation is not an accident or the failure of the system but its very possibility. It is perceived as an accident because the operations of the system are presumed to originate from a controlling centre such that at a certain point one particular supplementary effect comes to be recognised as breaking out of that control when in fact such a breaking out was always – 'always already' – in effect, from the beginning, within the origin itself.

The supplement receives special attention in Derrida's analysis of Rousseau in *Of Grammatology* because he, as it were unknowingly, alternately uses the verb *suppléer* in one of its senses or the other. Derrida thereby effects a comparison between masturbation as the 'dangerous' supplement to coital sex that risks replacing it, and writing as the supplement to speech, occluding the structure whereby all sex is a type of self-stimulation or *auto-affection* and that all language is a type of writing.

D. Wills

SYMBOLIC EXCHANGE A term adapted by Jean Baudrillard, from the way certain anthropologists have theorised the gift, to mark what is incontrovertible, heterogeneous and subversively other to simulation and to logics of exchange, use and sign value.

Social and anthropological theory in the tradition of Marcel Mauss (*Essay on the Gift*, 1925) valorises the gift as an extra-material social relation beyond the reductive constraints of value, utility and contract. Baudrillard's radical anthropology in *Symbolic Exchange and Death* (1976) proposes a notion of death through select examples of initiation rites as symbolic counter-gifts that force modern institutions – unilaterally giving the gifts of work as slow death, social security and consumerism – to receive and respond in kind with their own deaths. The failure to receive the counter-gift and repay in kind is loss of face – spirit, wealth, health, rank and power. Baudrillard underlines that death is not biological but initiatic, a rite involving a reciprocal-antagonistic exchange between the living and the dead. Baudrillard extends this analysis to the desocialisation of the dead in the West, where it is not normal to be dead but rather chronically alive.

Baudrillard's controversial response to the events of September 11th 2001 in *The Spirit of Terrorism* (2002) rehearses his theory of symbolic exchange: the suicide planes that embedded themselves in the twin towers of the Word Trade Center were symbolic forces of disorder issuing counter-gifts of mass death against a hegemonic world power whose ideal is 'zero death' and which tries to neutralise any symbolic stakes. According to Baudrillard's poetic anthropology, the towers collapsed by themselves as if responding in kind to the challenge of the suicide planes.

G. Genosko

SYMBOLIC ORDER In Lacan's theory, the set of signifiers. Lacan gives to the concept of signifier a tremendous extension, since any object in the human sphere is marked by the primacy of language and thus conceived as a signifier. Also, he stresses the supremacy of the symbolic order: for him, it is the foundation and beginning of all psychic mechanisms. For example, the universal prohibition of incest (and hence the change for animal instinct to human desire) depends on its formulation through the symbolic order. Lacan posits the symbolic order's radical otherness by designating it as the Other, at first external to subject, then interiorised: 'The exteriority of the Symbolic order in regard to the person is the notion of the unconscious itself' (*Écrits*, 1966). The symbolic order determines the subject by its signifying chains, undermining the ego's autonomy. Indeed, the ego is submitted to a radical determinacy that it chooses to largely ignore.

The symbolic order is a universal characteristic of humanity; a group can be said to be human only if it is subordinated to a symbolic structure.

At the same time, this mark of humanity is specified according to linguistic groups: any existing language determines a symbolic order particular to a certain community. At the level of the symbolic order resides the broadest level of generality: this is where general statements can be made, where, through a given language, societies put their signifiers in common; this is where the superego and cultural constraints function.

This notion does not make sense per se, but only in relationship to the other sets distinguished by Lacan, the imaginary order and the Real, and only in the mapping out of their respective positioning in the 'topology of the subject'.

A. Leupin

SYNTHETIC A PRIORI JUDGEMENT A special form of knowledge, the possibility of which forms the basic question of Kant's 'transcendental' philosophy. The account of such judgements is prepared in the *Critique of Pure Reason* by a distinction between analytical and synthetic judgements. The former is explicative, with the predicate implicit to the subject, while the latter is ampliative, with the predicate adding something that was not present in the subject of the judgement. What is added is an a priori element that is independent of the subject of the judgement. Kant claims there are two such a priori elements, namely a priori intuitions and a priori concepts.

An answer to the question of the possibility of a priori synthetic judgements would have to prove that a priori intuitions and concepts indeed exist and can be synthesised. Such proofs are offered in the 'Transcendental Aesthetic' and the 'Transcendental Analytic' of the first *Critique*. The synthetic a priori judgement is shown to consist in the synthesis of intuitions and concepts, or the subsumption of a manifold of intuition under a concept of the understanding. In the case of both concept and intuition the a priori element is not simply added to the perception of an object, but is a condition for its very appearance. All experience is thus only possible as an a priori synthesis, hence the crucial significance of the question of a priori synthetic propositions for the transcendental philosophy as a whole.

H. Caygill

TAYLOR, CHARLES (1931–) Canadian philosopher and political theorist. Born and raised in Montreal, Taylor spent most of his twenties in England, where he studied philosophy at Oxford and was active in the New Left movement. (Taylor was one of the founding editors of the influential *New Left Review*.) Taylor's doctoral dissertation, subsequently published as *The Explanation of Behaviour* (1964), exposed the epistemological extravagances and empirical shortcomings of behaviourism, in a manner reminiscent of earlier work by Merleau-Ponty (whose influence on Taylor has been profound). The book was the first of many attacks on naturalism – roughly speaking, the view that the objective, disengaged perspective of the modern natural sciences (such as physics) has unrestricted validity. The main problem with this view, according to Taylor, is that it generates an overly rationalistic, atomistic and simplistically reductionist conception of the human world. While naturalism has the surface appearance of scientific rigour and impartiality, Taylor argues that it has deeper roots in a normative conception of the human subject, a conception moreover that naturalism is incapable of articulating for itself.

Naturalism is important for Taylor not so much because it is an unspoken yet dubious assumption of much academic discourse, but because it represents the dominant 'spiritual' outlook of modern technological civilisation. In Taylor's terms, it is a facet of the 'modern identity'. In *Sources of the Self* (1989), Taylor offers a genealogy of modern (Enlightenment) naturalism that is at the same time a diagnosis of the times. Taylor's account is complex, but the gist of it is that while naturalism is driven by values that few in the modern world would repudiate – such as the intrinsic worth of 'ordinary life', the reduction of needless suffering and the equal dignity of all human beings – it is blind to the 'expressive' aspirations of the modern subject (as articulated paradigmatically by Romanticism and post-Romantic thought) and it lacks the resources to show why even the values it does recognise ultimately matter. Developing ideas first presented in his book *Hegel* (1975), Taylor thus identifies an internal fracture or 'intramural conflict' within the modern identity and vulnerability in regard to its 'moral sources'. Departing from both critics of modernity such as Foucault and defenders of an unfinished project of modernity such as Habermas, Taylor suggests that recovery from the malaise must involve a retrieval of the full range of goods that make up the modern identity.

In his political philosophy, Taylor tries to spell out the conditions for realising the key modern good of freedom. He does this by way of a critique of rights-based and 'proceduralist' models of liberalism on the one hand, and exclusionary nationalist and Jacobin models of self-rule on the other. In this vein, Taylor has written influentially on the 'politics of recognition' and he has diagnosed some of the self-undermining tendencies of modern liberal democracies. More recently, the focus of Taylor's research has turned to secularism, social imaginaries and the idea of alternative modernities.

N. Smith

TECHNIQUES OF THE SELF A phrase Foucault coined to name ascetic or disciplinary practices through which individuals seek to alter themselves (their souls, bodies, thoughts, desires or conduct) in order to make their lives more beautiful or pure or happy, or to make themselves more able and worthy to exercise certain forms of power, or to prepare themselves for some future state such as unification with the Logos or ascension into heaven. Such practices seem to exist in most societies, Foucault asserts, although the goals they serve vary greatly. In *The Use of Pleasure* (1984) and *The Care of the Self* (1984), Foucault studied ancient Greek and Roman ascetic practices that were designed to cultivate self-mastery and enable citizens and heads of households to perform their governing roles more effectively. He maintains that through these projects of self-cultivation, the ancients were not adhering to any rigid ethical code but rather were engaged in the creation of styles or ways of life. While Foucault never advocates a return to the past, he does suggest that in the present day, as belief in any universal ethical code or moral law has weakened, people might fruitfully experiment with techniques of the self so as to create new ways of life. Foucault sometimes refers to techniques of the self as 'practices of freedom', contrasting them to disciplinary regimes that are imposed on people through institutional managerial forces. Techniques of the self serve to strengthen the self and so might help people resist the normalising powers in contemporary society that render individuals docile.

L. McWhorter

TECHNOLOGY, PHILOSOPHY OF Until the late twentieth century, technology was not a widely attractive philosophical topic. Even today, certainly in North America and to a somewhat lesser extent in the UK, Scandinavia and the rest of Continental Europe, the philosophy of technology is still typically regarded as either a small and not especially prestigious area of specialisation or an interest most appropriately handled in an institute or programme outside of philosophy.

The reasons for this situation are partly historical. In the modern West, Anglo-American empiricist, French Enlightenment and European positivist traditions typically see technology as either a neutral or mostly beneficial force for human progress, but one that needs proper linkage with modern science to realise its promise. For these traditions, science tells us what there is; technology employs this knowledge for our benefit. Technology is 'applied science', and the primary philosophical issues thus lie either before or after technology itself. First, we must have reliable science – and of course a 'philosophy of' science that explains what method guarantees the objectivity of its results. Next, we must decide what are our most desirable goals; hence, the need for 'ethics' (in the broad sense, including socio-political issues). With philosophy properly focused on these two central topics – that is what we can verifiably know and legitimately do – technology falls uninterestingly between them, understood simply as the totality of means for applying scientific knowledge to effectuate the natural and social relations that ethics prescribes.

Romantic and post-Hegelian continental traditions, at least at first glance, have always seemed less willing to treat technology as applied science, for they are less inclined to conceive all knowledge on the model of science, or to see the use of science as mostly a force for good. Suspicious of a reductive scientism and false historical optimism that lurks here, these traditions tend to give science a restrictive (theoretical/cognitive and instrumental) definition, defining it as expressive of only one kind of human interest. Further, to secure space for other values and interests (beauty and artistic creativity, the 'understanding' of self and others, socio-political liberation), they tend to interpret the social application of scientific rationality in critical or sometimes even dystopian terms rather than in the progressive or utopian manner characteristic of the empiricist and positivist traditions. Yet precisely by curbing the scope and function of science in this fashion, Romantic and post-Hegelian thinkers in their own way continue to make technology philosophically inessential. For if the real problem is to avoid overrating science in order to serve other, non-instrumental purposes, then technology – though now reconceived as potentially serving several masters – is still understood as essentially the 'mere means' for enacting chosen purposes.

By the 1970s, however, this inherited understanding of both science and technology was under attack from several directions. Most influential among its opponents were historians and sociologists of science and technology, together with various new philosophical movements – phenomenology, hermeneutics, neo-Marxism and critical social theory, feminism (especially second- and third-wave), as well as post-analytic and neo-pragmatist Anglo-American philosophy. Regarding science, the main new tendency was to insist that it be treated as an actual human practice to be studied in context – on the grounds that neither science itself, nor its allegedly formalisable 'method', nor the philosophy 'of' science, nor any axiology is ever rightly to be construed as neutral, ahistorical or 'objectively' above the fray in the way the modern ideal depicts them. All the newer movements, echoing the Romantic and post-Hegelian traditions, argue in various ways that failure to see the metaphysically and epistemologically selective, sociopolitically, culturally and historically determinate character of all human activities, including science, is serious misperception.

What is true of science and its philosophy is, of course, true also of technology and its relation to science. Despite the long-standing assumption, there really is no factual support for the idea that technology is a mostly modern or science-driven phenomenon. As historians of technology have always known, the urge to develop useful artifacts, to 'mechanise' human practices and even to express a sheer love of gadgetry are all massively present in human history from the very beginning, often as catalysts for profound social change. Moreover, there is plenty of evidence that the rise of science itself depended crucially upon the prior existence of devices whose invention in the Middle Ages owed nothing to science.

'Philosophy of technology', then, became a recognisable enterprise in precisely the same measure as traditional philosophy of science began to suffer decline. As befits a situation in which a family of similarly but not identically minded movements are simultaneously responsible for intellectual change, no unified vision of either post-positivist philosophy of science or philosophy of technology has been produced. It does seem clear, however, that all the boundaries between philosophical, social-scientific and engineering interests in science and technology have become thoroughly porous. Regarding the development of the philosophy of technology specifically, the best one can do is identify certain phases and trends.

Until quite recently, most of the various post-positivist movements have tended to consider the relation between contemporary technology and modern science primarily at a 'global' level. Indeed, except for those inspired by the 'applied ethics' model of analytic philosophy, there has been the widespread feeling that as pressing and immediate as the issues of, say, technology transfer, medical patients' rights and biotechnology in agriculture clearly may be, debates that stay at the level of these issues have the effect of silently perpetuating long-standing, deeply held, but now hotly contested general assumptions about the nature of science, about the technological appropriations of science and about the proper place of science and technology within the larger scope of human affairs. Some have argued that the scientific conception of knowledge is essentially Baconian and manifests a drive for power (Habermas, Foucault). In this connection, some have been especially concerned about the seeming inevitability of the way scientifically informed technological practices increasingly define the nature and direction of human life (Ellul, Wiener) and its political economies (Horkheimer and Adorno, Marcuse). Some link this trend specifically with reductive conceptions of human intelligence (Dreyfus) or a fundamental disrespect for nature (Naess) that may also involve an equally deep-seated male gender bias (Merchant, Haraway). Others argue that even the ancient human concern for 'making' already anticipates the very development and eventual dominance of science itself (Marx, Heidegger, Mumford, Arendt, some pragmatists). Obviously, such issues simply cannot be addressed adequately if they are permitted to arise only between the lines in discussions focused primarily on issues of how to control, modify or conceptually clarify this or that specific political, ethical, aesthetic or engineering problem.

The *locus classicus* for many of these global studies is Heidegger's essay, 'The Question Concerning Technology' (1954), which presents what is probably the single most influential (though not, of course, a universally favoured) position in the field. In this famous essay, Heidegger considers what it is like to be 'in the midst' of our technological existence. He concludes that for the most part, our activities, the things we deal with and even we ourselves all seem to happen together in a world where everything is 'enframed' – that is, disclosed and understood as part of a 'standing-reserve' of materials and personnel available for technological purposes. He argues that only by reflecting on the very occurrence of this enframing might we open up the possibility of taking a 'free relation with technology' in which our technological engagements do not close us off from non-instrumental possibilities.

Heidegger's work was certainly not the only catalyst for exploration of these themes; but it is useful to see much recent work as one of three possible reactions to its outlook. One response, of course, is to continue working out, holistically/globally, the ontological, epistemological and socio-political consequences of the enframing situation itself (Reiner Schürmann, *Heidegger on Being and Acting*, 1987; Dominique Janicaud, *Powers of the Rational*, 1995). A second option is to explore in greater detail what it is to 'be with' technology. For some, this means working out countervailing possibilities more or less against the background of Heidegger's view of enframing (Albert Borgmann, *Holding on to Reality*, 1999; *Crossing the Postmodern Divide*, 1992; *Technology and the Character of Contemporary Life*,

1984). Others complain that Heidegger's global pessimism leads him, quite unphenomenologically, to overemphasise the negative experiences of being-with-technology (Don Ihde, *Bodies in Technology*, 2002; *Technology and the Lifeworld*, 1990). A third option is to develop political and social programmes that facilitate the transformation from the chained to the free relation with technology of which Heidegger speaks (Andrew Feenberg, *Questioning Technology*, 2003; Charles Spinosa et al., *Disclosing New Worlds*, 1997; Donna Haraway, *Modest_Witness@Second_Millennium.   FemaleMan©_Meets_Onco-Mouse™*, 1997; Lorenzo Simpson, *Technology, Time, and the Conversations of Modernity*, 1995).

What is noticeable in all these trends, however, is their steady enrichment of topics that are taken as included in any philosophical conception of contemporary 'technoscientific' life. Indeed, one strain of recent thought has actually identified this tendency as a praiseworthy 'empirical turn' in recent philosophy of technology (Hans Achterhuis (ed.), *American Philosophy of Technology*, 2001). Here – quite plausibly and for both North America and Western Europe – the continental movements of phenomenology, hermeneutics and critical social theory are depicted as converging with the social studies of science movement (Latour, Pickering, Bijker and Pinch) and the pragmatist tradition (Larry Hickman, *Philosophical Tools for a Technological Culture*, 2002) in a thoroughly interdisciplinary programme of 'technoscience studies'. Whether this marriage also foreshadows an eclipse of the more global critiques of technoscientifically saturated culture remains to be seen.

R. Scharff

See also: Ecocriticism; Environmental Philosophy; Nature, Philosophy of

TELEOLOGICAL JUDGEMENT The focus of the second part of Kant's *Critique of Judgement*, it explains an event in terms of 'final cause' or that for the sake of which it took place. It corresponds to the fourth of Aristotle's four causes – material, formal, efficient and final – and was largely supplanted by material and efficient cause in modern philosophy. Kant, however, sought to determine a limited field for the legitimate use of such judgements, seeking to justify such judgements as supplements to the determinate conceptual judgements of Newtonian physics. They are to serve as 'regulative principles' for the extension of knowledge, but not as objects of knowledge themselves. Teleological judgement must not introduce ends into nature, but can use the concept of an end for framing hypotheses that may extend the bounds of knowledge in terms of mechanical causality. In the third

Critique Kant correspondingly tries to sketch out the limits of the legitimate uses of teleological judgement and to distinguish them from their fallacious or dialectical applications.

In Kant's practical philosophy the concept of end plays an important role in explaining the will's determination to act. Moral judgements are defined almost by definition in terms of ends, but this does not make them strictly speaking teleological judgements, since ends serve as determinants of the will rather than as full explanations of given actions. Nevertheless, this affinity with teleology underlies Kant's teleological view of the 'ultimate end' of nature as the integration of human freedom and natural laws through culture.

H. Caygill

TELEOLOGICAL SUSPENSION OF THE ETHICAL A phrase coined by Kierkegaard for Abraham's willingness to sacrifice Isaac. Such willingness transgresses the universal ethical prohibition against murder. Yet Abraham was called by God, and so his suspension of the ethical thus had a higher ('teleological') justification. Kierkegaard is deeply aware that this could be used to justify any crime or antisocial act; only an exceptional individual could do such a thing. He set stringent conditions for such an exception: he must love the universal and accept its condemnation of his act. If, like Kierkegaard himself, he breaks a marriage contract he must not do so because he despises marriage and he must accept his guilt towards those he has ethically wronged. This problem haunted the nineteenth century. In Dostoevsky's *Crime and Punishment*, the murderer, though seeing himself as an exception, seeks to justify his act in utilitarian terms. In the doctrine of suicide preached by Dostoevsky's fictional nihilist Kirillov, the utilitarian element is removed, and the breaking of the prohibition is embraced as an assertion of an individual's absolute right over his own life. Nietzsche seeks to free the exception from any residual religious and ethical guilt; the strong have no law but the law they give themselves. If such acts require any justification at all, it must be aesthetic, not ethical. Lukács used the example of Abraham to justify his revolutionary communist acceptance of murder as a political means. For Sartre, the very idea of universal ethical requirements has fallen away and each individual is continually in the situation of having to create his own values.

G. Pattison

THOUGHT The question of thinking is a central question for twentieth-century continental philosophy; Deleuze calls it the 'arrow' shot

by Heidegger. Although Husserl had already turned philosophy towards thought when he defined consciousness as a correlation between
noesis and noema (literally, between thinking and thought-object), it is
indeed Heidegger who makes the question of thinking urgent. In his
1951–2 lecture course *Was heisst denken?* (*What is Called Thinking?*),
Heidegger seeks an answer to this complicated question, which entails
all the following: What does thinking mean? What calls for thinking?
What calls us to think? What directs thinking? Heidegger claims that
what calls for thinking, that is what is most thought-provoking, is that
we are not yet thinking. With this answer Heidegger shows that
thinking is not what we normally think it is: conscious mental activity
accessible by psychological self-reflection and expressed in propositions. With this negative definition of thinking, we can see that
Heidegger has broken with the Western tradition. Earlier, as with
Aristotle, the purest form of thought (*nous*) was concerned to think
itself. But with Heidegger thought is no longer defined by self-
reflection; it no longer thinks the same; it thinks what is other than
itself. Later, as with Descartes, thought was a natural ability possessed
by us as soon as we are conscious; it was a foundation guaranteeing the
certainty of our being. But with Heidegger thought is no longer defined
as a natural ability; it is no longer a foundation; thought happens to us
as a gift coming from existence itself.

So far, we have only a negative definition of thought. What then is
thinking? Heidegger tells us that it is 'memory' understood as that
which 'gathers up' what lies before us. This 'gathering up' is original
truth (in ancient Greek, *aletheia*). The 'gathering' (*Versammlung*) of
truth is central to Heidegger's thought in general. When Heidegger's
'arrow' reaches France in the 1960s, it is precisely this idea of
'gathering' that is questioned. Instead of gathering, we have multiplicity, which is probably the central concept of this philosophical
moment (1968 in France). How does multiplicity function within
thought?

Deleuze is clearest here. He criticises what he calls 'the natural image
of thought', which consists of two parts. On the one hand, there is
common sense, the received opinions (*doxa*) through which we naturally think, what 'everybody knows'. On the other hand, there is good
sense, the belief that everyone wants the truth and can get it. It is
correct thinking (*ortho-doxa*). Because the natural image of thought
consists in common opinions and in the truth, the natural image of
thought, for Deleuze, is indeed an image; it is copied from common
opinions and corresponds to the way things are. Even philosophical
thinking – as we can see in Kant and Husserl – is merely copied from

common opinions (*Urdoxa*). Being an image anchored in something else, natural thinking never produces anything new. In contrast, for Deleuze – but this true for Derrida and Foucault as well – thinking begins with *para-doxa*. Strangely, by starting from *para-doxa* (literally, that which is against opinion), the French philosophy of the 1960s (despite being an anti-Platonism) remains faithful to the Platonic inspiration for philosophy, which consists in escaping from *doxa*. In any case, as with Heidegger, with Deleuze thinking happens to us, and it happens when we undergo an ordeal (*une épreuve*). This ordeal is a sensation that cannot be sensed, for example the sensation of a blinding light. Because it cannot be sensed, it is precisely what cannot be thought. Thought always begins with the experience of powerlessness.

And here, with 'impuissance', Deleuze, Derrida and Foucault take their inspiration from both Maurice Blanchot and Antonin Artaud: we experience the powerlessness of thinking as an imperative to think and that imperative calls forth memory. Relying now on Proust, Deleuze claims that involuntary memory brings back many memories. In fact, it brings back so many that one could go mad or become stupid. That is why, for Deleuze, involuntary memory is not sufficient for thought. There must be voluntary memory, in which one works on the memories. Like the production of a novel, thinking produces something new. At times Deleuze calls the 'new' an idea and at other times a concept; in Foucault it is a statement, in Derrida an undecidable. We can speak of an undecidable concept because for Deleuze, Derrida and Foucault memory is a multiplicity. It contains no single origin or original – this lack of an origin is why Foucault calls this memory a 'counter-memory' – and the thought that it produces is not an image. Thought is imageless. But precisely because memory is a multiplicity, a clamour as Deleuze would say or a murmur as Foucault would say or voices as Derrida would say, the new concept is a variation that unifies disjunctively. The concept therefore is a dispersion.

For example, in Foucault, we have the concept of a battle between words and things; *Les mots et les choses* (words and things) is the original French title of what we have in English as *The Order of Things*. Why, in *The Archaeology of Knowledge*, does Foucault say that this title is ironic? With the phrase 'words and things', we have a very traditional opposition, which could just as well be expressed as saying and showing, naming and figuring, representing and stating, and so on. To say that there is a battle between them means indeed that we have opponents, even a duality, the French *or* the Prussians. No single strategy (no principle or *arche*) dominates the field because of this disjunction; there is no unity or gathering. But the battle also means that we have many combatants crossing the field and many attacks, many arrows shot. The many attacks make it impossible to decide who is French or who is Prussian, who is a word or who is a thing. The undecidability between words and things makes the title ironic. And yet, despite the undecidability, there is one formation, one layout (Deleuze and Foucault would say one *dispositif*), which produces more and more variation. With this idea of indefinite variation, we can see that, shot across the twentieth century, Heidegger's arrow has traveled far. Thought no longer concerns truth; it concerns the production of the new. And thus the arrow always demands to be shot again.

L. Lawlor

THROWNNESS (*Geworfenheit*) A term which in Heidegger's *Being and Time* designates one of the three basic structures of Dasein, also referred to as existentials. Existence is being-in-the-world, but being-in-the-world is itself a complex, threefold phenomenon. Dasein is always projecting itself towards a number of possibilities, and ultimately (which also means from the start) towards its own death, so that it is 'being-toward-death'. But Dasein also exists as 'thrown' in the world, in so far as it does not and cannot choose to be thrown in this or that way. This is the unsurpassable 'factical' dimension of existence, in which the world is disclosed to Dasein in a distinctive way, or in which Dasein finds itself 'attuned' to the world: as thrown into the world, I am disclosed to myself as well as to the world primarily through passive affects or dispositions (fear, anxiety, boredom, joy and so on).

M. de Beistegui

TIME In so far as time and its theoretical and practical modes – duration and eternity, mortality and immortality – are among the central concepts of the entire Western philosophical tradition, their importance in continental philosophy is assured. Since almost all the philosophers in this tradition have reflected on time, a comprehensive treatment cannot be attempted, and so we will present a highly selective treatment.

We begin by treating Kant in a strictly modern context, even though his relation to the ancients, like that of all the thinkers discussed in this article, was crucial. Striving to undercut both rationalists like Leibniz and Wolff, for whom time is a confused perception of a rational order, and empiricists like Locke, for whom time is a simple reflection on the facts of the succession of psychological states, in the *Critique of Pure Reason* (1781, 1787) Kant granted time both empirical reality (it necessarily accompanies our experience) and transcendental ideality (it is nothing in itself, but is only a condition of our experience). For Kant, time is a framework, a 'pure form of intuition': along with space, it coordinates our sensible intuitions. As such, time is the form of inner sense: all our experience, even non-spatial inner psychological experience, ineluctably occurs in time. The temporal orderings of appearances are rendered precise in the schemata, which are temporal 'translations' of the categories, the concepts of the understanding. By such temporal determination, schematised categories are able to determine intuitions, and in so doing they determine the limits of human knowledge, which is possible only to the extent that an intuition can be brought under a schematised category. In one of the most famous moves in Western philosophy, however, Kant offers a practical supplement to several now illegitimate objects of theoretical knowledge: God, the world and the soul. Kant tells us in the *Critique of Practical Reason* (1784) that along with the assumption of God as the moral author of the world, the assumption of 'immortality' is necessary to conceive of a fulfilment of the moral law, after which we can only strive in the time allotted to us on earth.

Although space and time are inseparable concepts, Kant asserts the subjective priority of time, as form of inner sense, over space, which is, along with time, one of the forms of outer sense. We will see this priority of time over space repeated with Heidegger, or more precisely the priority of Dasein's temporality over its spatiality. The bond of space and time is, however, for Hegel more intimate than for perhaps any philosopher prior to Derrida. For Hegel, time is, in nature, the 'truth of space'. In the *Encyclopedia* (1817, 1827, 1830), in the *Philosophy of Nature*, after the full concretion of the Idea at the end of the *Logic*, we find the pure self-othering of the Idea into pure abstract exteriority. The first and simplest natural exteriority is space, a pure exteriority which necessitates a determination by a self-negation in the point. The point negates and retains itself in lifting itself into the line, and the line in turn becomes the plane. Time is the 'truth' of space, the 'for itself' of the self-negations of point, line and plane. As the 'for itself' of negation, the being of time lies in its non-being, and time is thus 'intuited becoming', the transition between being and non-being. While there is in one sense a directionality to time, from not yet to no longer, in another sense time is simply a series of identical nows, and as a set of exteriorised identities, time is identical to space. The identity of space and time is place, and the movement of the immanent breakdown of natural concepts continues through motion and matter.

Beyond this somewhat tortured metaphysical treatment, Hegel's reflection on the temporality or historicality of human cognition and experience is perhaps the most noteworthy and influential aspect of his philosophy: 'Philosophy', he says in the preface to the *Philosophy of Right* (1821) 'is its own time raised to the level of thought'. In the *Phenomenology of Spirit* (1807) Hegel showed the way in which different historical epochs had different categorical structures resulting in different fundamental 'experiences'. Hegel also showed how these transcendental categorical changes occur in practice, not just in cognition. Thus he thought he had unified the theory–practice split in Kant.

Following Kant and Hegel, the nineteenth century saw a rich series of reflections on temporality and historicality from philosophical thinkers as diverse as Kierkegaard, Marx and Dilthey. The development of historicised biology is of course inseparable from the figure of Darwin, and debates over thermodynamics, entropy and the 'arrow of time' were among the most prominent scientific and cultural issues of the day. Let us reluctantly reserve these questions for another treatment, and resume our philosophical narrative with Nietzsche, for whom two temporal issues are primary. One is the theoretical issue of the privilege of being over becoming. This theoretical concern is translated into the ethical issue of the eternal return. Those stricken with resentment are tortured by the past, with which they can never be done and which constantly comes back to them in the form of memories of their injuries. The past is thus a monstrous weight of being that never becomes anything else. By contrast, the noble person can forget, and in so doing, shrugs off the weight of being and opens the door to self-overcoming, the prime example of which is the ability to affirm the eternal recurrence of all things in their ceaseless becoming.

Next, let us consider Bergson, whom one can consider in the 'vitalist' tradition of Nietzsche and Dilthey. Bergson's thought was neglected for a large part of the twentieth century, but is now being rehabilitated, perhaps due to interest in Deleuze, who, as we will see, incorporates Bergson's thought of the pure past in his own philosophy of time. For Bergson in *Time and Free Will* (1889) the key to thinking time is to criticise the way it is imaged as a line. Bergson proposes the notion of 'duration' as the only adequate way of thinking our lived time, which is 'intensive' (indivisible), rather than 'extensive' (divisible). In *Matter and Memory* (1896) Bergson introduces a notion of the pure past, a 'past which has never been present', but which always conditions the present, with which it coexists and causes to pass. The present is then only the most contracted degree of the past which coexists with it, forming a 'cone'; memory in the form of 'pure recollection' accesses a 'virtual' object which is actualised in reaching a specific level of this past. In *Creative Evolution* (1907) Bergson uses the notion of the *élan vital* as breaking open a future in which genuine novelty is possible, while in *Duration and Simultaneity* (1922) he criticises Einstein for having spatialised time once again by overlooking the difference between virtual and actual multiplicities.

One of the most important investigations of time in continental philosophy is produced by Husserlian phenomenology. For Husserl, echoing Kant, time consciousness is the most primordial and fundamental of all structures of consciousness. Unlike Kant's search for universal and necessary conditions to which objects must conform, Husserl begins his reflection with the concrete ego and through the reductions isolates the transcendental structures of intentionality and time-consciousness that result in the temporal constitution of objects and of the flow of conscious states. In the *Lectures on the Phenomenology of Internal Time-Consciousness* (1928) Husserl describes the form of all acts as the 'living present', which is built up of primal impression, retention and protention. In a move upon which Derrida will fasten, Husserl distinguishes recollection and retention, so that what appears in the concrete living present, including the contents of retention (which is said to be continuous with primal impression), is perceived, while it is this whole living present that is re-presented in recollection. The primal impression of the living present springs up again new, and the whole of perceived time slides along, as the former impressions are retained along with former retentions, which tail off and sink away. Thus we can describe a 'double intentionality' at work in time-consciousness. A 'transverse' intentionality constitutes temporal objects, while a 'longitudinal' intentionality allows time-constitution to appear to itself in a 'primordial consciousness'. The process by which new primal impressions are generated, however, the ultimate level of time-generation, is described by Husserl, bowing to the fear of an infinite regress, as atemporal. About this 'absolute subjectivity', Husserl says, 'all names are lacking', although we do seem able to say something of its paradoxical nature, both mobile and immobile. Finally, we can also talk about the construction of 'objective time', which possesses fixed positions and does not slide in the way perceived time does, and is made possible by re-presentation.

The description of internal time-consciousness is not the only aspect of Husserl's philosophy of interest to a discussion of time. A fundamental tension in Husserl is that between structural, or static, and genetic phenomenology. Static phenomenology investigates the constitution of stable objects in the temporal flow of consciousness, while genetic analyses describe the history of the ego and its constituting habits. Finally, Husserl's description in the *Crisis of the European Sciences* (1936) of the historicity of the life-world and of the constitution of scientific objects out of the life-world is also relevant to us. The establishment of scientific objectivity is a historical European project for Husserl, beginning with the Greeks. In modernity, however, science has entered a 'crisis' whereby it has lost its meaning for the culture as a whole, necessitating the reactivation, by a 'return inquiry', of the origins of science buried beneath cultural sedimentation, the taking for granted of established truths. Sedimentation is not always to be despised, however, for in a highly developed science like geometry the manipulation of symbols whose grounding one takes for granted is the condition for progress.

Certainly one of the most important works of the continental tradition, Heidegger's *Being and Time* (1927) establishes its author as a prime figure in our narrative. For Heidegger, time is the transcendental horizon for the question of the sense of Being. The temporal recapitulation of the existential analytic of Dasein culminates in the analysis of Dasein's temporality, in which Heidegger claims to break with the entire history of presence-focused 'metaphysics' in prioritising the future. The line of nows is only an abstraction and derivation from Dasein's temporality, characterised as a 'future that makes present in the process of having-been'. The rejection of the straight line model and the priority of the future will mark all of continental philosophy after Heidegger.

In the 1930s Heidegger developed a notion of the 'history of being', in which 'basic words' uttered in classic philosophy texts or poetry are clues to the fundamental experience of being in an age, a notion also described in politically charged terms of the 'destiny' of a 'people'. This notion of historically different categorical structures hearkens back to Hegel and forward to the early Foucault, with the key difference that in *Madness and Civilisation* (1961) Foucault will not only read philosophy and poetry but also obscure practical manuals in trying to elucidate the historically different categorical structures of the experience of madness.

We can note two developments of Heidegger's thought of temporality by other thinkers at mid-century. In *Time and the Other* (1947), Emmanuel Levinas proposes a generation of temporality through contact with the other, which breaks open the generation of nows by the individual and creates the openness to the future. In *The Human Condition* (1958), Hannah Arendt proposes an analysis of political temporality grounded in 'natality', the ability of humans to produce novelty, and in the ability to bind ourselves to future action through promises.

Derrida tackles time in Husserl in *Speech and Phenomena* (1967) and in Heidegger in 'Ousia and Grammè' (1968), two of his most important early works. In these and other works, Derrida develops the notion of *différance* as 'differing and deferring', as the 'becoming time of space and the becoming space of time'. In his work on practical and political philosophy, Derrida develops a moving meditation on love, death, memory and mourning in *Memoires: for Paul DeMan* (1986), showing that the necessary possibility of mourning that inaugurates friendship (I can only be friends with a fellow mortal) occurs in an absolute past that vitiates the living present: 'everything that we inscribe in the living present of our relation to others already carries, always, the signature of *memoirs-from-beyond-the-grave*'. Derrida's work on politics in the 1990s builds on the solidarity of mortals in thinking the futurity of justice and democracy, which are always 'to come' ('à-venir', a play on the French 'avenir', or 'future').

After Derrida, let us next consider Deleuze, who treats three syntheses of time in *Difference and Repetition* (1968), relying upon Hume, Bergson and Nietzsche respectively. The first synthesis is a passive synthesis of the living present. This synthesis of 'habit' is not psychological or subjective, but is comprised of 'organic syntheses' that we do not operate, but that 'we are'. The second synthesis is that of 'memory', of the Bergsonian pure past, while the third synthesis, 'the pure and empty form of time', is that of the future, a rereading of the notion of eternal recurrence in Nietzsche which emphasises the openness to novelty: 'only that which is different returns'. In *Logic of Sense* (1969) Deleuze returns to the Stoics to distinguish Chronos, or the actual time of the everyday, and Aion, or the time of the virtual. In the virtual realm 'events' or 'singularities' inhere and as it were lie in wait for bodies to come upon them. Singularities are actualised in states of affairs when bodies reach certain thresholds in their composition of forces: in this context Deleuze likes to quote Joe Bousquet: 'my wound existed before me; I was born to embody it'.

Let us conclude our discussion with a consideration of feminist analyses of time. Beginning with Beauvoir's analysis of the gendered future of the 'project', feminist work has produced challenging readings of the way time has been previously conceptualised; the relegation of women to space and/or place (the maternal nature of the *chora* brought forth by Plato in the *Timaeus* is often cited in this context), and subsequent exclusion from a time reserved for masculine endeavour, has been a special focus. In 'Women's Time' (1979), Julia Kristeva juxtaposes the 'cyclical' and 'monumental' mythological times that, based on reproduction, have been the basis for women's subjectivity, with the entry into linear historical time desired by the first generation of feminists. The second, post-1968, generation of feminists, Kristeva writes in passages not entirely devoid of polemic, desired the affirmation of women's radical difference from men and hence abjured linear historical time. A third, new, generation is now appearing, Kristeva claims, which has the task of reconciling all three forms of 'women's time'. Testifying to the need to rethink the relations of space and time, Kristeva specifies that 'generation' is 'less a chronology than a *signifying space*, a both corporeal and desiring mental space'.

Finally, Luce Irigaray's investigations of the topology of sexual difference always include references to time and space-time, especially with regard to creating a positive notion of the temporality of generation, contra its masculinist capture in the notion of the (circular) reproduction of the species. For example, in 'The Limits of the Transference (1981)', Irigaray writes: 'Woman must . . . give birth within herself to mother and daughter in a never-completed progression'. This interior giving birth is 'a story to do with time and the way we measure it'. But, Irigaray concludes, the time is not yet ripe for all to accept affirmatively generation as the 'gift of space-time'.

J. Protevi

TOTALITY A notion taken up by Levinas from Rosenzweig's characterisation of Hegelian Spirit as an 'All-One' that encompasses everything, leaving nothing exterior to thought. Similarly, the Husserlian thesis according to which every object is 'constituted' by consciousness and the Heideggerian thesis that every relationship to beings is a relation to them in their being suggest, for Levinas, a philosophical tradition which construes every relationship as mediated by the structures of the ego's consciousness and its modes of existing. This leaves no place for an unmediated relation to the other person which would be an 'experience' of the other in his or her absolute otherness. Western philosophy, on Levinas's view, has thus most often been an ontology that reduces difference to sameness. The 'face-to-face relation' (*rapport face-à-face*) serves Levinas as the singular instance of a relation whose terms do not form a totality, that is as an instance in which it is possible for the ego to be in a relation to an other without first subsuming the other under a concept, constituting it in consciousness, or comporting toward it on the basis of a prior understanding of the world (in the Heideggerian sense). The possibility of a relation to the other as an exteriority or as non-encompassable within the totality is necessary, on Levinas's view, for the possibility of ethics.

D. Perpich

TRANSCENDENTAL ANALYTIC The analysis, in Kant's *Critique of Pure Reason*, of the faculties of reason and understanding. The contents of the first *Critique* are divided into two main sections: the 'Transcendental Doctrine of the Elements' and the 'Transcendental Doctrine of Method'. Most of the argument is confined to the former, which is in turn divided into two main parts – the 'Transcendental Aesthetic' and the 'Transcendental Logic'. The first is dedicated to the analysis of the a priori forms of intuition – space and time – the latter to the elements of judgement. The Transcendental Logic is in turn divided into two parts, the 'Transcendental Analytic', followed by the exposure of the dialectical inferences of the metaphysical sciences of psychology, cosmology and theology in the 'Transcendental Dialectic'.

The task of the Transcendental Analytic is to provide a 'touchstone' or 'canon' for truth by providing 'rules for the exposition of appearances'. This is accomplished by means of an analysis of the faculties of reason and the understanding into their elements. The elements of the understanding may be divided into 'concepts' and 'principles'. The analysis of concepts yields the table of twelve a priori pure concepts of the understanding, the most basic elements of the judgements that make up experience. The principles, on the other hand, comprise the corresponding elements that permit the concepts of the understanding to be related to the spatio-temporal conditions of sensibility.

Kant's ambitions for the 'Transcendental Analytic' were very great. He regarded it as the successor to ontology – the 'general metaphysics' or pure reason that preceded the critical philosophy. The analytical scrutiny of the conditions of the possibility of experience took the place of ontology's exposition of being in general and prepared the way for the critique of the 'special metaphysics' of psychology, cosmology and theology carried out in the 'Transcendental Dialectic'.

H. Caygill

TRANSCENDENTAL DIALECTIC The part of Kant's *Critique of Pure Reason* in which he demonstrates the 'illusory' nature of metaphysical claims.

The dominant conception of the metaphysics in eighteenth-century Germany was elaborated by Christian Wolff, whose works provided the model for the 'pure reason' under critique in Kant's *Critique of Pure Reason*. Wolff regarded metaphysics as made up of a general metaphysics devoted to being in general or ontology followed by the three branches of special metaphysics devoted to the objects of God, the World and the Soul – namely theology, cosmology and psychology. In the first *Critique* Kant 'replaces' Wolff's ontology – an account of being based on the principle of non-contradiction – with the 'Transcendental Analytic' or the exposition of the spatio-temporal limits of experience. This is followed by the critique of the three sciences of 'special metaphysics' (theology, cosmology, psychology) in the 'Transcendental Dialectic'.

If the Transcendental Analytic offers a 'touchstone of truth', the Dialectic proceeds to a 'critique of dialectical illusion'. The necessary illusions in question arise from the transformation of the formal conditions for thinking absolute wholes (that is, wholes that lie beyond the limits of space and time) into supposedly existing objects, namely God, the universe and the soul. This procedures amounts to a conferral of being upon what for Kant are but the 'principles' and 'maxims' of the use of reason, namely that you must think to the completion of a series of syllogisms. But claiming that an existing object corresponds to the completion of a series of syllogisms pushes knowledge beyond the spatio-temporal limits of experience and hence generates dialectical inferences. Kant exposes the dialectical character of such inferences by showing that (1) theology must resort to ideals in its reasoning; while (2) cosmology falls into antinomies – equally plausible but contrary inferences concerning the universe; and (3) psychology relies on paralogism, or the fallacy of inferring the truth of a prior from a consequent premise – the unity of the 'I think' being used to infer the existence of a substantial and self-identical soul.

Although both the second and third *Critiques* possess sections on 'dialectical' practical and aesthetic or teleological inferences, these lack the focus of the 'Transcendental Dialectic' of the first *Critique*. On the whole they are confined to exposing the dialectical character of claims about practical and aesthetic or philosophy rather than forming an integral part of the critique of the contents of these philosophies as is the case with metaphysics in the *Critique of Pure Reason*.

H. Caygill

TRANSCENDENTAL EGO (1) That which grounds the act of self-consciousness, which for Fichte serves as the first principle of his philosophy. Fichte's theory is derived from Kant's notion that self-consciousness underlies our experience of objects. However, Kant left the nature of the relationship between experience and self-consciousness quite loose: the experience of objects only needs to conform to the conditions under which an experience of self is possible. That is, we are aware of objects only in so far as we can be aware of ourselves being aware of objects. Fichte thought the relationship was much more direct, indeed genetic. He believed that the conditions for object-consciousness – and, indeed, objectivity itself – can be exhaustively deduced from the act of self-consciousness. This is a form of idealism because it entails that the transcendental ego is the source of all reality. At the same time, Fichte's transcendental ego is not personal or finite. Since it makes experience possible it cannot itself be a feature of experience. It is known through transcendental deduction, not direct experience.

This transcendental ego also grounds moral action. It is self-determining, having nothing external to itself that might determine it and thus constrain its freedom. In determining itself, it creates a not-I as a foil or self-limitation. This accounts for the finitude of our empirical egos; at the same time, it is the moral duty of finite egos to forever strive to overcome this source of heteronomy. Our moral ground and destination is the infinite freedom of the transcendental ego.

J. Norman

TRANSCENDENTAL EGO (2) The pole of identity that functions to unify transcendental experience and to constitute the meaning and structure of mundane experience in Husserl's phenomenology. Access to the transcendental ego is achieved via the transcendental reduction, which manifests it to phenomenological reflection as the a priori source of the empirical ego (which, in turn, is the source of the unity of mundane experience). The parallelism between the empirical ego and the transcendental ego does not point to their being separate entities for Husserl, but to the different modes of access to the unity of experience that occurs in the different cognitive attitudes belonging to natural and transcendental reflection.

B. Hopkins

TRANSCENDENTAL EMPIRICISM A phrase used by Deleuze to describe the version of transcendental philosophy put forward in *Difference and Repetition*. It was Kant who first used the term 'transcendental' in its modern sense. His Copernican Revolution held that the conditions of objects were one and the same as the conditions of the knowledge of objects, and thus that those conditions were to be found in the subject. Kant's aim was to discover criteria immanent to the understanding so as to distinguish between the legitimate and illegitimate uses of the syntheses of consciousness. In the name of transcendental philosophy (immanence of criteria), Kant proposed a 'critique of pure reason' that would denounce the transcendent use of the synthesis as had appeared in traditional metaphysics (the Ideas of the Soul, the World and God).

Post-Kantian philosophers, while taking up the critical and immanent aims of Kant's philosophy, nonetheless broke with it on several key points. One of these issues concerned the nature of the 'transcendental field'. Kant had defined this field in terms of the transcendental subject; Fichte would define it in terms of the transcendental ego; Hegel in terms of the Absolute. All of these thinkers thus took consciousness as their model for the transcendental field: they modelled the transcendental structures of the mind on the empirical structures of consciousness. Deleuze rejects this move, and defines his own 'transcendental empiricism' in terms of two conditions: (1) the transcendental field must not be traced off the empirical (the transcendental must not resemble the empirical); and (2) it therefore cannot be defined in terms of consciousness, but rather as a field of pre-individual and impersonal singularities. For this reason, the transcendental field must be explored empirically, that is via 'experiments' (the French noun *expérience* means both 'experience' in the ordinary English sense of the term as well as 'experiment'). Such experiments are conducted by pushing systems to the thresholds at which their singularities come into play, triggering a qualitatively new behaviour. Deleuze's entire philosophy can in fact be seen as a development of a transcendental empiricism.

D. Smith

See also: actual/virtual distinction

TRANSCENDENTAL UNITY OF APPERCEPTION A concept which plays a crucial role in the Transcendental Analytic of Kant's *Critique of Pure Reason* in determining the formal conditions of the unity of experience, even though its precise character and function are not always transparent. The term 'apperception' was most widely used before Kant by Leibniz, who distinguished it from perception. While perception is a transitory unification of a multiplicity, apperception is the reflective knowledge of this unification. While Leibniz was prepared to entertain differences of degree between the two, Kant's distinction was far more rigorous. Indeed, in his pre-critical works he took the crucial step of aligning apperception with judgement. The ability to make representation itself the object of thought was for him a condition of legitimate judgement or unification of a manifold.

As a consequence, the *Critique of Pure Reason* reserves a crucial role in its justification of judgement for the transcendental unity of apperception. The spontaneity of the 'I think' is contrasted with the receptivity of the intuitions, identifying them as manifolds and making them available for judgement. Furthermore, the same spontaneous apperception enables the unification of the manifold in judgement, not immediately, but through the functions of unity that make up the pure concepts of the understanding. Yet, while the transcendental unity of apperception is crucial for experience, it is so as a formal condition – the assumption that such unification is carried out by a subject already in possession of an integrated soul is strongly criticised in the 'Transcendental Dialectic'.

H. Caygill

TRANSVERSALITY A concept wrested from Sartrean phenomenology and relaunched as a political tool by Félix Guattari in the essay 'Transversality' (1964), part of his analytical critique of and experimentation with institutional formations of subjectivity.

For Sartre in *The Transcendence of the Ego* (1937), transversality described consciousness's unification of temporal intentionalities within duration. Guattari opened up the Sartrean analysis by turning retention, or intentionality toward the past, toward protention, intentionality toward the future, giving mobility and openness to transversality. In other words, consciousness now was free to explore multiple dimensions of temporal relations. Guattari integrated transversality into analytic technique via borrowings from D. W. Winnicott, Melanie Klein and Jacques Lacan concerning transference (the movement of positive and negative affect back and forth from patient and doctor). Guattari's innovation was putting the rapport between patient and doctor in a collective clinical context beyond the dual analytical situation. If transference is the impulse for the unconscious becoming conscious, transversality is the measure of the institution's influence on all its denizens. Guattari foregrounded the institution so as to experiment with its organisation; his goal was to maximise an institution's 'therapeutic coefficient' by unfixing rigid roles, thawing frozen hierarchies and opening hitherto closed blinkers. He did this through an institutional technique called 'the grid', a complex rotating system of tasks and responsibilities.

Transversality effects institutional change and is available for ongoing analysis in a collective setting, especially concerning the consequences of the incorporation of institutional objects into the superego. The goal is to bring about the acceptance of new objects, primarily by answering new demands and setting up innovative points of reference. The modification of alienating fantasies allows for mobility, creativity and the self-engendering of subjectivity, the latter now conceived as a group or 'assemblage'.

G. Genosko

TRUTH A concept which, in its reception in continental philosophy, has two aspects. On the one hand, truth is that which designates the goal of inquiry, whatever it is that inquirers, philosophers in particular, consider themselves to be seeking. On the other hand, there is also a view, held by philosophers as diverse as Tarski ('The Semantic Conception of Truth', 1944) and Heidegger (*Being and Time*, 1927), that the history of philosophy exhibits adherence to what the former calls the 'classical Aristotelian conception of truth', and what the latter calls the 'traditional concept of truth'. According to this interpretation of the tradition, truth is a property first and foremost of judgements (or, as later unpacked, of propositions, beliefs or sentences), and designates either their correspondence to reality or their coherence with one another. Neither Heidegger nor Tarski cites any record of overt debate on the matter, however, and the 'traditional' or 'classical' view may be more myth than reality. Certainly truth in its other meaning, as signifying the goal of inquiry, especially philosophical inquiry, has had meanings that go far beyond the sort of judgement-based 'tradition' cited by Tarski and Heidegger.

Continental philosophers since Husserl have claimed to overcome the centrality of the judgement-based tradition with a variety of strategies. Husserl's 'phenomenological' account of truth in his *Philosophical Investigations*, while claiming to capture the traditional sense of truth as correspondence to an object, is couched in terms of the process of fulfilment of an 'intention' or of the directing of the mind upon an object. This view of truth as a process was developed, in different ways, by Heidegger's account of truth as the progressive 'disclosure' of an entity and by Gadamer's view of truth as the event of 'merging of horizons', in which interpretive expectations are actually fulfilled by an interpreted object such as a text.

The 'judgement-based tradition' against which these continental views are directed, however, may never have existed. Throughout Plato's writings, for example, *t'alēthē*, 'the true things', normally refers to the Forms, to which the Platonic philosopher seeks proximity. Platonic Forms, of course, are unchanging essences, not sentences or propositions. Aristotle himself, though he begins philosophy's tradition of correspondence theories of truth, has several mysterious discussions in *Metaphysics* 9.10 of the sense in which things, rather than propositions, are true. Augustine, in his *Soliloquies*, goes so far as to say that truth is being. Anselm's *De Veritate* follows him.

Though the Neoplatonist Proclus makes use of an apparently mathematical procedure in his *Elements of Theology*, and some of his formulations of the nature of truth sound very traditional, his commentary on Plato's *Parmenides* propounds a rather different view. There, he distinguishes falsity from error: if S is P, and I say 'S is not P', I have asserted a falsehood, because S is P. But *both* 'S is P' and 'S is not P' are in 'error', because in them the mind moves (*errare*) from the subject to the predicate of the sentence. Neither true nor false statements are adequate to the unity of the One, and that unity is the truth towards which Proclean inquiry moves. Question I, Article II of Thomas Aquinas' *De Veritate* begins with the assurance that truth is located, not in things, but in the intellect properly perceiving reality. But the intellect may be God's, in which case a thing is 'true' in so far as it 'fulfils the end to which it is ordained by God'. A statement which accurately depicts reality will be 'true' in this sense, but so will a great many non-statements. With respect to the human intellect, truth is indeed found in the conformity of intellect to thing; but something's being true in this sense, Aquinas teaches, follows from its being true in the other sense, that of divine teleology:

> Since everything is true according as it has the form proper to its nature, the intellect, insofar as it is knowing, must be true according as it has the likeness of the thing known, which is its form as a knowing power. For this reason truth is defined as the conformity of intellect and thing; and to know this conformity is to know truth. (*Summa Theologiae*, Part I, Question 16, Article 2)

For Aquinas, then, truth is primarily in the intellect – because it is the 'form' of the intellect itself. When the human intellect has its proper form, to be sure, it contains propositions it knows to be true. But that state, as far as truth is concerned, is derivative.

Dealing with the modern tradition, we can note that the first definition of truth in Spinoza's *Ethics* is 'adequate to its object', which sounds traditional enough. But 'adequacy' turns out to mean, not 'corresponding to an object', but 'existing as in the mind of God'. Spinoza emphasises that God knows an object in relation to its entire causal context, which is ultimately the entire universe: to know anything adequately is to know everything adequately. Kant, in his first Critique, 'granted' the view that truth is correspondence; but the grammar of the sentence, as Gerold Prauss has shown, is complex; Kant really means to say that the old definition is no longer adequate (Prauss, 'Zum Wahrheitsproblem bei Kant', 1969). Hegel's complex definition of truth, which he rightly asserts in his Science of Logic is 'completely different' (*ganz andere*) from the propositional or correspondence view, assigns truth to things such as words and experiences, rather than merely to sentences or propositions.

Nietzsche develops several celebrated positions on truth, all of which maintain the correspondence notion of truth while disputing the possibility of ever attaining it in an absolute rather than perspectival sense. In the 1873 fragment 'On Truth and Lies in an Extra-Moral Sense', he claims 'truth is a mobile army of metaphors'. In his *Will to Power*, which has been massively influential in spite of the fact that he himself never published it, truth is 'the kind of error without which a certain species could not live. The value for *life* is ultimately decisive'. Finally, some of Nietzsche's most important reflections are contained in his interrogation of the 'will-to-truth' he diagnoses in the activities of scholars and scientists. Perhaps it is his own virtue, he writes, that he alone dares to question the 'value' of truth.

In keeping with his criticism of the 'judgement-based tradition', Heidegger, too, criticises sentential truth in favour of a complex alternative which makes it a property of our encounters with things, rather than of sentences ('On the Essence of Truth', 1930). In *Being and Time*, a more fundamental truth is located in the opening in which things appear than in the correspondence of judgements with things. Later Heidegger will locate truth in the concealment from which things step forth; he takes up the Greek word *aletheia* for this interplay of revealing and concealing. In addition, a long investigation into the truth of the work of art is contained in 'The Origin of the Work of Art' (1935).

In recent continental philosophy, Foucault follows Nietzsche in suggesting that truth is established in communities by means of a complex interplay of 'power-knowledge'. In *History of Sexuality, Volume 1*, Foucault is particularly fascinated by the way in which contemporary people are incited to find our truth in examining our sexuality. Falling for this audacious gambit, he writes, enmeshes us ever deeper in networks of power.

It is unclear whether these challenges bring into question the possibility of obtaining truth in the traditional sense, or its status as the supreme goal of inquiry. Habermas undertakes to defend it in both senses (*The Philosophical Discourse of Modernity*, 1985).

J. McCumber

UNDECIDABILITY An aporia which, for Derrida, far from pre-empting or paralysing decision, renders decision possible and hence introduces the possibility of ethics and of political agency. As Derrida writes in *Limited Inc*, 'a decision can only come into being in a space that exceeds the calculable program that would destroy all responsibility by transforming it into a programmable effect of determinate causes. There can be no moral or political responsibility without this trial and this passage by way of the undecidable'. Without undecidability, without something akin to Kierkegaard's *madness* of the instant of decision (a non-rational or unknowable effect), a so-called decision is simply a form of programmed automation that leaves no room for responsibility and therefore for ethics. Although a decision brings undecidability to a close, that undecidability has nevertheless, and however contradictorily, to remain as a structure within the decision for it to retain any ethical content. Derrida goes so far as to insist that the only true decision must be 'passive', that it must come from the other, be unconscious: '*In sum, a decision is unconscious* – insane as that may seem, it involves the unconscious and nevertheless remains responsible' (*The Politics of Friendship*).

Derrida explicitly distinguishes undecidability from indeterminacy, which he considers to be insufficiently rigorous to account for what is always a choice between pragmatically determined possibilities. Even if it relies on the play of *différance*, undecidability is, like *différance*, but unlike the negativity of indeterminacy, what allows difference to be determined; it always carries that affirmative sense.

D. Wills

UNDERSTANDING (*Verstand*) (1) For Kant, the faculty of human knowledge functioning between sensibility and reason. It is usually aligned with reason as a 'higher faculty' opposed to the lower faculty of sensibility, from which it is distanced by a 'transcendental distinction'. Its anatomy is the main concern of the 'Transcendental Analytic' of the *Critique of Pure Reason*, where it is identified as the 'faculty of judgement'. Its intermediate character between sensibility and reason lends it some of its particular characteristics. Like reason, it is characterised by spontaneity, although in the case of the understanding this issues from the 'transcendental unity of apperception' – or function of unity in judgement which is distributed across the twelve 'pure concepts of the understanding'. The understanding is also described variously as a 'power' of thought and a faculty of concepts and of rules – indeed, it is often described as a legislator that gives law to the manifold or 'rabble' of the sensibility. Yet, while formally separated from sensibility, it nevertheless must be accommodated to it in order to allow experience to take place.

The unifying vocation of the understanding is distributed across the twelve pure concepts of experience or categories whose legitimacy is endorsed in the deduction of the pure concepts of the understanding. These are presented in four groups of three according to the forms of judgement in which they may be exhibited: quantity, quality, relation and modality. Between them the four groups comprise the 'table of categories' that form the a priori conditions for possible experience. However, the understanding is not only responsible for the justification of the categories, but also for their application to the manifolds presented by the spatio-temporal forms of intuition. The understanding does not simply apply its rules to pre-given manifolds, but, in its legislative role, contributes to their pre-conceptual shaping. The discussion of this aspect of the understanding in the section on the 'schematism' and in the 'analytic of principles' provide some of the most provocative and rewarding passages of argument in the entire critical philosophy.

H. Caygill

UNDERSTANDING (2) Sociologists have long been divided over the question of whether the discipline's goal is to promote understanding, explanation or both. The debate surrounding this question dates to the work of Weber, for whom understanding (*Verstehen*) was construed as a characteristic feature of sociological inquiry because humans are meaning-creating creatures. He promoted an interpretive sociology whose task it was to comprehend, not behaviour, but meaningful action. This necessitated an effort by researchers to place themselves in empathetic relationships with the subjects being studied in order to comprehend how they made sense of their social setting and why they acted as they did. Perhaps the best illustration of what Weber had in mind can be found in his analysis of the emergence of the Protestant ethic, where he sought to understand the world-view or fundamental belief system of the early entrepreneurial adherents to the Protestant Reformation. This approach to sociological inquiry can be found in various contemporary forms of interpretive or hermeneutical sociology, most prominently in phenomenological theory, symbolic interaction and various versions of cultural sociology. It is often opposed to a tradition that seeks to offer explanatory accounts of social causation without reference to the actors themselves, a position pioneered by Durkheim. This divide is depicted today in terms of those who emphasise agency versus those who emphasise structure. For his part, Weber thought it possible to reconcile understanding and explanation, as have such major subsequent theorists as Talcott Parsons and Anthony Giddens.

P. Kivisto

UNEVEN DEVELOPMENT A concept used to describe and explain the tendency of nations and individuals to develop asymmetrically in relation to one another and to a prescribed historical pattern of economic and cultural transformations by dint of their localised influences. Recognisable in *The German Ideology* (1846) as a concept informing its discussion of the economic, political and philosophical differences between France and Germany, the idea that every country could have its own idiosyncratic path to development was later explicitly rejected by Marx and Engels in favour of a theory emphasising the necessity of homogenous international development for socialist revolution. The concept was rehabilitated by Trotsky and Lenin in the early twentieth century to theorise the possibility of revolution in a country like Russia that lacked a developed capitalist infrastructure. Though originally in agreement, Marxists-Leninists and Trotskyites came to bitterly dispute what the 'law of uneven development' implied. For Marxists-Leninists, it justified the policy of 'socialism in one country' and buttressed their theory of imperialism. For Trotskyites, it showed exactly the opposite: the extreme interdependence and unevenness of the global economy made socialism in one country impossible. Though much debated, the concept was employed throughout the twentieth century by left-leaning economists, sociologists and politicians, especially those in developing nations. In the developed West, the notion enjoyed a brief revival in the 1960s when Althusser generalised it and used the concept to explain the existence of individual diversity within a specific socio-economic structure such as capitalism.

W. Lewis

UNIVERSAL PRAGMATICS A concept introduced by Habermas to designate the study of normative expectations underlying the production of any spoken utterance whatsoever. It differs somewhat from the transcendental pragmatics developed by Habermas's colleague Apel, which holds that such expectations are rationally necessary as well as factually universal. Both universal and transcendental pragmatics are inspired by Chomsky's theories regarding universal language learning competencies and by pragmatic philosophies of meaning, ranging from studies of language use pioneered by Wittgenstein and Buhler to the pragmatist semiotics of Pierce. The speech act theories developed by Wittgenstein and his followers, Austin and Searle, broaden the concept of linguistic meaning beyond the narrow compass of referential meaning (the designation and description of named objects) to include pragmatic meaning (the accomplishment of tasks built around shared expectations). In the somewhat different lexicon developed by Buhler, every speech act performs at least three distinctive but interrelated functions: the expression of speaker intentions; the representation of facts; and the establishment of mutual obligations between speaker and addressee. As reformulated by Habermas, these functions depend upon speaker and listener reaching agreement on three claims, regarding: (1) the speaker's sincerity; (2) the truth of his or her representation of the world; and (3) the rightness of his or her proposed interaction with the addressee. If agreement on any of these so-called 'validity claims' breaks down, speaker and listener must strive to reach agreement through impartial reasoning or discourse, which is itself premised on the presumed satisfaction of certain universal normative expectations associated with ideal speech.

D. Ingram

UTOPIA A term developed in Renaissance philosophy from Greek elements that literally mean 'no place' (*ou* + *topos*), or the place that does not exist. The term utopia is linked to the emergence of a distinctively modern ideal: political universalism. Sir Thomas More, who coined the term, used it in his *Utopia* (1516) to describe the perfect state, one in which all citizens have financial and juridical equality. The untimeliness of More's scheme made the meaning of utopia that of a noble ideal with no likely applicability. Tommaso Campanella's *The City of the Sun* (1602) and Francis Bacon's *New Atlantis* (1627) followed in More's footsteps. In the early nineteenth century, a generation of French political theorists, including Saint-Simon, Fourier and Proudhon, articulated a version of utopian socialism. Fourier develops a critique of the familial structure as the matrix of unbridled individualism and commerce that Marx and Engels will follow in their *The Holy Family* (1945).

Throughout the twentieth century, the concept of utopia assumed a new prominence, specifically among a group of German thinkers inspired by the boldness of the artistic avant-gardes and depressed by the alienating and homogenising effects of modern capitalism.

Bloch's *The Spirit of Utopia* (1918) and *The Principle of Hope* (1954–6), Adorno's *Negative Dialectics* (1966) and Marcuse's five lectures on *Psychoanalysis, Politics, and Utopia* (1970) all pursue these goals in different ways. More recent discussions of utopia include Agnes Heller's *Radical Philosophy* (1978), which provides a genealogy of modern philosophical utopia reaching back to Kant's definition of the regulative ideas, and Robert Nozick's *Anarchy, State and Utopia* (1974), for whom libertarianism, or the theory that minimal state interference with individual rights is best, can be viewed as a framework for utopia

G. Borradori

VARELA, FRANCISCO J. (1946–2001) Chilean biologist and theoretician. Best known as the co-originator of the theory of autopoiesis with Humberto Maturana, Varela concentrated on the modelling and understanding of autonomous systems. This focus led Varela to extend his work beyond the biological sciences proper to investigate figures of autonomy in psychology, cognitive science, phenomenology and Buddhism. While never abandoning his scientific research, mainly concerned with the neurophysiology of vision and the perception of colour, Varela's writings became more and more preoccupied with philosophical issues, taking him beyond the 'mechanism' of his work with Maturana to speculations on the limits of representation, the nature of first-person observation and the exploration of a non-foundational thought.

Varela's work with Maturana sought to provide a definition of 'living systems' as self-referential and operationally closed machines, obviating the resort to teleology in the study of the living. This research is summarised in *Autopoiesis and Cognition* (1980, which he wrote with Maturana), where the theory of autopoiesis receives its most exhaustive treatment. In *Principles of Biological Autonomy* (1979), Varela built on his work with Maturana to provide a critique of the conception of mind, psychology and perception forwarded by cognitivism. Chief among Varela's objections was that cognition in autonomous systems cannot be understood in terms of an input–output schema of information transfer and, furthermore, that the internal interactions within a cognitive system which give rise to perception and action cannot be usefully grasped in terms of a unified 'control' or central processing unit. Rather, cognitive behaviour is best modelled in terms of the reciprocal regulation and production of components within a topologically unified system in 'structural coupling' with the elements of its environment.

In the 1990s, Varela's espousal of the project of a 'naturalised phenomenology' brought his philosophical speculation to the foreground. This took the form of a return to the Merleau-Ponty of *The Structure of Behavior* (1939) and the advocacy of a Heideggerian notion of being-in-the-world, as applied to issues in cognitive science. Working with the French phenomenologist Nathalie Depraz, Varela also returned to Husserl on time-consciousness, trying to combine the insights of transcendental phenomenology with experimental neurophysiology. Following Merleau-Ponty, Varela eschewed the foundational aspects of the phenomenological reduction, preferring a far less theoretical and more descriptive definition of phenomenology.

Though never tempted by vitalism, Varela's work can be included in an anti-reductionist current of thought vis-à-vis the natural sciences. This is especially clear in his twin critique of the representationalist tendency in the cognitive sciences and the deterministic tendencies of neo-Darwinism. In both, Varela discerned a philosophical and foundationalist commitment to an objectivism at odds with his characterisation of autonomy and his later notion of enaction, both of which place great emphasis on the creative activities of autonomous beings. It should be noted in this regard that Varela was an enthusiastic proponent of artificial life and of the ultimate untenability of a distinction between life and artifice, as was clear from his collaboration with Paul Bourgine on the collective work *Towards a Practice of Autonomous Systems* (1990).

A. Toscano

See also: Asian Philosophy; autopoiesis; Biology, Philosophy of; Cognitive Science; enaction; Naturalising Phenomenology; organism

VATTIMO, GIANNI (1936–) Italian philosopher who has made important contributions to the reading of Heidegger and of Nietzsche and to the interpretation of postmodernity, art, religion, and political philosophy. Vattimo's thought is organised around his conception of hermeneutics and the task confronting it in the present day. He has taught for many years at the University of Turin and has more recently been active in Italian and European politics.

Throughout a dialogue with the works of Nietzsche that began in the early 1960s, Vattimo has delineated a distinct reading that presents a more moderate figure than the one often put forward today. Vattimo's reading of Nietzsche is developed in tandem with his interpretation of Heidegger, and of Heidegger's own reading of Nietzsche. Whereas Heidegger regards Nietzsche's conception of the will-to-power as the final stage in the history of metaphysics and therefore as a position to be superseded, Vattimo sees Nietzsche's nihilism as the occasion for a new affirmation through which history may continue in a more positive vein. In this way, Nietzsche's diagnosis of nihilism serves as a key for Vattimo's conception of postmodernity.

Joining Nietzsche in a rejection of metaphysical realism, Vattimo accepts the principle that truth is the fruit of interpretation, and moreover that there is an irresolvable conflict between interpretations. Yet for Vattimo, this situation should be viewed as an opportunity, not a crisis; although contemporary culture cannot simply abandon the language of the metaphysical tradition for some radically new beginning, in postmodernity we can acknowledge and accelerate the dissolution of traditional ontological categories as a positive step towards our liberation from the authority of metaphysics. In a move closely aligned with Nietzsche's own notion of convalescence and Heidegger's conception of the overcoming of metaphysics as a gradual release (*Verwindung*), Vattimo thereby affirms what he called a 'weak ontology'. This expression led others to describe his overall philosophical approach as 'weak thought' (*pensiero debole*), a term he adopted somewhat reluctantly for a period.

Engaging with Weber, Horkheimer, Adorno, Apel and the Frankfurt School, Vattimo dissents both from the idea that progressive rationalisation may make society more transparent to itself and from the gloomy picture that mass culture has given way to a shallow play of images and information in which our freedom is constrained or lost altogether. If the media and the human sciences are giving society a greater self-transparency, what is revealed is not some inner truth, but pluralism and a conflict of interpretations over which the old myths of truth and philosophy no longer have the power to prevail. In Vattimo's view, this is the world for which Nietzsche invented the overman.

For Vattimo, the necessity for interpretation arising from the absence of incontrovertible grounds means that hermeneutics is no longer just one methodology alongside others. It now names the milieu of contemporary thought as a whole. Vattimo translated Gadamer's *Truth and Method* into Italian, but it is Heidegger who most significantly shapes his own understanding of hermeneutics. He accepts Heidegger's formulation of the ontological difference and of the twofold conception of truth that follows from it, namely that prior to truth as correctness of judgement, there occurs an original event of truth as the unconcealment of beings, such that a propositional relation to the thing first becomes possible. For Vattimo, how being is given can only be understood as the outcome of the tradition of Western metaphysics to which we belong, which consists above all in the link between the interpretative essence of truth and nihilism. Hermeneutics, then, is itself an interpretative response to our own historical tradition; it is the best way we can make sense of the legacy handed down to us through art, literature, science, religion and philosophy.

Given that philosophy itself cannot discover a ground for our knowledge and experience, art takes on an important role, both as an interpretative activity and as an instance of the more original disclosure of being. Taking his lead from Heidegger's account of art and truth in 'The Origin of the Work of Art', Vattimo encourages us to leave aesthetic theory behind, and most especially the traditional appeal to formal perfection. If instead we take up a more direct relation to art as an event in which being is disclosed and a world opened, art can provide the jolt we need to expose ourselves to the plurality of perspectives in postmodernity. Drawing also on Benjamin, Vattimo presents aesthetic experience as an exercise in disorientation.

A similar valorisation of uncertainty runs through Vattimo's writing on religion. He attributes the apparent renewal of interest in religion to the dissolution of the categories in which the rationalist critique of religion has been couched. Although we no longer need the strong paternalistic religion that Nietzsche saw reaching its end, undone by the very commitment to truth it embodied, this does not mean that the religious dimension has entirely disappeared from our culture. Indeed, Vattimo insists that the secularisation of our culture that hastened the end of traditional religious discourse would itself have been impossible without the influence of Christianity. The principle of 'kenosis', in which God is incarnated in human form, is not just emblematic of a shift from the eternal to the temporal, but has contributed positively to the process of secularisation that has brought us to postmodernity, hermeneutics and the end of metaphysics. In so far as a hermeneutic response recognises this influence on its own becoming, religion is rehabilitated, but in a form that now acknowledges its own interpretative character and uncertainty.

In Vattimo's later writing, a political current that had always been present in his work has come to the fore in his elaboration of ideas of liberty, justice, law and peace within a broader conception of democracy consistent with his understanding of nihilism, art, technology, the ontological difference and postmodernity.

D. Webb

VIRILIO, PAUL (1932–) French urbanist and critic whose explorations of architecture, speed, war, cinema and technology examine a range of cultural and political themes his commentators have taken to calling 'hypermodernism'. Focusing on 'dromology' or the study of the compulsive logic of speed, Virilio's writings do not stem from the reaction against modernism in art, as in postmodernism, but from the 'war model', Virilio's approach to hypermodern culture.

In *Speed and Politics* (1977) Virilio analyses the dromocratic aspects of social history in examining, among other topics, Hitler's political mobilisation of proletarian sport and transportation. Virilio's hypermodern perspective on dromology, geopolitics and totalitarianism does not explain causes, but suggests what he calls the 'tendency' or a change of intensity in social processes.

In *The Aesthetics of Disappearance* (1980), Virilio considers modernist aesthetics and the evolution of vision technologies. Employing hypermodern and phenomenologically derived artistic concepts, Virilio interrogates the extraordinary bias hypermodern society retains for contemporary cinematic or televisual and videographic 'disappearance' over ancient 'appearance-based art' such as Greek marble sculptures. Drawing on the mathematician Mandelbrot, the filmmaker Méliès and the philosopher Bergson, Virilio argues that the current crises in contemporary 'motorised' and other cybernetic forms of art converge on their disappearance into vision technologies and the elimination of the difference between here and now.

In *Ground Zero* (2002), Virilio's focuses his dromological gaze on the terror attacks of September 11, 2001. With his characteristic flamboyance, Virilio condemns the terrorists who created 'ground zero' while pointing to the emergence of a global secret state, to the 'unknown quantity' of a private criminality. Yet in this book Virilio is equally preoccupied with advancing a hypermodern analysis of present-day conceptions of technological progress. Consequently, *Ground Zero* offers a powerful critical assessment of contemporary developments in medicine and technoscience. Indeed, according to Virilio, what might be termed the 'medical-scientific-complex' is set to discard the 'information bomb' (the dangerous energy activated by interactive information and communications technologies) for what he calls the 'genetic bomb' or the transformation of the human embryo into nothing more than a commercial product. In Virilio's estimation, then, the detonation of the genetic bomb by the medical-scientific-complex is merely one more illustration of the reduction of genuine human life to the status of a thing. In sum, human beings are everywhere subject to a kind of technological framing wherein human life becomes the raw material for the post-industrial production process. The hypermodern era of technological development as described by Virilio in *Ground Zero* is thus a time of human desolation in which humanity has forgotten the true nature of being.

J. Armitage

See also: dromology; information bomb

VITALISM A term referring to those scientific and philosophical approaches to biological phenomena that advocate the irreducibility of the latter to mechanistic explanation. Originating in Aristotle's speculations on the soul as the formal principle of living beings, vitalism became a prominent stance in eighteenth- and nineteenth-century biology and physiology. While often opposed to the kind of mechanistic explanation of living beings originating in the work of Descartes, as well as to the non-teleological processes of variation and selection adduced by Darwinism and neo-Darwinism, vitalism rarely entailed the stark and seemingly mystical separation from materialistic reduction that has so often turned it into a term of abuse. Its critical function has been to draw attention not to the existence of a separate substance, force or principle (what Kant called *Lebenskraft*) but to the functional, contextual and behavioural specificity of the living, and against merely technological models of organic life.

In philosophy, it can be seen as the attempt to give ontological valence to certain traits that have traditionally been ascribed to the living, such as productivity, self-reference and creativity. Though most philosophers have been understandably wary of the term vitalism, if we follow this definition we could divide 'vitalist' philosophers into three groupings: first, those philosophers who have tried to generalise the aforementioned traits to baseline ontological principles (Schelling, Ravaisson, Bergson); second, those who have affirmed the singularity of the living in terms of its normative character (Canguilhem); third, those who have sought to redefine vitalism against the centrality of organic life (Deleuze).

A. Toscano

VOID (*vide*) The fundamental category in Badiou's systematic ontology. In most formal terms, all that exists is pure multiplicity. Any existing entity (a natural being, a social institution, a historical phenomenon, etc.) is a multiple of multiples. Any such multiplicity, however, can appear, present itself, only in structured ways, such that individual elements are distinguished as individuals, counted as ones and organised with others in sets according to rules. At bottom, to exist is synonymous with 'being presented', that is being in a structure or 'situation' where structural laws grant multiplicity its modalities of appearance. But existence in situations is clearly not being itself if being is pure multiplicity. The proper name of being is therefore the Nothing, or the Void: despite being the condition of possibility of all structured situations, being cannot appear in its true form as pure multiplicity in situations where the multiple is always unified by laws. Any 'situation' is therefore structured around its own specific void, the pure multiplicity that cannot appear as such in it, yet must be retro- actively postulated as the condition of its possibility. Ontology, the science of being as being, is therefore the science of the void, and any entity, studied ontologically, is only a modality of the void. This means that thinking the true essence of anything, and in particular the truth about truth, knowledge and the subject, is to describe their specific connections with their void.

J.-P. Deranty

WAR MACHINE A term used by Deleuze and Guattari in *A Thousand Plateaus* to refer to a mode of organisation that is innovative, as opposed to those modelled on the state which are rigid and bureau- cratic. Deleuze and Guattari point to societies without state appara- tuses, non-state organisations, and especially to nomads as privileged, but not exclusive, examples.

Following the 'political anthropologist' Pierre Clastres, Deleuze and Guattari argue that the absence of a state apparatus does not mark a social organisation as primitive. Such groups actually have intricate mechanisms of distributed governance, including institutions appar- ently designed specifically to inhibit the concentration of power required for a state. Hostility to the state and all hierarchical organisa- tion is the primary characteristic of the war machine. But, confusingly enough, war is not at all intrinsic to the war machine. War is imposed on the war machine when it is captured by the state: war is the state's expression of the creativity of the war machine.

This apparently socio-political term is also imbued with a cross- disciplinary resonance. Nomad culture, for instance, is not only associated with the creative deployment of new weaponry against the ancient empires, but also with the development of metallurgy. This is a standing refutation of the doctrine of form and matter or 'hylomorphism' according to which technical production is applied to an inert matter. Rather, metalworking involves a careful exploration of the potentialities and thresholds immanent to matter itself, what Deleuze and Guattari describe as a 'technological vitalism'.

A. Welchman

WEBER, MAX (1864–1920) German sociologist, known for his analyses of rationalisation in modernity. One of the leading figures in the classical period of sociology, Weber produced a complex corpus that is difficult to summarise, but in terms of the substantive writings, as opposed to the strictly methodological work, might profitably be viewed as the product of a long and intense dialogue with the thought of Marx and Nietzsche. The master theme of his work is rationalisation, a concept that can be seen as shaping all of his major works from his famous essay on *The Protestant Ethic and the Spirit of Capitalism* (1904–5) until the end of his life.

The bulk of the Protestant ethic essay is devoted to an analysis of the rise of the inner worldly asceticism of the early capitalist adherents to Calvinism well before the Industrial Revolution. He understood there to be an 'elective affinity' between the ethical world-view of Protestantism and the spirit of capitalism; it was not by chance that Protestantism and capitalism arose in the same place at the same time. In this regard, by focusing on the realm of ideas, the essay offers a complement to Marx's materialism. Weber's subsequent comparative studies of the major world religions were designed to discern why the historical fate of Western civilisation differed so much from that of the rest of the world. Near the end of the *Protestant Ethic*, Weber turned his attention to the future, speculating pessimistically that increasingly the world would come to resemble an 'iron cage'. This metaphor is a reflection of Weber's deep concern that the modern world posed a threat to individuality and freedom, and that given the power of the capitalist economic system there was no way out.

Weber was suspicious of socialists who thought that by abolishing capitalism the problems of industrial society would be overcome. In his view, socialism would not simply share with capitalism the problems inherent in industrial society, but in fact would render them even more problematic. What both shared in common was the need to create a powerful administrative apparatus of control that he described as the modern bureaucratic organisation. In his view, rationalisation takes organisational form in the modern bureaucracy, which he believed is as central to the modern economy as is the machine. In order to succeed in a competitive marketplace, the capitalist had to institutionalise

rationalisation in order to make decisions based on efficiency, calculability, predictability and control. If one sought to abandon the market
for a command economy, the need for a bureaucratic apparatus would
only intensify.

Once in motion, industrial society no longer needed to rely on the
Protestant ethic. Instead, a society dominated by machine production
and bureaucratic organisation developed its own internal logic.
Although Weber generally agreed with Marx's understanding of the
class structure, he disputed the Marxist belief that the egalitarian
aspirations of socialism could be realised, since bureaucratic organisations were structured in terms of a hierarchal chain of command.
Likewise, freedom is jeopardised in so far as individuals are controlled
and constrained in the interests of the effective functioning of the
system. In describing bureaucracy, Weber often used the image of a
machine, viewing people as cogs in its mechanisms that lose their sense
of individuality, creativity and freedom.

Weber realised that rationalisation did not only occur in the economic realm, but rather could be seen increasingly in all facets of social
life. He was particularly concerned about the implications of bureaucratic rationalisation on politics. In his contribution to political
thought, Weber related power (*Macht*) to authority (*Herrschaft*). Power
refers to the ability to accomplish a goal regardless of the obstacles and
the capacity to get others to do what one wants them to do. Authority or
domination is viewed, in effect, as legitimated power. He depicts three
types of authority: traditional, charismatic and legal-rational.

Weber was concerned both with the prospects for democracy in an
increasingly bureaucratic world and with the need for strong leaders. In
the contemporary world, legal-rational authority is the type associated
with bureaucracy. It increasingly replaces traditional authority as the
principal form of order. Weber was interested in determining the
nature of the relationship between charismatic authority (with its
potential for disrupting the status quo) and legal-rational authority.
He was not an advocate of a position that sought to privilege charismatic authority, with its irrational devotion to the leader, vis-à-vis
legal-rational authority. Rather, he sought to find a way to effect a set of
trade-offs that minimise the negative impact of bureaucratic rationalisation by articulating a set of constructive oppositions: a working
parliament versus a government bureaucracy, the government bureaucracy versus political leadership, a political leadership selected by
plebiscite versus the party bureaucracy, and the party bureaucracy
versus an emotionalised population. In this analysis Weber is far more
pragmatic than he is pessimistic.

Weber's contribution to methodology is not always readily apparent in his substantive work, but his contribution to methodological debates is associated with the following: promoting a comparative historical sociology, value-neutrality, the construction of ideal types and a method that sought understanding (*Verstehen*). He was critical of theories of social evolution and the quest for law-like patterns of social development, arguing that the human sciences were distinct from the natural sciences due to the fact that the subjects of the former are meaning-creating creatures. Rationalisation is not construed to be an external social force, but rather is the product of long and complex historical processes that are to be comprehended by exploring the confluence between material conditions and structures of conscious-ness, the latter being comprehended by a process of understanding. To assist in this task, ideal types, distilled from empirical reality, are constructed in order to make comparative analyses possible. When Weber spoke about value neutrality, he did not mean that scholars were capable of readily divorcing their values from their research. Rather, it was necessary to be able to distinguish between what is the case and what one hopes might be the case. In his valedictory essay 'Scholarship as a Vocation' (1919), Weber made it clear that scholarship's value was in helping us to comprehend our situation; it could not, however, save us from it.

P. Kivisto

See also: ideal type; rationalisation; understanding (2)

WEIL, SIMONE (1909–43) French political philosopher and activist who devoted her short life to improving the conditions of the working class. Almost all of Weil's writings were published posthumously. The contours of a truly original thought are evident in her highly lucid critique of Marxism and of socialism, *Oppression and Liberty* (1955). Marx's error, Weil believed, was to have failed to pursue the philo-sophy of labour he had begun to outline early in his career; in consequence, his thought drifted into 'metaphysical clouds' and relied increasingly on the empty formulas of nineteenth-century utopian socialism. The task reserved for the twentieth century lay in taking up again the investigation into how labour under both the capitalist and the socialist systems tends to oppress workers and deny freedom. The ultimate goal would be to conceive of a state in which 'for each of us, our work would be an object of contemplation'.

Deeply influenced by ancient thought, especially the Stoicism of Marcus Aurelius, Weil believed philosophy to be a spiritual exercise that cannot be divorced from action. While working as a philosophy teacher in a number of high schools, she frequently joined the lines of striking workers or took part in demonstrations organised by the unemployed. In spite of poor physical health, she spent stints as a manual labourer in the Alsthom Electrical Works and the Renault factory at Boulogne-Billancourt, and as a farm-hand. Her journals relate her arduous and alienating experience in great detail. In 1936 she served briefly as a volunteer for the Republicans in the Spanish civil war; she died in London where she had joined De Gaulle's Free French Movement.

Weil's interest in the conditions of the working class led her to speculate in a general way on the ills besetting society in her time. In *The Need for Roots* (1949, prefaced by T. S. Eliot), she seeks the causes of contemporary spiritual rootlessness in the demeaning character of work in an era of specialisation. She insists also upon the deracinating effects of a culture in which knowledge and science are reduced to abstractions. The tone and the register of language in this and other works from the period (*Gravity and Grace*, 1947; *Waiting for God*, 1950) are often religious and even overtly Christian. Weil had indeed undergone a number of mystical experiences in Christian contexts and had entered into an important correspondence with Father Joseph-Marie Perrin (see *Letter to a Priest*, 1951). In 1938 she converted from Judaism to Christianity. Her later writings bear witness to a searching that takes her beyond the concepts and the traditional language of continental philosophy, leading her to reflect on the nature of grace, revelation, sin and other Christian subjects. She insists increasingly on the importance of 'detachment' and what she calls 'decreation' in the quest for reality. Always, however, these investigations are conducted in relation to the fundamental question of the *condition ouvrière* ('worker's condition') and the 'dignity of manual labour'.

P. Connor

WHITEHEAD, ALFRED NORTH (1861–1947) Anglo-American mathematician and philosopher who made major contributions to mathematics (*Universal Algebra*), mathematical logic (*Principia Mathematica*, with Bertrand Russell), applied mathematics (with a decided phenomenological bias in *Concept of Nature* and *Principles of Relativity*), philosophy (*Process and Reality, Adventures of Ideas*) and religion (*Religion in the Making*). Though his only formal training was in mathematics, Whitehead read Plato as a schoolboy and the latter's emphasis on becoming became his central theme. Taking his clue from *Timaeus*, Whitehead conceived the world as an ongoing creative matrix autoerotically responding to the lure of the Good. He said he knew

Kant 'by heart' when he went up to university. He was also deeply influenced by Bradley, James and Bergson.

When a proposed second volume of his *Universal Algebra* converged with Russell's proposal for a sequel to his *Principles of Mathematics,* they began a ten-year collaboration whose issue was *Principia.* The first of three volumes appeared in 1910. By logisticising Peano's axioms for number, they mistakenly though they could prove that logic is prior to mathematics. His friends report that he was displeased with Russell for rushing the text into print and for an introduction with which he disagreed.

In 1910 he retired from Cambridge and left for London with no prospects, but in 1912 he was appointed to the mathematics faculty of University College and in 1914 be became Professor and then Dean at the Imperial College of Science and Technology. Aside from his major work in the philosophy of science, his writing and lectures (appearing in the *Aims of Education*) as the chairman of the Royal Commission on Education helped save the centrality of classics, a reform that persisted to the Thatcher era.

After his second retirement, he was persuaded to come to Harvard and begin his third career as a philosopher and teacher, perhaps the most successful, if measured by the distinction and variety of creative responses he encouraged in his students. He never established a school, though his relatively few remarks in *Process and Reality* have had important consequences in Hartshorne and others in process theology. His influence has been seminal in developing philosophical reflection on complexity and chaos theory.

He began in 1918 by asserting that the fundamental fact was the passage of nature: sense terminates, not in things, but in something going on. In a protest against 'misplaced concreteness' in which the abstract is taken as prior to the concrete, he used extensive abstraction to define the basic concepts of mathematics and physics from this passage. In *Process and Reality* (1927) he rejected traditional terminology because it harboured substance assumptions; like Heidegger, he turned to what Greek shows us about the world. Moreover, he identified this feeling of passage with physical vectors and with Bradley's 'living emotion ever before me'. In this panpsychism, actual entities are windowed monads encapsulating emotion in a granular time discontinuous with its 'causal past' and pregnant with the future. Continuity becomes; there is no continuity of becoming.

C. Bigger

WILL-TO-POWER (*Wille-zur-Macht*) the name Nietzsche gives to his central cosmological hypothesis and to the active principle featured therein. First proposed as such in *Thus Spoke Zarathustra* (1883–5), the hypothesis of will-to-power maintains that every being, whether animate or inanimate, both shares in and articulates a will to express its native power. The hypothesis of will-to-power is thus meant to suggest an amoral, chaotic cosmos, whose constitutive 'quanta' continuously reorganise themselves into transient configurations that promise, at any given moment, the greatest possible expression of power.

Nietzsche also maintains that will-to-power is the essence of life itself, in that living beings blindly pursue the circumstances under which they might best express their native force (*Kraft*) and thereby participate in the natural process of self-overcoming (*Selbstüberwindung*). Nietzsche often presents his hypothesis of will-to-power as a more faithfully scientific alternative to the popular, 'Darwinian' notion that self-preservation is the cardinal instinct of life. What living beings seek above all else, he insists, is to secure the optimal conditions under which they might discharge their strength – even if doing so places them at mortal risk.

As this sensitivity to the influence of Social Darwinism indicates, Nietzsche was often concerned to apply his hypothesis of will-to-power to an explanation of *human* organisms and their behaviour. (Although best known for its contribution to the cosmology sketched by Zarathustra, the hypothesis of will-to-power was originally advanced by Nietzsche as a basic principle of human psychology.) While an appeal to an instinct for self-preservation may adequately account for the behaviour of most human beings, especially under conditions of pandemic decay, only the hypothesis of will-to-power can explain the behaviour of those exemplary human beings who 'squander' themselves while expressing their native stores of strength. Nietzsche thus promotes his hypothesis of will-to-power not only for its superior explanatory power, but also as a hedge against the continued reduction of humankind to its lowest common denominator.

D. Conway

WILL-TO-TRUTH (*Wille-zur-Wahrheit*) Nietzsche's term for the animating impulse behind the scientific scholarship that distinguishes the 'Alexandrian' culture of Western civilisation. That the pursuit of truth characteristically takes the form of a will is meant by Nietzsche to indicate a reliance on truth that remains to some extent unknown and unexamined. As an expression of will, in fact, scientific research remains irrational to an extent that practising scholars are typically reluctant to acknowledge. This is especially true of those scholars who maintain that the project of Alexandrian science is justified on the strength of its claim to a fully rational basis. According to Nietzsche, this means that the role played by truth in contemporary scholarly practices is defined as much by religious prejudice (or superstition) as by scientific designs. Truth is an ideal, he avers, whose status and value scholars have not yet been willing to interrogate.

While generally appreciative of scientific advances, and in no event dismissive of the value of truth, Nietzsche nevertheless exposes the unacknowledged faith on which the will-to-truth rests. This faith in the saving power of truth is most evident in the strength of the conviction, shared by most scholars (including Nietzsche himself), that the value of truth is simply inestimable. According to Nietzsche, this means that science continues to constitute its defining practices and expertise on a basis partially informed by ignorance and prejudice. 'We Alexandrians' tenaciously seek the truth, but we have never dared to question, much less to assay, its real value.

Although it may have been necessary in the past for scholars to turn a blind eye to their enabling faith in truth, Nietzsche believes that the time is now ripe to undertake a scholarly determination of the value of truth. Doing so may ultimately weaken our faith in truth, and thereby compromise the will to truth that informs Alexandrian science, but these are risks that Nietzsche is apparently willing to bear, in part because he believes that we can no longer endure the self-denial and self-deprivation that attends our faith in truth. For his own part, he aims to turn the will-to-truth against itself and thereby steer science into a confrontation with its own unscientific foundation. What we will learn in the process, he predicts, is that the value of truth has been generally overestimated. Under certain circumstances, he provocatively insists, untruth is more valuable than truth itself.

D. Conway

WITTGENSTEIN, LUDWIG (1889–1951) Austrian-born philosopher

whose works have greatly influenced philosophical reflection on logic and language in both the analytic and continental traditions. As a prisoner of war in the First World War Wittgenstein compiled most of what was to be the only book published in his lifetime: *Tractatus Logico-Philosophicus* (1922). Despite the paucity of publications, however, Wittgenstein was a prolific writer. Following his death his *Nachlass* was left in the hands of his literary executors for them to publish as they saw fit. From this more than sixteen books have been published, with *Philosophical Investigations* at their core. There is much more that might yet appear in book form and the whole *Nachlass* is slowly being made available by the Cambridge Wittgenstein Archive: www.wittgen-cam.ac.uk.

There is a fierce debate as to how one should read Wittgenstein's first book. The parties in the debate tend to fall into three groups which can be characterised along the following lines: doctrinal, elucidatory and therapeutic. Doctrinal readers see Wittgenstein as advancing (metaphysical) doctrines about how language hooks onto the world. Central to this claim is the idea that in the *Tractatus* Wittgenstein puts forward a 'picture theory of meaning'. Remarks such as §6.54 (where Wittgenstein tells the reader that anyone who understands *him* will see the propositions of the *Tractatus* as nonsense) are treated as the rhetorical flourishes of an otherwise brilliant logician who has become too enamoured with mysticism. Elucidatory readers claim that Wittgenstein sets forth a series of elucidatory though, ultimately (hence §6.54), nonsensical propositions in an attempt to elucidate the limits of logic and language. This reading, therefore, holds onto the idea that there are (in *Tractarian* terms) logical distinctions between nonsensical sentences. Therapeutic readers (sometimes referred to as resolute readers) take seriously Wittgenstein's claim in the *Tractatus* that the propositions of the body of the *Tractatus* are nonsense (6.54). Therefore, unlike the elucidatory readers, they claim no logical distinctions between nonsensical sentences; in other words, there is no elucidatory nonsense. However, there are psychological distinctions among nonsensical sentences. The activity of reading the *Tractatus* provides philosophers with a mirror whereby they can come to recognise their metaphysical tendencies, impulses and assumptions. While few Wittgenstein scholars would attempt to sustain a doctrinal reading now, variants of the other two readings vie for dominance, and the debate seems likely to continue for sometime.

The influence of philosophers from the continental tradition on the *Tractatus* is not easy to discern. Wittgenstein (in)famously rejected the suggestion he should include a bibliography, suggesting, in a letter to G. E. Moore, that either the work 'stands alone or I shall go to hell'. However, exegetes have variously aligned certain themes in the text with the philosophies of Kierkegaard, Kant and Schopenhauer. The *Tractatus*'s influence on subsequent continental philosophy is even more difficult to assess. As with any significant text in philosophy one will find references; however, these are often out of context and are not a good guide to the text. Unfortunately, the *Tractatus* is all too often taken as being a work of logical atomism and as one of the foundational texts in the analytic tradition, thus of little serious interest to more overtly 'continental' philosophers. The current exegetical debate should, if nothing else, show this thought to be erroneous.

As with *Tractatus* exegesis, how one should read Wittgenstein's later work has been disputed, sometimes hotly. However, while doctrinal readers exist, it is stretching the concept of 'reading' somewhat to call theirs a reading of *PI*, as it is a radically therapeutic text. Wittgenstein advances no theses and, explicitly, advises those who share his vision of philosophy to refrain from doing so. Indeed, for Wittgenstein, one cannot advance controversial theses in philosophy. The Wittgensteinian task is to practise therapy on one's philosophical interlocutor (or on oneself). This therapy ought to serve to facilitate an aspect-shift in one's interlocutor, so that they may be freed from the grip of a philosophical problem, a problem that has its roots in a temporary inability to acknowledge other aspects.

The first influence on Wittgenstein that might well come to mind with talk of therapy is Freud. Wittgenstein's relationship to Freud initially appears complicated. Throughout Wittgenstein's *Nachlass* there are many references to the psychologist. Wittgenstein is often contemptuous of Freud's claims, while at other times praises his brilliance. How does one understand these seemingly contradictory remarks? On close attention they turn out not to be contradictory. What Wittgenstein deplores in Freud is his scientism, while what he sees as 'brilliant' is Freud's devising of the therapeutic method. Freud is said to be emblematic of the 'darkness of the times' owing to his propensity to wrap up this insight with a metaphysics of mind which is then claimed to have scientific credentials. Wittgenstein, therefore, takes on none of Freud's psychological theory; he takes only the therapeutic method. The correct way of characterising the relationship of Wittgenstein to Freud might therefore begin with noting that the analogy is between Wittgenstein's method and psychotherapy and not between his philosophy and psychoanalysis.

Wittgenstein's later work has been compared to, affiliated with and explored in tandem with a number of philosophers in the continental tradition, such as Kierkegaard, Heidegger, Derrida and Marx. It should be noted that there is little biographical evidence of Wittgenstein having read in depth any of those of the above whose writings were available to him. However, there are some parallels discernable and of interest, though it is crucial, if one wishes to understand Wittgenstein, not to overplay these, for Wittgenstein is not open to affiliation to another 'school of thought'. For better or for worse his vision of philosophy marks a significant departure from what had gone under that name before (as he himself noted). As for the influence of Wittgenstein on contemporary continental philosophers, this is a more difficult question. As with the *Tractatus*, references to *PI* abound, many of which lack understanding and are misleading. However, Wittgenstein's influence is on the increase in France in the wake of Jacques Bouveresse's subtle and insightful work.

P. Hutchinson

WORLDHOOD (*Weltlichkeit*) A term which in Heidegger's *Being and Time* designates the distinctly ontological interpretation of the phenomenon of world, as characteristic of the being of Dasein. This worldhood of the world of Dasein is interpreted by looking at the everyday world of Dasein, the world (*Welt*) as environment (*Umwelt*). The world of Dasein is a world that is all around, a world that does not stand opposed to Dasein, but enfolds itself around it. This clearly suggests a distinct spatiality, which Heidegger is concerned to thematise. The spatiality of Dasein, of its world and of those beings encountered within it is not one that can be measured and represented mathematically (geometrically); it is not the spatiality of extended matter. Rather, it is an existential spatiality: things are close by or far away not according to their actual distance, but according to the manner in which they relate to our concerns, our aspirations, our needs and so on. The world of Dasein is not made of extended things, as in Descartes, but of things that emerge from a context that, for the most part, is practical. The world we live in is made of things of use, or of things that are ready-to-hand (*zuhandene*), manipulable. Yet these things emerge from a given context, which is always referential and meaningful: some particular thing becomes manifest and is used with a view to something else, some practical goal. All things have this structure of being 'for the sake of' (*um-willen*) some other thing. Yet the totality of goals and involvements that characterise the practical sphere ultimately refers back to a 'towards which' in which there is no further involvement, and which itself is not something that is ready-to-hand; in other words, all such involvements ultimately point in the direction of Dasein itself as the being whose very Being is at issue for it.

M. de Beistegui

Y

YOUNG HEGELIANS A group of scholars, journalists and reformers, also known as the 'Left Hegelians', who collectively sought to discern and to advance the radical current in Hegel's thought for philosophical and political ends. Following Hegel's death in 1831, there was a broad commitment to the orthodoxy and finality of his Absolute Idealism. This consensus fell apart rapidly, however, as the problems of doctrinal interpretation created disputes and opposition parties. Because of the extraordinary esteem Hegel had earned in official circles, and because of tumultuous political conditions in Germany at the time, the stakes that weighed upon the interpretation of his ideas were very great. One important line of contention was drawn through the aphorism 'All that is rational is real; and all that is real is rational'. Some of Hegel's followers adopted the second refrain and used it as an endorsement and as a rationalisation of the status quo. Others, who came to be known collectively as the Young Hegelians or the Left Hegelians, seized upon the first refrain, and used it as a point of attack against the irrational – and for that reason soon-to-be abolished – religious and political conditions prevailing in Germany at the time. The members of this group emphasised the legacy of Hegel's early and more liberal thought, exemplified in his admiration for the French Revolution.

The group included David Strauss, Ludwig Feuerbach, Bruno Bauer, Max Stirner, Moses Hess, Arnold Ruge and Karl Marx among others. Lasting and irreconcilable divisions quickly formed between various individuals and factions within this group, and by 1845 there was effectively no united front of Young Hegelians whatsoever. Despite the short life of the movement, however, its importance in the history of politics and in the history of ideas is very great. It was a movement that set much of the tone and orientation of German Idealism as a whole, producing the first important efforts toward the possible range of post-Hegelian philosophies. It established, especially through the work of Marx and Engels, a platform of political ideas that changed not only the history of Germany but of Europe and of the world.

The early orientation and vitality of the Young Hegelian movement was determined by the contributions of its various members to debates on the status of Christianity, which was then the official religion of the Prussian state. The publication of Strauss's *Life of Jesus* (1835) is often identified as the first decisive blow of criticism struck against the conventional Hegelian interpretation of religion and, by implication, against the existing German political order. Feuerbach, in his *Principles of the Philosophy of the Future* (1843), argued that 'the task of the modern era was the realisation and humanisation of God – the transformation and dissolution of theology into anthropology'. Bauer was initially a conservative Hegelian and a capable defender of the gospel. His religious and political views drifted toward the left, however, and following the publication of several controversial works.

As had happened to Strauss before him, Bauer was forbidden from teaching. He then moved swiftly with the current of his times and published openly atheistic tracts in radical Hegelian journals and newspapers. The generally humanistic, sceptical and materialistic approach of works such as these quickly stirred suspicion among the censors and potentates of the Prussian monarchy. A real war of ideas ensued, written works were suppressed, some of the more outspoken Young Hegelians were expelled from their academic posts and some were even deported.

Although the critical efforts of the Young Hegelians began as a fierce struggle to achieve some kind of emancipation from conservative religious orthodoxy, they did not end there. Johann Kaspar Schmidt, who wrote under the pseudonym Max Stirner, represented perhaps the most extreme anti-authoritarian tendency within the Young Hegelian movement, espousing a mixture of anarchism and egoism that assailed hierarchies of power as a matter of principle. 'The state', wrote Stirner in *The Ego and His Own* (1845), 'is a *despotism* whose sole purpose is to limit the individual, to master him and subordinate him'. Despite the extremity of his position, Stirner in fact aimed to subjectivise Hegel within the terms of the Hegelian philosophy itself. Whereas Hegel had begun his account of the history of human freedom with its most conspicuous illustration, the case of the tyrant and his subjects, Stirner completes his account with the solitary tyrant, the unconditional sovereignty of the individual, and the end of subjection to authority altogether.

Arnold Ruge was the co-founder and principal editor of the most influential Young Hegelian journals, which were continually being shut down by Prussian authorities. He was instrumental in transferring the critical attention of the Young Hegelian movement from the project of religious emancipation to the project of political emancipation. For his time Ruge was a radical democrat, affirming the legitimacy of the state in principle. In this he was initially an inspiration and later an irritant to the young Karl Marx, who soon came to realise the futility of attempting superficial political solutions to fundamentally economic problems. The two founded the *Deutsche-Französiche Jarbücher* but soon quarrelled, in print, over the significance of the textile workers' riots in Bohemia and Silesia. Ruge dismissed the uprisings while Marx saw in them a portent of the future. This seemingly trivial dispute turned out to be of some significance, as it pushed Marx further toward the dialectic of labour and capital and toward the political economy of class relations in general.

If anything united the diverse efforts of the Young Hegelians, in principle if not in practice, it was a commitment to overturn the conditions of human self-alienation in its myriad forms. For some, this amounted to a demystification of theology or of religion altogether; for others it amounted to the abolition of the Prussian monarchy; for others still it amounted to a revolution in the socio-economic order.

P. Lewis

ŽIŽEK, SLAVOJ (1949–) Leading figure of the Slovene School, a group of philosophers and social theorists centred in Ljubljana, Slovenia, heavily influenced by Lacanian psychoanalysis and German Idealism. Žižek has written extensively on ideology in *The Sublime Object of Ideology* (1989) and *Did Somebody Say Totalitarianism?* (2002); on German Idealism in *Tarrying With the Negative* (1991) and *The Indivisible Remainder* (1994); on Lacanian psychoanalysis in *Enjoy Your Symptom* (1992) and *The Plague of Fantasies* (1997); on feminist theory in *The Metastases of Enjoyment* (1994); on popular culture in *Looking Awry* (1991); and on religion in *The Fragile Absolute* (2000) and *On Belief* (2001). His work revolves around the trials and tribulations of subjectivity in a world characterised by fundamental psychic trauma and political alienation. In particular, two themes stand out: the mechanisms through which ideologies provide false understanding to those within their sway, and the way in which cultural formations both reveal and occlude these mechanisms.

Žižek's work relies heavily on his distinctive reinterpretation of both Hegel's dialectic and Lacan's psychoanalytic theory of subjectivity. Hegelian dialectic is often understood as an expression of rationalistic optimism about the possibilities of overcoming the philosophical, social and political antagonisms of modernity. On Žižek's reading Hegel is unique among classical modern philosophers in resisting such a flight from antagonism and instead turning such antagonisms into the primary object of his philosophical analyses. Much of Žižek's work, for example in *The Sublime Object of Ideology* (1989) and *Tarrying with the Negative* (1991), is an attempt to defend Hegelian dialectic and clear it of the charges of complicity with hegemonic metaphysics and politics levelled especially by contemporary French philosophers and critical theorists.

Similarly, Žižek's appropriation and interpretation of Lacanian psychoanalysis casts Lacan as an ally of liberatory politics in spite of the latter's reputation as an opponent of political and social radicalism and defender of a particularly misogynist version of psycho-analytic theory. Žižek's strategy in such works as *Looking Awry* (1991), *Enjoy Your Symptom* (1992) and *Plague of Fantasies* (1997) is to expound on the basic concepts of Lacan's theory of subjectivity and to use them in critical analysis of contemporary culture. Hence both of these books are introductions to, as well as defences of and applications of, Lacanian psychoanalytic theory in Žižek's distinctive idiom.

In addition to exploring the arcane details of a wide range of philosophers and theorists, Žižek's work's deliberately engages in contemporary political controversy in a self-conscious attempt to further the role of the 'critical intellectual' advocated by Marx, Adorno and other neo-Marxists. For example, *For They Know Not What They Do* (1991) addresses the question of the lure of nationalism in an age of increasing economic and cultural globalisation, especially in the context of the dissolution of Eastern European communism. Likewise, *Welcome to the Desert of the Real* is a commentary on political, cultural and theoretical responses to the terrorist attacks on the United States in 2001. This political engagement has been an important part of Žižek's career and is one of the unifying factors of the efforts of the whole of the Slovene school.

For a sample of the work of other members of Žižek's group, and fellow travellers from the US and France, see the collection of essays edited by Žižek, *Everything You Ever Wanted To Know About Lacan But Were Afraid To Ask Hitchcock* (1992).

G. Matthews

List of Contributors

John Armitage
School of Arts and Social Sciences
Northumbria University (UK)

Branka Arsić
Department of English
State University of New York at Albany (USA)

Miguel de Beistegui
Department of Philosophy
Warwick University (UK)
Università degli Studi di Milano (Italy)

Debra Bergoffen
Department of Philosophy
George Mason University (USA)

Charles Bigger
Emeritus, Department of Philosophy
Louisiana State University (USA)

Mark Bonta
Division of Social Sciences
Delta State University (USA)

Giovanna Borradori
Department of Philosophy
Vassar College (USA)

Constantin Boundas
Emeritus, Department of Philosophy
Trent University (Canada)

Patrick Bourgeois
Department of Philosophy
Loyola New Orleans (USA)

Zachary Braiterman
Department of Religion
Syracuse University (USA)

Michael Bray
Department of Philosophy
Southwestern University (USA)

Ronald Bruzina
Department of Philosophy
University of Kentucky (USA)

Howard Caygill
Historical and Cultural Studies
Goldsmiths College, University of London (UK)

Chambi Chachage
Centre of African Studies
University of Edinburgh (UK)

Daniel Chandler
Department of Theatre, Film and Television Studies
University of Wales, Aberystwyth (UK)

Peter Connor
Department of French
Barnard College, Columbia University (USA)

Dan Conway
Department of Philosophy
Pennsylvania State University (USA)

Jean-Philippe Deranty
Department of Philosophy
Macquarie University (Australia)

Max Deutscher
Emeritus, Department of Philosophy
Macquarie University (Australia)

Rosalyn Diprose
School of Philosophy
University of New South Wales (Australia)

Madeleine Dobie
Department of French and Romance Philology
Columbia University (USA)

Mark Dooley
Dublin (Ireland)

Robin Durie
Plymouth Medical School
University of Exeter (UK)

Fred Evans
Department of Philosophy
Duquesne University (USA)

Emmanuel Chukwudi Eze
Department of Philosophy
DePaul University (USA)

Edward F. Findlay
Arlington, Virginia (USA)

Bernard Flynn
Department of Philosophy
Empire State College (USA)

Bruce Foltz
Department of Philosophy
Eckerd College (USA)

Shaun Gallagher
Department of Philosophy
University of Central Florida (USA)

Stephen Gardner
Department of Philosophy
University of Tulsa (USA)

Gary Genosko
Department of Sociology
Lakehead University (Canada)

Simon Glendinning
European Institute
London School of Economics (UK)

Mark Hansen
Department of English
Princeton University (USA)

Sarah K. Hansen
Department of Philosophy
Vanderbilt University (USA)

Ben Highmore
Cultural Studies
University of the West of England (UK)

Jason Hill
Department of Philosophy
DePaul University (USA)

Burt C. Hopkins
Department of Philosophy
Seattle University (USA)

Alexandra Howson
Department of Sociology
University of Abertay (UK)

Jeff Humphries
Department of French Studies
Louisiana State University (USA)

Phil Hutchinson
Department of Philosophy
Manchester Metropolitan University (UK)

David Ingram
Department of Philosophy
Loyola University Chicago (USA)

Caren Irr
Department of English
Brandeis University (USA)

Virginia Lyle Jennings
Department of Philosophy
Loyola New Orleans (USA)

Vrasidas Karalis
Department of Modern Greek
University of Sydney (Australia)

Stacy Keltner
Department of Philosophy
Kennesaw State University (USA)

Bob Kinkead
Apollo, Pennsylvania (USA)

Peter Kivisto
Department of Sociology
Augustana College (USA)

David Kolb
Department of Philosophy
Bates College (USA)

Gregg Lambert
Department of English
Syracuse University (USA)

Alex Law
Department of Sociology
University of Abertay (UK)

Leonard Lawlor
Department of Philosophy
University of Memphis (USA)

Joseph P. Lawrence
Department of Philosophy
College of the Holy Cross (USA)

Alexandre Leupin
Department of French Studies
Louisiana State University (USA)

Paul Lewis
Department of Philosophy
University of the Incarnate Word (USA)

William Lewis
Department of Philosophy
Skidmore College (USA)

Iain Macdonald
Department of Philosophy
Université de Montréal (Canada)

William Mander
Harris Manchester College
University of Oxford (UK)

John Panteleimon Manoussakis
Department of Philosophy
Boston College (USA)

George Matthews
School of Integrated Studies
Pennsylvania College of Technology (USA)

William McBride
Department of Philosophy
Purdue University (USA)

John McCumber
Department of German
University of California at Los Angeles (USA)

Wallace McNeish
Department of Sociology
University of Abertay (USA)

Ladelle McWhorter
Department of Philosophy
University of Richmond (USA)

Ann Murphy
School of Philosophy
University of New South Wales (Australia)

Timothy S. Murphy
Department of English
University of Oklahoma (USA)

Eric Sean Nelson
Department of Philosophy
University of Massachusetts Lowell (USA)

Judith Norman
Department of Philosophy
Trinity University (USA)

Christopher Norris
Department of Philosophy
Cardiff University (UK)

Kelly Oliver
Department of Philosophy
Vanderbilt University (USA)

Dorothea Olkowski
Department of Philosophy
University of Colorado (USA)

Thomas O'Meara
Emeritus, Department of Theology
University of Notre Dame (USA)

George Pattison
Faculty of Theology
University of Oxford (UK)

Paul Patton
School of Philosophy
University of New South Wales (Australia)

Diane Perpich
Department of Philosophy
Vanderbilt University (USA)

Mary Pickering
Department of History
San Jose State University (USA)

Sadie Plant
Birmingham, England (UK)

Arkady Plotnitsky
Department of English
Purdue University (USA)

Elizabeth Potter
Department of Philosophy
Mills College (USA)

Jeffrey L. Powell
Department of Philosophy
Marshall University (USA)

John Protevi
Department of French Studies
Louisiana State University (USA)

François Raffoul
Department of Philosophy
Louisiana State University (USA)

Marcia Robinson
Department of Religion
Syracuse University (USA)

Tom Rockmore
Department of Philosophy
Duquesne University (USA)

David Roden
Department of Philosophy
Open University (UK)

Jaime de Salas
Department of Philosophy
Universidad Complutense de Madrid (Spain)

Sean Sayers
Department of Philosophy
University of Kent (UK)

Robert Scharff
Department of Philosophy
University of New Hampshire (USA)

Theodore Schatzki
Department of Philosophy
University of Kentucky (USA)

Louis G. Schwartz
Department of Cinema and Comparative Literature
University of Iowa (USA)

Linnell Secomb
Department of Gender Studies
University of Sydney (Australia)

Evan Selinger
Department of Philosophy
Rochester Institute of Technology (USA)

Daniel W. Smith
Department of Philosophy
Purdue University (USA)

Nicholas H. Smith
Department of Philosophy
Macquarie University (Australia)

Leonard Stanton
Department of Foreign Languages
Louisiana State University (USA)

Greg Stone
Department of French Studies
Louisiana State University (USA)

Rob Switzer
Department of Philosophy
American University in Cairo (Egypt)

Adam Thurschwell
Cleveland-Marshall School of Law
Cleveland State University (USA)

James Tiles
Department of Philosophy
University of Hawai'i at Manoā (USA)

Mary Tiles
Department of Philosophy
University of Hawai'i at Manoā (USA)

Alberto Toscano
Department of Sociology
Goldsmiths College, University of London (UK)

Peter Trawny
Department of Philosophy
Universität Wuppertal (Germany)

Nancy Tuana
Department of Philosophy
Pennsylvania State University (USA)

Robert Vallier
Department of Philosophy
DePaul University (USA)

Massimo Verdicchio
Department of Modern Languages
University of Alberta (Canada)

David Webb
Department of Philosophy
Staffordshire University (UK)

Phil Wegner
Department of English
University of Florida (USA)

Alistair Welchman
Austin, Texas (USA)

Brigitte Weltman-Aron
Department of Foreign Languages
University of Memphis (USA)

Ken Westphal
School of Philosophy
University of East Anglia (UK)

James Williams
Department of Philosophy
University of Dundee (UK)

David Wills
Department of Languages, Literatures and Cultures
State University of New York at Albany (USA)